JOHANN WOLFGANG von GOETHE

Wilhelm Meister's Apprenticeship

THE THOMAS CARLYLE TRANSLATION

With a new Introduction by Franz Schoenberner and

Illustrations by William Sharp

THE HERITAGE PRESS

New York

The special contents of this edition are copyright © 1959

by The George Macy Companies, Inc.

Contents

FRANZ SCHOENBERNER
The Adventure of Reading *Wilhelm Meister's Apprenticeship*   IX

THOMAS CARLYLE
The Translator's Preface   XXI

JOHANN WOLFGANG VON GOETHE
Wilhelm Meister's Apprenticeship

BOOK ONE   3
BOOK TWO   69
BOOK THREE   137
BOOK FOUR   193
BOOK FIVE   269
BOOK SIX   341
BOOK SEVEN   397
BOOK EIGHT   467

Color Plates

The puppet players   FRONTISPIECE

Wilhelm and Mariana   OPPOSITE PAGE   8

A serenade beneath Mariana's window   65

Wilhelm watches the minstrels prepare   89

Mignon performs her egg-dance   108

The count and the countess meet the players   144

Wilhelm embraces the countess   191

The players' vehicles are attacked   216

Serlo and Aurelia discuss *Hamlet* with Wilhelm   233

"I am thy father's spirit"   312

Narciss in a duel   352

Wilhelm has strange dreams   401

Wilhelm and Theresa   424

"Here is your indenture"   464

Mignon as an angel   481

Wilhelm and Natalia in the Hall of the Past   504

Wilhelm Meister's Apprenticeship

IT HAS been said that a classic is a book everybody talks about and nobody reads. This is not quite true, because there have always been, and in every country, certain classics which are read continuously by anybody who can claim a certain degree of education. Corneille and Racine are still living authors in France, and even today cantos from Dante or Tasso are recited by the Italian man-in-the-street at the slightest provocation.

Here in this country the tradition of being brought up with Shakespeare and the Bible was alive at least until the end of the nineteenth century. And in a similar way the slowly vanishing generation of Germans born around 1890 grew up with Goethe and Schiller and other famous classical authors whose complete works, or "Klassiker Ausgaben," usually bound in ugly cloth with gold filigree, belonged as much to the furniture of every gute Stube (drawing room) as the sofa in red plush.

There was even a typical expression indicating a special intimacy with Goethe: one used to speak of Goethe-Deutsche (Goethe-Germans), which may account for the strange phenomenon that so many German authors in their later years began to imitate the Olympian attitude, the style, and, if possible, even the imposing looks of the old Minister von Goethe.

I had not quite enough time to become a real Goethe-Deutscher, though it must be more than fifty years since I first read Wilhelm Meister's Apprenticeship. I read it a second time some twenty years ago, while living as a refugee in France, trying to recall the spiritual Germany where I was still at home.

Coming back to this classic now again and reading both the original as well as Carlyle's translation, I was delighted to find it as fascinating as ever — if not more so. Having long since become an American by adoption and adaptation, I understood perhaps better than before that Goethe's practical, almost pragmatic wisdom of life, with its emphasis on the *vita activa*, had a certain quite conscious affinity to the spirit of the New World.

There are, of course, a respectable number of Goethe scholars of my own or even a younger generation who have virtually never stopped reading Goethe in general and *Wilhelm Meister* in particular. These specialized philologists have produced, and are still producing, whole libraries about every line Goethe ever wrote, including his shopping lists. But even when studying the History of Literature at the University of Berlin as one of the last pupils of the great Germanist, Erich Schmidt, I felt rather disappointed with this kind of introduction into the spiritual and poetical world of a great genius. Perhaps it is, after all, a good thing that I did not become a Germanic scholar; this way I feel closer to the prospective readers of the new edition of *Wilhelm Meister's Apprenticeship*. Probably few of them will have read this great book more recently than about twenty years ago. So we are more or less in the same boat, and I can try to share with them my own intense pleasure of discovery or re-discovery.

Seen on the surface, the whole form and content of this eighteenth-century novel is certainly dated — which can be said of every great masterwork of the past, be it *Don Quixote* or *A Sentimental Journey* or *Tom Jones*. But there is, underneath, an astonishing, timeless freshness of feeling, an abundance of profound and original thought about the most divergent subjects. It is no wonder that this book became the prototype of the *Bildungsroman* or *Entwicklungsroman*, the novel of education or development (a translation which, like most translations, falls short of the original). *Bildung* means not only the training and the development of a young mind towards greater maturity or higher knowledge; it has also the connotation of *bilden* in the sense of the English word "to build" (which in Middle English, by the way, was exactly the same word as the German *bilden*).

There were other books of this kind long before *Wilhelm Meister's Apprenticeship*, as, for example, Wieland's *Agathon*, describing the education of a young Athenian, or perhaps Rousseau's *Émile*, which, it is true, was more a sort of educational textbook than a novel. But for whatever reasons, *Wilhelm Meister's Apprenticeship* influenced German and indeed all European literature as a model of such — mostly autobiographical — writing. There are, among others, the Swiss classic, Gottfried Keller's *Der Grüne Heinrich*, Stendhal's *La Chartreuse de Parme*, Flaubert's *Éducation Sentimentale*, and even Henry Adams's purely cerebral, almost dehydrated self-portrait used the word "education" in the Goethean sense.

Wilhelm Meister may be said to occupy in Goethe's life and work a place similar to that of his *Faust*. It is known that the young Goethe began the novel in 1777, three years after his *Sorrows of Young Werther*, in his late twenties, and that in 1785, not long before his first voyage to Italy, he had finished the first six books. It was approximately, as he thought, the first half of his novel, which significantly enough had originally the title *Wilhelm Meisters Theatralische Sendung (Wilhelm Meister's Theatrical Mission)*.

To the bitter regret of Goethe scholars, the original manuscript and its copies were lost, presumably burnt by the author himself. It was only in 1910 that by a strange coincidence a handwritten copy of *Wilhelm Meister's Theatrical Mission* was found in Switzerland. As it turned out, Barbara Schulthess of Zurich, one of the friends among whom the young Goethe used to circulate his works in progress, had received a transcript of the original manuscript and, with the help of her daughter, had hastily copied it before sending it back in the special little box built for this purpose. It took more than a year before the Goethe philologists had gone through with the painstaking elimination of all the little mistakes obviously or probably made by the copyists. But when finally this newly found fragment appeared in print, it was quite a sensation, because this first version — exactly as with the first draft of *Faust* — was rather different from the corresponding chapters of the novel which had appeared in 1795 and 1796 under the new title, *Wilhelm Meisters Lehrjahre*.

The fragment, *Wilhelm Meister's Theatrical Mission*, was a frankly autobiographical piece written with the whole freshness and narrative impetus of the young Goethe, who had hardly emerged from the period of *Sturm und Drang.* The story of the puppet theatre, for example, which played such a decisive role in the world of the little Wolfgang — a motive taken up again in *Dichtung und Wahrheit* — was here told at great length. But this part was severely cut in the work of the mature Goethe, who, with ironical detachment, now made Wilhelm Meister himself tell the shortened story while his lovely mistress Mariana, bored to death, falls asleep in his arms. But this is only one typical trait indicating the totally changed attitude of the author towards his work.

When in 1793 he took up the old fragment, in order to finish the novel after an interruption of almost eight years, Goethe himself had become an entirely different person and Wilhelm Meister was no longer his "beloved dramatic image," as he had said in his youth. There was no longer a real identification with the emotional, amorous, sentimental, and wildly enthusiastic young man, who in the first version believed so thoroughly in his theatrical mission and in the "German National Theatre." When Goethe wrote the Apprenticeship he had gone through a long phase of poetic dearth, and his new "puberty," as he called it, had really started only when his long-postponed friendship with Schiller came finally to fruition. Throughout his now very intensive work on the novel he discussed his writing with Schiller, often by letter, chapter after chapter, in every detail. The new ideas inspired by Schiller's more abstract and philosophical mind became incorporated, frequently in a somewhat forced manner, into his work. The whole plan had changed and the flow of the narration had now to be interrupted by long didactic essays about education, about the theatre, the drama, the art of acting, about Shakespeare, and especially about Hamlet — a topic which, it is true, played an important role even in the first version.

There was still enough left of the character of the picaresque novel of the eighteenth century to fill the story with the most improbable coincidences and fantastic adventures; with tales of attempted murder and arson, of insanity, incest, and suicide; with complicated romances and mistaken identities; with lost, stolen, or substituted children; with mystical messages, prophetic dreams, and, of course, a Secret Society.

This latter feature, it is true, does not belong to the realm of pure imagination. Actually secret societies of religious, political, or even criminal character flourished everywhere in the eighteenth and early nineteenth century. The Order of the Freemasons, to which Goethe as well as Schiller belonged, was only the most serious and most influential among them. Steeped in a deistic, philosophical, humanitarian spirit, this idealistic as well as utilitarian order with its complicated symbols and rituals, so magnificently reflected in Mozart's *Magic Flute*, served evidently as model for Goethe's Society of the Tower. Its aim is, as it turns out, purely educational. But the underlying principles of this education, developed by a few superior persons like the mysterious Abbé or the anonymous "Uncle," appear astonishingly modern, though they serve here only for the secret guidance of a few selected and somehow promising individuals, like Wilhelm Meister.

The method is almost as new and progressive as Dewey's theories: the learning by doing, by trial and error, by mistakes which, once recognized, will not be repeated, but need not be repented because they are only necessary detours, leading to the right goal: the forming of the personality, the free development of its highest potentialities.

Especially startling are the psychological and psychiatric, almost psychoanalytical insights, presented here by the country clergyman and the old physician, who try to cure the harper's mental derangement by a kind of occupational therapy. They recognize the psychosomatic element in Mignon's heart condition and in the fatal illness of the jilted Aurelia, who had the great misfortune "not to be lovable when she loved." They understand perfectly the neurotic guilt complex of the Countess when, against all medical evidence, she has the feeling of a cancerous induration in the spot where Wilhelm, parting from her with a first and last embrace, had accidentally pressed the jewelled miniature portrait of her husband into her breast. — And all this a century before Freud, who, himself, it is true, used to say that poets had always known what he tried to systematize.

But quite apart from all its romantic or anticipatory elements, the novel gives a vivid, true-to-life picture of actual social conditions in the second half of the eighteenth century. The strict caste division of the landed and military aristocracy, the middle class of burghers, especially merchants or professionals, and finally the rather dubious sphere of the theatrical world with its Bohemian actors and actresses, who are hardly one step above circus acrobats and gypsies, was a reality and quite naturally accepted by all concerned. (Goethe, who in 1791, sixteen years after his arrival in Weimar, had become director of the court theatre, had learned more about the great world, about the stage, and about actors, than he would have liked.)

Seen in the context of such a social order, it was an almost revolutionary idea that the artistically inclined burgher Wilhelm Meister, who has actually lost even his own caste by becoming an actor, should finally marry a highly distinguished noblewoman, the "beautiful amazon" Natalia. And Theresa, believed to be a born aristocrat, declares even more explicitly she would rather live with an honest farmer than in the world of conventional high society. In fact, the novel ends with no less than four so-called mésalliances. But it is perhaps even more daring and significant when Wilhelm Meister, trying to organize his company of actors, casually states that "among good people the republican form of government is certainly the best." His plan, including a president and a senate, freely elected, resembles very much the American Constitution, a document much admired by European intellectuals of that time.

I shall not try the impossible task of summarizing the complicated plot, the real story of this novel, but it may be desirable to prepare the reader for its heterogeneous elements. There is, for example, inserted in the middle of a highly dramatic action, the long and seemingly unrelated Book VI under the title: *"Die Geständnisse einer schönen Seele."* (Strangely enough, Carlyle did not translate this literally as "The Confessions of a Beautiful Soul," but — quite misleadingly — "The Confessions of a Fair Saint.") It is the story of Goethe's motherly friend, Susanna von Klettenberg, an aristocratic old lady who at a relatively early age had become converted to the pietistic religion of the so-called Herrnhuter. (Founded in the 1770s by Count Zinzendorf, this sect represented a revival of the old Moravian Church, going back to the Czech reformer John Huss, who was burnt at the stake in 1415. Congregations of these *Mährische Brüder* — Moravian Brethren — had settled in and around Bethlehem, Pennsylvania.) Based certainly on the personal autobiographical writings of Susanna von Klettenberg, Book VI appears as an alien body in the framework of the novel. But it serves intentionally as a sort of counterbalance to the highly secular world of the theatre and so-called high society.

It is typical that Leopold von Stolberg, the friend of Goethe's youth, or such a highly moral person as Goethe's brother-in-law Schlosser, cut Book VI out of their personal copies of the *Lehrjahre* to preserve it, while burning the other parts. Even years later Schlosser bitterly reproached Goethe for having put this story of such a pure and pious person in his "bordello." Poor old Schlosser was probably thinking in this context not only of Mariana, Wilhelm's first mistress, but primarily of one of Goethe's most charming figures, the pretty and completely amoral, though not immoral, young actress Philina. It is this "pleasing sinner," this "lighthearted beauty," who, loving Wilhelm Meister in her own way, says once in an amusingly equivocal situation a word of sublime feminine wisdom: *"Wenn ich dich lieb habe, was geht's dich an?"* — "If I love you, what does it matter to you?" (Carlyle's "If I have a touch of kindness for thee, what hast thou to do with it?" is a rather funny bowdlerization.) All of which goes to prove that even among his relatives and close friends, Goethe's intentions and the magnificent universality of his world view were often absolutely misunderstood. (Goethe's mother, the wonderful "Frau Aja," had, of course, not the slightest objection to seeing her old friend Susanna in rather worldly company.)

It is true, and easily explicable by the history of this novel, that even in its finished form *Wilhelm Meister's Apprenticeship* had to remain a kind of "patchwork," as Carlyle called it. But it reflects in its necessarily imperfect form the whole enormous scope of Goethe's mind, the strange convolutions and evolutions of his own development over almost twenty years. It is surprising that the same artist who created the romantic, touching, and deeply ambiguous figure of Mignon, a kind of ethereal being between girl and boy, should lead his hero towards an ideal of sober-practical, manly activity, in happy equilibrium between thought and action. Emerging from an atmosphere of rather sentimental feeling, of vague philosophical speculation, of adolescent confusion, Wilhelm Meister, after several false starts, ends up as the husband of the over-idealized, virtuous prodigy Natalia. He is free either to choose the administration of her (and his) large estates or to accept Jarno's plan of making a fresh start in the New World, which occupies such a significant place in the whole novel. Jarno, the former soldier and friend of princes, decides, mainly for practical reasons, to take up the challenge of a new country to which, he feels, the future will belong. And Lothario, Natalia's brother, has fought in the American War of Independence and has come back — temporarily, as it turns out — with the intention of applying the newly learned social principles of a free country on his own estates because he feels, "Here is America."

Actually, in *Wilhelm Meisters Wanderjahre* (*Wilhelm Meister's Travels*) — the continuation of the *Apprenticeship*, following after twenty-five years — the whole Society of the Tower is about to leave Europe behind, inspired by the hope of finding in America the possibility of living in freedom, according to their own ideas, without being hampered by the limitations and petrified traditions of Germany.

It would be tempting to follow this line of thought and to point out that Goethe's never-flagging interest in America goes as far back as 1775, a year before the Declaration of Independence and a year after *Werther*. The young genius of twenty-six, trying to break free from his fiancée Lily Schönemann, the beautiful society girl of Frankfurt, thinks seriously of going to America. And even at almost seventy he confesses wistfully that, were he twenty years younger, he would like to sail to the United States. It would be equally interesting to examine America's curious attitude towards Goethe, the man and his work.

The strangely differing aspects of this mutual relationship have been recently elucidated in an excellent little study by Johannes Urzidil.[1] But here it may suffice to say that Goethe for a long time suffered from two quite contradictory handicaps in the judgment of his American contemporaries as well as of later generations. On the one hand he was reproached for being a coldly arrogant, aristocratic courtier, a stuffy reactionary, opposed to freedom and democracy. On the other hand he was condemned for being a libertine and a licentious hedonist, whose classicist idealization of antiquity was pure paganism, immoral, anti-Christian, and so obviously subversive. It is true that Emerson

---

[1] *Das Glück der Gegenwart — Goethes Amerikabild*, Zürich and Stuttgart, Artemis Verlag, 1957. It is to be hoped that this distinguished Austrian-American scholar and author will publish for American readers a (perhaps enlarged) version of his highly valuable study.

as well as Longfellow showed a much better understanding. Interestingly enough, they both felt that Goethe, though endowed with much greater power of imagination, had many things in common with Franklin in his concrete common sense, his scientific interest, his wide tolerance and worldly wisdom. But it seems that even to this day Goethe has not become very popular among Americans, not even among professional literati. Not too long ago the book reviewer of a great metropolitan paper stated quite frankly in his regular column that he had "only a nodding acquaintance with Goethe."

There is, of course, one difficulty: Great books always lose very much in translation, while bad or indifferent books can often be improved by good translators. Carlyle himself was rather severe in judging his own translation, as the last, almost touchingly humble paragraph of his Preface of 1824 proves. And even later, in a short notice To the Reader, written for a reprint in 1839, he confessed that he had made many little changes, "but could not, unfortunately, change it into a right translation. It hung in many places, stiff and laboured, too like some unfortunate buckram cloak round the light, harmonious movement of the original; and, alas, still hangs so, here and there."

I personally think that Carlyle was a bit unjust towards himself. Translation, even at its best, is an almost impossible task, especially in the sphere of poetry. (The German Shakespeare translation by Schlegel and Tieck is a brilliant exception.) Undoubtedly, the wonderful verses sung by Mignon and the harper, which, set to music by great composers like Beethoven, Schubert, Schumann, Liszt, Tchaikovsky, Hugo Wolf, and others, soon gained the popularity of *Volkslieder* in Germany, sound rather stiff and stilted in Carlyle's version. Still, Goethe translations by contemporaries have always the one great advantage of conveying in their language something of the special atmosphere of the times, which even talented modern translators can rarely catch.

A rather amusing fact is that Carlyle, this dour Scot, despite his sincere admiration, evidently quite often disapproved of Goethe, as he says in his Preface: "In many points, both literary and moral, I may have wished devoutly that he had not written as he has done; but to alter anything was not in my commission." Nevertheless, as we mentioned before, Carlyle was not the only one to have all kinds of objections. It took men like Schiller or the Schlegels to expound in long thoughtful essays (much too long for any modern magazine!) the beauties and profundities of the novel. Certainly nobody will be surprised by contradictory judgments, since Goethe himself called *Wilhelm Meister* his "most incalculable work." We can only wish that the modern American reader will be curious enough to try to find out what he himself thinks of this strange, multiform, and in every respect deeply significant novel.

But in concluding I should like to warn the reader against the one subtle danger of becoming overawed, overwhelmed by the monumental figure of a genius who in his old age seemed sometimes to impersonate his own legend or perhaps a statue of classical antiquity. This danger is real. Even the rather irreverent Heine confessed in later life [1] that as a young student, seeing Goethe for the first and last time, he instinctively looked around for the eagle with lightning in its beak, the mythological companion of Jupiter.

It should be remembered, however, that the Father of the Gods himself proved time and again to be ardently human and highly susceptible to the beauty of merely mortal women. Goethe, without the divine gift of eternal youth, followed, up to the last, his own injunction: "As long as one lives, one should stay alive." He stayed so gloriously alive throughout his seventh and eighth decades that there were more Suleikas than the one celebrated in the glowing verses of *West-Östlicher Divan*. Other youthful beauties were to stir his ageless heart deeply and dangerously until by the magic of his genius they were safely enshrined in the golden perfection of immortal poetry. It was a miracle of both human and poetic vitality when, at seventy-four, he fell so passionately in love with an exquisite child of nineteen, that, in magnificent disregard of ridicule or censure, he tossed aside his priceless wisdom and sent his old friend the Grand Duke Charles Augustus to ask — in vain — for her hand. Out of the desperate, almost fatal pain of love and renunciation, Goethe saved himself and his unique creative power by one of his greatest, most deeply moved and moving poems, the tragically incandescent "Trilogie der Leidenschaft" ("Trilogy of Passion").

---

[1] See his brilliant Goethe essay in *The Romantic School.*

Introduction

In order not to overemphasize again an almost superhuman stature, it should be noted that at this point the old Goethe fell gravely ill. It took him many months to recover, but he still needed some more years of work to finish *Wilhelm Meister's Travels* and the second part of *Faust* and to edit the final edition of all his writings. When at eighty-three he finally "agreed to die," as he once said of an old friend, he was still human enough to leave with a touchingly simple last word. It was, as modern scholars luckily discovered, not the famous, slightly pompous and heavily symbolic "More light!" so dear to the Goethe legend. Instead, turning to his charming daughter-in-law Ottilie, he said, *"Gib mir dein Pfötchen"* ("Give me your little paw").

If this is not enough to put the most timid or intimidated Goethe readers at ease, I can do no more to prepare them for the keen enjoyment of Wilhelm Meister's — if not their own — Apprenticeship.

FRANZ SCHOENBERNER

New York, 1958

THE TRANSLATOR'S PREFACE

WHETHER IT BE that the quantity of genius among ourselves and the French, and the number of works more lasting than brass produced by it, have of late been so considerable as to make us independent of additional supplies; or that, in our ancient aristocracy of intellect, we disdain to be assisted by the Germans, whom, by a species of second sight, we have discovered, before knowing anything about them, to be a tumid, dreaming, extravagant, insane race of mortals — certain it is, that hitherto our literary intercourse with that nation has been very slight and precarious. After a brief period of not too judicious cordiality, the acquaintance on our part was altogether dropped: nor, in the few years since we partially resumed it, have our feelings of affection or esteem been materially increased. Our translators are unfortunate in their selection or execution, or the public is tasteless and absurd in its demands; for, with scarcely more than one or two exceptions, the best works of Germany have lain neglected, or worse than neglected: and the Germans are yet utterly unknown to us. Kotzebue still lives in our minds as the representative of a nation that despises him; Schiller is chiefly known to us by the monstrous production of his boyhood; and Klopstock by a hacked and mangled image of his *Messiah*, in which a beautiful poem is distorted into a theosophic rhapsody, and the brother of Virgil and Racine ranks little higher than the author of *Meditations Among the Tombs*.

But of all these people there is none that has been more unjustly dealt with than Johann Wolfgang von Goethe. For half a century the admiration — we might almost say the idol — of his countrymen, to us he is still a stranger. His name, long echoed and re-echoed through reviews and magazines, has become familiar to our ears; but it is a sound and nothing more: it excites no definite idea in almost any mind. To such as know him by the faint and garbled version of his *Werther*, Goethe figures as a sort of poetic Heraclitus; some woe-begone hypochondriac, whose eyes are overflowing with perpetual tears, whose long life has been spent in melting into ecstasy at the sight of waterfalls and clouds, and the moral sublime, or dissolving into hysterical wailings over hapless love-stories, and the miseries of human life. They are not aware that Goethe smiles at this performance of his youth, or that the German Werther, with all his faults, is a very different person from his English namesake; that his *Sorrows* are in the original recorded in a tone of strength and sarcastic emphasis, of which the other offers no vestige, and intermingled with touches of powerful thought, glimpses of a philosophy deep as it is bitter, which our sagacious translator has seen proper wholly to omit. Others, again, who have fallen in with Retsch's *Outlines* and the extracts from *Faust*, consider Goethe as a wild mystic, a dealer in demonology and osteology, who draws attention by the aid of skeletons and evil spirits, whose excellence it is to be extravagant, whose chief aim it is to do what no one but himself has tried. The tyro in German may tell us that the charm of *Faust* is altogether unconnected with its preternatural import; that the work delineates the fate of human enthusiasm struggling against doubts and errors from within, against scepticism, contempt, and selfishness from without; and that the witchcraft and magic, intended merely as a shadowy frame for so complex and mysterious a picture of the moral world and the human soul, are introduced for the purpose, not so much of being trembled at as laughed at. The voice of the tyro is not listened to; our indolence takes part with our ignorance; *Faust* continues to be called a monster; and Goethe is regarded as a man of "some genius," which he has perverted to produce all manner of misfashioned prodigies — things false, abortive, formless, Gorgons and Hydras and Chimæras dire.

Now, it must no doubt be granted, that, so long as our invaluable constitution is preserved in its pristine purity, the British nation may exist in a state of comparative prosperity with very inadequate ideas of Goethe; but, at the same time, the present arrangement is an evil in its kind — slight, it is true, and easy to be borne, yet still more easy to be remedied, and which, therefore, ought to have been remedied ere now. Minds like Goethe's are the common property of all nations; and, for many reasons, all should have correct impressions of them.

It is partly with the view of doing something to supply this want, that *Wilhelm Meister's Lehrjahre* is now presented to the English public. Written in its author's forty-fifth year, embracing hints or disquisitions on almost every leading point in life and literature, it affords us a more distinct view of his matured genius, his manner of thought, and favorite subjects, than any of his other works. Nor is it Goethe alone whom it portrays: the prevailing taste of Germany is likewise indicated by it. Since the year 1795, when it first appeared at Berlin, numerous editions of *Meister* have been printed: critics of all ranks, and some of them dissenting widely from its doctrines, have loaded it with encomiums; its songs and poems are familiar to every German ear; the people read it, and speak of it, with an admiration approaching in many cases to enthusiasm.

That it will be equally successful in England, I am far indeed from anticipating. Apart from the above considerations — from the curiosity, intelligent or idle, which it may awaken — the number of admiring, or even approving, judges it will find can scarcely fail of being very limited. To the great mass of readers, who read to drive away the tedium of mental vacancy, employing the crude phantasmagoria of a modern novel, as their grandfathers employed tobacco and diluted brandy, *Wilhelm Meister* will appear beyond endurance weary, flat, stale, and unprofitable. Those, in particular, who take delight in "King Cambyses' vein," and open *Meister* with the thought of *Werther* in their minds, will soon pause in utter dismay; and their paroxysm of dismay will pass by degrees into unspeakable contempt. Of romance interest there is next to none in *Meister*; the characters are samples to judge of, rather than persons to love or hate; the incidents are contrived for other objects than moving or affrighting us; the hero is a milksop, whom, with all his gifts, it takes an effort to avoid despising. The author himself, far from "doing it in a passion," wears a face of the most still indifference throughout the whole affair: often it is even wrinkled by a slight sardonic grin. For the friends of the sublime, then — for those who cannot do without heroical sentiments, and "moving accidents by flood and field," — there is nothing here that can be of any service.

Nor among readers of a far higher character can it be expected that many will take the praiseworthy pains of Germans, reverential of their favorite author, and anxious to hunt out his most elusive charms. Few among us will disturb themselves about the allegories and topical allusions of the work; will stop to inquire whether it includes a remote emblem of human culture, or includes no such matter; whether this is a light, airy sketch of the development of man in all his endowments and faculties, gradually proceeding from the first rude exhibitions of puppets and mountebanks, through the perfection of poetic and dramatic art, up to the unfolding of the principle of religion, and the greatest of all arts — the art of life — or is nothing more than a bungled piece of patchwork, presenting in the shape of a novel much that should have been suppressed entirely, or at least given out by way of lecture. Whether the characters do or do not represent distinct classes of men, including various stages of human nature, from the gay, material vivacity of Philina to the severe moral grandeur of the uncle and the splendid accomplishment of Lothario, will to most of us be of small importance; and the everlasting disquisitions about plays and players, and politeness and activity, and art and nature, will weary many a mind that knows not and heeds not whether they are true or false. Yet every man's judgment is, in this free country, a lamp to himself: whoever is displeased will censure; and many, it is to be feared, will insist on judging *Meister* by the common rule, and, what is worse, condemning it, let Schlegel bawl as loudly as he pleases. "To judge," says he, "of this book — new and peculiar as it is, and only to be understood and learned from itself, by our common notion of the novel, a notion pieced together and produced out of custom and belief, out of accidental and arbitrary requisitions — is as if a child should grasp at the moon and stars, and insist on packing them into its toy-box." [1] Unhappily the most of us have boxes, and some of them are very small.

Yet, independently of these its more recondite and dubious qualities, there are beauties in *Meister* which cannot but secure it some degree of favor at the hands of many. The philosophical discussions it contains; its keen glances into life and art; the minute and skilful delineation of men; the lively, genuine exhibition of the scenes they move in; the occasional touches of eloquence and tenderness, and even of poetry, the very essence of poetry; the quantity of thought and knowl-

---

[1] *Charakteristik des Meister.*

edge embodied in a style so rich in general felicities, of which, at least, the new and sometimes exquisitely happy metaphors have been preserved — cannot wholly escape an observing reader, even on the most cursory perusal. To those who have formed for themselves a picture of the world, who have drawn out, from the thousand variable circumstances of their being, a philosophy of life, it will be interesting and instructive to see how man and his concerns are represented in the first of European minds: to those who have penetrated to the limits of their own conceptions, and wrestled with thoughts and feelings too high for them, it will be pleasing and profitable to see the horizon of their certainties widened, or at least separated with a firmer line from the impalpable obscure which surrounds it on every side. Such persons I can fearlessly invite to study *Meister*. Across the disfigurement of a translation, they will not fail to discern indubitable traces of the greatest genius in our times. And the longer they study, they are likely to discern them the more distinctly. New charms will successively arise to view; and of the many apparent blemishes, while a few superficial ones may be confirmed, the greater and more important part will vanish, or even change from dark to bright. For, if I mistake not, it is with *Meister* as with every work of real and abiding excellence, — the first glance is the least favorable. A picture of Raphael, a Greek statue, a play of Sophocles or Shakspeare, appears insignificant to the unpractised eye; and not till after long and patient and intense examination, do we begin to descry the earnest features of that beauty, which has its foundation in the deepest nature of man, and will continue to be pleasing through all ages.

If this appear excessive praise, as applied in any sense to *Meister*, the curious sceptic is desired to read and weigh the whole performance, with all its references, relations, purposes, and to pronounce his verdict after he has clearly seized and appreciated them all. Or, if a more faint conviction will suffice, let him turn to the picture of Wilhelm's states of mind in the end of the first book, and the beginning of the second; the eulogies of commerce and poesy, which follow; the description of Hamlet; the character of histrionic life in Serlo and Aurelia; that of sedate and lofty manhood in the uncle and Lothario. But, above all, let him turn to the history of Mignon. This mysterious child, at first neglected by the reader, gradually forced on his attention, at length overpowers him with an emotion more deep and thrilling than any poet since the days of Shakspeare has succeeded in producing. The daughter of enthusiasm, rapture, passion, and despair, she is of the earth, but not earthly. When she glides before us through the light mazes of her fairy dance, or twangs her cithern to the notes of her homesick verses, or whirls her tambourine and hurries round us like an antique Mænad, we could almost fancy her a spirit; so pure is she, so full of fervor, so disengaged from the clay of this world. And when all the fearful particulars of her story are at length laid together, and we behold in connected order the image of her hapless existence, there is, in those dim recollections — those feelings so simple, so impassioned and unspeakable, consuming the closely shrouded, woe-struck, yet ethereal spirit of the poor creature — something which searches into the inmost recesses of the soul. It is not tears which her fate calls forth, but a feeling far too deep for tears. The very fire of heaven seems miserably quenched among the obstructions of this earth. Her little heart, so noble and so helpless, perishes before the smallest of its many beauties is unfolded; and all its loves and thoughts and longings do but add another pang to death, and sink to silence utter and eternal. It is as if the gloomy porch of Dis, and his pale kingdoms, were realized and set before us, and we heard the ineffectual wail of infants reverberating from within their prison-walls forever.

> *Continuo auditae voces, vagitus et ingens,*
> *Infantumque animae flentes in limine primo :*
> *Quos dulcis vitae exsortes, et ab ubere raptos,*
> *Abstulit atra dies, et funere mersit acerbo.*

The history of Mignon runs like a thread of gold through the tissue of the narrative, connecting with the heart much that were else addressed only to the head. Philosophy and eloquence might have done the rest, but this is poetry in the highest meaning of the word. It must be for the power of producing such creations and emotions, that Goethe is by many of his countrymen ranked at the side of Homer and Shakspeare, as one of the only three men of genius that have ever lived.

But my business here is not to judge of *Meister* or its author, it is only to prepare others for judging it; and for this purpose the most that I had room to say is said. All I ask in the name of this illustrious

foreigner is that the court which tries him be pure, and the jury instructed in the cause; that the work be not condemned for wanting
what it was not meant to have, and by persons nowise called to pass
sentence on it.

Respecting my own humble share in the adventure, it is scarcely
necessary to say anything. Fidelity is all the merit I have aimed at: to
convey the author's sentiments, as he himself expressed them; to follow the original, in all the variations of its style — has been my constant endeavor. In many points, both literary and moral, I could have
wished devoutly that he had not written as he has done; but to alter
anything was not in my commission. The literary and moral persuasions of a man like Goethe are objects of a rational curiosity, and the
duty of a translator is simple and distinct. Accordingly, except a few
phrases and sentences, not in all amounting to a page, which I have
dropped as evidently unfit for the English taste, I have studied to
present the work exactly as it stands in German. That my success has
been indifferent, I already know too well. In rendering the ideas of
Goethe, often so subtle, so capriciously expressive, the meaning was
not always easy to seize, or to convey with adequate effect. There were
thin tints of style, shades of ridicule or tenderness or solemnity, resting
over large spaces, and so slight as almost to be evanescent: some of
these I may have failed to see; to many of them I could do no justice.
Nor, even in plainer matters, can I pride myself in having always
imitated his colloquial familiarity without falling into sentences bald
and rugged, into idioms harsh or foreign; or in having copied the flowing oratory of other passages, without at times exaggerating or defacing
the swelling cadences and phrases of my original. But what work,
from the translating of a German novel to the writing of an epic, was
ever as the workman wished and meant it? This version of *Meister*,
with whatever faults it may have, I honestly present to my countrymen: if, while it makes any portion of them more familiar with the richest, most gifted of living minds, it increase their knowledge, or even
afford them a transient amusement, they will excuse its errors, and I
shall be far more than paid for all my labor.

THOMAS CARLYLE

Edinburgh, 1824

JOHANN WOLFGANG VON GOETHE

Wilhelm Meister's Apprenticeship

Book One

CHAPTER ONE

THE PLAY was late in breaking up: old Barbara went more than once to the window, and listened for the sound of carriages. She was waiting for Mariana, her pretty mistress, who had that night, in the afterpiece, been acting the part of a young officer, to the no small delight of the public. Barbara's impatience was greater than it used to be, when she had nothing but a frugal supper to present: on this occasion Mariana was to be surprised with a packet, which Norberg, a young and wealthy merchant, had sent by the post, to show that in absence he still thought of his love.

As an old servant, as confidante, counsellor, manager, and house-keeper, Barbara assumed the privilege of opening seals; and this evening she had the less been able to restrain her curiosity, as the favor of the open-handed gallant was more a matter of anxiety with herself than with her mistress. On breaking up the packet, she had found, with unfeigned satisfaction, that it held a piece of fine muslin and some ribbons of the newest fashion, for Mariana; with a quantity of calico, two or three neckerchiefs, and a moderate *rouleau* of money, for herself. Her esteem for the absent Norberg was of course unbounded: she meditated only how she might best present him to the mind of Mariana, best bring to her recollection what she owed him, and what he had a right to expect from her fidelity and thankfulness.

The muslin, with the ribbons half unrolled, to set it off by their colors, lay like a Christmas present on the small table; the position of the lights increased the glitter of the gilt; all was in order, when the old woman heard Mariana's step on the stairs, and hastened to meet her. But what was her disappointment, when the little female officer, without deigning to regard her caresses, rushed past her with unusual speed and agitation, threw her hat and sword upon the table, and walked hastily up and down, bestowing not a look on the lights, or any portion of the apparatus.

"What ails thee, my darling?" exclaimed the astonished Barbara. "For Heaven's sake, what is the matter? Look here, my pretty child! See what a present! And who could have sent it but thy kindest of friends? Norberg has given thee the muslin to make a night-gown of; he will soon be here himself; he seems to be fonder and more generous than ever."

Barbara went to the table, that she might exhibit the memorials with which Norberg had likewise honored *her*, when Mariana, turning away from the presents, exclaimed with vehemence, "Off! off! Not a word of all this to-night. I have yielded to thee; thou hast willed it; be it so! When Norberg comes, I am his, am thine, am any one's; make of me what thou pleasest; but till then I will be my own; and, if thou hadst a thousand tongues, thou shouldst never talk me from my purpose. All, all that *is* my own will I give up to him who loves me, whom I love. No sour faces! I will abandon myself to this affection, as if it were to last forever."

The old damsel had abundance of objections and serious considerations to allege: in the progress of this dialogue, she was growing bitter and keen, when Mariana sprang at her, and seized her by the breast. The old damsel laughed aloud. "I must have a care," she cried, "that you don't get into pantaloons again, if I mean to be sure of my life. Come, doff you! The girl will beg my pardon for the foolish things the boy is doing to me. Off with the frock. Off with them all. The dress beseems you not; it is dangerous for you, I observe; the epaulets make you too bold."

Thus speaking, she laid hands upon her mistress: Mariana pushed her off, exclaiming, "Not so fast! I expect a visit tonight."

"Visit!" rejoined Barbara: "you surely do not look for Meister, the young, soft-hearted, callow merchant's son?"

"Just for him," replied Mariana.

"Generosity appears to be growing your ruling passion," said the old woman with a grin: "you connect yourself with minors and moneyless people, as if they were the chosen of the earth. Doubtless it is charming to be worshipped as a benefactress."

"Jeer as thou pleasest. I love him! I love him! With what rapture do I now, for the first time, speak the word! *This* is the passion I have mimicked so often, when I knew not what it meant. Yes! I will throw myself about his neck: I will clasp him as if I could hold him forever. I will show him all my love, will enjoy all his in its whole extent."

"Moderate yourself," said the old dame coolly, "moderate yourself. A single word will interrupt your rapture: Norberg is coming! Coming in a fortnight! Here is the letter that arrived with the packet."

"And, though the morrow were to rob me of my friend, I would conceal it from myself and him. A fortnight! An age! Within a fortnight, what may not happen, what may not alter?"

Here Wilhelm entered. We need not say how fast she flew to meet him, with what rapture he clasped the red uniform, and pressed the beautiful wearer of it to his bosom. It is not for us to describe the blessedness of two lovers. Old Barbara went grumbling away: we shall retire with her, and leave the happy two alone.

WHEN WILHELM saluted his mother next morning, she informed him that his father was very greatly discontented with him, and meant to forbid him these daily visits to the playhouse. "Though I myself often go with pleasure to the theatre," she continued, "I could almost detest it entirely, when I think that our fireside-peace is broken by your excessive passion for that amusement. Your father is ever repeating, 'What is the use of it? How can any one waste his time so?' "

"He has told me this already," said Wilhelm, "and perhaps I answered him too hastily; but, for Heaven's sake, mother, is nothing, then, of use but what immediately puts money in our purse? but what procures us some property that we can lay our hands on? Had we not, for instance, room enough in the old house? and was it indispensable to build a new one? Does not my father every year expend a large part of his profit in ornamenting his chambers? Are these silk carpets, this English furniture, likewise of no use? Might we not content ourselves with worse? For my own part, I confess, these striped walls, these hundred times repeated flowers and knots and baskets and figures, produce a really disagreeable effect upon me. At best, they but remind me of the front curtain of our theatre. But what a different thing it is to sit and look at that! There, if you must wait for a while, you are always sure that it will rise at last, and disclose to you a thousand curious objects to entertain, to instruct, and to exalt you."

"But you go to excess with it," said the mother. "Your father wishes to be entertained in the evenings as well as you: besides, he thinks it diverts your attention; and, when he grows ill-humored on the subject, it is I that must bear the blame. How often have I been upbraided with that miserable puppet-show, which I was unlucky enough to provide for you at Christmas, twelve years ago! It was the first thing that put these plays into your head."

"Oh, do not blame the poor puppets! do not repent of your love and motherly care! It was the only happy hour I had enjoyed in the new empty house. I never can forget that hour; I see it still before me; I recollect how surprised I was, when, after we had got our customary

· 6 ·

presents, you made us seat ourselves before the door that leads to the other room. The door opened, but not, as formerly, to let us pass and repass: the entrance was occupied by an unexpected show. Within it rose a porch, concealed by a mysterious curtain. All of us were standing at a distance: our eagerness to see what glittering or jingling article lay hid behind the half-transparent veil was mounting higher and higher, when you bade us each sit down upon his stool, and wait with patience.

"At length all of us were seated and silent: a whistle gave the signal; the curtain rolled aloft, and showed us the interior of the temple, painted in deep-red colors. The high-priest Samuel appeared with Jonathan, and their strange alternating voices seemed to me the most striking thing on earth. Shortly after entered Saul, overwhelmed with confusion at the impertinence of that heavy-limbed warrior, who had defied him and all his people. But how glad was I when the little dapper son of Jesse, with his crook and shepherd's pouch and sling, came hopping forth, and said, 'Dread king and sovereign lord, let no one's heart sink down because of this: if your Majesty will grant me leave, I will go out to battle with this blustering giant!' Here ended the first act, leaving the spectators more curious than ever to see what further would happen; each praying that the music might soon be done. At last the curtain rose again. David devoted the flesh of the monster to the fowls of the air and the beasts of the field: the Philistine scorned and bullied him, stamped mightily with both his feet, and at length fell like a mass of clay, affording a splendid termination to the piece. And then the virgins sang, 'Saul hath slain his thousands, but David his ten thousands!' The giant's head was borne before his little victor, who received the king's beautiful daughter to wife. Yet withal, I remember, I was vexed at the dwarfish stature of this lucky prince; for the great Goliath and the small David had both been formed, according to the common notion, with a due regard to their figures and proportions. I pray you, mother, tell me what has now become of those puppets? I promised to show them to a friend, whom I was lately entertaining with a history of all this child's work."

"I can easily conceive," said the mother, "how these things should stick so firmly in your mind: I well remember what an interest you took in them, — how you stole the little book from me, and learned the whole piece by heart. I first noticed it one evening when you had made a Goliath and a David of wax : you set them both to declaim against each other, and at length gave a deadly stab to the giant, fixing his shapeless head, stuck upon a large pin with a wax handle, in little David's hand. I then felt such a motherly contentment at your fine recitation and good memory, that I resolved to give you up the whole wooden troop to your own disposal. I did not then foresee that it would cause me so many heavy hours."

"Do not repent of it,' said Wilhelm : "this little sport has often made us happy." So saying, he got the keys, made haste to find the puppets, and, for a moment, was transported back into those times when they almost seemed to him alive, when he felt as if he himself could give them life by the cunning of his voice and the movements of his hands. He took them to his room, and locked them up with care.

CHAPTER THREE

IF THE first love is indeed, as I hear it everywhere maintained to be, the most delicious feeling which the heart of man, before it or after, can experience, then our hero must be reckoned doubly happy, as permitted to enjoy the pleasure of this chosen period in all its fulness. Few men are so peculiarly favored : by far the greater part are led by the feelings of their youth into nothing but a school of hardship, where, after a stinted and checkered season of enjoyment, they are at length constrained to renounce their dearest wishes, and to learn forever to dispense with what once hovered before them as the highest happiness of existence.

Wilhelm's passion for that charming girl now soared aloft on the wings of imagination. After a short acquaintance, he had gained her affections : he found himself in possession of a being, whom, with all his heart, he not only loved, but honored; for she had first appeared

Wilhelm and Mariana

before him in the flattering light of theatric pomp, and his passion for the stage combined itself with his earliest love for woman. His youth allowed him to enjoy rich pleasures, which the activity of his fancy exalted and maintained. The situation of his mistress, too, gave a turn to her conduct which greatly enlivened his emotions. The fear lest her lover might, before the time, detect the real state in which she stood, diffused over all her conduct an interesting tinge of anxiety and bashfulness; her attachment to the youth was deep; her very inquietude appeared but to augment her tenderness; she was the loveliest of creatures while beside him.

When the first tumult of joy had passed, and our friend began to look back upon his life and its concerns, every thing appeared new to him: his duties seemed holier, his inclinations keener, his knowledge clearer, his talents stronger, his purposes more decided. Accordingly, he soon fell upon a plan to avoid the reproaches of his father, to still the cares of his mother, and, at the same time, to enjoy Mariana's love without disturbance. Through the day he punctually transacted his business, commonly forbore attending the theatre, strove to be entertaining at table in the evening; and, when all were asleep, he glided softly out into the garden, and hastened, wrapped up in his mantle, with all the feelings of Leander in his bosom, to meet his mistress without delay.

"What is this you bring?" inquired Mariana, as he entered one evening, with a bundle, which Barbara, in hopes it might turn out to be some valuable present, fixed her eyes upon with great attention. "You will never guess," said Wilhelm.

Great was the surprise of Mariana, great the scorn of Barbara, when the napkin, being loosened, gave to view a perplexed multitude of span-long puppets. Mariana laughed aloud, as Wilhelm set himself to disentangle the confusion of the wires, and show her each figure by itself. Barbara glided sulkily out of the room.

A very little thing will entertain two lovers; and accordingly our friends, this evening, were as happy as they wished to be. The little troop was mustered: each figure was minutely examined, and laughed at, in its turn. King Saul, with his golden crown and his black velvet robe, Mariana did not like: he looked, she said, too stiff and pedantic. She was far better pleased with Jonathan, his sleek chin, his turban, his cloak of red and yellow. She soon got the art of turning him deftly on his wire: she made him bow, and repeat declarations of love. On the other hand, she refused to give the least attention to the prophet Samuel; though Wilhelm commended the pontifical breastplate, and told her that the taffeta of the cassock had been taken from a gown of his own grandmother's. David she thought too small; Goliath was too big; she held by Jonathan. She grew to manage him so featly, and at last to extend her caresses from the puppet to its owner, that, on this occasion, as on others, a silly sport became the introduction to happy hours.

Their soft, sweet dreams were broken in upon by a noise which arose on the street. Mariana called for the old dame, who, as usual, was occupied in furbishing the changeful materials of the playhouse wardrobe for the service of the play next to be acted. Barbara said the disturbance arose from a set of jolly companions, who were just then sallying out of the Italian tavern hard by, where they had been busy discussing fresh oysters, a cargo of which had just arrived, and by no means sparing their champagne.

"Pity," Mariana said, "that we did not think of it in time: we might have had some entertainment to ourselves."

"It is not yet too late," said Wilhelm, giving Barbara a *louis-d'or*: "get us what we want, then come and take a share with us."

The old dame made speedy work: erelong a trimly covered table, with a neat collation, stood before the lovers. They made Barbara sit with them: they ate and drank, and enjoyed themselves.

On such occasions, there is never want of enough to say. Mariana soon took up little Jonathan again, and the old dame turned the conversation upon Wilhelm's favorite topic. "You were once telling us," she said, "about the first exhibition of a puppet-show on Christmas Eve: I remember you were interrupted just as the ballet was going to begin. We have now the pleasure of a personal acquaintance with the honorable company by whom those wonderful effects were brought about."

"Oh, yes!" cried Mariana: "do tell us how it all went on, and how you felt then."

"It is a fine emotion, Mariana," said the youth, "when we bethink ourselves of old times, and old, harmless errors, especially if this is at a period when we have happily gained some elevation, from which we can look around us, and survey the path we have left behind. It is so pleasant to think, with composure and satisfaction, of many obstacles, which often with painful feelings we may have regarded as invincible, — pleasant to compare what we now are with what we then were struggling to become. But I am happy above others in this matter, that I speak to you about the past, at a moment when I can also look forth into the blooming country, which we are yet to wander through together, hand in hand."

"But how was it with the ballet?" said Barbara. "I fear it did not quite go off as it should have done."

"I assure you," said Wilhelm, "it went off quite well. And certainly the strange caperings of these Moors and Mooresses, these shepherds and shepherdesses, these dwarfs and dwarfesses, will never altogether leave my recollection while I live. When the curtain dropped, and the door closed, our little party skipped away, frolicking as if they had been tipsy, to their beds. For myself, however, I remember that I could not go to sleep: still wanting to have something told me on the subject, I continued putting questions to every one, and would hardly let the maid away who had brought me up to bed.

"Next morning, alas! the magic apparatus had altogether vanished; the mysterious veil was carried off; the door permitted us again to go and come through it without obstruction; the manifold adventures of the evening had passed away, and left no trace behind. My brothers and sisters were running up and down with their playthings; I alone kept gliding to and fro: it seemed to me impossible that two bare doorposts could be all that now remained, where the night before so much enchantment had been displayed. Alas! the man that seeks a lost love can hardly be unhappier than I then thought myself."

A rapturous look, which he cast on Mariana, convinced her that he was not afraid of such ever being his case.

CHAPTER FOUR

"MY SOLE wish now," continued Wilhelm, "was to witness a second exhibition of the play. For this purpose I had recourse, by constant entreaties, to my mother; and she attempted in a favorable hour to persuade my father. Her labor, however, was in vain. My father's principle was, that none but enjoyments of rare occurrence were adequately prized; that neither young nor old could set a proper value on pleasures which they tasted every day.

"We might have waited long, perhaps till Christmas returned, had not the contriver and secret director of the spectacle himself felt a pleasure in repeating the display of it, partly incited, I suppose, by the wish to produce a brand-new harlequin expressly prepared for the afterpiece.

"A young officer of the artillery, a person of great gifts in all sorts of mechanical contrivance, had served my father in many essential particulars during the building of the house; for which, having been handsomely rewarded, he felt desirous of expressing his thankfulness to the family of his patron, and so made us young ones a present of this complete theatre, which, in hours of leisure, he had already carved and painted, and strung together. It was this young man, who, with the help of a servant, had himself managed the puppets, disguising his voice to pronounce their various speeches. He had no great difficulty in persuading my father, who granted, out of complaisance to a friend, what he had denied from conviction to his children. In short, our theatre was again set up, some little ones of the neighborhood were invited, and the play was again represented.

"If I had formerly experienced the delights of surprise and astonishment, I enjoyed on this second occasion the pleasure of examining and scrutinizing. *How* all this happened was my present concern. That the puppets themselves did not speak, I had already decided; that of themselves they did not move, I also conjectured; but, then, how came it all to be so pretty, and to look just as if they both spoke and moved of themselves? and where were the lights, and the people that managed the deception? These enigmas perplexed me the more, as I wished to be at the same time among the enchanters and the enchanted, at the same time to have a secret hand in the play, and to enjoy, as a looker-on, the pleasure of illusion.

"The play being finished, preparations were making for the farce: the spectators had risen, and were all busy talking together. I squeezed myself closer to the door, and heard, by the rattling within, that the people were packing up some articles. I lifted the lowest screen, and poked in my head between the posts. As our mother noticed it, she drew me back: but I had seen well enough that here friends and foes, Saul and Goliath, and whatever else their names might be, were lying quietly down together in a drawer; and thus my half-contented curiosity received a fresh excitement. To my great surprise, moreover, I had noticed the lieutenant very diligently occupied in the interior of the shrine. Henceforth, Jack-pudding, however he might clatter with his heels, could not any longer entertain me. I sank into deep meditation: my discovery made me both more satisfied, and less so, than before. After a little, it first struck me that I yet comprehended nothing: and here I was right; for the connection of the parts with each other was entirely unknown to me, and every thing depends on that."

CHAPTER FIVE

"IN WELL adjusted and regulated houses," continued Wilhelm, "children have a feeling not unlike what I conceive rats and mice to have: they keep a sharp eye on all crevices and holes, where they may come at any forbidden dainty; they enjoy it also with a fearful, stolen satisfaction, which forms no small part of the happiness of childhood.

"More than any other of the young ones, I was in the habit of looking out attentively, to see if I could notice any cupboard left open, or key standing in its lock. The more reverence I bore in my heart for those closed doors, on the outside of which I had to pass by for weeks and months, catching only a furtive glance when our mother now and then opened the consecrated place to take something from it, the quicker was I to make use of any opportunities which the forgetfulness of our housekeepers at times afforded me.

"Among all the doors, that of the storeroom was, of course, the one I watched most narrowly. Few of the joyful anticipations in life can equal the feeling which I used to have when my mother happened to call me, that I might help her to carry out something, whereupon I might pick up a few dried plums, either with her kind permission, or by help of my own dexterity. The accumulated treasures of this chamber took hold of my imagination by their magnitude: the very fragrance exhaled by so multifarious a collection of sweet-smelling spices produced such a craving effect on me, that I never failed, when passing near, to linger for a little, and regale myself at least on the unbolted atmosphere. At length, one Sunday morning, my mother, being hurried by the ringing of the church-bells, forgot to take this precious key with her on shutting the door, and went away, leaving all the house in a deep Sabbath stillness. No sooner had I marked this oversight than, gliding softly once or twice to and from the place, I at last approached very gingerly, opened the door, and felt myself, after a single step, in immediate contact with these manifold and long-wished-for means of happiness. I glanced over glasses, chests, and bags, and drawers and boxes, with a quick and doubtful eye, considering what I ought to choose and take; turned finally to my dear withered plums, provided myself also with a few dried apples, and completed the forage with an orange-chip. I was quietly retreating with my plunder, when some little chests, lying piled over one another, caught my attention, — the more so as I noticed a wire, with hooks at the end of it, sticking through the joint of the lid in one of them. Full of eager hopes, I opened this singular package; and judge of my emotions, when I found my glad world of heroes all sleeping safe within! I meant to pick out the topmost, and, having examined them, to pull up those below; but in this attempt the wires got very soon entangled: and I fell into a fright and flutter, more particularly as the cook just then began making some stir in the kitchen, which was close by; so that I had nothing for it but to squeeze the whole together the best way I could, and to shut the chest, having stolen from it nothing but a little written book, which happened to be lying above, and contained the whole drama of Goliath and David. With this booty I made good my retreat into the garret.

"Henceforth all my stolen hours of solitude were devoted to perusing the play, to learning it by heart, and picturing in thought how glorious it would be, could I but get the figures, to make them move along with it. In idea I myself became David and Goliath by turns. In every corner of the court-yard, of the stables, of the garden, under all kinds of circumstances, I labored to stamp the whole piece upon my mind; laid hold of all the characters, and learned their speeches by heart, most commonly, however, taking up the parts of the chief personages, and allowing all the rest to move along with them, but as satellites, across my memory. Thus day and night the heroic words of David, wherewith he challenged the braggart giant, Goliath of Gath, kept their place in my thoughts. I often muttered them to myself; while no one gave heed to me, except my father, who, frequently observing some such detached exclamation, would in secret praise the excellent memory of his boy, that had retained so much from only two recitations.

"By this means growing bolder and bolder, I one evening repeated almost the entire piece before my mother, whilst I was busied in fashioning some bits of wax into players. She observed it, questioned me hard; and I confessed.

"By good fortune, this detection happened at a time when the lieutenant had himself been expressing a wish to initiate me in the mysteries of the art. My mother forthwith gave him notice of these unexpected talents; and he now contrived to make my parents offer him a couple of chambers in the top story, which commonly stood empty, that he might accommodate the spectators in the one, while the other held his actors, the proscenium again filling up the opening of the door: my father had allowed his friend to arrange all this; himself, in the mean time, seeming only to look at the transaction, as it were, through his fingers; for his maxim was, that children should not be allowed to see the kindness which is felt towards them, lest their pretensions come to extend too far. He was of opinion, that, in the enjoyments of the young, one should assume a serious air; often interrupting the course of their festivities, to prevent their satisfaction from degenerating into excess and presumption."

CHAPTER SIX

"THE LIEUTENANT now set up his theatre, and managed all the rest. During the week I readily observed that he often came into the house at unusual hours, and I soon guessed the cause. My eagerness increased immensely; for I well understood, that, till Sunday evening, I could have no share in what was going on. At last the wished-for day arrived.

At five in the evening my conductor came, and took me up with him. Quivering with joy, I entered, and descried, on both sides of the frame-work, the puppets all hanging in order as they were to advance to view. I considered them narrowly, and mounted on the steps, which raised them above the scene, and allowed me to hover aloft over all that little world. Not without reverence did I look down between the pieces of board, and recollect what a glorious effect the whole would produce, and feel into what mighty secrets I was now admitted. We made a trial, which succeeded well.

"Next day a party of children were invited: we performed rarely; except that once, in the fire of action, I let poor Jonathan fall, and was obliged to reach down with my hand, and pick him up, — an accident which sadly marred the illusion, produced a peal of laughter, and vexed me unspeakably. My father, however, seemed to relish this misfortune not a little. Prudently shrouding up the contentment he felt at the expertness of his little boy, after the play was finished, he dwelt on the mistakes we had committed, saying it would all have been very pretty had not this or that gone wrong with us.

"I was vexed to the heart at these things, and sad for all the evening. By next morning, however, I had quite slept off my sorrow, and was blessed in the persuasion, that, but for this one fault, I had acted delightfully. The spectators also flattered me with their unanimous approval: they all maintained, that though the lieutenant, in regard to the coarse and the fine voices, had done great things, yet his declamation was in general too stiff and affected; whereas the new aspirant spoke his Jonathan and David with exquisite grace. My mother in particular commended the gallant tone in which I had challenged Goliath, and acted the modest victor before the king.

"From this time, to my extreme delight, the theatre continued open; and as the spring advanced, so that fires could be dispensed with, I passed all my hours of recreation lying in the garret, and making the puppets caper and play together. Often I invited up my comrades, or my brothers and sisters; but, when they would not come, I staid by myself not the less. My imagination brooded over that tiny world, which soon afterwards acquired another form.

"Scarcely had I once or twice exhibited the first play, for which my scenery and actors had been formed and decorated, when it ceased to give me any pleasure. On the other hand, among some of my grandfather's books, I had happened to fall in with 'The German Theatre,' and a few translations of Italian operas; in which works I soon got very deeply immersed, on each occasion first reckoning up the characters, and then, without further ceremony, proceeding to exhibit the play. King Saul, with his black velvet cloak, was therefore now obliged to personate Darius or Cato, or some other pagan hero; in which cases, it may be observed, the plays were never wholly represented, — for most part, only the fifth acts, where the cutting and stabbing lay.

"It was natural that the operas, with their manifold adventures and vicissitudes, should attract me more than any thing beside. In these compositions I found stormy seas, gods descending in chariots of cloud, and, what most of all delighted me, abundance of thunder and lightning. I did my best with pasteboard, paint, and paper: I could make night very prettily; my lightning was fearful to behold; only my thunder did not always prosper, which, however, was of less importance. In operas, moreover, I found frequent opportunities of introducing my David and Goliath, — persons whom the regular drama would hardly admit. Daily I felt more attachment for the hampered spot where I enjoyed so many pleasures; and, I must confess, the fragrance which the puppets had acquired from the storeroom added not a little to my satisfaction.

"The decorations of my theatre were now in a tolerable state of completeness. I had always had the knack of drawing with compasses, and clipping pasteboard, and coloring figures; and here it served me in good stead. But the more sorry was I, on the other hand, when, as frequently happened, my stock of actors would not suffice for representing great affairs.

"My sisters, dressing and undressing their dolls, awoke in me the project of furnishing my heroes by and by with garments which might also be put off and on. Accordingly, I slit the scraps of cloth from off their bodies, tacked the fragments together as well as possible, saved a particle of money to buy new ribbons and lace, begged many a rag of taffeta, and so formed, by degrees, a full theatrical wardrobe, in which hoop-petticoats for the ladies were especially remembered.

"My troop was now fairly provided with dresses for the most important play, and you might have expected that henceforth one exhibition would follow close upon the heels of another; but it happened with me, as it often happens with children, — they embrace wide plans, make mighty preparations, then a few trials, and the whole undertaking is abandoned. I was guilty of this fault. My greatest pleasure lay in the inventive part, and the employment of my fancy. This or that piece inspired me with interest for a few scenes of it, and immediately I set about providing new apparel suitable for the occasion. In such fluctuating operations, many parts of the primary dresses of my heroes had fallen into disorder, or totally gone out of sight; so that now the first great play could no longer be exhibited. I surrendered myself to my imagination; I rehearsed and prepared forever; built a thousand castles in the air, and failed to see that I was at the same time undermining the foundations of these little edifices."

During this recital, Mariana had called up and put in action all her courtesy for Wilhelm, that she might conceal her sleepiness. Diverting as the matter seemed on one side, it was too simple for her taste, and her lover's view of it too serious. She softly pressed her foot on his, however, and gave him all visible signs of attention and approval. She drank out of his glass: Wilhelm was convinced that no word of his history had fallen to the ground. After a short pause, he said, "It is now your turn, Mariana, to tell me what were your first childish joys. Till now we have always been too busy with the present to trouble ourselves, on either side, about our previous way of life. Let me hear, Mariana, under what circumstances you were reared: what are the first lively impressions which you still remember?"

These questions would have very much embarrassed Mariana, had not Barbara made haste to help her. "Think you," said the cunning old woman, "we have been so mindful of what happened to us long ago, that we have merry things like these to talk about, and, though we had, that we could give them such an air in talking of them?"

"As if they needed it!" cried Wilhelm. "I love this soft, good, amiable creature so much, that I regret every instant of my life which has not been spent beside her. Allow me, at least in fancy, to have a share in thy by-gone life; tell me everything; I will tell everything to thee! If possible, we will deceive ourselves, and win back those days that have been lost to love."

"If you require it so eagerly," replied the old dame, "we can easily content you. Only, in the first place, let us hear how your taste for the theatre gradually reached a head; how you practised, how you improved so happily, that now you can pass for a superior actor. No doubt you must have met with droll adventures in your progress. It is not worth while to go to bed now: I have still one flask in reserve; and who knows whether we shall soon all sit together so quiet and cheery again?"

Mariana cast upon her a mournful look, not noticed by Wilhelm, who proceeded with his narrative.

CHAPTER SEVEN

"The recreations of youth, as my companions began to increase in number, interfered with this solitary, still enjoyment. I was by turns a hunter, a soldier, a knight, as our games required; and constantly I had this small advantage above the rest, that I was qualified to furnish them suitably with the necessary equipments. The swords, for example, were generally of my manufacture; I gilded and decorated the scabbards; and a secret instinct allowed me not to stop till our militia was accoutred according to the antique model. Helmets, with plumes of paper, were got ready; shields, even coats of mail, were provided; undertakings in which such of the servants as had aught of the tailor in them, and the seamstresses of the house, broke many a needle.

"A part of my comrades I had now got well equipped; by degrees, the rest were likewise furbished up, though on a thriftier plan; and so a very seemly corps at length was mustered. We marched about the court-yards and gardens, smote fearfully upon each other's shields and heads: many flaws of discord rose among us, but none that lasted.

"This diversion greatly entertained my fellows; but scarcely had it been twice or thrice repeated, when it ceased to content me. The aspect of so many harnessed figures naturally stimulated in my mind those ideas of chivalry, which for some time, since I had commenced the reading of old romances, were filling my imagination.

"Koppen's translation of 'Jerusalem Delivered' at length fell into my hands, and gave these wandering thoughts a settled direction. The whole poem, it is true, I could not read; but there were passages which I learned by heart, and the images expressed in these hovered round me. Particularly was I captivated with Clorinda, and all her deeds and bearing. The masculine womanhood, the peaceful completeness of her being, had a greater influence upon my mind, just beginning to unfold itself, than the factitious charms of Armida; though the garden of that enchantress was by no means an object of my contempt.

"But a hundred and a hundred times, while walking in the evenings on the balcony which stretches along the front of the house, and looking over the neighborhood, as the quivering splendor streamed up at the horizon from the departed sun, and the stars came forth, and night pressed forward from every cleft and hollow, and the small, shrill tone of the cricket tinkled through the solemn stillness, — a hundred and a hundred times have I repeated to myself the history of the mournful duel between Tancred and Clorinda.

"However strongly I inclined by nature to the party of the Christians, I could not help declaring for the Paynim heroine with all my heart when she engaged to set on fire the great tower of the besiegers. And when Tancred in the darkness met the supposed knight, and the strife began between them under that veil of gloom, and the two battled fiercely, I could never pronounce the words, —

> " 'But now the sure and fated hour is nigh:
> Clorinda's course is ended, — she must die;' —

without tears rushing into my eyes, which flowed plentifully when the hapless lover, plunging his sword into her breast, opened the departing warrior's helmet, recognized the lady of his heart, and, shuddering, brought water to baptize her.

"How my heart ran over when Tancred struck with his sword that tree in the enchanted wood; when blood flowed from the gash, and a voice sounded in his ears, that now again he was wounding Clorinda; that Destiny had marked him out ever unwittingly to injure what he loved beyond all else.

"The recital took such hold of my imagination, that what I had read of the poem began dimly, in my mind, to conglomerate into a whole; wherewith I was so taken that I could not but propose to have it some way represented. I meant to have Tancred and Rinaldo acted; and, for this purpose, two coats of mail, which I had before manufactured, seemed expressly suitable. The one, formed of dark-gray paper with scales, was to serve for the solemn Tancred; the other, of silver and gilt paper, for the magnificent Rinaldo. In the vivacity of my anticipations, I told the whole project to my comrades, who felt quite charmed with it, except that they could not well comprehend how so glorious a thing could be exhibited, and, above all, exhibited by them.

"Such scruples I easily set aside. Without hesitation, I took upon me, in idea, the management of two rooms in the house of a neighboring playmate; not calculating that his venerable aunt would never give them up, or considering how a theatre could be made of them, whereof I had no settled notion, except that it was to be fixed on beams, to have side-scenes made of parted folding-screens, and on the floor a large piece of cloth. From what quarter these materials and furnishings were to come, I had not determined.

"So far as concerned the forest, we fell upon a good expedient. We betook ourselves to an old servant of one of our families, who had now become a woodman, with many entreaties that he would get us a few young firs and birches; which actually arrived more speedily than we had reason to expect. But, in the next place, great was our embarrassment as to how the piece should be got up before the trees were withered. Now was the time for prudent counsel. We had no house, no scenery, no curtain: the folding-screens were all we had.

"In this forlorn condition we again applied to the lieutenant, giving him a copious description of all the glorious things we meant to do. Little as he understood us, he was very helpful: he piled all the tables he could get in the house or neighborhood, one above the other, in a little room: to these he fixed our folding-screens, and made a back-view with green curtains, sticking up our trees along with it.

"At length the appointed evening came: the candles were lit, the maids and children were sitting in their places, the piece was to go forward, the whole corps of heroes was equipped and dressed, — when each for the first time discovered that he knew not what he was to say.

In the heat of invention, being quite immersed in present difficulties, I had forgotten the necessity of each understanding what and where he was to speak; nor, in the midst of our bustling preparations, had it once occurred to the rest; each believing he could easily enact a hero, easily so speak and bear himself, as became the personage into whose world I had transplanted him. They all stood wonder-struck, asking, What was to come first? I alone, having previously got ready Tancred's part, entered *solus* on the scene, and began reciting some verses of the epic. But as the passage soon changed into narrative, and I, while speaking, was at once transformed into a third party, and the bold Godfredo, when his turn came, would not venture forth, I was at last obliged to take leave of my spectators under peals of laughter, — a disaster which cut me to the heart. Thus had our undertaking proved abortive; but the company still kept their places, still wishing to see something. All of us were dressed: I screwed my courage up, and determined, foul or fair, to give them David and Goliath. Some of my companions had before this helped me to exhibit the puppet-play; all of them had often seen it; we shared the characters among us; each promised to do his best; and one small, grinning urchin painted a black beard upon his chin, and undertook, if any *lacuna* should occur, to fill it with drollery as harlequin, — an arrangement to which, as contradicting the solemnity of the piece, I did not consent without extreme reluctance; and I vowed within myself, that, if once delivered out of this perplexity, I would think long and well before risking the exhibition of another play."

CHAPTER EIGHT

MARIANA, OVERPOWERED with sleep, leaned upon her lover, who clasped her close to him, and proceeded in his narrative; while the old damsel prudently sipped up the remainder of the wine.

"The embarrassment," he said, "into which, along with my companions, I had fallen, by attempting to act a play that did not anywhere exist, was soon forgotten. My passion for representing each romance I read, each story that was told me, would not yield before the most unmanageable materials. I felt convinced that whatever gave delight in narrative must produce a far deeper impression when exhibited: I wanted to have every thing before my eyes, every thing brought forth upon the stage. At school, when the elements of general history were related to us, I carefully marked the passages where any person had been slain or poisoned in a singular way; and my imagination, glancing rapidly along the exposition and intrigue, hastened to the interesting fifth act. Indeed, I actually began to write some plays from the end backwards, without, however, in any of them reaching the beginning.

"At the same time, partly by inclination, partly by the counsel of my good friends, who had caught the fancy of acting plays, I read a whole wilderness of theatrical productions, as chance put them into my hands. I was still in those happy years when all things please us, when number and variety yield us abundant satisfaction. Unfortunately, too, my taste was corrupted by another circumstance. Any piece delighted me especially, in which I could hope to give delight; there were few which I did not peruse in this agreeable delusion: and my lively conceptive power enabling me to transfer myself into all the characters, seduced me to believe that I might likewise represent them all. Hence, in the distribution of the parts, I commonly selected such as did not fit me, and always more than one part, if I could by any means accomplish more.

"In their games, children can make all things out of any: a staff becomes a musket, a splinter of wood a sword, any bunch of cloth a puppet, any crevice a chamber. Upon this principle was our private theatre got up. Totally unacquainted with the measure of our strength, we undertook all: we stuck at no *quid pro quo*, and felt convinced that every one would take us for what we gave ourselves out to be. Now, however, our affairs went on so soberly and smoothly, that I have not even a curious insipidity to tell you of. We first acted all the few plays in which only males are requisite, next we travestied some of ourselves, and at last took our sisters into the concern along with us. In one or two houses, our amusement was looked upon as profitable;

and company was invited to see it. Nor did our lieutenant of artillery now turn his back upon us. He showed us how we ought to make our exits and our entrances; how we should declaim, and with what attitudes and gestures. Yet generally he earned small thanks for his toil, we conceiving ourselves to be much deeper in the secrets of theatrical art than he himself was.

"We very soon began to grow tired of tragedy; for all of us believed, as we had often heard, that it was easier to write or represent a tragedy than to attain proficiency in comedy. In our first attempts, accordingly, we had felt as if exactly in our element: dignity of rank, elevation of character, we studied to approach by stiffness and affectation, and imagined that we succeeded rarely; but our happiness was not complete, except we might rave outright, might stamp with our feet, and, full of fury and despair, cast ourselves upon the ground.

"Boys and girls had not long carried on these amusements in concert, till Nature began to take her course; and our society branched itself off into sundry little love-associations, as generally more than one sort of comedy is acted in the playhouse. Behind the scenes, each happy pair pressed hands in the most tender style; they floated in blessedness, appearing to one another quite ideal persons, when so transformed and decorated; whilst, on the other hand, unlucky rivals consumed themselves with envy, and out of malice and spite worked every species of mischief.

"Our amusements, though undertaken without judgment, and carried on without instruction, were not without their use to us. We trained our memories and persons, and acquired more dexterity in speech and gesture than is usually met with at so early an age. But, for me in particular, this time was in truth an epoch: my mind turned all its faculties exclusively to the theatre; and my highest happiness was in reading, in writing, or in acting, plays.

"Meanwhile the labors of my regular teachers continued: I had been set apart for the mercantile life, and placed under the guidance of our neighbor in the counting-house; yet my spirit at this very time recoiled more forcibly than ever from all that was to bind me to a low profession. It was to the stage that I aimed at consecrating all my powers, — on the stage that I meant to seek all my happiness and satisfaction.

"I recollect a poem, which must be among my papers, where the Muse of tragic art and another female form, by which I personified Commerce, were made to strive very bravely for my most important self. The idea is common, nor do I recollect that the verses were of any worth; but you shall see it, for the sake of the fear, the abhorrence, the love and passion, which are prominent in it. How repulsively did I paint the old housewife, with the distaff in her girdle, the bunch of keys by her side, the spectacles on her nose, ever toiling, ever restless, quarrelsome and penurious, pitiful and dissatisfied! How feelingly did I describe the condition of that poor man who has to cringe beneath her rod, and earn his slavish day's wages by the sweat of his brow!

"And how differently advanced the other! What an apparition for the overclouded mind! Formed as a queen, in her thoughts and looks she announced herself the child of freedom. The feeling of her own worth gave her dignity without pride: her apparel became her, it veiled her form without constraining it; and the rich folds repeated, like a thousand-voiced echo, the graceful movements of the goddess. What a contrast! How easy for me to decide! Nor had I forgotten the more peculiar characteristics of my Muse. Crowns and daggers, chains and masks, as my predecessors had delivered them, were here produced once more. The contention was keen: the speeches of both were palpably enough contrasted, for at fourteen years of age one usually paints the black lines and the white pretty near each other. The old lady spoke as beseemed a person that would pick up a pin from her path; the other, like one that could give away kingdoms. The warning threats of the housewife were disregarded; I turned my back upon her promised riches: disinherited and naked, I gave myself up to the Muse; she threw her golden veil over me, and called me hers.

"Could I have thought, my dearest," he exclaimed, pressing Mariana close to him, "that another, a more lovely goddess would come to encourage me in my purpose, to travel with me on my journey, the poem might have had a finer turn, a far more interesting end. Yet it is no poetry, it is truth and life that I feel in thy arms: let us prize the sweet happiness, and consciously enjoy it."

The pressure of his arms, the emotion of his elevated voice, awoke Mariana, who hastened by caresses to conceal her embarrassment; for no word of the last part of his story had reached her. It is to be wished, that in future, our hero, when recounting his favorite histories, may find more attentive hearers.

CHAPTER NINE

THUS WILHELM passed his nights in the enjoyment of confiding love, his days in the expectation of new happy hours. When desire and hope had first attracted him to Mariana, he already felt as if inspired with new life; felt as if he were beginning to be another man: he was now united to her; the contentment of his wishes had become a delicious habitude. His heart strove to ennoble the object of his passion; his spirit, to exalt with it the young creature whom he loved. In the shortest absence, thoughts of her arose within him. If she had once been necessary to him, she was now grown indispensable, now that he was bound to her by all the ties of nature. His pure soul felt that she was the half, more than the half, of himself. He was grateful and devoted without limit.

Mariana, too, succeeded in deceiving herself for a season: she shared with him the feeling of his liveliest blessedness. Alas! if but the cold hand of self-reproach had not often come across her heart! She was not secure from it, even in Wilhelm's bosom, even under the wings of his love. And when she was again left alone, again left to sink from the clouds, to which passion had exalted her, into the consciousness of her real condition, then she was indeed to be pitied. So long as she had lived among degrading perplexities, disguising from herself her real situation, or rather never thinking of it, frivolity had helped her through; the incidents she was exposed to had come upon her each by itself; satisfaction and vexation had cancelled one another; humiliation had been compensated by vanity; want by frequent, though momentary, superfluity: she could plead necessity and custom as a law or an excuse; and hitherto all painful emotions from hour to hour, and from day to day, had by these means been shaken off. But now, for some instants, the poor girl had felt herself transported to a better world; aloft, as it were, in the midst of light and joy, she had looked down upon the abject desert of her life, had felt what a miserable creature is the woman, who, inspiring desire, does not also inspire reverence and love: she regretted and repented, but found herself outwardly or inwardly no better for regret. She had nothing that she could accomplish or resolve upon. When she looked into and searched herself, all was waste and void within her soul: her heart had no place of strength or refuge. But the more sorrowful her state was, the more vehemently did her feelings cling to the man she loved: her passion for him even waxed stronger daily, as the danger of losing him came daily nearer.

Wilhelm, on the other hand, soared serenely happy in higher regions: to him also a new world had been disclosed, but a world rich in the most glorious prospects. Scarcely had the first excess of joy subsided, when all that had long been gliding dimly through his soul stood up in bright distinctness before it. She is mine! She has given herself up to me! She, the loved, the wished for, the adored, has given herself up to me in truth and faith: she shall not find me ungrateful for the gift. Standing or walking, he talked to himself; his heart constantly overflowed; with a copiousness of splendid words, he uttered to himself the loftiest emotions. He imagined that he understood the visible beckoning of Fate, reaching out its hand by Mariana to save him from the stagnant, weary, drudging life, out of which he had so often wished for deliverance. To leave his father's house and people, now appeared a light matter. He was young, and had not tried the world: his eagerness to range over its expanses, seeking fortune and contentment, was stimulated by his love. His vocation for the theatre was now clear to him: the high goal, which he saw raised before him, seemed nearer whilst he was advancing to it with Mariana's hand in his; and, in his comfortable prudence, he beheld in himself the embryo of a great actor, — the future founder of that national theatre, for which he heard so much and various sighing on every side. All that till now had slumbered in the innermost corners of his soul, at length awoke. He painted for himself a picture of his manifold ideas, in the colors of love, upon a canvas of cloud: the figures of it, indeed, ran sadly into one another; yet the whole had an air but the more brilliant on that account.

HE WAS now in his chamber at home, ransacking his papers, making ready for departure. Whatever savored of his previous employment he threw aside, meaning at his entrance upon life to be free, even from recollections that could pain him. Works of taste alone, poets and critics, were, as acknowledged friends, placed among the chosen few. Heretofore he had given little heed to the critical authors; his desire for instruction now revived, when, again looking through his books, he found the theoretical part of them lying generally still uncut. In the full persuasion that such works were absolutely necessary, he had bought a number of them; but, with the best disposition in the world, he had not reached midway in any.

The more steadfastly, on the other hand, he had dwelt upon examples, and, in every kind that was known to him, had made attempts himself.

Werner entered the room; and, seeing his friend busied with the well-known sheets, he exclaimed, "Again among your papers? And without intending, I dare swear, to finish any one of them! You look them through and through once or twice, then throw them by, and begin something new."

"To finish is not the scholar's care: it is enough if he improves himself by practice."

"But also completes according to his best ability."

"And still the question might be asked, 'Is there not good hope of a youth, who, on commencing some unsuitable affair, soon discovers its unsuitableness, and discontinues his exertions, not choosing to spend toil and time on what never can be of any value?' "

"I know well enough it was never your concern to bring aught to a conclusion: you have always sickened on it before it came half way. When you were the director of our puppet-show, for instance, how many times were fresh clothes got ready for the dwarfish troop, fresh decorations furbished up? Now this tragedy was to be acted, now that; and at the very best you gave us some fifth act, where all was going topsy-turvy, and people cutting one another's throats."

"If you talk of those times, whose blame really was it that we ripped off from our puppets the clothes that fitted them, and were fast stitched to their bodies, and laid out money for a large and useless wardrobe? Was it not yours, my good friend, who had always some fragment of ribbon to traffic with; and skill, at the same time, to stimulate my taste, and turn it to your profit?"

Werner laughed, and continued, "I still recollect, with pleasure, how I used to extract gain from your theatrical campaigns, as army contractors do from war. When you mustered for the 'Deliverance of Jerusalem,' I, for my part, made a pretty thing of profit, like the Venetians in the corresponding case. I know of nothing in the world more rational than to turn the folly of others to our own advantage."

"Perhaps it were a nobler satisfaction to cure men of their follies."

"From the little I know of men, this might seem a vain endeavor. But something towards it is always done, when any individual man grows wise and rich; and generally this happens at the cost of others."

"Well, here is 'The Youth at the Parting of the Ways': it has just come into my hand," said Wilhelm, drawing out a bunch of papers from the rest; "this at least is finished, whatever else it may be."

"Away with it! to the fire with it!" cried Werner. "The invention does not deserve the smallest praise: that affair has plagued me enough already, and drawn upon yourself your father's wrath. The verses may be altogether beautiful, but the meaning of them is fundamentally false. I still recollect your Commerce personified: a shrivelled, wretched-looking sibyl she was. I suppose you picked up the image of her from some miserable huckster's shop. At that time you had no true idea at all of trade; whilst I could not think of any man whose spirit was, or needed to be, more enlarged than the spirit of a genuine merchant. What a thing is it to see the order which prevails throughout his business! By means of this he can at any time survey the general whole, without needing to perplex himself in the details. What advantages does he derive from the system of book-keeping by double entry! It is among the finest inventions of the human mind: every prudent master of a house should introduce it into his economy."

"Pardon me," said Wilhelm, smiling; "you begin by the form, as if it were the matter: you traders commonly, in your additions and balancings, forget what is the proper net result of life."

"My good friend, you do not see how form and matter are in this case one, how neither can exist without the other. Order and arrangement increase the desire to save and get. A man embarrassed in his circumstances, and conducting them imprudently, likes best to continue in the dark: he will not gladly reckon up the debtor entries he is charged with. But, on the other hand, there is nothing to a prudent manager more pleasant than daily to set before himself the sums of his growing fortune. Even a mischance, if it surprise and vex, will not affright, him; for he knows at once what gains he has acquired to cast into the other scale. I am convinced, my friend, that, if you once had a proper taste for our employments, you would grant that many faculties of the mind are called into full and vigorous play by them."

"Possibly this journey I am thinking of may bring me to other thoughts."

"Oh, certainly! Believe me, you want but to look upon some

great scene of activity to make you ours forever; and, when you come back, you will joyfully enroll yourself among that class of men whose art it is to draw towards themselves a portion of the money, and materials of enjoyment, which circulate in their appointed courses through the world. Cast a look on the natural and artificial productions of all the regions of the earth; consider how they have become, one here, another there, articles of necessity for men. How pleasant and how intellectual a task is it to calculate, at any moment, what is most required, and yet is wanting, or hard to find; to procure for each easily and soon what he demands; to lay in your stock prudently beforehand, and then to enjoy the profit of every pulse in that mighty circulation. This, it appears to me, is what no man that has a head can attend to without pleasure."

Wilhelm seemed to acquiesce, and Werner continued.

"Do but visit one or two great trading-towns, one or two sea-ports, and see if you can withstand the impression. When you observe how many men are busied, whence so many things have come, and whither they are going, you will feel as if you, too, could gladly mingle in the business. You will then see the smallest piece of ware in its connection with the whole mercantile concern; and for that very reason you will reckon nothing paltry, because every thing augments the circulation by which you yourself are supported."

Werner had formed his solid understanding in constant intercourse with Wilhelm: he was thus accustomed to think also of *his* profession, of *his* employments, with elevation of soul; and he firmly believed that he did so with more justice than his otherwise more gifted and valued friend, who, as it seemed to him, had placed his dearest hopes, and directed all the force of his mind, upon the most imaginary objects in the world. Many a time he thought his false enthusiasm would infallibly be got the better of, and so excellent a soul be brought back to the right path. So hoping in the present instance, he continued, "The great ones of the world have taken this earth of ours to themselves: they live in the midst of splendor and superfluity. The smallest nook of the land is already a possession which none may touch or meddle with: offices and civil callings bring in little profit. Where, then, will you find more honest acquisitions, juster conquests, than those of trade? If the princes of this world hold the rivers, the highways, the havens, in their power, and take a heavy tribute from every thing that passes through them, may not we embrace with joy the opportunity of levying tax and toll, by *our* activity, on those commodities which the real or imaginary wants of men have rendered indispensable? I can promise you, if you would rightly apply your poetic view, my goddess might be represented as an invincible, victorious queen, and boldly opposed to yours. It is true, she bears the olive rather than the sword: dagger or chain she knows not. But she, too, gives crowns to her favorites; which, without offence to yours be it said, are of true gold from the furnace and the mine, and glance with genuine pearls, which she brings up from the depths of the ocean by the hands of her unwearied servants."

This sally somewhat nettled Wilhelm; but he concealed his sentiments, remembering that Werner used to listen with composure to *his* apostrophes. Besides, he had fairness enough to be pleased at seeing each man think the best of his own peculiar craft, provided only *his*, of which he was so passionately fond, were likewise left in peace.

"And for you," exclaimed Werner, "who take so warm an interest in human concerns, what a sight will it be to behold the fortune, which accompanies bold undertakings, distributed to men before your eyes! What is more spirit-stirring than the aspect of a ship arriving from a lucky voyage, or soon returning with a rich capture? Not only the relatives, the acquaintances, and those that share with the adventurers, but every unconcerned spectator also, is excited, when he sees the joy with which the long-imprisoned shipman springs on land before his keel has wholly reached it, feeling that he is free once more, and now can trust what he has rescued from the false sea to the firm and faithful earth. It is not, my friend, in figures of arithmetic alone that gain presents itself before us. Fortune is the goddess of breathing men: to feel her favors truly, we must live and be men who toil with their living minds and bodies, and enjoy with them also."

CHAPTER ELEVEN

IT IS now time that we should know something more of Wilhelm's father and of Werner's, — two men of very different modes of thinking, but whose opinions so far coincided, that both regarded commerce as the noblest calling; and both were peculiarly attentive to every advantage which any kind of speculation might produce to them. Old Meister, when his father died, had turned into money a valuable collection of pictures, drawings, copper-plates, and antiquities: he had entirely rebuilt and furnished his house in the newest style, and turned his other property to profit in all possible ways. A considerable portion of it he had embarked in trade, under the direction of the elder Werner, — a man noted as an active merchant, whose speculations were commonly favored by fortune. But nothing was so much desired by Meister as to confer upon his son those qualities of which himself was destitute, and to leave his children advantages which he reckoned it of the highest importance to possess. Withal, he felt a peculiar inclination for magnificence, — for whatever catches the eye, and possesses at the same time real worth and durability. In his house he would have all things solid and massive: his stores must be copious and rich, all his plate must be heavy, the furniture of his table must be costly. On the other hand, his guests were seldom invited; for every dinner was a festival, which, both for its expense and for its inconvenience, could not often be repeated. The economy of his house went on at a settled, uniform rate; and every thing that moved or had place in it was just what yielded no one any real enjoyment.

The elder Werner, in his dark and hampered house, led quite another sort of life. The business of the day, in his narrow counting-house, at his ancient desk, once done, Werner liked to eat well, and, if possible, to drink better. Nor could he fully enjoy good things in solitude: with his family he must always see at table his friends, and any stranger that had the slightest connection with his house. His chairs were of unknown age and antic fashion, but he daily invited some to sit on them. The dainty victuals arrested the attention of his guests, and none remarked that they were served up in common ware. His cellar held no great stock of wine, but the emptied niches were usually filled by more of a superior sort.

So lived these two fathers, often meeting to take counsel about their common concerns. On the day we are speaking of, it had been determined to send Wilhelm out from home, for the despatch of some commercial affairs.

"Let him look about him in the world," said old Meister, "and at the same time carry on our business in distant parts. One cannot do a young man any greater kindness than initiate him early in the future business of his life. Your son returned so happily from his first expedition, and transacted his affairs so cleverly, that I am very curious to see how mine will do: *his* experience, I fear, will cost him dearer."

Old Meister had a high notion of his son's faculties and capabilities: he said this in the hope that his friend would contradict him, and hold up to view the admirable gifts of the youth. Here, however, he deceived himself. Old Werner, who, in practical concerns, would trust no man but such as he had proved, answered placidly, "One must try all things. We can send him on the same journey: we shall give him a paper of directions to conduct him. There are sundry debts to be gathered in, old connections are to be renewed, new ones to be made. He may likewise help the speculation I was lately talking of; without punctual intelligence gathered on the spot, there is little to be done in it."

"He must prepare," said Meister, "and set forth as soon as possible. Where shall we get a horse for him to suit this business?"

"We shall not seek far. The shopkeeper in H———, who owes us somewhat, but is withal a good man, has offered me a horse instead of payment. My son knows it, and tells me it is a serviceable beast."

"He may fetch it himself. Let him go with the diligence; the day after to-morrow he is back again betimes; we have his saddle-bags and letters made ready in the mean time; he can set out on Monday morning."

Wilhelm was sent for, and informed of their determination. Who so glad as he, now seeing the means of executing his purpose put into his hands, the opportunity made ready for him, without co-operation of his own! So intense was his love, so full was his conviction of the perfect rectitude of his intention to escape from the pressure of his actual mode of life, and follow a new and nobler career, that his conscience did not in the least rebel; no anxiety arose within him; he even reckoned the deception he was meditating holy. He felt certain, that, in the long-run, parents and relations would praise and bless him for this resolution: he acknowledged in these concurring circumstances the signal of a guiding fate.

How slowly the time passed with him till night, till the hour when he should again see his Mariana! He sat in his chamber, and revolved the plan of his journey; as a conjurer, or a cunning thief in durance, often draws out his feet from the fast-locked irons, to cherish in himself the conviction that his deliverance is possible, nay nearer than short-sighted turnkeys believe.

At last the appointed hour struck: he went out, shook off all anxiety, and hastened through the silent streets. In the middle of the great square he raised his hands to the sky, feeling as if all was behind him and below him: he had freed himself from all. One moment he figured himself as in the arms of his beloved, the next as glancing with her at the splendors of the stage: he soared aloft in a world of hopes, only now and then the call of some watchman brought to his recollection that he was still wandering on the vulgar earth.

Mariana came to the stairs to meet him, — and how beautiful, how lovely! She received him in the new white *négligé:* he thought he had never seen her so charming. Thus did she handsel the gift of her absent lover in the arms of a present one; with true passion she lavished on her darling the whole treasure of those caresses which nature suggested, or art had taught: need we ask if he was happy, if he was blessed?

He disclosed to her what had passed, and showed her, in general terms, his plan and his wishes. He would try, he said, to find a residence, then come back for her: he hoped she would not refuse him her hand. The poor girl was silent: she concealed her tears, and pressed her friend against her bosom. Wilhelm, though interpreting her silence in the most favorable manner, could have wished for a distinct reply; and still more, when at last he inquired of her in the tenderest and most delicate terms, if he might not think himself a father. But to this she answered only with a sigh, with a kiss.

CHAPTER TWELVE

NEXT MORNING Mariana awoke only to new despondency; she felt herself very solitary; she wished not to see the light of day, but staid in bed, and wept. Old Barbara sat down by her, and tried to persuade and console her; but it was not in her power so soon to heal the wounded heart. The moment was now at hand to which the poor girl had been looking forward as to the last of her life. Who could be placed in a more painful situation? The man she loved was departing; a disagreeable lover was threatening to come; and the most fearful mischiefs were to be anticipated, if the two, as might easily happen, should meet together.

"Calm yourself, my dear," said the old woman: "do not spoil your pretty eyes with crying. Is it, then, so terrible a thing to have two lovers? And though you can bestow your love but on the one, yet be thankful to the other, who, caring for you as he does, certainly deserves to be named your friend."

"My poor Wilhelm," said the other, all in tears, "had warning that a separation was at hand. A dream discovered to him what we strove so much to hide. He was sleeping calmly at my side; on a sudden I heard him mutter some unintelligible sounds: I grew frightened, and awoke him. Ah! with what love and tenderness and warmth did he clasp me! 'O Mariana!' cried he, 'what a horrid fate have you freed me from! How shall I thank you for deliverance from such torment? I dreamed that I was far from you in an unknown country, but your figure hovered before me; I saw you on a beautiful hill, the sunshine was glancing over it all; how charming you looked! But it had not lasted long, before I observed your image sinking down, sinking, sinking: I stretched out my arms towards you; they could not reach you through the distance. Your image still kept gliding down: it approached a great sea that lay far extended at the foot of the hill, — a marsh rather than a sea. All at once a man gave you his hand, and seemed meaning to conduct you upwards; but he led you sidewards, and appeared to draw you after him. I cried out: as I could not reach you, I hoped to warn you. If I tried to walk, the ground seemed to hold me fast; if I could walk, the water hindered me; and even my cries were smothered in my breast.' So said the poor youth, while recovering from his terror, and reckoning himself happy to see a frightful dream thrust aside by the most delicious reality."

Barbara made every effort to reduce, by her prose, the poetry of her friend to the domain of common life; employing, in the present case, the ingenious craft which so often succeeds with bird-catchers, when they imitate with a whistle the tones of those luckless creatures they soon hope to see by dozens safely lodged in their nets. She praised Wilhelm: she expatiated on his figure, his eyes, his love. The poor girl heard her with a gratified heart, then arose, let herself be dressed, and appeared calmer. "My child, my darling," continued the old woman, in a cozening tone, "I will not trouble you or injure you: I cannot think of tearing from you your dearest happiness. Could you mistake my intention? Have you forgotten that on all occasions I have cared for you more than for myself? Tell me only what you wish: we shall soon see how it may be brought about."

"What can I wish?" said Mariana; "I am miserable, miserable for life: I love him, and he loves me; yet I see that I must part with him, and know not how I shall survive it. Norberg is coming, to whom we owe our whole subsistence, whom we cannot live without. Wilhelm is straitened in his fortune: he can do nothing for me."

"Yes, unfortunately, he is of those lovers who bring nothing but their hearts; and these people, too, have the highest pretensions of any."

"No jesting! The unhappy youth thinks of leaving his home, of going upon the stage, of offering me his hand."

"Of empty hands we have already four."

"I have no choice," continued Mariana: "do you decide for me. Cast me away to this side or to that: mark only one thing, — I think I carry in my bosom a pledge that ought to unite me with him still more closely. Consider and determine: whom shall I forsake? whom shall I follow?"

After a short silence, Barbara exclaimed, "Strange, that youth should always be for extremes! To my view, nothing would be easier than for us to combine both the profit and the enjoyment. Do you love the one, let the other pay for it: all we have to mind, is being sharp enough to keep the two from meeting."

"Do as you please: I can imagine nothing, but I will obey."

"We have this advantage: we can humor the manager's caprice and pride about the morals of his troop. Both lovers are accustomed already to go secretly and cautiously to work. For hours and opportunity I will take thought: only henceforth you must act the part that I prescribe to you. Who knows what circumstances may arise to help us? If Norberg would arrive even now, when Wilhelm is away! Who can hinder you from thinking of the one in the arms of the other? I wish you a son, and good fortune with him: he will have a rich father."

These projects lightened Mariana's despondency only for a very short time. She could not bring her situation into harmony with her feelings, with her convictions: she would fain have forgotten the painful relations in which she stood, and a thousand little circumstances forced them back every moment to her recollection.

IN THE mean time, Wilhelm had completed the short preliminary journey. His merchant being from home, he delivered the letter of introduction to the mistress of the house. But neither did this lady give him much furtherance in his purposes: she was in a violent passion, and her whole economy was in confusion.

He had not waited long when she disclosed to him, what in truth could not be kept a secret, that her step-daughter had run off with a player, — a person who had parted lately from a small strolling company, and had staid in the place, and commenced teaching French. The father, distracted with grief and vexation, had run to the *Amt* to have the fugitives pursued. She blamed her daughter bitterly, and vilified the lover, till she left no tolerable quality with either: she deplored at great length the shame thus brought upon the family; embarrassing our hero not a little, who here felt his own private scheme beforehand judged and punished, in the spirit of prophecy as it were, by this frenzied sibyl. Still stronger and deeper was the interest he took in the sorrows of the father, who now returned from the *Amt,* and with fixed sorrow, in broken sentences, gave his wife an account of the errand, and strove to hide the embarrassment and distraction of his mind; while, after looking at the letter, he directed that the horse it spoke of should be given to Wilhelm.

Our friend thought it best to mount his steed immediately, and quit a house where, in its present state, he could not possibly be comfortable; but the honest man would not allow the son of one to whom he had so many obligations to depart without tasting of his hospitality, without remaining at least a night beneath his roof.

Wilhelm had partaken of a melancholy supper, worn out a restless night, and hastened, early in the morning, to get rid of these people, who, without knowing it, had, by their narratives and utterances, been constantly wounding him to the quick.

In a musing mood, he was riding slowly along, when all at once he observed a number of armed men coming through the fields. By their long, loose coats, with enormous cuffs; by their shapeless hats, clumsy muskets; by their unpretending gait, and contented bearing of the body, — he recognized in these people a detachment of provincial militia. They halted beneath an old oak, set down their fire-arms, and placed themselves at their ease upon the sward, to smoke a pipe of tobacco. Wilhelm lingered near them, and entered into conversation with a young man who came up on horseback. The history of the two runaways, which he knew but too well, was again detailed to him, and that with comments not particularly flattering, either to the young pair themselves, or to the parents. He also learned that the military had come hither to take into custody the loving couple, who had already been seized and detained in a neighboring village. After some time, accordingly, a cart was seen advancing to the place, encircled with a city guard more ludicrous than appalling. An amorphous town-clerk rode forth, and made his compliments to the *Actuarius* (for such was the young man Wilhelm had been speaking to), on the border of their several districts, with great conscientiousness and queer grimaces; as perhaps the ghost and the conjurer do, when they meet, the one within the circle and the other out of it, in their dismal midnight operations.

But the chief attention of the lookers-on was directed to the cart: they could not behold, without compassion, the poor, misguided creatures, who were sitting upon bundles of straw, looking tenderly at one another, and scarcely seeming to observe the by-standers. Accident had forced their conductors to bring them from the last village in that unseemly style; the old chaise, which had previously transported the lady, having there broken down. On that occurrence she had begged for permission to sit beside her friend; whom, in the conviction that his crime was of a capital sort, the rustic bailiffs had so far brought along in irons. These irons certainly contributed to give the tender group a more interesting appearance, particularly as the young man moved and bore himself with great dignity, while he kissed more than once the hands of his fair companion.

"We are unfortunate," she cried to the by-standers, "but not so guilty as we seem. It is thus that cruel men reward true love; and parents, who entirely neglect the happiness of their children, tear them with fury from the arms of joy, when it has found them after many weary days."

The spectators were expressing their sympathy in various ways, when, the officers of law having finished their ceremonial, the cart went on; and Wilhelm, who took a deep interest in the fate of the lovers, hastened forward by a foot path to get some acquaintance with the *Amtmann* before the procession should arrive. But scarcely had he reached the *Amthaus*, where all was in motion, and ready to receive the fugitives, when his new friend, the *Actuarius*, laid hold of him; and giving him a circumstantial detail of the whole proceedings, and then launching out into a comprehensive eulogy of his own horse, which he had got by barter the night before, put a stop to every other sort of conversation.

The luckless pair, in the mean time, had been set down behind, at the garden, which communicated by a little door with the *Amthaus*, and thus brought in unobserved. The *Actuarius*, for this mild and handsome treatment, accepted of a just encomium from Wilhelm; though in truth his sole object had been to mortify the crowd collected in front of the *Amthaus*, by denying them the satisfaction of looking at a neighbor in disgrace.

The *Amtmann*, who had no particular taste for such extraordinary occurrences, being wont on these occasions to commit frequent errors, and, with the best intentions, to be often paid with sour admonitions from the higher powers, went with heavy steps into his office-room; the *Actuarius* with Wilhelm and a few respectable citizens following him.

The lady was first produced: she advanced without pertness, calm and self-possessed. The manner of her dress, the way in which she bore herself, showed that she was a person not without value in her own eyes. She accordingly began, without any questions being put, to speak, not unskilfully, about her situation.

The *Actuarius* bade her be silent, and held his pen over the folded sheet. The *Amtmann* gathered up his resolution, looked at his assistant, cleared his throat by two or three hems, and asked the poor girl what was her name, and how old she was.

"I beg your pardon, sir," said she, "but it seems very strange to me that you ask my name and age, seeing you know very well what my name is, and that I am just of the age of your oldest son. What you do want to know of me, and need to know, I will tell freely without circumlocution.

"Since my father's second marriage, my situation in his house has not been of the most enviable sort. Oftener than once I have had it in my power to make a suitable marriage, had not my step-mother, dreading the expense of my portion, taken care to thwart all such proposals. At length I grew acquainted with the young Melina; I felt constrained to love him; and, as we both foresaw the obstacles that stood in the way of our regular union, we determined to go forth together, and seek in the wide world the happiness denied us at home. I took nothing with me that was not my own: we did not run away like thieves and robbers; and my lover does not merit to be hauled about in this way, with chains and handcuffs. The prince is just, and will not sanction such severity. If we are liable to punishment, it is not punishment of this kind."

The old *Amtmann* hereupon fell into double and treble confusion. Sounds of the most gracious eulogies were already humming through his brain, and the girl's voluble speech had entirely confounded the plan of his protocol. The mischief increased, when to repeated official questions she refused giving any answer, but constantly referred to what she had already said.

"I am no criminal," she said. "They have brought me hither on bundles of straw to put me to shame, but there is a higher court that will bring us back to honor."

The *Actuarius*, in the mean time, had kept writing down her words: he whispered the *Amtmann*, "just to go on, — a formal protocol might be made out by and by."

The senior then again took heart, and began, with his heavy words, in dry prescribed formulas, to seek information about the sweet secrets of love.

The red mounted into Wilhelm's cheeks, and those of the pretty criminal likewise glowed with the charming tinge of modesty. She was silent, she stammered, till at last her embarrassment itself seemed to exalt her courage.

"Be assured," she cried, "that I should have strength enough to confess the truth, though it made against myself; and shall I now hesitate and stammer, when it does me honor? Yes: from the moment when I first felt certain of his love and faith, I looked upon him as my husband; I freely gave him all that love requires, — that a heart once convinced cannot long refuse. Now do with me what you please. If I hesitated for a moment to confess, it was solely owing to fear lest the admission might prove hurtful to my lover."

On hearing this confession, Wilhelm formed a high opinion of the young woman's feelings, while her judges marked her as an impudent strumpet; and the townsfolk present thanked God that in their families no such scandal had occurred, or at least been brought to light.

Wilhelm transported his Mariana into this conjuncture, answering at the bar: he put still finer words in her mouth, making her uprightness yet more affecting, her confession still nobler. The most violent desire to help the two lovers took possession of him. Nor did he conceal this feeling, but signified in private to the wavering *Amtmann*, that it were better to end the business; all being clear as possible, and requiring no further investigation.

This was so far of service that the young woman was allowed

to retire; though, in her stead, the lover was brought in, his fetters having previously been taken off him at the door. This person seemed a little more concerned about his fate. His answers were more careful; and, if he showed less heroic generosity, he recommended himself by the precision and distinctness of his expressions.

When this audience also was finished, and found to agree in all points with the former, except that, from regard for his mistress, Melina stubbornly denied what had already been confessed by herself, the young woman was again brought forward; and a scene took place between the two, which made the heart of our friend entirely their own.

What usually occurs nowhere but in romances and plays, he saw here in a paltry court-room before his eyes, — the contest of reciprocal magnanimity, the strength of love in misfortune.

"Is it, then, true," said he internally, "that timorous affection, which conceals itself from the eye of the sun and of men, not daring to taste of enjoyment save in remote solitude and deep secrecy, yet, if torn rudely by some cruel chance into light, will show itself more courageous, strong, and resolute than any of our loud and ostentatious passions?"

To his comfort, the business now soon came to a conclusion. The lovers were detained in tolerable quarters: had it been possible, he would that very evening have brought back the young lady to her parents. For he firmly determined to act as intercessor in this case, and to forward a happy and lawful union between the lovers.

He begged permission of the *Amtmann* to speak in private with Melina, a request which was granted without difficulty.

CHAPTER FOURTEEN

THE CONVERSATION of these new acquaintances very soon grew confidential and lively. When Wilhelm told the downcast youth of his connection with the lady's parents, and offered to mediate in the affair, showing at the same time the strongest expectation of success, a light was shed across the dreary and anxious mind of the prisoner: he felt himself already free, already reconciled with the parents of his bride, and now began to speak about his future occupation and support.

"On this point," said our friend, "you cannot long be in difficulty; for you seem to me directed, not more by your circumstances than by nature, to make your fortune in the noble profession you have chosen. A pleasing figure, a sonorous voice, a feeling heart! Could an actor be better furnished? If I can serve you with a few introductions, it will give me the greatest pleasure."

"I thank you with all my heart," replied the other, "but I shall hardly be able to make use of them; for it is my purpose, if possible, not to return to the stage."

"Here you are certainly to blame," said Wilhelm, after a pause, during which he had partly recovered out of his astonishment; for it had never once entered his head, but that the player, the moment his young wife and he were out of durance, would repair to some theatre. It seemed to him as natural and as necessary as for the frog to seek pools of water. He had not doubted of it for a moment, and he now heard the contrary with boundless surprise.

"Yes," replied Melina, "I have it in view not to re-appear upon the stage, but rather to take up some civil calling, be it what it will, so that I can but obtain one."

"This is a strange resolution, which I cannot give my approbation to. Without especial reasons, it can never be advisable to change the mode of life we have begun with; and, besides, I know of no condition that presents so much allurement, so many charming prospects, as the condition of an actor."

"It is easy to see that you have never been one," said the other.

"Alas, sir," answered Wilhelm, "how seldom is any man contented with the station where he happens to be placed! He is ever coveting that of his neighbor, from which the neighbor in his turn is longing to be free."

"Yet still there is a difference," said Melina, "between bad and worse. Experience, not impatience, makes me determine as you see. Is there in the world any creature whose morsel of bread is attended with such vexation, uncertainty, and toil? It were almost as good to take the staff and wallet, and beg from door to door. What things to be endured from the envy of rivals, from the partiality of managers, from the ever-altering caprices of the public! In truth, one would need to have a hide like a bear's, that is led about in a chain along with apes, and dogs of knowledge, and cudgelled into dancing at the sound of a bagpipe before the populace and children."

Wilhelm thought a thousand things, which he would not vex the worthy man by uttering. He merely, therefore, led the conversation round them at a distance. His friend explained himself the more candidly and circumstantially on that account. "Is not the manager obliged," said he, "to fall down at the feet of every little *Stadtrath*, that he may get permission, for a month between the fairs, to cause another *groschen* or two to circulate in the place? Ours, on the whole, a worthy man, I have often pitied; though at other times he gave me cause enough for discontentment. A good actor drains him by extortion; of the bad he cannot rid himself; and, should he try to make his income at all equal to his outlay, the public immediately takes umbrage, the house stands empty; and, not to go to wreck entirely, he must continue acting in the midst of sorrow and vexation. No, no, sir! Since you are so good as to undertake to help me, have the kindness, I entreat you, to plead with the parents of my bride: let them get me a little post of clerk or collector, and I shall think myself well dealt with."

After exchanging a few words more, Wilhelm went away with the promise to visit the parents early in the morning, and see what could be done. Scarcely was he by himself, when he gave utterance to his thoughts in these exclamations: "Unhappy Melina! not in thy condition, but in thyself, lies the mean impediment over which thou canst not gain the mastery. What mortal in the world, if without inward calling he take up a trade, an art, or any mode of life, will not feel his situation miserable? But he who is born with capacities for any undertaking, finds in executing this the fairest portion of his being. Nothing upon earth without its difficulties! It is the secret impulse within, it is the love and the delight we feel, that help us to conquer obstacles, to clear out new paths, and to overleap the bounds of that narrow circle in which others poorly toil. For *thee* the stage is but a few boards: the parts assigned thee are but what a task is to a school-boy. The spectators thou regardest as on work-days they regard each other. For thee, then, it may be well to wish thyself behind a desk, over ruled ledgers, collecting tolls, and picking out reversions. Thou feelest not the co-operating, co-inspiring whole, which the mind alone can invent, comprehend, and complete: thou feelest not that in man there lives a spark of purer fire, which, when it is not fed, when it is not fanned, gets covered by the ashes of indifference and daily wants, yet not till late, perhaps never, can be altogether quenched. Thou feelest in thy soul no strength to fan this spark into a flame, no riches in thy heart to feed it when aroused. Hunger drives thee on, inconveniences withstand thee; and it is hidden from thee, that, in every human condition, foes lie in wait for us, invincible except by cheerfulness and equanimity. Thou doest well to wish thyself within the limits of a common station, for what station that required soul and resolution couldst thou rightly fill? Give a soldier, a statesman, a divine, thy sentiments, and as justly will he fret himself about the miseries of *his* condition. Nay, have there not been men so totally forsaken by all feeling of existence, that they have held the life and nature of mortals as a nothing, a painful, short, and tarnished gleam of being? Did the forms of active men rise up living in thy soul; were thy breast warmed by a sympathetic fire; did the vocation which proceeds from within diffuse itself over all thy frame; were the tones of thy voice, the words of thy mouth, delightful to hear; didst thou feel thy own being sufficient for thyself, — then wouldst thou doubtless seek place and opportunity likewise to feel it in others."

Amid such words and thoughts, our friend undressed himself, and went to bed, with feelings of the deepest satisfaction. A whole romance of what he now hoped to do, instead of the worthless occupations which should have filled the approaching day, arose within his mind: pleasant fantasies softly conducted him into the kingdom of sleep, and then gave him up to their sisters, sweet dreams, who received him with open arms, and encircled his reposing head with the images of heaven.

Early in the morning he was awake again, and thinking of the business that lay before him. He revisited the house of the forsaken family, where his presence caused no small surprise. He introduced his proposal in the most prudent manner, and soon found both more and fewer difficulties than he had anticipated. For one thing, the evil was already *done*: and though people of a singularly strict and harsh temper are wont to set themselves forcibly against the past, and thus to increase the evil that cannot now be remedied; yet, on the other hand, what is actually done exerts an irresistible effect upon most minds: an event which lately appeared impossible takes its place, so soon as it has really occurred, with what occurs daily. It was accordingly soon settled, that Herr Melina was to wed the daughter; who, however, in return, because of her misconduct, was to take no marriage-portion with her, and to promise that she would leave her aunt's legacy, for a few years more, at an easy interest, in her father's hands. But the second point, touching a civil provision for Melina, was attended with greater difficulties. They liked not to have the luckless pair continually living in their sight: they would not have a present object ever calling to their minds the connection of a mean vagabond with so respectable a family, — a family which could number even a superintendent among its relatives; nay, it was not to be looked for, that the government would trust him with a charge. Both parents were alike inflexible in this matter; and Wilhelm, who pleaded very hard, unwilling that a man whom he contemned should return to the stage, and convinced that he deserved not such a happiness, could not, with all his rhetoric, produce the slenderest impression. Had he known the secret springs of the business, he would have spared himself the labor of attempting to persuade. The father would gladly have kept his daughter near him; but he hated the young man, because his wife herself had cast an eye upon him: while the latter could not bear to have, in her step-daughter, a happy rival constantly before her eyes. So Melina with his young wife, who already manifested no dislike to go and see the world, and be seen of it, was obliged, against his will, to set forth in a few days, and seek some place in any acting company where he could find one.

HAPPY SEASON of youth! Happy times of the first wish of love! A man is then like a child that can for hours delight itself with an echo, can support alone the charges of conversation, and be well contented with its entertainment, if the unseen interlocutor will but repeat the concluding syllables of the words addressed to it.

So was it with Wilhelm in the earlier and still more in the later period of his passion for Mariana; he transferred the whole wealth of his own emotions to her, and looked upon himself as a beggar that lived upon her alms: and as a landscape is more delightful, nay, is delightful only, when it is enlightened by the sun; so likewise in his eyes were all things beautified and glorified which lay round her or related to her.

Often would he stand in the theatre behind the scenes, to which he had obtained the freedom of access from the manager. In such cases, it is true, the perspective magic was away; but the far mightier sorcery of love then first began to act. For hours he could stand by the sooty light-frame, inhaling the vapor of tallow lamps, looking out at his mistress; and when she returned, and cast a kindly glance upon him, he could feel himself lost in ecstasy; and, though close upon laths and bare spars, he seemed transported into paradise. The stuffed bunches of wool denominated lambs, the waterfalls of tin, the paper roses, and the one-sided huts of straw, awoke in him fair poetic visions of an old pastoral world. Nay, the very dancing-girls, ugly as they were when seen at hand, did not always inspire him with disgust: they trod the same floor with Mariana. So true is it, that love, which alone can give their full charm to rose-bowers, myrtle-groves, and moonshine, can also communicate, even to shavings of wood, and paper-clippings, the aspect of animated nature. It is so strong a spice, that tasteless or even nauseous soups are by it rendered palatable.

So potent a spice was certainly required to render tolerable, nay, at last agreeable, the state in which he usually found her chamber, not to say herself.

Brought up in a substantial burgher's house, cleanliness and order were the elements in which he breathed; and, inheriting as he did a portion of his father's taste for finery, it had always been his care, in boyhood, to furbish up his chamber, which he regarded as his little kingdom, in the stateliest fashion. His bed-curtains were drawn together in large, massy folds, and fastened with tassels, as they are usually seen in thrones; he had got himself a carpet for the middle of his chamber, and a finer one for his table; his books and apparatus he had, almost instinctively, arranged in such a manner, that a Dutch painter might have imitated them for groups in his still-life scenes. He had a white cap, which he wore straight up like a turban; and the sleeves of his night-gown he had caused to be cut short, in the mode of the Orientals. By way of reason for this, he pretended that long, wide sleeves encumbered him in writing. When, at night, the boy was quite alone, and no longer dreaded any interruption, he usually wore a silk sash tied round his body: and often, it is said, he would fix in his girdle a sword, which he had appropriated from an old armory, and thus repeat and declaim his tragic parts; nay, in the same trim he would kneel down and say his evening prayer.

In those times, how happy did he think the players, whom he saw possessed of so many splendid garments, trappings, and arms; and in the constant practice of a lofty demeanor, the spirit of which seemed to hold up a mirror of whatever, in the opinions, relations, and passions of men, was stateliest and most magnificent. Of a piece with this, thought Wilhelm, is also the player's domestic life, — a series of dignified transactions and employments, whereof their appearance on the stage is but the outmost portion; like as a mass of silver, long simmering about in the purifying furnace, at length gleams with a bright and beautiful tinge in the eye of the refiner, and shows him, at the same time, that the metal now is cleansed of all foreign mixture.

Great, accordingly, was his surprise at first, when he found himself beside his mistress, and looked down, through the cloud that environed him, on tables, stools, and floor. The wrecks of a transient, light, and false decoration lay, like the glittering coat of a skinned fish, dispersed in wild disorder. The implements of personal cleanliness, — combs, soap, towels, — with the traces of their use, were not concealed. Music, portions of plays and pairs of shoes, washes and Italian flowers, pin-cushions, hair-skewers, rouge-pots, and ribbons, books and straw hats, — no article despised the neighborhood of another: all were united by a common element, — powder and dust. Yet as Wilhelm scarcely noticed in her presence aught except herself; nay, as all that had belonged to her, that she had touched, was dear to him, — he came at last to feel, in this chaotic housekeeping, a charm which the proud pomp of his own habitation never had communicated. When, on this hand, he lifted aside her bodice, to get at the harpsichord; on that, threw her gown upon the bed, that he might find a seat; when she herself, with careless freedom, did not seek to hide from him many a natural office, which, out of respect for the presence of a second person, is usually concealed, — he felt as if by all this he was coming nearer to her every moment, as if the communion betwixt them was fastening by invisible ties.

It was not so easy to reconcile with his previous ideas the behavior of the other players, whom, on his first visits, he often met with in her house. Ever busied in being idle, they seemed to think least of all on their employment and object: the poetic worth of a piece they were never heard to speak of, or to judge of, right or wrong; their continual question was simply, How much will it *bring*? Is it a stock-piece? How long will it run? How often think you it may be played? and other inquiries and observations of the same description. Then commonly they broke out against the manager, that he was stinted with his salaries, and especially unjust to this one or to that; then against the public, how seldom it recompensed the right man with its approval, how the German theatre was daily improving, how the player was ever growing more honored, and never could be honored enough. Then they would descant largely about wine-gardens and coffee-houses; how much debt one of their comrades had contracted, and must suffer a deduction from his wages on account of; about the disproportion of their weekly salaries; about the cabals of some rival company: on which occasions, they would pass again to the great and merited attention which the public now bestowed upon them; not forgetting the importance of the theatre to the improvement of the nation and the world.

All this, which had already given Wilhelm many a restless hour, came again into his memory, as he walked his horse slowly homewards, and contemplated the various occurrences in which he had so lately been engaged. The commotion produced by a girl's elopement, not only in a decent family, but in a whole town, he had seen with his own eyes: the scenes upon the highway and in the *Amthaus*, the views entertained by Melina, and whatever else he had witnessed, again arose before him, and brought his keen, forecasting mind into a sort of anxious disquietude; which no longer to endure, he struck the spurs into his horse, and hastened towards home.

By this expedient, however, he but ran to meet new vexations. Werner, his friend and future brother-in-law, was waiting for him, to begin a serious, important, unexpected conversation.

Werner was one of those tried, sedate persons, with fixed principles and habits, whom we usually denominate cold characters, because on emergencies they do not burst forth quickly or very visibly. Accordingly, his intercourse with Wilhelm was a perpetual contest; which, however, only served to knit their mutual affection the more firmly; for, notwithstanding their very opposite modes of thinking, each found his account in communicating with the other. Werner was very well contented with himself, that he could now and then lay a bridle on the exalted but commonly extravagant spirit of his friend; and Wilhelm often felt a glorious triumph, when the staid and thinking Werner could be hurried on with him in warm ebullience. Thus each exercised himself upon the other; they had been accustomed to see each other daily; and you would have said, their eagerness to meet and talk together had even been augmented by the inability of each to understand the other. At bottom, however, being both good-hearted men, they were both travelling together towards one goal; and they could never understand how it was that neither of the two could bring the other over to his own persuasion.

For some time Werner had observed that Wilhelm's visits had been rarer; that in his favorite discussions he was brief and absent-minded; that he no longer abandoned himself to the vivid depicting of singular conceptions, — tokens by which, in truth, a mind getting rest and contentment in the presence of a friend is most clearly indicated. The considerate and punctual Werner first sought for the root of the evil in his own conduct; till some rumors of the neighborhood set him on the proper trace, and some unguarded proceedings on the part of Wilhelm brought him nearer to the certainty. He began his investigation, and erelong discovered, that for some time Wilhelm had been openly visiting an actress, had often spoken with her at the theatre, and accompanied her home. On discovering the nightly visits of his friend, Werner's anxiety increased to a painful extent: for he heard that Mariana was a most seductive girl, who probably was draining the youth of his money; while, at the same time, she herself was supported by another and a very worthless lover.

Having pushed his suspicions as near certainty as possible, he had resolved to make a sharp attack on Wilhelm: he was now in full readiness with all his preparations, when his friend returned, discontented and unsettled, from his journey.

That very evening Werner laid the whole of what he knew before him, first calmly, then with the emphatic earnestness of a well-meaning friendship. He left no point of the subject undiscussed, and made Wilhelm taste abundance of those bitter things which men at ease are accustomed, with virtuous spite, to dispense so liberally to men in love. Yet, as might have been expected, he accomplished little. Wilhelm answered with interior commotion, though with great confidence, "You know not the girl! Appearances, perhaps, are not to her advantage; but I am certain of her faithfulness and virtue, as of my love."

Werner maintained his accusations, and offered to bring proofs and witnesses. Wilhelm waived these offers, and parted with his friend out of humor and unhinged, like a man in whose jaw some unskilful dentist has been seizing a diseased, yet fast-rooted, tooth, and tugging at it harshly to no purpose.

It exceedingly dissatisfied Wilhelm to see the fair image of Mariana overclouded and almost deformed in his soul, first by the capricious fancies of his journey, and then by the unfriendliness of Werner. He adopted the surest means of restoring it to complete brilliancy and beauty, by setting out at night, and hastening to his wonted destination. She received him with extreme joy: on entering the town, he had ridden past her window; she had been expecting his company; and it is easy to conceive that all scruples were soon driven from his heart. Nay, her tenderness again opened up the whole stores of his confidence; and he told her how deeply the public, how deeply his friend, had sinned against her.

Much lively talking led them at length to speak about the earliest period of their acquaintance, the recollection of which forms always one of the most delightful topics between two lovers. The first steps that introduce us to the enchanted garden of love are so full of pleasure, the first prospects so charming, that every one is willing to recall them to his memory. Each party seeks a preference above the other; each has loved sooner, more devotedly; and each, in this contest, would rather be conquered than conquer.

Wilhelm repeated to his mistress, what he had so often told her before, how she soon abstracted his attention from the play, and fixed it on herself; how her form, her acting, her voice, inspired him; how at last he went only on the nights when *she* was to appear; how, in fine, having ventured behind the scenes, he had often stood by her unheeded; and he spoke with rapture of the happy evening when he found an opportunity to do her some civility, and lead her into conversation.

Mariana, on the other hand, would not allow that she had failed so long to notice him: she declared that she had seen him in the public walk, and for proof she described the clothes which he wore on that occasion; she affirmed that even then he pleased her before all others, and made her long for his acquaintance.

How gladly did Wilhelm credit all this! How gladly did he catch at the persuasion, that, when he used to approach her, she had felt herself drawn towards him by some resistless influence; that she had gone with him between the side-scenes on purpose to see him more closely, and get acquainted with him; and that, in fine, when his backwardness and modesty were not to be conquered, she had herself afforded him an opportunity, and, as it were, compelled him to hand her a glass of lemonade.

In this affectionate contest, which they pursued through all the little circumstances of their brief romance, the hours passed rapidly away; and Wilhelm left his mistress with his heart at peace, and firmly determined on proceeding forthwith to the execution of his project.

CHAPTER SIXTEEN

THE NECESSARY preparations for his journey his father and mother had attended to: some little matters, that were yet wanting to his equipage, delayed his departure for a few days. Wilhelm took advantage of this opportunity to write to Mariana, meaning thus to bring to a decision the proposal, about which she had hitherto avoided speaking with him. The letter was as follows: —

"Under the kind veil of night, which has often over-shadowed us together, I sit and think, and write to thee: all that I meditate and do is solely on thy account. O Mariana! with me, the happiest of men, it is as with a bridegroom who stands in the festive chamber, dreaming of the new universe that is to be unfolded to him, and by means of him, and, while the holy ceremonies are proceeding, transports himself in longing thought before the mysterious curtains, from which the loveliness of love whispers out to him.

"I have constrained myself not to see thee for a few days: the sacrifice was easy, when united with the hope of such a recompense, of being always with thee, of remaining ever thine! Need I repeat what I desire? I must! for it seems as if yet thou hadst never understood me.

"How often, in the low tones of true love, which, though wishing to gain all, dares speak but little, have I sought in thy heart for the desire of a perpetual union. Thou hast understood me, doubtless; for in thy own heart the same wish must have arisen: thou *didst* comprehend me, in that kiss, in the intoxicating peace of that happy evening. Thy silence testified to me thy modest honor; and how did it increase my love! Another woman would have had recourse to artifice, that she might ripen by superfluous sunshine the purpose of her lover's heart, might elicit a proposal, and secure a firm promise. Mariana, on the contrary, drew back: she repelled the half-opened confidence of him she loved, and sought to conceal her approving feelings by apparent indifference. But I have understood thee! What a miserable creature must I be, if I did not by these tokens recognize the pure and generous love that cares not for itself, but for its object! Confide in me, and fear nothing. We belong to one another; and neither of us leaves aught or forsakes aught, if we live for one another.

"Take it, then, this hand! Solemnly I offer this unnecessary pledge! All the joys of love we have already felt, but there is a new blessedness in the firm thought of duration. Ask not how, — care not. Fate takes care of love, and the more certainly as love is easy to provide for.

"My heart has long ago forsaken my paternal home: it is with thee, as my spirit hovers on the stage. O my darling! to what other man has it been given to unite all his wishes, as it is to me? No sleep falls upon my eyes: like the redness of an everlasting dawn, thy love and thy happiness still glow around me.

"Scarcely can I hold myself from springing up, from rushing forth to thee, and forcing thy consent, and, with the first light of to-morrow, pressing forward into the world for the mark I aim at. But, no! I will restrain myself; I will not act like a thoughtless fool, will do nothing rashly: my plan is laid, and I will execute it calmly.

"I am acquainted with the manager Serlo: my journey leads me directly to the place where he is. For above a year he has frequently been wishing that his people had a touch of my vivacity, and my delight in theatrical affairs: I shall doubtless be very kindly received. Into your company I cannot enter, for more than one reason. Serlo's theatre, moreover, is at such a distance from this, that I may there begin my undertaking without any apprehension of discovery. With him I shall thus at once find a tolerable maintenance: I shall look about me in the public, get acquainted with the company, and then come back for thee.

"Mariana, thou seest what I can force myself to do, that I may certainly obtain thee. For such a period not to see thee; for such a period to know thee in the wide world! I dare not view it closely. But yet if I recall to memory thy love, which assures me of all; if thou shalt not disdain my prayer, and give me, ere we part, thy hand, before the priest, — I may then depart in peace. It is but a form between us, yet a form so touching, — the blessing of Heaven to the blessing of the earth. Close by thy house, in the Ritterschaftliche Chapel, the ceremony will be soon and secretly performed.

"For the beginning I have gold enough; we will share it between us; it will suffice for both; and, before that is finished, Heaven will send us more.

"No, my darling, I am not downcast about the issue. What is begun with so much cheerfulness must reach a happy end. I have never doubted that a man may force his way through the world, if he really is in earnest about it; and I feel strength enough within me to provide a liberal support for two, and many more. The world, we are often told, is unthankful: I have never yet discovered that it was unthankful, if one knew how, in the proper way, to do it service. My whole soul burns at the idea, that I shall at length step forth, and speak to the hearts of men something they have long been yearning to hear. How many thousand times has a feeling of disgust passed through me, alive as I am to the nobleness of the stage, when I have seen the poorest creatures fancying they could speak a word of power to the hearts of the people! The tone of a man's voice singing treble sounds far pleasanter and purer to my ear: it is incredible how these blockheads, in their coarse ineptitude, deform things beautiful and venerable.

"The theatre has often been at variance with the pulpit: they ought not, I think, to quarrel. How much is it to be wished, that in both, the celebration of nature and of God were intrusted to none but men of noble minds! These are no dreams, my darling! As I have felt in thy heart that thou couldst love, I seize the dazzling thought, and say, — no, I will not say, but I will hope and trust, — that we two shall yet appear to men as a pair of chosen spirits, to unlock their hearts, to touch the recesses of their nature, and prepare for them celestial joys, as surely as the joys I have tasted with thee deserved to be named celestial, since they drew us from ourselves, and exalted us above ourselves.

"I cannot end. I have already said too much, and know not whether I have yet said all, all that concerns *thy* interests; for to express the agitations of the vortex that whirls round within myself, is beyond the power of words.

"Yet take this sheet, my love! I have again read it over: I observe it ought to have begun more cautiously; but it contains in it all that thou hast need to know, — enough to prepare thee for the hour when I shall return with the lightness of love to thy bosom. I seem to myself like a prisoner that is secretly filing his irons asunder. I bid good night to my soundly sleeping parents. Farewell, my beloved, farewell! For this time I conclude; my eyelids have more than once dropped together; it is now deep in the night."

CHAPTER SEVENTEEN

IT SEEMED as if the day would never end, while Wilhelm, with the letter beautifully folded in his pocket, longed to meet with Mariana. The darkness had scarcely come on, when, contrary to custom, he glided forth to her house. His plan was, to announce himself for the night; then to quit his mistress for a short time, leaving the letter with her ere he went away; and, returning at a late hour, to obtain her reply, her consent, or to force it from her by the power of his caresses. He flew into her arms, and pressed her in rapture to his bosom. The vehemence of his emotions prevented him at first from noticing, that, on this occasion, she did not receive him with her wonted heartiness; yet she could not long conceal her painful situation, but imputed it to slight indisposition. She complained of a headache, and would not by any means consent to his proposal of coming back that night. Suspecting nothing wrong, he ceased to urge her, but felt that this was not the moment for delivering his letter. He retained it, therefore; and, as several of her movements and observations courteously compelled him to take his leave, in the tumult of unsatiable love he snatched up one of her neckerchiefs, squeezed it into his pocket, and forced himself away from her lips and her door. He returned home, but could not rest there: he again dressed himself, and went out into the open air.

After walking up and down several streets, he was accosted by a stranger inquiring for a certain inn. Wilhelm offered to conduct him to the house. In the way, his new acquaintance asked about the names of the streets, the owners of various extensive edifices, then about some police regulations of the town; so that, by the time they reached the door of the inn, they had fallen into quite an interesting conversation. The stranger politely compelled his guide to enter, and drink a glass of punch with him. Ere long he had told his name and place of abode, as well as the business that had brought him hither; and he seemed to expect a like confidence from Wilhelm. Our friend, without any hesitation, mentioned his name, and the place where he lived.

"Are you not a grandson of the old Meister, who possessed that beautiful collection of pictures and statues?" inquired the stranger.

"Yes, I am. I was ten years old when my grandfather died, and it grieved me very much to see these fine things sold."

"Your father got a fine sum of money for them."

"You know of it, then?"

"Yes, indeed: I saw that treasure ere it left your house. Your grandfather was not merely a collector, he had a thorough knowledge of art. In his younger happy years he had been in Italy, and had brought back with him such treasures as could not now be got for any price. He possessed some exquisite pictures by the best masters. When you looked through his drawings, you would scarcely have believed your eyes. Among his marbles were some invaluable fragments; his series of bronzes was instructive and well chosen; he had also collected medals, in considerable quantity, relating to history and art; his few gems deserved the greatest praise. In addition to all which, the whole was tastefully arranged; although the rooms and hall of the old house had not been symmetrically built."

"You may conceive," said Wilhelm, "what we young ones lost, when all these articles were taken down and sent away. It was the first mournful period of my life. I cannot tell you how empty the chambers looked when we saw those objects vanish one by one, which had amused us from our earliest years, and which we considered as unalterable as the house, or the town itself."

"If I mistake not, your father put the capital produced by the sale into some neighbor's stock, with whom he commenced a sort of partnership in trade."

"Quite right; and their joint speculations have prospered in their hands. Within the last twelve years, they have greatly increased their fortunes, and are now the more vehemently bent on gaining. Old Werner also has a son, who suits that sort of occupation much better than I."

"I am sorry the place should have lost such an ornament as your grandfather's cabinet was to it. I saw it but a short time prior to the sale; and I may say, I was myself the cause of its being then disposed of. A rich nobleman, a great amateur, but one who, in such important transactions, does not trust to his own solitary judgment, had sent me hither, and requested my advice. For six days I examined the collection: on the seventh, I advised my friend to pay down the required sum without delay. You were then a lively boy, often running about me: you explained to me the subjects of the pictures, and in general, I recollect, could give a very good account of the whole cabinet."

"I remember such a person, but I should not have recognized him in you."

"It is a good while ago, and we all change more or less. You had, if I mistake not, a favorite piece among them, to which you were ever calling my attention."

"Oh, yes! it represented the history of that king's son dying of a secret love for his father's bride."

"It was not, certainly, the best picture, — badly grouped, of no superiority in coloring, and executed altogether with great mannerism."

"This I did not understand, and do not yet: it is the subject that charms me in a picture, not the art."

"Your grandfather seemed to have thought otherwise. The greater part of his collection consisted of excellent pieces; in which, represent what they might, one constantly admired the talent of the master. This picture of yours had accordingly been hung in the outermost room, — a proof that he valued it slightly."

"It was in that room where we young ones used to play, and where the piece you mention made on me a deep impression; which not even your criticism, greatly as I honor it, could obliterate, if we stood before the picture at this moment. What a melancholy object is a youth that must shut up within himself the sweet impulse, the fairest inheritance which nature has given us, and conceal in his own bosom the fire which should warm and animate himself and others, so that his vitals are wasted away by unutterable pains! I feel a pity for the ill-fated man that would consecrate himself to another, when the heart of that other has already found a worthy object of true and pure affection."

"Such feelings are, however, very foreign to the principles by which a lover of art examines the works of great painters; and most probably you, too, had the cabinet continued in your family, would have by and by acquired a relish for the works themselves, and have learned to see in the performances of art something more than yourself and your individual inclinations."

"In truth, the sale of that cabinet grieved me very much at the time; and often since I have thought of it with regret: but when I consider that it was a necessary means of awakening a taste in me, of developing a talent, which will operate far more powerfully on my history than ever those lifeless pictures could have done, I easily content myself, and honor destiny, which knows how to bring about what is best for me, and what is best for every one."

"It gives me pain to hear this word destiny in the mouth of a young person, just at the age when men are commonly accustomed to ascribe their own violent inclinations to the will of higher natures."

"You, then, do not believe in destiny? No power that rules over us and directs all for our ultimate advantage?"

"The question is not now of my belief, nor is this the place to explain how I may have attempted to form for myself some not impossible conception of things which are incomprehensible to all of us: the question here is, What mode of viewing them will profit us the most? The fabric of our life is formed of necessity and chance: the reason of man takes its station between them, and may rule them both; it treats the necessary as the groundwork of its being; the accidental it can direct and guide, and employ for its own purposes: and only while this principle of reason stands firm and inexpugnable, does man deserve to be named the god of this lower world. But woe to him who, from his youth, has used himself to search in necessity for something of arbitrary will; to ascribe to chance a sort of reason, which it is a matter of religion to obey. Is conduct like this aught else than to renounce one's understanding, and give unrestricted scope to one's inclinations? We think it is a kind of piety to move along without consideration; to let accidents that please us determine our conduct; and, finally, to bestow on the result of such a vacillating life the name of providential guidance."

"Was it never your case that some little circumstance induced you to strike into a certain path, where some accidental occurrence erelong met you, and a series of unexpected incidents at length brought you to some point which you yourself had scarcely once contemplated? Should not lessons of this kind teach us obedience to destiny, confidence in some such guide?"

"With opinions like these, no woman could maintain her virtue, no man keep the money in his purse; for occasions enough are occurring to get rid of both. He alone is worthy of respect, who knows what is of use to himself and others, and who labors to control his self-will. Each man has his own fortune in his hands; as the artist has a piece of rude matter, which he is to fashion to a certain shape. But the art of living rightly is like all arts: the capacity alone is born with us; it must be learned, and practised with incessant care."

These discussions our two speculators carried on between them to considerable length: at last they parted without seeming to have

A serenade beneath Mariana's window

wrought any special conviction in each other, but engaging to meet at an appointed place next day.

Wilhelm walked up and down the streets for a time: he heard a sound of clarinets, hunting-horns, and bassoons; it swelled his bosom with delightful feelings. It was some travelling showmen that produced this pleasant music. He spoke with them: for a piece of coin they followed him to Mariana's house. The space in front of the door was adorned with lofty trees; under them he placed his artists; and, himself resting on a bench at some distance, he surrendered his mind without restraint to the hovering tones which floated round him in the cool mellow night. Stretched out beneath the kind stars, he felt his existence like a golden dream. "She, too, hears these flutes," said he within his heart: "she feels whose remembrance, whose love of her, it is that makes the night full of music. In distance, even, we are united by these melodies, as in every separation, by the ethereal accordance of love. Ah! two hearts that love each other are as two magnetic needles: whatever moves the one must move the other with it; for it is one power that works in both, one principle that pervades them. Can I in her arms conceive the possibility of parting from her? And yet I am soon to be far from her, to seek out a sanctuary for our love, and then to have her ever with me.

"How often, when absent from her, and lost in thoughts about her, happening to touch a book, a piece of dress or aught else, have I thought I felt her hand, so entirely was I invested with her presence! And to recollect those moments which shunned the light of day and the eye of the cold spectator; which, to enjoy, the gods might determine to forsake the painless condition of their pure blessedness! To recollect them! As if by memory we could renew the tumultuous thrilling of that cup of joy, which encircles our senses with celestial bonds, and lifts them beyond all earthly hinderances. And her form" — He lost himself in thoughts of her; his rest passed away into longing; he leaned against a tree, and cooled his warm cheek on its bark; and the winds of the night wafted speedily aside the breath, which proceeded in sighs from his pure and impassioned bosom. He groped for the neckerchief he had taken from her; but it was forgotten, it lay in his other clothes. His frame quivered with emotion.

The music ceased, and he felt as if fallen from the element in which his thoughts had hitherto been soaring. His restlessness increased, as his feelings were no longer nourished and assuaged by the melody. He sat down upon her threshold, and felt more peace. He kissed the brass knocker of her door: he kissed the threshold over which her feet went out and in, and warmed it by the fire of his breast. He again sat still for a moment, and figured her behind her curtains in the white night-gown, with the red ribbon round her head, in sweet repose: he almost fancied that he was himself so near her, she must needs be dreaming of him. His thoughts were beautiful, like the spirits of the twilight; rest and desire alternated within him; love ran with a quivering hand, in a thousand moods, over all the chords of his soul; it was as if the spheres stood mute above him, suspending their eternal song to watch the low melodies of his heart.

Had he then had about him the master-key with which he used to open Mariana's door, he could not have restrained himself from penetrating into the sanctuary of love. Yet he went away slowly; he slanted, half-dreaming, in beneath the trees, set himself for home, and constantly turned round again; at last, with an effort, he constrained himself, and actually departed. At the corner of the street, looking back yet once, he imagined that he saw Mariana's door open, and a dark figure issue from it. He was too distant for seeing clearly; and, before he could exert himself and look sharply, the appearance was already lost in the night; yet afar off he thought he saw it again gliding past a white house. He stood, and strained his eyes; but, ere he could arouse himself and follow the phantom, it had vanished. Whither should he pursue it? What street had the man taken, if it were a man?

A nightly traveller, when at some turn of his path he has seen the country for an instant illuminated by a flash of lightning, will, with dazzled eyes, next moment, seek in vain for the preceding forms and the connection of his road; so was it in the eyes and the heart of Wilhelm. And as a spirit of midnight, which awakens unutterable terror, is, in the succeeding moments of composure, regarded as a child of imagination, and the fearful vision leaves doubts without end behind it in the soul; so likewise was Wilhelm in extreme disquietude, as, leaning on the corner-stone of the street, he heeded not the clear gray of the morning, and the crowing of the cocks; till the early trades began to stir, and drove him home.

On his way, he had almost effaced the unexpected delusion from his mind by the most sufficient reasons; yet the fine harmonious feelings of the night, on which he now looked back as if they too had been a vision, were also gone. To soothe his heart, and put the last seal on his returning belief, he took the neckerchief from the pocket of the dress he had been last wearing. The rustling of a letter which fell out of it took the kerchief away from his lips: he lifted and read, —

"As I love thee, little fool, what ailed thee last night? This evening I will come again. I can easily suppose that thou art sick of staying here so long: but have patience; at the fair I will return for thee. And observe, never more put me on that abominable black-green-brown jacket: thou lookest in it like the witch of Endor. Did I not send the white night-gown, that I might have a snowy little lamb-kin in my arms? Send thy letters always by the ancient sibyl: the Devil himself has selected her as Iris."

Book Two

WHOEVER STRIVES in our sight with vehement force to reach an object, be it one that we praise or that we blame, may count on exciting an interest in our minds; but, when once the matter is decided, we turn our eyes away from him: whatever once lies finished and done, can no longer at all fix our attention, especially if we at first prophesied an evil issue to the undertaking.

Therefore we shall not try to entertain our readers with any circumstantial account of the grief and desperation into which our ill-fated friend was cast, when he saw his hopes so unexpectedly and instantaneously ruined. On the contrary, we shall even pass over several years, and again take up our friend, where we hope to find him in some sort of activity and comfort. First, however, we must shortly set forth a few matters necessary for maintaining the connection of our narrative.

The pestilence, or a malignant fever, rages with more fierceness, and speedier effect, if the frame which it attacks was before healthy and full of vigor; and in like manner, when a luckless, unlooked-for fate overtook the wretched Wilhelm, his whole being in a moment was laid waste. As when by chance, in the preparation of some artificial fire-work, any part of the composition kindles before its time; and the skilfully bored and loaded barrels, which, arranged, and burning after a settled plan, would have painted in the air a magnificently varying series of flaming images, now hissing and roaring, promiscuously explode with a confused and dangerous crash, — so, in our hero's case, did happiness and hope, pleasure and joys, realities and dreams, clash together with destructive tumult, all at once in his bosom. In such desolate moments, the friend that has hastened to deliverance stands fixed in astonishment; and for him who suffers, it is a benefit that sense forsakes him.

Days of pain, unmixed, ever-returning, and purposely renewed, succeeded next: still, even these are to be regarded as a grace from nature. In such hours Wilhelm had not yet quite lost his mistress: his pains were indefatigable struggles, still to hold fast the happiness that was gliding from his soul; again to luxuriate in thought on the possibility of it; to procure a brief after-life for his joys that had departed forever. Thus one may look upon a body as not utterly dead while the putrefaction lasts; while the forces that in vain seek to work by their old appointment, still labor in dissevering the particles of that frame which they once animated; and not till all is disunited and inert, till we see the whole mouldered down into indifferent dust, — not till then does there rise in us the mournful, vacant sentiment of death, — death, not to be recalled, save by the breath of Him that lives forever.

In a temper so new, so entire, so full of love, there was much to tear asunder, to desolate, to kill; and even the healing force of youth gave nourishment and violence to the power of sorrow. The stroke had extended to the roots of his whole existence. Werner, by necessity his confidant, attacked the hated passion itself with fire and sword, resolutely zealous to search into the monster's inmost life. The opportunity was lucky, the evidence at hand, and many were the histories and narratives with which he backed it out. With such unrelenting vehemence did he make his advances, leaving his friend not even the respite of the smallest momentary self-deception, but treading down every lurking-place in which he might have saved himself from desperation, that Nature, not inclined to let her darling perish utterly, visited him with sickness, to make an outlet for him on the other side.

A violent fever, with its train of consequences, medicines, overstraining, and exhaustion, besides the unwearied attentions of his family, the love of his brothers and sisters, which first becomes truly sensible in times of distress and want, were so many fresh occupations to his mind, and thus formed a kind of painful entertainment. It was not till he grew better, in other words, till his strength was exhausted, that Wilhelm first looked down with horror into the gloomy abyss of a barren misery, as one looks down into the hollow crater of an extinguished volcano.

He now bitterly reproached himself, that, after so great a loss, he could yet enjoy one painless, restful, indifferent moment. He despised his own heart, and longed for the balm of tears and lamentation.

To awaken these again within him, he would recall to memory the scenes of his by-gone happiness. He would paint them to his fancy in the liveliest colors, transport himself again into the days when they were real; and when standing on the highest elevation he could reach, when the sunshine of past times again seemed to animate his limbs and heave his bosom, he would look back into the fearful chasm, would feast his eye on its dismembering depth, then plunge down into its horrors, and thus force from nature the bitterest pains. With such repeated cruelty did he tear himself in pieces; for youth, which is so rich in undeveloped force, knows not what it squanders when, to the anguish which a loss occasions, it adds so many sorrows of its own production, as if it meant then first to give the right value to what is gone forever. He likewise felt so convinced that his present loss was the sole, the first, the last, he ever could experience in life, that he turned away from every consolation which aimed at showing that his sorrows might be less than endless.

CHAPTER TWO

ACCUSTOMED IN this way to torment himself, he now also attacked what still remained to him; what next to love, and along with it, had given him the highest joys and hopes, — his talent as a poet and actor, with spiteful criticisms on every side. In his labors he could see nothing but a shallow imitation of prescribed forms, without intrinsic worth: he looked on them as stiff school-exercises, destitute of any spark of nature, truth, or inspiration. His poems now appeared nothing more than a monotonous arrangement of syllables, in which the most trite emotions and thoughts were dragged along and kept together by a miserable rhyme. And thus did he also deprive himself of every expectation, every pleasure, which on this quarter at least might have aided the recovery of his peace.

With his theatric talent it fared no better. He blamed himself for not having sooner detected the vanity on which alone this pretension had been founded. His figure, his gait, his movements, his mode of declamation, were severally taxed: he decisively renounced every species of advantage or merit that might have raised him above the common run of men, and so doing he increased his mute despair to the highest pitch. For, if it is hard to give up a woman's love, no less painful is the task to part from the fellowship of the Muses, to declare ourselves forever undeserving to be of their community, and to forego the fairest and most immediate kind of approbation, what is openly bestowed on our person, our voice, and our demeanor.

Thus, then, our friend had long ago entirely resigned himself, and set about devoting his powers with the greatest zeal to the business of trade. To the surprise of friends, and to the great contentment of his father, no one was now more diligent than Wilhelm, on the exchange or in the counting-house, in the sales-room or the warehouses: correspondence and calculations, all that was intrusted to his charge, he attended to and managed with the greatest diligence and zeal. Not, in truth, with that warm diligence which to the busy man is its own reward, when he follows with constancy and order the employment he was born for, but with the silent diligence of duty, which has the best principle for its foundation; which is nourished by conviction, and rewarded by conscience; yet which oft, even when the clearest testimony of our minds is crowning it with approbation, can scarcely repress a struggling sigh.

In this manner he lived for a time, assiduously busied, and at last persuaded that his former hard trial had been ordained by fate for the best. He felt glad at having thus been timefully, though somewhat harshly, warned about the proper path of life; while many are constrained to expiate more heavily, and at a later age, the misconceptions into which their youthful inexperience has betrayed them. For each man commonly defends himself as long as possible from casting out the idols which he worships in his soul, from acknowledging a master error, and admitting any truth which brings him to despair.

Determined as he was to abandon his dearest projects, some time was still necessary to convince him fully of his misfortune. At last, however, he had so completely succeeded, by irrefragable reasons, in annihilating every hope of love, or poetical performance, or stage representation, that he took courage to obliterate entirely all the traces of his folly, — all that could in any way remind him of it. For this purpose he had lit a fire in his chamber, one cool evening, and brought out a little chest of relics, among which were multitudes of small articles, that, in memorable moments, he had begged or stolen from Mariana. Each withered flower brought to his mind the time when it bloomed fresh among her hair; each little note the happy hour to which it had invited him; each ribbon-knot the lovely resting-place of his head, —

her beautiful bosom. So occupied, was it not to be expected that each emotion which he thought long since quite dead, should again begin to move? Was it not to be expected that the passion over which, when separated from his mistress, he had gained the victory, should, in the presence of these memorials, again gather strength? We first observe how dreary and disagreeable an overclouded day is when a single sunbeam pierces through, and offers to us the exhilarating splendor of a serene hour.

Accordingly, it was not without disturbance that he saw these relics, long preserved as sacred, fade away from before him in smoke and flame. Sometimes he shuddered and hesitated in his task: he had still a pearl necklace and a flowered neckerchief in his hands, when he resolved to quicken the decaying fire with the poetical attempts of his youth.

Till now he had carefully laid up whatever had proceeded from his pen, since the earliest unfolding of his mind. His papers yet lay tied up in a bundle at the bottom of the chest, where he had packed them; purposing to take them with him in his elopement. How altogether different were his feelings now in opening them, and his feelings then in tying them together!

If we happen, under certain circumstances, to have written and sealed and despatched a letter to a friend, which, however, does not find him, but is brought back to us, and we open it at the distance of some considerable time, a singular emotion is produced in us, on breaking up our own seal, and conversing with our altered self as with a third person. A similar and deep feeling seized our friend, as he now opened this packet, and threw the scattered leaves into the fire; which was flaming fiercely with its offerings, when Werner entered, expressed his wonder at the blaze, and asked what was the matter.

"I am now giving proof," said Wilhelm, "that I am serious in abandoning a trade for which I was not born." And, with these words, he cast the second packet likewise into the fire. Werner made a motion to prevent him, but the business was already done.

"I cannot see how thou shouldst bring thyself to such extremities," said Werner. "Why must these labors, because they are not excellent, be annihilated?"

"Because either a poem is excellent, or it should not be allowed to exist. Because each man who has no gift for producing first-rate works, should entirely abstain from the pursuit of art, and seriously guard himself against every deception on that subject. For it must be owned, that in all men there is a certain vague desire to imitate whatever is presented to them; and such desires do not prove at all that we possess within us the force necessary for succeeding in these enterprises. Look at boys, how, whenever any rope-dancers have been visiting the town, they go scrambling up and down, and balancing on all the planks and beams within their reach, till some other charm calls them off to other sports, for which perhaps they are as little suited. Hast thou never marked it in the circle of our friends? No sooner does a *dilettante* introduce himself to notice, than numbers of them set themselves to learn playing on his instrument. How many wander back and forward on this bootless way! Happy they who soon detect the chasm that lies between their wishes and their powers!"

Werner contradicted this opinion: their discussion became lively, and Wilhelm could not without emotion employ against his friend the arguments with which he had already so frequently tormented himself. Werner maintained that it was not reasonable wholly to re-linquish a pursuit for which a man had some propensity and talent, merely because he never could succeed in it to full perfection. There were many vacant hours, he said, which might be filled up by it; and then by and by some result might be produced which would yield a certain satisfaction to himself and others.

Wilhelm, who in this matter was of quite a different opinion, here interrupted him, and said with great vivacity, —

"How immensely, dear friend, do you err in believing that a work, the first presentation of which is to fill the whole soul, can be pro-duced in broken hours scraped together from other extraneous em-ployment. No: the poet must live wholly for himself, wholly in the objects that delight him. Heaven has furnished him internally with precious gifts; he carries in his bosom a treasure that is ever of itself increasing; he must also live with this treasure, undisturbed from without, in that still blessedness which the rich seek in vain to pur-chase with their accumulated stores. Look at men, how they struggle after happiness and satisfaction! Their wishes, their toil, their gold, are ever hunting restlessly, — and after what? After that which the poet has received from nature, — the right enjoyment of the world, the feeling of himself in others, the harmonious conjunction of many things that will seldom exist together.

"What is it that keeps men in continual discontent and agitation? It is, that they cannot make realities correspond with their conceptions, that enjoyment steals away from among their hands, that the wished-for comes too late, and nothing reached and acquired produces on the heart the effect which their longing for it at a distance led them to anticipate. Now, fate has exalted the poet above all this, as if he were a god. He views the conflicting tumult of the passions; sees families and kingdoms raging in aimless commotion; sees those inexplicable enigmas of misunderstanding, which frequently a single monosyllable would suffice to explain, occasioning convulsions unutterably baleful. He has a fellow-feeling of the mournful and the joyful in the fate of all human beings. When the man of the world is devoting his days to wasting melancholy, for some deep disappointment, or, in the ebullience of joy, is going out to meet his happy destiny, the lightly moved and all-conceiving spirit of the poet steps forth, like the sun from night to day, and with soft transitions tunes his harp to joy or woe. From his heart, its native soil, springs up the lovely flower of wisdom; and if others, while waking, dream, and are pained with fantastic delusions from their every sense, he passes the dream of life like one awake; and the strangest of incidents is to him a part both of the past and of the future. And thus the poet is at once a teacher, a prophet, a friend of gods and men. What! thou wouldst have him descend from his height to some paltry occupation! He who is fashioned like the bird to hover round the world, to nestle on the lofty summits, to feed on buds and fruits, exchanging gayly one bough for another, *he* ought also to work at the plough like an ox; like a dog to train himself to the harness and draught; or perhaps, tied up in a chain, to guard a farmyard by his barking!"

Werner, it may well be supposed, had listened with the greatest surprise. "All true," he rejoined, "if men were but made like birds, and, though they neither spun nor weaved, could yet spend peaceful days in perpetual enjoyment; if, at the approach of winter, they could as easily betake themselves to distant regions, could retire before scarcity, and fortify themselves against frost."

"Poets have lived so," exclaimed Wilhelm, "in times when true nobleness was better reverenced; and so should they ever live! Sufficiently provided for within, they had need of little from without: the gift of communicating lofty emotions and glorious images to men, in melodies and words that charmed the ear, and fixed themselves inseparably on whatever objects they referred to, of old enraptured the world, and served the gifted as a rich inheritance. At the courts of kings, at the tables of the great, beneath the windows of the fair, the sound of them was heard; while the ear and the soul were shut for all beside: and men felt as we do when delight comes over us, and we stop with rapture if, among the dingles we are crossing, the voice of the nightingale starts out touching and strong. They found a home in every habitation of the world, and the lowliness of their condition but exalted them the more. The hero listened to their songs, and the conqueror of the earth did reverence to a poet; for he felt, that, without poets, his own wild and vast existence would pass away like a whirlwind, and be forgotten forever. The lover wished that he could feel his longings and his joys so variedly and so harmoniously as the poet's inspired lips had skill to show them forth; and even the rich man could not of himself discern such costliness in his idol grandeurs, as when they were presented to him shining in the splendor of the poet's spirit, sensible to all worth, and exalting all. Nay, if thou wilt have it, who but the poet was it that first formed gods for us, that exalted us to them, and brought them down to us?"

"My friend," said Werner, after some reflection, "it has often grieved me that thou shouldst strive by force to banish from thy soul what thou feelest so vividly. I am greatly mistaken, if it were not better for thee in some degree to yield to these propensities, than to waste thyself by the contradictions of so hard a piece of self-denial, and with the enjoyment of this one guiltless pleasure to renounce the enjoyment of all others."

"Shall I confess it," said the other, "and wilt not thou laugh at me if I acknowledge, that these ideas pursue me constantly; that, let me flee from them as I will, when I explore my heart, I find all my early wishes yet rooted there, firmly, — nay, more firmly than ever? Yet what now remains for me, wretched as I am? Ah! whoever should have told me that the arms of my spirit, with which I was grasping at infinity, and hoping with certainty to clasp something great and glorious, would so soon be crushed and smote in pieces, — whoever should have told me this, would have brought me to despair. And yet now, when judgment has been passed against me; now, when *she*, that was to be as my divinity to guide me to my wishes, is gone forever, — what remains but that I yield up my soul to the bitterest woes? O my brother! I will not deceive you: in my secret purposes, she was as the hook on which the ladder of my hopes was fixed. See! With daring aim the mountain adventurer hovers in the air: the iron breaks, and he lies broken and dismembered on the earth. No, there is no hope, no comfort for me more! I will not," he cried out, springing to his feet, "leave a single fragment of these wretched papers from the flames." He then seized one or two packets of them, tore them up, and threw them into the fire. Werner endeavored to restrain him, but in vain. "Let me alone!" cried Wilhelm: "what should these miserable leaves do here? To me they give neither pleasant recollections nor pleasant hopes. Shall they remain behind to vex me to the end of my life? Shall they perhaps one day serve the world for a jest, instead of awakening sympathy and horror? Woe to me! my doom is woe! Now I comprehend the wailings of the poets, of the wretched whom necessity has rendered wise. How long did I look upon myself as invulnerable and invincible; and alas! I am now made to see that a deep and early sorrow can never heal, can never pass away: I feel that I shall take it with me to my grave. No! not a day of my life shall escape this anguish, which at last must crush me down; and *her* image too shall stay with me, shall live and die with me, the image of the worthless, — O my friend! if I must speak the feeling of my heart, — the perhaps not altogether worthless! Her situation, the crookedness of her destiny, have a thousand times excused her in my mind. I have been too cruel; you steeled me in your own cold unrelenting harshness; you held my wavering senses captive, and hindered me from doing for myself and her what I owed to both. Who knows to what a state I may have brought her! my conscience by degrees presents to me, in all its heaviness, in what helplessness, in what despair, I may have left her. Was it not possible that she might clear herself? Was it not possible? How many misconceptions throw the world into perplexity! how many circumstances may extort forgiveness for the greatest fault! Often do I figure her as sitting by herself in silence, leaning on her elbows. 'This,' she says, 'is the faith, the love, he swore to me! With this hard stroke to end the delicious life which made us one!' " He broke out into a stream of tears; while he threw himself down with his face upon the table, and wetted the remaining papers with his weeping.

Werner stood beside him in the deepest perplexity. He had not anticipated this fierce ebullition of feeling. More than once he had tried to interrupt his friend, more than once to lead the conversation elsewhere, but in vain: the current was too strong for him. It remained that long-suffering friendship should again take up her office. Werner allowed the first shock of sorrow to pass over, while by his silent presence he testified a pure and honest sympathy. And thus they both remained that evening, — Wilhelm sunk in the dull feeling of old sorrows; and the other terrified at this new outbreaking of a passion which he thought his prudent councils and keen persuasion had long since mastered and destroyed.

CHAPTER THREE

AFTER SUCH relapses, Wilhelm usually applied himself to business and activity with augmented ardor; and he found it the best means to escape the labyrinth into which he had again been tempted to enter. His attractive way of treating strangers, the ease with which he carried on a correspondence in any living language, more and more increased the hopes of his father and his trading-friends, and comforted them in their sorrow for his sickness, — the origin of which had not been known, — and for the pause which had thus interrupted their plan. They determined a second time on Wilhelm's setting out to travel; and we now find him on horseback, with his saddle-bags behind him, exhilarated by the motion and the free air, approaching the mountains, where he had some affairs to settle.

He winded slowly on his path, through dales and over hills, with a feeling of the greatest satisfaction. Overhanging cliffs, roaring brooks, moss-grown rocky walls, deep precipices, he here saw for the first time; yet his earliest dreams of youth had wandered among such regions. In these scenes he felt his age renewed; all the sorrows he had undergone were obliterated from his soul; with unbroken cheerfulness he repeated to himself passages of various poems, particularly of the "Pastor Fido," which, in these solitary places, flocked in crowds into his mind. He also recollected many pieces of his own songs, and recited them with a peculiar contentment. He peopled the world which lay before him with all the forms of the past, and each step into the future was to him full of augury of important operations and remarkable events.

Several men, who came behind him in succession, and saluted him as they passed by to continue their hasty way into the mountains, by steep footpaths, sometimes interrupted his thoughts without attracting his attention to themselves. At last a communicative traveller joined him, and explained the reason of this general pilgrimage.

"At Hochdorf," he said, "there is a play to be acted to-night; and the whole neighborhood is gathering to see it."

"What!" cried Wilhelm. "In these solitary hills, among these impenetrable forests, has theatric art sought out a place, and built herself a temple? And I am journeying to her festivities!"

"You will wonder more," said the other, "when you learn by whom the play is to be acted. There is in the place a large manufactory, which employs many people. The proprietor, who lives, so to speak, remote from all human society, can find no better means of entertaining his workmen during winter, than allowing them to act plays. He suffers no cards among them, and wishes also to withdraw them from all coarse rustic practices. Thus they pass the long evenings; and to-day, being the old gentleman's birthday, they are giving a particular festival in honor of him."

Wilhelm came to Hochdorf, where he was to pass the night, and alighted at the manufactory, the proprietor of which stood as a debtor in his list.

When he gave his name, the old man cried in a glad surprise, "Aye, sir, are you the son of that worthy man to whom I owe so many thanks, — so long have owed money? Your good father has had so much patience with me, I should be a knave if I did not pay you speedily and cheerfully. You come at the proper time to see that I am fully in earnest about it."

He then called out his wife, who seemed no less delighted than himself to see the youth: she declared that he was very like his father, and lamented, that, having such a multitude of guests already in the house, she could not lodge him for the night.

The account was clear, and quickly settled: Wilhelm put the roll of gold into his pocket, and wished that all his other business might go on so smoothly. At last the play-hour came: they now waited nothing but the coming of the head forester, who at length also arrived, entered with a few hunters, and was received with the greatest reverence.

The company was then led into the playhouse, formed out of a barn that lay close upon the garden. Without any extraordinary taste, both seats and stage were yet decked out in a cheerful and pretty way. One of the painters employed in the manufactory had formerly worked as an understrapper at the prince's theatre: he had now represented woods and streets and chambers, somewhat rudely, it is true, yet so as to be recognized for such. The play itself they had borrowed from a strolling company, and shaped it aright, according to their own ideas. As it was, it did not fail to yield some entertainment. The plot of two lovers wishing to carry off a girl from her guardian, and mutually from one another, produced a great variety of interesting situations. Being the first play our friend had witnessed for so long a time, it suggested several reflections to him. It was full of action, but without any true delineation of character. It pleased and delighted. Such are always the beginnings of the scenic art. The rude man is contented if he see but something going on; the man of more refinement must be made to feel; the man entirely refined, desires to reflect.

The players he would willingly have helped here and there, for a very little would have made them greatly better.

His silent meditations were somewhat broken in upon by the tobacco-smoke, which now began to rise in great and greater copiousness. Soon after the commencement of the play, the head forester had lit his pipe: by and by others took the same liberty. The large dogs, too, which followed these gentlemen, introduced themselves in no pleasant style. At first they had been bolted out; but, soon finding the backdoor passage, they entered on the stage, ran against the actors, and at last, jumping over the orchestra, joined their masters, who had taken up the front seats in the pit.

For afterpiece an oblation was represented. A portrait of the old gentleman in his bridegroom-dress stood upon an altar, hung with garlands. All the players paid their reverence to it in the most submissive postures. The youngest child came forward dressed in white, and made a speech in verse; by which the whole family, and even the head forester himself, whom it brought in mind of his own children, were melted into tears. Thus ended the play; and Wilhelm could not help stepping on the stage, to have a closer view of the actresses, to praise them for their good performance, and give them a little counsel for the future.

The remaining business, which our friend in the following days had to transact in various quarters of the hill-country, was not all so pleasant, or so easy to conclude with satisfaction. Many of his debtors entreated for delay, many were uncourteous, many lied. In conformity with his instructions, he had to sue some of them at law: he was thus obliged to seek out advocates, and give instructions to them, to appear before judges, and go through many other sorry duties of the same sort.

His case was hardly bettered when people chanced to incline showing some attention to him. He found very few that could any way instruct him, few with whom he could hope to establish a useful commercial correspondence. Unhappily, moreover, the weather now grew rainy; and travelling on horseback in this district came to be attended with insufferable difficulties. He therefore thanked his stars on again getting near the level country; and at the foot of the mountains, looking out into a fertile and beautiful plain, intersected by a smooth-flowing river, and seeing a cheerful little town lying on its banks, all glittering in the sunshine, he resolved, though without any special business in the place, to pass a day or two there, that he might refresh both himself and his horse, which the bad roads had considerably injured.

ON ALIGHTING at an inn, upon the market-place, he found matters going on very joyously, — at least very stirringly. A large company of rope-dancers, leapers, and jugglers, having a strong man along with them, had just arrived with their wives and children, and, while preparing for a grand exhibition, kept up a perpetual racket. They first quarrelled with the landlord, then with one another; and, if their contention was intolerable, the expressions of their satisfaction were infinitely more so. Undetermined whether he should go or stay, he was standing in the door looking at some workmen, who had just begun to erect a stage in the middle of the square.

A girl with roses and other flowers for sale, coming by, held out her basket to him, and he purchased a beautiful nosegay; which, like one that had a taste for these things, he tied up in a different fashion, and was looking at it with a satisfied air, when the window of another inn on the opposite side of the square flew open, and a handsome woman looked out from it. Notwithstanding the distance, he observed that her face was animated by a pleasant cheerfulness; her fair hair fell carelessly streaming about her neck; she seemed to be looking at the stranger. In a short time afterwards, a boy with a white jacket, and a barber's apron on, came out from the door of her house towards Wilhelm, saluted him, and said, "The lady at the window bids me ask if you will not favor her with a share of your beautiful flowers." — "They are all at her service," answered Wilhelm, giving the nosegay to this nimble messenger, and making a bow to the fair one, who returned it with a friendly courtesy, and then withdrew from the window.

Amused with this small adventure, he was going up-stairs to his chamber, when a young creature sprang against him, and attracted his attention. A short silk waistcoat with slashed Spanish sleeves, tight trousers with puffs, looked very pretty on the child. Its long black hair was curled, and wound in locks and plaits about the head. He looked at the figure with astonishment, and could not determine whether to take it for a boy or a girl. However, he decided for the latter: and, as the child ran by, he took her up in his arms, bade her good-day, and asked her to whom she belonged; though he easily perceived that she must be a member of the vaulting and dancing company lately arrived. She viewed him with a dark, sharp side-look, as she pushed herself out of his arms, and ran into the kitchen without making any answer.

On coming up-stairs, he found in the large parlor two men practising the small sword, or seeming rather to make trial which was the better fencer. One of them plainly enough belonged to the vaulting company: the other had a somewhat less savage aspect. Wilhelm looked at them, and had reason to admire them both; and as the black-bearded, sturdy contender soon afterwards forsook the place of action, the other with extreme complaisance offered Wilhelm the rapier.

"If you want to take a scholar under your inspection," said our friend, "I am well content to risk a few passes with you."

Accordingly they fought together; and, although the stranger greatly overmatched his new competitor, he politely kept declaring that it all depended upon practice: in fact, Wilhelm, inferior as he was, had made it evident that he had got his first instructions from a good, solid, thorough-paced German fencing-master.

Their entertainment was disturbed by the uproar with which the party-colored brotherhood issued from the inn, to make proclamation of the show, and awaken a desire to see their art, throughout the town. Preceded by a drum, the manager advanced on horseback: he was followed by a female dancer mounted on a corresponding hack, and holding a child before her, all bedizened with ribbons and spangles. Next came the remainder of the troop on foot, some of them carrying children on their shoulders in dangerous postures, yet smoothly and lightly: among these the young, dark, black-haired figure again attracted Wilhelm's notice.

Pickleherring ran gayly up and down the crowded multitude, distributing his handbills with much practical fun, — here smacking the lips of a girl, there breeching a boy, and awakening generally among the people an invincible desire to know more of him.

On the painted flags, the manifold science of the company was visibly delineated, particularly of the Monsieur Narciss and the Demoiselle Landrinette: both of whom, being main characters, had prudently kept back from the procession, thereby to acquire a more dignified consideration, and excite a greater curiosity.

During the procession, Wilhelm's fair neighbor had again appeared at the window; and he did not fail to inquire about her of his new companion. This person, whom for the present we shall call Laertes, offered to take Wilhelm over and introduce him. "I and the lady," said he laughing, "are two fragments of an acting company that made shipwreck here a short while ago. The pleasantness of the place has induced us to stay in it, and consume our little stock of cash in peace; while one of our friends is out seeking some situation for himself and us."

Laertes immediately accompanied his new acquaintance to Philina's door; where he left him for a moment, and ran to a shop hard by for a few sweetmeats. "I am sure you will thank me," said he, on returning, "for procuring you so pleasant an acquaintance."

The lady came out from her room, in a pair of tight little slippers with high heels, to give them welcome. She had thrown a black mantle over her, above a white *negligée*, not indeed superstitiously clean; which, however, for that very reason, gave her a more frank and domestic air. Her short dress did not hide a pair of the prettiest feet and ankles in the world.

"You are welcome," she cried to Wilhelm, "and I thank you for your charming flowers." She led him into her chamber with the one hand, pressing the nosegay to her breast with the other. Being all seated, and got into a pleasant train of general talk, to which she had the art of giving a delightful turn, Laertes threw a handful of gingerbread-nuts into her lap; and she immediately began to eat them.

"Look what a child this young gallant is!" she said: "he wants to persuade you that I am fond of such confectionery, and it is himself that cannot live without licking his lips over something of the kind."

"Let us confess," replied Laertes, "that in this point, as in others, you and I go hand in hand. For example," he continued, "the weather is delightful to-day: what if we should take a drive into the country, and eat our dinner at the Mill?"

"With all my heart," said Philina: "we must give our new acquaintance some diversion."

Laertes sprang out, for he never walked: and Wilhelm motioned to return for a minute to his lodgings, to have his hair put in order; for at present it was all dishevelled with riding. "You can do it here," she said, then called her little servant, and constrained Wilhelm in the politest manner to lay off his coat, to throw her powder-mantle over him, and to have his head dressed in her presence. "We must lose no time," said she: "who knows how short a while we may all be together?"

The boy, out of sulkiness and ill nature more than want of skill, went on but indifferently with his task: he pulled the hair with his implements, and seemed as if he would not soon be done. Philina more than once reproved him for his blunders, and at last sharply packed him off, and chased him to the door. She then undertook the business herself, and frizzled Wilhelm's locks with great dexterity and grace; though she, too, appeared to be in no exceeding haste, but found always this and that to improve and put to rights; while at the same time she could not help touching his knees with hers, and holding her nosegay and bosom so near his lips, that he was strongly tempted more than once to imprint a kiss on it.

When Wilhelm had cleaned his brow with a little powder-knife, she said to him, "Put it in your pocket, and think of me when you see it." It was a pretty knife: the haft, of inlaid steel, had these friendly words wrought on it, "Think of me." Wilhelm put it up, and thanked her, begging permission at the same time to make her a little present in return.

At last they were in readiness. Laertes had brought round the coach, and they commenced a very gay excursion. To every beggar, Philina threw out money from the window: giving along with it a merry and friendly word.

Scarcely had they reached the Mill, and ordered dinner, when a strain of music struck up before the house. It was some miners singing various pretty songs, and accompanying their clear and shrill voices with a cithern and triangle. In a short while the gathering crowd had formed a ring about them, and our company nodded approbation to them from the windows. Observing this attention, they expanded their circle, and seemed making preparation for their grandest piece. After some pause, a miner stepped forward with a mattock in his hand; and, while the others played a serious tune, he set himself to represent the action of digging.

Ere long a peasant came from among the crowd, and, by pantomimic threats, let the former know that he must cease and remove. Our company were greatly surprised at this: they did not discover that the peasant was a miner in disguise, till he opened his mouth, and, in a sort of recitative, rebuked the other for daring to meddle with his field. The latter did not lose his composure of mind, but began to inform the husbandman about his right to break ground there; giving him withal some primary conceptions of mineralogy. The peasant, not being master of his foreign terminology, asked all manner of silly questions; whereat the spectators, as themselves more knowing, set up many a hearty laugh. The miner endeavored to instruct him, and showed him the advantage, which, in the long-run, would reach even him, if the deep-lying treasures of the land were dug out from their secret beds. The peasant, who at first had threatened his instructor with blows, was gradually pacified; and they parted good friends at last, though it was the miner chiefly that got out of this contention with honor.

"In this little dialogue," said Wilhelm, when seated at the table, "we have a lively proof how useful the theatre might be to all ranks; what advantage even the state might procure from it, if the occupations, trades, and undertakings of men were brought upon the stage, and presented on their praiseworthy side, in that point of view in which the state itself should honor and protect them. As matters stand, we exhibit only the ridiculous side of men: the comic poet is, as it were, but a spiteful tax-gatherer, who keeps a watchful eye over the errors of his fellow-subjects, and seems gratified when he can fix any charge upon them. Might it not be a worthy and pleasing task for a statesman to survey the natural and reciprocal influence of all classes on each other, and to guide some poet, gifted with sufficient humor, in such labors as these? In this way, I am persuaded, many very entertaining, both agreeable and useful, pieces, might be executed."

Wilhelm watches the minstrels prepare

"So far," said Laertes, "as I, in wandering about the world, have been able to observe, statesmen are accustomed merely to forbid, to hinder, to refuse, but very rarely to invite, to further, to reward. They let all things go along, till some mischief happens: then they get into a rage, and lay about them."

"A truce with state and statesmen!" said Philina: "I cannot form a notion of statesmen except in periwigs; and a periwig, wear it who will, always gives my fingers a spasmodic motion: I could like to pluck it off the venerable gentleman, to skip up and down the room with it, and laugh at the bald head."

So, with a few lively songs, which she could sing very beautifully, Philina cut short their conversation, and urged them to a quick return homewards, that they might arrive in time for seeing the performance of the rope-dancers in the evening. On the road back she continued her lavish generosity, in a style of gayety reaching to extravagance; for at last, every coin belonging to herself or her companions being spent, she threw her straw hat from the window to a girl, and her neckerchief to an old woman, who asked her for alms.

Philina invited both of her attendants to her own apartments, because, she said, the spectacle could be seen more conveniently from her windows than from theirs.

On arriving, they found the stage set up, and the background decked with suspended carpets. The swing-boards were already fastened, the slack-rope fixed to posts, the tight-rope bound over trestles. The square was moderately filled with people, and the windows with spectators of some quality.

Pickleherring, with a few insipidities, at which the lookers-on are generally kind enough to laugh, first prepared the meeting to attention and good-humor. Some children, whose bodies were made to exhibit the strangest contortions, awakened astonishment or horror; and Wilhelm could not, without the deepest sympathy, see the child he had at the first glance felt an interest in, go through her fantastic positions with considerable difficulty. But the merry tumblers soon changed the feeling into that of lively satisfaction, when they first singly, then in rows, and at last all together, vaulted up into the air, making somersets backwards and forwards. A loud clapping of hands and a strong huzza echoed from the whole assembly.

The general attention was next directed to quite a different object. The children in succession had to mount the rope, — the learners first, that by practising they might prolong the spectacle, and show the difficulties of the art more clearly. Some men and full-grown women likewise exhibited their skill to moderate advantage; but still there was no Monsieur Narciss, no Demoiselle Landrinette.

At last this worthy pair came forth: they issued from a kind of tent with red spread curtains, and, by their agreeable forms and glittering decorations, fulfilled the hitherto increasing hopes of the spectators. He, a hearty knave, of middle stature, with black eyes and a strong head of hair; she, formed with not inferior symmetry, — exhibited themselves successively upon the rope, with delicate movements, leaping, and singular postures. Her airy lightness, his audacity; the exactitude with which they both performed their feats of art, — raised the universal satisfaction higher at every step and spring. The stateliness with which they bore themselves, the seeming attentions of the rest to them, gave them the appearance of king and queen of the whole troop; and all held them worthy of the rank.

The animation of the people spread to the spectators at the

windows: the ladies looked incessantly at Narciss, the gentlemen at Landrinette. The populace hurrahed, the more cultivated public could not keep from clapping of the hands: Pickleherring now could scarcely raise a laugh. A few, however, slunk away when some members of the troop began to press through the crowd with their tin plates to collect money.

"They have made their purpose good, I imagine," said Wilhelm to Philina, who was leaning over the window beside him. "I admire the ingenuity with which they have turned to advantage even the meanest parts of their performance: out of the unskilfulness of their children, and exquisiteness of their chief actors, they have made up a whole which at first excited our attention, and then gave us very fine entertainment."

The people by degrees dispersed; and the square was again become empty, while Philina and Laertes were disputing about the forms and the skill of Narciss and Landrinette, and rallying each other on the subject at great length. Wilhelm noticed the wonderful child standing on the street near some other children at play: he showed her to Philina, who, in her lively way, immediately called and beckoned to the little one, and, this not succeeding, tripped singing down-stairs, and led her up by the hand.

"Here is the enigma," said she, as she brought her to the door. The child stood upon the threshold, as if she meant again to run off; laid her right hand on her breast, the left on her brow, and bowed deeply. "Fear nothing, my little dear," said Wilhelm, rising, and going towards her. She viewed him with a doubting look, and came a few steps nearer.

"What is thy name?" he asked. "They call me Mignon." — "How old art thou?" — "No one has counted." — "Who was thy father?" — "The Great Devil is dead."

"Well! this is singular enough," said Philina. They asked her a few more questions: she gave her answers in a kind of broken German, and with a strangely solemn manner; every time laying her hands on her breast and brow, and bowing deeply.

Wilhelm could not satisfy himself with looking at her. His eyes and his heart were irresistibly attracted by the mysterious condition of this being. He reckoned her about twelve or thirteen years of age: her body was well formed, only her limbs gave promise of a stronger growth, or else announced a stunted one. Her countenance was not regular, but striking; her brow full of mystery; her nose extremely beautiful; her mouth, although it seemed too closely shut for one of her age, and though she often threw it to a side, had yet an air of frankness, and was very lovely. Her brownish complexion could scarcely be discerned through the paint. This form stamped itself deeply in Wilhelm's soul: he kept looking at her earnestly, and forgot the present scene in the multitude of his reflections. Philina waked him from his half-dream, by holding out the remainder of her sweet-meats to the child, and giving her a sign to go away. She made her little bow as formerly, and darted like lightning through the door.

As the time drew on when our new friends had to part for the evening, they planned a fresh excursion for the morrow. They pur-posed now to have their dinner at a neighboring *Jägerhaus*. Before taking leave of Laertes, Wilhelm said many things in Philina's praise, to which the other made only brief and careless answers.

Next morning, having once more exercised themselves in fencing for an hour, they went over to Philina's lodging, towards which they had seen their expected coach passing by. But how surprised was Wilhelm, when the coach seemed altogether to have vanished; and how much more so, when Philina was not to be found at home! She had placed herself in the carriage, they were told, with a couple of strangers who had come that morning, and was gone with them. Wilhelm had been promising himself some pleasant entertainment from her company, and could not hide his irritation. Laertes, on the other hand, but laughed at it, and cried, "I love her for this: it looks so like herself! Let us, however, go directly to the *Jägerhaus*: be Philina where she pleases, we will not lose our promenade on her account."

As Wilhelm, while they walked, continued censuring the in-consistency of such conduct, Laertes said, "I cannot reckon it incon-sistent so long as one keeps faithful to his character. If this Philina plans you any thing, or promises you any thing, she does it under the tacit condition that it shall be quite convenient for her to fulfil her plan, to keep her promise. She gives willingly, but you must ever hold yourself in readiness to return her gifts."

"That seems a singular character," said Wilhelm.

"Any thing but singular: only she is not a hypocrite. I like her on that account. Yes: I am her friend, because she represents the sex so truly, which I have so much cause to hate. To me she is another genuine Eve, the great mother of womankind: so are they all, only they will not all confess it."

With abundance of such talk, in which Laertes very vehemently exhibited his spleen against the fair sex, without, however, giving any cause for it, they arrived at the forest; into which Wilhelm entered in no joyful mood, the speeches of Laertes having again revived in him the memory of his relation to Mariana. Not far from a shady well, among some old and noble trees, they found Philina sitting by herself at a stone table. Seeing them, she struck up a merry song; and, when Laertes asked for her companions, she cried out, "I have already cozened them: I have already had my laugh at them, and sent them a-travelling, as they deserved. By the way hither I had put to proof their liberality; and, finding that they were a couple of your close-fisted gentry, I immediately determined to have amends of them. On arriving at the inn, they asked the waiter what was to be had. He, with his customary glibness of tongue, reckoned over all that could be found in the house, and more than could be found. I noticed their perplexity: they looked at one another, stammered, and inquired about the cost. "What is the use of all this studying?" said I. "The table is the lady's business: allow me to manage it." I immediately began ordering a most unconscionable dinner, for which many necessary articles would require to be sent for from the neighborhood. The waiter, of whom, by a wry mouth or two, I had made a confidant, at last helped me out; and so, by the image of a sumptuous feast, we tortured them to such a degree that they fairly determined on having a walk in the forest, from which I imagine we shall look with clear eyes if we see them come again. I have laughed a quarter of an hour for my own behoof; I shall laugh forever when I think of the looks they had." At table, Laertes told of similar adventures: they got into the track of recounting ludicrous stories, mistakes, and dexterous cheats.

A young man of their acquaintance, from the town, came gliding through the wood with a book in his hand: he sat down by them, and began praising the beauty of the place. He directed their attention to the murmuring of the brook, to the waving of the boughs, to the checkered lights and shadows, and the music of the birds. Philina commenced a little song of the cuckoo, which did not seem at all to exhilarate the man of taste: he very soon made his compliments, and went on.

"Oh that I might never hear more of nature, and scenes of nature!" cried Philina, so soon as he was gone: "there is nothing in the world more intolerable than to hear people reckon up the pleasures you enjoy. When the day is bright you go to walk, as to dance when you hear a tune played. But who would think a moment on the music or the weather? It is the dancer that interests us, not the violin; and to look upon a pair of bright black eyes is the life of a pair of blue ones. But what on earth have we to do with wells and brooks, and old rotten lindens?" She was sitting opposite to Wilhelm; and, while speaking so, she looked into his eyes with a glance which he could not hinder from piercing at least to the very door of his heart.

"You are right," replied he, not without embarrassment: "man is ever the most interesting object to man, and perhaps should be the only one that interests. Whatever else surrounds us is but the element in which we live, or else the instrument which we employ. The more we devote ourselves to such things, the more we attend to and feel concern in them, the weaker will our sense of our own dignity become, the weaker our feelings for society. Men who put a great value on gardens, buildings, clothes, ornaments, or any other sort of property, grow less social and pleasant: they lose sight of their brethren, whom very few can succeed in collecting about them and entertaining. Have you not observed it on the stage? A good actor makes us very soon forget the awkwardness and meanness of paltry decorations, but a splendid theatre is the very thing which first makes us truly feel the want of proper actors."

After dinner Philina sat down among the long, overshaded grass, and commanded both her friends to fetch her flowers in great quantities. She wreathed a complete garland, and put it round her head: it made her look extremely charming. The flowers were still sufficient for another: this, too, she plaited, while both the young men sat beside her. When, at last, amid infinite mirth and sportfulness, it was completed, she pressed it on Wilhelm's head with the greatest dignity, and shifted the posture of it more than once, till it seemed to her properly adjusted. "And I, it appears, must go empty," said Laertes.

"Not by any means: you shall not have reason to complain," replied Philina, taking off the garland from her own head, and putting it on his.

"If we were rivals," said Laertes, "we might now dispute very warmly which of us stood higher in thy favor."

"And the more fools you," said she, while she bent herself towards him, and offered him her lips to kiss; and then immediately turned round, threw her arm about Wilhelm, and bestowed a kind salute on him also. "Which of them tastes best?" said she archly.

"Surprisingly!" exclaimed Laertes: "it seems as if nothing else had ever such a tang of wormwood in it."

"As little wormwood," she replied, "as any gift that a man may enjoy without envy and without conceit. But now," cried she, "I should like to have an hour's dancing; and after that we must look to our vaulters."

Accordingly, they went into the house, and there found music in readiness. Philina was a beautiful dancer: she animated both her companions. Nor was Wilhelm without skill; but he wanted careful practice, a defect which his two friends voluntarily took charge of remedying.

In these amusements the time passed on insensibly. It was already late when they returned. The rope-dancers had commenced their operations. A multitude of people had again assembled in the square; and our friends, on alighting, were struck by the appearance of a tumult in the crowd, occasioned by a throng of men rushing towards the door of the inn, which Wilhelm had now turned his face to. He sprang forward to see what it was; and, pressing through the people, he was struck with horror to observe the master of the rope-dancing company dragging poor Mignon by the hair out of the house, and unmercifully beating her little body with the handle of a whip.

Wilhelm darted on the man like lightning, and seized him by the collar. "Quit the child!" he cried, in a furious tone, "or one of us shall never leave this spot!" and, so speaking, he grasped the fellow by the throat with a force which only rage could have lent him. The showman, on the point of choking, let go the child, and endeavored to defend himself against his new assailant. But some people, who had felt compassion for Mignon, yet had not dared to begin a quarrel for her, now laid hold of the rope-dancer, wrenched his whip away, and threatened him with great fierceness and abuse. Being now reduced to the weapons of his mouth, he began bullying, and cursing horribly. The lazy, worthless urchin, he said, would not do her duty; refused to perform the egg-dance, which he had promised to the public; he would beat her to death, and no one should hinder him. He tried to get loose, and seek the child, who had crept away among the crowd. Wilhelm held him back, and said sternly, "You shall neither see nor touch her, till you have explained before a magistrate where you stole her. I will pursue you to every extremity. You shall not escape me." These words, which Wilhelm uttered in heat, without thought or purpose, out of some vague feeling, or, if you will, out of inspiration, soon brought the raging showman to composure. "What have I to do with the useless brat?" cried he. "Pay me what her clothes cost, and make of her what you please. We shall settle it to-night." And, being liberated, he made haste to resume his interrupted operations, and to calm the irritation of the public by some striking displays of his craft.

As soon as all was still again, Wilhelm commenced a search for Mignon, whom, however, he could nowhere find. Some said they had seen her on the street, others on the roofs of the adjoining houses; but, after seeking unsuccessfully in all quarters, he was forced to content himself, and wait to see if she would not again turn up of herself.

In the mean time, Narciss had come into the house; and Wilhelm set to question him about the birthplace and history of the child. Monsieur Narciss knew nothing about these things, for he had not long been in the company; but in return he recited, with much volubility and levity, various particulars of his own fortune. Upon Wilhelm's wishing him joy of the great approbation he had gained, Narciss expressed himself as if exceedingly indifferent on that point. "People laugh at us," he said, "and admire our feats of skill; but their admiration does nothing for us. The master has to pay us, and may raise the funds where he pleases." He then took his leave, and was setting off in great haste.

At the question, whither he was bent so fast, the dog gave a smile, and admitted that his figure and talents had acquired for him a more solid species of favor than the huzzaing of the multitude. He had been invited by some young ladies, who desired much to become acquainted with him; and he was afraid it would be midnight before he could get all his visits over. He proceeded with the greatest candor to detail his adventures. He would have given the names of his patronesses, their streets and houses, had not Wilhelm waived such indiscretion, and politely dismissed him.

Laertes had meanwhile been entertaining Landrinette: he declared that she was fully worthy to be and to remain a woman.

Our friend next proceeded to his bargain with the showman for Mignon. Thirty crowns was the price set upon her; and for this sum the black-bearded, hot Italian entirely surrendered all his claims: but of her history or parentage he would discover nothing, only that she had fallen into his hands at the death of his brother, who, by reason of his admirable skill, had usually been named the "Great Devil."

Next morning was chiefly spent in searching for the child. It was in vain that they rummaged every hole and corner of the house and neighborhood: the child had vanished; and Wilhelm was afraid she might have leaped into some pool of water, or destroyed herself in some other way.

Philina's charm could not divert his inquietude. He passed a dreary, thoughtful day. Nor at evening could the utmost efforts of the tumblers and dancers, exerting all their powers to gratify the public, divert the current of his thoughts, or clear away the clouds from his mind.

By the concourse of people flocking from all places round, the numbers had greatly increased on this occasion: the general approbation was like a snowball rolling itself into a monstrous size. The feat of leaping over swords, and through the cask with paper ends, made a great sensation.

The strong man, too, produced a universal feeling of mingled astonishment and horror, when he laid his head and feet on a couple of separate stools, and then allowed some sturdy smiths to place a stithy on the unsupported part of his body, and hammer a horseshoe till it was completely made by means of it.

The Hercules' Strength, as they called it, was a no less wonderful affair. A row of men stood up; then another row, upon their shoulders; then women and young lads, supported in like manner on the second row; so that finally a living pyramid was formed; the peak being ornamented by a child, placed on its head, and dressed out in the shape of a ball and weather-vane. Such a sight, never witnessed in those parts before, gave a worthy termination to the whole performance. Narciss and Landrinette were then borne in litters, on the shoulders of the rest, along the chief streets of the town, amid the triumphant shouts of the people. Ribbon, nosegays, silks, were thrown upon them: all pressed to get a sight of them. Each thought himself happy if he could behold them, and be honored with a look of theirs.

"What actor, what author, nay, what man of any class, would not regard himself as on the summit of his wishes, could he, by a noble saying or a worthy action, produce so universal an impression? What a precious emotion would it give, if one could disseminate generous, exalted, manly feelings with electric force and speed, and rouse assembled thousands into such rapture, as these people, by their bodily alertness, have done! If one could communicate to thronging multitudes a fellow-feeling in all that belongs to man, by the portraying of happiness and misery, of wisdom and folly, nay, of absurdity and silliness; could kindle and thrill their inmost souls, and set their stagnant nature into movement, free, vehement, and pure!" So said our friend; and, as neither Laertes nor Philina showed any disposition to take part in such a strain, he entertained himself with these darling speculations, walking up and down the streets till late at night, and again pursuing, with all the force and vivacity of a liberated imagination, his old desire to have all that was good and noble and great embodied and shown forth by the theatric art.

CHAPTER FIVE

NEXT MORNING, the rope-dancers, not without much parade and bustle, having gone away, Mignon immediately appeared, and came into the parlor as Wilhelm and Laertes were busy fencing. "Where hast thou been hid?" said Wilhelm, in a friendly tone. "Thou hast given us a great deal of anxiety." The child looked at him, and answered nothing. "Thou art ours now," cried Laertes: "we have bought thee." — "For how much?" inquired the child quite coolly. "For a hundred ducats," said the other: "pay them again, and thou art free." — "Is that very much?" she asked. "Oh, yes! thou must now be a good child." — "I will try," she said.

From that moment she observed strictly what services the waiter had to do for both her friends; and, after next day, she would not any more let him enter the room. She persisted in doing every thing herself, and accordingly went through her duties, slowly, indeed, and sometimes awkwardly, yet completely, and with the greatest care.

She was frequently observed going to a basin of water, and washing her face with such diligence and violence, that she almost wore the skin from her cheeks; till Laertes, by dint of questions and reproofs, learned that she was striving by all means to get the paint from her skin, and that, in her zealous endeavors towards this object, she had mistaken the redness produced by rubbing for the most obdurate dye. They set her right on this point, and she ceased her efforts; after which, having come again to her natural state, she exhibited a fine brown complexion, beautiful, though sparingly intermingled with red.

The siren charms of Philina, the mysterious presence of the child, produced more impression on our friend than he liked to confess: he passed several days in that strange society, endeavoring to elude self-reproaches by a diligent practice of fencing and dancing, — accomplishments which he believed might not again be put within his reach so conveniently.

It was with great surprise, and not without a certain satisfaction, that he one day observed Herr Melina and his wife alight at the inn. After the first glad salutation, they inquired about "the lady-manager and the other actors," and learned, with astonishment and terror, that the lady-manager had long since gone away, and her actors, to a very few, dispersed themselves about the country.

This couple, subsequently to their marriage, in which, as we know, our friend did his best to serve them, had been travelling about in various quarters, seeking an engagement, without finding any, and had at last been directed to this little town by some persons who met them on their journey, and said there was a good theatre in the place.

Melina by no means pleased the lively Laertes, when introduced to him, any more than his wife did Philina. Both heartily wished to be rid of these new-comers; and Wilhelm could inspire them with no favorable feelings on the subject, though he more than once assured them that the Melinas were very worthy people.

Indeed, the previous merry life of our three adventurers was interfered with by this extension of their society, in more ways than one. Melina had taken up his quarters in the inn where Philina staid, and he very soon began a system of cheapening and higgling. He would have better lodging, more sumptuous diet, and readier attendance, for a smaller charge. In a short while, the landlord and waiter showed very rueful looks; for whereas the others, to get pleasantly along, had expressed no discontent with any thing, and paid instantly, that they might avoid thinking longer of payment, Melina now insisted on regulating every meal, and investigating its contents beforehand, — a species of service for which Philina named him, without scruple, a ruminating animal.

Yet more did the merry girl hate Melina's wife. Frau Melina was a young woman not without culture, but wofully defective in soul and spirit. She could declaim not badly, and kept declaiming constantly; but it was easy to observe that her performances were little more than recitations of words. She labored a few detached passages, but never could express the feeling of the whole. Withal, however, she was seldom disagreeable to any one, especially to men. On the contrary, people who enjoyed her acquaintance commonly ascribed to her a fine understanding; for she was what might be called a kind of *spiritual chameleon*, or *taker-on*. Any friend whose favor she had need of she could flatter with peculiar adroitness, could give in to his ideas so long as she could understand them, and, when they went beyond her own horizon, could hail with ecstasy such new and brilliant visions. She understood well when to speak and when to keep silence; and, though her disposition was not spiteful, she could spy out with great expertness where another's weak side lay.

CHAPTER SIX

MELINA, IN the mean time, had been making strict inquiry about the wrecks of the late theatrical establishment. The wardrobe, as well as decorations, had been pawned with some traders; and a notary had been empowered, under certain conditions, to dispose of them by sale, should purchasers occur. Melina wished to see this ware, and he took Wilhelm with him. No sooner was the room opened, than our friend felt towards its contents a kind of inclination, which he would not confess to himself. Sad as was the state of the blotched and tarnished decorations; little showy as the Turkish and pagan garments, the old farce-coats for men and women, the cowls for enchanters, priests, and Jews, might be, — he was not able to exclude the feeling, that the happiest moments of his life had been spent in a similar magazine of frippery. Could Melina have seen into his heart, he would have urged him more pressingly to lay out a sum of money in liberating these scattered fragments, in furbishing them up, and again combining them into a beautiful whole. "What a happy man could I be," cried Melina, "had I but two hundred crowns, to get into my hands, for a beginning, these fundamental necessaries of a theatre! How soon should I get up a little playhouse, that would draw contributions from the town and neighborhood, and maintain us all!" Wilhelm was silent. They left these treasures of the stage to be again locked up, and both went away in a reflective mood.

Thenceforth Melina talked of nothing else but projects and plans for setting up a theatre, and gaining profit by it. He tried to interest Philina and Laertes in his schemes; and proposals were made to Wilhelm about advancing money, and taking them as his security. On this occasion, Wilhelm first clearly perceived that he was lingering too long here: he excused himself, and set about making preparations for departure.

In the mean time, Mignon's form, and manner of existence, were growing more attractive to him every day. In her whole system of proceedings there was something very singular. She never walked up or down the stairs, but jumped. She would spring along by the railing, and before you were aware would be sitting quietly above upon the landing. Wilhelm had observed, also, that she had a different sort of salutation for each individual. For himself, it had of late been with her arms crossed upon her breast. Often for the whole day she was mute. At times she answered various questions more freely, yet always strangely: so that you could not determine whether it was caused by shrewd sense, or ignorance of the language; for she spoke in broken German interlaced with French and Italian. In Wilhelm's service she was indefatigable, and up before the sun. On the other hand, she vanished early in the evening, went to sleep in a little room upon the bare floor, and could not by any means be induced to take a bed or even a *paillasse*. He often found her washing herself. Her clothes, too, were kept scrupulously clean; though nearly all about her was quilted two or three plies thick. Wilhelm was moreover told, that she went every morning early to hear mass. He followed her on one occasion, and saw her kneeling down with a rosary in a corner of the church, and praying devoutly. She did not observe him; and he returned home, forming many a conjecture about this appearance, yet unable to arrive at any probable conclusion.

A new application from Melina for a sum of money to redeem the often-mentioned stage apparatus caused Wilhelm to think more seriously than ever about setting off. He proposed writing to his people, who for a long time had heard no tidings of him, by the very earliest post. He accordingly commenced a letter to Werner, and had advanced a considerable way with the history of his adventures, in recounting which he had more than once unintentionally swerved a little from the truth, when, to his vexation and surprise, he observed, upon the back of his sheet, some verses which he had been copying from his album for Madam Melina. Out of humor at this mistake, he tore the paper in pieces, and put off repeating his confession till the next post-day.

CHAPTER SEVEN

OUR PARTY was now again collected; and Philina, who always kept a sharp lookout on every horse or carriage that passed by, exclaimed with great eagerness, "Our Pedant! Here comes our dearest Pedant! Who the deuce is it he has with him?" Speaking thus, she beckoned at the window; and the vehicle drew up.

A woful-looking genius, whom by his shabby coat of grayish brown, and his ill-conditioned lower garments, you must have taken for some unprosperous preceptor, of the sort that moulder in our universities, now descended from the carriage, and, taking off his hat to salute Philina, discovered an ill-powdered, but yet very stiff, periwig; while Philina threw a hundred kisses of the hand towards him.

As Philina's chief enjoyment lay in loving one class of men, and being loved by them; so there was a second and hardly inferior satisfaction, wherewith she entertained herself as frequently as possible; and this consisted in hoodwinking and passing jokes upon the other class, whom at such moments she happened not to love, — all which she could accomplish in a very sprightly style.

Amid the flourish which she made in receiving this old friend, no attention was bestowed upon the rest who followed him. Yet among the party were an oldish man and two young girls, whom Wilhelm thought he knew. Accordingly it turned out, that he had often seen them all, some years ago, in a company then playing in his native town. The daughters had grown since that period: the old man was a little altered. He commonly enacted those good-hearted, boisterous old gentlemen, whom the German theatre is never without and whom, in common life, one also frequently enough falls in with. For as it is the character of our countrymen to do good, and cause it, without pomp or circumstance; so they seldom consider that there is likewise a mode of doing what is right with grace and dignity: more frequently, indeed, they yield to the spirit of contradiction, and fall into the error of deforming their dearest virtue by a surly mode of putting it in practice.

Such parts our actor could play very well; and he played them so often and exclusively, that he had himself taken up the same turn of proceeding in his ordinary life.

On recognizing him, Wilhelm was seized with a strong commotion; for he recollected how often he had seen this man on the stage with his beloved Mariana: he still heard him scolding, still heard the small, soothing voice, with which in many characters she had to meet his rugged temper.

The first anxious question put to the strangers, — Whether they had heard of any situation in their travels? — was answered, alas, with No! and, to complete the information, it was further added, that all the companies they had fallen in with were not only supplied with actors, but many of them were afraid lest, on account of the approaching war, they should be forced to separate. Old Boisterous, with his daughters, moved by spleen and love of change, had given up an advantageous engagement: then, meeting with the Pedant by the way, they had hired a carriage to come hither; where, as they found, good counsel was still dear, needful to have, and difficult to get.

The time while the rest were talking very keenly of their circumstances, Wilhelm spent in thought. He longed to speak in private with the old man: he wished and feared to hear of Mariana, and felt the greatest disquietude.

The pretty looks of the stranger damsels could not call him from his dream; but a war of words, which now arose, awakened his attention. It was Friedrich, the fair-haired boy who used to attend Philina, stubbornly refusing, on this occasion, to cover the table and bring up dinner. "I engaged to serve you," he cried, "but not to wait on everybody." They fell into a hot contest. Philina insisted that he should do his duty; and, as he obstinately refused, she told him plainly he might go about his business.

"You think, perhaps, I cannot leave you!" cried he sturdily, then went to pack up his bundle, and soon hastily quitted the house.

"Go, Mignon," said Philina, "and get us what we want: tell the waiter, and help him to attend us."

Mignon came before Wilhelm, and asked in her laconic way, "Shall I? May I?" To which Wilhelm answered, "Do all the lady bids thee, child."

She accordingly took charge of every thing, and waited on the guests the whole evening, with the utmost carefulness. After dinner, Wilhelm proposed to have a walk with the old man alone. Succeeding in this, after many questions about his late wanderings, the conversation turned upon the former company; and Wilhelm hazarded a question touching Mariana.

"Do not speak to me of that despicable creature!" cried the old man: "I have sworn to think of her no more." Terrified at this speech, Wilhelm felt still more embarrassed, as the old man proceeded to vituperate her fickleness and wantonness. Most gladly would our friend have broken off the conversation, but now it was impossible: he was obliged to undergo the whole tumultuous effusions of this strange old gentleman.

"I am ashamed," continued he, "that I felt such a friendship for her. Yet, had you known the girl better, you would excuse me. She was so pretty, so natural and good, so pleasing, in every sense so tolerable, I could never have supposed that ingratitude and impudence were to prove the chief features of her character."

Wilhelm had nerved himself to hear the worst of her; when all at once he observed, with astonishment, that the old man's tones grew milder, his voice faltered, and he took out his handkerchief to dry the tears, which at last began to trickle down his cheeks.

"What is the matter with you?" cried Wilhelm. "What is it that suddenly so changes the current of your feelings? Conceal it not from me. I take a deeper interest in the fate of this girl than you suppose. Only tell me all."

"I have not much to say," replied the old man, again taking up his earnest, angry tone. "I have suffered more from her than I shall ever forgive. She had always a kind of trust in me. I loved her as my own daughter; indeed, while my wife lived, I had formed a resolution to take the creature to my own house, and save her from the hands of that old crone, from whose guidance I boded no good. But my wife died, and the project went to nothing.

"About the end of our stay in your native town, — it is not quite three years ago, — I noticed a visible sadness about her. I questioned her, but she evaded me. At last we set out on our journey. She travelled in the same coach with me; and I soon observed, what she herself did not long deny, that she was with child, and suffering the greatest terror lest our manager might turn her off. In fact, in a short while he did make the discovery; immediately threw up her contract, which at any rate was only for six weeks; paid off her arrears; and, in spite of all entreaties, left her behind, in the miserable inn of a little village.

"Devil take all wanton jilts!" cried the old man, with a splenetic tone, "and especially this one, that has spoiled me so many hours of my life! Why should I keep talking how I myself took charge of her, what I did for her, what I spent on her, how in absence I provided for her? I would rather throw my purse into the ditch, and spend my time in nursing mangy whelps, than ever more bestow the smallest care on such a thing. Pshaw! At first I got letters of thanks, notices of places she was staying at; and, finally, no word at all, — not even an acknowledgment for the money I had sent to pay the expenses of her lying-in. Oh! the treachery and the fickleness of women are rightly matched, to get a comfortable living for themselves, and to give an honest fellow many heavy hours."

WILHELM'S feelings, on returning home after this conversation, may be easily conceived. All his old wounds had been torn up afresh, and the sentiment that Mariana was not wholly unworthy of his love had again been brought to life. The interest the old man had shown about her fate, the praises he gave her against his will, displayed her again in all her attractiveness. Nay, even the bitter accusations brought against her contained nothing that could lower her in Wilhelm's estimation; for he, as well as she, was guilty in all her aberrations. Nor did even her final silence seem greatly blamable: it rather inspired him with mournful thoughts. He saw her as a frail, ill-succored mother, wandering helplessly about the world, — wandering, perhaps, with his own child. What he knew, and what he knew not, awoke in him the painfullest emotions.

Mignon had been waiting for him: she lighted him up-stairs. On setting down the light, she begged he would allow her, that evening, to compliment him with a piece of her art. He would rather have declined this, particularly as he knew not what it was; but he had not the heart to refuse any thing this kind creature wished. After a little while she again came in. She carried below her arm a little carpet, which she then spread out upon the floor. Wilhelm said she might proceed. She thereupon brought four candles, and placed one upon each corner of the carpet. A little basket of eggs, which she next carried in, made her purpose clearer. Carefully measuring her steps, she then walked to and fro on the carpet, spreading out the eggs in certain figures and positions; which done, she called in a man that was waiting in the house, and could play on the violin. He retired with his instrument into a corner: she tied a band about her eyes, gave a signal; and, like a piece of wheel-work set a-going, she began moving the same instant as the music, accompanying her beats and the notes of the tune with the strokes of a pair of castanets.

Lightly, nimbly, quickly, and with hair's-breadth accuracy, she carried on the dance. She skipped so sharply and surely along between the eggs, and trod so closely down beside them, that you would have

Mignon performs her egg-dance

thought every instant she must trample one of them in pieces, or kick the rest away in her rapid turns. By no means! She touched no one of them, though winding herself through their mazes with all kinds of steps, wide and narrow, nay, even with leaps, and at last half kneeling.

Constant as the movement of a clock, she ran her course; and the strange music, at each repetition of the tune, gave a new impulse to the dance, recommencing and again rushing off as at first. Wilhelm was quite led away by this singular spectacle; he forgot his cares; he followed every movement of the dear little creature, and felt surprised to see how finely her character unfolded itself as she proceeded in the dance.

Rigid, sharp, cold, vehement, and in soft postures, stately rather than attractive, — such was the light in which it showed her. At this moment he experienced at once all the emotions he had ever felt for Mignon. He longed to incorporate this forsaken being with his own heart, to take her in his arms, and with a father's love to awaken in her the joy of existence.

The dance being ended, she rolled the eggs together softly with her foot into a little heap, left none behind, harmed none; then placed herself beside it, taking the bandage from her eyes, and concluding her performance with a little bow.

Wilhelm thanked her for having executed, so prettily and unexpectedly, a dance he had long wished to see. He patted her; was sorry she had tired herself so much. He promised her a new suit of clothes; to which she vehemently replied, "Thy color!" This, too, he promised her, though not well knowing what she meant by it. She then lifted up the eggs, took the carpet under her arm, asked if he wanted any thing further, and skipped out of the room.

The musician, being questioned, said, that for some time she had taken much trouble in often singing over the tune of this dance, the well-known fandango, to him, and training him till he could play it accurately. For his labor she had likewise offered him some money; which, however, he would not accept.

AFTER A restless night, which our friend spent, sometimes waking, sometimes oppressed with unpleasant dreams, seeing Mariana now in all her beauty, now in woful case, at one time with a child on her arm, then soon bereaved of it, the morning had scarcely dawned, when Mignon entered with a tailor. She brought some gray cloth and blue taffeta; signifying in her own way that she wished to have a new jacket and sailor's trousers, such as she had seen the boys of the town wear, with blue cuffs and tiers.

Since the loss of Mariana, Wilhelm had laid aside all gay colors. He had used himself to gray, — the garment of the shades; and only perhaps a sky-blue lining, or little collar of that dye, in some degree enlivened his sober garb. Mignon, eager to wear his colors, hurried on the tailor, who engaged to have his work soon ready.

The exercise in dancing and fencing, which our friend took this day with Laertes, did not prosper in their hands. Indeed, it was soon interrupted by Melina, who came to show them circumstantially how a little company was now of itself collected, sufficient to exhibit plays in abundance. He renewed the proposal that Wilhelm should advance a little money for setting them in motion; which, however, Wilhelm still declined.

Ere long Philina and the girls came in, racketing and laughing as usual. They had now devised a fresh excursion, for change of place and objects was a pleasure after which they always longed. To eat daily in a different spot was their highest wish. On this occasion they proposed a sail.

The boat in which they were to fall down the pleasant windings of the river had already been engaged by the Pedant. Philina urged them on: the party did not linger, and were soon on board.

"What shall we take to now?" said Philina, when all had placed themselves upon the benches.

"The readiest thing," replied Laertes, "were for us to extemporize a play. Let each take a part that suits his character, and we shall see how we get along."

"Excellent!" said Wilhelm. "In a society where there is no dis-simulation, but where each without disguise pursues the bent of his own humor, elegance and satisfaction cannot long continue; and, where dissimulation always reigns, they do not enter at all. It will not be amiss, then, that we take up dissimulation to begin with, and then, behind our masks, be as candid as we please."

"Yes," said Laertes: "it is on this account that one goes on so pleasantly with women; they never show themselves in their natural form."

"That is to say," replied Madam Melina, "they are not so vain as men, who conceive themselves to be always amiable enough, just as nature has produced them."

In the mean time the river led them between pleasant groves and hills, between gardens and vineyards; and the young women, especially Madam Melina, expressed their rapture at the landscape. The latter even began to recite, in solemn style, a pretty poem of the descriptive sort, upon a similar scene of nature; but Philina interrupted her with the proposal of a law, that no one should presume to speak of any inanimate object. On the other hand, she zealously urged on their project of an extempore play. Old Boisterous was to be a half-pay officer; Laertes a fencing-master, taking his vacation; the Pedant, a Jew; she herself would act a Tyrolese; leaving to the rest to choose characters according to their several pleasures. They would suppose themselves to be a party of total strangers to each other, who had just met on board a merchant-ship.

She immediately began to play her part with the Jew, and a universal cheerfulness diffused itself among them.

They had not sailed far, when the skipper stopped in his course, asking permission of the company to take in a person standing on the shore, who had made a sign to him.

"That is just what we needed," cried Philina: "a chance passenger was wanting to complete the travelling-party."

A handsome man came on board; whom, by his dress and his dignified mien, you might have taken for a clergyman. He saluted the party, who thanked him in their own way, and soon made known to him the nature of their game. The stranger immediately engaged to act the part of a country parson; which, in fact, he accomplished in the adroitest manner, to the admiration of all, — now admonishing, now telling stories, showing some weak points, yet never losing their respect.

In the mean time, every one who had made a false step in his part, or swerved from his character, had been obliged to forfeit a pledge: Philina had gathered them with the greatest care, and especially threatened the reverend gentleman with many kisses; though he himself had never been at fault. Melina, on the other hand, was completely fleeced: shirt-buttons, buckles, every movable about his person, was in Philina's hands. He was trying to enact an English traveller, and could not by any means get into the spirit of his part.

Meanwhile the time had passed away very pleasantly. Each had strained his fancy and his wit to the utmost, and each had garnished his part with agreeable and entertaining jests. Thus comfortably occupied, they reached the place where they meant to pass the day; and Wilhelm, going out to walk with the clergyman, as both from his appearance and late character he persisted in naming him, soon fell into an interesting conversation.

"I think this practice," said the stranger, "very useful among actors, and even in the company of friends and acquaintances. It is the best mode of drawing men out of themselves, and leading them, by a circuitous path, back into themselves again. It should be a custom with every troop of players to practice in this manner: and the public would assuredly be no loser if every month an unwritten piece were brought forward; in which, of course, the players had prepared themselves by several rehearsals."

"One should not, then," replied our friend, "consider an extempore piece as, strictly speaking, composed on the spur of the moment, but as a piece, of which the plan, action, and division of the scenes were given; the filling up of all this being left to the player."

"Quite right," said the stranger; "and, in regard to this very filling up, such a piece, were the players once trained to these performances, would profit greatly. Not in regard to the mere words, it is true; for, by a careful selection of these, the studious writer may certainly adorn his work; but in regard to the gestures, looks, exclamations, and every thing of that nature; in short, to the mute and half-mute play of the dialogue, which seems by degrees fading away among us altogether. There are indeed some players in Germany whose bodies figure what they think and feel; who by their silence, their delays, their looks, their slight, graceful movements, can prepare the audience for a speech, and, by a pleasant sort of pantomime, combine the pauses of the dialogue with the general whole; but such a practice as this, co-operating with a happy natural turn, and training it to compete with the author, is far from being so habitual as, for the comfort of play-going people, were to be desired."

"But will not a happy natural turn," said Wilhelm, "as the first and last requisite, of itself conduct the player, like every other artist, — nay, perhaps every other man, — to the lofty mark he aims at?"

"The first and the last, the beginning and the end, it may well be; but, in the middle, many things will still be wanting to an artist, if instruction, and early instruction too, have not previously made that of him which he was meant to be: and perhaps for the man of genius it is worse in this respect than for the man possessed of only common capabilities; the one may much more easily be misinstructed, and be driven far more violently into false courses, than the other."

"But," said Wilhelm, "will not genius save itself, not heal the wounds which itself has inflicted?"

"Only to a very small extent, and with great difficulty," said the other, "or perhaps not at all. Let no one think that he can conquer the first impressions of his youth. If he has grown up in enviable freedom, surrounded with beautiful and noble objects, in constant intercourse with worthy men; if his masters have taught him what he needed first to know, for comprehending more easily what followed; if he has never learned any thing which he requires to unlearn; if his first operations have been so guided, that, without altering any of his habits, he can more easily produce what is excellent in future, — then such a one will lead a purer, more perfect and happier, life, than another man who has wasted the force of his youth in opposition and error. A great deal is said and written about education; yet I meet with very few who can comprehend, and transfer to practice, this simple yet vast idea, which includes within itself all others connected with the subject."

"That may well be true," said Wilhelm; "for the generality of men are limited enough in their conceptions to suppose that every other should be fashioned by education, according to the pattern of themselves. Happy, then, are those whom Fate takes charge of, and educates according to their several natures!"

"Fate," said the other, smiling, "is an excellent but most expensive schoolmaster. In all cases, I would rather trust to the reason of a human tutor. Fate, for whose wisdom I entertain all imaginable reverence, often finds in Chance, by which it works, an instrument not over manageable. At least the latter very seldom seems to execute precisely and accurately what the former had determined."

"You seem to express a very singular opinion," said Wilhelm.

"Not at all," replied the other. "Most of what happens in the world confirms my opinion. Do not many incidents at their commencement show some mighty purport, and generally terminate in something paltry?"

"You mean to jest."

"And as to what concerns the individual man," pursued the other, "is it not so with this likewise? Suppose Fate had appointed one to be a good player; and why should it not provide us with good players as well as other good things? Chance would perhaps conduct the youth into some puppet-show, where, at such an early age, he could not help taking interest in what was tasteless and despicable, reckoning insipidities endurable or even pleasing, and thus corrupting and misdirecting his primary impressions, — impressions which can never be effaced, and whose influence, in spite of all our efforts, cling to us in some degree to the very last."

"What makes you think of puppet-shows?" said Wilhelm, not without some consternation.

"It was an accidental instance: if it does not please you, we shall take another. Suppose Fate had appointed any one to be a great painter, and it pleased Chance that he should pass his youth in sooty huts, in barns and stables: do you think that such a man would ever be enabled to exalt himself to purity, to nobleness, to freedom of soul? The more keenly he may in his youth have seized on the impure, and tried in his own manner to ennoble it, the more powerfully in the remainder of his life will it be revenged on him; because, while he was endeavoring to conquer it, his whole being has become inseparably combined with it. Whoever spends his early years in mean and pitiful society, though at an after period he may have the choice of better, will yet constantly look back with longing towards that which he enjoyed of old, and which has left its impression blended with the memory of all his young and unreturning pleasures."

From conversation of this sort, it is easy to imagine, the rest of the company had gradually withdrawn. Philina, in particular, had stepped aside at the very outset. Wilhelm and his comrade now rejoined them by a cross-path. Philina brought out her forfeits, and they had to be redeemed in many different ways. During which business, the stranger, by the most ingenious devices, and by his frank participation in their sports, recommended himself much to all the party, and particularly to the ladies; and thus, amid joking, singing, kissing, and railleries of all sorts, the hours passed away in the most pleasant manner.

CHAPTER TEN

WHEN OUR friends began to think of going home, they looked about them for their clergyman; but he had vanished, and was nowhere to be found.

"It is not polite in the man, who otherwise displayed good breeding," said Madam Melina, "to desert a company that welcomed him so kindly, without taking leave."

"I have all the time been thinking," said Laertes, "where I can have seen this singular man before. I fully intended to ask him about it at parting."

"I, too, had the same feeling," said Wilhelm; "and certainly I should not have let him go, till he had told us something more about his circumstances. I am much mistaken if I have not ere now spoken with him somewhere."

"And you may in truth," said Philina, "be mistaken there. This person seems to have the air of an acquaintance, because he looks like a *man*, and not like Jack or Kit."

"What is this?" said Laertes. "Do not we, too, look like men?"

"I know what I am saying," cried Philina; "and, if you cannot understand me, never mind. In the end my words will be found to require no commentary."

Two coaches now drove up. All praised the attention of Laertes, who had ordered them. Philina, with Madam Melina, took her place opposite to Wilhelm: the rest bestowed themselves as they best could. Laertes rode back on Wilhelm's horse, which had likewise been brought out.

Philina was scarcely seated in the coach, when she began to sing some pretty songs, and gradually led the conversation to some stories, which she said might be successfully treated in the form of dramas. By this cunning turn, she very soon put her young friend into his finest humor: from the wealth of his living imaginative store, he forthwith constructed a complete play, with all its acts, scenes, characters, and plots. It was thought proper to insert a few catches and songs; they composed them; and Philina, who entered into every part of it, immediately fitted them with well-known tunes, and sang them on the spot.

It was one of her beautiful, most beautiful, days: she had skill to enliven our friend with all manner of diverting wiles; he felt in spirits such as he had not for many a month enjoyed.

Since that shocking discovery had torn him from the side of Mariana, he had continued true to his vow to be on his guard against the encircling arms of woman; to avoid the faithless sex; to lock up his inclinations, his sweet wishes, in his own bosom. The conscientiousness with which he had observed this vow gave his whole nature a secret nourishment; and, as his heart could not remain without affection, some loving sympathy had now become a want with him. He went along once more, as if environed by the first cloudy glories of youth; his eye fixed joyfully on every charming object, and never had his judgment of a lovely form been more favorable. How dangerous, in such a situation, this wild girl must have been to him, is but too easy to conceive.

Arrived at home, they found Wilhelm's chamber all ready to receive them; the chairs set right for a public reading; in midst of them the table, on which the punch-bowl was in due time to take its place.

The German chivalry-plays were new at this period, and had just excited the attention and the inclination of the public. Old Boisterous had brought one of this sort with him: the reading of it had already been determined on. They all sat down: Wilhelm took possession of the pamphlet, and began to read.

The harnessed knights, the ancient keeps, the true-heartedness, honesty, and downrightness, but especially the independence of the acting characters, were received with the greatest approbation. The reader did his utmost, and the audience gradually mounted into rapture. Between the third and fourth acts, the punch arrived in an ample bowl; and, there being much fighting and drinking in the piece itself, nothing was more natural than that, on every such occurrence, the company should transport themselves into the situation of the heroes, should flourish and strike along with them, and drink long life to their favorites among the *dramatis personæ*.

Each individual of the party was inflamed with the noblest fire of national spirit. How it gratified this German company to be poetically entertained, according to their own character, on stuff of their own manufacture! In particular, the vaults and caverns, the ruined castles, the moss and hollow trees, but above all the nocturnal gypsy scenes, and the Secret Tribunal, produced a quite incredible effect. Every actor now figured to himself how, erelong, in helm and harness, he; every actress how, with a monstrous spreading ruff, she, — would present their Germanship before the public. Each would appropriate to himself without delay some name taken from the piece or from German history; and Madam Melina declared that the son or daughter she was then expecting should not be christened otherwise than by the name of Adelbert or of Mathilde.

Towards the fifth act, the approbation became more impetuous and louder; and at last, when the hero actually trampled down his oppressor, and the tyrant met his doom, the ecstasy increased to such a height, that all averred they had never passed such happy moments. Melina, whom the liquor had inspired, was the noisiest: and when the second bowl was emptied, and midnight near, Laertes swore through thick and thin, that no living mortal was worthy ever more to put these glasses to his lips; and, so swearing, he pitched his own right over his head, through a window-pane, out into the street. The rest followed his example; and notwithstanding the protestations of the landlord, who came running in at the noise, the punch-bowl itself, never after this festivity to be polluted by unholy drink, was dashed into a thousand shreds. Philina, whose exhilaration was the least noticed, — the other two girls by that time having laid themselves upon the sofa in no very elegant positions, — maliciously encouraged her companions in their tumult. Madam Melina recited some spirit-stirring poems; and her husband, not too amiable in the uproar, began to cavil at the insufficient preparation of the punch, declaring that he could arrange an entertainment altogether in a different style, and at last becoming sulkier and louder as Laertes commanded silence, till the latter, without much consideration, threw the fragments of the punch-bowl about his head, and thereby not a little deepened the confusion.

Meanwhile the town-guard had arrived, and were demanding admission to the house. Wilhelm, much heated by his reading, though he had drunk but little, had enough to do, with the landlord's help, to content these people by money and good words, and afterwards to get the various members of his party sent home in that unseemly case. On coming back, overpowered with sleep and full of chagrin, he threw himself upon his bed without undressing; and nothing could exceed his disgust, when, opening his eyes next morning, he looked out with dull sight upon the devastations of the bygone day, and saw the uncleanness, and the many bad effects, of which that ingenious, lively, and well-intentioned poetical performance had been the cause.

AFTER A SHORT consideration, he called the landlord, and bade him mark to his account both the damage and the regular charge. At the same time he learned, not without vexation, that his horse had been so hard ridden by Laertes last night, that, in all probability, it was foundered, as they term it; the farrier having little hope of its recovering.

A salute from Philina, which she threw him from her window, restored him in some degree to a more cheerful humor: he went forthwith into the nearest shop to buy her a little present, which, in return for the powder-knife, he still owed her; and it must be owned, that, in selecting his gift, he did not keep himself within the limits of proportional value. He not only purchased her a pair of earrings, but added likewise a hat and neckerchief, and some other little articles, which he had seen her lavishly throw from her on the first day of their acquaintance.

Madam Melina, happening to observe him as he was delivering his presents, took an opportunity before breakfast to rate him very earnestly about his inclination for this girl; at which he felt the more astonished, the less he thought it merited. He swore solemnly, that he had never once entertained the slightest notion of attaching himself to such a person, whose whole manner of proceeding was well known to him. He excused himself as well as possible for his friendly and polite conduct towards her, yet did not by any means content Madam Melina, whose spite grew ever more determined, as she could not but observe that the flatteries, by which she had acquired for herself a sort of partial regard from our friend, were not sufficient to defend this conquest from the attacks of a lively, younger, and more gifted rival.

As they sat down to table, her husband joined them, likewise in a very fretful humor; which he was beginning to display on many little things, when the landlord entered to announce a player on the harp. "You will certainly," he said, "find pleasure in the music and the songs of this man: no one who hears him can forbear to admire him, and bestow something on him."

"Let him go about his business," said Melina: "I am any thing but in a trim for hearing fiddlers, and we have singers constantly among ourselves disposed to gain a little by their talent." He accompanied these words with a sarcastic side-look at Philina: she understood his meaning, and immediately prepared to punish him, by taking up the cause of the harper. Turning towards Wilhelm, "Shall we not hear the man?" said she: "shall we do nothing to save ourselves from this miserable *ennui?*"

Melina was going to reply, and the strife would have grown keener, had not the person it related to at that moment entered. Wilhelm saluted him, and beckoned him to come near.

The figure of this singular guest set the whole party in astonishment: he had found a chair before any one took heart to ask him a question, or make any observation. His bald crown was encircled by a few gray hairs, and a pair of large blue eye looked out softly from beneath his long white eyebrows. To a nose of beautiful proportions was subjoined a flowing, hoary beard, which did not hide the fine shape and position of his lips; and a long dark-brown garment wrapped his thin body from the neck to the feet. He began to prelude on the harp, which he had placed before him.

The sweet tones which he drew from his instrument very soon inspirited the company.

"You can sing, too, my good old man," said Philina.

"Give us something that shall entertain the spirit and the heart as well as the senses," said Wilhelm. "The instrument should but accompany the voice; for tunes and melodies without words and meaning seem to me like butterflies or finely variegated birds, which hover round us in the air, which we could wish to catch and make our own: whereas song is like a blessed genius that exalts us towards heaven, and allures the better self in us to attend him."

The old man looked at Wilhelm, then aloft, then gave some trills upon his harp, and began his song. It contained a eulogy on minstrelsy, — described the happiness of minstrels, and reminded men to honor them. He produced his song with so much life and truth, that it seemed as if he had composed it at the moment, for this special occasion. Wilhelm could scarcely refrain from clasping him in his arms: but the fear of awakening a peal of laughter detained him in his chair; for the rest were already in half-whispers making sundry very shallow observations, and debating if the harper was a Papist or a Jew.

When asked about the author of the song, the man gave no distinct reply; declaring only that he was rich in songs, and anxious that they should please. Most of the party were now merry and joyful; even Melina was grown frank in his way; and, whilst they talked and joked together, the old man began to sing the praise of social life in the most sprightly style. He described the loveliness of unity and courtesy, in soft, soothing tones. Suddenly his music became cold, harsh, and jarring, as he turned to deplore repulsive selfishness, short-sighted enmity, and baleful division; and every heart willingly threw off those galling fetters, while, borne on the wings of a piercing melody, he launched forth in praise of peacemakers, and sang the happiness of souls, that, having parted, meet again in love.

Scarcely had he ended, when Wilhelm cried to him, "Whoever thou art, that as a helping spirit comest to us with a voice which blesses and revives, accept my reverence and my thanks! Feel that we all admire thee, and confide in us if thou wantest any thing."

The old man spoke not: he threw his fingers softly across the strings, then struck more sharply, and sang, —

> " 'What notes are those without the wall,
>   Across the portal sounding?
> Let's have the music in our hall,
>   Back from its roof rebounding.'
> So spoke the king, the henchman flies:
> His answer heard, the monarch cries,
>   'Bring in that ancient minstrel.'
>
> 'Hail, gracious king! each noble knight,
>   Each lovely dame, I greet you!
> What glittering stars salute my sight!
>   What heart unmoved may meet you!
> Such lordly pomp is not for me,
> Far other scenes my eyes must see:
>   Yet deign to list my harping.'
>
> The singer turns him to his art,
>   A thrilling strain he raises:
> Each warrior hears with glowing heart,
>   And on his loved one gazes.
> The king, who liked his playing well,
> Commands, for such a kindly spell,
>   A golden chain be given him.
>
> 'The golden chain give not to me;
>   Thy boldest knight may wear it,
> Who, 'cross the battle's purple sea,
>   On lion breast may bear it:
> Or let it be thy chancellor's prize,
> Amid his heaps to feast his eyes;
>   Its yellow glance will please him.'

"I sing but as the linnet sings,
  That on the green bough dwelleth;
A rich reward his music brings,
  As from his throat it swelleth:
Yet might I ask, I'd ask of thine
One sparkling draught of purest wine,
  To drink it here before you.'

He viewed the wine: he quaffed it up.
  'O draught of sweetest savor!
O happy house, where such a cup
  Is thought a little favor!
If well you fare, remember me,
And thank kind Heaven, from envy free,
  As now for this I thank you.' "

When the harper, on finishing his song, took up a glass of wine that stood poured out for him, and, turning with a friendly mien to his entertainers, drank it off, a buzz of joyful approbation rose from all the party. They clapped hands, and wished him health from that glass, and strength to his aged limbs. He sang a few other ballads, exciting more and more hilarity among the company.

"Old man," said Philina, "dost thou know the tune, 'The shepherd decked him for the dance'?" [1]

"Oh, yes!" said he: "if you will sing the words, I shall not fail for my part of it."

Philina then stood up, and held herself in readiness. The old man commenced the tune; and she sang a song, which we cannot impart to our readers, lest they might think it insipid, or perhaps undignified.

Meanwhile the company were growing merrier and merrier: they had already emptied several flasks of wine, and were now beginning to get very loud. But our friend, having fresh in his remembrance the bad consequences of their late exhilaration, determined to break up the sitting; he slipped into the old man's hand a liberal remuneration for his trouble, the rest did something likewise; they gave him leave to go and take repose, promising themselves another entertainment from his skill in the evening.

---

[1] *Der Schäfer putzte sich zum Tanz,* — a song of Goethe's. — ED.

When he had retired, our friend said to Philina, "In this favorite song of yours I certainly find no merit, either moral or poetical; yet if you were to bring forward any proper composition on the stage, with the same arch simplicity, the same propriety and gracefulness, I should engage that strong and universal approbation would be the result."

"Yes," said Philina: "it would be a charming thing indeed to warm one's self at ice."

"After all," said Wilhelm, "this old man might put many a player to the blush. Did you notice how correctly the dramatic part of his ballads was expressed? I maintain there was more living true representation in his singing than in many of our starched characters upon the stage. You would take the acting of many plays for a narrative, and you might ascribe to these musical narratives a sensible presence."

"You are hardly just," replied Laertes. "I pretend to no great skill, either as a player or as a singer; yet I know well enough, that when music guides the movements of the body, at once affording to them animation and a scale to measure it; when declamation and expression are furnished me by the composer, — I feel quite a different man from what I do when, in prose dramas, I have all this to create for myself, — have both gesture and declamation to invent, and am, perhaps, disturbed in it, too, by the awkwardness of some partner in the dialogue."

"Thus much I know," said Melina: "the man certainly puts us to the blush in one point, and that a main point. The strength of his talent is shown by the profit he derives from it. Even us, who perhaps erelong shall be embarrassed where to get a meal, he persuades to share our pittance with him. He has skill enough to wile the money from our pockets with an old song, — the money that we should have used to find ourselves employment. So pleasant an affair is it to squander the means which might procure subsistence to one's self and others."

This remark gave the conversation not the most delightful turn. Wilhelm, for whom the reproach was peculiarly intended, replied with some heat; and Melina, at no time over studious of delicacy and politeness, explained his grievances at last in words more plain than courteous. "It is now a fortnight," said he, "since we looked at the theatrical machinery and wardrobe which is lying pawned here: the whole might be redeemed for a very tolerable sum. You then gave me hopes that you would lend me so much; and hitherto I do not see that you have thought more of the matter, or come any nearer a determination. Had you then consented, we should ere now have been under way. Nor has your intention to leave the place been executed, nor has your money in the mean time been spared: at least there are people who have always skill to create opportunities for scattering it faster and faster away."

Such upbraidings, not altogether undeserved, touched Wilhelm to the quick. He replied with keenness, nay, with anger; and, as the company rose to part, he took hold of the door, and gave them not obscurely to understand that he would no longer continue with such unfriendly and ungrateful people. He hastened down, in no kindly humor, and seated himself upon the stone bench without the door of his inn; not observing, that, first out of mirth, then out of spleen, he had drunk more wine than usual.

CHAPTER TWELVE

AFTER A short time, which he passed sitting looking out before him, disquieted by many thoughts, Philina came singing and skipping along through the front door. She sat down by him, nay, we might almost say, on him, so close did she press herself towards him: she leaned upon his shoulders, began playing with his hair, patted him, and gave him the best words in the world. She begged of him to stay with them, and not leave her alone in that company, or she must die of tedium: she could not live any longer in the same house with Melina, and had come over to lodge in the other inn for that reason.

He tried in vain to satisfy her with denials, — to make her understand that he neither could nor would remain any longer. She did not cease with her entreaties; nay, suddenly she threw her arm round his neck, and kissed him with the liveliest expression of fondness.

"Are you mad, Philina?" cried Wilhelm, endeavoring to disengage himself; "to make the open street the scene of such caresses, which I nowise merit! Let me go! I can not and I will not stay."

"And I will hold thee fast," said she, "and kiss thee here on the open street, and kiss thee till thou promise what I want. I shall die of laughing," she continued: "by this familiarity the good people here must take me for thy wife of four weeks' standing; and husbands, who witness this touching scene, will commend me to their wives as a pattern of childlike, simple tenderness."

Some persons were just then going by: she caressed him in the most graceful way; and he, to avoid giving scandal, was constrained to play the part of the patient husband. Then she made faces at the people, when their backs were turned, and, in the wildest humor, continued to commit all sorts of improprieties, till at last he was obliged to promise that he would not go that day, or the morrow, or the next day.

"You are a true clod!" said she, quitting him; "and I am but a fool to spend so much kindness on you." She arose with some vexation, and walked a few steps, then turned round laughing, and cried, "I believe it is just that, after all, that makes me so crazy about thee. I will but go and seek my knitting-needles and my stocking, that I may have something to do. Stay there, and let me find the stone man still upon the stone bench when I come back."

She cast a sparkling glance on him, and went into the house. He had no call to follow her; on the contrary, her conduct had excited fresh aversion in him; yet he rose from the bench to go after her, not well knowing why.

He was just entering the door, when Melina passed by, and spoke to him in a respectful tone, asking his pardon for the somewhat too harsh expressions he had used in their late discussion. "You will not take it ill of me," continued he, "if I appear perhaps too fretful in my present circumstances. The charge of providing for a wife, perhaps soon for a child, forbids me from day to day to live at peace, or spend my time as you may do, in the enjoyment of pleasant feelings. Consider, I pray you, and, if possible, do put me in possession of that stage machinery that is lying here. I shall not be your debtor long, and I will be obliged to you while I live."

Our friend, unwilling to be kept upon the threshold, over which an irresistible impulse was drawing him at that moment to Philina, answered, with an absent mind, eager to be gone, and surprised into a transient feeling of good will, "If I can make you happy and contented by doing this, I will hesitate no longer. Go you and put every thing to rights. I shall be prepared this evening, or to-morrow morning, to pay the money." He then gave his hand to Melina in confirmation of his promise, and was very glad to see him hastily proceed along the street; but, alas! his entrance, which he now thought sure, was a second time prohibited, and more disagreeably than at first.

A young man, with a bundle on his back, came walking fast along the street, and advanced to Wilhelm, who at once recognized him for Friedrich.

"Here am I again!" cried he, looking with his large blue eyes joyfully up and down, over all the windows of the house. "Where is Mamsell? Devil take me, if I can stroll about the world any longer without seeing her!"

The landlord, joining them at this instant, replied that she was above; Friedrich, with a few bounds, was up-stairs; and Wilhelm continued standing, as if rooted to the threshold. At the first instant he was tempted to pluck the younker back, and drag him down by the hair; then all at once the spasm of a sharp jealousy stopped the current of his spirits and ideas; and, as he gradually recovered from this stupefaction, there came over him a splenetic fit of restlessness, a general discomfort, such as he had never felt in his life before.

He went up to his room, and found Mignon busy writing. For some time the creature had been laboring with great diligence in writing every thing she knew by heart, giving always to her master and friend the papers to correct. She was indefatigable, and of good comprehension; but still, her letters were irregular, and her lines crooked. Here, too, the body seemed to contradict the mind. In his usual moods, Wilhelm took no small pleasure in the child's attention; but, at the present moment, he regarded little what she showed him, — a piece of neglect which she felt the more acutely, as on this occasion she conceived her work had been accomplished with peculiar success.

Wilhelm's unrest drove him up and down the passages of the house, and finally again to the street-door. A rider was just prancing towards it, — a man of good appearance, of middle age, and a brisk, contented look. The landlord ran to meet him, holding out his hand as to an old acquaintance. "Ay, *Herr Stallmeister*," cried he, "have we the pleasure to see you again?"

"I am only just going to bait with you," replied the stranger, "and then along to the estate, to get matters put in order as soon as possible. The count is coming over to-morrow with his lady; they mean to stay a while to entertain the Prince von —— in their best style: he intends to fix his headquarters in this neighborhood for some time."

"It is pity," said the landlord, "that you cannot stop with us: we have good company in the house." The hostler came running out, and took the horse from the *Stallmeister*, who continued talking in the door with the landlord, and now and then giving a look at Wilhelm.

Our friend, observing that he formed the topic of their conversation, went away, and walked up and down the streets.

CHAPTER THIRTEEN

IN THE restless vexation of his present humor, it came into his head to go and see the old harper; hoping by his music to scare away the evil spirits that tormented him. On asking for the man, he was directed to a mean public house, in a remote corner of the little town; and, having mounted up-stairs there to the very garret, his ear caught the fine twanging of the harp coming from a little room before him. They were heart-moving, mournful tones, accompanied by a sad and dreary singing. Wilhelm glided to the door; and as the good old man was performing a sort of voluntary, the few stanzas of which, sometimes chanted, sometimes in recitative, were repeated more than once, our friend succeeded, after listening for a while, in gathering nearly this: —

> Who never ate his bread in sorrow,
> Who never spent the darksome hours
> Weeping and watching for the morrow,
> He knows ye not, ye gloomy Powers.
>
> To earth, this weary earth, ye bring us,
> To guilt ye let us heedless go,
> Then leave repentance fierce to wring us:
> A moment's guilt, an age of woe!

The heart-sick, plaintive sound of this lament pierced deep into the soul of the hearer. It seemed to him as if the old man were often stopped from proceeding by his tears: his harp would alone be heard for a time, till his voice again joined it in low, broken tones. Wilhelm stood by the door; he was much moved; the mourning of this stranger had again opened the avenues of his heart; he could not resist the claim of sympathy, or restrain the tears which this woe-begone complaint at last called forth. All the pains that pressed upon his soul seemed now at once to loosen from their hold: he abandoned himself without reserve to the feelings of the moment. Pushing up the door, he stood before the harper. The old man was sitting on a mean bed, the only seat, or article of furniture, which his miserable room afforded.

"What feelings thou hast awakened in me, good old man!" exclaimed he. "All that was lying frozen at my heart thou hast melted, and put in motion. Let me not disturb thee, but continue, in solacing thy own sorrows, to confer happiness upon a friend." The harper was about to rise, and say something; but Wilhelm hindered him, for he had noticed in the morning that the old man did not like to speak. He sat down by him on the straw bed.

The old man wiped his eyes, and asked, with a friendly smile, "How came you hither? I meant to wait upon you in the evening again."

"We are more quiet here," said Wilhelm. "Sing to me what thou pleasest, what accords with thy own mood of mind, only proceed as if I were not by. It seems to me, that to-day thou canst not fail to suit me. I think thee very happy, that, in solitude, thou canst employ and entertain thyself so pleasantly; that, being everywhere a stranger, thou findest in thy own heart the most agreeable society."

The old man looked upon his strings; and after touching them softly, by way of prelude, he commenced and sang, —

"Who longs in solitude to live,
   Ah! soon his wish will gain:
Men hope and love, men get and give,
   And leave him to his pain.
Yes, leave me to my moan!
   When from my bed
   You all are fled,
I still am not alone.

The lover glides with footstep light:
   His love, is she not waiting there?
So glides to meet me, day and night,
   In solitude my care,
   In solitude my woe:
True solitude I then shall know
   When lying in my grave,
   When lying in my grave,
And grief has let me go."

We might describe with great prolixity, and yet fail to express the charms of, the singular conversation which Wilhelm carried on with this wayfaring stranger. To every observation our friend addressed to him, the old man, with the nicest accordance, answered in some melody, which awakened all the cognate emotions, and opened a wide field to the imagination.

Whoever has happened to be present at a meeting of certain devout people, who conceive, that, in a state of separation from the Church, they can edify each other in a purer, more affecting, and more spiritual manner, may form to himself some conception of the present scene. He will recollect how the leader of the meeting would append to his words some verse of a song, that raised the soul till, as he wished, she took wing; how another of the flock would erelong subjoin, in a different tune, some verse of a different song; and to this again a third would link some verse of a third song, — by which means the kindred ideas of the songs to which the verses belonged were indeed suggested, yet each passage by its new combination became new and individualized, as if it had been first composed that moment; and thus from a well-known circle of ideas, from well-known songs and sayings, there was formed for that particular society, in that particular time, an original whole, by means of which their minds were animated, strengthened, and refreshed. So, likewise, did the old man edify his guest: by known and unknown songs and passages, he brought feelings near and distant, emotions sleeping and awake, pleasant and painful, into a circulation, from which, in Wilhelm's actual state, the best effects might be anticipated.

CHAPTER FOURTEEN

ACCORDINGLY, in walking back, he began to think with greater earnestness than ever on his present situation: he had reached home with the firm purpose of altering it, when the landlord disclosed to him, by way of secret, that Mademoiselle Philina had made a conquest of the count's *Stallmeister*, who, after executing his commission at his master's estate, had returned in the greatest haste, and was even now partaking of a good supper with her up in her chamber.

At this very moment Melina came in with a notary: they went into Wilhelm's chamber together, where the latter, though with some hesitation, made his promise good; gave a draft of three hundred crowns to Melina, who, handing it to the lawyer, received in return a note acknowledging the sale of the whole theatrical apparatus, and engaging to deliver it next morning.

Scarcely had they parted, when Wilhelm heard a cry of horror rising from some quarter of the house. He caught the sound of a young voice, uttering menacing and furious tones, which were ever and anon choked by immoderate weeping and howling. He observed this frantic noise move hastily from above, go past his door, and down to the lower part of the house.

Curiosity enticing our friend to follow it, he found Friedrich in a species of delirium. The boy was weeping, grinding his teeth, stamping with his feet, threatening with clenched fists: he appeared beside himself from fury and vexation. Mignon was standing opposite him, looking on with astonishment. The landlord, in some degree, explained this phenomenon.

The boy, he said, being well received at his return by Philina, seemed quite merry and contented: he had kept singing and jumping about, till the time when Philina grew acquainted with the *Stallmeister*. Then, however, this half-grown younker had begun to show his indignation, to slam the doors, and run up and down in the highest dudgeon. Philina had ordered him to wait at table that evening, upon which he had grown still sulkier and more indignant; till at last, carrying up a plate with a ragout, instead of setting it upon the table, he had thrown the whole between Mademoiselle and her guest, who were sitting moderately close together at the time: and the *Stallmeister*, after two or three hearty cuffs, had then kicked him out of the room. He, the landlord, had himself helped to clean both of them; and certainly their clothes had suffered much.

On hearing of the good effect of his revenge, the boy began to laugh aloud, whilst the tears were still running down his cheeks. He heartily rejoiced for a time, till the disgrace which he had suffered from the stronger party once more came into his head, and he began afresh to howl and threaten.

Wilhelm stood meditating, and ashamed at this spectacle. It reflected back to him his own feelings, in coarser and exaggerated features: he, too, was inflamed with a fierce jealousy; and, had not decency restrained him, he would willingly have satisfied his wild humor; with malicious spleen would have abused the object of his passion, and called out his rival; he could have crushed in pieces all the people round him; they seemed as if standing there but to vex him.

Laertes also had come in, and heard the story: he roguishly spurred on the irritated boy, who was now asserting with oaths that he would make the *Stallmeister* give him satisfaction; that he had never yet let any injury abide with him; that, should the man refuse, there were other ways of taking vengeance.

This was the very business for Laertes. He went up-stairs, with a solemn countenance, to call out the *Stallmeister* in the boy's name.

"This is a pleasant thing," said the *Stallmeister*: "such a joke as this I had scarcely promised myself to-night." They went down, and Philina followed them. "My son," said the *Stallmeister* to Friedrich, "thou art a brave lad, and I do not hesitate to fight thee. Only as our years and strength are unequal, and the attempt a little dangerous on that account, I propose a pair of foils in preference to other weapons. We can rub the buttons of them with a piece of chalk; and whoever marks upon the other's coat the first or the most thrusts, shall be held the victor, and be treated by the other with the best wine that can be had in town."

Laertes decided that the proposition might be listened to: Friedrich obeyed him, as his tutor. The foils were produced: Philina took a seat, went on with her knitting, and looked at the contending parties with the greatest peace of mind.

The *Stallmeister*, who could fence very prettily, was complaisant enough to spare his adversary, and to let a few chalk scores be marked upon his coat; after which the two embraced, and wine was ordered. The *Stallmeister* took the liberty of asking Friedrich's parentage and history; and Friedrich told him a long story, which had often been repeated already, and which, at some other opportunity, we purpose communicating to our readers.

To Wilhelm, in the mean time, this contest completed the representation of his own state of mind. He could not but perceive that he would willingly have taken up a foil against the *Stallmeister*, — a sword still more willingly, though evidently much his inferior in the science of defence. Yet he deigned not to cast one look on Philina; he was on his guard against any word or movement that could possibly betray his feelings: and, after having once or twice done justice to the health of the duellists, he hastened to his own room, where a thousand painful thoughts came pressing round him.

He called to memory the time when his spirit, rich in hope, and full of boundless aims, was raised aloft, and encircled with the liveliest enjoyments of every kind as with its proper element. He now clearly saw, that of late he had fallen into a broken, wandering path, where, if he tasted, it was but in drops what he once quaffed in unrestricted measure. But he could not clearly see what insatiable want it was that nature had made the law of his being, and how this want had been only set on edge, half satisfied, and misdirected by the circumstances of his life.

It will not surprise us, therefore, that, in considering his situation, and laboring to extricate himself, he fell into the greatest perplexity. It was not enough, that by his friendship for Laertes, his attachment to Philina, his concern for Mignon, he had been detained longer than was proper in a place and a society where he could cherish his darling inclination, content his wishes as it were by stealth, and, without proposing any object, again pursue his early dreams. These ties he believed himself possessed of force enough to break asunder: had there been nothing more to hold him, he could have gone at once. But, only a few moments ago, he had entered into money transactions with Melina: he had seen that mysterious old man, the enigma of whose history he longed with unspeakable desire to clear. Yet of this too, after much balancing of reasons, he at length determined, or thought he had determined, that it should not keep him back. "I must go." He threw himself into a chair: he felt greatly moved. Mignon came in, and asked whether she might help to undress him. Her manner was still and shy: it had grieved her to the quick to be so abruptly dismissed by him before.

Nothing is more touching than the first disclosure of a love which has been nursed in silence, of a faith grown strong in secret, and which at last comes forth in the hour of need, and reveals itself to him who formerly has reckoned it of small account. The bud, which had been closed so long and firmly, was now ripe to burst its swathings; and Wilhelm's heart could never have been readier to welcome the impressions of affection.

She stood before him, and noticed his disquietude. "Master!" she cried, "if thou art unhappy, what will become of Mignon?" — "Dear little creature," said he, taking her hands, "thou, too, art part of my anxieties. I must go hence." She looked at his eyes, glistening with restrained tears, and knelt down with vehemence before him. He kept her hands: she laid her head upon his knees, and remained quite still. He played with her hair, patted her, and spoke kindly to her. She continued motionless for a considerable time. At last he felt a sort of palpitating movement in her, which began very softly, and then by degrees, with increasing violence, diffused itself over all her frame. "What ails thee, Mignon?" cried he: "What ails thee?" She raised her little head, looked at him, and all at once laid her hand upon her heart, with the countenance of one repressing the utterance of pain. He raised her up, and she fell upon his breast: he pressed her towards him, and kissed her. She replied not by any pressure of the hand, by any motion whatever. She held firmly against her heart, and all at once gave a cry, which was accompanied by spasmodic movements of the body. She started up, and immediately fell down before him, as if broken in every joint. It was an excruciating moment. "My child!" cried he, raising her up, and clasping her fast, "my child, what ails thee?" The palpitations continued, spreading from the heart over all the lax and powerless limbs: she was merely hanging in his arms. All at once she again became quite stiff, like one enduring the sharpest corporeal agony; and soon with a new vehemence all her frame once more became alive; and she threw herself about his neck, like a bent spring that is closing; while in her soul, as it were, a strong rent took place, and at the same moment a stream of tears flowed from her shut eyes into his bosom. He held her fast. She wept, and no tongue can express the force of these tears. Her long hair had loosened, and was hanging down before her: it seemed as if her whole being was melting incessantly into a brook of tears. Her rigid limbs were again become relaxed; her inmost soul was pouring itself forth; in the wild confusion of the moment Wilhelm was afraid she would dissolve in his arms, and leave nothing there for him to grasp. He held her faster and faster. "My child!" cried he, "my child! thou art indeed mine, if that word can comfort thee. Thou art mine! I will keep thee, I will never forsake thee!" Her tears continued flowing. At last she raised herself: a faint gladness shone upon her face. "My father!" cried she, "thou wilt not forsake me? Wilt be my father? I am thy child!"

Softly, at this moment, the harp began to sound before the door: the old man brought his most affecting songs as an evening offering to our friend, who, holding his child ever faster in his arms, enjoyed the most pure and undescribable felicity.

Book Three

Know'st thou the land where citron-apples bloom,
And oranges like gold in leafy gloom;
A gentle wind from deep blue heaven blows,
The myrtle thick, and high the laurel grows?
Know'st thou it, then?
            'Tis there! 'tis there,
O my belov'd one, thou with me must go!

Know'st thou the house, its porch with pillars tall?
The rooms do glitter, glitters bright the hall,
And marble statues stand, and look each one:
What's this, poor child, to thee they've done?
Know'st thou it, then?
            'Tis there! 'tis there,
O my protector, thou with me must go!

Know'st thou the hill, the bridge that hangs on cloud?
The mules in mist grope o'er the torrent loud,
In caves lie coil'd the dragon's ancient brood,
The crag leaps down and over it the flood:
Know'st thou it, then?
            'Tis there! 'tis there
Our way runs; O my father, wilt thou go?

NEXT MORNING, on looking for Mignon about the house, Wilhelm did not find her, but was informed that she had gone out early with Melina, who had risen betimes to receive the wardrobe and other apparatus of his theatre.

After the space of some hours, Wilhelm heard the sound of music before his door. At first he thought it was the harper come again to visit him; but he soon distinguished the tones of a cithern, and the voice which began to sing was Mignon's. Wilhelm opened the door: the child came in, and sang him the song we have just given above.

The music and general expression of it pleased our friend extremely, though he could not understand all the words. He made her once more repeat the stanzas, and explain them: he wrote them down, and translated them into his native language. But the originality of its turns he could imitate only from afar: its childlike innocence of expression vanished from it in the process of reducing its broken phraseology to uniformity, and combining its disjointed parts. The charm of the tune, moreover, was entirely incomparable.

She began every verse in a stately and solemn manner, as if she wished to draw attention towards something wonderful, as if she had something weighty to communicate. In the third line, her tones became deeper and gloomier; the words, *"Dost know?"* were uttered with a show of mystery and eager circumspectness; in *" 'Tis there! 'tis there!"* lay an irresistible longing; and her *"Let us go!"* she modified at each repetition, so that now it appeared to entreat and implore, now to impel and persuade.

On finishing her song for the second time, she stood silent for a moment, looked keenly at Wilhelm, and asked him, *"Know'st thou the land?"* — "It must mean Italy," said Wilhelm: "where didst thou get the little song?" — "Italy!" said Mignon, with an earnest air. "If thou go to Italy, take me along with thee; for I am too cold here." — "Hast thou been there already, little dear?" said Wilhelm. But the child was silent, and nothing more could be got out of her.

Melina entered now: he looked at the cithern, — was glad that she had rigged it up again so prettily. The instrument had been among Melina's stage-gear: Mignon had begged it of him in the morning, and then gone to the old harper. On this occasion she had shown a talent she was not before suspected of possessing.

Melina had already got possession of his wardrobe, with all that pertained to it: some members of the town magistracy had promised him permission to act, for a time, in the place. He was now returning with a merry heart and a cheerful look. His nature seemed altogether changed: he was soft, courteous to every one, — nay, fond of obliging, and almost attractive. He was happy, he said, at now being able to afford employment to his friends, who had hitherto lain idle and embarrassed; sorry, however, that at first he could not have it in his power to remunerate the excellent actors whom fortune had offered him, in a style corresponding to their talents and capacities; being under the necessity, before all other things, of discharging his debt to so generous a friend as Wilhelm had proved himself to be.

"I cannot describe," said he to Wilhelm, "the friendliness which you have shown, in helping me forward to the management of a theatre. When I found you here, I was in a very curious predicament. You recollect how strongly I displayed to you, on our first acquaintance, my aversion to the stage; and yet, on being married, I was forced to look about for a place in some theatre, out of love to my wife, who promised to herself much joy and great applause if so engaged. I could find none, at least no constant one; but in return I luckily fell in with some commercial men, who, in extraordinary cases, were enabled to employ a person that could handle his pen, that understood French, and was not without a little skill in ciphering. I managed pretty well in this way for a time; I was tolerably paid; got about me many things which I had need of, and did not feel ashamed of my work. But these commissions of my patrons came to an end; they could afford me no permanent establishment: and, ever since, my wife has continued urging me still more to go upon the stage again; though, at present, alas! her own situation is none of the favorablest for exhibiting herself with honor in the eyes of the public. But now, I hope, the establishment which by your kind help I have the means of setting up, will prove a good beginning for me and mine: you I shall thank for all my future happiness, let matters turn out as they will."

Wilhelm listened to him with contentment: the whole fraternity of players were likewise moderately satisfied with the declarations of the new manager; they secretly rejoiced that an offer of employment had occurred so soon, and were disposed to put up at first with a smaller salary, the rather, that most of them regarded the present one, so unexpectedly placed within their reach, as a kind of supplement, on which a short while ago they could not count. Melina made haste to profit by this favorable temper: he endeavored in a sly way to get a little talk with each in private, and erelong had, by various methods, so cockered them all, that they did not hesitate to strike a bargain with him without loss of time; scarcely thinking of this new engagement, or reckoning themselves secure at worst of getting free again after six-weeks' warning.

The terms were now to be reduced to proper form; and Melina was considering with what pieces he would first entice the public, when a courier riding up informed the *Stallmeister* that his lord and lady were at hand; on which the latter ordered out his horses.

In a short time after this, the coach with its masses of luggage rolled in; two servants sprang down from the coachbox before the inn; and Philina, according to her custom, foremost in the way of novelties, placed herself within the door.

"Who are you?" said the countess, entering the house.

"An actress, at your Excellency's service," was the answer; while the cheat, with a most innocent air, and looks of great humility, courtesied, and kissed the lady's gown.

The count, on seeing some other persons standing round, who also signified that they were players, inquired about the strength of their company, their last place of residence, their manager. "Had they but been Frenchmen," said he to his lady, "we might have treated the prince with an unexpected enjoyment, and entertained him with his favorite pastime at our house."

"And could we not," said the countess, "get these people, though unluckily they are but Germans, to exhibit with us at the castle while the prince stays there? Without doubt they have some degree of skill. A large party can never be so well amused with any thing as with a theatre: besides, the baron would assist them."

So speaking, they went up-stairs; and Melina presented himself above, as manager. "Call your folk together," said the count, "and place them before me, that I may see what is in them. I must also have the list of pieces you profess to act."

Melina, with a low bow, hastened from the room, and soon returned with his actors. They advanced in promiscuous succession: some, out of too great anxiety to please, introduced themselves in a rather sorry style; the others, not much better, by assuming an air of unconcern. Philina showed the deepest reverence to the countess, who behaved with extreme graciousness and condescension: the count, in the mean time, was mustering the rest. He questioned each about his special province of acting, and signified to Melina that he must rigorously keep them to their several provinces, — a precept which the manager received with the greatest devotion.

The count then stated to each in particular what he ought especially to study, what about his figure or his postures ought to be amended; showed them luminously in what points the Germans always fail; and displayed such extraordinary knowledge, that all stood in the deepest humility, scarcely daring to draw their breath before so enlightened a critic and so right honorable a patron.

"What fellow is that in the corner?" said the count, looking at a subject who had not yet been presented to him, and who now approached, — a lean, shambling figure, with a rusty coat, patched at the elbows, and a woful periwig covering his submissive head.

This person, whom, from the last Book, we know already as Philina's darling, had been wont to enact pedants, tutors, and poets, — generally undertaking parts in which any cudgelling or ducking was to be endured. He had trained himself to certain crouching, ludicrous, timid bows; and his faltering, stammering speech befitted the characters he played, and created laughter in the audience; so that he was always looked on as a useful member of the company, being moreover very serviceable and obliging. He approached the count in his own peculiar way, bent himself before him, and answered every question with the grimaces and gestures he was used to on the stage. The count looked at him for some time with an air of attentive satisfaction and studious observation; then, turning to the countess, "Child," said he, "consider this man well: I will engage for it he is a great actor, or may become so." The creature here, in the fulness of his heart, made an idiotic bow: the count burst into laughing, and exclaimed, "He does it excellently well! I bet this fellow can act any thing he likes: it is pity that he has not been already used to something better."

So singular a prepossession was extremely galling to the rest: Melina alone felt no vexation, but completely coincided with the count, and answered, with a prostrate look, "Alas! it is too true: both he and others of us have long stood in need of such encouragement, and such a judge, as we now find in your Excellency."

"Is this the whole company?" inquired the count.

"Some of them are absent," said the crafty Melina; "and at any rate, if we should meet with support, we could soon collect abundant numbers from the neighborhood."

Philina in the mean while was saying to the countess, "There is a very pretty young man above, who without doubt would shortly become a first-rate amateur."

"Why does he not appear?" said the countess.

"I will bring him," cried Philina, hastening to the door.

She found our friend still occupied with Mignon: she persuaded him to come down. He followed her with some reluctance: yet curiosity impelled him; for, hearing that the family were people of rank, he longed much to know more of them. On entering the room, his eyes met those of the countess, which were directed towards him. Philina led him to the lady, while the count was busied with the rest. Wilhelm made his bow, and replied to several questions from the fair dame, not without confusion of mind. Her beauty and youth, her graceful dignity and refined manner, made the most delightful impression on him; and the more so, as her words and looks were accompanied with a certain bashfulness, one might almost say embarrassment. He was likewise introduced to the count, who, however, took no special notice of him, but went to the window with his lady, and seemed to ask her about something. It was easy to observe that her opinion accorded strongly with his own; that she even tried to persuade him, and strengthen him in his intentions.

In a short while he turned round to the company, and said, "I must not stay at present, but I will send a friend to you; and if you make reasonable proposals, and will take very great pains, I am not disinclined to let you play at the castle."

All testified their joy at this: Philina in particular kissed the hands of the countess with the greatest vivacity.

"Look you, little thing," said the lady, patting the cheeks of the light-minded girl, "look you, child, you shall come to me again: I will keep my promise; only you must dress better." Philina stated in excuse that she had little to lay out upon her wardrobe; and the countess immediately ordered her waiting-maids to bring from the carriage a silk neckerchief and an English hat, the articles easiest to come at, and give them to her new favorite. The countess herself then decked Philina, who continued very neatly to support, by her looks and conduct, that saintlike, guiltless character she had assumed at first.

The count took his lady's hand, and led her down. She bowed to the whole company with a friendly air, in passing by them: she turned round again towards Wilhelm, and said to him, with the most gracious mien, "We shall soon meet again."

These happy prospects enlivened the whole party: every one of them gave free course to his hopes, his wishes, his imaginations; spoke of the parts he would play, and the applause he would acquire. Melina was considering how he might still, by a few speedy exhibitions, gain a little money from the people of the town before he left it; while others went into the kitchen, to order a better dinner than of late they had been used to.

CHAPTER TWO

AFTER a few days the baron came, and it was not without fear that Melina received him. The count had spoken of him as a critic: and it might be dreaded, he would speedily detect the weakness of the little party, and see that it formed no efficient troop; there being scarcely a play which they could act in a suitable manner. But the manager, as well as all the members, were soon delivered from their cares, on finding that the baron was a man who viewed the German stage with a most patriotic enthusiasm, to whom every player, and every company of players, was welcome and agreeable. He saluted them all with great solemnity; was happy to come upon a German theatre so unexpectedly, to get connected with it, and to introduce their native Muses to the mansion of his relative. He then pulled out from his pocket a bundle of stitched papers, in which Melina hoped to find the terms of their contract specified; but it proved something very different. It was a drama, which the baron himself had composed, and wished to have played by them: he requested their attention while he read it. Willingly they formed a circle round him, charmed at being able with so little trouble to secure the favor of a man so important; though, judging by the thickness of the manuscript, it was clear that a very long rehearsal might be dreaded. Their apprehensions were not groundless: the piece was written in five acts, and that sort of acts which never have an end.

The hero was an excellent, virtuous, magnanimous, and at the same time misunderstood and persecuted, man: this worthy person, after many trials, gained the victory at last over all his enemies; on whom, in consequence, the most rigorous poetic justice would have been exercised, had he not pardoned them on the spot.

While this piece was rehearsing, each of the auditors had leisure enough to think of himself, and to mount up quite softly from the humble prostration of mind, to which, a little while ago, he had felt disposed, into a comfortable state of contentment with his own gifts and advantages, and, from this elevation, to discover the most pleasing prospects in the future. Such of them as found in the play no parts adapted for their own acting, internally pronounced it bad, and viewed the baron as a miserable author; while the others, every time they noticed any passage which they hoped might procure them a little clapping of the hands, exalted it with the greatest praise, to the immeasurable satisfaction of the author.

The commercial part of their affair was soon completed. Melina made an advantageous bargain with the baron, and contrived to keep it secret from the rest.

Of our friend, Melina took occasion to declare in passing, that he seemed to be successfully qualifying himself for becoming a dramatic poet, and even to have some capacities for being an actor. The

The count and the countess meet the players

baron introduced himself to Wilhelm as a colleague; and the latter by and by produced some short pieces, which, with a few other relics, had escaped by chance, on the day when he threw the greater part of his works into the flames. The baron lauded both his pieces and delivery: he spoke of it as a settled thing, that Wilhelm should come over to the castle with the rest. For all, at his departure, he engaged to find the best reception, comfortable quarters, a good table, applauses, and presents; and Melina further gave the promise of a certain modicum of pocket-money to each.

It is easy to conceive how this visit raised the spirits of the party: instead of a low and harassing situation, they now at once saw honors and enjoyment before them. On the score of these great hopes they already made merry, and each thought it needless and stingy to retain a single *groschen* of money in his purse.

Meanwhile our friend was taking counsel with himself about accompanying the troop to the castle; and he found it, in more than one sense, advisable to do so. Melina was in hopes of paying off his debt, at least in part, by this engagement; and Wilhelm, who had come from home to study men, was unwilling to let slip this opportunity of examining the great world, where he expected to obtain much insight into life, into himself, and the dramatic art. With all this, he durst not confess how greatly he wished again to be near the beautiful countess. He rather sought to persuade himself in general of the mighty advantages which a more intimate acquaintance with the world of rank and wealth would procure for him. He pursued his reflections on the count, the countess, the baron; on the security, the grace, and propriety of their demeanor: he exclaimed with rapture when alone, —

"Thrice happy are they to be esteemed, whom their birth of itself exalts above the lower stages of mankind; who do not need to traverse those perplexities, not even to skirt them, in which many worthy men so painfully consume the whole period of life. Far-extending and unerring must their vision be, on that higher station; easy each step of their progress in the world. From their very birth, they are placed, as it were, in a ship, which, in this voyage we have all to make, enables them to profit by the favorable winds, and to ride out the cross ones; while others, bare of help, must wear their strength away in swimming, can derive little profit from the favorable breeze, and in the storm must soon become exhausted, and sink to the bottom. What convenience, what ease of movement, does a fortune we are born to confer upon us! How securely does a traffic flourish, which is founded on a solid capital, where the failure of one or of many enterprises does not of necessity reduce us to inaction! Who can better know the worth and worthlessness of earthly things, than he that has had within his choice the enjoyment of them from youth upwards? and who can earlier guide his mind to the useful, the necessary, the true, than he that may convince himself of so many errors in an age when his strength is yet fresh to begin a new career?"

Thus did our friend cry joy to all inhabitants of the upper regions, and, not to them only, but to all that were permitted to approach their circle, and draw water from their wells. So he thanked his own happy stars, that seemed preparing to grant this mighty blessing to himself.

Melina, in the mean time, was torturing his brains to get the company arranged according to their several provinces, and each of them appointed to produce his own peculiar effect. In compliance with the count's injunctions and his own persuasions, he made many efforts; but at last, when it came to the point of execution, he was forced to be content, if, in so small a troop, he found his people willing to adjust themselves to this or that part as they best were able. When matters would admit of it, Laertes played the lover; Philina the lady's maid; the two young girls took up between them the characters of the artless and tender loved ones; the boisterous old gentleman of the piece was sure to be the best acted. Melina himself thought he might come forth as chevalier; Madam Melina, to her no small sorrow, was obliged to satisfy herself with personating young wives, or even affectionate mothers; and as in the newer plays, a poet or pedant is rarely introduced, and still more rarely for the purpose of being laughed at, the well-known favorite of the count was now usually transformed into president or minister, — these being commonly set forth as knaves, and severely handled in the fifth act. Melina, too, in the part of chamberlain or the like, introduced, with great satisfaction, the ineptitudes put into his hands by various honest Germans, according to use and wont, in many well-accepted plays: he delighted in these characters, because he had an opportunity of decking himself out in a fashionable style, and was called upon to assume the airs of a courtier, which he conceived himself to possess in great perfection.

It was not long till they were joined by several actors from different quarters; who, being received without very strict examination, were also retained without very burdensome conditions.

Wilhelm had been more than once assailed with persuasions from Melina to undertake an amateur part. This he declined; yet he interested and occupied himself about the general cause with great alacrity, without our new manager's acknowledging his labors in the smallest. On the contrary, it seemed to be Melina's opinion, that with his office he had at the same time picked up all the necessary skill for carrying it on. In particular, the task of curtailment formed one of his most pleasing occupations: he would succeed in reducing any given piece down to the regular measure of time, without the slightest respect to proprieties or proportions, or any thing whatever, but his watch. He met with great encouragement; the public was very much delighted; the most knowing inhabitants of the burgh maintained, that the prince's theatre itself was not so well conducted as theirs.

CHAPTER THREE

AT LAST the time arrived when the company had to prepare for travelling, and to expect the coaches and other vehicles that were to carry them to the count's mansion. Much altercation now took place about the mode of travelling, and who should sit with whom. The ordering and distribution of the whole was at length settled and concluded, with great labor, and, alas! without effect. At the appointed hour, fewer coaches came than were expected: they had to accommodate themselves as the case would admit. The baron, who followed shortly afterwards on horseback, assigned, as the reason, that all was in motion at the castle, not only because the prince was to arrive a few days earlier than had been looked for, but also because an unexpected party of visitors were already come: the place, he said, was in great confusion; on this account perhaps they would not lodge so comfortably as had been intended, — a change which grieved him very much.

Our travellers packed themselves into the carriages the best way they could; and the weather being tolerable, and the castle but a few leagues distant, the heartiest of the troop preferred setting out on foot to waiting the return of the coaches. The caravan got under way with great jubilee, for the first time without caring how the landlord's bill was to be paid. The count's mansion rose on their souls like a palace of the fairies: they were the happiest and merriest mortals in the world. Each throughout the journey, in his own peculiar mode, kept fastening a continued chain of fortune, honor, and prosperity to that auspicious day.

A heavy rain, which fell unexpectedly, did not banish these delightful contemplations; though, as it incessantly continued with more and more violence, many of the party began to show traces of uneasiness. The night came on; and no sight could be more welcome than the palace of the count, which shone upon them from a hill at some distance, glancing with light in all its stories, so that they could reckon every window.

On approaching nearer, they found all the windows in the wings illuminated also. Each of the party thought within himself what chamber would be his; and most of them prudently determined to be satisfied with a room in the attic, or some of the side buildings.

They were now proceeding through the village, past the inn. Wilhelm stopped the coach, in the mind to alight there; but the landlord protested that it was not in his power to afford the least accommodation: his lordship the count, he said, being visited by some unexpected guests, had immediately engaged the whole inn; every chamber in the house had been marked with chalk last night, specifying who was to lodge there. Our friend was accordingly obliged, against his will, to travel forward to the castle with the rest of the company.

In one of the side buildings, round the kitchen fire, they noticed several cooks running busily about, — a sight which refreshed them not a little. Servants came jumping hastily with lights to the staircase of the main door, and the hearts of the worthy pilgrims overflowed at the aspect of such honors. But how great was their surprise, when this cordial reception changed into a storm of curses. The servants scouted the coachman for driving in hither; they must wheel out again, it was bawled, and take their loading round to the old castle; there was no room here for such guests! To this unfriendly and unexpected dismissal, they joined all manner of jeering, and laughed aloud at each other for leaping out in the rain on so false an errand. It was still pouring; no star was visible in the sky; while our company were dragged along a rough, jolting road, between two walls, into the old mansion, which stood behind, inhabited by none since the present count's father had built the new residence in front of it. The carriages drew up, partly in the court-yard, partly in a long, arched gateway; and the postilions, people hired from the village, unyoked their horses, and rode off.

As nobody came forward to receive the travellers, they alighted from their places, they shouted, and searched. In vain! All continued dark and still. The wind swept through the lofty gate: the court and the old towers were lying gray and dreary, and so dim that their forms could scarcely be distinguished in the gloom. The people were all shuddering and freezing; the women were becoming frightened; the children began to cry; the general impatience was increasing every minute; so quick a revolution of fortune, for which no one of them had been at all prepared, entirely destroyed their equanimity.

Expecting every minute that some person would appear and unbolt the doors, mistaking at one time the pattering of rain, at another the rocking of the wind, for the much-desired footstep of the castle bailiff, they continued downcast and inactive: it occurred to none of them to go into the new mansion, and there solicit help from charitable souls. They could not understand where their friend the baron was lingering: they were in the most disconsolate condition.

At last some people actually arrived: by their voices, they were recognized as the pedestrians who had fallen behind the others on the journey. They intimated that the baron had tumbled with his horse, and hurt his leg severely; and that, on calling at the castle, they, too, had been roughly directed hither.

The whole company were in extreme perplexity: they guessed and speculated as to what should now be done, but they could fix on nothing. At length they noticed from afar a lantern advancing, and took fresh breath at sight of it; but their hopes of quick deliverance again evaporated, when the object approached, and came to be distinctly seen. A groom was lighting the well-known *Stallmeister* of the castle towards them: this gentleman, on coming nearer, very anxiously inquired for Mademoiselle Philina. No sooner had she stepped forth from the crowd, than he very pressingly offered to conduct her to the new mansion, where a little place had been provided for her with the countess's maids. She did not hesitate long about accepting his proposal; she caught his arm, and, recommending her trunk to the care of the rest, was going to hasten off with him directly: but the others intercepted them, asking, entreating, conjuring the *Stallmeister*, till at last, to get away with his fair one, he promised every thing, assuring them, that, in a little while, the castle should be opened, and they lodged in the most comfortable manner. In a few moments they saw the glimmer of his lantern vanish: they long looked in vain for another gleam of light. At last, after much watching, scolding, and reviling, it actually appeared, and revived them with a touch of hope and consolation.

An ancient footman opened the door of the old edifice, into which they rushed with violence. Each of them now strove to have his trunk unfastened, and brought in beside him. Most of this luggage, like the persons of its owners, was thoroughly wetted. Having but a single light, the process of unpacking went on very slowly. In the dark passages they pushed against each other, they stumbled, they fell. They begged to have more lights, they begged to have some fuel. The monosyllabic footman, with much ado, consented to put down his own lantern; then went his way, and came not again.

They now began to investigate the edifice. The doors of all the rooms were open: large stoves, tapestry hangings, inlaid floors, yet bore witness to its former pomp; but of other house-gear there was none to be seen, — no table, chair, or mirror, nothing but a few monstrous, empty bedsteads, stripped of every ornament and every necessary. The wet trunks and knapsacks were adopted as seats: a part of the tired wanderers placed themselves upon the floor. Wilhelm had sat down upon some steps: Mignon lay upon his knees. The child was restless; and, when he asked what ailed her, she answered, "I am hungry." He himself had nothing that could still the craving of the child: the rest of the party had consumed their whole provision, so he was obliged to leave the little traveller without refreshment. Through the whole adventure he had been inactive, silently immersed in thought. He was very sullen, and full of indignant regret that he had not kept by his first determination, and remained at the inn, though he should have slept in the garret.

The rest demeaned themselves in various ways. Some of them had got a heap of old wood collected within a vast, gaping chimney in the hall: they set fire to the pile with great huzzaing. Unhappily, however, their hopes of warming and drying themselves by means of it were mocked in the most frightful manner. The chimney, it appeared, was there for ornament alone, and was walled up above; so the smoke rushed quickly back, and at once filled the whole chamber. The dry wood rose crackling into flames; the flame was also driven back; the draught sweeping through the broken windows gave it a wavering direction. Terrified lest the castle should catch fire, the unhappy guests had to tear the burning sticks asunder, to smother and trample them under their feet; the smoke increased; their case was rendered more intolerable than before; they were driven to the brink of desperation.

Wilhelm had retreated from the smoke into a distant chamber, to which Mignon soon followed him, leading in a well-dressed servant, with a high, clear, double-lighted lantern in his hand. He turned to Wilhelm, and, holding out to him some fruits and confectionery on a beautiful porcelain plate, "The young lady up-stairs," said he, "sends you this, with the request that you would join her party: she bids me tell you," added the lackey, with a sort of grin, "that she is very well off yonder, and wishes to divide her enjoyments with her friends."

Wilhelm had not at all expected such a message; for, ever since the adventure on the stone bench, he had treated Philina with the most decided contempt. He was still so resolute to have no more concern with her that he thought of sending back her dainty gifts untasted, when a supplicating look of Mignon's induced him to accept them. He returned his thanks in the name of the child. The invitation he entirely rejected. He desired the servant to exert himself a little for the stranger company, and made inquiry for the baron. The latter, he was told, had gone to bed, but had already, as the lackey understood, given orders to some other person to take charge of these unfortunate and ill-lodged gentlemen.

The servant went away, leaving one of his lights, which Wilhelm, in the absence of a candlestick, contrived to fix upon the window-casement; and now, at least in his meditations, he could see the four walls of his chamber. Nor was it long till preparations were commenced for conducting our travellers to rest. Candles arrived by degrees, though without snuffers; then a few chairs; an hour afterwards came bed-clothes; then pillows, all well steeped in rain. It was far past midnight when straw beds and mattresses were produced, which, if sent at first, would have been extremely welcome.

In the interim, also, somewhat to eat and drink had been brought in: it was enjoyed without much criticism; though it looked like a most disorderly collection of remains, and offered no very singular proof of the esteem in which our guests were held.

CHAPTER FOUR

THE DISORDERS and mischievous tricks of some frolicsome companions still further augmented the disquietudes and distresses of the night: these gay people woke each other; each played a thousand giddy pranks to plague his fellow. The next morning dawned amid loud complaints against their friend the baron, for having so deceived them, for having given so very false a notion of the order and comfort that awaited their arrival. However, to their great surprise and consolation, at an early hour the count himself, attended by a few servants, made his entrance, and inquired about their circumstances. He appeared much vexed on discovering how badly they had fared; and the baron, who came limping along, supported on the arm of a servant, bitterly accused the steward for neglecting his commands on this occasion, — showing great anxiety to have that person punished for his disobedience.

The count gave immediate orders that every thing should be arranged, in his presence, to the utmost possible convenience of the guests. While this was going on, some officers arrived, who forthwith scraped acquaintance with the actresses. The count assembled all the company before him, spoke to each by name, introduced a few jokes among his observations; so that every one was charmed at the gracious condescension of his lordship. At last it came to Wilhelm's turn. He appeared with Mignon holding by his hand. Our friend excused himself, in the best terms he could, for the freedom he had taken. The count, on the other hand, spoke as if the visit had been looked for.

A gentleman, who stood beside the count, and who, although he wore no uniform, appeared to be an officer, conversed with Wilhelm: he was evidently not a common man. His large, keen blue eyes, looking out from beneath a high brow; his light-colored hair, thrown carelessly back; his middle stature; every thing about him, — showed an active, firm, and decisive mode of being. His questions were lively. He seemed to be at home in all that he inquired about.

Wilhelm asked the baron what this person was, but found that he had little good to say of him. "He held the rank of major, was the special favorite of the prince; managed his most secret affairs; was, in short, regarded as his right arm, — nay, there was reason to believe him the prince's natural son. He had been on embassies in France, England, Italy. In all those places he had greatly distinguished himself, by which means he was grown conceited; imagining, among other pretensions, that he thoroughly understood the literature of Germany, and allowing himself to vent all kinds of sorry jests upon it. He, the baron, was in the habit of avoiding all intercourse with him; and Wilhelm would do well to imitate that conduct, for it somehow happened that no one could be near him without being punished for it. He was called Jarno, though nobody knew rightly what to make of such a name."

Wilhelm had nothing to urge against all this: he had felt a sort of inclination for the stranger, though he noticed in him something cold and repulsive.

The company being arranged and distributed throughout the castle, Melina issued the strictest orders that they should behave themselves with decency, the women live in a separate quarter, and each direct his whole attention to the study of dramatic art, and of the characters he had to play. He posted up written ordinances, consisting of many articles, upon all the doors. He settled the amount of fine which should be levied upon each transgressor, and put into a common box.

This edict was but little heeded. Young officers went out and in; they jested, not in the most modest fashion, with the actresses; made game of the actors, and annihilated the whole system of police before it had the smallest time to take root in the community. The people ran chasing one another through the rooms; they changed clothes; they disguised themselves. Melina, attempting to be rigorous with a few at first, was exasperated by every sort of insolence; and, when the count soon after sent for him to come and view the place where his theatre was to be erected, matters grew worse and worse. The young gentry devised a thousand broad jokes: by the help of some actors, they became yet coarser. It seemed as if the old castle had been altogether given up to an infuriate host, and the racket did not end till dinner.

Meanwhile, the count had led Melina over to a large hall, which, though belonging to the old castle, communicated by a gallery with the new one: it seemed very well adapted for being changed into a little theatre. Here the sagacious lord of the mansion pointed out in person how he wanted every thing to be.

The labor now commenced in the greatest haste; the stage apparatus was erected and furbished up; what decorations they had brought along with them and could employ were set in order, and what was wanting was prepared by some skilful workmen of the count's. Wilhelm likewise put his hand to the business; he assisted in settling the perspective, in laying off the outlines of the scenery: he was very anxious that nothing should be executed clumsily. The count, who frequently came in to inspect their progress, was highly satisfied: he showed particularly how they should proceed in every case, displaying an uncommon knowledge of all the arts they were concerned with.

Next began the business of rehearsing, in good earnest; and there would have been enough of space and leisure for this undertaking, had the actors not continually been interrupted by the presence of visitors. Some new guests were daily arriving, and each insisted on viewing the operations of the company.

CHAPTER FIVE

THE BARON had, for several days, been cheering Wilhelm with the hope of being formally presented to the countess. "I have told this excellent lady," said he, "so much about the talent and fine sentiment displayed in your compositions, that she feels quite impatient to see you, and hear one or two of them read. Be prepared, therefore, to come over at a moment's notice; for, the first morning she is at leisure, you will certainly be called on." He then pointed out to him the afterpiece it would be proper to produce on that occasion; adding, that doubtless it would recommend him to no usual degree of favor. The lady, he declared, was extremely sorry that a guest like him had happened to arrive at a time of such confusion, when they could not entertain him in a style more suitable to his merits and their own wishes.

In consequence of this information, Wilhelm, with the most sedulous attention, set about preparing the piece, which was to usher him into the great world. "Hitherto," said he, "thou hast labored in silence for thyself, applauded only by a small circle of friends. Thou hast for a time despaired of thy abilities, and are yet full of anxious doubts whether even thy present path is the right one, and whether thy talent for the stage at all corresponds with thy inclination for it. In the hearing of such practised judges, in the closet where no illusion can take place, the attempt is far more hazardous than elsewhere; and yet I would not willingly recoil from the experiment: I could wish to add this pleasure to my former enjoyments, and, if it might be, to give extension and stability to my hopes from the future."

He accordingly went through some pieces; read them with the keenest critical eye; made corrections here and there; recited them aloud, that he might be perfect in his tones and expression: and finally selected the work which he was best acquainted with, and hoped to gain most honor by. He put it in his pocket, one morning, on being summoned to attend the countess.

The baron had assured him that there would be no one present but the lady herself and a worthy female friend of hers. On entering the chamber, the Baroness von C—— advanced with great friendliness to meet him, expressed her happiness at gaining his acquaintance, and introduced him to the countess, who was then under the hands of her hair-dresser. The countess received him with kind words and looks. But it vexed him to see Philina kneeling at her chair, and playing a thousand fooleries. "The poor child," said the baroness, "has just been singing to us. Finish the song you were in the midst of: we should not like to lose it."

Wilhelm listened to her quavering with great patience, being anxious for the *friseur's* departure before he should begin to read. They offered him a cup of chocolate, the baroness herself handing him the biscuit. Yet, in spite of these civilities, he relished not his breakfast: he was longing too eagerly to lay before the lovely countess some performance that might interest and gratify her. Philina, too, stood somewhat in his way: on former occasions, while listening to him, she had more than once been troublesome. He looked at the *friseur* with a painful feeling, hoping every moment that the tower of curls would be complete.

Meanwhile the count came in, and began to talk of the fresh visitors he was expecting, of the day's occupations or amusements, and of various domestic matters that were started. On his retiring, some officers sent to ask permission of the countess to pay their respects to her, as they had to leave the castle before dinner. The footman having come to his post at the door, she permitted him to usher in the gentlemen.

The baroness, amid these interruptions, took pains to entertain our friend, and showed him much consideration; all which he accepted with becoming reverence, though not without a little absence of mind. He often felt for the manuscript in his pocket, and hoped for his deliverance every instant. He was almost losing patience, when a man-milliner was introduced, and immediately began without mercy to open his papers, bags, and bandboxes; pressing all his various wares upon the ladies, with an importunity peculiar to that species of creature.

The company increased. The baroness cast a look at Wilhelm, and then whispered with the countess: he noticed this, but did not understand the purpose of it. The whole, however, became clear enough, when, after an hour of painful and fruitless endurance, he went away. He then found a beautiful pocket-book, of English manufacture, in his pocket. The baroness had dexterously put it there without his notice; and soon afterwards the countess's little black came out, and handed him an elegantly flowered waistcoat, without very clearly saying whence it came.

THIS mingled feeling of vexation and gratitude spoiled the remainder of his day; till, towards evening, he once more found employment. Melina informed him that the count had been speaking of a little prelude, which he wished to have produced in honor of the prince, on the day of his Highness's arrival. He meant to have the great qualities of this noble hero and philanthropist personified in the piece. These Virtues were to advance together, to recite his praises, and finally to encircle his bust with garlands of flowers and laurels; behind which a transparency might be inserted, representing the princely Hat, and his name illuminated on it. The count, Melina said, had ordered him to take charge of getting ready the verses and other arrangements; and Wilhelm, he hoped, to whom it must be an easy matter, would stand by him on this occasion.

"What!" exclaimed our friend, in a splenetic tone, "have we nothing but portraits, illuminated names, and allegorical figures, to show in honor of a prince, who, in my opinion, merits quite a different eulogy? How can it flatter any reasonable man to see himself set up in effigy, and his name glimmering on oiled paper? I am very much afraid that your allegories, particularly in the present state of the wardrobe, will furnish occasion for many ambiguities and jestings. If you mean, however, to compose the play, or have it composed, I can have nothing to object; only I desire to have no part or lot in the matter."

Melina excused himself; alleging this to be only a casual hint of his lordship the count, who for the rest had left the arrangement of the piece entirely in their own hands. "With all my heart," replied our friend, "will I contribute something to the pleasure of this noble family: my Muse has never had so pleasant an employment as to sing, though in broken numbers, the praises of a prince who merits so much veneration. I will think of the matter: perhaps I may be able to contrive some way of bringing out our little troop, so as at least to produce some effect."

From this moment Wilhelm eagerly reflected on his undertaking. Before going to sleep he had got it all reduced to some degree of order;

early next morning his plan was ready, the scenes laid out; a few of the most striking passages and songs were even versified and written down.

As soon as he was dressed, our friend made haste to wait upon the baron, to submit the plan to his inspection, and take his advice upon certain points connected with it. The baron testified his approbation of it, but not without considerable surprise. For, on the previous evening, he had heard his lordship talk of having ordered some quite different piece to be prepared and versified.

"To me it seems improbable," replied our friend, "that it could be his lordship's wish to have the piece got ready, exactly as he gave it to Melina. If I am not mistaken, he intended merely to point out to us from a distance the path we were to follow. The amateur and critic shows the artist what is wanted, and then leaves to him the care of producing it by his own means."

"Not at all," replied the baron: "his lordship understands that the piece shall be composed according to that and no other plan which he has himself prescribed. Yours has, indeed, a remote similarity with his idea; but if we mean to accomplish our purpose, and get the count diverted from his first thought, we shall need to employ the ladies in the matter. The baroness especially contrives to execute such operations in the most masterly manner: the question is now, whether your plan shall so please her, that she will undertake the business; in that case it will certainly succeed."

"We need the assistance of the ladies," said our friend, "at any rate; for neither our company nor our wardrobe would suffice without them. I have counted on some pretty children, that are running up and down the house, and belong to certain of the servants."

He then desired the baron to communicate his plan to the ladies. The baron soon returned with intelligence that they wished to speak with Wilhelm personally. That same evening, when the gentlemen sat down to play, which, owing to the arrival of a certain general, was expected to be deeper and keener than usual, the countess and her friend, under pretext of some indisposition, would retire to their chamber, where Wilhelm, being introduced by a secret staircase, might submit his project without interruption. This sort of mystery, the baron said, would give the adventure a peculiar charm; in particular

the baroness was rejoicing like a child in the prospect of their rendezvous, and the more so, because it was to be accomplished secretly, and
against the inclination of the count.

Towards evening, at the appointed time, Wilhelm was sent for,
and led in with caution. As the baroness advanced to meet him in a
small cabinet, the manner of their interview brought former happy
scenes for a moment to his mind. She conducted him along to the
countess's chamber, and they now proceeded earnestly to question and
investigate. He exhibited his plan with the utmost warmth and vivacity,
so that his fair audience were quite decided in its favor. Our readers
also will permit us to present a brief sketch of it here.

The play was to open with a dance of children in some rural
scene, — their dance representing that particular game wherein each
has to wheel round, and gain the other's place. This was to be followed by several variations of their play; till at last, in performing a
dance of the repeating kind, they were all to sing a merry song.

Here the old harper with Mignon was to enter, and, by the
curiosity which they excited, gather several country-people round
them; the harper would sing various songs in praise of peace, repose,
and joy; and Mignon would then dance the egg-dance.

In these innocent delights, they are disturbed by the sound of
martial music; and the party are surprised by a troop of soldiers. The
men stand on the defensive, and are overcome: the girls flee, and are
overtaken. In the tumult all seems going to destruction, when a
person (about whose form and qualities the poet was not yet determined) enters, and, by signifying that the general is near, restores
composure. Whereupon the hero's character is painted in the finest
colors; security is promised in the midst of arms; violence and lawless
disorder are now to be restrained. A universal festival is held in honor
of the noble-minded captain.

The countess and her friend expressed great satisfaction with the
plan; only they maintained that there must of necessity be something
of allegory introduced, to make it palatable to his lordship. The baron
proposed that the leader of the soldiers should be represented as the
Genius of Dissension and Violence; that Minerva should then advance to bind fetters on him, to give notice of the hero's approach,
and celebrate his praise. The baroness undertook the task of persuad-

ing the count that this plan was the one proposed by himself, with a few alterations; at the same time expressly stipulating, that without fail, at the conclusion of the piece, the bust, the illuminated name, and the princely Hat should be exhibited in due order; since otherwise, her attempt was vain.

Wilhelm had already figured in his mind how delicately and how nobly he would have the praises of his hero celebrated in the mouth of Minerva, and it was not without a long struggle that he yielded in this point. Yet he felt himself delightfully constrained to yield. The beautiful eyes of the countess, and her lovely demeanor, would easily have moved him to sin against his conscience as a poet; to abandon the finest and most interesting invention, the keenly wished-for unity of his composition, and all its most suitable details. His conscience as a burgher had a trial no less hard to undergo, when the ladies, in distributing the characters, pointedly insisted that he must undertake one himself.

Laertes had received for his allotment the part of that violent war-god; Wilhelm was to represent the leader of the peasants, who had some very pretty and tender verses to recite. After long resistance he was forced to comply: he could find no excuse, when the baroness protested that their stage was in all respects to be regarded as a private one, and that she herself would very gladly play on it, if they could find her a fit occasion. On receiving his consent, they parted with our friend on the kindest terms. The baroness assured him that he was an incomparable man: she accompanied him to the little stairs, and wished him good-night with a squeeze of the hand.

CHAPTER SEVEN

THE INTEREST in his undertakings, which the countess and her friend expressed and felt so warmly, quickened Wilhelm's faculties and zeal: the plan of his piece, which the process of describing it had rendered more distinct, was now present in the most brilliant vivid-ness before his mind. He spent the greater part of that night, and the whole of next morning, in the sedulous versification of the dialogue and songs.

He had proceeded a considerable way, when a message came, requiring his attendance in the castle: the noble company, who were then at breakfast, wished to speak with him. As he entered the parlor, the baroness advanced to meet him, and, under pretext of wishing him good-morning, whispered cunningly, "Say nothing of your piece but what you shall be asked."

"I hear," cried the count to him, "that you are very busy work-ing at my prelude, which I mean to present in honor of the prince. I consent that you introduce a Minerva into it; and we are just thinking beforehand how the goddess shall be dressed, that we may not blunder in costume. For this purpose I am causing them to fetch from the library all the books that contain any figures of her."

At the same instant, one or two servants entered the parlor, with a huge basket full of books of every shape and appearance.

Montfaucon, the collections of antique statues, gems, and coins, all sorts of mythological writings, were turned up, and their plates compared. But this was not enough. The count's faithful memory recalled to him all the Minervas to be found in frontispieces, vignettes, or anywhere else; and book after book was, in consequence, carried from the library, till finally the count was sitting in a chaos of volumes. Unable at last to recollect any other figure of Minerva, he observed with a smile, "I durst bet, that now there is not a single Minerva in all the library; and perhaps it is the first time that a collection of books has been so totally deprived of the presence of its patron god-dess."

The whole company were merry at this thought: Jarno particu-larly, who had all along been spurring on the count to call for more and more books, laughed quite immoderately.

"Now," said the count, turning to Wilhelm, "one chief point is, — which goddess do you mean? Minerva, or Pallas? The goddess of war, or of the arts?"

"Would it not be best, your Excellency," said Wilhelm, "if we were not clearly to express ourselves on this head; if, since the goddess plays a double part in the ancient mythology, we also exhibited her here in a double quality? She announces a warrior, but only to calm the tumults of the people; she celebrates a hero by exalting his humanity; she conquers violence, and restores peace and security."

The baroness, afraid lest Wilhelm might betray himself, hastily pushed forward the countess's tailor, to give his opinion how such an antique robe could best be got ready. This man, being frequently employed in making masquerade dresses, very easily contrived the business: and as Madam Melina, notwithstanding her advanced state of pregnancy, had undertaken to enact the celestial virgin, the tailor was directed to take her measure; and the countess, though with some reluctance, selected from the wardrobe the clothes he was to cut up for that purpose.

The baroness, in her dexterous way, again contrived to lead Wilhelm aside, and let him know that she had been providing all the other necessaries. Shortly afterwards she sent him the musician, who had charge of the count's private band; and this professor set about composing what airs were wanted, or choosing from his actual stock such tunes as appeared suitable. From this time all went on according to the wishes of our friend: the count made no more inquiries about the piece; being altogether occupied with the transparent decoration, destined to surprise the spectators at the conclusion of the play. His inventive genius, aided by the skill of his confectioner, produced, in fact, a very pretty article. In the course of his travels, the count had witnessed the most splendid exhibitions of this sort: he had also brought home with him a number of copper-plates and drawings, and could sketch such things with considerable taste.

Meanwhile Wilhelm finished the play, gave every one his part, and began the study of his own. The musician also, having great skill in dancing, prepared the ballet; so that every thing proceeded as it ought.

Yet one unexpected obstacle occurred, which threatened to occasion an unpleasant gap in the performance. He had promised to himself a striking effect from Mignon's egg-dance, and was much surprised when the child, with her customary dryness of manner, refused to dance; saying she was now his, and would no more go upon the stage. He sought to move her by every sort of persuasion, and did not discontinue his attempt till she began weeping bitterly, fell at his feet, and cried out, "Dearest father! stay thou from the boards thyself!" Little heeding this caution, he studied how to give the scene some other turn that might be equally interesting.

Philina, whose appointment was to act one of the peasant girls, and in the concluding dance to give the single-voice part of the song, and lead the chorus, felt exceedingly delighted that it had been so ordered. In other respects, too, her present life was altogether to her mind: she had her separate chamber; was constantly beside the countess, entertaining her with fooleries, and daily received some present for her pains. Among other things, a dress had been expressly made for her wearing in this prelude. And being of a light, imitative nature, she quickly marked in the procedure of the ladies whatever would befit herself: she had of late grown all politeness and decorum. The attentions of the *Stallmeister* augmented rather than diminished; and as the officers also paid zealous court to her, living in so genial an element, it came into her head for once in her life to play the prude, and, in a quiet, gradual way, to take upon herself a certain dignity of manner to which she had not before aspired. Cool and sharp-sighted as she was, eight days had not elapsed till she knew the weak side of every person in the house; so that, had she possessed the power of acting from any constant motive, she might very easily have made her fortune. But on this occasion, as on all others, she employed her advantages merely to divert herself, — to procure a bright to-day, and be impertinent, wherever she observed that impertinence was not attended with danger.

The parts were now committed to memory: a rehearsal of the piece was ordered; the count purposed to be present at it, and his lady began to feel anxious how he might receive it. The baroness called Wilhelm to her privately. The nearer the hour approached, they all displayed the more perplexity; for the truth was, that, of the count's original idea, nothing whatever had been introduced. Jarno, who joined them while consulting together, was admitted to the secret. He felt amused at the contrivance, and was heartily disposed to offer the ladies his good services in carrying it through. "It will go hard," said he, "if you cannot extricate yourselves without help from this affair; but, at all events, I will wait, as a body of reserve." The baroness then told them how she had on various occasions recited the whole piece to the count, but only in fragments and without order; that consequently he was prepared for each individual passage, yet certainly possessed with the idea that the whole would coincide with his original conception. "I will sit by him," said she, "to-night at the rehearsal, and study to divert his attention. The confectioner I have engaged already to make the decoration as beautiful as possible, but as yet he has not quite completed it."

"I know of a court," said Jarno, "where I wish we had a few such active and prudent friends as you. If your skill to-night will not suffice, give me a signal: I will take out the count, and not let him in again till Minerva enter; and you have speedy aid to expect from the illumination. For a day or two I have had something to report to him about his cousin, which for various reasons I have hitherto postponed. It will give his thoughts another turn, and that none of the pleasantest."

Business hindered the count from being present when the play began; the baroness amused him after his arrival: Jarno's help was not required. For as the count had abundance of employment in pointing out improvements, rectifying and arranging the detached parts, he entirely forgot the purport of the whole; and, as at last Madam Melina advanced, and spoke according to his heart, and the transparency did well, he seemed completely satisfied. It was not till the whole was finished, and his guests were sitting down to cards, that the difference appeared to strike him; and he began to think whether after all this piece was actually of his invention. At a signal from the baroness, Jarno then came forward into action; the evening passed away; the intelligence of the prince's approach was confirmed; the people rode out more than once to see his vanguard encamping in the neighborhood; the house was full of noise and tumult; and our actors, not always served in the handsomest manner by unwilling servants, had to pass their time in practisings and expectations at their quarters in the old mansion, without any one particularly taking thought about them.

AT LENGTH the prince arrived, with all his generals, staff-officers, and suite accompanying him. These, and the multitude of people coming to visit or do business with him, made the castle like a beehive on the point of swarming. All pressed forward to behold a man no less distinguished by his rank than by his great qualities, and all admired his urbanity and condescension: all were astonished at finding the hero and leader of armies also the most accomplished and attractive courtier.

By the count's orders, the inmates of the castle were required to be all at their posts when the prince arrived: not a player was allowed to show himself, that his Highness might have no anticipation of the spectacle prepared to welcome him. Accordingly, when at evening he was led into the lofty hall, glowing with light, and adorned with tapestries of the previous century, he seemed not at all prepared to expect a play, and still less a prelude in honor of himself. Every thing went off as it should have done: at the conclusion of the show, the whole troop were called and presented individually to the prince, who contrived, with the most pleasing and friendly air, to put some question, or make some remark, to every one of them. Wilhelm, as author of the piece, was particularly noticed, and had his tribute of applause liberally paid him.

The prelude being fairly over, no one asked another word about it: in a few days, it was as if it never had existed; except that occasionally Jarno spoke of it to Wilhelm, judiciously praised it, adding, however, "It is pity you should play with hollow nuts, for a stake of hollow nuts." This expression stuck in Wilhelm's mind for several days: he knew not how to explain it, or what to infer from it.

Meanwhile the company kept acting every night, as well as their capacities permitted; each doing his utmost to attract the attention of spectators. Undeserved applauses cheered them on: in their old castle they fully believed, that the great assemblage was crowding thither solely on their account; that the multitude of strangers was allured by their exhibitions; that *they* were the centre round which, and by means of which, the whole was moving and revolving.

Wilhelm alone discovered, to his sorrow, that directly the reverse was true. For although the prince had waited out the first exhibitions, sitting on his chair, with the greatest conscientiousness, yet by degrees he grew remiss in his attendance, and seized every plausible occasion of withdrawing. And those very people whom Wilhelm, in conversation, had found to be the best informed and most sensible, with Jarno at their head, were wont to spend but a few transitory moments in the hall of the theatre; sitting for the rest of their time in the ante-chamber, gaming, or seeming to employ themselves in business.

Amid all his persevering efforts, to want the wished and hoped for approbation grieved Wilhelm very deeply. In the choice of plays, in transcribing the parts, in numerous rehearsals, and whatever further could be done, he zealously co-operated with Melina, who, being in secret conscious of his own insufficiency, at length acknowledged and pursued these counsels. His own parts Wilhelm diligently studied, and executed with vivacity and feeling, and with all the propriety the little training he had yet received would allow.

At the same time, the unwearied interest the baron took in their performances obliterated every doubt from the minds of the rest of the company: he assured them that their exhibitions were producing the deepest effect, especially while one of his own pieces had been representing; only he was grieved to say, the prince showed an exclusive inclination for the French theatre; while a part of his people, among whom Jarno was especially distinguished, gave a passionate preference to the monstrous productions of the English stage.

If in this way the art of our players was not adequately noticed and admired, their persons on the other hand grew not entirely indifferent to all the gentlemen and all the ladies of the audience. We observed above, that, from the very first, our actresses had drawn upon them the attention of the young officers: in the sequel they were luckier, and made more important conquests. But, omitting these, we shall merely observe, that Wilhelm every day appeared more interesting to the countess; while in him, too, a silent inclination towards her was beginning to take root. Whenever he was on the stage, she could not turn her eyes from him; and, erelong, he seemed to play and to recite with his face towards her alone. To look upon each other, was to them the sweetest satisfaction; to which their harmless souls yielded without reserve, without cherishing a bolder wish, or thinking about any consequence.

As two hostile outposts will sometimes peacefully and pleasantly converse together across the river which divides them, not thinking of the war in which both their countries are engaged: so did the countess exchange looks full of meaning with our friend, across the vast chasm of birth and rank; both believing for themselves that they might safely cherish their several emotions.

The baroness, in the mean time, had selected Laertes, who, being a spirited and lively young man, pleased her very much; and who, woman-hater as he was, felt unwilling to refuse a passing adventure. He would actually on this occasion have been fettered, against his will, by the courteous and attractive nature of the baroness, had not the baron done him accidentally a piece of good, or, if you will, of bad, service, by instructing him a little in the habits and temper of this lady.

Laertes, happening once to celebrate her praises, and give her the preference to every other of her sex, the baron, with a grin, replied, "I see how matters stand: our fair friend has got a fresh inmate for her stalls." This luckless comparison, which pointed too clearly to the dangerous caresses of the Circe, grieved poor Laertes to the heart: he could not listen to the baron without spite and anger, as the latter continued without mercy, —

"Every stranger thinks he is the first whom this delightful manner of proceeding has concerned, but he is grievously mistaken; for we have all, at one time or another, been trotted round this course. Man, youth, or boy, be who he like, each must devote himself to her service for a season, must hang about her, and toil and long to gain her favor."

To the happy man just entering the garden of an enchantress, and welcomed by all the pleasures of an artificial spring, nothing can form a more unpleasant surprise, than if, while his ear is watching and drinking in the music of the nightingales, some transformed predecessor on a sudden grunts at his feet.

After this discovery, Laertes felt heartily ashamed that vanity should have again misled him to think well, even in the smallest degree, of any woman whatsoever. He now entirely forsook the baroness;

kept by the *Stallmeister*, with whom he diligently fenced and hunted; conducting himself at rehearsals and representations as if these were but secondary matters.

The count and his lady would often in the mornings send for some of the company to attend them, and all had continual cause to envy the undeserved good fortune of Philina. The count kept his favorite, the Pedant, frequently for hours together, at his toilet. This genius had been dressed out by degrees: he was now equipped and furnished, even to watch and snuff-box.

Many times, too, particularly after dinner, the whole company were called out before the noble guests, — an honor which the artists regarded as the most flattering in the world; not observing, that on these very occasions the servants and huntsmen were ordered to bring in a multitude of hounds, and to lead strings of horses about the court of the castle.

Wilhelm had been counselled to praise Racine, the prince's favorite, and thereby to attract some portion of his Highness's favor to himself. On one of these afternoons, being summoned with the rest, he found an opportunity to introduce this topic. The prince asked him if he diligently read the great French dramatic writers, to which Wilhelm answered with a very eager "Yes." He did not observe that his Highness, without waiting for the answer, was already on the point of turning round to some one else: he fixed upon him, on the contrary, almost stepping in his way, and proceeded to declare that he valued the French theatre very highly, and read the works of their great masters with delight; particularly he had learned with true joy that his Highness did complete justice to the great talents of Racine. "I can easily conceive," continued he, "how people of high breeding and exalted rank must value a poet who has painted so excellently and so truly the circumstances of their lofty station. Corneille, if I may say so, has delineated great men; Racine, men of eminent rank. In reading his plays, I can always figure to myself the poet as living at a splendid court, with a great king before his eyes, in constant inter-course with the most distinguished persons, and penetrating into the secrets of human nature, as it works concealed behind the gorgeous tapestry of palaces. When I study his 'Britannicus,' his 'Bérénice,' it seems as if I were transported in person to the court, were initiated into the great and the little, in the habitations of these earthly gods: through the fine and delicate organs of my author, I see kings whom a nation adores, courtiers whom thousands envy, in their natural forms, with their failings and their pains. The anecdote of Racine's dying of a broken heart, because Louis Fourteenth would no longer attend to him, and had shown him his dissatisfaction, is to me the key to all his works. It was impossible that a poet of his talents, whose life and death depended on the looks of a king, should not write such works as a king and a prince might applaud."

Jarno had stepped near, and was listening with astonishment. The prince, who had made no answer, and had only shown his approbation by an assenting look, now turned aside; though Wilhelm, who did not know that it was contrary to etiquette to continue a discussion under such circumstances, and exhaust a subject, would gladly have spoken more, and convinced the prince that he had not read his favorite poet without sensibility and profit.

"Have you never," said Jarno, taking him aside, "read one of Shakspeare's plays?"

"No," replied Wilhelm: "since the time when they became more known in Germany, I have myself grown unacquainted with the theatre; and I know not whether I should now rejoice that an old taste, and occupation of my youth, has been by chance renewed. In the mean time, all I have heard of these plays has excited no wish to become acquainted with such extraordinary monsters, which appear to set probability and dignity alike at defiance."

"I would advise you," said the other, "to make a trial, notwithstanding: it can do one no harm to look at what is extraordinary with one's own eyes. I will lend you a volume or two; and you cannot better spend your time, than by casting every thing aside, and retiring to the solitude of your old habitation, to look into the magic-lantern of that unknown world. It is sinful of you to waste your hours in dressing out these apes to look more human, and teaching dogs to dance. One thing only I require, — you must not cavil at the form: the rest I can leave to your own good sense and feeling."

The horses were standing at the door; and Jarno mounted with some other cavaliers, to go and hunt. Wilhelm looked after him with sadness. He would fain have spoken much with this man, who, though in a harsh, unfriendly way, gave him new ideas, — ideas he had need of.

Oftentimes a man, when approaching some development of his powers, capacities, and conceptions, gets into a perplexity, from which a prudent friend might easily deliver him. He resembles a traveller who, at but a short distance from the inn he is to rest at, falls into the water: were any one to catch him then, and pull him to the bank, with one good wetting it were over; whereas, though he struggles out himself, it is often at the side where he tumbled in; and he has to make a wide and dreary circuit before reaching his appointed object.

Wilhelm now began to have an inkling that things went forward in the world differently from what he had supposed. He now viewed close at hand the solemn and imposing life of the great and distinguished, and wondered at the easy dignity which they contrived to give it. An army on its march, a princely hero at the head of it, such a multitude of co-operating warriors, such a multitude of crowding worshippers, exalted his imagination. In this mood he received the promised books; and erelong, as may be easily supposed, the stream of that mighty genius laid hold of him, and led him down to a shoreless ocean, where he soon completely forgot and lost himself.

CHAPTER NINE

THE CONNECTION between the baron and the actors had suffered various changes since the arrival of the latter. At the commencement it had been productive of great satisfaction to both parties. As the baron for the first time in his life now saw one of those plays, with which he had already graced a private theatre, put into the hands of real actors, and in the fair way for a decent exhibition, he showed the benignest humor in the world. He was liberal in gifts: he bought little presents for the actresses from every millinery hawker, and contrived to send over many an odd bottle of champagne to the actors. In return for all this, our company took every sort of trouble with his play; and Wilhelm spared no diligence in learning, with extreme correctness, the sublime speeches of that very eminent hero, whose part had fallen to his share.

But, in spite of all these kind reciprocities, some clouds by degrees arose between the players and their patron. The baron's preference for certain actors became daily more observable: this of necessity chagrined the rest. He exalted his favorites quite exclusively, and thus, of course, introduced disunion and jealousy among the company. Melina, without skill to help himself in dubious junctures, felt his situation very vexing. The persons eulogized accepted of their praise, without being singularly thankful for it; while the neglected gentlemen showed traces of their spleen by a thousand methods, and constantly found means to make it very disagreeable for their once much-honored patron to appear among them. Their spite received no little nourishment from a certain poem, by an unknown author, which made a great sensation in the castle. Previously to this the baron's intercourse with the company had given rise to many little strokes of merriment; several stories had been raised about him; certain little incidents, adorned with suitable additions, and presented in the proper light, had been talked of, and made the subject of much bantering and laughter. At last it began to be said that a certain rivalry of trade was arising between him and some of the actors, who also looked upon themselves as writers. The poem we spoke of was founded upon this report: it ran as follows: —

> I, poor devil, dear Lord Baron,
> Must envy you your crest of arms,
> The coach you ride in, coat you've on,
> Your copses, ponds, and rack-rent farms,
> Your father's polish'd ashlar house,
> And all his hounds and hares and grouse.
>
> Me, poor devil, dear Lord Baron,
> You envy my small shred of wit;
> Because it seems, as things have gone,
> Old Nature had a hand in it;
> She made me light of heart and gay,
> With long-necked purse, not brain of clay.

Look you now, my dear Lord Baron,
What if we both should cease to fret,
You being his Lordship's eldest son,
And I being mother Nature's brat?
Let's live in peace, all envy chase,
And heed not which o' th' two surpasses;
I in the Herald's Books no place,
You having none about Parnassus.

Upon this poem, which various persons were possessed of, in copies scarcely legible, opinions were exceedingly divided. But who the author was, no one could guess; and, as some began to draw a spiteful mirth from it, our friend expressed himself against it very keenly.

"We Germans," he exclaimed, "deserve to have our Muses still continue in the low contempt wherein they have languished so long; since we cannot value men of rank who take a share in our literature, no matter how! Birth, rank, and fortune are no wise incompatible with genius and taste; as foreign nations, reckoning among their best minds a great number of noblemen, can fully testify. Hitherto, indeed, it has been rare in Germany for men of high station to devote themselves to science; hitherto few famous names have become more famous by their love of art and learning; while many, on the other hand, have mounted out of darkness to distinction, and risen like unknown stars on the horizon. Yet such will not always be the case; and I greatly err, if the first classes of the nation are not even now in the way of also employing their advantages to earn the fairest laurels of the Muses, at no distant date. Nothing, therefore, grieves me more than to see the burgher jeering at the noble who can value literature; nay, even men of rank themselves, with inconsiderate caprice, maliciously scaring off their equal from a path where honor and contentment wait on all."

Apparently this latter observation pointed at the count, of whom Wilhelm had heard that he liked the poem very much. In truth, this nobleman, accustomed to rally the baron in his own peculiar way, was extremely glad of such an opportunity to plague his kinsman more effectually. As to who the writer of the squib might be, each formed his own hypothesis; and the count, never willing that another should surpass him in acuteness, fell upon a thought, which, in a short time, he would have sworn to the truth of. The verses could be written, he believed, by no one but his Pedant, who was a very shrewd knave, and in whom, for a long while, he had noticed some touches of poetic genius. By way of proper treat, he therefore caused the Pedant one morning to be sent for, and made him read the poem, in his own manner, in presence of the countess, the baroness, and Jarno, — a service he was paid for by applauses, praises, and a present; and, on the count's inquiring if he had not still some other poems of an earlier time, he cunningly contrived to evade the question. Thus did the Pedant get invested with the reputation of a poet and a wit, and, in the eyes of the baron's friends, of a pasquinader and a bad-hearted man. From that period, play as he might, the count applauded him with greater zeal than ever; so that the poor wight grew at last inflated till he nearly lost his senses, and began to meditate having a chamber in the castle, like Philina.

Had this project been fulfilled at once, a great mishap might have been spared him. As he was returning late one evening from the castle, groping about in the dark, narrow way, he was suddenly laid hold of, and kept on the spot by some persons, while some others rained a shower of blows upon him, and battered him so stoutly, that in a few seconds he was lying almost dead upon the place, and could not without difficulty crawl in to his companions. These, indignant as they seemed to be at such an outrage, felt their secret joy in the adventure: they could hardly keep from laughing, at seeing him so thoroughly curried, and his new brown coat bedusted through and through, and bedaubed with white, as if he had had to do with millers.

The count, who soon got notice of the business, broke into a boundless rage. He treated this act as the most heinous crime, called it an infringement of the *Burgfried*, or peace of the castle, and caused his judge to make the strictest inquisition touching it. The whited coat, it was imagined, would afford a leading proof. Every creature that possibly could have the smallest trade with flour or powder in the castle was submitted to investigation, but in vain.

The baron solemnly protested on his honor, that although this sort of jesting had considerably displeased him, and the conduct of his lordship the count had not been the friendliest, yet he had got over the affair; and with respect to the misfortune which had come upon the poet, or pasquinader, or whatsoever his title might be, he knew absolutely nothing, and had not the most remote concern in it.

The operations of the strangers, and the general commotion of the house, soon effaced all recollection of the matter; and so, without redress, the unlucky favorite had to pay dear for the satisfaction of pluming himself, a short while, in feathers not his own.

Our troop, regularly acting every night, and on the whole very decently treated, now began to make more clamorous demands, the better they were dealt with. Erelong their victuals, drink, attendance, lodging, grew inadequate; and they called upon the baron, their protector, to provide more liberally for them, and at last make good those promises of comfortable entertainment, which he had been giving them so long. Their complaints grew louder, and the efforts of our friend to still them more and more abortive.

Meanwhile, excepting in rehearsals and hours of acting, Wilhelm scarcely ever came abroad. Shut up in one of the remotest chambers, to which Mignon and the harper alone had free access, he lived and moved in the Shakspearian world, feeling or knowing nothing but the movements of his own mind.

We have heard of some enchanter summoning, by magic formulas, a vast multitude of spiritual shapes into his cell. The conjurations are so powerful that the whole space of the apartment is quickly full; and the spirits, crowding on to the verge of the little circle which they must not pass, around this, and above the master's head, keep increasing in number, and ever whirling in perpetual transformation. Every corner is crammed, every crevice is possessed. Embryos expand themselves, and giant-forms contract into the size of nuts. Unhappily the black-artist has forgot the counterword, with which he might command this flood of sprites again to ebb.

So sat Wilhelm in his privacy: with unknown movements, a thousand feelings and capacities awoke in him, of which he formerly had neither notion nor anticipation. Nothing could allure him from this state: he was vexed and restless if any one presumed to come to him, and talk of news or what was passing in the world.

Accordingly, he scarce took notice of the circumstance, when told that a judicial sentence was about being executed in the castle-yard, — the flogging of a boy, who had incurred suspicions of nocturnal housebreaking, and who, as he wore a peruke-maker's coat, had most probably been one of the assaulters of the Pedant. The boy indeed, it seemed, denied most obstinately; so that they could not inflict a formal punishment, but meant to give him a slight memorial as a vagabond, and send him about his business; he having prowled about the neighborhood for several days, lain at night in the mills, and at last clapped a ladder to the garden-wall, and mounted over by it.

Our friend saw nothing very strange in the transaction, and was dismissing it altogether, when Mignon came running in, and assured him that the criminal was Friedrich, who, since the rencounter with the *Stallmeister*, had vanished from the company, and not again been heard of.

Feeling an interest in the boy, Wilhelm hastily arose: he found, in the court-yard of the castle, the preparations almost finished. The count loved solemnity on these occasions. The boy being now led out, our friend stepped forward, and entreated for delay, as he knew the boy, and had various things to say which might, perhaps, throw light on the affair. He had difficulty in succeeding, notwithstanding all his statements; at length, however, he did get permission to speak with the culprit in private. Friedrich averred, that, concerning the assault in which the Pedant had been used so harshly, he knew nothing whatever. He had merely been lurking about, and had come in at night to see Philina, whose room he had discovered, and would certainly have reached, had he not been taken by the way.

For the credit of the company, Wilhelm felt desirous not to have the truth of his adventure published. He hastened to the *Stallmeister*: he begged him to show favor, and, with his intimate knowledge of men and things about the castle, to find some means of quashing the affair, and dismissing the boy.

This whimsical gentleman, by Wilhelm's help, invented a little story, — how the boy had belonged to the troop, had run away from it, but soon wished to get back, and be received again into his place; how he had accordingly been trying in the night to come at certain of his well-wishers, and solicit their assistance. It was testified by others that his former behavior had been good: the ladies put their hands to the work, and Friedrich was let go.

Wilhelm took him in, — a third person in that strange family, which for some time he had looked on as his own. The old man and little Mignon received the returning wanderer kindly; and all the three combined to serve their friend and guardian with attention, and procure him all the pleasure in their power.

CHAPTER TEN

PHILINA now succeeded in insinuating farther every day into the favor of the ladies. Whenever they were by themselves, she was wont to lead the conversation on the men whom they saw about the castle; and our friend was not the last or least important that engaged them.

The cunning girl was well aware that he had made a deep impression on the countess: she therefore talked about him often, telling much that she knew or did not know, only taking care to speak of nothing that might be interpreted against him; eulogizing, on the contrary, his nobleness of mind, his generosity, and, more than all, his modest and respectful conduct to the fair sex. To all inquiries made about him she replied with equal prudence; and the baroness, when she observed the growing inclination of her amiable friend, was likewise very glad at the discovery. Her own intrigues with several men, especially of late with Jarno, had not remained hidden from the countess, whose pure soul could not look upon such levities without disapprobation, and meek, though earnest, censures.

In this way both Philina and the baroness were personally interested in establishing a closer intercourse between the countess and our friend. Philina hoped, moreover, that there would occur some opportunity when she might once more labor for herself, and, if possible, get back the favor of the young man she had lost.

One day his lordship, with his guests, had ridden out to hunt; and their return was not expected till the morrow. On this the baroness devised a frolic, which was altogether in her way, for she loved disguises, and, in order to surprise her friends, would suddenly appear among them as a peasant-girl at one time, at another as a page, at another as a hunter's boy. By which means she almost gave herself the air of a little fairy, that is present everywhere, and exactly in the place where it is least expected. Nothing could exceed this lady's joy, if, without being recognized, she could contrive to wait upon the company for some time as a servant, or mix among them anyhow, and then at last in some sportful way disclose herself.

Towards night she sent for Wilhelm to her chamber, and, happening to have something else to do just then, left Philina to receive and prepare him.

He arrived, and found to his surprise, not the honorable lady, but the giddy girl, in the room. She received him with a certain dignified openness of manner, which she had of late been practising, and so constrained him likewise to be courteous.

At first she rallied him in general on the good fortune which pursued him everywhere, and which, as she could not but see, had led him hither in the present case. Then she delicately set before him the treatment with which of late he had afflicted her; she blamed and up-braided herself; confessed that she had but too well deserved such punishment; described with the greatest candor what she called her *former* situation; adding, that she would despise herself, if she were not capable of altering, and making herself worthy of his friendship.

Wilhelm was struck with this oration. He had too little knowl-edge of the world to understand that persons quite unstable, and incapable of all improvement, frequently accuse themselves in the bitterest manner, confessing and deploring their faults with extreme ingenuousness, though they possess not the smallest power within them to retire from that course, along which the irresistible tendency of their nature is dragging them forward. Accordingly, he could not find in his heart to behave inexorably to the graceful sinner: he entered into con-versation, and learned from her the project of a singular disguisement, wherewith it was intended to surprise the countess.

He found some room for hesitation here, nor did he hide his scruples from Philina: but the baroness, entering at this moment, left him not an instant for reflection; she hurried him away with her, declaring it was just the proper hour.

It was now grown dark. She took him to the count's wardrobe, made him change his own coat with his lordship's silk night-gown, and put the cap with red trimmings on his head. She then led him forward to the cabinet; and bidding him sit down upon the large chair, and take a book, she lit the Argand lamp which stood before him, and showed him what he was to do, and what kind of part he had to play.

They would inform the countess, she said, of her husband's un-expected arrival, and that he was in very bad humor. The countess would come in, walk up and down the room once or twice, then place herself beside the back of his chair, lay her arm upon his shoulder, and speak a few words. He was to play the cross husband as long and as well as possible; and, when obliged to disclose himself, he must behave politely, handsomely, and gallantly.

Wilhelm was left sitting, restlessly enough, in this singular mask. The proposal had come upon him by surprise: the execution of it got the start of the deliberation. The baroness had vanished from the room, before he saw how dangerous the post was which he had engaged to fill. He could not deny that the beauty, the youth, the gracefulness, of the countess had made some impression on him: but his nature was entirely averse to all empty gallantry, and his principles forbade any thought of more serious enterprises; so that his perplexity at this moment was in truth extreme. The fear of displeasing the countess, and that of pleasing her too well, were equally busy in his mind.

Every female charm that had ever acted on him, now showed itself again to his imagination. Mariana rose before him in her white morning-gown, and entreated his remembrance. Philina's loveliness, her beautiful hair, her insinuating blandishments, had again become attractive by her late presence. Yet all this retired as if behind the veil of distance, when he figured to himself the noble, blooming countess, whose arm in a few minutes he would feel upon his neck, whose innocent caresses he was there to answer.

The strange mode in which he was to be delivered out of this perplexity he certainly did not anticipate. We may judge of his astonishment, nay, his terror, when the door opened behind him; and, at the first stolen look in the mirror, he quite clearly discerned the count coming in with a light in his hand. His doubt what he should do, whether he should sit still or rise, should flee, confess, deny, or beg forgiveness, lasted but a few instants. The count, who had remained motionless standing in the door, retired, and shut it softly. At the same moment, the baroness sprang forward by the side-door, extinguished the lamp, tore Wilhelm from his chair, and hurried him with her into the closet. Instantly he threw off the night-gown, and put it in its former place. The baroness took his coat under her arm, and hastened with him through several rooms, passages, and partitions into her chamber, where Wilhelm, so soon as she recovered breath, was informed, that on her going to the countess, and delivering the fictitious intelligence about her husband's arrival, the countess had answered, "I know it already: what can have happened? I saw him riding in, at the postern, even now." On which the baroness, in an excessive panic, had run to the count's chamber to give warning.

"Unhappily you came too late!" said Wilhelm. "The count was in the room before you, and saw me sitting."

"And recognized you?"

"That I know not. He was looking at me in the glass, as I at him; and, before I could well determine whether it was he or a spirit, he drew back, and closed the door behind him."

The anxiety of the baroness increased, when a servant came to call her, signifying that the count was with his lady. She went with no light heart, and found the count silent and thoughtful, indeed, but milder and kinder in his words than usual. She knew not what to think of it. They spoke about the incidents of the chase, and the causes of his quick return. The conversation soon ran out. The count became taciturn; and it struck the baroness particularly, when he asked for Wilhelm, and expressed a wish that he were sent for, to come and read something.

Wilhelm, who had now dressed himself in the baroness's chamber, and in some degree recovered his composure, obeyed the order, not without anxiety. The count gave him a book, out of which he read an adventurous tale, very little at his ease. His voice had a certain inconstancy and quivering in it, which fortunately corresponded with the import of the story. The count more than once gave kindly tokens of approval, and at last dismissed our friend, with praises of his exquisite manner of reading.

CHAPTER ELEVEN

WILHELM had scarcely read one or two of Shakspeare's plays, till their effect on him became so strong that he could go no farther. His whole soul was in commotion. He sought an opportunity to speak with Jarno; to whom, on meeting with him, he expressed his boundless gratitude for such delicious entertainment.

"I clearly enough foresaw," said Jarno, "that you would not remain insensible to the charms of the most extraordinary and most admirable of all writers."

"Yes!" exclaimed our friend: " I cannot recollect that any book, any man, any incident of my life, has produced such important effects on me, as the precious works to which by your kindness I have been directed. They seem as if they were performances of some celestial genius, descending among men, to make them, by the mildest instructions, acquainted with themselves. They are no fictions! You would think, while reading them, you stood before the unclosed awful Books of Fate, while the whirlwind of most impassioned life was howling through the leaves, and tossing them fiercely to and fro. The strength and tenderness, the power and peacefulness, of this man, have so astonished and transported me, that I long vehemently for the time when I shall have it in my power to read farther."

"Bravo!" said Jarno, holding out his hand, and squeezing our friend's. "This is as it should be! And the consequences, which I hope for, will likewise surely follow."

"I wish," said Wilhelm, "I could but disclose to you all that is going on within me even now. All the anticipations I have ever had regarding man and his destiny, which have accompanied me from youth upwards, often unobserved by myself, I find developed and fulfilled in Shakspeare's writings. It seems as if he cleared up every one of our enigmas to us, though we cannot say, Here or there is the word of solution.His men appear like natural men, and yet they are not. These, the most mysterious and complex productions of creation, here act before us as if they were watches, whose dial-plates and cases were of crystal, which pointed out, according to their use, the course of the hours and minutes; while, at the same time, you could discern the combination of wheels and springs that turned them. The few glances I have cast over Shakspeare's world incite me, more than any thing beside, to quicken my footsteps forward into the actual world, to mingle in the flood of destinies that is suspended over it, and at length, if I shall prosper, to draw a few cups from the great ocean of true nature, and to distribute them from off the stage among the thirsting people of my native land."

"I feel delighted with the temper of mind in which I now behold you," answered Jarno, laying his hand upon the shoulder of the excited youth: "renounce not the purpose of embarking in active life. Make haste to employ with alacrity the years that are granted you.

If I can serve you, I will with all my heart. As yet I have not asked you how you came into this troop, for which you certainly were neither born nor bred. So much I hope and see, — you long to be out of it. I know nothing of your parentage, of your domestic circumstances: consider what you shall confide to me. Thus much only I can say: the times of war we live in may produce quick turns of fortune; did you incline devoting your strength and talents to our service, not fearing labor, and, if need were, danger, I might even now have an opportunity to put you in a situation, which you would not afterwards be sorry to have filled for a time." Wilhelm could not sufficiently express his gratitude: he was ready to impart to his friend and patron the whole history of his life.

In the course of this conversation, they had wandered far into the park, and at last came upon the highway that crossed it. Jarno stood silent for a moment, and then said, "Deliberate on my proposal, determine, give me your answer in a few days, and then let me have the narrative you mean to trust me with. I assure you, it has all along to me seemed quite incomprehensible how you ever could have any thing to do with such a class of people. I have often thought with spleen and disgust, how, in order to gain a paltry living, you must fix your heart on a wandering ballad-monger, and a silly mongrel, neither male nor female."

He had not yet concluded, when an officer on horseback came hastily along; a groom following him with a led horse. Jarno shouted a warm salutation to him. The officer sprang from his horse; Jarno and he embraced and talked together; while Wilhelm, confounded at the last expressions of his war-like friend, stood thoughtfully at a side. Jarno turned over some papers which the stranger had delivered to him; while the latter came to Wilhelm, held out his hand, and said with emphasis, "I find you in worthy company: follow the counsel of your friend, and, by doing so, accomplish likewise the desire of an unknown man, who takes a genuine interest in you." So saying, he embraced Wilhelm, and pressed him cordially to his breast. At the same instant Jarno advanced, and said to the stranger, "It is best that I ride on with you: by this means you may get the necessary orders, and set out again before night." Both then leaped into their saddles, and left our astonished friend to his own reflections.

Jarno's last words were still ringing in his ears. It galled him to see the two human beings that had most innocently won his affections so grievously disparaged by a man whom he honored so much. The strange embracing of the officer, whom he knew not, made but a slight impression on him; it occupied his curiosity and his imagination for a moment: but Jarno's speech had cut him to the heart; he was deeply hurt by it: and now, in his way homewards, he broke out into reproaches against himself, that he should for a single instant have mistaken or forgotten the unfeeling coldness of Jarno, which looked out from his very eyes, and spoke in all his gestures. "No!" exclaimed he, "thou conceivest, dead-hearted worldling, that thou canst be a friend! All that thou hast power to offer me is not worth the sentiment which binds me to these forlorn beings. How fortunate that I have discovered in time what I had to expect from thee!"

Mignon came to meet him as he entered: he clasped her in his arms, exclaiming, "Nothing, nothing, shall part us, thou good little creature! The seeming prudence of the world shall never cause me to forsake thee, or forget what I owe thee!"

The child, whose warm caresses he had been accustomed to avoid, rejoiced with all her heart at this unlooked-for show of tenderness, and clung so fast to him that he had some difficulty to get loose from her.

From this period he kept a stricter eye on Jarno's conduct: many parts of it he did not think quite praiseworthy; nay, several things came out which totally displeased him. He had strong suspicions, for example, that the verses on the baron, which the poor Pedant had so dearly paid for, were composed by Jarno. And as the latter, in Wilhelm's presence, had made sport of the adventure, our friend thought here was certainly a symptom of a most corrupted heart; for what could be more depraved than to treat a guiltless person, whose griefs one's self had occasioned, with jeering and mockery, instead of trying to satisfy or to indemnify him? In this matter Wilhelm would himself willingly have brought about reparation; and erelong a very curious accident led him to obtain some traces of the persons concerned in that nocturnal outrage.

Hitherto his friends had contrived to keep him unacquainted with the fact, that some of the young officers were in the habit of passing whole nights in merriment and jollity, with certain actors and actresses, in the lower hall of the old castle. One morning, having risen early, according to his custom, he happened to visit this chamber, and found the gallant gentlemen just in the act of performing rather a singular operation. They had mixed a bowl of water with a quantity of chalk, and were plastering this gruel with a brush upon their waistcoats and pantaloons, without stripping; thus very expeditiously restoring the spotlessness of their apparel. On witnessing this piece of ingenuity, our friend was at once struck with the recollection of the poor Pedant's whited and bedusted coat: his suspicions gathered strength when he learned that some relations of the baron were among the party.

To throw some light on his doubts, he engaged the youths to breakfast with him. They were very lively, and told a multitude of pleasant stories. One of them especially, who for a time had been on the recruiting-service, was loud in praising the craft and activity of his captain; who, it appeared, understood the art of alluring men of all kinds towards him, and overreaching every one by the deception proper for him. He circumstantially described how several young people of good families and careful education had been cozened, by playing off to them a thousand promises of honor and preferment; and he heartily laughed at the simpletons, who felt so gratified, when first enlisted, at the thought of being esteemed and introduced to notice by so reputable, prudent, bold, and munificent an officer.

Wilhelm blessed his better genius for having drawn him back in time from the abyss to whose brink he had approached so near. Jarno he now looked upon as nothing better than a crimp: the embrace of the stranger officer was easily explained. He viewed the feelings and opinions of these men with contempt and disgust; from that moment he carefully avoided coming into contact with any one that wore a uniform; and, when he heard that the army was about to move its quarters, the news would have been extremely welcome to him, if he had not feared, that, immediately on its departure, he himself must be banished from the neighborhood of his lovely friend, perhaps forever.

MEANWHILE the baroness had spent several days disquieted by anxious fears and unsatisfied curiosity. Since the late adventure, the count's demeanor had been altogether an enigma to her. His manner was changed: none of his customary jokes were to be heard. His demands on the company and the servants had very much abated. Little pedantry or imperiousness was now to be discerned in him; he was silent and thoughtful, yet withal he seemed composed and placid; in short, he was quite another man. In choosing the books, which now and then he caused to be read to him, those of a serious, often a religious, cast, were pitched upon; and the baroness lived in perpetual fright lest, beneath this apparent serenity, a secret rancor might be lurking, — a silent purpose to revenge the offence he had so accidentally discovered. She determined, therefore, to make Jarno her confidant; and this the more freely, as that gentleman and she already stood in a relation to each other where it is not usual to be very cautious in keeping secrets. For some time Jarno had been her dearest friend, yet they had been dexterous enough to conceal their attachment and joys from the noisy world in which they moved. To the countess alone this new romance had not remained unknown; and very possibly the baroness might wish to get her fair friend occupied with some similar engagement, and thus to escape the silent reproaches she had often to endure from that noble-minded woman.

Scarcely had the baroness related the occurrence to her lover, when he cried out laughing, "To a certainty the old fool believes that he has seen his ghost! He dreads that the vision may betoken some misfortune, perhaps death, to him; and so he is become quite tame, as all half-men do, in thinking of that consummation which no one has escaped or will escape. Softly a little! As I hope he will live long enough, we may now train him at least, so that he shall not again give disturbance to his wife and household."

They accordingly, as soon as any opportunity occurred, began talking, in the presence of the count, about warnings, visions, apparitions, and the like. Jarno played the sceptic, the baroness likewise;

and they carried it so far, that his lordship at last took Jarno aside, reproved him for his free-thinking, and produced his own experience to prove the possibility, nay, actual occurrence, of such preternatural events. Jarno affected to be struck, to be in doubt, and finally to be convinced; but, in private with his friend, he made himself so much the merrier at the credulous weakling, who had thus been cured of his evil habits by a bugbear, but who, they admitted, still deserved some praise for expecting dire calamity, or death itself, with such composure.

"The natural result which the present apparition might have had, would possibly have ruffled him!" exclaimed the baroness, with her wonted vivacity; to which, when anxiety was taken from her heart, she had instantly returned. Jarno was richly rewarded; and the two contrived fresh projects for frightening the count still further, and still further exciting and confirming the affection of the countess for Wilhelm.

With this intention, the whole story was related to the countess. She, indeed, expressed her displeasure at such conduct; but from that time she became more thoughtful, and in peaceful moments seemed to be considering, pursuing, and painting out that scene which had been prepared for her.

The preparations now going forward on every side left no room for doubt that the armies were soon to move in advance, and the prince at the same time to change his headquarters. It was even said that the count intended leaving his castle, and returning to the city. Our players could therefore, without difficulty, calculate the aspect of their stars; yet none of them, except Melina, took any measures in consequence: the rest strove only to catch as much enjoyment as they could from the moment that was passing over them.

Wilhelm, in the mean time, was engaged with a peculiar task. The countess had required from him a copy of his writings, and he looked on this request as the noblest recompense for his labors.

A young author, who has not yet seen himself in print, will, in such a case, apply no ordinary care to provide a clear and beautiful transcript of his works. It is like the golden age of authorship: he feels transported into those centuries when the press had not inundated the world with so many useless writings, when none but excellent performances were copied, and kept by the noblest men; and he easily admits the illusion, that his own accurately ruled and measured manuscript may itself prove an excellent performance, worthy to be kept and valued by some future critic.

The prince being shortly to depart, a great entertainment had been appointed in honor of him. Many ladies of the neighborhood were invited, and the countess had dressed betimes. On this occasion she had taken a costlier suit than usual. Her head-dress, and the decorations of her hair, were more exquisite and studied: she wore all her jewels. The baroness, too, had done her utmost to appear with becoming taste and splendor.

Philina, observing that both ladies, in expectation of their guests, felt the time rather tedious, proposed to send for Wilhelm, who was wishing to present his manuscript, now completed, and to read them some other little pieces. He came, and on his entrance was astonished at the form and the graces of the countess, which her decorations had but made more visible and striking. Being ordered by the ladies, he began to read; but with so much absence of mind, and so badly, that, had not his audience been excessively indulgent, they would very soon have dismissed him.

Every time he looked at the countess, it seemed to him as if a spark of electric fire were glancing before his eyes. In the end he knew not where to find the breath he wanted for his reading. The countess had always pleased him, but now it appeared as if he never had beheld a being so perfect and so lovely. A thousand thoughts flitted up and down his soul: what follows might be nearly their substance.

"How foolish is it in so many poets, and men of sentiment as they are called, to make war on pomp and decoration; requiring that women of all ranks should wear no dress but what is simple, and conformable to nature! They rail at decoration, without once considering, that, when we see a plain or positively ugly person clothed in a costly and gorgeous fashion, it is not the poor decoration that displeases us. I would assemble all the judges in the world, and ask them here if they wished to see one of these folds, of these ribbons and laces, these braids, ringlets, and glancing stones, removed? Would they not dread disturbing the delightful impression that so naturally and spontaneously meets us here? Yes, naturally I will say! As Minerva sprang in complete armor from the head of Jove; so does this goddess seem to have stepped forth with a light foot, in all her ornaments, from the bosom of some flower."

While reading, he turned his eyes upon her frequently, as if he wished to stamp this image on his soul forever: he more than once read wrong, yet without falling into confusion of mind; though, at other times, he used to feel the mistaking of a word or a letter as a painful deformity, which spoiled a whole recitation.

A false alarm of the arrival of the guests put an end to the reading; the baroness went out; and the countess, while about to shut her writing-desk, which was standing open, took up her casket, and put some other rings upon her finger. "We are soon to part," said she, keeping her eyes upon the casket: "accept a memorial of a true friend, who wishes nothing more earnestly than that you may always prosper." She then took out a ring, which, underneath a crystal, bore a little plait of woven hair beautifully set with diamonds. She held it out to Wilhelm, who, on taking it, knew neither what to say nor do, but stood as if rooted to the ground. The countess shut her desk, and sat down upon the sofa.

"And I must go empty?" said Philina, kneeling down at the countess's right hand. "Do but look at the man: he carries such a store of words in his mouth, when no one wants to hear them; and now he cannot stammer out the poorest syllable of thanks. Quick, sir! Express your services by way of pantomime at least; and if to-day you can invent nothing, then, for Heaven's sake, be my imitator."

Philina seized the right hand of the countess, and kissed it warmly. Wilhelm sank upon his knee, laid hold of the left, and pressed it to his lips. The countess seemed embarrassed, yet without displeasure.

"Ah!" cried Philina, "so much splendor of attire, I may have seen before, but never one so fit to wear it. What bracelets, but also what a hand! What a neckdress, but also what a bosom."

"Peace, little cozener!" said the countess.

"Is this his lordship, then?" said Philina, pointing to a rich medallion, which the countess wore on her left side, by a particular chain.

"He is painted in his bridegroom-dress," replied the countess.

"Was he, then, so young?" inquired Philina: "I know it is but a year or two since you were married."

"His youth must be placed to the artist's account," replied the lady.

"He is a handsome man," observed Philina. "But was there never," she continued, placing her hand on the countess's heart, "never any other image that found its way in secret hither?"

"Thou art very bold, Philina," cried she: "I have spoiled thee. Let me never hear the like again."

"If you are angry, then am I unhappy," said Philina, springing up, and hastening from the room.

Wilhelm still held that lovely hand in both of his. His eyes were fixed on the bracelet-clasp: he noticed, with extreme surprise, that his initials were traced on it, in lines of brilliants.

"Have I, then," he modestly inquired, "your own hair in this precious ring?"

Wilhelm embraces the countess

"Yes," replied she, in a faint voice: then, suddenly collecting herself, she said, and pressed his hand, "Arise, and fare you well!"

"Here is my name," cried he, "by the most curious chance!" He pointed to the bracelet-clasp.

"How?" cried the countess: "it is the cipher of a female friend!"

"They are the initials of my name. Forget me not. Your image is engraven on my heart, and will never be effaced. Farewell! I must be gone."

He kissed her hand, and meant to rise; but, as in dreams, some strange thing fades and changes into something stranger, and the succeeding wonder takes us by surprise; so, without knowing how it happened, he found the countess in his arms: her lips were resting upon his, and their warm mutual kisses were yielding them that blessedness which mortals sip from the topmost sparkling foam on the freshly poured cup of love.

Her head lay on his shoulder: the disordered ringlets and ruffles were forgotten. She had thrown her arm round him: he clasped her with vivacity, and pressed her again and again to his breast. Oh that such a moment could but last forever! And woe to envious Fate that shortened even this brief moment to our friends!

How terrified was Wilhelm, how astounded did he start from his happy dream, when the countess, with a shriek, on a sudden tore herself away, and hastily pressed her hand against her heart.

He stood confounded before her: she held the other hand upon her eyes, and, after a moment's pause, exclaimed, "Away! leave me! delay not!"

He continued standing.

"Leave me!" she cried; and, taking off her hand from her eyes, she looked at him with an indescribable expression of countenance, and added, in the most tender and affecting voice, "Flee, if you love me."

Wilhelm was out of the chamber, and again in his room, before he knew what he was doing.

Unhappy creatures! What singular warning of chance or of destiny tore them asunder?

Book Four

L AERTES was standing at the window in a thoughtful mood, resting on his arm, and looking out into the fields. Philina came gliding towards him, across the large hall: she leaned upon him, and began to mock him for his serious looks.

"Do not laugh," replied he: "it is frightful to think how time goes on, how all things change and have an end. See here! A little while ago there was a stately camp: how pleasantly the tents looked! what restless life and motion was within them! how carefully they watched the whole enclosure! And, behold, it is all vanished in a day! For a short while, that trampled straw, those holes which the cooks have dug, will show a trace of what was here; and soon the whole will be ploughed and reaped as formerly, and the presence of so many thousand gallant fellows in this quarter will but glimmer in the memories of one or two old men."

Philina began to sing, and dragged forth her friend to dance with her in the hall. "Since Time is not a person we can overtake when he is past," cried she, "let us honor him with mirth and cheerfulness of heart while he is passing."

They had scarcely made a step or two, when Frau Melina came walking through the hall. Philina was wicked enough to invite her to join them in the dance, and thus to bring her in mind of the shape to which her pregnancy had reduced her.

"That I might never more see a woman *in an interesting situation!*" said Philina, when her back was turned.

"Yet she feels an *interest* in it," said Laertes.

"But she manages so shockingly. Didst thou notice that wabbling fold of her shortened petticoat, which always travels out before her

when she moves? She has not the smallest knack or skill to trim herself a little, and conceal her state."

"Let her be," said Laertes. "Time will soon come to her aid."

"It were prettier, however," cried Philina, "if we could shake
children from the trees."

The baron entered, and spoke some kind words to them, adding
a few presents, in the name of the count and the countess, who had
left the place very early in the morning. He then went to Wilhelm,
who was busy in the side-chamber with Mignon. She had been extremely affectionate and taking; had asked minutely about Wilhelm's
parents, brothers, sisters, and relations; and so brought to his mind
the duty he owed his people, to send them some tidings of himself.

With the farewell compliments of the family, the baron delivered
him an assurance from the count, that his lordship had been exceedingly obliged by his acting, his poetical labors, and theatrical exertions.
For proof of this statement, the baron then drew forth a purse, through
whose beautiful texture the bright glance of new gold coin was sparkling out. Wilhelm drew back, refusing to accept of it.

"Look upon this gift," said the baron, "as a compensation for
your time, as an acknowledgment of your trouble, not as the reward
of your talents. If genius procures us a good name and good will from
men, it is fair likewise, that, by our diligence and efforts, we should
earn the means to satisfy our wants; since, after all, we are not wholly
spirit. Had we been in town, where every thing is to be got, we should
have changed this little sum into a watch, a ring, or something of
that sort; but, as it is, I must place the magic rod in your own hands;
procure a trinket with it, such as may please you best and be of
greatest use, and keep it for our sakes. At the same time, you must not
forget to hold the purse in honor. It was knit by the fingers of our
ladies: they meant that the cover should give to its contents the most
pleasing form."

"Forgive my embarrassment," said Wilhelm, "and my doubts
about accepting this present. It, as it were, annihilates the little I have
done, and hinders the free play of happy recollection. Money is a
fine thing, when any matter is to be completely settled and abolished:
I feel unwilling to be so entirely abolished from the recollection of
your house."

"That is not the case," replied the baron; "but, feeling so tenderly yourself, you could not wish that the count should be obliged to consider himself wholly your debtor, especially when I assure you that his lordship's highest ambition has always consisted in being punctual and just. He is not uninformed of the labor you have undergone, or of the zeal with which you have devoted all your time to execute his views; nay, he is aware, that, to quicken certain operations, you have even expended money of your own. With what face shall I appear before him, then, if I cannot say that his acknowledgment has given you satisfaction?"

"If I thought only of myself," said Wilhelm, "if I might follow merely the dictates of my own feelings, I should certainly, in spite of all these reasons, steadfastly refuse this gift, generous and honorable as it is; but I will not deny, that, at the very moment when it brings me into one perplexity, it frees me from another, into which I have lately fallen with regard to my relations, and which has in secret caused me much uneasiness. My management, not only of the time, but also of the money, for which I have to give account, has not been the best; and now, by the kindness of his lordship, I shall be enabled, with confidence, to give my people news of the good fortune to which this curious by-path has led me. I therefore sacrifice those feelings of delicacy, which, like a tender conscience, admonish us on such occasions, to a higher duty; and, that I may appear courageously before my father, I must consent to stand ashamed before you."

"It is singular," replied the baron, "to see what a world of hesitation people feel about accepting money from their friends and patrons, though ready to receive any other gift with joy and thankfulness. Human nature manifests some other such peculiarities, by which many scruples of a similar kind are produced and carefully cherished."

"Is it not the same with all points of honor?" said our friend.

"It is so," replied the baron, "and with several other prejudices. We must not root them out, lest in doing so we tear up noble plants along with them. Yet I am always glad when I meet with men that feel superior to such objections, when the case requires it; and I recall with pleasure the story of that ingenious poet who had written several plays for the court-theatre, which met with the monarch's warmest approbation. 'I must give him a distinguished recompense,' said the generous prince: 'ask him whether he would choose to have some jewel given him, or if he would disdain to accept a sum of money.' In his humorous way, the poet answered the inquiring courtier, 'I am thankful, with all my heart, for these gracious purposes; and, as the emperor is daily taking money from us, I see not wherefore I should feel ashamed of taking some from him.' "

Scarcely had the baron left the room, when Wilhelm eagerly began to count the cash, which had come to him so unexpectedly, and, as he thought, so undeservedly. It seemed as if the worth and dignity of gold, not usually felt till later years, had now, by anticipation, twinkled in his eyes for the first time, as the fine, glancing coins rolled out from the beautiful purse. He reckoned up, and found, that, particularly as Melina had engaged immediately to pay the loan, he had now as much or more on the right side of his account as on that day when Philina first asked him for the nosegay. With a little secret satisfaction, he looked upon his talents; with a little pride, upon the fortune which had led and attended him. He now seized the pen, with an assured mind, to write a letter which might free his family from their anxieties, and set his late proceedings in the most favorable light. He abstained from any special narrative, and only by significant and mysterious hints left them room for guessing at what had befallen him. The good condition of his cash-book, the advantage he had earned by his talents, the favor of the great and of the fair, acquaintance with a wider circle, the improvement of his bodily and mental gifts, his hopes from the future, altogether formed such a fair cloud-picture, that Fata Morgana itself could scarcely have thrown together a stranger or a better.

In this happy exaltation, the letter being folded up, he went on to maintain a conversation with himself, recapitulating what he had been writing, and pointing out for himself an active and glorious future. The example of so many gallant warriors had fired him; the poetry of Shakspeare had opened a new world to him; from the lips of the beautiful countess he had inhaled an inexpressible inspiration. All this could not and would not be without effect.

The *Stallmeister* came to inquire whether they were ready with their packing. Alas! with the single exception of Melina, no one of them had thought of it. Now, however, they were speedily to be in motion. The count had engaged to have the whole party conveyed forward a few days' journey on their way: the horses were now in readiness, and could not long be wanted. Wilhelm asked for his trunk: Frau Melina had taken it to put her own things in. He asked for money: Herr Melina had stowed it all far down at the bottom of his box. Philina said she had still some room in hers: she took Wilhelm's clothes, and bade Mignon bring the rest. Wilhelm, not without reluctance, was obliged to let it be so.

While they were loading, and getting all things ready, Melina said, "I am sorry we should travel like mountebanks and rope-dancers. I could wish that Mignon would put on girl's clothes, and that the harper would let his beard be shorn." Mignon clung firmly to Wilhelm, and cried, with great vivacity, "I am a boy — I will be no girl!" The old man held his peace; and Philina, on this suggestion, made some merry observations on the singularity of their protector, the count. "If the harper should cut off his beard," said she, " let him sew it carefully upon a ribbon, and keep it by him, that he may put it on again whenever his lordship the count falls in with him in any quarter of the world. It was this beard alone that procured him the favor of his lordship."

On being pressed to give an explanation of this singular speech, Philina said to them, "The count thinks it contributes very much to the completeness of theatrical illusion if the actor continues to play his part, and to sustain his character, even in common life. It was for this reason that he showed such favor to the Pedant: and he judged it, in like manner, very fitting that the harper not only wore his false beard at nights on the stage, but also constantly by day; and he used to be delighted at the natural appearance of the mask."

While the rest were laughing at this error, and the other strange opinions of the count, the harper led our friend aside, took leave of him, and begged, with tears, that he would even now let him go. Wilhelm spoke to him, declaring that he would protect him against all the world; that no one should touch a hair of his head, much less send him off against his will.

The old man seemed affected deeply: an unwonted fire was glowing in his eyes. "It is not that," cried he, "which drives me away. I have long been reproaching myself in secret for staying with you. I ought to linger nowhere; for misfortune flies to overtake me, and injures all that are connected with me. Dread every thing, unless you dismiss me; but ask me no questions. I belong not to myself. I cannot stay."

"To whom dost thou belong? Who can exert such a power on thee?"

"Leave me my horrid secret, and let me go! The vengeance which pursues me is not of the earthly judge. I belong to an inexorable destiny. I cannot stay, and I dare not."

"In the situation I see thee in, I shall certainly not let thee go."

"It were high treason against you, my benefactor, if I should delay. I am secure while with you, but you are in peril. You know not whom you keep beside you. I am guilty, but more wretched than guilty. My presence scares happiness away, and good deeds grow powerless when I become concerned in them. Fugitive, unresting I should be, that my evil genius might not seize me, which pursues but at a distance, and only appears when I have found a place, and am laying down my head to seek repose. More grateful I cannot show myself than by forsaking you."

"Strange man! Thou canst neither take away the confidence I place in thee, nor the hope I feel to see thee happy. I wish not to penetrate the secrets of thy superstition; but if thou livest in belief of wonderful forebodings, and entanglements of fate, then, to cheer and hearten thee, I say, unite thyself to my good fortune, and let us see which genius is the stronger, thy dark or my bright one."

Wilhelm seized this opportunity of suggesting to him many other comfortable things; for of late our friend had begun to imagine that this singular attendant of his must be a man, who, by chance or destiny, had been led into some weighty crime, the remembrance of which he was ever bearing on his conscience.

A few days ago Wilhelm, listening to his singing, had observed attentively the following lines: —

> "For him the light of ruddy morn
>   But paints the horizon red with flame;
> And voices, from the depths of nature borne,
>   Woe! woe! upon his guilty head proclaim."

But, let the old man urge what arguments he pleased, our friend had constantly a stronger argument at hand. He turned every thing on its fairest side; spoke so bravely, heartily, and cheerily, that even the old man seemed again to gather spirits, and to throw aside his whims.

CHAPTER TWO

MELINA was in hopes to get established, with his company, in a small but thriving town at some distance. They had already reached the place where the count's horses were to turn, and now they looked about for other carriages and cattle to transport them onward. Melina had engaged to provide them a conveyance: he showed himself but niggardly, according to his custom. Wilhelm, on the contrary, had the shining ducats of the countess in his pocket, and thought he had the fullest right to spend them merrily; forgetting very soon how ostentatiously he had produced them in the stately balance transmitted to his father.

His friend Shakspeare, whom with the greatest joy he acknowledged as his godfather, and rejoiced the more that his name was Wilhelm, had introduced him to a prince, who frolicked for a time among mean, nay, vicious companions, and who, notwithstanding his nobleness of nature, found pleasure in the rudeness, indecency, and coarse intemperance of these altogether sensual knaves. This ideal likeness, which he figured as the type and the excuse of his own actual condition, was most welcome to our friend; and the process of self-deception, to which already he displayed an almost invincible tendency, was thereby very much facilitated.

He now began to think about his dress. It struck him that a waistcoat, over which, in case of need, one could throw a little short mantle, was a very fit thing for a traveller. Long knit pantaloons, and a pair of lacing-boots, seemed the true garb of a pedestrian. He next procured a fine silk sash, which he tied about him, under the pretence at first of securing warmth for his person. On the other hand, he freed his neck from the tyranny of stocks, and got a few stripes of muslin sewed upon his shirt; making the pieces of considerable breadth, so that they presented the complete appearance of an ancient ruff. The beautiful silk neckerchief, the memorial of Mariana, which had once been saved from burning, now lay slackly tied beneath this muslin collar. A round hat, with a party-colored band, and a large feather, perfected the mask.

The women all asserted that this garb became him very well. Philina in particular appeared enchanted with it. She solicited his hair for herself, — beautiful locks, which, the closer to approach the natural ideal, he had unmercifully clipped. By so doing she recommended herself not amiss to his favor; and our friend, who by his open-handedness had acquired the right of treating his companions somewhat in Prince Harry's manner, erelong fell into the humor of himself contriving a few wild tricks, and presiding in the execution of them. The people fenced, they danced, they devised all kinds of sports, and, in their gayety of heart, partook of what tolerable wine they could fall in with in copious proportions; while, amid the disorder of this tumultuous life, Philina lay in wait for the coy hero, — over whom let his better genius keep watch!

One chief diversion, which yielded the company a frequent and very pleasing entertainment, consisted in producing an extempore play, in which their late benefactors and patrons were mimicked, and turned into ridicule. Some of our actors had seized very neatly whatever was peculiar in the outward manner of several distinguished people in the count's establishment; their imitation of these was received by the rest of the party with the greatest approbation: and when Philina produced, from the secret archives of her experience, certain peculiar declarations of love that had been made to her, the audience were like to die with laughing and malicious joy.

Wilhelm censured their ingratitude; but they told him in reply that these gentry well deserved what they were getting, their general conduct toward such deserving people, as our friends believed themselves, not having been by any means the best imaginable. The little consideration, the neglect they had experienced, were now described with many aggravations. The jesting, bantering, and mimicry proceeded as before: our party were growing bitterer and more unjust every minute.

"I wish," observed Wilhelm, "there were no envy or selfishness lurking under what you say, but that you would regard those persons and their station in the proper point of view. It is a peculiar thing to be placed, by one's very birth, in an elevated situation in society. The man for whom inherited wealth has secured a perfect freedom of existence; who finds himself from his youth upwards abundantly encompassed with all the secondary essentials, so to speak, of human life, — will generally become accustomed to consider these qualifications as the first and greatest of all; while the worth of that mode of human life, which nature from her own stores equips and furnishes, will strike him much more faintly. The behavior of noblemen to their inferiors, and likewise to each other, is regulated by external preferences. They give each credit for his title, his rank, his clothes, and equipage; but his individual merits come not into play."

This speech was honored with the company's unbounded applause. They declared it to be shameful,that men of merit should constantly be pushed into the background; and that, in the great world, there should not be a trace of natural and hearty intercourse. On this latter point particularly they overshot all bounds.

"Blame them not for it," said Wilhelm, "rather pity them! They have seldom an exalted feeling of that happiness which we admit to be the highest that can flow from the inward abundance of nature. Only to us poor creatures is it granted to enjoy the happiness of friendship in its richest fulness. Those dear to us we cannot elevate by our countenance, or advance by our favor, or make happy by our presents. We have nothing but ourselves. This whole self we must give away; and, if it is to be of any value, we must make our friend secure of it forever. What an enjoyment, what a happiness, for giver and receiver! With what blessedness does truth of affection invest our situation! It gives to the transitory life of man a heavenly certainty: it forms the crown and capital of all that we possess."

While he spoke thus, Mignon had come near him: she threw her little arms round him, and stood with her cheek resting on his breast. He laid his hand on the child's head, and proceeded, "It is easy for a great man to win our minds to him, easy to make our hearts his own. A mild and pleasant manner, a manner only not inhuman, will of itself do wonders, — and how many means does he possess of holding fast the affections he has once conquered? To us, all this occurs less frequently; to us it is all more difficult; and we naturally, therefore, put a greater value on whatever, in the way of mutual kindness, we acquire and accomplish. What touching examples of faithful servants giving themselves up to danger and death for their masters? How finely has Shakspeare painted out such things to us! Fidelity, in this case, is the effort of a noble soul, struggling to become equal with one exalted above it. By steadfast attachment and love, the servant is made equal to his lord, who, but for this, is justified in looking on him as a hired slave. Yes, these virtues belong to the lower class of men alone: that class cannot do without them, and with them it has a beauty of its own. Whoever is enabled to requite all favors easily will likewise easily be tempted to raise himself above the habit of acknowledgment. Nay, in this sense, I am of opinion it might almost be maintained, that a great man may possess friends, but cannot be one."

Mignon clung more and more closely to him.

"It may be so," replied one of the party: "we do not need their friendship, and do not ask it. But it were well if they understood a little more about the arts, which they affect to patronize. When we played in the best style, there was none to mind us: it was all sheer partiality. Any one they chose to favor, pleased; and they did not choose to favor those that merited to please. It was intolerable to observe how often silliness and mere stupidity attracted notice and applause."

"When I abate from this," said Wilhelm, "what seemed to spring from irony and malice, I think we may nearly say, that one fares in art as he does in love. And, after all, how shall a fashionable man of the world, with his dissipated habits, attain that intimate presence with a special object, which an artist must long continue in, if he would produce any thing approaching to perfection, — a state of feeling without which it is impossible for any one to take such an interest, as the artist hopes and wishes, in his work?

"Believe me, my friends, it is with talents as with virtue: one must love them for their own sake, or entirely renounce them. And neither of them is acknowledged and rewarded, except when their possessor can practise them unseen, like a dangerous secret."

"Meanwhile, until some proper judge discovers us, we may all die of hunger," cried a fellow in the corner.

"Not quite inevitably," answered Wilhelm. "I have observed, that, so long as one stirs and lives, one always finds food and raiment, though they be not of the richest sort. And why should we repine? Were we not, altogether unexpectedly, and when our prospects were the very worst, taken kindly by the hand, and substantially entertained? And now, when we are in want of nothing, does it once occur to us to attempt any thing for our improvement, or to strive, though never so faintly, towards advancement in our art? We are busied about indifferent matters; and, like schoolboys, we are casting all aside that might bring our lesson to our thoughts."

"In sad truth," said Philina, "it is even so! Let us choose a play: we will go through it on the spot. Each of us must do his best, as if he stood before the largest audience."

They did not long deliberate: a play was fixed on. It was one of those which at that time were meeting great applause in Germany, and have now passed away. Some of the party whistled a symphony; each speedily bethought him of his part; they commenced, and acted the entire play with the greatest attention, and really well beyond expectation. Mutual applauses circulated: our friends had seldom been so pleasantly diverted.

On finishing, they all felt exceedingly contented, partly on account of their time being spent so well, partly because each of them experienced some degree of satisfaction with his own performance. Wilhelm expressed himself copiously in their praise: the conversation grew cheerful and merry.

"You would see," cried our friend, "what advances we should make, if we continued this sort of training, and ceased to confine our attention to mere learning by heart, rehearsing and playing mechanically, as if it were a barren duty, or some handicraft employment. How different a character do our musical professors merit! What interest they take in their art! how correct are they in the practisings they undertake in common! What pains they are at in tuning their instruments; how exactly they observe time; how delicately they express the strength and the weakness of their tones! No one there thinks of gaining credit to himself by a loud accompaniment of the solo of another. Each tries to play in the spirit of the composer, each to express well whatever is committed to him, be it much or little.

"Should not we, too, go as strictly and as ingeniously to work, seeing we practise an art far more delicate than that of music, — seeing we are called on to express the commonest and the strangest emotions of human nature, with elegance, and so as to delight? Can any thing be more shocking than to slur over our rehearsal, and in our acting to depend on good luck, or the capricious choice of the moment? We ought to place our highest happiness and satisfaction in mutually desiring to gain each other's approbation: we should even value the applauses of the public only in so far as we have previously sanctioned them among ourselves. Why is the master of the band more secure about his music than the manager about his play? Because, in the orchestra, each individual would feel ashamed of his mistakes, which offend the outward ear; but how seldom have I found an actor disposed to acknowledge or feel ashamed of mistakes, pardonable or the contrary, by which the inward ear is so outrageously offended! I could wish, for my part, that our theatre were as narrow as the wire of a rope-dancer, that so no inept fellow might dare to venture on it, instead of being, as it is, a place where every one discovers in himself capacity enough to flourish and parade."

The company gave this apostrophe a kind reception; each being convinced that the censure conveyed in it could not apply to him, after acting a little while ago so excellently with the rest. On the other hand, it was agreed, that during this journey, and for the future if they remained together, they would regularly proceed with their training in the manner just adopted. Only it was thought, that, as this was a thing of good humor and free will, no formal manager must be allowed to have a hand in it. Taking it for an established fact, that, among good men, the republican form of government is the best, they declared that the post of manager should go round among them: he must be chosen by universal suffrage, and every time have a sort of little senate joined in authority along with him. So delighted did they feel with this idea, that they longed to put it instantly in practice.

"I have no objection," said Melina, "if you incline making such an experiment while we are travelling: I shall willingly suspend my own directorship until we reach some settled place." He was in hopes of saving cash by this arrangement, and of casting many small expenses on the shoulders of the little senate or of the interim manager. This fixed, they went very earnestly to counsel how the form of the new commonwealth might best be adjusted.

"'Tis an itinerating kingdom," said Laertes: "we shall at least have no quarrels about frontiers."

They directly proceeded to the business, and elected Wilhelm as their first manager. The senate also was appointed, the women having seat and vote in it: laws were propounded, were rejected, were agreed to. In such playing, the time passed on unnoticed; and, as our friends had spent it pleasantly, they also conceived that they had really been effecting something useful, and, by their new constitution, had been opening a new prospect for the stage of their native country.

CHAPTER THREE

SEEING the company so favorably disposed, Wilhelm now hoped he might further have it in his power to converse with them on the poetic merit of the plays which might come before them. "It is not enough," said he next day, when they were all again assembled, "for the actor merely to glance over a dramatic work, to judge of it by his first impression, and thus, without investigation, to declare his satisfaction or dissatisfaction with it. Such things may be allowed in a spectator, whose purpose it is rather to be entertained and moved than formally to criticise. But the actor, on the other hand, should be prepared to give a reason for his praise or censure; and how shall he do this, if he have not taught himself to penetrate the sense, the views, and feelings of his author? A common error is, to form a judgment of a drama from a single part in it, and to look upon this part itself in an isolated point of view, not in its connection with the whole. I have noticed this within a few days, so clearly in my own conduct, that I will give you the account as an example, if you please to hear me patiently.

"You all know Shakspeare's incomparable 'Hamlet': our public reading of it at the castle yielded every one of us the greatest satisfaction. On that occasion we proposed to act the play; and I, not knowing what I undertook, engaged to play the prince's part. This I conceived that I was studying, while I began to get by heart the strongest passages, the soliloquies, and those scenes in which force of soul, vehemence and elevation of feeling, have the freest scope; where the agitated heart is allowed to display itself with touching expressiveness.

"I further conceived that I was penetrating quite into the spirit of the character, while I endeavored, as it were, to take upon myself the load of deep melancholy under which my prototype was laboring, and in this humor to pursue him through the strange labyrinths of his caprices and his singularities. Thus learning, thus practising, I doubted not but I should by and by become one person with my hero.

"But, the farther I advanced, the more difficult did it become for me to form any image of the whole, in its general bearings; till at last it seemed as if impossible. I next went through the entire piece, without interruption; but here, too, I found much that I could not away with. At one time the characters, at another time the manner of displaying them, seemed inconsistent; and I almost despaired of finding any general tint, in which I might present my whole part with all its shadings and variations. In such devious paths I toiled, and wandered long in vain; till at length a hope arose that I might reach my aim in quite a new way.

"I set about investigating every trace of Hamlet's character, as it had shown itself before his father's death: I endeavored to distinguish what in it was independent of this mournful event, independent of the terrible events that followed; and what most probably the young man would have been, had no such thing occurred.

"Soft, and from a noble stem, this royal flower had sprung up under the immediate influences of majesty: the idea of moral rectitude with that of princely elevation, the feeling of the good and dignified with the consciousness of high birth, had in him been unfolded simultaneously. He was a prince, by birth a prince; and he wished to reign, only that good men might be good without obstruction. Pleasing in form, polished by nature, courteous from the heart, he was meant to be the pattern of youth and the joy of the world.

"Without any prominent passion, his love for Ophelia was a still presentiment of sweet wants. His zeal in knightly accomplishments was not entirely his own: it needed to be quickened and inflamed by praise bestowed on others for excelling in them. Pure in sentiment, he knew the honorable-minded, and could prize the rest which an upright spirit tastes on the bosom of a friend. To a certain degree, he had learned to discern and value the good and the beautiful in arts and sciences; the mean, the vulgar, was offensive to him; and, if hatred could take root in his tender soul, it was only so far as to make him properly despise the false and changeful insects of a court, and play with them in easy scorn. He was calm in his temper, artless in his conduct, neither pleased with idleness, nor too violently eager for employment. The routine of a university he seemed to continue when at court. He possessed more mirth of humor than of heart: he was a good companion, pliant, courteous, discreet, and able to forget and forgive an injury, yet never able to unite himself with those who over-stepped the limits of the right, the good, and the becoming.

"When we read the piece again, you shall judge whether I am yet on the proper track. I hope at least to bring forward passages that shall support my opinion in its main points."

This delineation was received with warm approval; the company imagined they foresaw that Hamlet's manner of proceeding might now be very satisfactorily explained; they applauded this method of pene-trating into the spirit of a writer. Each of them proposed to himself to take up some piece, and study it on these principles, and so unfold the author's meaning.

CHAPTER FOUR

OUR FRIENDS had to continue in the place for a day or two, and it was not long ere sundry of them got engaged in adventures of a rather pleasant kind. Laertes in particular was challenged by a lady of the neighborhood, a person of some property; but he received her blandishments with extreme, nay, unhandsome, coldness, and had in consequence to undergo a multitude of jibes from Philina. She took this opportunity of detailing to our friend the hapless love-story which had made the youth so bitter a foe to womankind. "Who can take it ill of him," she cried, "that he hates a sex which has played him so foul, and given him to swallow, in one stoutly concentrated potion, all the miseries that man can fear from woman? Do but conceive it: within four and twenty hours, he was lover, bridegroom, husband, cuckold, patient, and widower! I wot not how you could use a man worse."

Laertes hastened from the room half vexed, half laughing; and Philina in her sprightliest style began to relate the story: how Laertes, a young man of eighteen, on joining a company of actors, found in it a girl of fourteen on the point of departing with her father, who had quarrelled with the manager. How, on the instant, he had fallen mortally in love; had conjured the father by all possible considerations to remain, promising at length to marry the young woman. How, after a few pleasing hours of groomship, he had accordingly been wedded, and been happy as he ought; whereupon, next day, while he was occupied at the rehearsal, his wife, according to professional rule, had honored him with a pair of horns; and how as he, out of excessive tenderness, hastening home far too soon, had, alas! found a former lover in his place, he had struck into the affair with thoughtless indignation, had called out both father and lover, and sustained a grievous wound in the duel. How father and daughter had thereupon set off by night, leaving him behind to labor with a double hurt. How the leech he applied to was unhappily the worst in nature, and the poor fellow had got out of the adventure with blackened teeth and watering eyes. That he was greatly to be pitied, being otherwise the bravest young man on the surface of the earth. "Especially," said she, "it grieves me that the poor soul now hates women; for, hating women, how can one keep living?"

Melina interrupted them with news, that, all things being now ready for the journey, they would set out to-morrow morning. He handed them a plan, arranging how they were to travel.

"If any good friend take me on his lap," said Philina, "I shall be content, though we sit crammed together never so close and sorrily: 'tis all one to me."

"It does not signify," observed Laertes, who now entered.

"It is pitiful," said Wilhelm, hastening away. By the aid of money, he secured another very comfortable coach; though Melina had pretended that there were no more. A new distribution then took place; and our friends were rejoicing in the thought that they should now travel pleasantly, when intelligence arrived that a party of military volunteers had been seen upon the road, from whom little good could be expected.

In the town these tidings were received with great attention, though they were but variable and ambiguous. As the contending armies were at that time placed, it seemed impossible that any hostile corps could have advanced, or any friendly one hung a-rear, so far. Yet every man was eager to exhibit to our travellers the danger that awaited them as truly dangerous: every man was eager to suggest that some other route might be adopted.

By these means, most of our friends had been seized with anxiety and fear; and when, according to the new republican constitution, the whole members of the state had been called together to take counsel on this extraordinary case, they were almost unanimously of opinion that it would be proper either to keep back the mischief by abiding where they were, or to evade it by choosing another road.

Wilhelm alone, not participating in the panic, regarded it as mean to abandon, for the sake of mere rumors, a plan they had not entered on without much thought. He endeavored to put heart into them: his reasons were manly and convincing.

"It is but a rumor," he observed; "and how many such arise in time of war! Well-informed people say that the occurrence is exceedingly improbable, nay, almost impossible. Shall we, in so important a matter, allow a vague report to determine our proceedings? The route pointed out to us by the count, and to which our passport was adapted, is the shortest and in the best condition. It leads us to the town, where you see acquaintances, friends, before you, and may hope for a good reception. The other way will also bring us thither; but by what a circuit, and along what miserable roads! Have we any right to hope, that, in this late season of the year, we shall get on at all? and what time and money shall we squander in the mean while!" He added many more considerations, presenting the matter on so many advantageous sides, that their fear began to dissipate, and their courage to increase. He talked to them so much about the discipline of regular troops, he painted the marauders and wandering rabble so contemptuously, and represented the danger itself as so pleasant and inspiring, that the spirits of the party were altogether cheered.

Laertes from the first had been of his opinion: he now declared that he would not flinch or fail. Old Boisterous found a consenting phrase or two to utter, in his own vein; Philina laughed at them all; and Madam Melina, who, notwithstanding her advanced state of pregnancy, had lost nothing of her natural stout-heartedness, regarded the proposal as heroic. Herr Melina, moved by this harmonious feeling, hoping also to save somewhat by travelling the short road which had been first contemplated, did not withstand the general consent; and the project was agreed to with universal alacrity.

They next began to make some preparations for defence at all hazards. They bought large hangers, and slung them in well-quilted straps over their shoulders. Wilhelm further stuck a pair of pistols in his girdle. Laertes, independently of this occurrence, had a good gun. They all took the road in the highest glee.

On the second day of their journey, the drivers, who knew the country well, proposed to take their noon's rest in a certain woody spot of the hills; since the town was far off, and in good weather the hill-road was generally preferred.

The day being beautiful, all easily agreed to the proposal. Wilhelm, on foot, went on before them through the hills; making every one that met him stare with astonishment at his singular figure. He hastened with quick and contented steps across the forest; Laertes walked whistling after him; none but the women continued to be dragged along in the carriages. Mignon, too, ran forward by his side, proud of the hanger, which, when the party were all arming, she would not go without. Around her hat she had bound the pearl necklace, one of Mariana's relics, which Wilhelm still possessed. Friedrich, the fair-haired boy, carried Laertes's gun. The harper had the most pacific look; his long cloak was tucked up within his girdle, to let him walk more freely; he leaned upon a knotty staff; his harp had been left behind him in the carriage.

Immediately on reaching the summit of the height, a task not without its difficulties, our party recognized the appointed spot, by the fine beech-trees which encircled and screened it. A spacious green, sloping softly in the middle of the forest, invited one to tarry; a trimly bordered well offered the most grateful refreshment; and on the farther side, through chasms in the mountains, and over the tops of the woods, appeared a landscape distant, lovely, full of hope. Hamlets and mills were lying in the bottoms, villages upon the plain: and a new chain of mountains, visible in the distance, made the prospect still more significant of hope; for they entered only like a soft limitation.

The first comers took possession of the place, rested a while in the shade, lighted a fire, and so awaited, singing as they worked, the remainder of the party, who by degrees arrived, and with one accord saluted the place, the lovely weather, and still lovelier scene.

CHAPTER FIVE

IF OUR FRIENDS had frequently enjoyed a good and merry hour together while within four walls, they were naturally much gayer here, where the freedom of the sky and the beauty of the place seemed, as it were, to purify the feelings of every one. All felt nearer to each other: all wished that they might pass their whole lives in so pleasant an abode. They envied hunters, charcoal-men, and wood-cutters, — people whom their calling constantly retains in such happy places, — but prized, above all, the delicious economy of a band of gypsies. They envied these wonderful companions, entitled to enjoy in blissful idleness all the adventurous charms of nature: they rejoiced at being in some degree like them.

Meanwhile the women had begun to boil potatoes, and to unwrap and get ready the victuals brought along with them. Some pots were standing by the fire. The party had placed themselves in groups, under the trees and bushes. Their singular apparel, their various weapons, gave them a foreign aspect. The horses were eating their provender at a side. Could one have concealed the coaches, the look of this little horde would have been romantic, even to complete illusion.

Wilhelm enjoyed a pleasure he had never felt before. He could now imagine his present company to be a wandering colony, and himself the leader of it. In this character he talked with those around him, and figured out the fantasy of the moment as poetically as he could. The feelings of the party rose in cheerfulness: they ate and drank and made merry, and repeatedly declared that they had never passed more pleasant moments.

Their contentment had not long gone on increasing, till activity awoke among the younger part of them. Wilhelm and Laertes seized their rapiers, and began to practise on this occasion with theatrical intentions. They undertook to represent the duel in which Hamlet and his adversary find so tragical an end. Both were persuaded, that, in this powerful scene, it was not enough merely to keep pushing awkwardly hither and thither, as it is generally exhibited in theatres: they were in hopes to show by example how, in presenting it, a worthy spectacle might also be afforded to the critic in the art of fencing. The rest made a circle round them. Both fought with skill and ardor. The interest of the spectators rose higher every pass.

But all at once, in the nearest bush, a shot went off, and immediately another; and the party flew asunder in terror. Next moment armed men were to be seen pressing forward to the spot where the horses were eating their fodder, not far from the coaches that were packed with luggage.

A universal scream proceeded from the women: our heroes threw away their rapiers, seized their pistols, and ran towards the robbers; demanding, with violent threats, the meaning of such conduct.

This question being answered laconically, with a couple of musket-shots, Wilhelm fired his pistol at a crisp-headed knave, who had got upon the top of the coach, and was cutting the cords of the package. Rightly hit, this artist instantly came tumbling down; nor had Laertes missed. Both, encouraged by success, drew their side-arms; when a number of the plundering party rushed out upon them, with curses and loud bellowing, fired a few shots at them, and fronted their impetuosity with glittering sabres. Our young heroes made a bold resistance. They called upon their other comrades, and endeavored to excite them to a general resistance. But, erelong, Wilhelm lost the sight of day, and the consciousness of what was passing. Stupefied by a shot that wounded him between the breast and the left arm, by a stroke that split his hat in two, and almost penetrated to his brain, he sank down, and only by the narratives of others came afterwards to understand the luckless end of this adventure.

On again opening his eyes, he found himself in the strangest posture. The first thing that pierced the dimness, which yet swam before his vision, was Philina's face bent down over his. He felt weak, and, making a movement to rise, discovered that he was in Philina's lap; into which, indeed, he again sank down. She was sitting on the sward. She had softly pressed towards her the head of the fallen young man, and made for him an easy couch, as far as in her power. Mignon was kneeling with dishevelled and bloody hair at his feet, which she embraced with many tears.

On noticing his bloody clothes, Wilhelm asked, in a broken voice, where he was, and what had happened to him and the rest. Philina begged him to be quiet: the others, she said, were all in safety, and none but he and Laertes wounded. Further she would tell him nothing, but earnestly entreated him to keep still, as his wounds had been but slightly and hastily bound. He stretched out his hand to Mignon, and inquired about the bloody locks of the child, who he supposed was also wounded.

For the sake of quietness, Philina let him know that this true-hearted creature, seeing her friend wounded, and in the hurry of the instant being able to think of nothing which would stanch the blood, had taken her own hair, that was flowing round her head, and tried to stop the wounds with it, but had soon been obliged to give up the vain attempt; that afterwards they had bound him with moss and dry mushrooms, Philina giving up her neckerchief for that purpose.

Wilhelm noticed that Philina was sitting with her back against her own trunk, which still looked firmly locked and quite uninjured. He inquired if the rest also had been so lucky as to save their goods. She answered with a shrug of the shoulders, and a look over the green, where broken chests, and coffers beaten into fragments, and knapsacks ripped up, and a multitude of little wares, lay scattered all round. No person was to be seen in the place, this strange group thus being alone in the solitude.

Inquiring further, our friend learned more and more particulars. The rest of the men, it appeared, who, at all events, might still have made resistance, were struck with terror, and soon overpowered. Some fled, some looked with horror at the accident. The drivers, for the sake of their cattle, had held out more obstinately; but they, too, were at last thrown down and tied; after which, in a few minutes, every thing was thoroughly ransacked, and the booty carried off. The hapless travellers, their fear of death being over, had begun to mourn their loss; had hastened with the greatest speed to the neighboring village, taking with them Laertes, whose wounds were slight, and carrying off but a very few fragments of their property. The harper, having placed his damaged instrument against a tree, had proceeded in their company to the place, to seek a surgeon, and return with his utmost rapidity to help his benefactor, whom he had left apparently upon the brink of death.

CHAPTER SIX

MEANWHILE our three adventurers continued yet a space in their strange position, no one returning to their aid. Evening was advancing: the darkness threatened to come on. Philina's indifference was changing to anxiety; Mignon ran to and fro, her impatience increasing every moment; and at last, when their prayer was granted, and human creatures did approach, a new alarm fell upon them. They distinctly heard a troop of horses coming up the road they had lately travelled: they dreaded lest a second time some company of unbidden guests might be purposing to visit this scene of battle, and gather up the gleanings.

The more agreeable was their surprise, when, after a few moments, a lady issued from the thickets, riding on a gray courser, and accompanied by an elderly gentleman and some cavaliers, followed by grooms, servants, and a troop of hussars.

Philina started at this phenomenon, and was about to call, and entreat the fair Amazon for help, when the latter turned her astonished eyes on the group, instantly checked her horse, rode up to them, and halted. She inquired eagerly about the wounded man, whose posture in the lap of this light-minded Samaritan seemed to strike her as peculiarly strange.

"Is he your husband?" she inquired of Philina. "Only a friend," replied the other, with a tone Wilhelm liked not at all. He had fixed his eyes upon the soft, elevated, calm, sympathizing features of the stranger: he thought he had never seen aught nobler or more lovely. Her shape he could not see: it was hid by a man's white great-coat, which she seemed to have borrowed from some of her attendants, to screen her from the chill evening air.

By this the horsemen also had come near. Some of them dismounted: the lady did so likewise. She asked, with humane sympathy, concerning every circumstance of the mishap which had befallen the travellers, but especially concerning the wounds of the poor youth who lay before her. Thereupon she turned quickly round, and went aside with the old gentleman to some carriages, which were slowly coming up the hill, and which at length stopped upon the scene of action.

The young lady having stood with her conductor a short time at the door of one of the coaches, and talked with the people in it, a man of a squat figure stepped out, and came along with them to our wounded hero. By the little box which he held in his hand, and the leathern pouch with instruments in it, you soon recognized him for a surgeon. His manners were rude rather than attractive; but his hand was light, and his help welcome.

Having examined strictly, he declared that none of the wounds were dangerous. He would dress them, he said, on the spot; after which the patient might be carried to the nearest village.

The young lady's anxiety seemed to augment. "Do but look," she said, after going to and fro once or twice, and again bringing the old gentleman to the place: "look how they have treated him! And is it not on our account that he is suffering?" Wilhelm heard these words, but did not understand them. She went restlessly up and down: it seemed as if she could not tear herself away from the presence of the wounded man; while at the same time she feared to violate decorum by remaining, when they had begun, though not without difficulty, to remove some part of his apparel. The surgeon was just cutting off the left sleeve of his patient's coat, when the old gentleman came near, and represented to the lady, in a serious tone, the necessity of proceeding on their journey. Wilhelm kept his eyes bent on her, and was so enchanted with her looks, that he scarcely felt what he was suffering or doing.

Philina, in the mean time, had risen to kiss the lady's hand. While they stood beside each other, Wilhelm thought he had never seen such a contrast. Philina had never till now appeared in so unfavorable a light. She had no right, as it seemed to him, to come near that noble creature, still less to touch her.

The lady asked Philina various things, but in an undertone. At length she turned to the old gentleman, and said, "Dear uncle, may I be generous at your expense?" She took off the great-coat, with the visible intention to give it to the stripped and wounded youth.

Wilhelm, whom the healing look of her eyes had hitherto held fixed, was now, as the surtout fell away, astonished at her lovely

The players' vehicles are attacked

figure. She came near, and softly laid the coat above him. At this moment, as he tried to open his mouth and stammer out some words of gratitude, the lively impression of her presence worked so strongly on his senses, already caught and bewildered, that all at once it appeared to him as if her head were encircled with rays; and a glancing light seemed by degrees to spread itself over all her form. At this moment the surgeon, making preparations to extract the ball from his wound, gave him a sharper twinge; the angel faded away from the eyes of the fainting patient; he lost all consciousness; and, on returning to himself, the horsemen and coaches, the fair one with her attendants, had vanished like a dream.

CHAPTER SEVEN

WILHELM's wounds once dressed, and his clothes put on, the surgeon hastened off, just as the harper with a number of peasants arrived. Out of some cut boughs, which they speedily wattled with twigs, a kind of litter was constructed, upon which they placed the wounded youth, and under the conduct of a mounted huntsman, whom the noble company had left behind them, carried him softly down the mountain. The harper, silent, and shrouded in his own thoughts, bore with him his broken instrument. Some men brought on Philina's box, herself following with a bundle. Mignon skipped along through copse and thicket, now before the party, now beside them, and looked up with longing eyes at her hurt protector.

He, meanwhile, wrapped in his warm surtout, was lying peacefully upon the litter. An electric warmth seemed to flow from the fine wool into his body: in short, he felt in the most delightful frame of mind. The lovely being, whom this garment lately covered, had affected him to the very heart. He still saw the coat falling down from her shoulders; saw that noble form, begirt with radiance, stand beside him; and his soul hied over rocks and forests on the footsteps of his vanished benefactress.

It was nightfall when the party reached the village, and halted at the door of the inn where the rest of the company, in the gloom of despondency, were bewailing their irreparable loss. The one little chamber of the house was crammed with people. Some of them were lying upon straw, some were occupying benches, some had squeezed themselves behind the stove. Frau Melina, in a neighboring room, was painfully expecting her delivery. Fright had accelerated this event. With the sole assistance of the landlady, a young, inexperienced woman, nothing good could be expected.

As the party just arrived required admission, there arose a universal murmur. All now maintained, that by Wilhelm's advice alone, and under his especial guidance, they had entered on this dangerous road, and exposed themselves to such misfortunes. They threw the blame of the disaster wholly on him: they stuck themselves in the door, to oppose his entrance; declaring that he must go elsewhere and seek quarters. Philina they received with still greater indignation, nor did Mignon and the harper escape their share.

The huntsman, to whom the care of the forsaken party had been earnestly and strictly recommended by his beautiful mistress, soon grew tired of this discussion: he rushed upon the company with oaths and menaces; commanding them to fall to the right and left, and make way for this new arrival. They now began to pacify themselves. He made a place for Wilhelm on a table, which he shoved into a corner: Philina had her box put there, and then sat down upon it. All packed themselves as they best could, and the huntsman went away to see if he could not find for "the young couple" a more convenient lodging.

Scarcely was he gone, when spite again grew noisy, and one reproach began to follow close upon another. Each described and magnified his loss, censuring the foolhardiness they had so keenly smarted for. They did not even hide the malicious satisfaction they felt at Wilhelm's wounds: they jeered Philina, and imputed to her as a crime the means by which she had saved her trunk. From a multitude of jibes and bitter innuendoes, you were required to conclude, that, during the plundering and discomfiture, she had endeavored to work herself into favor with the captain of the band, and had persuaded him, Heaven knew by what arts and complaisance, to give her back the chest unhurt. To all this she answered nothing, only clanked with the large padlocks of her box, to impress her censurers completely with its presence, and by her own good fortune to augment their desperation.

Though our friend was weak from loss of blood, and though, ever since the appearance of that helpful angel, his feelings had been soft and mild, yet at last he could not help getting vexed at the harsh and unjust speeches which, as he continued silent, the discontented company went on uttering against him. Feeling himself strong enough to sit up, and expostulate on the annoyance they were causing to their friend and leader, he raised his bandaged head, and propping himself with some difficulty, and leaning against the wall, he began to speak as follows: —

"Considering the pain your losses occasion, I forgive you for assailing me with injuries at a moment when you should condole with me; for opposing and casting me from you the first time I have needed to look to you for help. The services I did you, the complaisance I showed you, I regarded as sufficiently repaid by your thanks, by your friendly conduct: do not warp my thoughts, do not force my heart to go back and calculate what I have done for you; the calculation would be painful to me. Chance brought me near you, circumstances and a secret inclination kept me with you. I participated in your labors and your pleasures: my slender abilities were ever at your service. If you now blame me with bitterness for the mishap that has befallen us, you do not recollect that the first project of taking this road came to us from stranger people, was weighed by all of you, and sanctioned by every one as well as by me.

"Had our journey ended happily, each would have taken credit to himself for the happy thought of suggesting this plan, and preferring it to others; each would joyfully have put us in mind of our deliberations, and of the vote he gave: but now you make me alone responsible; you force a piece of blame upon me, which I would willingly submit to, if my conscience, with a clear voice, did not pronounce me innocent, nay, if I might not appeal with safety even to yourselves. If you have aught to say against me, bring it forward in order, and I shall defend myself; if you have nothing reasonable to allege, then be silent, and do not torment me now, when I have such pressing need of rest."

By way of answer, the girls once more began whimpering and whining, and describing their losses circumstantially. Melina was quite beside himself; for he had suffered more in purse than any of them, — more, indeed, than we can rightly estimate. He stamped like a madman up and down the little room, he knocked his head against the wall, he swore and scolded in the most unseemly manner; and the landlady entering at this very time with news that his wife had been delivered of a dead child, he yielded to the most furious ebullitions; while, in accordance with him, all howled and shrieked, and bellowed and uproared, with double vigor.

Wilhelm, touched to the heart at the same time with sympathy for their sorrows and with vexation at their mean way of thinking, felt all the vigor of his soul awakened, notwithstanding the weakness of his body. "Deplorable as your case may be," exclaimed he, "I shall almost be compelled to despise you! No misfortune gives us right to load an innocent man with reproaches. If I had share in this false step, am not I suffering my share? I lie wounded here; and, if the company has come to loss, I myself have come to most. The wardrobe of which we have been robbed, the decorations that are gone, were mine; for you, Herr Melina, have not yet paid me; and I here fully acquit you of all obligation in that matter."

"It is well to give what none of us will ever see again," replied Melina. "Your money was lying in my wife's coffer, and it is your own blame that you have lost it. But, ah! if that were all!" And thereupon he began anew to stamp and scold and squeal. Every one recalled to memory the superb clothes from the count's wardrobe; the buckles, watches, snuff-boxes, hats, for which Melina had so happily transacted with the head valet. Each, then, thought also of his own, though far inferior, treasures. They looked with spleen at Philina's box, and gave Wilhelm to understand that he had indeed done wisely to connect himself with that fair personage, and to save his own goods also, under the shadow of her fortune.

"Do you think," he exclaimed at last, "that I shall keep any thing apart while you are starving? And is this the first time I have honestly shared with you in a season of need? Open the trunk: all that is mine shall go to supply the common wants."

"It is *my* trunk," observed Philina, "and I will not open it till I please. Your rag or two of clothes, which I have saved for you, could amount to little, though they were sold to the most conscientious of Jews. Think of yourself, — what your cure will cost, what may befall you in a strange country."

"You, Philina," answered Wilhelm, "will keep back from me nothing that is mine; and that little will help us out of the first perplexity. But a man possesses many things besides coined money to assist his friends with. All that is in me shall be devoted to these hapless persons, who, doubtless, on returning to their senses, will repent their present conduct. Yes," continued he, "I feel that you have need of help; and, what is mine to do, I will perform. Give me your confidence again; compose yourselves for a moment, and accept of what I promise. Who will receive the engagement of me in the name of all?"

Here he stretched out his hand, and cried, "I promise not to flinch from you, never to forsake you till each shall see his losses doubly and trebly repaired; till the situation you are fallen into, by whose blame soever, shall be totally forgotten by all of you, and changed with a better."

He kept his hand still stretched out, but no one would take hold of it. "I promise it again," cried he, sinking back upon his pillow. All continued silent: they felt ashamed, but nothing comforted: and Philina, sitting on her chest, kept cracking nuts, a stock of which she had discovered in her pocket.

CHAPTER NINE

THE HUNTSMAN now came back with several people, and made preparations for carrying away the wounded youth. He had persuaded the parson of the place to receive the "young couple" into his house; Philina's trunk was taken out; she followed with a natural air of dignity. Mignon ran before; and, when the patient reached the parsonage, a wide couch, which had long been standing ready as guest's bed and bed of honor, was assigned him. Here it was first discovered that his wound had opened, and bled profusely. A new bandage was required for it. He fell into a feverish state: Philina waited on him faithfully; and, when fatigue overpowered her, she was relieved by the harper. Mignon, with the firmest purpose to watch, had fallen asleep in a corner.

Next morning Wilhelm, who felt himself in some degree refreshed, learned, by inquiring of the huntsman, that the honorable persons who last night assisted him so nobly, had shortly before left their estates, in order to avoid the movements of the contending armies, and remain, till the time of peace, in some more quiet district. He named the elderly nobleman, as well as his niece, mentioned the place they were first going to, and told how the young lady had charged him to take care of Wilhelm.

The entrance of the surgeon interrupted the warm expressions of gratitude our friend was giving vent to. He made a circumstantial description of the wounds, and certified that they would soon heal, if the patient took care of them, and kept himself at peace.

When the huntsman was gone, Philina signified that he had left with her a purse of twenty *louis-d'or;* that he had given the parson a remuneration for their lodging, and left with him money to defray the surgeon's bill when the cure should be completed. She added, that she herself passed everywhere for Wilhelm's wife; that she now begged leave to introduce herself once for all to him in this capacity, and would not allow him to look out for any other sick-nurse.

"Philina," said Wilhelm, "in this disaster that has overtaken us, I am already deeply in your debt, for kindness shown me; and I should not wish to see my obligations increased. I am uneasy so long as you are about me, for I know of nothing by which I can repay your labor. Give me what things of mine you have saved in your trunk; join the rest of the company; seek another lodging; take my thanks, and the gold watch as a small acknowledgment: only leave me; your presence disturbs me more than you can fancy."

She laughed in his face when he had ended. "Thou art a fool," she said: "thou wilt not gather wisdom. I know better what is good for thee: I will stay, I will not budge from the spot. I have never counted on the gratitude of men, and therefore not on thine; and, if I have a touch of kindness for thee, what hast thou to do with it?"

She staid accordingly, and soon wormed herself into favor with the parson and his household; being always cheerful, having the knack of giving little presents, and of talking to each in his own vein; at the same time always contriving to do exactly what she pleased. Wilhelm's state was not uncomfortable: the surgeon, an ignorant but not unskilful man, let nature have sway; and the patient was soon on the road to recovery. For such a consummation he vehemently longed, being eager to pursue his plans and wishes.

Incessantly he kept recalling that event, which had made an ineffaceable impression on his heart. He saw the beautiful Amazon again come riding out of the thickets: she approached him, dismounted, went to and fro, and strove to serve him. He saw the garment she was wrapped in fall down from her shoulders: he saw her countenance, her figure, vanish in their radiance. All the dreams of his youth now fastened on this image. Here he conceived he had at length beheld the noble, the heroic, Clorinda with his own eyes; and again he bethought him of that royal youth, to whose sickbed the lovely, sympathizing princess came in her modest meekness.

"May it not be," said he often to himself in secret, "that, in youth as in sleep, the images of coming things hover round us, and mysteriously become visible to our unobstructed eyes? May not the seeds of what is to betide us be already scattered by the hand of Fate? may not a foretaste of the fruits we yet hope to gather possibly be given us?"

His sick-bed gave him leisure to repeat those scenes in every mood. A thousand times he called back the tone of that sweet voice: a thousand times he envied Philina, who had kissed that helpful hand. Often the whole incident appeared before him as a dream; and he would have reckoned it a fiction, if the white surtout had not been left behind to convince him that the vision had a real existence.

With the greatest care for this piece of apparel, he combined the most ardent wish to wear it. The first time he arose, he put it on, and was kept in fear all day lest it might be hurt by some stain or other injury.

CHAPTER TEN

Laertes visited his friend. He had not been present during that lively scene at the inn, being then confined to bed in an upper chamber. For his loss he was already in a great degree consoled: he helped himself with his customary, "What does it signify?" He detailed various laughable particulars about the company; particularly charging Frau Melina with lamenting the loss of her stillborn daughter, solely because she herself could not on that account enjoy the Old-German satisfaction of having a Mechthilde christened. As for her husband, it now appeared that he had been possessed of abundant cash, and even at first had by no means needed the advances which he had cajoled from Wilhelm. Melina's present plan was, to set off by the next post-wagon, and he meant to require of Wilhelm an introductory letter to his friend, Manager Serlo, in whose company, the present undertaking having gone to wreck, he now wished to establish himself.

For some days Mignon had been singularly quiet: when pressed with questions, she at length admitted that her right arm was out of joint. "Thou hast thy own folly to thank for that," observed Philina, and then told how the child had drawn her sword in the battle, and, seeing her friend in peril, had struck fiercely at the freebooters, one of whom had at length seized her by the arm, and pitched her to a side. They chid her for not sooner speaking of her ailment; but they easily saw that she was apprehensive of the surgeon, who had hitherto looked on her as a boy. With a view to remove the mischief, she was made to keep her arm in a sling, which arrangement, too, displeased her; for now she was obliged to surrender most part of her share in the management and nursing of our friend to Philina. That pleasing sinner but showed herself the more active and attentive on this account.

One morning, on awakening, Wilhelm found himself strangely near to her. In the movements of sleep, he had hitched himself quite to the back of the spacious bed. Philina was lying across from the front part of it: she seemed to have fallen asleep on the bed while sitting there and reading. A book had dropped from her hand: she had sunk back; and her head was lying near his breast, over which her fair and now loosened hair was spread in streams. The disorder of sleep enlivened her charms more than art or purpose could have done: a childlike smiling rest hovered on her countenance. He looked at her for a time, and seemed to blame himself for the pleasure this gave him. He had viewed her attentively for some moments, when she began to awake. He softly closed his eyes, but could not help glimmering at her through his eyelashes, as she trimmed herself again, and went away to see about breakfast.

All the actors had at length successively announced themselves to Wilhelm; asking introductory letters, requiring money for their journey with more or less impatience and ill-breeding, and constantly receiving it, against Philina's will. It was in vain for her to tell our friend that the huntsman had already left a handsome sum with these people, and that accordingly they did but cozen him. To these remonstrances he gave no heed: on the contrary, the two had a sharp quarrel about it; which ended by Wilhelm signifying, once for all, that Philina must now join the rest of the company, and seek her fortune with Serlo.

For an instant or two she lost temper; but, speedily recovering her composure, she cried, "If I had but my fair-haired boy again, I should not care a fig for any of you." She meant Friedrich, who had vanished from the scene of battle, and never since appeared.

Next morning Mignon brought news to the bedside, that Philina had gone off by night; leaving all that belonged to Wilhelm very neatly laid out in the next room. He felt her absence; he had lost in her a faithful nurse, a cheerful companion; he was no longer used to be alone. But Mignon soon filled up the blank.

Ever since that light-minded beauty had been near the patient with her friendly cares, the little creature had by degrees drawn back, and remained silent and secluded in herself; but, the field being clear once more, she again came forth with her attentions and her love, again was eager in serving, and lively in entertaining, him.

CHAPTER ELEVEN

WILHELM was rapidly approaching complete recovery: he now hoped to be upon his journey in a few days. He proposed no more to lead an aimless routine of existence: the steps of his career were henceforth to be calculated for an end. In the first place, he purposed to seek out that beneficent lady, and express the gratitude he felt to her; then to proceed without delay to his friend the manager, that he might do his utmost to assist the luckless company; intending, at the same time, to visit the commercial friends whom he had letters for, and to transact the business which had been intrusted to him. He was not without hope that fortune, as formerly, would favor him, and give him opportunity, by some lucky speculation, to repair his losses, and fill up the vacuity of his coffer.

The desire of again beholding his beautiful deliverer augmented every day. To settle his route, he took counsel with the clergyman, — a person well skilled in statistics and geography, and possessing a fine collection of charts and books. They two searched for the place which this noble family had chosen as their residence while the war continued: they searched for information respecting the family itself. But their place was to be found in no geography or map, and the heraldic manuals made no mention of their name.

Wilhelm grew uneasy; and, having mentioned the cause of his anxiety, the harper told him he had reason to believe that the huntsman, from whatever motive, had concealed the real designations.

Conceiving himself now to be in the immediate neighborhood of his lovely benefactress, Wilhelm hoped he might obtain some tidings of her if he sent out the harper; but in this, too, he was deceived. Diligently as the old man kept inquiring, he could find no trace of her. Of late days a number of quick movements and unforeseen marches had taken place in that quarter; no one had particularly noticed the travelling party; and the ancient messenger, to avoid being taken for a Jewish spy, was obliged to return, and appear without any olive-leaf before his master and friend. He gave a strict account of his conduct in this commission, striving to keep far from him all suspicions of remissness. He endeavored by every means to mitigate the trouble of our friend; bethought him of every thing that he had learned from the huntsman, and advanced a number of conjectures; out of all which, one circumstance at length came to light, whereby Wilhelm could explain some enigmatic words of his vanished benefactress.

The freebooters, it appeared, had lain in wait, not for the wandering troop, but for that noble company, whom they rightly guessed to be provided with store of gold and valuables, and of whose movements they must have had precise intelligence. Whether the attack should be imputed to some free corps, to marauders, or to robbers, was uncertain. It was clear, however, that, by good fortune for the high and rich company, the poor and low had first arrived upon the place, and undergone the fate which was provided for the others. It was to this that the lady's words referred, which Wilhelm yet well recollected. If he might now be happy and contented, that a prescient Genius had selected him for the sacrifice, which saved a perfect mortal, he was, on the other hand, nigh desperate, when he thought that all hope of finding her and seeing her again was, at least for the present, completely gone.

What increased this singular emotion still further, was the likeness which he thought he had observed between the countess and the beautiful unknown. They resembled one another as two sisters may, of whom neither can be called the younger or the elder, for they seem to be twins.

The recollection of the amiable countess was to Wilhelm infinitely sweet. He recalled her image but too willingly into his memory. But anon the figure of the noble Amazon would step between: one vision melted and changed into the other, and the form of neither would abide with him.

A new resemblance — the similarity of their handwritings — naturally struck him with still greater wonder. He had a charming song in the countess's hand laid up in his portfolio; and in the surtout he had found a little note, inquiring with much tender care about the health of an uncle.

Wilhelm was convinced that his benefactress must have penned this billet; that it must have been sent from one chamber to another, at some inn during their journey, and put into the coat-pocket by the uncle. He held both papers together; and, if the regular and graceful letters of the countess had already pleased him much, he found in the similar but freer lines of the stranger a flowing harmony which could not be described. The note contained nothing; yet the strokes of it seemed to affect him, as the presence of their fancied writer once had done.

He fell into a dreamy longing; and well accordant with his feelings was the song which at that instant Mignon and the harper began to sing, with a touching expression, in the form of an irregular duet.

" 'Tis but who longing knows,   Ah! far is he who knows
My grief can measure.   Me, and doth treasure.
Alone, reft of repose,   I faint, my bosom glows
All joy, all pleasure,   'Neath pain's sore pressure.
I thither look to those   'Tis but who longing knows,
Soft lines of azure.   My grief can measure."

THE SOFT allurements of his dear presiding angel, far from leading our friend to any one determined path, did but nourish and increase the unrest he had previously experienced. A secret fire was gliding through his veins: objects distinct and indistinct alternated within his soul, and awoke unspeakable desire. At one time he wished for a horse, at another for wings; and not till it seemed impossible that he could stay, did he look round him to discover whither he was wanting to go.

The threads of his destiny had become so strangely entangled, he wished to see its curious knots unravelled, or cut in two. Often when he heard the tramp of a horse, or the rolling of a carriage, he would run to the window, and look out, in hopes it might be some one seeking him, — some one, even though it were by chance, bringing him intelligence and certainty and joy. He told stories to himself, how his friend Werner might visit these parts, and come upon him; how, perhaps, Mariana might appear. The sound of every post's horn threw him into agitation. It would be Melina sending news to him of his adventures: above all, it would be the huntsman coming back to carry him to the beauty he worshipped.

Of all these possibilities, unhappily no one occurred: he was forced at last to return to the company of himself; and, in again looking through the past, there was one circumstance which, the more he viewed and weighed it, grew the more offensive and intolerable to him. It was his unprosperous generalship, of which he never thought without vexation. For although, on the evening of that luckless day, he had produced a pretty fair defence of his conduct when accused by the company, yet he could not hide from himself that he was guilty. On the contrary, in hypochondriac moments, he took the blame of the whole misfortune.

Self-love exaggerates our faults as well as our virtues. Wilhelm though he had awakened confidence in himself, had guided the will of the rest; that, led by inexperience and rashness, they had ventured on, till a danger seized them, for which they were no match. Loud as

well as silent reproaches had then assailed him; and if, in their sorrowful condition, he had promised the company, misguided by him, never
to forsake them till their loss had been repaid with usury, this was but
another folly for which he had to blame himself, — the folly of presuming to take upon his single shoulders a misfortune that was spread
over many. One instant he accused himself of uttering this promise,
under the excitement and the pressure of the moment; the next, he
again felt that this generous presentation of his hand, which no one
deigned to accept, was but a light formality compared with the vow
his heart had taken. He meditated means of being kind and useful to
them: he found every cause conspire to quicken his visit to Serlo. Accordingly he packed his things together; and without waiting his
complete recovery, without listening to the counsel of the parson or
of the surgeon, he hastened, in the strange society of Mignon and the
harper, to escape the inactivity in which his fate had once more too
long detained him.

CHAPTER THIRTEEN

SERLO received him with open arms, crying as he met him, "Is it you?
Do I see you again? You have scarcely changed at all. Is your love
for that noblest of arts still as lively and strong? So glad am I at your
arrival, that I even feel no longer the mistrust your last letters had excited in me."

Wilhelm asked with surprise for a clearer explanation.

"You have treated me," said Serlo, "not like an old friend, but
as if I were a great lord, to whom with a safe conscience you might
recommend useless people. Our destiny depends on the opinion of the
public; and I fear Herr Melina and his suite can hardly be received
among us."

Wilhelm tried to say something in their favor; but Serlo began to draw so merciless a picture of them, that our friend was happy when a lady came into the room, and put a stop to the discussion. She was introduced to him as Aurelia, the sister of his friend; she received him with extreme kindness; and her conversation was so pleasing, that he did not even remark a shade of sorrow visible on her expressive countenance, to which it lent peculiar interest.

For the first time during many months, Wilhelm felt once more in his proper element. Of late in talking, he had merely found submissive listeners, and even these not always; but now he had the happiness to speak with critics and artists, who not only fully understood him, but repaid his observations by others equally instructive. With wonderful vivacity they travelled through the latest plays, with wonderful correctness judged them. The decisions of the public they could try and estimate: they speedily threw light on each other's thoughts.

Loving Shakspeare as our friend did, he failed not to lead round the conversation to the merits of that dramatist. Expressing, as he entertained, the liveliest hopes of the new epoch which these exquisite productions must form in Germany, he erelong introduced his "Hamlet," which play had busied him so much of late.

Serlo declared that he would long ago have represented the play, had it at all been possible, and that he himself would willingly engage to act Polonius. He added, with a smile, "An Ophelia, too, will certainly turn up, if we had but a Prince."

Wilhelm did not notice that Aurelia seemed a little hurt at her brother's sarcasm. Our friend was in his proper vein, becoming copious and didactic, expounding how he would have "Hamlet" played. He circumstantially delivered to his hearers the opinions we before saw him busied with; taking all the trouble possible to make his notion of the matter acceptable, sceptical as Serlo showed himself regarding it. "Well, then," said the latter finally, "suppose we grant you all this, what will you explain by it?"

"Much, every thing," said Wilhelm. "Conceive a prince such as I have painted him, and that his father suddenly dies. Ambition and the love of rule are not the passions that inspire him. As a king's son, he would not have been contented; but now he is first constrained to consider the difference which separates a sovereign from a subject.

Serlo and Aurelia discuss HAMLET *with Wilhelm*

The crown was not hereditary; yet his father's longer possession of it would have strengthened the pretensions of an only son, and secured his hopes of succession. In place of this, he now beholds himself excluded by his uncle, in spite of specious promises, most probably forever. He is now poor in goods and favor, and a stranger in the scene which from youth he had looked upon as his inheritance. His temper here assumes its first mournful tinge. He feels that now he is not more, that he is less, than a private nobleman; he offers himself as the servant of every one; he is not courteous and condescending, he is needy and degraded.

"His past condition he remembers as a vanished dream. It is in vain that his uncle strives to cheer him, to present his situation in another point of view. The feeling of his nothingness will not leave him.

"The second stroke that came upon him wounded deeper, bowed still more. It was the marriage of his mother. The faithful, tender son had yet a mother, when his father passed away. He hoped, in the company of his surviving noble-minded parent, to reverence the heroic form of the departed: but his mother, too, he loses; and it is something worse than death that robs him of her. The trustful image, which a good child loves to form of its parents, is gone. With the dead there is no help, on the living no hold. Moreover, she is a woman; and her name is Frailty, like that of all her sex.

"Now only does he feel completely bowed down, now only orphaned; and no happiness of life can repay what he has lost. Not reflective or sorrowful by nature, reflection and sorrow have become for him a heavy obligation. It is thus that we see him first enter on the scene. I do not think that I have mixed aught foreign with the play, or overcharged a single feature of it."

Serlo looked at his sister, and said, "Did I give thee a false picture of our friend? He begins well: he has still many things to tell us, many to persuade us of." Wilhelm asseverated loudly, that he meant not to persuade, but to convince: he begged for another moment's patience.

"Figure to yourselves this youth," cried he, "this son of princes; conceive him vividly, bring his state before your eyes, and then observe him when he learns that his father's spirit walks; stand by him in the terrors of the night, when even the venerable ghost appears before him. He is seized with boundless horror; he speaks to the mysterious form; he sees it beckon him; he follows and hears. The fearful accusation of his uncle rings in his ears, the summons to revenge, and the piercing, oft-repeated prayer, Remember me!

"And, when the ghost has vanished, who is it that stands before us? A young hero panting for vengeance? A prince by birth, rejoicing to be called to punish the usurper of his crown? No! trouble and astonishment take hold of the solitary young man: he grows bitter against smiling villains, swears that he will not forget the spirit, and concludes with the significant ejaculation, —

> " 'The time is out of joint: O cursed spite,
> That ever I was born to set it right!'

"In these words, I imagine, will be found the key to Hamlet's whole procedure. To me it is clear that Shakspeare meant, in the present case, to represent the effects of a great action laid upon a soul unfit for the performance of it. In this view the whole play seems to me to be composed. There is an oak-tree planted in a costly jar, which should have borne only pleasant flowers in its bosom: the roots expand, the jar is shivered.

"A lovely, pure, noble, and most moral nature, without the strength of nerve which forms a hero, sinks beneath a burden it cannot bear and must not cast away. All duties are holy for him: the present is too hard. Impossibilities have been required of him, — not in themselves impossibilities, but such for him. He winds and turns, and torments himself; he advances and recoils; is ever put in mind, ever puts himself in mind; at last does all but lose his purpose from his thoughts, yet still without recovering his peace of mind."

SEVERAL PEOPLE entering interrupted the discussion. They were musical *dilettanti*, who commonly assembled at Serlo's once a week, and formed a little concert. Serlo himself loved music much: he used to maintain, that a player without taste for it never could attain a distinct conception and feeling of the scenic art. "As a man performs," he would observe, "with far more ease and dignity when his gestures are accompanied and guided by a tune; so the player ought, in idea as it were, to set to music even his prose parts, that he may not monotonously slight them over in his individual style, but treat them in suitable alternation by time and measure."

Aurelia seemed to give but little heed to what was passing: at last she conducted Wilhelm to another room; and going to the window, and looking out at the starry sky, she said to him, "You have more to tell us about Hamlet: I will not hurry you, — my brother must hear it as well as I; but let me beg to know your thoughts about Ophelia."

"Of her there cannot much be said," he answered: "for a few master-strokes complete her character. The whole being of Ophelia floats in sweet and ripe sensation. Kindness for the prince, to whose hand she may aspire, flows so spontaneously, her tender heart obeys its impulses so unresistingly, that both father and brother are afraid: both give her warning harshly and directly. Decorum, like the thin lawn upon her bosom, cannot hide the soft, still movements of her heart: it, on the contrary, betrays them. Her fancy is smit; her silent modesty breathes amiable desire; and, if the friendly goddess Opportunity should shake the tree, its fruit would fall."

"And then," said Aurelia, "when she beholds herself forsaken, cast away, despised; when all is inverted in the soul of her crazed lover, and the highest changes to the lowest, and, instead of the sweet cup of love, he offers her the bitter cup of woe" —

"Her heart breaks," cried Wilhelm; "the whole structure of her being is loosened from its joinings; her father's death strikes fiercely against it, and the fair edifice altogether crumbles into fragments."

Our friend had not observed with what expressiveness Aurelia pronounced those words. Looking only at this work of art, at its connection and completeness, he dreamed not that his auditress was feeling quite a different influence; that a deep sorrow of her own was vividly awakened in her breast by these dramatic shadows.

Aurelia's head was still resting on her arms; and her eyes, now full of tears, were turned to the sky. At last, no longer able to conceal her secret grief, she seized both hands of her friend, and exclaimed, while he stood surprised before her, "Forgive, forgive a heavy heart! I am girt and pressed together by these people; from my hard-hearted brother I must seek to hide myself; your presence has untied these bonds. My friend!" continued she, "it is but a few minutes since we saw each other first, and already you are going to become my confidant." She could scarcely end the words, and sank upon his shoulder. "Think not worse of me," she said, with sobs, "that I disclose myself to you so hastily, that I am so weak before you. Be my friend, remain my friend: I shall deserve it." He spoke to her in his kindest manner, but in vain: her tears still flowed, and choked her words.

At this moment Serlo entered, most unwelcomely, and, most unexpectedly, Philina, with her hand in his. "Here is your friend," said he to her: "he will be glad to welcome you."

"What!" cried Wilhelm in astonishment: "are you here?" With a modest, settled mien, she went up to him; bade him welcome; praised Serlo's goodness, who, she said, without merit on her part, but purely in the hope of her improvement, had agreed to admit her into his accomplished troop. She behaved, all the while, in a friendly manner towards Wilhelm, yet with a dignified distance.

But this dissimulation lasted only till the other two were gone. Aurelia having left them, that she might conceal her trouble, and Serlo being called away, Philina first looked very sharply at the doors, to see that both were really out; then began skipping to and fro about the room, as if she had been mad; at last dropped down upon the floor, like to die of giggling and laughing. She then sprang up, patted and flattered our friend; rejoicing above measure that she had been clever enough to go before, and spy the land, and get herself nestled in.

"Pretty things are going on here," she said; "just of the sort I like. Aurelia has had a hapless love-affair with some nobleman, who seems to be a very stately person, one whom I myself could like to see some day. He has left her a memorial, or I much mistake. There is a boy running about the house, of three years old or so: the papa must be a very pretty fellow. Commonly I cannot suffer children, but this brat quite delights me. I have calculated Aurelia's business. The death of her husband, the new acquaintance, the child's age, — all things agree.

"But now her spark has gone his ways: for a year she has not seen a glimpse of him. She is beside herself and inconsolable on this account. The more fool she! Her brother has a dancing-girl in his troop, with whom he stands on pretty terms; an actress with whom he is intimate; in the town, some other women whom he courts; I, too, am on his list. The more fool he! Of the rest thou shalt hear to-morrow. And now one word about Philina, whom thou knowest: the arch-fool is fallen in love with thee." She swore it was true and prime sport. She earnestly requested Wilhelm to fall in love with Aurelia, for then the chase would be worth beholding. "She pursues her faithless swain, thou her, I thee, her brother me. If that will not divert us for a quarter of a year, I engage to die at the first episode which occurs in this four times complicated tale." She begged of him not to spoil her trade, and to show her such respect as her external conduct should deserve.

CHAPTER FIFTEEN

NEXT MORNING Wilhelm went to visit Frau Melina, but found her not at home. On inquiring here for the other members of the wandering community, he learned that Philina had invited them to breakfast. Out of curiosity, he hastened thither, and found them all in very good spirits and of good comfort. The cunning creature had collected them, was treating them with chocolate, and giving them to understand that some prospects still remained for them; that, by her influence, she hoped to convince the manager how advantageous it would be for him to introduce so many clever hands among his company. They listened to her with attention; swallowed cup after cup of her chocolate; thought the girl was not so bad, after all, and went away proposing to themselves to speak whatever good of her they could.

"Do you think, then," said our friend, who staid behind, "that Serlo will determine to retain our comrades?" — "Not at all," replied Philina; "nor do I care a fig for it. The sooner they are gone, the better! Laertes alone I could wish to keep: the rest we shall by and by pack off."

Next she signified to Wilhelm her firm persuasion that he should no longer hide his talent, but, under the direction of a Serlo, go upon the boards. She was lavish in her praises of the order, the taste, the spirit, which prevailed in this establishment: she spoke so flatteringly to Wilhelm, with such admiration of his gifts, that his heart and his imagination were advancing towards this proposal as fast as his understanding and his reason were retreating from it. He concealed his inclination from himself and from Philina, and passed a restless day, unable to resolve on visiting his trading correspondents, to receive the letters which might there be lying for him. The anxieties of his people during all this time he easily conceived; yet he shrank from the precise account of them, particularly at the present time, as he promised to himself a great and pure enjoyment from the exhibition of a new play that evening.

Serlo had refused to let him witness the rehearsal. "You must see us on the best side," he observed, "before we can allow you to look into our cards."

The performance, however, where our friend did not fail to be present, yielded him a high satisfaction. It was the first time he had ever seen a theatre in such perfection. The actors were evidently all possessed of excellent gifts, superior capacities, and a high, clear notion of their art; they were not equal, but they mutually restrained and supported one another; each breathed ardor into those around him; throughout all their acting, they showed themselves decided and correct. You soon felt that Serlo was the soul of the whole: as an individual, he appeared to much advantage. A merry humor, a measured vivacity, a settled feeling of propriety, combined with a great gift of imitation, were to be observed in him the moment he appeared upon the stage. The inward contentment of his being seemed to spread itself over all that looked on him; and the intellectual style in which he could so easily and gracefully express the finest shadings of his part, excited more delight, as he could conceal the art which, by long-continued practice, he had made his own.

Aurelia, his sister, was not inferior: she obtained still greater approbation; for she touched the souls of the audience, which he had it in his power to exhilarate and amuse.

After a few days had passed pleasantly enough, Aurelia sent to inquire for our friend. He hastened to her: she was lying on a sofa; she seemed to be suffering from headache; her whole frame had visibly a feverish movement. Her eye lighted up as she noticed Wilhelm. "Pardon me!" she cried, as he entered: "the trust you have inspired me with has made me weak. Till now I have contrived to bear up against my woes in secret; nay, they gave me strength and consolation: but now, I know not how it is, you have loosened the bands of silence.

You will now, even against your will, take part in the battle I am fighting with myself!"

Wilhelm answered her in kind and obliging terms. He declared that her image and her sorrows had not ceased to hover in his thoughts; that he longed for her confidence, and devoted himself to be her friend.

While he spoke, his eyes were attracted to the boy, who sat before her on the floor, and was busy rattling a multitude of playthings. This child, as Philina had observed, might be about three years of age; and Wilhelm now conceived how that giddy creature, seldom elevated in her phraseology, had likened it to the sun. For its cheerful eyes and full countenance were shaded by the finest golden locks, which flowed round in copious curls; dark, slender, softly bending eyebrows showed themselves upon a brow of dazzling whiteness; and the living tinge of health was glancing on its cheeks. "Sit by me," said Aurelia: "you are looking at the happy child with admiration; in truth, I took it into my arms with joy; I keep it carefully; yet, by it, too, I can measure the extent of my sufferings; for they seldom let me feel the worth of such a gift.

W.S.

"Allow me," she continued, "to speak to you about myself and my destiny; for I have it much at heart that you should not misunderstand me. I thought I should have a few calm instants; and, accordingly, I sent for you. You are now here, and the thread of my narrative is lost.

"'One more forsaken woman in the world!' you will say. You are a man. You are thinking, 'What a noise she makes, the fool, about a necessary evil; which, certainly as death, awaits a woman, when such is the fidelity of men!' O my friend! if my fate were common, I would gladly undergo a common evil; but it is so singular! why cannot I present it to you in a mirror, — why not command some one to tell it you? Oh! had I, had I been seduced, surprised, and afterwards forsaken, there would then still be comfort in despair; but I am far more miserable. I have been my own deceiver; I have wittingly betrayed myself; and this, this, is what shall never be forgiven me."

"With noble feelings, such as yours," said Wilhelm, "you cannot be entirely unhappy."

"And do you know to what I am indebted for my feelings?" asked Aurelia. "To the worst education that ever threatened to contaminate a girl; to the vilest examples for misleading the senses and inclinations.

"My mother dying early, the fairest years of my youth were spent with an aunt, whose principle it was to despise the laws of decency. She resigned herself headlong to every impulse, careless whether the object of it proved her tyrant or her slave, so she might forget herself in wild enjoyment.

"By children, with the pure, clear vision of innocence, what ideas of men were necessarily formed in such a scene! How stolid, brutally bold, importunate, unmannerly, was every one she allured! How sated, empty, insolent, and insipid, as soon as he had had his wishes gratified! I have seen this woman live, for years, humbled under the control of the meanest creatures. What incidents she had to undergo! With what a front she contrived to accommodate herself to her destiny; nay, with how much skill, to wear these shameful fetters!

"It was thus, my friend, that I became acquainted with your sex; and deeply did I hate it, when, as I imagined, I observed that even tolerable men, in their conduct to ours, appeared to renounce every honest feeling, of which nature might otherwise have made them capable.

"Unhappily, moreover, on such occasions, a multitude of painful discoveries about my own sex were forced upon me; and, in truth, I was then wiser, as a girl of sixteen, than I now am, now that I scarcely understand myself. Why are we so wise when young, — so wise, and ever growing less so?"

The boy began to make a noise: Aurelia became impatient, and rang. An old woman came to take him out. "Hast thou toothache still?" said Aurelia to the crone, whose face was wrapped in cloth. "Unsufferable," said the other, with a muffled voice, then lifted the boy, who seemed to like going with her, and carried him away.

Scarcely was he gone, when Aurelia began bitterly to weep. "I am good for nothing," cried she, "but lamenting and complaining; and I feel ashamed to lie before you like a miserable worm. My recollection is already fled: I can relate no more." She faltered, and was silent. Her friend, unwilling to reply with a commonplace, and unable to reply with any thing particularly applicable, pressed her hand, and looked at her for some time without speaking. Thus embarrassed, he at length took up a book, which he noticed lying on the table before him: it was Shakspeare's works, and open at "Hamlet."

Serlo, at this moment entering, inquired about his sister, and, looking in the book which our friend had hold of, cried, "So you are again at 'Hamlet'? Very good! Many doubts have arisen in me, which seem not a little to impair the canonical aspect of the play as you would have it viewed. The English themselves have admitted that its chief interest concludes with the third act; the last two lagging sorrily on, and scarcely uniting with the rest: and certainly about the end it seems to stand stock-still."

"It is very possible," said Wilhelm, "that some individuals of a nation, which has so many masterpieces to feel proud of, may be led by prejudice and narrowness of mind to form false judgments; but this cannot hinder us from looking with our own eyes, and doing justice where we see it due. I am very far from censuring the plan of 'Hamlet': on the other hand, I believe there never was a grander one invented; nay, it is not invented, it is real."

"How do you demonstrate that?" inquired Serlo.

"I will not demonstrate any thing," said Wilhelm: "I will merely show you what my own conceptions of it are."

Aurelia raised herself from her cushion, leaned upon her hand, and looked at Wilhelm, who, with the firmest assurance that he was in the right, went on as follows: "It pleases us, it flatters us, to see a hero acting on his own strength, loving and hating at the bidding of his heart, undertaking and completing, casting every obstacle aside, and attaining some great end. Poets and historians would willingly persuade us that so proud a lot may fall to man. In 'Hamlet' we are taught another lesson: the hero is without a plan, but the play is full of plan. Here we have no villain punished on some self-conceived and rigidly accomplished scheme of vengeance: a horrid deed is done; it rolls along with all its consequences, dragging with it even the guiltless: the guilty perpetrator would, as it seems, evade the abyss made ready for him; yet he plunges in, at the very point by which he thinks he shall escape, and happily complete his course.

"For it is the property of crime to extend its mischief over innocence, as it is of virtue to extend its blessings over many that deserve them not; while frequently the author of the one or of the other is not punished or rewarded at all. Here in this play of ours, how strange! The Pit of darkness sends its spirit and demands revenge: in vain! All circumstances tend one way, and hurry to revenge: in vain! Neither earthly nor infernal thing may bring about what is reserved for Fate alone. The hour of judgment comes; the wicked falls with the good; one race is mowed away, that another may spring up."

After a pause, in which they looked at one another, Serlo said, "You pay no great compliment to Providence, in thus exalting Shakspeare; and besides, it appears to me, that for the honor of your poet, as others for the honor of Providence, you ascribe to him an object and a plan such as he himself had never thought of."

"LET ME also put a question," said Aurelia. "I have looked at Ophelia's part again: I am contented with it, and confident, that, under certain circumstances, I could play it. But tell me, should not the poet have furnished the insane maiden with another sort of songs? Could not some fragments out of melancholy ballads be selected for this purpose! Why put double meanings and lascivious insipidities in the mouth of this noble-minded girl?"

"Dear friend," said Wilhelm, "even here I cannot yield you one iota. In these singularities, in this apparent impropriety, a deep sense is hid. Do we not understand from the very first what the mind of the good, soft-hearted girl was busied with? Silently she lived within herself, yet she scarce concealed her wishes, her longing: the tones of desire were in secret ringing through her soul; and how often may she have attempted, like an unskilful nurse, to lull her senses to repose with songs which only kept them more awake? But at last, when her self-command is altogether gone, when the secrets of her heart are hovering on her tongue, that tongue betrays her; and in the innocence of insanity she solaces herself, unmindful of king or queen, with the echo of her loose and well-beloved songs, — 'To-morrow is Saint Valentine's Day,' and 'By Gis and by Saint Charity.'"

He had not finished speaking, when all at once an extraordinary scene took place before him, which he could not in any way explain.

Serlo had walked once or twice up and down the room, without evincing any special object. On a sudden, he stepped forward to Aurelia's dressing-table, caught hastily at something that was lying there, and hastened to the door with his booty. No sooner did Aurelia notice this, than, springing up, she threw herself in his way, laid hold of him with boundless vehemence, and had dexterity enough to clutch an end of the article he was carrying off. They struggled and wrestled with great obstinacy, twisted and threw each other sharply round; he laughed; she exerted all her strength; and as Wilhelm hastened towards them, to separate and soothe them, Aurelia sprang aside with a naked dagger in her hand; while Serlo cast the scabbard,

which had staid with him, angrily upon the floor. Wilhelm started
back astonished; and his dumb wonder seemed to ask the cause why
so violent a strife, about so strange an implement, had taken place
between them.

"You shall judge betwixt us," said the brother. "What business
she with sharp steel? Do but look at it. That dagger is unfit for any
actress, — point like a needle's, edge like a razor's! What good's the
farce? Passionate as she is, she will one day chance to do herself a
mischief. I have a heart's hatred at such singularities: a serious thought
of that sort is insane, and so dangerous a plaything is not in taste."

"I have it back!" exclaimed Aurelia, and held the polished blade
aloft: "I will now keep my faithful friend more carefully. Pardon me,"
she cried, and kissed the steel, "that I have so neglected thee."

Serlo was like to grow seriously angry. "Take it as thou wilt,
brother," she continued: "how knowest thou but, under this form, a
precious talisman may have been given me, so that, in extreme need, I

may find help and counsel in it? Must all be hurtful that looks dangerous?"

"Such talk without a meaning might drive one mad," said Serlo, and left the room with suppressed indignation. Aurelia put the dagger carefully into its sheath, and placed it in her bosom. "Let us now resume the conversation which our foolish brother has disturbed," said she, as Wilhelm was beginning to put questions on the subject of this quarrel.

"I must admit your picture of Ophelia to be just," continued she; "I cannot now misunderstand the object of the poet: I must pity; though, as you paint her, I shall rather pity her than sympathize with her. But allow me here to offer a remark, which in these few days you have frequently suggested to me. I observe with admiration the correct, keen, penetrating glance with which you judge of poetry, especially dramatic poetry: the deepest abysses of invention are not hidden from you, the finest touches of representation cannot escape you. Without ever having viewed the objects in nature, you recognize the truth of their images: there seems, as it were, a presentiment of all the universe to lie in you, which by the harmonious touch of poetry is awakened and unfolded. For in truth," continued she, "from without, you receive not much: I have scarcely seen a person that so little knew, so totally misknew, the people he lived with, as you do. Allow me to say it; in hearing you expound the mysteries of Shakspeare, one would think you had just descended from a synod of the gods, and had listened there while they were taking counsel how to form men; in seeing you transact with your fellows, I could imagine you to be the first large-born child of the Creation, standing agape, and gazing with strange wonderment and edifying good nature at lions and apes and sheep and elephants, and true-heartedly addressing them as your equals, simply because they were there, and in motion like yourself."

"The feeling of my ignorance in this respect," said Wilhelm, "often gives me pain; and I should thank you, worthy friend, if you would help me to get a little better insight into life. From youth, I have been accustomed to direct the eyes of my spirit inwards rather than outwards; and hence it is very natural, that, to a certain extent, I should be acquainted with man, while of men I have not the smallest knowledge."

"In truth," said Aurelia, "I at first suspected, that, in giving such accounts of the people whom you sent to my brother, you meant to make sport of us: when I compared your letters with the merits of these persons, it seemed very strange."

Aurelia's remarks, well founded as they might be, and willing as our friend was to confess himself deficient in this matter, carried with them something painful, nay, offensive, to him; so that he grew silent, and retired within himself, partly to avoid showing any irritated feeling, partly to search his mind for the truth or error of the charge.

"Let not this alarm you," said Aurelia: "the light of the understanding it is always in our power to reach, but this fulness of the heart no one can give us. If you are destined for an artist, you cannot long enough retain the dim-sightedness and innocence of which I speak; it is the beautiful hull upon the young bud; woe to us if we are forced too soon to burst it! Surely it were well, if we never knew what the people are for whom we work and study.

"Oh! I, too, was in that happy case, when I first betrod the stage, with the loftiest opinion of myself and of my nation. What a people, in my fancy, were the Germans! what a people might they yet become! I addressed this people, raised above them by a little joinery, separated from them by a row of lamps, whose glancing and vapor threw an indistinctness over every thing before me. How welcome was the tumult of applause which sounded to me from the crowd! how gratefully did I accept the present offered me unanimously by so many hands! For a time I rocked myself in these ideas: I affected the multitude, and was again affected by them. With my public I was on the fairest footing: I imagined that I felt a perfect harmony betwixt us, and that on each occasion I beheld before me the best and noblest of the land.

"Unhappily it was not the actress alone that inspired these friends of the stage with interest: they likewise made pretensions to the young and lively girl. They gave me to understand, in terms distinct enough, that my duty was, not only to excite emotion in them, but to share it with them personally. This, unluckily, was not my business: I wished to elevate their minds; but, to what they called their hearts, I had not the slightest claim. Yet now men of all ranks, ages, and characters, by turns afflicted me with their addresses; and it did seem hard that I could not, like an honest young woman, shut my door, and spare myself such a quantity of labor.

"The men appeared, for most part, much the same as I had been accustomed to about my aunt; and here again I should have felt disgusted with them, had not their peculiarities and insipidities amused me. As I was compelled to see them, in the theatre, in open places, in my house, I formed the project of spying out their follies; and my brother helped me with alacrity to execute it. And if you reflect, that up from the whisking shopman and the conceited merchant's son, to the polished, calculating man of the world, the bold soldier, and the impetuous prince, all in succession passed in review before me, each in his way endeavoring to found his small romance, you will pardon me if I conceived that I had gained some acquaintance with my nation.

"The fantastically dizened student; the awkward, humbly proud man of letters; the sleek-fed, gouty canon; the solemn, heedful man of office; the heavy country-baron; the smirking, vapid courtier; the young, erring parson; the cool as well as the quick and sharply speculating merchant, — all these I have seen in motion; and I swear to you, that there were few among them fitted to inspire me even with a sentiment of toleration: on the contrary, I felt it altogether irksome to collect, with tedium and annoyance, the suffrages of fools; to pocket those applauses in detail, which in their accumulated state had so delighted me, which in the gross I had appropriated with such pleasure.

"If I expected a rational compliment upon my acting, if I hoped that they would praise an author whom I valued, they were sure to make one empty observation on the back of another, and to name some vapid play in which they wished to see me act. If I listened in their company, to hear if some noble, brilliant, witty thought had met with a response among them, and would re-appear from some of them in proper season, it was rare that I could catch an echo of it. An error that had happened, a mispronunciation, a provincialism of some actor, such were the weighty points by which they held fast, beyond which they could not pass. I knew not, in the end, to what hand I should turn: themselves they thought too clever to be entertained; and me they imagined they were well entertaining, if they romped and made noise enough about me. I began very cordially to despise them all: I felt as if the whole nation had, on purpose, deputed these people to debase it in my eyes. They appeared to me so clownish, so ill-bred, so wretchedly instructed, so void of pleasing qualities, so tasteless, I frequently exclaimed, 'No German can buckle his shoes, till he has learned to do it of some foreign nation!'

"You perceive how blind, how unjust and splenetic, I was; and, the longer it lasted, my spleen increased. I might have killed myself with these things, but I fell into the contrary extreme: I married, or, rather, let myself be married. My brother, who had undertaken to conduct the theatre, wished much to have a helper. His choice lighted on a young man, who was not offensive to me, who wanted all that my brother had, — genius, vivacity, spirit, and impetuosity of mind; but who also in return had all my brother wanted, — love of order, diligence, and precious gifts in housekeeping and management of money.

"He became my husband, I know not how: we lived together, I do not well know why. Suffice it to say, our affairs went prosperously forward. We drew a large income: of this my brother's activity was the cause. We lived with a moderate expenditure, and that was the merit of my husband. I thought no more about world or nation. With the world I had nothing to participate: my idea of the nation had faded away. When I entered on the scene, I did so that I might subsist: I opened my lips because I durst not continue silent, because I had come out to speak.

"Yet let me do the matter justice. I had altogether given myself up to the disposal of my brother. His objects were, applause and money; for, between ourselves, he has no dislike to hear his own praises; and his outlay is always great. I no longer played according to my own feeling, to my own conviction, but as he directed me; and, if I did it to his satisfaction, I was content. He steered entirely by the caprices of the public. Money flowed upon us: he could live according to his humor, and so we had good times with him.

"Thus had I fallen into a dull, handicraft routine. I spun out my days without joy or sympathy. My marriage was childless, and not of long continuance. My husband grew sick; his strength was visibly decaying; anxiety for him interrupted my general indifference. It was at this time that I formed an acquaintance which opened a new life for me, — a new and quicker one, for it will soon be done."

She kept silence for a time, and then continued, "All at once my prattling humor alters: I have not the courage to go on. Let me rest a little. You shall not go, till you have learned the whole extent of my misfortune. Meanwhile, call in Mignon, and ask her what she wants."

The child had more than once been in the room, while Aurelia and our friend were talking. As they spoke lower on her entrance, she had glided out again, and was now sitting quietly in the hall, and waiting. Being bid return, she brought a book with her, which its form and binding showed to be a small geographical atlas. She had seen some maps, for the first time, at the parson's house, with great astonishment; had asked him many questions, and informed herself so far as possible about them. Her desire to learn seemed much excited by this new branch of knowledge. She now earnestly requested Wilhelm to purchase her the book; saying she had pawned her large silver buckle with the print-seller for it, and wished to have back the pledge to-morrow morning, as this evening it was late. Her request was granted; and she then began repeating several things she had already learned; at the same time, in her own way, making many very strange inquiries. Here again one might observe, that, with a mighty effort, she could comprehend but little and laboriously. So likewise was it with her writing, at which she still kept busied. She yet spoke very broken German: it was only when she opened her mouth to sing, when she touched her cithern, that she seemed to be employing an organ by which, in some degree, the workings of her mind could be disclosed and communicated.

Since we are at present on the subject, we may also mention the perplexity which Wilhelm had of late experienced from certain parts of her procedure. When she came or went, wished him good-morning or good-night, she clasped him so firmly in her arms, and kissed him with such ardor, that often the violence of this expanding nature gave him serious fears. The spasmodic vivacity of her demeanor seemed daily to increase: her whole being moved in a restless stillness. She would never be without some piece of packthread to twist in her hands, some napkin to tie in knots, some paper or wood to chew. All her sports seemed but the channels which drained off some inward violent commotion. The only thing that seemed to cause her any cheerfulness was being near the boy Felix, with whom she could go on in a very dainty manner.

Aurelia, after a little rest, being now ready to explain to her friend a matter which lay very near her heart, grew impatient at the little girl's delay, and signified that she must go, — a hint, however, which the latter did not take; and at last, when nothing else would do, they sent her off expressly and against her will.

"Now or never," said Aurelia, "must I tell you the remainder of my story. Were my tenderly beloved and unjust friend but a few miles distant, I would say to you, 'Mount on horseback, seek by some means to get acquainted with him: on returning, you will certainly forgive me, and pity me with all your heart.' As it is, I can only tell you with words how amiable he was, and how much I loved him.

"It was at the critical season, when care for the illness of my husband had depressed my spirits, that I first became acquainted with this stranger. He had just returned from America, where, in company with some Frenchmen, he had served with much distinction under the colors of the United States.

"He addressed me with an easy dignity, a frank kindliness: he spoke about myself, my state, my acting, like an old acquaintance, so affectionately and distinctly, that now for the first time I enjoyed the pleasure of perceiving my existence reflected in the being of another. His judgments were just, though not severe; penetrating, yet not void of love. He showed no harshness: his pleasantry was courteous, with all his humor. He seemed accustomed to success with women; this excited my attention: he was never in the least importunate or flattering; this put me off my guard.

"In the town, he had intercourse with few: he was often on horseback, visiting his many friends in the neighborhood, and managing the business of his house. On returning, he would frequently alight at my apartments; he treated my ever-ailing husband with warm attention, he procured him mitigation of his sickness by a good physician. And, taking part in all that interested me, he allowed me to take part in all that interested him. He told me the history of his campaigns: he spoke of his invincible attachment to military life, of his family relations, of his present business. He kept no secret from me; he displayed to me his inmost thoughts, allowed me to behold the most secret corners of his soul: I became acquainted with his passions and his capabilities. It was the first time in my life that I enjoyed a cordial, intellectual intercourse with any living creature. I was attracted by him, borne along by him, before I thought about inquiring how it stood with me.

"Meanwhile I lost my husband, nearly just as I had taken him. The burden of theatrical affairs now fell entirely on me. My brother, not to be surpassed on the stage, was never good for any thing in economical concerns: I took the charge of all, at the same time studying my parts with greater diligence than ever. I again played as of old, — nay, with new life, with quite another force. It was by reason of my friend, it was on his account, that I did so; yet my success was not always best when I knew him to be present. Once or twice he listened to me unobserved, and how pleasantly his unexpected applauses surprised me you may conceive.

"Certainly I am a strange creature. In every part I played, it seemed as if I had been speaking it in praise of him; for that was the temper of my heart, the words might be any thing they pleased. Did I understand him to be present in the audience, I durst not venture to speak out with all my force; just as I would not press my love or praise on him to his face: was he absent, I had then free scope; I did my best, with a certain peacefulness, with a contentment not to be described. Applause once more delighted me; and, when I charmed the people, I longed to call down among them, 'This you owe to him!'

"Yes: my relation to the public, to the nation, had been altered by a wonder. On a sudden they again appeared to me in the most favorable light: I felt astonished at my former blindness.

" 'How foolish,' said I often to myself, 'was it to revile a nation, — foolish, simply because it was a nation. Is it necessary, is it possible, that individual men should generally interest us much? Not at all! The only question is, whether in the great mass there exists a sufficient quantity of talent, force, and capability, which lucky circumstances may develop, which men of lofty minds may direct upon a common object.' I now rejoiced in discovering so little prominent originality among my countrymen; I rejoiced that they disdained not to accept of guidance from without; I rejoiced that they had found a leader.

"Lothario, — allow me to designate my friend by this, his first name, which I loved, — Lothario had always presented the Germans to my mind on the side of valor, and shown me, that, when well commanded, there was no braver nation on the face of the earth; and I felt ashamed that I had never thought of this, the first quality of a people. History was known to him: he was in connection and correspondence with the most distinguished persons of the age. Young as he was, his eye was open to the budding youthhood of his native country, to the silent labors of active and busy men in so many provinces of art. He afforded me a glimpse of Germany, — what it was and what it might be; and I blushed at having formed my judgment of a nation from the motley crowd that squeeze into the wardrobe of a theatre. He made me look upon it as a duty that I too, in my own department, should be true, spirited, enlivening. I now felt as if inspired every time I stepped upon the boards. Mediocre passages grew golden in my mouth: had any poet been at hand to support me adequately, I might have produced the most astonishing effects.

"So lived the young widow for a series of months. He could not do without me, and I felt exceedingly unhappy when he staid away. He showed me the letters he received from his relations, from his amiable sister. He took an interest in the smallest circumstance that concerned me: more complete, more intimate, no union ever was than ours. The name of love was not mentioned. He went and came, came and went. And now, my friend, it is high time that you, too, should go."

CHAPTER SEVENTEEN

WILHELM could put off no longer the visiting of his commercial friends. He proceeded to their place with some anxiety, knowing he should there find letters from his people. He dreaded the reproofs which these would of course contain: it seemed likely also that notice had been given to his trading correspondents, concerning the perplexities and fears which his late silence had occasioned. After such a series of knightly adventures, he recoiled from the school-boy aspect in which he must appear: he proposed within his mind to act with an air of sternness and defiance, and thus hide his embarrassment.

To his great wonder and contentment, however, all went off very easily and well. In the vast, stirring, busy counting-room, the men had scarcely time to seek him out his packet: his delay was but alluded to in passing. And on opening the letters of his father, and his friend Werner, he found them all of very innocent contents. His father, in hopes of an extensive journal, the keeping of which he had strongly recommended to his son at parting, giving him also a tabulary scheme for that purpose, seemed pretty well pacified about the silence of the first period; complaining only of a certain enigmatical obscurity in the last and only letter despatched, as we have seen, from the castle of the count. Werner joked in his way; told merry anecdotes, facetious burgh-news; and requested intelligence of friends and acquaintances, whom Wilhelm, in the large trading-city, would now meet with in great numbers. Our friend, extremely pleased at getting off so well, answered without loss of a moment, in some very cheerful letters; promising his father a copious journal of his travels, with all the re-quired geographical, statistical, and mercantile remarks. He had seen much on his journey, he said, and hoped to make a tolerably large manuscript out of these materials. He did not observe that he was almost in the same case as he had once experienced before, when he assembled an audience and lit his lamps to represent a play which was not written, still less got by heart. Accordingly, so soon as he com-menced the actual work of composition, he became aware that he had much to say about emotions and thoughts, and many experiences of the heart and spirit, but not a word concerning outward objects, on which, as he now discovered, he had not bestowed the least attention.

In this embarrassment, the acquisitions of his friend Laertes came very seasonably to his aid. Custom had united these young people, unlike one another as they were; and Laertes, with all his fail-ings and singularities, was actually an interesting man. Endowed with warm and pleasurable senses, he might have reached old age without reflecting for a moment on his situation. But his ill-fortune and his sickness had robbed him of the pure feelings of youth, and opened for him instead of it a view into the transitoriness, the discontinuity, of man's existence. Hence had arisen a humorous, flighty, rhapsodical way of thinking about all things, or, rather, of uttering the immediate impressions they produced on him. He did not like to be alone; he strolled about all the coffee-houses and *tables-d'hôte*; and, when he did stay at home, books of travels were his favorite, nay, his only, kind of reading. Having lately found a large circulating library, he had been enabled to content his taste in this respect to the full; and erelong half the world was figuring in his faithful memory.

It was easy for him, therefore, to speak comfort to his friend, when the latter had disclosed his utter lack of matter for the narrative so solemnly promised by him. "Now is the time for a stroke of art," said Laertes, "that shall have no fellow!

"Has not Germany been travelled over, cruised over, walked, crept, and flown over, repeatedly from end to end? And has not every German traveller the royal privilege of drawing from the public a repayment of the great or small expenses he may have incurred while travelling? Give me your route previous to our meeting: the rest I know already. I will find you helps and sources of information: of miles that were never measured, populations that were never counted, we shall give them plenty. The revenues of provinces we will take from almanacs and tables, which, as all men know, are the most authentic documents. On these we will ground our political discussions: we shall not fail in side-glances at the ruling powers. One or two princes we will paint as true fathers of their country, that we may gain more ready credence in our allegations against others. If we do not travel through the residence of any noted man, we shall take care to meet such persons at the inn, and make them utter the most foolish stuff to us. Particularly, let us not forget to insert, with all its graces and sentiments, some love-story with a pastoral bar-maid. I tell you, it shall be a composition which will not only fill father and mother with delight, but which booksellers themselves shall gladly pay you current money for."

They went accordingly to work, and both of them found pleasure in their labor. Wilhelm, in the mean time, frequenting the play at night, and conversing with Serlo and Aurelia by day, experienced the greatest satisfaction, and was daily more and more expanding his ideas, which had been too long revolving in the same narrow circle.

IT WAS NOT without deep interest that he became acquainted with the history of Serlo's career. Piecemeal he learned it; for it was not the fashion of that extraordinary man to be confidential, or to speak of any thing connectively. He had been, one may say, born and suckled in the theatre. While yet literally an infant, he had been produced upon the stage to move spectators, merely by his presence; for authors even then were acquainted with this natural and very guiltless mode of doing so. Thus his first "Father!" or "Mother!" in favorite pieces, procured him approbation, before he understood what was meant by that clapping of the hands. In the character of Cupid, he more than once descended, with terror, in his flying-gear; as harlequin, he used to issue from the egg; and, as a little chimney-sweep, to play the sharpest tricks.

Unhappily, the plaudits of these glancing nights were too bitterly repaid by sufferings in the intervening seasons. His father was persuaded that the minds of children could be kept awake and steadfast by no other means than blows: hence, in the studying of any part, he used to thrash him at stated periods, not because the boy was awkward, but that he might become more certainly and constantly expert. It was thus that in former times, while putting down a landmark, people were accustomed to bestow a hearty drubbing on the children who had followed them; and these, it was supposed, would recollect the place exactly to the latest day of their lives. Serlo waxed in stature, and showed the finest capabilities of spirit and of body, — in particular, an admirable pliancy at once in his thoughts, looks, movements, and gestures. His gift of imitation was beyond belief. When still a boy, he could mimic persons, so that you would think you saw them; though in form, age, and disposition, they might be entirely unlike him, and unlike each other. Nor with all this, did he want the knack of suiting himself to his circumstances, and picking out his way in life. Accordingly, so soon as he had grown in some degree acquainted with his strength, he very naturally eloped from his father, who, as the boy's understanding and dexterity increased, still thought it needful to forward their perfection by the harshest treatment.

Happy was the wild boy, now roaming free about the world, where his feats of waggery never failed to secure him a good reception. His lucky star first led him in the Christmas season to a cloister, where the friar, whose business it had been to arrange processions, and to entertain the Christian community by spiritual masquerades, having just died, Serlo was welcomed as a helping angel. On the instant he took up the part of Gabriel in the Annunciation, and did not by any means displease the pretty girl, who, acting the Virgin, very gracefully received his most obliging kiss, with external humility and inward pride. In their Mysteries, he continued to perform the most important parts, and thought himself no slender personage, when at last, in the character of Martyr, he was mocked of the world, and beaten, and fixed upon the cross.

Some pagan soldiers had, on this occasion, played their parts a little *too* naturally. To be avenged on these heathen in the proper style, he took care at the Day of Judgment to have them decked out in gaudy clothes as emperors and kings; and at that moment when they, exceedingly contented with their situation, were about to take precedence of the rest in heaven, as they had done on earth, he, on a sudden, rushed upon them in the shape of the Devil; and to the cordial edification of all the beggars and spectators, having thoroughly curried them with his oven-fork, he pushed them without mercy back into the chasm, where, in the midst of waving flame, they met with the sorriest welcome.

He was acute enough, however, to perceive that these crowned heads might feel offended at such bold procedure, and perhaps forget the reverence due to his privileged office of Accuser and Turnkey. So in all silence, before the Millennium commenced, he withdrew, and betook him to a neighboring town. Here a society of persons, denominated Children of Joy, received him with open arms. They were a set of clever, strong-headed, lively geniuses, who saw well enough that the sum of our existence, divided by reason, never gives an integer number, but that a surprising fraction is always left behind. At stated times, to get rid of this fraction, which impedes, and, if it is diffused over all the mass of our conduct, endangers us, was the object of the Children of Joy. For one day a week each of them in succession was a fool on purpose; and, during this, he in his turn exhibited to ridicule, in allegorical representations, whatever folly he had noticed in himself, or the rest, throughout the other six. This practice might be somewhat ruder than that constant training, in the course of which a man of ordinary morals is accustomed to observe, to warn, to punish, himself daily; but it was also merrier and surer. For as no Child of Joy concealed his bosom-folly, so he and those about him held it for simply what it was; whereas, on the other plan, by the help of self-deception, this same bosom-folly often gains the head authority within, and binds down reason to a secret servitude, at the very time when reason fondly hopes that she has long since chased it out of doors. The mask of folly circulated round in this society; and each member was allowed, in his particular day, to decorate and characterize it with his own attributes or those of others. At the time of Carnival, they assumed the greatest freedom, vying with the clergy in attempts to instruct and entertain the multitude. Their solemn figurative processions of Virtues and Vices, Arts and Sciences, Quarters of the World, and Seasons of the Year, bodied forth a number of conceptions, and gave images of many distant objects to the people, and hence were not without their use; while, on the other hand, the mummeries of the priesthood tended but to strengthen a tasteless superstition, already strong enough.

Here again young Serlo was altogether in his element. Invention in its strictest sense, it is true, he had not; but, on the other hand, he had the most consummate skill in employing what he found before him, in ordering it, and shadowing it forth. His roguish turns, his gift of mimicry; his biting wit, which at least one day weekly he might use with entire freedom, even against his benefactors, — made him precious, or rather indispensable, to the whole society.

Yet his restless mind soon drove him from this favorable scene to other quarters of his country, where other means of instruction awaited him. He came into the polished, but also barren, part of Germany, where, in worshipping the good and the beautiful, there is indeed no want of truth, but frequently a grievous want of spirit. His masks would here do nothing for him: he had now to aim at working on the heart and mind. For short periods, he attached himself to small or to extensive companies of actors, and marked, on these occasions, what were the distinctive properties, both of the pieces and the players. The monotony which then reigned on the German theatre, the mawkish sound and cadence of their Alexandrines, the flat and yet distorted dialogue, the shallowness and commonness of these undisguised preachers of morality, he was not long in comprehending, or in seizing, at the same time, what little there was that moved and pleased.

Not only single parts in the current pieces, but the pieces themselves, remained easily and wholly in his memory, and, along with them, the special tone of any player who had represented them with approbation. At length, in the course of his rambles, his money being altogether done, the project struck him of acting entire pieces by himself, especially in villages and noblemen's houses, and thus in all places making sure at least of entertainment and lodging. In any tavern, any room, or any garden, he would accordingly at once set up his theatre: with a roguish seriousness and a show of enthusiasm, he would contrive to gain the imaginations of his audience, to deceive their senses, and before their eyes to make an old press into a tower, or a fan into a dagger. His youthful warmth supplied the place of deep feeling: his vehemence seemed strength, and his flattery tenderness. Such of the spectators as already knew a theatre, he put in mind of all that they had seen and heard: in the rest he awakened a presentiment of something wonderful, and a wish to be more acquainted with it. What produced an effect in one place he did not fail to repeat in others; and his mind overflowed with a wicked pleasure when, by the same means, on the spur of the moment, he could make gulls of all the world.

His spirit was lively, brisk, and unimpeded: by frequently repeating parts and pieces, he improved very fast. Erelong he could recite and play with more conformity to the sense than the models whom he had at first imitated. Proceeding thus, he arrived by degrees at playing naturally; though he did not cease to feign. He seemed transported, yet he lay in wait for the effect; and his greatest pride was in moving, by successive touches, the passions of men. The mad trade he drove did itself soon force him to proceed with a certain moderation; and thus, partly by constraint, partly by instinct, he learned the art of which so few players seemed to have a notion, — the art of being frugal in the use of voice and gestures.

Thus did he contrive to tame, and to inspire with interest for him, even rude and unfriendly men. Being always contented with food and shelter; thankfully accepting presents of any kind as readily as money, which latter, when he reckoned that he had enough of it, he frequently declined, — he became a general favorite, was sent about from one to another with recommendatory letters; and thus he wandered many a day from castle to castle, exciting much festivity, enjoying much, and meeting in his travels with the most agreeable and curious adventures.

With such inward coldness of temper, he could not properly be said to love any one; with such clearness of vision, he could respect no one; in fact, he never looked beyond the external peculiarities of men; and he merely carried their characters in his mimical collection. Yet withal, his selfishness was keenly wounded if he did not please every one and call forth universal applause. How this might be attained, he had studied in the course of time so accurately, and so sharpened his sense of the matter, that not only on the stage, but also in common life, he no longer could do otherwise than flatter and deceive. And thus did his disposition, his talent, and his way of life, work reciprocally on each other, till by this means he had imperceptibly been formed into a perfect actor. Nay, by a mode of action and re-action, which is quite natural, though it seems paradoxical, his recitation, declamation, and gesture improved, by critical discernment and practice, to a high degree of truth, ease, and frankness; while, in his life and intercourse with men, he seemed to grow continually more secret, artful, or even hypocritical and constrained.

Of his fortunes and adventures we perhaps shall speak in another place: it is enough to remark at present, that in later times, when he had become a man of circumstance, in possession of a distinct reputation, and of a very good, though not entirely secure, employment and rank, he was wont, in conversation, partly in the way of irony, partly of mockery, in a delicate style, to act the sophist, and thus to destroy almost all serious discussion. This kind of speech he seemed peculiarly fond of using towards Wilhelm, particularly when the latter took a fancy, as often happened, for introducing any of his general and theoretical disquisitions. Yet still they liked well to be together: with such different modes of thinking, the conversation could not fail to be lively. Wilhelm always wished to deduce every thing from abstract ideas which he had arrived at: he wanted to have art viewed in all its connections as a whole. He wanted to promulgate and fix down universal laws; to settle what was right, beautiful, and good: in short, he treated all things in a serious manner. Serlo, on the other hand, took up the matter very lightly: never answering directly to any question, he would contrive, by some anecdote or laughable turn, to give the finest and most satisfactory illustrations, and thus to instruct his audience while he made them merry.

WHILE our friend was in this way living very happily, Melina and the rest were in quite a different case. Wilhelm they haunted like evil spirits; and not only by their presence, but frequently by rueful faces and bitter words, they caused him many a sorry moment. Serlo had not admitted them to the most trifling part, far less held out to them any hope of a permanent engagement; and yet he had contrived, by degrees, to get acquainted with the capabilities of every one of them. Whenever any actors were assembled in leisure hours about him, he was wont to make them read, and frequently to read along with them. On such occasions he took plays which were by and by to be acted, which for a long time had remained unacted; and generally by portions. In like manner, after any first representation, he caused such passages to be repeated as he had any thing to say upon: by which means he sharpened the discernment of his actors, and strengthened their certainty of hitting the proper point. And as a person of slender but correct understanding may produce more agreeable effect on others than a perplexed and unpurified genius, he would frequently exalt men of mediocre talents, by the clear views which he imperceptibly afforded them, to a wonderful extent of power. Nor was it an unimportant item in his scheme, that he likewise had poems read before him in their meetings; for by these he nourished in his people the feeling of that charm which a well-pronounced rhythm is calculated to awaken in the soul: whereas, in other companies, those prose compositions were already getting introduced for which any tyro was adequate.

On occasions such as these, he had contrived to make himself acquainted with the new-come players: he had decided what they were, and what they might be, and silently made up his mind to take advantage of their talents, in a revolution which was now threatening his own company. For a while he let the matter rest; declined every one of Wilhelm's intercessions for his comrades, with a shrug of the shoulders; till at last he saw his time, and altogether unexpectedly made the proposal to our friend, "that he himself should come upon the stage; that, on this condition, the others, too, might be admitted."

"These people must not be so useless as you formerly described them," answered Wilhelm, "if they can now be all received at once; and I suppose their talents would remain the same without me as with me."

Under seal of secrecy, Serlo hereupon explained his situation, — how his first actor was giving hints about a rise of salary at the renewal of their contract; how he himself did not incline conceding this, the rather as the individual in question was no longer in such favor with the public; how, if he dismissed him, a whole train would follow; whereby, it was true, his company would lose some good, but likewise some indifferent, actors. He then showed Wilhelm what he hoped to gain in him, in Laertes, Old Boisterous, and even Frau Melina. Nay, he promised to procure for the silly Pedant himself, in the character of Jew, minister, but chiefly of villain, a decided approbation.

Wilhelm faltered; the proposal fluttered him; he knew not what to say. That he might say something, he rejoined, with a deep-drawn breath, "You speak very graciously about the good you find and hope to find in us; but how is it with our weak points, which certainly have not escaped your penetration?"

"These," said Serlo, "by diligence, practice, and reflection, we shall soon make strong points. Though you are yet but freshmen and bunglers, there is not one among you that does not warrant expectation more or less: for, so far as I can judge, no stick, properly so called, is to be met with in the company; and your stick is the only person that can never be improved, never bent or guided, whether it be self-conceit, stupidity, or hypochondria, that renders him unpliant."

The manager next stated, in a few words, the terms he meant to offer; requested Wilhelm to determine soon, and left him in no small perplexity.

In the marvellous composition of those travels, which he had at first engaged with, as it were, in jest, and was now carrying on in conjunction with Laertes, his mind had by degrees grown more attentive to the circumstances and the every-day life of the actual world than it was wont. He now first understood the object of his father in so earnestly recommending him to keep a journal. He now, for the first time, felt how pleasant and how useful it might be to become participator in so many trades and requisitions, and to take a hand in diffusing activity and life into the deepest nooks of the mountains and forests of Europe. The busy trading-town in which he was; the unrest of Laertes, who dragged him about to examine every thing, — afforded him the most impressive image of a mighty centre, from which every thing was flowing out, to which every thing was coming back; and it was the first time that his spirit, in contemplating this species of activity, had really felt delight. At such a juncture Serlo's offer had been made him; had again awakened his desires, his tendencies, his faith in a natural talent, and again brought into mind his solemn obligation to his helpless comrades.

"Here standest thou once more," said he within himself, "at the Parting of the Ways, between the two women who appeared before thee in thy youth. The one no longer looks so pitiful as then, nor does the other look so glorious. To obey the one, or to obey the other, thou art not without a kind of inward calling: outward reasons are on both sides strong enough, and to decide appears to thee impossible. Thou wishest some preponderancy from without would fix thy choice; and yet, if thou consider well, it is external circumstances only that inspire thee with a wish to trade, to gather, to possess; whilst it is thy inmost want that has created, that has nourished, the desire still further to unfold and perfect what endowments soever for the beautiful and good, be they mental or bodily, may lie within thee. And ought I not to honor Fate, which, without furtherance of mine, has led me hither to the goal of all my wishes? Has not all that I, in old times, meditated and forecast, now happened accidentally, and without my co-operation? Singular enough! We seem to be so intimate with nothing as we are with our own wishes and hopes, which have long been kept and cherished in our hearts; yet when they meet us, when they, as it were, press forward to us, then we know them not, then we recoil from them. All that, since the hapless night which severed me from Mariana, I have but allowed myself to dream, now stands before me, entreating my acceptance. Hither I intended to escape by flight; hither I am softly guided: with Serlo I meant to seek a place; he now seeks me, and offers me conditions, which, as a beginner, I could not have looked for. Was it, then, mere love to Mariana that bound me to the stage? Or love to art that bound me to her? Was that prospect, that outlet, which the theatre presented me, nothing but the project of a restless, disorderly, and disobedient boy, wishing to lead a life which the customs of the civic world would not admit of? Or was all this different, worthier, purer? If so, what moved thee to alter the persuasions of that period? Hast thou not hitherto, even without knowing it, pursued thy plan? Is not the concluding step still further to be justified, now that no side-purposes combine with it; now that in making it thou mayest fulfil a solemn promise, and nobly free thyself from a heavy debt?"

All that could affect his heart and his imagination was now moving, and conflicting in the liveliest strife within him. The thought that he might retain Mignon, that he should not need to put away the harper, was not an inconsiderable item in the balance, which, however, had not ceased to waver to the one and to the other side, when he went, as he was wont, to see his friend Aurelia.

CHAPTER TWENTY

SHE WAS LYING on the sofa: she seemed quiet. "Do you think you will be fit to act to-morrow?" he inquired. "Oh, yes!" cried she with vivacity: "you know there is nothing to prevent me. If I but knew a way," continued she "to rid myself of those applauses! The people mean it well, but they will kill me. Last night I thought my very heart would break! Once, when I used to please myself, I could endure this gladly: when I had studied long, and well prepared myself, it gave me joy to hear the sound, 'It has succeeded!' pealing back to me from every corner. But now I speak not what I like, nor as I like; I am swept along, I get confused, I scarce know what I do; and the impression I make is far deeper. The applause grows louder; and I think, Did you but know what charms you! These dark, vague, vehement tones of passion move you, force you to admire; and you feel not that they are the cries of agony, wrung from the miserable being whom you praise.

"I learned my part this morning: just now I have been repeating it and trying it. I am tired, broken down; and to-morrow I must do the same. To-morrow evening is the play. Thus do I drag myself to and fro: it is wearisome to rise, it is wearisome to go to bed. All moves within me in an everlasting circle. Then come their dreary consolations, and present themselves before me; and I cast them out, and execrate them. I will not surrender, not surrender to necessity: why should that be necessary which crushes me to the dust? Might it not be otherwise? I am paying the penalty of being born a German: it is the nature of the Germans, that they bear heavily on every thing, that every thing bears heavily on them."

"O my friend!" cried Wilhelm, "could you cease to whet the dagger wherewith you are ever wounding me! Does nothing, then, remain for you? Are your youth, your form, your health, your talents, nothing? Having lost one blessing, without blame of yours, must you throw all the others after it? Is that also necessary?"

She was silent for a few moments, and then burst forth, "I know well, it is a waste of time, nothing but a waste of time, this love! What might not, should not, I have done! And now it is all vanished into air. I am a poor, wretched, lovelorn creature, — lovelorn, that is all! Oh, have compassion on me! God knows I am poor and wretched!"

She sank in thought: then, after a brief pause, she exclaimed with violence, "You are accustomed to have all things fly into your arms. No: you cannot feel, no man is qualified to feel, the worth of a woman that can reverence herself. By all the holy angels, by all the images of blessedness, which a pure and kindly heart creates, there is not any thing more heavenly than the soul of a woman giving herself to the man she loves!

"We are cold, proud, high, clear-sighted, wise, while we deserve the name of women; and all these qualities we lay down at your feet, the instant that we love, that we hope to excite a return of love. Oh, how have I cast away my whole existence wittingly and willingly! But now will I despair, purposely despair. There is no drop of blood within me but shall suffer, no fibre that I will not punish. Smile, I pray you; laugh at this theatrical display of passion."

Wilhelm was far enough from any tendency to laugh. This horrible, half-natural, half-factitious condition of his friend afflicted him but too deeply. He sympathized in the tortures of that racking misery: his thoughts were wandering in painful perplexities, his blood was in a feverish tumult.

She had risen, and was walking up and down the room. "I see before me," she exclaimed, "all manner of reasons why I should not love him. I know he is not worthy of it; I turn my mind aside, this way and that; I seize upon whatever business I can find. At one time I take up a part, though I have not to play it; at another, I begin to practise old ones, though I know them through and through; I practise them more diligently, more minutely, — I toil and toil at them. My friend, my confidant, what a horrid task is it to tear away one's thoughts from one's self! My reason suffers, my brain is racked and strained: to save myself from madness, I again admit the feeling that I love him. Yes, I love him, I love him!" cried she, with a shower of tears: "I love him, I shall die loving him!"

He took her by the hand, and entreated her in the most earnest manner not to waste herself in such self-torments. "Oh! it seems hard," said he, "that not only so much that is impossible should be denied us, but so much also that is possible! It was not your lot to meet with a faithful heart that would have formed your perfect happiness. It was mine to fix the welfare of my life upon a hapless creature, whom, by the weight of my fidelity, I drew to the bottom like a reed, perhaps even broke in pieces!"

He had told Aurelia of his intercourse with Mariana, and could therefore now refer to it. She looked him intently in the face, and asked, "Can you say that you never yet betrayed a woman, that you never tried with thoughtless gallantry, with false asseverations, with cajoling oaths, to wheedle favor from her?"

"I can," said Wilhelm, "and indeed without much vanity: my life has been so simple and sequestered, I have had but few enticements to attempt such things. And what a warning, my beautiful, my noble, friend, is this melancholy state in which I see you! Accept of me a vow, which is suited to my heart; which, under the emotion you have caused me, has settled into words and shape, and will be hallowed by the hour in which I utter it. Each transitory inclination I will study to withstand, and even the most earnest I will keep within my bosom: no woman shall receive an acknowledgment of love from my lips to whom I cannot consecrate my life!"

She looked at him with a wild indifference, and drew back some steps as he offered her his hand. " 'Tis of no moment!" cried she: "so many women's tears, more or fewer; the ocean will not swell by reason of them. And yet," continued she, "among thousands, one woman saved; that still is something: among thousands, one honest man discovered; this is not to be refused. Do you know, then, what you promise?"

"I know it," answered Wilhelm, with a smile, and holding out his hand.

"I accept it, then," said she, and made a movement with her right hand, as if meaning to take hold of his; but instantly she darted it into her pocket, pulled out her dagger quick as lightning, and scored with the edge and point of it across his hand. He hastily drew it back, but the blood was already running down.

"One must mark you men rather sharply, if one would have you take heed," cried she, with a wild mirth, which soon passed into a quick assiduity. She took her handkerchief, and bound his hand with it to stanch the fast-flowing blood. "Forgive a half-crazed being," cried she, "and regret not these few drops of blood. I am appeased. I am again myself. On my knees will I crave your pardon: leave me the comfort of healing you."

She ran to her drawer, brought lint, with other apparatus, stanched the blood, and viewed the wound attentively. It went across the palm, close under the thumb, dividing the life-line, and running towards the little finger. She bound it up in silence, with a significant, reflective look. He asked, once or twice, "Aurelia, how could you hurt your friend?"

"Hush!" replied she, laying her finger on her mouth: "Hush!"

Book Five

CHAPTER ONE

THUS WILHELM, to his pair of former wounds, which were yet scarcely healed, had now got the accession of a third, which was fresh and not a little disagreeable. Aurelia would not suffer him to call a surgeon: she dressed the hand with all manner of strange speeches, saws, and ceremonies, and so placed him in a very painful situation. Yet not he alone, but all persons who came near her, suffered by her restlessness and singularity, and no one more than little Felix. This stirring child was exceedingly impatient under such oppression, and showed himself still naughtier the more she censured and instructed him.

He delighted in some practices which commonly are thought bad habits, and in which she would not by any means indulge him. He would drink, for example, rather from the bottle than the glass; and his food seemed visibly to have a better relish when eaten from the bowl than from the plate. Such ill-breeding was not overlooked: if he left the door standing open, or slammed it to; if, when bid do any thing, he stood stock-still, or ran off violently, — he was sure to have a long lecture inflicted on him for the fault. Yet he showed no symptoms of improvement from this training: on the other hand, his affection for Aurelia seemed daily to diminish; there was nothing tender in his tone when he called her mother; whereas he passionately clung to the old nurse, who let him have his will in every thing.

But she likewise had of late become so sick, that they had at last been obliged to take her from the house into a quiet lodging; and Felix would have been entirely alone if Mignon had not, like a kindly guardian spirit, come to help him. The two children talked together, and amused each other in the prettiest style. She taught him little songs; and he, having an excellent memory, frequently recited them, to the surprise of those about him. She attempted also to explain her maps to him. With these she was still very busy, though she did not seem to take the fittest method. For, in studying countries, she appeared to care little about any other point than whether they were cold or warm. Of the north and south poles, of the horrid ice which reigns there, and of the increasing heat the farther one retires from them, she could give a very clear account. When any one was travelling, she merely asked whether he was going northward or southward, and strove to find his route in her little charts. Especially when Wilhelm spoke of travelling, she was all attention, and seemed vexed when any thing occurred to change the subject. Though she could not be prevailed upon to undertake a part, or even to enter the theatre when any play was acting, yet she willingly and zealously committed many odes and songs to memory; and by unexpectedly, and, as it were, on the spur of the moment, reciting some such poem, generally of the earnest and solemn kind, she would often cause astonishment in every one.

Serlo, accustomed to regard with favor every trace of opening talent, encouraged her in such performances; but what pleased him most in Mignon was her sprightly, various, and often even mirthful, singing. By means of a similar gift, the harper likewise had acquired his favor.

Without himself possessing genius for music, or playing on any instrument, Serlo could rightly prize the value of the art: he failed not, as often as he could, to enjoy this pleasure, which cannot be compared with any other. He held a concert once a week; and now, with Mignon, the harper, and Laertes, who was not unskilful on the violin, he had formed a very curious domestic band.

He was wont to say, "Men are so inclined to content themselves with what is commonest; the spirit and the senses so easily grow dead to the impressions of the beautiful and perfect, — that every one should study, by all methods, to nourish in his mind the faculty of feeling these things. For no man can bear to be entirely deprived of such enjoyments: it is only because they are not used to taste of what is excellent that the generality of people take delight in silly and insipid things, provided they be new. For this reason," he would add, "one ought, every day at least, to hear a little song, read a good poem, see a fine picture, and, if it were possible, to speak a few reasonable words." With such a turn of thought in Serlo, which in some degree was natural to him, the persons who frequented his society could scarcely be in want of pleasant conversation.

It was in the midst of these instructive entertainments, that Wilhelm one day received a letter sealed in black. Werner's hand betokened mournful news; and our friend was not a little shocked when, opening the sheet, he found it to contain the tidings of his father's death, conveyed in a very few words. After a short and sudden illness, he had parted from the world, leaving his domestic affairs in the best possible order.

This unlooked-for intelligence struck Wilhelm to the heart. He deeply felt how careless and negligent we often are of friends and relations while they inhabit with us this terrestrial sojourn; and how we first repent of our insensibility when the fair union, at least for this side of time, is finally cut asunder. His grief for the early death of this honest parent was mitigated only by the feeling that he had loved but little in the world, and the conviction that he had enjoyed but little.

Wilhelm's thoughts soon turned to his own predicament, and he felt himself extremely discomposed. A person can scarcely be put into a more dangerous position, than when external circumstances have produced some striking change in his condition, without his manner of feeling and of thinking having undergone any preparation for it. There is, then, an epoch without epoch; and the contradiction which arises is the greater the less the person feels that he is not trained for this new manner of existence.

Wilhelm saw himself in freedom, at a moment when he could not yet be at one with himself. His thoughts were noble, his motives pure, his purposes were not to be despised. All this he could, with some degree of confidence, acknowledge to himself: but he had of late been frequently enough compelled to notice, that experience was sadly wanting to him; and hence, on the experience of others, and on the results which they deduced from it, he put a value far beyond its real one, and thus led himself still deeper into error. What he wanted, he conceived he might most readily acquire if he undertook to collect and retain whatever memorable thought he should meet with in reading or in conversation. He accordingly recorded his own or other men's opinions, nay, wrote whole dialogues, when they chanced to interest him. But unhappily by this means he held fast the false no less firmly than the true; he dwelt far too long on one idea, particularly when it was of an aphoristic shape; and thus he left his natural mode of thought and action, and frequently took foreign lights for his loadstars. Aurelia's bitterness, and Laertes's cold contempt for men, warped his judgment oftener than they should have done: but no one, in his present case, would have been so dangerous as Jarno, a man whose clear intellect could form a just and rigorous decision about present things, but who erred, withal, in enunciating these particular decisions with a kind of universal application; whereas, in truth, the judgments of the understanding are properly of force but once, and that in the strictest cases, and become inaccurate in some degree when applied to any other.

Thus Wilhelm, striving to become consistent with himself, was deviating farther and farther from wholesome consistency; and this confusion made it easier for his passions to employ their whole artillery against him, and thus still farther to perplex his views of duty.

Serlo did not fail to take advantage of the late tidings; and in truth he daily had more reason to be anxious about some fresh arrangement of his people. Either he must soon renew his old contracts, — a measure he was not specially fond of; for several of his actors, who reckoned themselves indispensable, were growing more and more arrogant, — or else he must entirely new-model and re-form his company; which plan he looked upon as preferable.

Though he did not personally importune our friend, he set

Aurelia and Philina on him; and the other wanderers, longing for some kind of settlement, on their side, gave Wilhelm not a moment's rest; so that he stood hesitating in his choice, in no slight embarrassment till he should decide. Who would have thought that a letter of Werner's, written with quite different views, should have forced him on resolving? We shall omit the introduction, and give the rest of it with little alteration.

CHAPTER TWO

"IT WAS, therefore, and it always must be, right for every one, on any opportunity, to follow his vocation and exhibit his activity. Scarcely had the good old man been gone a quarter of an hour, when every thing in the house began moving by a different plan than his. Friends, acquaintances, relations, crowded forward, especially all sorts of people who on such occasions use to gain any thing. They fetched and carried, they counted, wrote, and reckoned; some brought wine and meat, others ate and drank; and none seemed busier than the women getting out the mournings.

"Such being the case, thou wilt not blame me, that, in this emergency, I likewise thought of *my* advantage. I made myself as active, and as helpful to thy sister, as I could, and, so soon as it was any way decorous, signified to her that it had now become our business to accelerate a union which our parents, in their too great circumspection, had hitherto postponed.

"Do not suppose, however, that it came into our heads to take possession of that monstrous empty house. We are more modest and more rational. Thou shalt hear our plan; thy sister, so soon as we are married, comes to our house; and thy mother comes along with her. 'How can that be?' thou wilt say: 'you have scarcely room for yourselves in that hampered nest.' There lies the art of it, my friend. Good packing renders all things possible: thou wouldst not believe what space one finds when one desires to occupy but little. The large house we shall sell, — an opportunity occurs for this; and the money we shall draw for it will produce a hundred-fold.

"I hope this meets thy views: I hope also thou hast not inherited the smallest particle of those unprofitable tastes for which thy father and thy grandfather were noted. The latter placed his greatest happiness in having about him a multitude of dull-looking works of art, which no one, I may well say no one, could enjoy with him: the former lived in a stately pomp, which he suffered no one to enjoy with him. We mean to manage otherwise, and we expect thy approbation.

"It is true, I myself in all the house have no place whatever but the stool before my writing-desk; and I see not clearly where they will be able to put a cradle down: but, in return, the room we shall have out of doors will be the more abundant. Coffee-houses and clubs for the husband, walks and drives for the wife, and pleasant country jaunts for both. But the chief advantage in our plan is, that, the round table being now completely filled, our father cannot ask his friends to dinner, who, the more he strove to entertain them, used to laugh at him the more.

"Now no superfluity for us! Not too much furniture and apparatus; no coach, no horses! Nothing but money, and the liberty, day after day, to do what you like in reason. No wardrobe; still the best and newest on your back: the man may wear his coat till it is done; the wife may truck her gown, the moment it is going out of fashion. There is nothing so unsufferable to me as an old huckster's shop of property. If you would offer me a jewel, on condition of my wearing it daily on my finger, I would not accept it; for how can one conceive any pleasure in a dead capital? This, then, is my confession of faith: To transact your business, to make money, to be merry with your household; and about the rest of the earth to trouble yourself no farther than where you can be of service to it.

"But ere now thou art saying, 'And, pray, what is to be done with me in this sage plan of yours? Where shall I find shelter when you have sold my own house, and not the smallest room remains in yours?'

"This is, in truth, the main point, brother; and in this, too, I shall have it in my power to serve thee. But first I must present the just tribute of my praise for time so spent as thine has been.

"Tell me, how hast thou within a few weeks become so skilled in every useful, interesting object? Highly as I thought of thy powers, I did not reckon such attention and such diligence among the number. Thy journal shows us with what profit thou art travelling. The description of the iron and the copper forges is exquisite: it evinces a complete knowledge of the subject. I myself was once there; but my relation, compared with this, has but a very bungled look. The whole letter on the linen-trade is full of information: the remarks on commercial competition are at once just and striking. In one or two places, there are errors in addition, which indeed are very pardonable.

"But what most delights my father and myself, is thy thorough knowledge of husbandry, and the improvement of landed property. We have thoughts of purchasing a large estate, at present under sequestration, in a very fruitful district. For paying it, we mean to use the money realized by the sale of the house; another portion we shall borrow; a portion may remain unpaid. And we count on thee for going thither, and superintending the improvement of it; by which means, before many years are passed, the land, to speak in moderation, will have risen above a third in value. We shall then bring it to the market again, seek out a larger piece, improve and trade as formerly. For all this thou art the man. Our pens, meanwhile, will not lie idle here; and so by and by we shall rise to be enviable people.

"For the present, fare thee well! Enjoy life on thy journey, and turn thy face wherever thou canst find contentment and advantage. For the next half-year we shall not need thee; thou canst look about thee in the world as thou pleasest: a judicious person finds his best instruction in his travels. Farewell! I rejoice at being connected with thee so closely by relation, and now united with thee in the spirit of activity."

Well as this letter might be penned, and full of economical truths as it was, Wilhelm felt displeased with it for more than one reason. The praise bestowed on him for his pretended statistical, technological, and rural knowledge was a silent reprimand. The ideal of the happiness of civic life, which his worthy brother sketched, by no means charmed him: on the contrary, a secret spirit of contradiction dragged him forcibly the other way. He convinced himself, that, except on the stage, he could nowhere find that mental culture which he longed to give himself: he seemed to grow the more decided in his resolution, the more strongly Werner, without knowing it, opposed him. Thus assailed, he collected all his arguments together, and buttressed his opinions in his mind the more carefully, the more desirable he reckoned it to show them in a favorable light to Werner; and in this manner he produced an answer, which also we insert.

CHAPTER THREE

"THY LETTER is so well written, and so prudently and wisely conceived, that no objection can be made to it. Only thou must pardon me, when I declare that one may think, maintain, and do directly the reverse, and yet be in the right as well as thou. Thy mode of being and imagining appears to turn on boundless acquisition, and a light, mirthful manner of enjoyment: I need scarcely tell thee, that in all this I find little that can charm me.

"First, however, I am sorry to admit, that my journal is none of mine. Under the pressure of necessity, and to satisfy my father, it was patched together by a friend's help, out of many books: and though in words I know the objects it relates to, and more of the like sort, I by no means understand them, or can occupy myself about them. What good were it for me to manufacture perfect iron while my own breast is full of dross? What would it stead me to put properties of land in order, while I am at variance with myself?

"To speak it in a word, the cultivation of my individual self, here as I am, has from my youth upwards been constantly though dimly my wish and my purpose. The same intention I still cherish, but the means of realizing it are now grown somewhat clearer. I have seen more of life than thou believest, and profited more by it also.

Give some attention, then, to what I say, though it should not altogether tally with thy own opinions.

"Had I been a nobleman, our dispute would soon have been decided; but, being a simple burgher, I must take a path of my own: and I fear it may be difficult to make thee understand me. I know not how it is in foreign countries, but in Germany, a universal, and, if I may say so, personal, cultivation is beyond the reach of any one except a nobleman. A burgher may acquire merit; by excessive efforts he may even educate his mind; but his personal qualities are lost, or worse than lost, let him struggle as he will. Since the nobleman, frequenting the society of the most polished, is compelled to give himself a polished manner; since this manner, neither door nor gate being shut against him, grows at last an unconstrained one; since, in court or camp, his figure, his person, are a part of his possessions, and, it may be, the most necessary part, — he has reason enough to put some value on them, and to show that he puts some. A certain stately grace in common things, a sort of gay elegance in earnest and important ones, becomes him well; for it shows him to be everywhere in equilibrium. He is a public person; and the more cultivated his movements, the more sonorous his voice, the more staid and measured his whole being is, the more perfect is he. If to high and low, to friends and relations, he continues still the same, then nothing can be said against him, none may wish him otherwise. His coldness must be reckoned clearness of head, his dissimulation prudence. If he can rule himself externally at every moment of his life, no man has aught more to demand of him; and, whatever else there may be in him or about him, capacities, talents, wealth, all seem gifts of supererogation.

"Now, imagine any burgher offering ever to pretend to these advantages, he will utterly fail, and the more completely, the greater inclination and the more endowments nature may have given him for that mode of being.

"Since, in common life, the nobleman is hampered by no limits; since kings, or kinglike figures, do not differ from him, — he can everywhere advance with a silent consciousness, as if before his equals: everywhere he is entitled to press forward, whereas nothing more beseems the burgher than the quiet feeling of the limits that are drawn round him. The burgher may not ask himself, 'What art thou?' He can only ask, 'What hast thou? What discernment, knowledge, talent, wealth?' If the nobleman, merely by his personal carriage, offers all that can be asked of him, the burgher by his personal carriage offers nothing, and can offer nothing. The former has a right to *seem*: the latter is compelled to *be*, and what he aims at seeming becomes ludicrous and tasteless. The former does and makes, the latter but effects and procures; he must cultivate some single gifts in order to be useful; and it is beforehand settled, that, in his manner of existence, there is no harmony, and can be none, since he is bound to make himself of use in one department, and so has to relinquish all the others.

"Perhaps the reason of this difference is not the usurpation of the nobles, and the submission of the burghers, but the constitution of society itself. Whether it will ever alter, and how, is to me of small importance: my present business is to meet my own case, as matters actually stand; to consider by what means I may save myself, and reach the object which I cannot live in peace without.

"Now, this harmonious cultivation of my nature, which has been denied me by birth, is exactly what I most long for. Since leaving thee, I have gained much by voluntary practice: I have laid aside much of my wonted embarrassment, and can bear myself in very tolerable style. My speech and voice I have likewise been attending to; and I may say, without much vanity, that in society I do not cause displeasure. But I will not conceal from thee, that my inclination to become a public person, and to please and influence in a larger circle, is daily growing more insuperable. With this, there is combined my love for poetry and all that is related to it; and the necessity I feel to cultivate my mental faculties and tastes, that so, in this enjoyment henceforth indispensable, I may esteem as good the good alone, as beautiful the beautiful alone. Thou seest well, that for me all this is nowhere to be met with except upon the stage; that in this element alone can I effect and cultivate myself according to my wishes. On the boards a polished man appears in his splendor with personal accomplishments, just as he does so in the upper classes of society; body and spirit must advance with equal steps in all his studies; and there I shall have it in my power at once to be and seem as well as anywhere. If I further long for solid occupations, we have there mechanical vexations in abundance: I may give my patience daily exercise.

"Dispute not with me on this subject; for, ere thou writest, the step is taken. In compliance with the ruling prejudices, I will change my name; as, indeed, that of Meister, or Master, does not suit me. Farewell! Our fortune is in good hands: on that subject I shall not disturb myself. What I need I will, as occasion calls, require from thee: it will not be much, for I hope my art will be sufficient to maintain me."

Scarcely was the letter sent away, when our friend made good his words. To the great surprise of Serlo and the rest, he at once declared that he was ready to become an actor, and bind himself by a contract on reasonable terms. With regard to these they were soon agreed; for Serlo had before made offers, with which Wilhelm and his comrades had good reason to be satisfied. The whole of that unlucky company, wherewith we have had so long to occupy ourselves, was now at once received; and, except perhaps Laertes, not a member of it showed the smallest thankfulness to Wilhelm. As they had entreated without confidence, so they accepted without gratitude. Most of them preferred ascribing their appointment to the influence of Philina, and directed their thanks to her. Meanwhile the contracts had been written out, and were now a-signing. At the moment when our friend was subscribing his assumed designation, by some inexplicable concatenation of ideas, there arose before his mind's eye the image of that green in the forest where he lay wounded in Philina's lap. The lovely Amazon came riding on her gray palfrey from the bushes of the wood: she approached him and dismounted. Her humane anxiety made her come and go: at length she stood before him. The white surtout fell down from her shoulders: her countenance, her form, began to glance in radiance; and she vanished from his sight. He wrote his name mechanically only, not knowing what he did, and felt not, till after he had signed, that Mignon was standing at his side, was holding by his arm, and had softly tried to stop him, and pull back his hand.

ONE of the conditions under which our friend had gone upon the stage was not acceded to by Serlo without some limitations. Wilhelm had required that "Hamlet" should be played entire and unmutilated: the other had agreed to this strange stipulation, in so far as it was *possible*. On this point they had many a contest; for as to what was possible or not possible, and what parts of the piece could be omitted without mutilating it, the two were of very different opinions.

Wilhelm was still in that happy season when one cannot understand how, in the woman one loves, in the writer one honors, there should be any thing defective. The feeling they excite in us is so entire, so accordant with itself, that we cannot help attributing the same perfect harmony to the objects themselves. Serlo again was willing to discriminate, perhaps too willing: his acute understanding could usually discern in any work of art nothing but a more or less *imperfect* whole. He thought, that as pieces usually stood, there was little reason to be chary about meddling with them; that of course Shakspeare, and particularly "Hamlet," would need to suffer much curtailment.

But, when Serlo talked of separating the wheat from the chaff, Wilhelm would not hear of it. "It is not chaff and wheat together," said he: "it is a trunk with boughs, twigs, leaves, buds, blossoms, and fruit. Is not the one there with the others, and by means of them?" To which Serlo would reply, that people did not bring a whole tree upon the table; that the artist was required to present his guests with silver apples in platters of silver. They exhausted their invention in similitudes, and their opinions seemed still farther to diverge.

Our friend was on the borders of despair, when on one occasion, after much debating, Serlo counselled him to take the simple plan, — to make a brief resolution, to grasp his pen, to peruse the tragedy; dashing out whatever would not answer, compressing several personages into one: and if he was not skilled in such proceedings, or had not heart enough for going through with them, he might leave the task to him, the manager, who would engage to make short work with it.

"That is not our bargain," answered Wilhelm. "How can you, with all your taste, show so much levity?"

"My friend," cried Serlo, "you yourself will erelong feel it and show it. I know too well how shocking such a mode of treating works is : perhaps it never was allowed on any theatre till now. But where, indeed, was ever one so slighted as ours? Authors force us on this wretched clipping system, and the public tolerates it. How many pieces have we, pray, which do not overstep the measure of our numbers, of our decorations and theatrical machinery, of the proper time, of the fit alternation of dialogue, and the physical strength of the actor? And yet we are to play, and play, and constantly give novelties. Ought we not to profit by our privilege, then, since we accomplish just as much by mutilated works as by entire ones? It is the public itself that grants the privilege. Few Germans, perhaps few men of any modern nation, have a proper sense of an æsthetic whole : — they praise and blame by passages; they are charmed by passages; and who has greater reason to rejoice at this than actors, since the stage is ever but a patched and piece-work matter?"

"Is!" cried Wilhelm; "but *must* it ever be so? Must every thing that is continue? Convince me not that you are right, for no power on earth should force me to abide by any contract which I had concluded with the grossest misconceptions."

Serlo gave a merry turn to the business, and persuaded Wilhelm to review once more the many conversations they had had together about "Hamlet," and himself to invent some means of properly reforming the piece.

After a few days, which he had spent alone, our friend returned with a cheerful look. "I am much mistaken," cried he, "if I have not now discovered how the whole is to be managed: nay, I am convinced that Shakspeare himself would have arranged it so, had not his mind been too exclusively directed to the ruling interest, and perhaps misled by the novels which furnished him with his materials."

"Let us hear," said Serlo, placing himself with an air of solemnity upon the sofa: "I will listen calmly, but judge with rigor."

"I am not afraid of you," said Wilhelm: "only hear me. In the composition of this play, after the most accurate investigation and the most mature reflection, I distinguish two classes of objects. The first are the grand internal relations of the persons and events, the powerful effects which arise from the characters and proceedings of the main figures: these, I hold, are individually excellent; and the order in which they are presented cannot be improved. No kind of interference must be suffered to destroy them, or even essentially to change their form. These are the things which stamp themselves deep into the soul, which all men long to see, which no one dares to meddle with. Accordingly, I understand, they have almost wholly been retained in all our German theatres. But our countrymen have erred, in my opinion, with regard to the second class of objects, which may be observed in this tragedy: I allude to the external relations of the persons, whereby they are brought from place to place, or combined in various ways, by certain accidental incidents. These they have looked upon as very unimportant; have spoken of them only in passing, or left them out altogether. Now, indeed, it must be owned, these threads are slack and slender; yet they run through the entire piece, and bind together much that would otherwise fall asunder, and does actually fall asunder, when you cut them off, and imagine you have done enough and more, if you have left the ends hanging.

"Among these external relations I include the disturbances in Norway, the war with young Fortinbras, the embassy to his uncle, the settling of that feud, the march of young Fortinbras to Poland, and his coming back at the end; of the same sort are Horatio's return from Wittenberg, Hamlet's wish to go thither, the journey of Laertes to France, his return, the despatch of Hamlet into England, his capture by pirates, the death of the two courtiers by the letter which they carried. All these circumstances and events would be very fit for expanding and lengthening a novel; but here they injure exceedingly the unity of the piece, particularly as the hero has no plan, and are, in consequence, entirely out of place."

"For once in the right!" cried Serlo.

"Do not interrupt me," answered Wilhelm: "perhaps you will not always think me right. These errors are like temporary props of an edifice: they must not be removed till we have built a firm wall in their stead. My project, therefore, is, not at all to change those first-mentioned grand situations, or at least as much as possible to spare them, both collectively and individually; but with respect to these external, single, dissipated, and dissipating motives, to cast them all at once away, and substitute a solitary one instead of them."

"And this?" inquired Serlo, springing up from his recumbent posture.

"It lies in the piece itself," answered Wilhelm, "only I employ it rightly. There are disturbances in Norway. You shall hear my plan, and try it:

"After the death of Hamlet the father, the Norwegians, lately conquered, grow unruly. The viceroy of that country sends his son, Horatio, an old school-friend of Hamlet's, and distinguished above every other for his bravery and prudence, to Denmark, to press forward the equipment of the fleet, which, under the new luxurious king, proceeds but slowly. Horatio has known the former king, having fought in his battles, having even stood in favor with him, — a circumstance by which the first ghost-scene will be nothing injured. The new sovereign gives Horatio audience, and sends Laertes into Norway with intelligence that the fleet will soon arrive; whilst Horatio is commissioned to accelerate the preparation of it: and the Queen, on the other hand, will not consent that Hamlet, as he wishes, should go to sea along with him."

"Heaven be praised!" cried Serlo: "we shall now get rid of Wittenberg and the university, which was always a sorry piece of business. I think your idea extremely good; for, except these two distant objects, Norway and the fleet, the spectator will not be required to *fancy* any thing: the rest he will *see*, the rest takes place before him; whereas, his imagination, on the other plan, was hunted over all the world."

"You easily perceive," said Wilhelm, "how I shall contrive to keep the other parts together. When Hamlet tells Horatio of his uncle's crime, Horatio counsels him to go to Norway in his company, to secure the affections of the army, and return in warlike force. Hamlet also is becoming dangerous to the King and Queen; they find no readier method of deliverance, than to send him in the fleet, with Rosencrantz and Guildenstern to be spies upon him; and, as Laertes in the mean time comes from France, they determine that this youth, exasperated even to murder, shall go after him. Unfavorable winds detain the fleet: Hamlet returns; for his wandering through the churchyard, perhaps some lucky motive may be thought of; his meeting with Laertes in Ophelia's grave is a grand moment, which he must not part with. After this, the King resolves that it is better to get quit of Hamlet on the spot: the festival of his departure, the pretended reconcilement with Laertes, are now solemnized; on which occasion knightly sports are held, and Laertes fights with Hamlet. Without the four corpses, I cannot end the play: no one must survive. The right of popular election now again comes in force; and Hamlet, while dying, gives his vote to Horatio."

"Quick! quick!" said Serlo, "sit down and work the play: your plan has my entire approbation; only let not your zeal evaporate."

CHAPTER FIVE

WILHELM HAD already been for some time busied with translating "Hamlet"; making use, as he labored, of Wieland's spirited performance, through which he had first become acquainted with Shakspeare. What had been omitted in Wieland's work he replaced, and had secured a complete version, at the very time when Serlo and he were pretty well agreed about the way of treating it. He now began, according to his plan, to cut out and insert, to separate and unite, to alter, and often to restore; for, satisfied as he was with his own conception, it still appeared to him as if, in executing it, he were but spoiling the original.

When all was finished, he read his work to Serlo and the rest. They declared themselves exceedingly contented with it: Serlo, in particular, made many flattering observations.

"You have felt very justly," said he, among other things, "that some external circumstances must accompany this play, but that they must be simpler than those which the great poet has employed. What takes place without the theatre, what the spectator does not see, but must imagine, is like a background, in front of which the acting figures move. Your large and simple prospect of the fleet and Norway will do much to improve the play; if this were altogether taken from it, we should have but a family scene remaining; and the great idea, that here a kingly house, by internal crimes and incongruities, goes down to ruin, would not be presented with its proper dignity. But if the former background were left standing, so manifold, so fluctuating and confused, it would hurt the impression of the figures."

Wilhelm again took Shakspeare's part; alleging that he wrote for islanders, for Englishmen, who generally, in the distance, were accustomed to see little else than ships and voyages, the coast of France and privateers; and thus what perplexed and distracted others was to them quite natural.

Serlo assented; and both were of opinion, that, as the play was now to be produced upon the German stage, this more serious and simple background was the best adapted for the German mind.

The parts had been distributed before : Serlo undertook Polonius; Aurelia, Ophelia; Laertes was already designated by his name; a young, thick-set, jolly new-comer was to be Horatio; the King and Ghost alone occasioned some perplexity, for both of these no one but Old Boisterous remaining. Serlo proposed to make the Pedant, King; but against this our friend protested in the strongest terms. They could resolve on nothing.

Wilhelm had also allowed both Rosencrantz and Guildenstern to continue in his play. "Why not compress them into one?" said Serlo. "This abbreviation will not cost you much."

"Heaven keep me from all such curtailments!" answered Wilhelm : "they destroy at once the sense and the effect. What these two persons are and do it is impossible to represent by one. In such small matters we discover Shakspeare's greatness. These soft approaches, this smirking and bowing, this assenting, wheedling, flattering, this whisking agility, this wagging of the tail, this allness and emptiness, this legal knavery, this ineptitude and insipidity, — how can they be expressed by a single man? There ought to be at least a dozen of these people, if they could be had; for it is only in society that they are any thing; they are society itself; and Shakspeare showed no little wisdom and discernment in bringing in a pair of them. Besides, I need them as a couple that may be contrasted with the single, noble, excellent Horatio."

"I understand you," answered Serlo, "and we can arrange it. One of them we shall hand over to Elmira, Old Boisterous's eldest daughter: it will all be right, if they look well enough; and I will deck and trim the puppets so that it shall be first-rate fun to behold them."

Philina was rejoicing not a little, that she had to act the Duchess in the small subordinate play. "I will show it so natural," cried she, "how you wed a second husband, without loss of time, when you have loved the first immensely. I mean to win the loudest plaudits, and every man shall wish to be the third."

Aurelia gave a frown: her spleen against Philina was increasing every day.

" 'Tis a pity, I declare," said Serlo, "that we have no ballet; else you should dance me a *pas de deux* with your first, and then another with your second husband, — and the first might dance himself to sleep by the measure; and your bits of feet and ankles would look so pretty, tripping to and fro upon the side stage."

"Of my ankles you do not know much," replied she pertly; "and as to my bits of feet," cried she, hastily reaching below the table, pulling off her slippers, and holding them together out to Serlo, "here are the cases of them; and I challenge you to find me more dainty ones."

"I was in earnest," said he, looking at the elegant half-shoes. "In truth, one does not often meet with any thing so dainty."

They were of Parisian workmanship: Philina had received them as a present from the countess, a lady whose foot was celebrated for its beauty.

"A charming thing!" cried Serlo: "my heart leaps at the sight of them."

"What gallant throbs!" replied Philina.

"There is nothing in the world beyond a pair of slippers," said he, "of such pretty manufacture, in their proper time and place, when" —

Philina took her slippers from his hands, crying, "You have squeezed them all! They are far too wide for me!" She played with them, and rubbed the soles of them together. "How hot it is!" cried she, clapping the sole upon her cheek, then again rubbing, and holding it to Serlo. He was innocent enough to stretch out his hand to feel the warmth. "Clip! clap!" cried she, giving him a smart rap over the knuckles with the heel; so that he screamed, and drew back his hand. "That's for indulging in thoughts of your own at the sight of my slippers."

"And that's for using old folk like children," cried the other; then sprang up, seized her, and plundered many a kiss, every one of which she artfully contested with a show of serious reluctance. In this romping, her long hair got loose, and floated round the group; the chair overset; and Aurelia, inwardly indignant at such rioting, arose in great vexation.

CHAPTER SIX

THOUGH in this remoulding of "Hamlet" many characters had been cut off, a sufficient number of them still remained, — a number which the company was scarcely adequate to meet.

"If this is the way of it," said Serlo, "our prompter himself must issue from his den, and mount the stage, and become a personage like one of us."

"In his own station," answered Wilhelm, "I have frequently admired him."

"I do not think," said Serlo, "that there is in the world a more perfect artist of his kind. No spectator ever hears him: we upon the stage catch every syllable. He has formed in himself, as it were, a peculiar set of vocal organs for this purpose: he is like a Genius that whispers intelligibly to us in the hour of need. He feels, as if by instinct, what portion of his task an actor is completely master of, and anticipates from afar where his memory will fail him. I have known cases in which I myself had scarcely read my part: he said it over to me word for word, and I played happily. Yet he has some peculiarities which would make another in his place quite useless. For example, he takes such an interest in the plays, that, in giving any moving passage, he does not indeed declaim it, but he reads it with all pomp and pathos. By this ill habit he has nonplussed me on more than one occasion."

"As with another of his singularities," observed Aurelia, "he once left me sticking fast in a very dangerous passage."

"How could this happen, with the man's attentiveness?" said Wilhelm.

"He is so affected," said Aurelia, "by certain passages, that he weeps warm tears, and for a few moments loses all reflection; and it is not properly passages such as we should call affecting that produce this impression on him; but, if I express myself clearly, the *beautiful* passages, those out of which the pure spirit of the poet looks forth, as it were, through open, sparkling eyes, — passages which others at most rejoice over, and which many thousands altogether overlook."

"And with a soul so tender, why does he never venture on the stage?"

"A hoarse voice," said Serlo, "and a stiff carriage, exclude him from it; as his melancholic temper excludes him from society. What trouble have I taken, and in vain, to make him take to me! But he is a charming reader; such another I have never heard; no one can observe like him the narrow limit between declamation and graceful recital."

"The very man!" exclaimed our friend, "the very man! What a fortunate discovery! We have now the proper hand for delivering the passage of 'The rugged Pyrrhus.' "

"One requires your eagerness," said Serlo, "before he can employ every object in the use it was meant for."

"In truth," said Wilhelm, "I was very much afraid we should be obliged to leave this passage out: the omission would have lamed the whole play."

"Well! That is what I cannot understand," observed Aurelia.

"I hope you will erelong be of my opinion," answered Wilhelm. "Shakspeare has introduced these travelling players with a double purpose. The person who recites the death of Priam with such feeling, in the *first* place, makes a deep impression on the prince himself; he sharpens the conscience of the wavering youth: and, accordingly, this scene becomes a prelude to that other, where, in the *second* place, the little play produces such effect upon the King. Hamlet sees himself reproved and put to shame by the player, who feels so deep a sympathy in foreign and fictitious woes; and the thought of making an experiment upon the conscience of his stepfather is in consequence suggested to him. What a royal monologue is that, which ends the second act! How charming it will be to speak it!

> " 'Oh, what a rogue and peasant slave am I!
> Is it not monstrous that this player here,
> But in a fiction, in a dream of passion,
> Could force his soul so to his own conceit,
> That, from her working, all his visage wann'd;
> Tears in his eyes, distraction in's aspect,
> A broken voice, and his whole function suiting
> With forms to his conceit? and all for nothing!
> For Hecuba!
> What's Hecuba to him, or he to Hecuba,
> That he should weep for her?' "

"If we can but persuade our man to come upon the stage," observed Aurelia.

"We must lead him to it by degrees," said Serlo. "At the rehearsal he may read the passage: we shall tell him that an actor whom we are expecting is to play it; and so, by and by, we shall lead him nearer to the point."

Having agreed on this affair, the conversation next turned upon the Ghost. Wilhelm could not bring himself to give the part of the living King to the Pedant, that so Old Boisterous might play the Ghost: he was of opinion that they ought to wait a while; because some other actors had announced themselves, and among these it was probable they would find a fitter man.

We can easily conceive, then, how astonished Wilhelm must have been when, returning home that evening, he found a billet lying on his table, sealed with singular figures, and containing what follows: —

"Strange youth! we know thou art in great perplexity. For thy Hamlet thou canst hardly find men enough, not to speak of ghosts. Thy zeal deserves a miracle: miracles we cannot work, but somewhat marvellous shall happen. If thou have faith, the Ghost shall arise at the proper hour! Be of courage and keep firm! This needs no answer: thy determination will be known to us."

With this curious sheet he hastened back to Serlo, who read and re-read it, and at last declared, with a thoughtful look, that it seemed a matter of some moment; that they must consider well and seriously whether they could risk it. They talked the subject over at some length; Aurelia was silent, only smiling now and then; and a few days after, when speaking of the incident again, she gave our friend, not obscurely, to understand that she held it all a joke of Serlo's. She desired him to cast away anxiety, and to expect the Ghost with patience.

Serlo, for most part, was in excellent humor: the actors that were going to leave him took all possible pains to play well, that their absence might be much regretted; and this, combined with the new-fangled zeal of the others, gave promise of the best results.

His intercourse with Wilhelm had not failed to exert some influence on him. He began to speak more about art: for, after all, he was a German; and Germans like to give themselves account of what they do. Wilhelm wrote down many of their conversations; which, as our narrative must not be so often interrupted here, we shall communicate to such of our readers as feel an interest in dramaturgic matters, by some other opportunity.

In particular, one evening, the manager was very merry in speaking of the part of Polonius, and how he meant to take it up. "I engage," said he, "on this occasion, to present a very meritorious person in his best aspect. The repose and security of this old gentleman, his emptiness and his significance, his exterior gracefulness and interior meanness, his frankness and sycophancy, his sincere roguery and deceitful truth, I will introduce with all due elegance in their fit proportions. This respectable, gray-haired, enduring, time-serving half-knave, I will represent in the most courtly style: the occasional roughness and coarseness of our author's strokes will further me here. I will speak like a book when I am prepared beforehand, and like an ass when I utter the overflowings of my heart. I will be insipid and absurd enough to chime in with every one, and acute enough never to observe when people make a mock of me. I have seldom taken up a part with so much zeal and roguishness."

"Could I but hope as much from mine!" exclaimed Aurelia. "I have neither youth nor softness enough to be at home in this character. One thing alone I am too sure of, — the feeling that turns Ophelia's brain, I shall not want."

"We must not take the matter up so strictly," said our friend. "For my share, I am certain, that the wish to act the character of Hamlet has led me exceedingly astray, throughout my study of the play. And now, the more I look into the part, the more clearly do I see, that, in my whole form and physiognomy, there is not one feature such as Shakspeare meant for Hamlet. When I consider with what nicety the various circumstances are adapted to each other, I can scarcely hope to produce even a tolerable effect."

"You are entering on your new career with becoming conscientiousness," said Serlo. "The actor fits himself to his part as he can, and the part to him as it must. But how has Shakspeare drawn his Hamlet? Is he so utterly unlike you?"

"In the first place," answered Wilhelm, "he is fair-haired."

"That I call far-fetched," observed Aurelia. "How do you infer that?"

"As a Dane, as a Northman, he is fair-haired and blue-eyed by descent."

"And you think Shakspeare had this in view?"

"I do not find it specially expressed; but, by comparison of passages, I think it incontestable. The fencing tires him; the sweat is running from his brow; and the Queen remarks, '*He's fat, and scant of breath.*' Can you conceive him to be otherwise than plump and fair-haired? Brown-complexioned people, in their youth, are seldom plump. And does not his wavering melancholy, his soft lamenting, his irresolute activity, accord with such a figure? From a dark-haired young man, you would look for more decision and impetuosity."

"You are spoiling my imagination," cried Aurelia: "away with your fat Hamlets! Do not set your well-fed prince before us! Give us rather any *succedaneum* that will move us, will delight us. The intention of the author is of less importance to us than our own enjoyment, and we need a charm that is adapted for us."

CHAPTER SEVEN

ONE EVENING a dispute arose among our friends about the novel and the drama, and which of them deserved the preference. Serlo said it was a fruitless and misunderstood debate: both might be superior in their kinds, only each must keep within the limits proper to it.

"About their limits and their kinds," said Wilhelm, "I confess myself not altogether clear."

"Who *is* so?" said the other; "and yet perhaps it were worth while to come a little closer to the business."

They conversed together long upon the matter; and, in fine, the following was nearly the result of their discussion: —

"In the novel as well as in the drama, it is human nature and human action that we see. The difference between these sorts of fiction lies not merely in their outward form, — not merely in the circumstance that the personages of the one are made to speak, while those of the other have commonly their history narrated. Unfortunately many dramas are but novels, which proceed by dialogue; and it would not be impossible to write a drama in the shape of letters.

"But, in the novel, it is chiefly *sentiments* and *events* that are exhibited; in the drama, it is *characters* and *deeds*. The novel must go slowly forward; and the sentiments of the hero, by some means or another, must restrain the tendency of the whole to unfold itself and to conclude. The drama, on the other hand, must hasten; and the character of the hero must press forward to the end: it does not restrain, but is restrained. The novel-hero must be suffering, — at least he must not in a high degree be active: in the dramatic one, we look for activity and deeds. Grandison, Clarissa, Pamela, the Vicar of Wakefield, Tom Jones himself, are, if not suffering, at least retarding, personages; and the incidents are all in some sort modelled by their sentiments. In the drama the hero models nothing by himself; all things withstand him; and he clears and casts away the hinderances from off his path, or else sinks under them."

Our friends were also of opinion, that, in the novel, some degree of scope may be allowed to Chance, but that it must always be led and guided by the sentiments of the personages: on the other hand, that Fate, which, by means of outward, unconnected circumstances, carries forward men, without their own concurrence, to an unforeseen catastrophe, can have place only in the drama; that Chance may produce pathetic situations, but never tragic ones; Fate, on the other hand, ought always to be terrible, — and is, in the highest sense, tragic, when it brings into a ruinous concatenation the guilty man, and the guiltless that was unconcerned with him.

These considerations led them back to the play of "Hamlet," and the peculiarities of its composition. The hero in this case, it was observed, is endowed more properly with sentiments than with a character: it is events alone that push him on, and accordingly the play has in some measure the expansion of a novel. But as it is Fate that draws the plan, as the story issues from a deed of terror, and the hero is continually driven forward to a deed of terror, the work is tragic in the highest sense, and admits of no other than a tragic end.

The book-rehearsal was now to take place, to which Wilhelm had looked forward as to a festival. Having previously collated all the parts, no obstacle on this side could oppose him. The whole of the actors were acquainted with the piece: he endeavored to impress their minds with the importance of these book-rehearsals. "As you require," said he, "of every musical performer, that he shall, in some degree, be able to play from the book: so every actor, every educated man, should train himself to recite from the book, to catch immediately the character of any drama, any poem, any tale he may be reading, and exhibit it with grace and readiness. No committing to memory will be of service, if the actor have not, in the first place, penetrated into the sense and spirit of his author: the mere letter will avail him nothing."

Serlo declared that he would overlook all subsequent rehearsals, — the last rehearsal itself, — if justice were but done to these rehearsals from the book. "For, commonly," said he, "there is nothing more amusing than to hear an actor speak of study: it is as if freemasons were to talk of building."

The rehearsal passed according to their wishes; and we may assert, that the fame and favor which our company acquired afterwards had their foundation in these few but well-spent hours.

"You did right, my friend," said Serlo, when they were alone, "in speaking to our fellow-laborers so earnestly; and yet I am afraid they will scarcely fulfil your wishes."

"How so?" asked Wilhelm.

"I have noticed," answered Serlo, "that, as easily as you may set in motion the imaginations of men, gladly as they listen to your tales and fictions, it is yet very seldom that you find among them any touch of an imagination you can call productive. In actors this remark is strikingly exemplified. Any one of them is well content to undertake a beautiful, praiseworthy, brilliant part; and seldom will any one of them do more than self-complacently transport himself into his hero's place, without in the smallest troubling his head whether other people view him so or not. But to seize with vivacity what the author's feeling was in writing; what portion of your individual qualities you must cast off, in order to do justice to a part; how, by your own conviction that you are become another man, you may carry with you the convictions of the audience; how, by the inward truth of your conceptive power, you can change these boards into a temple, this pasteboard into woods, — to seize and execute all this, is given to very few. That internal strength of soul, by which alone deception can be brought about; that lying truth, without which nothing will affect us rightly, — have, by most men, never even been imagined.

"Let us not, then, press too hard for spirit and feeling in our friends. The surest way is first coolly to instruct them in the sense and letter of the play, — if possible, to open their understandings. Whoever has the talent will then, of his own accord, eagerly adopt the spirited feeling and manner of expression; and those who have it not will at least be prevented from acting or reciting altogether falsely. And among actors, as indeed in all cases, there is no worse arrangement than for any one to make pretensions to the spirit of a thing, while the sense and letter of it are not ready and clear to him."

CHAPTER EIGHT

COMING to the first stage-rehearsal very early, Wilhelm found himself alone upon the boards. The appearance of the place surprised him, and awoke the strangest recollections. A forest and village scene stood exactly represented as he once had seen it in the theatre of his native town. On that occasion also, a rehearsal was proceeding; and it was the morning when Mariana first confessed her love to him, and promised him a happy interview. The peasants' cottages resembled one another on the two stages, as they did in nature : the true morning sun, beaming through a half-closed window-shutter, fell upon a part of a bench ill joined to a cottage door; but unhappily it did not now enlighten Mariana's waist and bosom. He sat down, reflecting on this strange coincidence : he almost thought that perhaps on this very spot he would soon see her again. And, alas! the truth was nothing more, than that an afterpiece, to which this scene belonged, was at that time very often played upon the German stage.

Out of these meditations he was roused by the other actors, along with whom two amateurs, frequenters of the wardrobe and the stage, came in, and saluted Wilhelm with a show of great enthusiasm. One of these was in some degree attached to Frau Melina, but the other was entirely a lover of the art, and both were of the kind which a good company should always wish to have about it. It was difficult to say whether their love for the stage, or their knowledge of it, was the greater. They loved it too much to know it perfectly: they knew it well enough to prize the good and to discard the bad. But, their inclination being so powerful, they could tolerate the mediocre; and the glorious joy which they experienced from the foretaste and the aftertaste of excellence surpassed expression. The mechanical department gave them pleasure, the intellectual charmed them; and so strong was their susceptibility, that even a discontinuous rehearsal afforded them a species of illusion. Deficiencies appeared in their eyes to fade away in distance: the successful touched them like an object near at hand. In a word, they were judges such as every artist wishes in his own department. Their favorite movement was from the side-scenes to the pit, and from the pit to the side-scenes; their happiest place was in the wardrobe; their busiest employment was in trying to improve the dress, position, recitation, gesture, of the actor; their liveliest conversation was on the effect produced by him; their most constant effort was to keep him accurate, active, and attentive, to do him service or kindness, and, without squandering, to procure for the company a series of enjoyments. The two had obtained the exclusive privilege of being present on the stage at rehearsals as well as exhibitions. In regard to "Hamlet," they had not in all points agreed with Wilhelm: here and there he had yielded; but, for most part, he had stood by his opinion: and, upon the whole, these discussions had been very useful in the forming of his taste. He showed both gentlemen how much he valued them; and they again predicted nothing less, from these combined endeavors, than a new epoch for the German theatre.

The presence of these persons was of great service during the rehearsals. In particular they labored to convince our players, that, throughout the whole of their preparations, the posture and action, as they were intended ultimately to appear, should always be combined with the words, and thus the whole be mechanically united by

habit. In rehearsing a tragedy especially, they said, no common movement with the hands should be allowed: a tragic actor that took snuff
in the rehearsal always frightened them; for, in all probability, on
coming to the same passage in the exhibition, he would miss his pinch.
Nay, on the same principles, they maintained that no one should rehearse in boots, if his part were to be played in shoes. But nothing, they
declared, afflicted them so much as when the women, in rehearsing,
stuck their hands into the folds of their gowns.

By the persuasion of our friends, another very good effect was
brought about: the actors all began to learn the use of arms. Since
military parts occur so frequently, said they, can any thing look more
absurd than men, without the smallest particle of discipline, trolling
about the stage in captains' and majors' uniforms?

Wilhelm and Laertes were the first that took lessons of a sub-
altern: they continued their practising of fence with the greatest zeal.

Such pains did these two men take for perfecting a company
which had so fortunately come together. They were thus providing
for the future satisfaction of the public, while the public was usually
laughing at their taste. People did not know what gratitude they owed
our friends, particularly for performing one service, — the service of
frequently impressing on the actor the fundamental point, that it was
his duty to speak so loud as to be heard. In this simple matter, they
experienced more opposition and repugnance than could have been
expected. Most part maintained that they were heard well enough
already; some laid the blame upon the building; others said, one could
not yell and bellow, when one had to speak naturally, secretly, or
tenderly.

Our two friends, having an immeasurable stock of patience, tried
every means of undoing this delusion, of getting round this obstinate
self-will. They spared neither arguments nor flatteries; and at last
they reached their object, being aided not a little by the good example
of Wilhelm. By him they were requested to sit down in the remotest
corners of the house, and, every time they did not hear him perfectly,
to rap on the bench with a key. He articulated well, spoke out in a
measured manner, raised his tones gradually, and did not overcry
himself in the most vehement passages. The rapping of the keys was
heard less and less every new rehearsal: by and by the rest submitted

to the same operation, and at last it seemed rational to hope that the piece would be heard by every one in all the nooks of the house.

From this example we may see how desirous people are to reach their object in their own way; what need there often is of enforcing on them truths which are self-evident; and how difficult it may be to reduce the man who aims at effecting something to admit the primary conditions under which alone his enterprise is possible.

CHAPTER NINE

THE NECESSARY preparations for scenery and dresses, and whatever else was requisite, were now proceeding. In regard to certain scenes and passages, our friend had whims of his own, which Serlo humored, partly in consideration of their bargain, partly from conviction, and because he hoped by these civilities to gain Wilhelm, and to lead him according to his own purposes the more implicitly in time to come.

Thus, for example, the King and Queen were, at the first audience, to appear sitting on the throne, with the courtiers at the sides, and Hamlet standing undistinguished in the crowd. "Hamlet," said he, "must keep himself quiet: his sable dress will sufficiently point him out. He should rather shun remark than seek it. Not till the audience is ended, and the King speaks with him as with a son, should he advance, and allow the scene to take its course."

A formidable obstacle still remained, in regard to the two pictures which Hamlet so passionately refers to in the scene with his mother. "We ought," said Wilhelm, "to have both of them visible, at full length, in the bottom of the chamber, near the main door; and the former king must be clad in armor, like the Ghost, and hang at the side where it enters. I could wish that the figure held its right hand in a commanding attitude, were somewhat turned away, and, as it were, looked over its shoulder, that so it might perfectly resemble the

Ghost at the moment when he issues from the door. It will produce a great effect, when at this instant Hamlet looks upon the Ghost, and the Queen upon the picture. The stepfather may be painted in royal ornaments, but not so striking."

There were several other points of this sort, about which we shall, perhaps, elsewhere have opportunity to speak.

"Are you, then, inexorably bent on Hamlet's dying at the end?" inquired Serlo.

"How can I keep him alive," said Wilhelm, "when the whole play is pressing him to death? We have already talked at large on that matter."

"But the public wishes him to live."

"I will show the public any other complaisance; but, as to this, I cannot. We often wish that some gallant, useful man, who is dying of a chronical disease, might yet live longer. The family weep, and conjure the physician; but he cannot stay him: and no more than this physician can withstand the necessity of nature, can we give law to an acknowledged necessity of art. It is a false compliance with the multitude, to raise in them emotions which they *wish*, when these are not emotions which they *ought*, to feel."

"Whoever pays the cash," said Serlo, "may require the ware according to his liking."

"Doubtless, in some degree," replied our friend; "but a great public should be reverenced, not used as children are, when pedlers wish to hook the money from them. By presenting excellence to the people, you should gradually excite in them a taste and feeling for the excellent; and they will pay their money with double satisfaction when reason itself has nothing to object against this outlay. The public you may flatter, as you do a well-beloved child, to better, to enlighten, it; not as you do a pampered child of quality, to perpetuate the error you profit from."

In this manner various other topics were discussed relating to the question, What might still be changed in the play, and what must of necessity remain untouched? We shall not enter farther on those points at present; but, perhaps, at some future time we may submit this altered "Hamlet" itself to such of our readers as feel any interest in the subject.

CHAPTER TEN

THE MAIN rehearsal was at length concluded: it had lasted very long. Serlo and Wilhelm still found much to care for: notwithstanding all the time which had already been consumed in preparation, some highly necessary matters had been left to the very last moment.

Thus, the pictures of the kings, for instance, were not ready: and the scene between Hamlet and his mother, from which so powerful an effect was looked for, had a very helpless aspect, as the business stood; for neither Ghost nor painted image of him was at present forthcoming. Serlo made a jest of this perplexity: "We should be in a pretty scrape," said he, "if the Ghost were to decline appearing, and the guard had nothing to fight with but the air, and our prompter were obliged to speak the spirit's part from the side-scenes."

"We will not scare away our strange friend by unbelief," said Wilhelm: "doubtless at the proper season he will come, and astonish us as much as the spectators."

"Well, certainly," said Serlo, "I shall be a happy man to-morrow night, when once the play will have been acted. It costs us more arrangement than I dreamed of."

"But none of you," exclaimed Philina, "will be happier than I, little as my part disturbs me. Really, to hear a single subject talked of forever and forever, when, after all, there is nothing to come of it beyond an exhibition, which will be forgotten like so many hundred others, this is what I have not patience for. In Heaven's name, not so many *pros* and *cons!* The guests you entertain have always something to object against the dinner; nay, if you could hear them talk of it at home, they cannot understand how it was possible to undergo so sad a business."

"Let me turn your illustration, pretty one, to my own advantage," answered Wilhelm. "Consider how much must be done by art and nature, by traffickers and tradesmen, before an entertainment can be given. How many years the stag must wander in the forest, the fish in the river or the sea, before they can deserve to grace our table! And what cares and consultations with her cooks and servants has the lady of the house submitted to! Observe with what indifference the people swallow the production of the distant vintager, the seaman, and the vintner, as if it were a thing of course. And ought these men to cease from laboring, providing, and preparing; ought the master of the house to cease from purchasing and laying up the fruit of their exertions, — because at last the enjoyment it affords is transitory? But no enjoyment can be transitory; the impression which it leaves is permanent: and what is done with diligence and effort communicates to the spectator a hidden force, of which we cannot say how far its influence may reach."

" 'Tis all one to me," replied Philina: "only here again I must observe, that you men are constantly at variance with yourselves. With all this conscientious horror at curtailing Shakspeare, you have missed the finest thought there was in 'Hamlet'!"

"The finest?" cried our friend.

"Certainly the finest," said Philina: "the prince himself takes pleasure in it."

"And it is?" inquired Serlo.

"If you wore a wig," replied Philina, "I would pluck it very coolly off you; for I think you need to have your understanding opened."

The rest began to think what she could mean: the conversation paused. The party arose; it was now grown late; they seemed about to separate. While they were standing in this undetermined mood, Philina all at once struck up a song, with a very graceful, pleasing tune: —

> "Sing me not with such emotion,
>   How the night so lonesome is:
> Pretty maids, I've got a notion
>   It is the reverse of this.
>
> For as wife and man are plighted,
>   And the better half the wife;
> So is night to day united:
>   Night's the better half of life.

Can you joy in bustling daytime,
   Day when none can get his will?
It is good for work, for haytime;
   For much other it is ill.

But when, in the nightly glooming,
   Social lamp on table glows,
Face for faces dear illuming,
   And such jest and joyance goes;

When the fiery, pert young fellow,
   Wont by day to run or ride,
Whispering now some tale would tell O,
   All so gentle by your side;

When the nightingale to lovers
   Lovingly her songlet sings,
Which for exiles and sad rovers
   Like mere woe and wailing rings, —

With a heart how lightsome feeling,
   Do ye count the kindly clock,
Which twelve times deliberate pealing,
   Tells you none to-night shall knock!

Therefore, on all fit occasions,
   Mark it, maidens, what I sing:
Every day its own vexations,
   And the night its joys, will bring."

She made a slight courtesy on concluding, and Serlo gave a loud "Bravo!" She scuttled off, and left the room with a teehee of laughter. They heard her singing and skipping as she went down-stairs.

Serlo passed into another room: Wilhelm bade Aurelia good-night; but she continued looking at him for a few moments, and said, —

"How I dislike that woman! Dislike her from my heart, and to her very slightest qualities! Those brown eyelashes, with her fair hair, which our brother thinks so charming, I cannot bear to look at; and that scar upon her brow has something in it so repulsive, so low and base, that I could recoil ten paces every time I meet her. She was lately telling as a joke, that her father, when she was a child, threw a plate at her head, of which this is the mark. It is well that she is marked in the eyes and brow, that those about her may be on their guard."

Wilhelm made no answer; and Aurelia went on, apparently with greater spleen, —

"It is next to impossible for me to speak a kind, civil word to her, so deeply do I hate her, with all her wheedling. Would that we were rid of her! And you, too, my friend, have a certain complaisance for the creature, a way of acting towards her, that grieves me to the soul, — an attention which borders on respect; which, by Heaven! she does not merit."

"Whatever she may be," replied our friend, "I owe her thanks. Her upbringing is to blame: to her natural character I would do justice."

"Character!" exclaimed Aurelia; "and do you think such a creature has a character? O you men! It is so like you! These are the women you deserve!"

"My friend, can you suspect me?" answered Wilhelm. "I will give account of every minute I have spent beside her."

"Come, come," replied Aurelia: "it is late, we will not quarrel. All like each, and each like all! Good-night, my friend! Good-night, my sparkling bird-of-paradise!"

Wilhelm asked how he had earned this title.

"Another time," cried she; "another time. They say it has no feet, but hovers in the air, and lives on ether. That, however, is a story, a poetic fiction. Good-night! Dream sweetly, if you are in luck!"

She proceeded to her room; and he, being left alone, made haste to his.

Half angrily he walked along his chamber to and fro. The jesting but decided tone of Aurelia had hurt him: he felt deeply how unjust she was. Could he treat Philina with unkindness or ill-nature? She had done no evil to him; but, for any love to her, he could proudly and confidently take his conscience to witness that it was not so.

On the point of beginning to undress, he was going forward to his bed to draw aside the curtains, when, not without extreme astonishment, he saw a pair of women's slippers lying on the floor before it. One of them was resting on its sole, the other on its edge. They were Philina's slippers: he recognized them but too well. He thought he noticed some disorder in the curtains; nay, it seemed as if they moved. He stood, and looked with unaverted eyes.

A new impulse, which he took for anger, cut his breath: after a short pause, he recovered, and cried in a firm tone, —

"Come out, Philina! What do you mean by this? Where is your sense, your modesty? Are we to be the speech of the house to-morrow?"

Nothing stirred.

"I do not jest," continued he: "these pranks are little to my taste."

No sound! No motion!

Irritated and determined, he at last went forward to the bed, and tore the curtains asunder. "Arise," said he, "if I am not to give you up my room to-night."

With great surprise, he found his bed unoccupied; the sheets and pillows in the sleekest rest. He looked around: he searched and searched, but found no traces of the rogue. Behind the bed, the stove, the drawers, there was nothing to be seen: he sought with great and greater diligence; a spiteful looker-on might have believed that he was seeking in the hope of finding.

All thought of sleep was gone. He put the slippers on his table; went past it, up and down; often paused before it; and a wicked sprite that watched him has asserted that our friend employed himself for several hours about these dainty little shoes; that he viewed them with a certain interest; that he handled them and played with them; and it was not till towards morning that he threw himself on the bed, without undressing, where he fell asleep amidst a world of curious fantasies.

He was still slumbering, when Serlo entered hastily. "Where are you?" cried he: "still in bed? Impossible! I want you in the theatre: we have a thousand things to do."

THE FORENOON and the afternoon fled rapidly away. The playhouse was already full: our friend hastened to dress. It was not with the joy which it had given him when he first essayed it, that he now put on the garb of Hamlet: he only dressed that he might be in readiness. On his joining the women in the stage-room, they unanimously cried that nothing sat upon him right; the fine feather stood awry; the buckle of his belt did not fit: they began to slit, to sew, and piece together. The music started: Philina still objected somewhat to his ruff; Aurelia had much to say against his mantle. "Leave me alone, good people," cried he: "this negligence will make me liker Hamlet." The women would not let him go, but continued trimming him. The music ceased: the acting was begun. He looked at himself in the glass, pressed his hat closer down upon his face, and retouched the painting of his cheeks.

At this instant somebody came rushing in, and cried, "The Ghost! the Ghost!"

Wilhelm had not once had time all day to think of the Ghost, and whether it would come or not. His anxiety on that head was at length removed, and now some strange assistant was to be expected. The stage-manager came in, inquiring after various matters: Wilhelm had not time to ask about the Ghost; he hastened to present himself before the throne, where King and Queen, surrounded with their court, were already glancing in all the splendors of royalty, and waiting till the scene in front of them should be concluded. He caught the last words of Horatio, who was speaking of the Ghost, in extreme confusion, and seemed to have almost forgotten his part.

The intermediate curtain went aloft, and Hamlet saw the crowded house before him. Horatio, having spoken his address, and been dismissed by the King, pressed through to Hamlet; and, as if presenting himself to the Prince, he said, "The Devil is in harness: he has put us all in fright."

In the mean while, two men of large stature, in white cloaks and capouches, were observed standing in the side-scenes. Our friend, in the distraction, embarrassment, and hurry of the moment, had failed in the first soliloquy; at least, such was his own opinion, though loud plaudits had attended his exit. Accordingly, he made his next entrance in no pleasant mood, with the dreary wintry feeling of dramatic condemnation. Yet he girded up his mind, and spoke that appropriate passage on the "rouse and wassail," the "heavy-headed revel" of the Danes, with suitable indifference; he had, like the audience, in thinking of it, quite forgotten the Ghost; and he started, in real terror, when Horatio cried out, "Look, my lord! it comes!" He whirled violently round; and the tall, noble figure, the low, inaudible tread, the light movement in the heavy-looking armor, made such an impression on him, that he stood as if transformed to stone, and could utter only in a half-voice his "Angels and ministers of grace defend us!" He glared at the form, drew a deep breathing once or twice, and pronounced his address to the Ghost in a manner so confused, so broken, so constrained, that the highest art could not have hit the mark so well.

His translation of this passage now stood him in good stead. He had kept very close to the original, in which the arrangement of the words appeared to him expressive of a mind confounded, terrified, and seized with horror: —

> " 'Be thou a spirit of health, or goblin damn'd,
>   Bring with thee airs from heaven, or blasts from hell,
>   Be thy intents wicked or charitable,
>   Thou com'st in such a questionable shape,
>   That I will speak to thee: I'll call thee Hamlet,
>   King, father, royal Dane: oh, answer me!' "

A deep effect was visible in the audience. The Ghost beckoned, the Prince followed him amid the loudest plaudits.

The scene changed: and, when the two had re-appeared, the Ghost, on a sudden, stopped, and turned round; by which means Hamlet came to be a little too close upon it. With a longing curiosity, he looked in at the lowered visor; but except two deep-lying eyes, and a well-formed nose, he could discern nothing. Gazing timidly, he stood before the Ghost; but when the first tones issued from the helmet, and a somewhat hoarse, yet deep and penetrating, voice, pronounced the words, "I am thy father's spirit," Wilhelm, shuddering, started back some paces; and the audience shuddered with him. Each imagined that he knew the voice: Wilhelm thought he noticed in it some resemblance to his father's. These strange emotions and remembrances, the curiosity he felt about discovering his secret friend, the anxiety about offending him, even the theatric impropriety of coming too near him in the present situation, all this affected Wilhelm with powerful and conflicting impulses. During the long speech of the Ghost, he changed his place so frequently, he seemed so unsettled and perplexed, so attentive and so absent-minded, that his acting caused a universal admiration, as the Spirit caused a universal horror. The latter spoke with a feeling of melancholy anger, rather than of sorrow; but of an anger spiritual, slow, and inexhaustible. It was the mistemper of a noble soul, that is severed from all earthly things, and yet devoted to unbounded woe. At last he vanished, but in a curious manner; for a thin, gray, transparent gauze arose from the place of descent, like a vapor, spread itself over him, and sank along with him.

Hamlet's friends now entered, and swore upon the sword. Old Truepenny, in the mean time, was so busy under ground, that, wherever they might take their station, he was sure to call out right beneath them, "Swear!" and they started, as if the soil had taken fire below them, and hastened to another spot. On each of these occasions, too, a little flame pierced through at the place where they were standing. The whole produced on the spectators a profound impression.

After this, the play proceeded calmly on its course: nothing failed; all prospered; the audience manifested their contentment, and the actors seemed to rise in heart and spirits every scene.

CHAPTER TWELVE

THE CURTAIN fell, and rapturous applauses sounded out of every corner of the house. The four princely corpses sprang aloft, and embraced each other. Polonius and Ophelia likewise issued from their graves, and listened with extreme satisfaction, as Horatio, who had stepped before the curtain to announce the following play, was welcomed with the most thundering plaudits. The people would not hear of any other play, but violently required the repetition of the present.

"We have won," cried Serlo, "and so not another reasonable word this night! Every thing depends on the first impression: we should never take it ill of any actor, that, on occasion of his first appearance, he is provident, and even self-willed."

The box-keeper came, and delivered him a heavy sum. "We have made a good beginning," cried the manager, "and prejudice itself will now be on our side. But where is the supper you promised us? To-night we may be allowed to relish it a little."

It had been agreed that all the party were to stay together in their stage-dresses, and enjoy a little feast among themselves. Wilhelm had engaged to have the place in readiness, and Frau Melina to provide the victuals.

A room, which commonly was occupied by scene-painters, had accordingly been polished up as well as possible: our friends had hung it round with little decorations, and so decked and trimmed it, that it looked half like a garden, half like a colonnade. On entering it, the company were dazzled with the glitter of a multitude of lights, which, across the vapors of the sweetest and most copious perfumes, spread a stately splendor over a well-decorated and well-furnished table. These preparations were hailed with joyful interjections by the party; all took their places with a certain genuine dignity; it seemed as if some royal family had met together in the Kingdom of the Shades. Wilhelm sat between Aurelia and the Frau Melina; Serlo between Philina and Elmira; nobody was discontented with himself or with his place.

Our two theatric amateurs, who had from the first been present, now increased the pleasure of the meeting. While the exhibition was proceeding, they had several times stepped round, and come upon the stage, expressing, in the warmest terms, the delight which they and the audience felt. They now descended to particulars, and each was richly rewarded for his efforts.

With boundless animation, the company extolled man after man, and passage after passage. To the prompter, who had modestly sat down at the bottom of the table, they gave a liberal commendation for his "rugged Pyrrhus;" the fencing of Hamlet and Laertes was beyond all praise; Ophelia's mourning had been inexpressibly exalted and affecting; of Polonius they would not trust themselves to speak.

Every individual present heard himself commended through the rest and by them, nor was the absent Ghost defrauded of his share of praise and admiration. He had played the part, it was asserted, with a very happy voice, and in a lofty style; but what surprised them most, was the information which he seemed to have about their own affairs. He entirely resembled the painted figure, as if he had sat to the painter of it; and the two amateurs described, in glowing language, how awful it had looked when the spirit entered near the picture, and stepped across before his own image. Truth and error, they declared, had been commingled in the strangest manner: they had felt as if the Queen really did not see the Ghost. And Frau Melina was especially commended, because on this occasion she had gazed upwards at the picture, while Hamlet was pointing downwards at the Spectre.

Inquiry was now made how the apparition could have entered. The stage-manager reported that a back-door, usually blocked up by decorations, had that evening, as the Gothic hall was occupied, been opened; that two large figures in white cloaks and hoods, one of whom was not to be distinguished from the other, had entered by this passage; and by the same, it was likely, they had issued when the third act was over.

Serlo praised the Ghost for one merit, — that he had not whined and lamented like a tailor; nay, to animate his son, had even introduced a passage at the end, which more beseemed such a hero. Wilhelm had kept it in memory: he promised to insert it in his manuscript.

Amid the pleasures of the entertainment, it had not been noticed that the children and the harper were absent. Erelong they made their entrance, and were blithely welcomed by the company. They came in together, very strangely decked: Felix was beating a triangle, Mignon a tambourine; the old man had his large harp hung round his neck, and was playing on it whilst he carried it before him. They marched round and round the table, and sang a multitude of songs. Eatables were handed them; and the guests seemed to think they could not do a greater kindness to the children, than by giving them as much sweet wine as they chose to have. For the company themselves had not by any means neglected a stock of savory flasks, presented by the two amateurs, which had arrived that evening in baskets. The children tripped about, and sang: Mignon, in particular, was frolicsome beyond all wont. She beat the tambourine with the greatest liveliness and grace: now, with her finger pressed against the parchment, she hummed across it swiftly to and fro; now rattled on it with her knuckles, now with the back of her hand; nay, sometimes, with alternating rhythm, she struck it first against her knee and then against her head; and anon twirling it in her hand, she made the shells jingle by themselves; and thus, from the simplest instrument, elicited a great variety of tones. After she and Felix had long rioted about, they sat down upon an elbow-chair which was standing empty at the table, exactly opposite to Wilhelm.

"Keep out of the chair!" cried Serlo: "it is waiting for the Ghost, I think; and, when he comes, it will be worse for you."

"I do not fear him," answered Mignon: "if he come, we can rise. He is my uncle, and will not harm me." To those who did not know that her reputed father had been named the Great Devil, this speech was unintelligible.

The party looked at one another: they were more and more confirmed in their suspicion that the manager was in the secret of the Ghost. They talked and tippled, and the girls from time to time cast timid glances towards the door.

The children, who, sitting in the big chair, looked from over the table but like puppets in their box, did actually at length start a little drama in the style of Punch. The screeching tone of these people Mignon imitated very well; and Felix and she began to knock their heads together, and against the edges of the table, in such a way as only wooden puppets could endure. Mignon, in particular, grew frantic with gayety: the company, much as they had laughed at her at first, were in fine obliged to curb her. But persuasion was of small avail; for she now sprang up, and raved, and shook her tambourine, and capered round the table. With her hair flying out behind her, with her head thrown back, and her limbs, as it were, cast into the air, she seemed like one of those antique Mænads, whose wild and all but impossible positions still, on classic monuments, often strike us with amazement.

Incited by the talents and the uproar of the children, each endeavored to contribute something to the entertainment of the night. The girls sung several canons! Laertes whistled in the manner of a nightingale; and the Pedant gave a symphony *pianissimo* upon the Jew's-harp. Meanwhile the youths and damsels, who sat near each other, had begun a great variety of games; in which, as the hands often crossed and met, some pairs were favored with a transient squeeze, the emblem of a hopeful kindness. Madam Melina in particular seemed scarcely to conceal a decided tenderness for Wilhelm. It was late; and Aurelia, perhaps the only one retaining self-possession in the party, now stood up, and signified that it was time to go.

By way of termination, Serlo gave a firework, or what resembled one; for he could imitate the sound of crackers, rockets, and firewheels, with his mouth, in a style of nearly inconceivable correctness. You had only to shut your eyes, and the deception was complete. In the mean time, they had all risen: the men gave their arms to the women to escort them home. Wilhelm was walking last with Aurelia. The stage-manager met him on the stairs, and said to him, "Here is the veil our Ghost vanished in; it was hanging fixed to the place where he sank; we found it this moment." — "A curious relic!" said our friend, and took it with him.

At this instant his left arm was laid hold of, and he felt a smart twinge of pain in it. Mignon had hid herself in the place: she had seized him, and bit his arm. She rushed past him, down stairs, and disappeared.

On reaching the open air, almost all of them discovered that they had drunk too liberally. They glided asunder without taking leave.

The instant Wilhelm gained his room, he stripped, and, extinguishing his candle, hastened into bed. Sleep was overpowering him without delay, when a noise, that seemed to issue from behind the stove, aroused him. In the eye of his heated fancy, the image of the harnessed King was hovering there: he sat up that he might address the Spectre; but he felt himself encircled with soft arms, and his mouth was shut with kisses, which he had not force to push away.

"I am thy father's spirit"

NEXT MORNING Wilhelm started up with an unpleasant feeling, and found himself alone. His head was still dim with the tumult, which he had not yet entirely slept off; and the recollection of his nightly visitant disquieted his mind. His first suspicion lighted on Philina; but, on second thoughts, he conceived that it could not have been she. He sprang out of bed: and, while putting on his clothes, he noticed that the door, which commonly he used to bolt, was now ajar; though whether he had shut it on the previous night, or not, he could not recollect.

But what surprised him most was the Spirit's veil, which he found lying on his bed. Having brought it up with him, he had most probably thrown it there himself. It was a gray gauze: on the hem of it he noticed an inscription broidered in dark letters. He unfolded it, and read the words, "FOR THE FIRST AND THE LAST TIME! FLEE, YOUTH! FLEE!" He was struck with it, and knew not what to think or say.

At this moment Mignon entered with his breakfast. The aspect of the child astonished Wilhelm, we may almost say frightened him. She appeared to have grown taller over night: she entered with a stately, noble air, and looked him in the face so earnestly, that he could not endure her glances. She did not touch him, as at other times, when, for morning salutation, she would press his hand, or kiss his cheek, his lips, his arm, or shoulder; but, having put his things in order, she retired in silence.

The appointed time of a first rehearsal now arrived: our friends assembled, all of them entirely out of tune from yesternight's debauch. Wilhelm roused himself as much as possible, that he might not at the very outset violate the principles he had preached so lately with such emphasis. His practice in the matter helped him through; for practice and habit must, in every art, fill up the voids which genius and temper in their fluctuations will so often leave.

But, in the present case, our friends had especial reason to admit the truth of the remark, that no one should begin with a festivity any situation that is meant to last, particularly that is meant to be a trade, a mode of living. Festivities are fit for what is happily concluded: at the commencement, they but waste the force and zeal which should inspire us in the struggle, and support us through a long-continued labor. Of all festivities, the marriage festival appears the most unsuitable: calmness, humility, and silent hope befit no ceremony more than this.

So passed the day, which to Wilhelm seemed the most insipid he had ever spent. Instead of their accustomed conversation in the evening, the company began to yawn: the interest of Hamlet was exhausted; they rather felt it disagreeable than otherwise that the play was to be repeated next night. Wilhelm showed the veil which the royal Dane had left: it was to be inferred from this, that he would not come again. Serlo was of that opinion; he appeared to be deep in the secrets of the Ghost: but, on the other hand, the inscription, "Flee, youth! Flee!" seemed inconsistent with the rest. How could Serlo be in league with any one whose aim it was to take away the finest actor of his troop?

It had now become a matter of necessity to confer on Boisterous the Ghost's part, and on the Pedant that of the King. Both declared that they had studied these sufficiently: nor was it wonderful; for in such a number of rehearsals, and so copious a treatment of the subject, all of them had grown familiar with it: each could have exchanged his part with any other. Yet they rehearsed a little here and there, and prepared the new adventurers, as fully as the hurry would admit. When the company was breaking up at a pretty late hour, Philina softly whispered Wilhelm as she passed, "I must have my slippers back: thou wilt not bolt the door?" These words excited some perplexity in Wilhelm, when he reached his chamber; they strengthened the suspicion that Philina was the secret visitant: and we ourselves are forced to coincide with this idea; particularly as the causes, which awakened in our friend another and a stranger supposition, cannot be disclosed. He kept walking up and down his chamber in no quiet frame: his door was actually not yet bolted.

On a sudden Mignon rushed into the room, laid hold of him, and cried, "Master! save the house! It is on fire!" Wilhelm sprang through the door, and a strong smoke came rushing down upon him from the upper story. On the street he heard the cry of fire; and the harper, with his instrument in his hand, came down-stairs breathless through the smoke. Aurelia hurried out of her chamber, and threw little Felix into Wilhelm's arms.

"Save the child!" cried she, "and we will mind the rest."

Wilhelm did not look upon the danger as so great: his first thought was, to penetrate to the source of the fire, and try to stifle it before it reached a head. He gave Felix to the harper; commanding him to hasten down the stone stairs, which led across a little garden-vault out into the garden, and to wait with the children in the open air. Mignon took a light to show the way. He begged Aurelia to secure her things there also. He himself pierced upwards through the smoke, but it was in vain that he exposed himself to such danger. The flame appeared to issue from a neighboring house; it had already caught the wooden floor and staircase: some others, who had hastened to his help, were suffering like himself from fire and vapor. Yet he kept inciting them; he called for water; he conjured them to dispute every inch with the flame, and promised to abide by them to the last. At this instant, Mignon came springing up, and cried, "Master! save thy Felix! The old man is mad! He is killing him." Scarcely knowing what he did, Wilhelm darted down-stairs; and Mignon followed close behind him.

On the last steps, which led into the garden-vault, he paused with horror. Some heaps of fire-wood branches, and large masses of straw, which had been stowed in the place, were burning with a clear flame; Felix was lying on the ground, and screaming; the harper stood aside, holding down his head, and leaned against the wall. "Unhappy creature! what is this?" said Wilhelm. The old man spoke not; Mignon lifted Felix, and carried him with difficulty to the garden; while Wilhelm strove to pull the fire asunder and extinguish it, but only by his efforts made the flame more violent. At last he, too, was forced to flee into the garden, with his hair and his eyelashes burned; tearing the harper with him through the conflagration, who, with singed beard, unwillingly accompanied him.

Wilhelm hastened instantly to seek the children. He found them on the threshold of a summer-house at some distance: Mignon was trying every effort to pacify her comrade. Wilhelm took him on his knee: he questioned him, felt him, but could obtain no satisfactory account from either him or Mignon.

Meanwhile, the fire had fiercely seized on several houses: it was now enlightening all the neighborhood. Wilhelm looked at the child in the red glare of the flames: he could find no wound, no blood, no hurt of any kind. He groped over all the little creature's body, but the boy gave no sign of pain: on the contrary, he by degrees grew calm, and began to wonder at the blazing houses, and express his pleasure at the spectacle of beams and rafters burning all in order, like a grand illumination, so beautifully there.

Wilhelm thought not of the clothes or goods he might have lost: he felt deeply how inestimable to him was this pair of human beings, who had just escaped so great a danger. He pressed little Felix to his heart with a new emotion: Mignon, too, he was about to clasp with joyful tenderness; but she softly avoided this: she took him by the hand, and held it fast.

"Master," said she (till the present evening she had hardly ever named him master; at first she used to name him sir, and afterwards to call him father), — "Master! we have escaped an awful danger: thy Felix was on the point of death."

By many inquiries, Wilhelm learned from her at last, that, when they came into the vault, the harper tore the light from her hand, and set on fire the straw. That he then put Felix down, laid his hands with strange gestures on the head of the child, and drew a knife as if he meant to sacrifice him. That she sprang forward, and snatched it from him; that she screamed; and some one from the house, who was carrying something down into the garden, came to her help, but must have gone away again in the confusion, and left the old man and the child alone.

Two or even three houses were now flaming in a general blaze. Owing to the conflagration in the vault, no person had been able to take shelter in the garden. Wilhelm was distressed about his friends, and in a less degree about his property. Not venturing to quit the children, he was forced to sit, and see the mischief spreading more and more.

In this anxious state he passed some hours. Felix had fallen asleep on his bosom: Mignon was lying at his side, and holding fast his hand. The efforts of the people finally subdued the fire. The burned houses sank, with successive crashes, into heaps; the morning was advancing; the children awoke, and complained of bitter cold; even Wilhelm, in his light dress, could scarcely brook the chillness of the falling dew. He took the young ones to the rubbish of the prostrate building, where, among the ashes and the embers, they found a very grateful warmth.

The opening day collected, by degrees, the various individuals of the party. All of them had got away unhurt: no one had lost much. Wilhelm's trunk was saved among the rest.

Towards ten o'clock Serlo called them to rehearse their "Hamlet," at least some scenes, in which fresh players were to act. He had some debates to manage, on this point, with the municipal authorities. The clergy required, that, after such a visitation of Providence, the playhouse should be shut for some time; and Serlo, on the other hand, maintained, that both for the purpose of repairing the damage he had suffered, and of exhilarating the depressed and terrified spirits of the people, nothing could be more in place than the exhibition of some interesting play. His opinion in the end prevailed, and the house was full. The actors played with singular fire, with more of a passionate freedom than at first. The feelings of the audience had been heightened by the horrors of the previous night, and their appetite for entertainment had been sharpened by the tedium of a wasted and dissipated day: every one had more than usual susceptibility for what was strange and moving. Most of them were new spectators, invited by the fame of the play: they could not compare the present with the preceding evening. Boisterous played altogether in the style of the unknown Ghost: the Pedant, too, had accurately seized the manner of his predecessor; nor was his own woful aspect without its use to him; for it seemed as if, in spite of his purple cloak and his ermine collar, Hamlet were fully justified in calling him a "king of shreds and patches."

Few have ever reached the throne by a path more singular than his had been. But although the rest, and especially Philina, made sport of his preferment, he himself signified that the count, a consummate judge, had at the first glance predicted this and much more of him. Philina, on the other hand, recommended lowliness of mind to him; saying, she would now and then powder the sleeves of his coat, that he might remember that unhappy night in the castle, and wear his crown with meekness.

CHAPTER FOURTEEN

OUR FRIENDS had sought out other lodgings, on the spur of the moment, and were by this means much dispersed. Wilhelm had conceived a liking for the garden-house, where he had spent the night of the conflagration: he easily obtained the key, and settled himself there.

But Aurelia being greatly hampered in her new abode, he was obliged to retain little Felix with him. Mignon, indeed, would not part with the boy.

He had placed the children in a neat chamber on the upper floor : he himself was in the lower parlor. The young ones were asleep at this time : Wilhelm could not sleep.

Adjoining the lovely garden, which the full moon had just risen to illuminate, the black ruins of the fire were visible; and here and there a streak of vapor was still mounting from them. The air was soft, the night extremely beautiful. Philina, in issuing from the theatre, had jogged him with her elbow, and whispered something to him, which he did not understand. He felt perplexed and out of humor : he knew not what he should expect or do. For a day or two Philina had avoided him : it was not till to-night that she had given him any second signal. Unhappily the doors, that he was not to bolt, were now consumed : the slippers had evaporated into smoke. How the girl would gain admission to the garden, if her aim was such, he knew not. He wished she might not come, and yet he longed to have some explanation with her.

But what lay heavier at his heart than this, was the fate of the harper, whom, since the fire, no one had seen. Wilhelm was afraid, that, in clearing off the rubbish, they would find him buried under it. Our friend had carefully concealed the suspicion which he entertained, that it was the harper who had fired the house. The old man had been first seen, as he rushed from the burning and smoking floor, and his desperation in the vault appeared a natural consequence of such a deed. Yet, from the inquiry which the magistrates had instituted touching the affair, it seemed likely that the fire had not originated in the house where Wilhelm lived, but had accidentally been kindled in the third from that, and had crept along beneath the roofs before it burst into activity.

Seated in a grove, our friend was meditating all these things, when he heard a low footfall in a neighboring walk. By the melancholy song which arose along with it, he recognized the harper. He caught the words of the song without difficulty : it turned on the consolations of a miserable man, conscious of being on the borders of insanity. Unhappily our friend forgot the whole of it except the last verse : —

"Wheresoe'er my steps may lead me,
 Meekly at the door I'll stay:
Pious hands will come to feed me,
 And I'll wander on my way.
Each will feel a touch of gladness
 When my aged form appears:
Each will shed a tear of sadness,
 Though I reck not of his tears."

So singing, he had reached the garden-door, which led into an unfrequented street. Finding it bolted, he was making an attempt to climb the railing, when Wilhelm held him back, and addressed some kindly words to him. The old man begged to have the door unlocked, declaring that he would and must escape. Wilhelm represented to him that he might indeed escape from the garden, but could not from the town; showing, at the same time, what suspicions he must needs incur by such a step. But it was in vain: the old man held by his opinion. Our friend, however, would not yield; and at last he brought him, half by force, into the garden-house, in which he locked himself along with him. The two carried on a strange conversation; which, however, not to afflict our readers with repeating unconnected thoughts and dolorous emotions, we had rather pass in silence than detail at large.

CHAPTER FIFTEEN

UNDETERMINED what to do with this unhappy man, who displayed such indubitable symptoms of madness, Wilhelm would have been in great perplexity, had not Laertes come that very morning, and delivered him from his uncertainty. Laertes, as usual, rambling everywhere about the town, had happened, in some coffee-house, to meet with a man, who, a short time ago, had suffered under violent attacks of melancholy. This person, it appeared, had been intrusted to the care of some country clergyman, who made it his peculiar business to attend to people in such situations. In the present instance, as in many others, his treatment had succeeded: he was still in town, and the friends of the patient were showing him the greatest honor.

Wilhelm hastened to find out this person: he disclosed the case to him, and agreed with him about the terms. The harper was to be brought over to him, under certain pretexts. The separation deeply pained our friend; so used was he to see the man beside him, and to hear his spirited and touching strains. The hope of soon beholding him recovered, served, in some degree, to moderate this feeling. The old man's harp had been destroyed in the burning of the house: they purchased him another, and gave it him when he departed.

Mignon's little wardrobe had in like manner been consumed. As Wilhelm was about providing her with new apparel, Aurelia proposed that now at last they should dress her as a girl.

"No! no! not at all!" cried Mignon, and insisted on it with such earnestness, that they let her have her way.

The company had not much leisure for reflection: the exhibitions followed close on one another.

Wilhelm often mingled with the audience, to ascertain their feelings; but he seldom heard a criticism of the kind he wished: more frequently the observations he listened to distressed or angered him. Thus, for instance, shortly after "Hamlet" had been acted for the first time, a youth was telling, with considerable animation, how happy he had been that evening in the playhouse. Wilhelm hearkened, and was scandalized to learn that his neighbor had, on that occasion, in contempt of those behind him, kept his hat on, stubbornly refusing to remove it till the play was done; to which heroical transaction he still looked back with great contentment.

Another gentleman declared that Wilhelm played Laertes very well, but that the actor who had undertaken Hamlet did not seem too happy in *his* part. This permutation was not quite unnatural; for Wilhelm and Laertes did resemble one another, though in a very distant manner.

A third critic warmly praised his acting, particularly in the scene with his mother; only he regretted much, that, in this fiery moment, a white strap had peered out from below the Prince's waistcoat, whereby the illusion had been greatly marred.

Meanwhile, in the interior of the company, a multitude of alterations were occurring. Philina, since the evening subsequent to that of the fire, had never given our friend the smallest sign of closer intimacy. She had, as it seemed on purpose, hired a remote lodging: she associated with Elmira, and came seldomer to Serlo, — an arrangement very gratifying to Aurelia. Serlo continued still to like her, and often visited her quarters, particularly when he hoped to find Elmira there. One evening he took Wilhelm with him. At their entrance, both of them were much surprised to see Philina, in the inner room, sitting in close contact with a young officer. He wore a red uniform with white pantaloons; but, his face being turned away, they could not see it. Philina came into the outer room to meet her visitors, and shut the door behind her. "You surprise me in the middle of a very strange adventure," cried she.

"It does not appear so strange," said Serlo; "but let us see this handsome, young, enviable gallant. You have us in such training, that we dare not show any jealousy, however it may be."

"I must leave you to suspicion for a time," replied Philina in a jesting tone; "yet I can assure you, the gallant is a lady of my friends, who wishes to remain a few days undiscovered. You shall know her history in due season; nay, perhaps you shall even behold the beautiful spinster in person; and then most probably I shall have need of all my prudence and discretion, for it seems too likely that your new acquaintance will drive your old friend out of favor."

Wilhelm stood as if transformed to stone. At the first glance, the red uniform had reminded him of Mariana: the figure, too, was hers; the fair hair was hers; only the present individual seemed to be a little taller.

"For Heaven's sake," cried he, "let us know something more about your friend! let us see this lady in disguise! We are now partakers of your secret: we will promise, we will swear; only let us see the lady!"

"What a fire he is in!" cried Philina: "but be cool, be calm; for to-day there will nothing come of it."

"Let us only know her name!" cried Wilhelm.

"It were a fine secret, then," replied Philina.

"At least her first name!"

"If you can guess it, be it so. Three guesses I will give you, — not a fourth. You might lead me through the whole calendar."

"Well!" said Wilhelm: "Cecilia, then?"

"None of your Cecilias!"

"Henrietta?"

"Not at all! Have a care, I pray you: guess better, or your curiosity will have to sleep unsatisfied."

Wilhelm paused and shivered: he tried to speak, but the sound died away within him. "Mariana?" stammered he at last, "Mariana?"

"Bravo!" cried Philina. "Hit to a hair's-breadth!" said she, whirling round upon her heel, as she was wont on such occasions.

Wilhelm could not utter a word; and Serlo, not observing his emotion, urged Philina more and more to let them in.

Conceive the astonishment of both, when Wilhelm, suddenly and vehemently interrupting their raillery, threw himself at Philina's feet, and, with an air and tone of the deepest passion, begged and conjured her, "Let me see the stranger," cried he: "she is mine; she is my Mariana! She for whom I have longed all the days of my life, she who is still more to me than all the women in this world! Go in to her at least, and tell her that I am here, — that the man is here who linked to her his earliest love, and all the happiness of his youth. Say that he will justify himself, though he left her so unkindly; he will pray for pardon of her; and will grant her pardon, whatsoever she may have done to him; he will even make no pretensions further, if he may but see her, if he may but see that she is living and in happiness."

Philina shook her head, and said, "Speak low! Do not betray us! If the lady is indeed your friend, her feelings must be spared; for she does not in the least suspect that you are here. Quite a different sort of business brings her hither; and you know well enough, one had rather see a spectre than a former lover at an inconvenient time. I will ask her, and prepare her: we will then consider what is further to be done. To-morrow I shall write you a note, saying when you are to come, or whether you may come at all. Obey me punctually; for I protest, that, without her own and my consent, no eye shall see this lovely creature. I shall keep my doors better bolted; and, with axe and crow, you surely will not visit me."

Our friend conjured her, Serlo begged of her; but all in vain:

they were obliged to yield, and leave the chamber and the house.

With what feelings Wilhelm passed the night is easy to conceive. How slowly the hours of the day flowed on, while he sat expecting a message from Philina, may also be imagined. Unhappily he had to play that evening: such mental pain he had never endured. The moment his part was done, he hastened to Philina's house, without inquiring whether he had got her leave or not. He found her doors bolted: and the people of the house informed him that mademoiselle had set out early in the morning, in company with a young officer; that she had talked about returning shortly; but they had not believed her, she having paid her debts, and taken every thing along with her.

This intelligence drove Wilhelm almost frantic. He hastened to Laertes, that he might take measures for pursuing her, and, cost what it would, for attaining certainty regarding her attendant. Laertes, however, represented to him the imprudence of such passion and credulity. "I dare wager, after all," said he, "that it is no one else but Friedrich. The boy is of a high family, I know; he is madly in love with Philina; it is likely he has cozened from his friends a fresh supply of money, so that he can once more live with her in peace for a while."

These considerations, though they did not quite convince our friend, sufficed to make him waver. Laertes showed him how improbable the story was with which Philina had amused them; reminded him how well the stranger's hair and figure answered Friedrich; that with the start of him by twelve hours, they could not easily be overtaken; and, what was more than all, that Serlo could not do without him at the theatre.

By so many reasons, Wilhelm was at last persuaded to postpone the execution of his project. That night Laertes got an active man, to whom they gave the charge of following the runaways. It was a steady person, who had often officiated as courier and guide to travelling-parties, and was at present without employment. They gave him money, they informed him of the whole affair; instructing him to seek and overtake the fugitives, to keep them in his eye, and instantly to send intelligence to Wilhelm where and how he found them. That very hour he mounted horse, pursuing this ambiguous pair; by which exertions, Wilhelm was in some degree at least, composed.

THE DEPARTURE of Philina did not make a deep sensation, either in the theatre or in the public. She never was in earnest with any thing: the women universally detested her; the men rather wished to see her *tête-à-tête* than on the boards. Thus her fine, and, for the stage, even happy, talents were of no avail to her. The other members of the company took greater labor on them to supply her place: the Frau Melina, in particular, was much distinguished by her diligence and zeal. She noted down, as formerly, the principles of Wilhelm; she guided herself according to his theory and his example; there was of late a something in her nature that rendered her more interesting. She soon acquired an accurate mode of acting: she attained the natural tone of conversation altogether, that of keen emotion she attained in some degree. She contrived, moreover, to adapt herself to Serlo's humors: she took pains in singing for his pleasure, and succeeded in that matter moderately well.

By the accession of some other players, the company was rendered more complete: and while Wilhelm and Serlo were busied each in his degree, the former insisting on the general tone and spirit of the whole, the latter faithfully elaborating the separate passages, a laudable ardor likewise inspired the actors; and the public took a lively interest in their concerns.

"We are on the right path," said Serlo once: "if we can continue thus, the public, too, will soon be on it. Men are easily astonished and misled by wild and barbarous exhibitions; yet lay before them anything rational and polished, in an interesting manner, and doubt not they will catch at it.

"What forms the chief defect of our German theatre, what prevents both actor and spectator from obtaining proper views, is the vague and variegated nature of the objects it contains. You nowhere find a barrier on which to prop your judgment. In my opinion, it is far from an advantage to us that we have expanded our stage into, as it were, a boundless arena for the whole of nature; yet neither manager nor actor need attempt contracting it, until the taste of the nation shall itself mark out the proper circle. Every good society submits to certain conditions and restrictions; so also must every good theatre. Certain manners, certain modes of speech, certain objects, and fashions of proceeding, must altogether be excluded. You do not grow poorer by limiting your household expenditure."

On these points our friends were more or less accordant or at variance. The majority, with Wilhelm at their head, were for the English theatre; Serlo and a few others for the French.

It was also settled, that in vacant hours, of which unhappily an actor has too many, they should in company peruse the finest plays in both these languages; examining what parts of them seemed best and worthiest of imitation. They accordingly commenced with some French pieces. On these occasions, it was soon observed, Aurelia went away whenever they began to read. At first they supposed she had been sick: Wilhelm once questioned her about it.

"I would not assist at such a reading," said she, "for how could I hear and judge, when my heart was torn in pieces? I hate the French language from the bottom of my soul."

"How can you be hostile to a language," cried our friend, "to which we Germans are indebted for the greater part of our accomplishments; to which we must become indebted still more, if our natural qualities are ever to assume their proper form?"

"It is no prejudice!" replied Aurelia, "a painful impression, a hated recollection of my faithless friend, has robbed me of all enjoyment in that beautiful and cultivated tongue. How I hate it now with my whole strength and heart! During the period of our kindliest connection, he wrote in German; and what genuine, powerful, cordial German! It was not till he wanted to get quit of me that he began seriously to write in French. I marked, I felt, what he meant. What he would have blushed to utter in his mother tongue, he could by this means write with a quiet conscience. It is the language of reservations, equivocations, and lies: it is a *perfidious* language. Heaven be praised! I cannot find another word to express this *perfide* of theirs in all its compass. Our poor *treulos*, the *faithless* of the English, are innocent as babes beside it. *Perfide* means faithless with pleasure, with insolence and malice. How enviable is the culture of a nation that can figure out so many shades of meaning by a single word! French is exactly the language of the world, — worthy to become the universal language, that all may have it in their power to cheat and cozen and betray each other! His French letters were always smooth and pleasant, while you read them. If you chose to believe it, they sounded warmly, even passionately; but, if you examined narrowly, they were but phrases, — accursed phrases! He has spoiled my feeling to the whole language, to French literature, even to the beautiful, delicious expressions of noble souls which may be found in it. I shudder when a French word is spoken in my hearing."

In such terms she could for hours continue to give utterance to her chagrin, interrupting or disturbing every other kind of conversation. Sooner or later, Serlo used to put an end to such peevish lamentations by some bitter sally; but by this means, commonly, the talk for the evening was destroyed.

In all provinces of life, it is unhappily the case, that whatever is to be accomplished by a number of co-operating men and circumstances cannot long continue perfect. Of an acting company as well as of a kingdom, of a circle of friends as well as of an army, you may commonly select the moment when it may be said that all was standing on the highest pinnacle of harmony, perfection, contentment, and activity. But alterations will ere long occur; the individuals that compose the body often change; new members are added; the persons are no longer suited to the circumstances, or the circumstances to the persons; what was formerly united quickly falls asunder. Thus it was with Serlo's company. For a time you might have called it as complete as any German company could ever boast of being. Most of the actors were occupying their proper places: all had enough to do, and all did it willingly. Their private personal condition was not bad; and each appeared to promise great things in his art, for each commenced with animation and alacrity. But it soon became apparent that a part of them were mere automatons, who could not reach beyond what was attainable without the aid of feeling. Nor was it long till grudgings and envyings arose among them, such as commonly obstruct every good arrangement, and easily distort and tear in pieces every thing that reasonable and thinking men would wish to keep united.

The departure of Philina was not quite so insignificant as it had at first appeared. She had always skilfully contrived to entertain the manager, and keep the others in good humor. She had endured Aurelia's violence with amazing patience, and her dearest task had been to flatter Wilhelm. Thus she was, in some respects, a bond of union for the whole: the loss of her was quickly felt.

Serlo could not live without some little passion of the love sort. Elmira was of late grown up, we might almost say grown beautiful; for some time she had been attracting his attention: and Philina, with her usual dexterity, had favored this attachment so soon as she observed it. "We should train ourselves in time," she would say, "to the business of procuress: nothing else remains for us when we are old." Serlo and Elmira had by this means so approximated to each other, that, shortly after the departure of Philina, both were of a mind: and their small romance was rendered doubly interesting, as they had to hide it sedulously from the father; Old Boisterous not understanding jokes of that description. Elmira's sister had been admitted to the secret; and Serlo was, in consequence, obliged to overlook a multitude of things in both of them. One of their worst habits was an excessive love of junketing, — nay, if you will, an intolerable gluttony. In this respect they altogether differed from Philina, to whom it gave a new tint of loveliness, that she seemed, as it were, to live on air, eating very little; and, for drink, merely skimming off, with all imaginable grace, the foam from a glass of champagne.

Now, however, Serlo, if he meant to please his doxies, was obliged to join breakfast with dinner; and with this, by a substantial bever, to connect the supper. But, amid gormandizing, Serlo entertained another plan, which he longed to have fulfilled. He imagined that he saw a kind of attachment between Wilhelm and Aurelia, and he anxiously wished that it might assume a serious shape. He hoped to cast the whole mechanical department of his theatrical economy on Wilhelm's shoulders; to find in him, as in the former brother, a faithful and industrious tool. Already he had, by degrees, shifted over to him most of the cares of management; Aurelia kept the strong-box; and Serlo once more lived as he had done of old, entirely according to his humor. Yet there was a circumstance which vexed him in secret, as it did his sister likewise.

The world has a particular way of acting towards public persons of acknowledged merit: it gradually begins to be indifferent to them, and to favor talents which are new, though far inferior; it makes excessive requisitions of the former, and accepts of any thing with approbation from the latter.

Serlo and Aurelia had opportunity enough to meditate on this peculiarity. The strangers, especially the young and handsome ones, had drawn the whole attention and applause upon themselves; and Serlo and his sister, in spite of the most zealous efforts, had in general to make their exits without the welcome sound of clapping hands. It is true, some special causes were at work on this occasion. Aurelia's pride was palpable, and her contempt for the public was known to many. Serlo, indeed, flattered every individual; but his cutting jibes against the whole were often circulated and repeated. The new members, again, were not only strangers, unknown, and wanting help, but some of them were likewise young and amiable: thus all of them found patrons.

Erelong, too, there arose internal discontents, and many bickerings, among the actors. Scarcely had they noticed that our friend was acting as director, when most of them began to grow the more remiss, the more he strove to introduce a better order, greater accuracy, and chiefly to insist that every thing mechanical should be performed in the most strict and regular manner.

Thus, by and by, the whole concern, which actually for a time had nearly looked ideal, grew as vulgar in its attributes as any mere itinerating theatre. And, unhappily, just as Wilhelm, by his labor, diligence, and vigorous efforts, had made himself acquainted with the requisitions of the art, and trained completely both his person and his habits to comply with them, he began to feel, in melancholy hours, that this craft deserved the necessary outlay of time and talents less than any other. The task was burdensome, the recompense was small. He would rather have engaged with any occupation in which, when the period of exertion is passed, one can enjoy repose of mind, than with this, wherein, after undergoing much mechanical drudgery, the aim of one's activity cannot still be attained but by the strongest effort of thought and emotion. Besides, he had to listen to Aurelia's complaints about her brother's wastefulness: he had to misconceive the winks and nods of Serlo, trying from afar to lead him to a marriage with Aurelia. He had, withal, to hide his own secret sorrow, which pressed heavy on his heart, because of that ambiguous officer whom he had sent in quest of. The messenger returned not, sent no tidings; and Wilhelm feared that his Mariana was lost to him a second time.

About this period, there occurred a public mourning, which obliged our friends to shut their theatre for several weeks. Wilhelm seized this opportunity to pay a visit to the clergyman with whom the harper had been placed to board. He found him in a pleasant district; and the first thing that he noticed in the parsonage was the old man teaching a boy to play upon his instrument. The harper showed great joy at sight of Wilhelm: he rose, held out his hand, and said, "You see, I am still good for something in the world; permit me to continue; for my hours are all distributed, and full of business."

The clergyman saluted Wilhelm very kindly, and told him that the harper promised well, already giving hopes of a complete recovery.

Their conversation naturally turned upon the various modes of treating the insane.

"Except physical derangements," observed the clergyman, "which often place insuperable difficulties in the way, and in regard to which I follow the prescriptions of a wise physician, the means of curing madness seem to me extremely simple. They are the very means by which you hinder sane persons from becoming mad. Awaken their activity; accustom them to order; bring them to perceive that they hold their being and their fate in common with many millions; that extraordinary talents, the highest happiness, the deepest misery, are but slight variations from the general lot: in this way, no insanity will enter, or, if it has entered, will gradually disappear. I have portioned out the old man's hours: he gives lessons to some children on the harp; he works in the garden; he is already much more cheerful. He wishes to enjoy the cabbages he plants: my son, to whom in case of death he has bequeathed his harp, he is ardent to instruct, that the boy may be able to make use of his inheritance. I have said but little to him, as a clergyman, about his wild, mysterious scruples; but a busy life brings on so many incidents, that erelong he must feel how true it is, that doubt of any kind can be removed by nothing but activity. I go softly to work: yet, if I could get his beard and hood removed, I should reckon it a weighty point; for nothing more exposes us to madness than distinguishing ourselves from others, and nothing more contributes to maintain our common sense than living in the universal way with multitudes of men. Alas! how much there is in education, in our social institutions, to prepare us and our children for insanity!"

Wilhelm staid some days with this intelligent divine; heard from him many curious narratives, not of the insane alone, but of persons such as commonly are reckoned wise and rational, though they may have peculiarities which border on insanity.

The conversation became doubly animated, on the entrance of the doctor, with whom it was a custom to pay frequent visits to his friend the clergyman, and to assist him in his labors of humanity. The physician was an oldish man, who, though in weak health, had spent many years in the practice of the noblest virtues. He was a strong advocate for country life, being himself scarcely able to exist except in the open air. Withal, he was extremely active and companionable. For several years he had shown a special inclination to make friends with all the country clergymen within his reach. Such of these as were employed in any useful occupation he strove by every means to help;

into others, who were still unsettled in their aims, he endeavored to infuse a taste for some profitable species of exertion. Being at the same time in connection with a multitude of noblemen, magistrates, judges, he had in the space of twenty years, in secret, accomplished much towards the advancement of many branches of husbandry: he had done his best to put in motion every project that seemed capable of benefiting agriculture, animals, or men, and had thus forwarded improvement in its truest sense. "For man," he used to say, "there is but one misfortune, — when some idea lays hold of him, which exerts no influence upon active life, or, still more, which withdraws him from it. At the present time," continued he, on this occasion, "I have such a case before me: it concerns a rich and noble couple, and hitherto has baffled all my skill. The affair belongs in part to your department, worthy pastor; and your friend here will forbear to mention it again.

"In the absence of a certain nobleman, some persons of the house, in a frolic not entirely commendable, disguised a young man in the master's clothes. The lady was to be imposed upon by this deception; and, although it was described to me as nothing but a joke, I am much afraid the purpose of it was to lead this noble and most amiable lady from the path of honor. Her husband, however, unexpectedly returns; enters his chamber; thinks he sees his spirit; and from that time falls into a melancholy temper, firmly believing that his death is near.

"He has now abandoned himself to men who pamper him with religious ideas; and I see not how he is to be prevented from going among the Herrnhuters with his lady, and, as he has no children, from depriving his relations of the chief part of his fortune."

"With his lady?" cried our friend in great agitation; for this story had frightened him extremely.

"And, alas!" replied the doctor, who regarded Wilhelm's exclamation only as the voice of common sympathy, "this lady is herself possessed with a deeper sorrow, which renders a removal from the world desirable to her also. The same young man was taking leave of her; she was not circumspect enough to hide a nascent inclination towards him; the youth grew bolder, clasped her in his arms, and pressed a large portrait of her husband, which was set with diamonds, forcibly against her breast. She felt a sharp pain, which gradually went off, leaving first a little redness, then no trace at all. As a man, I am convinced that she has nothing further to reproach herself with, in this affair; as a physician, I am certain that this pressure could not have the smallest ill effect. Yet she will not be persuaded that an induration is not taking place in the part; and, if you try to overcome her notion by the evidence of feeling, she maintains, that, though the evil is away this moment, it will return the next. She conceives that the disease will end in cancer, and thus her youth and loveliness be altogether lost to others and herself."

"Wretch that I am!" cried Wilhelm, striking his brow, and rushing from the company into the fields. He had never felt himself in such a miserable case.

The clergyman and the physician were of course exceedingly astonished at this singular discovery. In the evening all their skill was called for, when our friend returned, and, with a circumstantial disclosure of the whole occurrence, uttered the most violent accusations of himself. Both took interest in him: both felt a real concern about his general condition, particularly as he painted it in the gloomy colors which arose from the humor of the moment.

Next day the physician, without much entreaty, was prevailed upon to accompany him in his return; both that he might bear him company, and that he might, if possible, do something for Aurelia, whom our friend had left in rather dangerous circumstances.

In fact, they found her worse than they expected. She was afflicted with a sort of intermittent fever, which could the less be mastered, as she purposely maintained and aggravated the attacks of it. The stranger was not introduced as a physician: he behaved with great courteousness and prudence. They conversed about her situation, bodily and mental: her new friend related many anecdotes of persons who, in spite of lingering disorders, had attained a good old age; adding, that, in such cases, nothing could be more injurious than the intentional recalling of passionate and disagreeable emotions. In particular he stated, that, for persons laboring under chronical and partly incurable distempers, he had always found it a very happy circumstance when they chanced to entertain, and cherish in their minds, true feelings of religion. This he signified in the most unobtrusive manner, as it were historically; promising Aurelia at the same time the reading of a very interesting manuscript, which he said he had received from the hands of an excellent lady of his friends, who was now deceased. "To me," he said, "it is of uncommon value; and I shall trust you even with the original. Nothing but the title is in my handwriting: I have called it, 'Confessions of a Fair Saint.' "

Touching the medical and dietetic treatment of the racked and hapless patient, he also left his best advice with Wilhelm. He then departed; promising to write, and, if possible, to come again in person.

Meanwhile, in Wilhelm's absence, there had changes been preparing such as he was not aware of. During his directorship, our friend had managed all things with a certain liberality and freedom; looking chiefly at the main result. Whatever was required for dresses, decorations, and the like, he had usually provided in a plentiful and handsome style; and, for securing the co-operation of his people, he had flattered their self-interest, since he could not reach them by nobler motives. In this he felt his conduct justified the more; as Serlo for his own part never aimed at being a strict economist, but liked to hear the beauty of his theatre commended, and was contented if Aurelia, who conducted the domestic matters, on defraying all expenses, signified that she was free from debt, and could besides afford the necessary sums for clearing off such scores as Serlo in the interim, by lavish kindness to his mistresses or otherwise, might have incurred.

Melina, who was charged with managing the wardrobe, had all the while been silently considering these things, with the cold, spiteful temper peculiar to him. On occasion of our friend's departure, and Aurelia's increasing sickness, he contrived to signify to Serlo, that more money might be raised and less expended, and, consequently, something be laid up, or at least a merrier life be led. Serlo hearkened gladly to such allegations, and Melina risked the exhibition of his plan.

"I will not say," continued he, "that any of your actors has at present too much salary: they are meritorious people, they would find a welcome anywhere; but, for the income which they bring us in, they have too much. My project would be, to set up an opera; and, as to what concerns the playhouse, I may be allowed to say it, you are the person for maintaining that establishment upon your single strength. Observe how at present your merits are neglected; and justice is refused you, not because your fellow-actors are excellent, but merely good.

"Come out alone, as used to be the case; endeavor to attract around you middling, I will even say inferior people, for a slender salary; regale the public with mechanical displays, as you can so cleverly do; apply your remaining means to the opera, which I am talking of; and you will quickly see, that, with the same labor and expense, you will give greater satisfaction, while you draw incomparably more money than at present."

These observations were so flattering to Serlo, that they could not fail of making some impression on him. He readily admitted, that, loving music as he did, he had long wished for some arrangement such as this; though he could not but perceive that the public taste would thus be still more widely led astray, and that with such a mongrel theatre, not properly an opera, not properly a playhouse, any residue of true feeling for regular and perfect works of art must shortly disappear.

Melina ridiculed, in terms more plain than delicate, our friend's pedantic notions in this matter, and his vain attempts to form the public mind, instead of being formed by it : Serlo and he at last agreed, with full conviction, that the sole concern was, how to gather money, and grow rich, or live a joyous life; and they scarcely concealed their wish to be delivered from those persons who at present hindered them. Melina took occasion to lament Aurelia's weak health, and the speedy end which it threatened; thinking all the while directly the reverse. Serlo affected to regret that Wilhelm could not sing, thus signifying that his presence was by no means indispensable. Melina then came forward with a whole catalogue of savings, which, he said, might be effected; and Serlo saw in him his brother-in-law replaced threefold. They both felt that secrecy was necessary in the matter, but this mutual obligation only joined them closer in their interests. They failed not to converse together privately on every thing that happened; to blame whatever Wilhelm or Aurelia undertook; and to elaborate their own project, and prepare it more and more for execution.

Silent as they both might be about their plan, little as their words betrayed them, in their conduct they were not so politic as constantly to hide their purposes. Melina now opposed our friend in many points that lay within the province of the latter; and Serlo, who had never acted smoothly to his sister, seemed to grow more bitter the more her sickness deepened, the more her passionate and variable humors would have needed toleration.

About this period they took up the "Emilie Galotti" of Lessing. The parts were very happily distributed and filled: within the narrow circle of this tragedy, the company found room for showing all the complex riches of their acting. Serlo, in the character of Marinelli, was altogether in his place; Odoardo was very well exhibited; Madam Melina played the Mother with considerable skill; Elmira gained distinction as Emilie; Laertes made a stately Appiani; and Wilhelm had bestowed the study of some months upon the Prince's part. On this occasion, both internally and with Aurelia and Serlo, he had often come upon this question: What is the distinction between a noble and a well-bred manner? and how far must the former be included in the latter, though the latter is not in the former?

Serlo, who himself in Marinelli had to act the courtier accurately, without caricature, afforded him some valuable thoughts on this. "A well-bred carriage," he would say, "is difficult to imitate; for in strictness it is negative, and it implies a long-continued previous training. You are not required to exhibit in your manner any thing that specially betokens dignity; for, by this means, you are like to run into formality and haughtiness: you are rather to avoid whatever is undignified and vulgar. You are never to forget yourself; are to keep a constant watch upon yourself and others; to forgive nothing that is faulty in your own conduct, in that of others neither to forgive too little nor too much. Nothing must appear to touch you, nothing to agitate: you must never overhaste yourself, must ever keep yourself composed, retaining still an outward calmness, whatever storms may rage within. The noble character at certain moments may resign himself to his emotions; the well-bred never. The latter is like a man dressed out in fair and spotless clothes: he will not lean on any thing; every person will beware of rubbing on him. He distinguishes himself from others, yet he may not stand apart; for as in all arts, so in this, the hardest must at length be done with ease: the well-bred man of rank, in spite of every separation, always seems united with the people round him; he is never to be stiff or uncomplying; he is always to appear the first, and never to insist on so appearing.

"It is clear, then, that, to seem well-bred, a man must actually be so. It is also clear why women generally are more expert at taking up the air of breeding than the other sex; why courtiers and soldiers catch it more easily than other men."

Wilhelm now despaired of doing justice to his part; but Serlo aided and encouraged him, communicated the acutest observations on detached points, and furnished him so well, that, on the exhibition of the piece, the public reckoned him a very proper Prince.

Serlo had engaged to give him, when the play was over, such remarks as might occur upon his acting: a disagreeable contention with Aurelia prevented any conversation of that kind. Aurelia had acted the character of Orsina, in such a style as few have ever done. She was well acquainted with the part, and during the rehearsals she had treated it indifferently: but, in the exhibition of the piece, she had opened, as it were, all the sluices of her personal sorrow; and the character was represented so as never poet in the first glow of invention could have figured it. A boundless applause rewarded her painful efforts; but her friends, on visiting her when the play was finished, found her half fainting in her chair.

Serlo had already signified his anger at her overcharged acting, as he called it; at this disclosure of her inmost heart before the public, to many individuals of which the history of her fatal passion was more or less completely known. He had spoken bitterly and fiercely; grinding with his teeth and stamping with his feet, as was his custom when enraged. "Never mind her," cried he, when he saw her in the chair, surrounded by the rest: "she will go upon the stage stark-naked one of these days, and then the approbation will be perfect."

"Ungrateful, inhuman man!" exclaimed she: "soon shall I be carried naked to the place where approbation or disapprobation can no longer reach our ears!" With these words she started up, and hastened to the door. The maid had not yet brought her mantle; the sedan was not in waiting; it had been raining lately; a cold, raw wind was blowing through the streets. They endeavored to persuade her to remain, for she was very warm. But in vain: she purposely walked slow; she praised the coolness, seemed to inhale it with peculiar eagerness. No sooner was she home, than she became so hoarse that she could hardly speak a word: she did not mention that there was a total stiffness in her neck and along her back. Shortly afterwards a sort of palsy in the tongue came on, so that she pronounced one word instead of another. They put her to bed: by numerous and copious remedies, the evil changed its form, but was not mastered. The fever gathered strength: her case was dangerous.

Next morning she enjoyed a quiet hour. She sent for Wilhelm, and delivered him a letter. "This sheet," said she, "has long been waiting for the present moment. I feel that my end is drawing nigh: promise me that you yourself will take this paper; that, by a word or two, you will avenge my sorrows on the faithless man. He is not void of feeling: my death will pain him for a moment."

Wilhelm took the letter; still endeavoring to console her, and to drive away the thought of death.

"No," said she: "do not deprive me of my nearest hope. I have waited for him long: I will joyfully clasp him when he comes."

Shortly after this the manuscript arrived which the physician had engaged to send her. She called for Wilhelm, — made him read it to her. The effect which it produced upon her, the reader will be better able to appreciate after looking at the following Book. The violent and stubborn temper of our poor Aurelia was mollified by hearing it. She took back the letter, and wrote another, as it seemed, in a meeker tone, charging Wilhelm at the same time to console her friend, if he should be distressed about her death; to assure him that she had forgiven him, and wished him every kind of happiness.

From this time she was very quiet, and appeared to occupy herself with but a few ideas, which she endeavored to extract and appropriate from the manuscript, out of which she frequently made Wilhelm read to her. The decay of her strength was not perceptible: nor had Wilhelm been anticipating the event, when one morning, as he went to visit her, he found that she was dead.

Entertaining such respect for her as he had done, and accustomed as he was to live in her society, the loss of her affected him with no common sorrow. She was the only person that had truly wished him well: the coldness of Serlo he had felt of late but too keenly. He hastened, therefore, to perform the service she had intrusted to him: he wished to be absent for a time.

On the other hand, this journey was exceedingly convenient for Melina: in the course of his extensive correspondence, he had lately entered upon terms with a male and a female singer, who, it was intended, should, by their performances in interludes, prepare the public for his future opera. The loss of Aurelia, and Wilhelm's absence, were to be supplied in this manner; and our friend was satisfied with any thing that could facilitate his setting out.

He had formed, within himself, a singular idea of the importance of his errand. The death of his unhappy friend had moved him deeply; and, having seen her pass so early from the scene, he could not but be hostilely inclined against the man who had abridged her life, and made that shortened term so full of woe.

Notwithstanding the last mild words of the dying woman, he resolved, that, on delivering his letter, he would pass a strict sentence on her faithless friend; and, not wishing to depend upon the temper of the moment, he studied an address, which, in the course of preparation, became more pathetic than just. Having fully convinced himself of the good composition of his essay, he began committing it to memory, and at the same time making ready for departure. Mignon was present as he packed his articles: she asked him whether he intended travelling south or north; and, learning that it was the latter, she replied, "Then, I will wait here for thee." She begged of him the pearl necklace which had once been Mariana's. He could not refuse to gratify the dear little creature, and he gave it her: the neckerchief she had already. On the other hand, she put the veil of Hamlet's Ghost into his travelling-bag; though he told her it could not be of any service to him.

Melina took upon him the directorship: his wife engaged to keep a mother's eye upon the children, whom Wilhelm parted with unwillingly. Felix was very merry at the setting out; and, when asked what pretty thing he wished to have brought back for him, he said, "Hark you! bring me a papa!" Mignon seized the traveller's hand; then, standing on her tiptoes, she pressed a warm and cordial, though not a tender, kiss upon his lips, and cried, "Master! forget us not, and come soon back."

And so we leave our friend, entering on his journey, amid a thousand different thoughts and feelings; and here subjoin, by way of close, a little poem, which Mignon had recited once or twice with great expressiveness, and which the hurry of so many singular occurrences prevented us from inserting sooner: —

O, ask me not to speak, I pray thee!
It must not be reveal'd but hid;
How gladly would my tongue obey thee,
Did not the voice of Fate forbid!

At his appointed time revolving,
The sun these shades of night dispels;
The rock, its rugged breast dissolving,
Gives up to Earth its hidden wells.

In Friendship's arms each heart reposes;
There soul to soul pours out its woe:
My lips an oath forever closes,
My sorrows God alone can know.

Book Six

TILL MY eighth year I was always a healthy child, but of that period I can recollect no more than of the day when I was born. About the beginning of my eighth year, I was seized with a hemorrhage; and from that moment my soul became all feeling, all memory. The smallest circumstances of that accident are yet before my eyes as if they had occurred but yesterday.

During the nine months which I then spent patiently upon a sick-bed, it appears to me the groundwork of my whole turn of thought was laid; as the first means were then afforded my mind of developing itself in its own manner.

I suffered and I loved: this was the peculiar form of my heart. In the most violent fits of coughing, in the depressing pains of fever, I lay quiet, like a snail drawn back within its house: the moment I obtained a respite, I wanted to enjoy something pleasant; and, as every other pleasure was denied me, I endeavored to amuse myself with the innocent delights of eye and ear. The people brought me dolls and picture-books, and whoever would sit by my bed was obliged to tell me something.

From my mother I rejoiced to hear the Bible histories, and my father entertained me with natural curiosities. He had a very pretty cabinet, from which he brought me first one drawer and then another, as occasion served; showing me the articles, and pointing out their properties. Dried plants and insects, with many kinds of anatomical preparations, such as human skin, bones, mummies, and the like, were in succession laid upon the sick-bed of the little one; the birds and animals he killed in hunting were shown to me, before they passed into the kitchen; and, that the Prince of the World might also have a voice in this assembly, my aunt related to me love-adventures out of fairy-tales. All was accepted, all took root. There were hours in which I vividly conversed with the Invisible Power. I can still repeat some verses which I then dictated, and my mother wrote down.

Often I would tell my father back again what I had learned from him. Rarely did I take any physic without asking where the simples it was made of grew, what look they had, what names they bore. Nor had the stories of my aunt lighted on stony ground. I figured myself out in pretty clothes, and met the most delightful princes, who could find no peace or rest till they discovered who the unknown beauty was. One adventure of this kind, with a charming little angel dressed in white, with golden wings, who warmly courted me, I dwelt upon so long, that my imagination painted out his form almost to visibility.

After a year I was pretty well restored to health, but nothing of the giddiness of childhood remained with me. I could not play with dolls: I longed for beings able to return my love. Dogs, cats, and birds, of which my father kept a great variety, afforded me delight; but what would I have given for such a creature as my aunt once told me of! It was a lamb which a peasant-girl took up and nourished in a wood; but, in the guise of this pretty beast, an enchanted prince was hid, who at length appeared in his native shape, a lovely youth, and rewarded his benefactress by his hand. Such a lamb I would have given the world for.

But there was none to be had; and, as every thing about me went on in such a quite natural manner, I by degrees all but abandoned nearly all hopes of such a treasure. Meanwhile I comforted myself by reading books in which the strangest incidents were set forth. Among them all, my favorite was the "Christian German Hercules": that devout love-history was altogether in my way. Whenever any thing befell his dear Valiska, and cruel things befell her, he always prayed before hastening to her aid; and the prayers stood there *verbatim*. My longing after the Invisible, which I had always dimly felt, was strengthened by such means; for, in short, it was ordained that God should also be my confidant.

As I grew older I continued reading, Heaven knows what, in

chaotic order. The "Roman Octavia" was the book I liked beyond all others. The persecutions of the first Christians, decorated with the charms of a romance, awoke the deepest interest in me.

But my mother now began to murmur at my constant reading; and, to humor her, my father took away my books to-day, but gave them back to-morrow. She was wise enough to see that nothing could be done in this way: she next insisted merely that my Bible should be read with equal diligence. To this I was not disinclined, and I accordingly perused the sacred volume with a lively interest. Withal my mother was extremely careful that no books of a corruptive tendency should come into my hands: immodest writings I would, of my own accord, have cast away; for my princes and my princesses were all extremely virtuous.

To my mother, and my zeal for knowledge, it was owing, that, with all my love of books, I also learned to cook; for much was to be seen in cookery. To cut up a hen, a pig, was quite a feast for me. I used to bring the entrails to my father, and he talked with me about them as if I had been a student of anatomy. With suppressed joy he would often call me his misfashioned son.

I had passed my twelfth year. I learned French, dancing, and drawing: I received the usual instructions in religion. In the latter, many thoughts and feelings were awakened, but nothing properly relating to my own condition. I liked to hear the people speak of God: I was proud that I could speak on these points better than my equals. I zealously read many books which put me in a condition to talk about religion; but it never once struck me to think how matters stood with *me*, whether *my* soul was formed according to these holy precepts, whether it was like a glass from which the everlasting sun could be reflected in its glancing. From the first I had presupposed all this.

My French I learned with eagerness. My teacher was a clever man. He was not a vain empiric, not a dry grammarian: he had learning, he had seen the world. Instructing me in language, he satisfied my zeal for knowledge in a thousand ways. I loved him so much, that I used to wait his coming with a palpitating heart. Drawing was not hard for me: I should have made greater progress had my teacher possessed head and science; he had only hands and practice.

Dancing was at first one of my smallest amusements; my body

was too sensitive for it; I learned it only in the company of my sisters. But our dancing-master took a thought of gathering all his scholars, male and female, and giving them a ball. This event gave dancing quite another charm for me.

Amid a throng of boys and girls, the most remarkable were two sons of the marshal of the court. The youngest was of my age; the other, two years older: they were children of such beauty, that, according to the universal voice, no one had seen their like. For my part, scarcely had I noticed them when I lost sight of all the other crowd. From that moment I began to dance with care, and to wish that I could dance with grace. How came it, on the other hand, that these two boys distinguished me from all the rest? No matter: before an hour had passed we had become the warmest friends, and our little entertainment did not end till we had fixed upon the time and place where we were next to meet. What a joy for me! And how charmed was I next morning when both of them inquired for my health, each in a gallant note, accompanied with a nosegay! I have never since felt as I then did. Compliment was met by compliment: letter answered letter. The church and the public-walks were grown a rendezvous; our young acquaintances, in all their little parties, now invited us together; while, at the same time, we were sly enough to veil the business from our parents, so that they saw no more of it than we thought good.

Thus had I at once got a pair of lovers. I had yet decided upon neither: they both pleased me, and we did extremely well together. All at once the eldest of the two fell very sick. I myself had often been sick; and thus I was enabled, by rendering him many little dainties and delicacies suited for a sick person, to afford some solace to the sufferer. His parents thankfully acknowledged my attention: in compliance with the prayer of their beloved son, they invited me, with all my sisters, to their house so soon as he had arisen from his sick-bed. The tenderness which he displayed on meeting me was not the feeling of a child: from that day I gave the preference to him. He warned me to keep our secret from his brother; but the flame could no longer be concealed, and the jealousy of the younger completed our romance. He played us a thousand tricks: eager to annihilate our joys, he but increased the passion he was seeking to destroy.

At last I had actually found the wished-for lamb, and this attachment acted on me like my sickness: it made me calm, and drew me back from noisy pleasures. I was solitary, I was moved; and thoughts of God again occurred to me. He was again my confidant; and I well remember with what tears I often prayed for this poor boy, who still continued sickly.

The more childishness there was in this adventure, the more did it contribute to the forming of my heart. Our French teacher had now turned us from translating into daily writing him some letter of our own invention. I brought my little history to market, shrouded in the names of Phyllis and Damon. The old man soon saw through it, and, to render me communicative, praised my labor very much. I still waxed bolder; came openly out with the affair, adhering, even in the minute details, to truth. I do not now remember what the passage was at which he took occasion to remark, "How pretty, how natural, it is! But the good Phyllis had better have a care: the thing may soon grow serious."

I felt vexed that he did not look upon the matter as already serious; and I asked him, with an air of pique, what he meant by serious. I had not to repeat the question: he explained himself so clearly, that I could scarcely hide my terror. Yet as anger came along with it, as I took it ill that he should entertain such thoughts, I kept myself composed: I tried to justify my nymph, and said, with glowing cheeks, "But, sir, Phyllis is an honorable girl."

He was rogue enough to banter me about my honorable heroine. While we were speaking French, he played upon the word *honnête*, and hunted the honorableness of Phyllis over all its meanings. I felt the ridicule of this, and extremely puzzled. He, not to frighten me, broke off, but afterwards often led the conversation to such topics. Plays, and little histories, such as I was reading and translating with him, gave him frequent opportunity to show how feeble a security against the calls of inclination our boasted virtue was. I no longer contradicted him, but I was in secret scandalized; and his remarks became a burden to me.

With my worthy Damon, too, I by degrees fell out of all connection. The chicanery of the younger boy destroyed our intercourse. Soon after, both these blooming creatures died. I lamented sore: however, in a short time, I forgot.

But Phyllis rapidly increased in stature, was altogether healthy, and began to see the world. The hereditary prince now married, and a short time after, on his father's death, began his rule. Court and town were in the liveliest motion : my curiosity had copious nourishment. There were plays and balls, with all their usual accompaniments; and, though my parents kept retired as much as possible, they were obliged to show themselves at court, where I was of course introduced. Strangers were pouring in from every side; high company was in every house; even to us some cavaliers were recommended, others introduced; and, at my uncle's, men of every nation might be met with.

My honest mentor still continued, in a modest and yet striking way, to warn me, and I in secret to take it ill of him. With regard to his assertion, that women under every circumstance were weak, I did not feel at all convinced; and here, perhaps, I was in the right, and my mentor in the wrong: but he spoke so earnestly that once I grew afraid he might be right, and said to him, with much vivacity, "Since the danger is so great, and the human heart so weak, I will pray to God that he may keep me."

This simple answer seemed to please him, for he praised my purpose; but, on my side, it was any thing but seriously meant. It was, in truth, but an empty word; for my feelings towards the Invisible were almost totally extinguished. The hurry and the crowd I lived in dissipated my attention, and carried me along as in a rapid stream. These were the emptiest years of my life. All day long to speak of nothing, to have no solid thought, never to do any thing but revel, — such was my employment. On my beloved books I never once bestowed a thought. The people I lived among had not the slightest tinge of literature or science : they were German courtiers, a class of men at that time altogether destitute of culture.

Such society, it may be thought, must naturally have led me to the brink of ruin. I lived away in mere corporeal cheerfulness: I never took myself to task, I never prayed, I never thought about myself or God. Yet I look upon it as a providential guidance, that none of these many handsome, rich, and well-dressed men could take my fancy. They were rakes, and did not conceal it; this scared me back: they adorned their speech with double meanings; this offended me, made me act with coldness towards them. Many times their improprieties exceeded belief, and I did not restrain myself from being rude.

Besides, my ancient counsellor had once in confidence contrived to tell me, that, with the greater part of these lewd fellows, health, as well as virtue, was in danger. I now shuddered at the sight of them: I was afraid if one of them in any way approached too near me. I would not touch their cups or glasses, — even the chairs they had been sitting on. Thus, morally and physically, I remained apart from them: all the compliments they paid me I haughtily accepted, as incense that was due.

Among the strangers then resident among us was one young man peculiarly distinguished, whom we used in sport to call Narciss. He had gained a reputation in the diplomatic line; and, among the various changes now occurring at court, he was in hopes of meeting with some advantageous place. He soon became acquainted with my father: his acquirements and manners opened for him the way to a select society of most accomplished men. My father often spoke in praise of him: his figure, which was very handsome, would have made a still better impression, had it not been for something of self-complacency which breathed from the whole carriage of the man. I had seen him, I thought well of him; but we had never spoken.

At a great ball, where we chanced to be in company, I danced a minuet with him; but this, too, passed without results. The more violent dances, in compliance with my father, who felt anxious about my health, I was accustomed to avoid: in the present case, when these came on, I retired to an adjoining room, and began to talk with certain of my friends, elderly ladies, who had set themselves to cards.

Narciss, who had jigged it for a while, at last came into the room where I was; and having got the better of a bleeding at the nose, which had overtaken him in dancing, he began speaking with me about a multitude of things. In half an hour the talk had grown so interesting, that neither of us could think of dancing any more. We were rallied by our friends, but we did not let their bantering disturb us. Next evening we recommenced our conversation, and were very careful not to hurt our health.

The acquaintance then was made. Narciss was often with my sisters and myself; and I now once more began to reckon over and consider what I knew, what I thought of, what I had felt, and what I could express myself about in conversation. My new friend had mingled in the best society; besides the department of history and politics, with every part of which he was familiar, he had gained extensive literary knowledge; there was nothing new that issued from the press, especially in France, that he was unacquainted with. He brought or sent me many a pleasant book, but this we had to keep as secret as forbidden love. Learned women had been made ridiculous, nor were well-informed women tolerated, — apparently because it would have been uncivil to put so many ill-informed men to shame. Even my father, much as he delighted in this new opportunity of cultivating my mind, expressly stipulated that our literary commerce should remain secret.

Thus our intercourse continued for almost year and day; and still I could not say, that, in any wise, Narciss had ever shown me aught of love or tenderness. He was always complaisant and kind, but manifested nothing like attachment: on the contrary, he even seemed to be in some degree affected by the charms of my youngest sister, who was then extremely beautiful. In sport, he gave her many little friendly names out of foreign tongues; for he could speak two or three of these extremely well, and loved to mix their idiomatic phrases with his German. Such compliments she did not answer very liberally; she was entangled in a different noose: and being very sharp, while he was very sensitive, the two were often quarrelling about trifles. With my mother and my aunt he kept on very pleasant terms; and thus, by gradual advances, he was grown to be a member of the family.

Who knows how long we might have lived in this way, had not a curious accident altered our relations all at once? My sisters and I were invited to a certain house, to which we did not like to go. The company was too mixed; and persons of the stupidest, if not the rudest, stamp were often to be met there. Narciss, on this occasion, was invited also; and on his account I felt inclined to go, for I was sure of finding one, at least, whom I could converse with as I desired. Even at table we had many things to suffer, for several of the gentlemen had drunk too much: then, in the drawing-room, they insisted on a game at forfeits. It went on with great vivacity and tumult. Narciss had lost a forfeit: they ordered him, by way of penalty, to whisper something pleasant in the ear of every member of the company. It seems he staid too long beside my next neighbor, the lady of a captain. The latter on a sudden struck him such a box with his fist, that the powder flew about me, into my eyes. When I had got my eyes cleared, and in some degree recovered from my terror, I saw that both gentlemen had drawn their swords. Narciss was bleeding; and the other, mad with wine and rage and jealousy, could scarcely be held back by all the company. I seized Narciss, led him by the arm upstairs; and, as I did not think my friend safe even here from his frantic enemy, I shut the door and bolted it.

Neither of us considered the wound serious, for a slight cut across the hand was all we saw. Soon, however, I discovered that there was a stream of blood running down his back, that there was a deep wound on the head. I now began to be afraid. I hastened to the lobby, to get help: but I could see no person; every one had staid below to calm the raving captain. At last a daughter of the family came skipping up: her mirth annoyed me; she was like to die with laughing at the bedlam spectacle. I conjured her, for the sake of Heaven, to get a surgeon; and she, in her wild way, sprang down-stairs to fetch me one herself.

Returning to my wounded friend, I found my handkerchief about his hand, and a neckerchief, that was hanging on the door, about his head. He was still bleeding copiously: he now grew pale, and seemed as if he were about to faint. There was none at hand to aid me: I very freely put my arm round him, patted his cheek, and tried to cheer him by little flatteries. It seemed to act on him like a spiritual remedy: he kept his senses, but sat as pale as death.

At last the active housewife arrived: it is easy to conceive her terror when she saw my friend in this predicament, lying in my arms, and both of us bestreamed with blood. No one had supposed he was wounded: all imagined I had carried him away in safety.

Now smelling-bottles, wine, and every thing that could support and stimulate, were copiously produced. The surgeon also came, and I might easily have been dispensed with. Narciss, however, held me firmly by the hand: I would have staid without holding. During the dressing of his wounds, I continued wetting his lips with wine: I minded not, though all the company were now about us. The surgeon having finished, his patient took a mute but tender leave of me, and was conducted home.

The mistress of the house now led me to her bedroom: she had to strip me altogether; and I must confess, while they washed the blood from me, I saw with pleasure, for the first time, in a mirror, that I might be reckoned beautiful without help of dress. No portion of my clothes could be put on again; and, as the people of the house were all either less or larger than myself, I was taken home in a strange disguise. My parents were, of course, astonished. They felt exceedingly indignant at my fright, at the wounds of their friend, at the captain's madness, at the whole occurrence. A very little would have made my father send the captain a challenge, that he might avenge his friend without delay. He blamed the gentlemen that had been there, because they had not punished on the spot such a murderous attempt; for it was but too clear, that the captain, instantly on striking, had drawn his sword, and wounded the other from behind. The cut across the hand had been given just when Narciss himself was grasping at his sword. I felt unspeakably affected, altered; or how shall I express it? The passion which was sleeping at the deepest bottom of my heart had at once broken loose, like a flame getting air. And if joy and pleasure are well suited for the first producing and the silent nourishing of love, yet this passion, bold by nature, is most easily impelled by terror to decide and to declare itself. My mother gave her little flurried daughter some medicine, and made her go to bed. With the earliest morrow my father hastened to Narciss, whom he found lying very sick of a wound-fever.

He told me little of what passed between them, but tried to quiet me about the probable results of this event. They were now considering whether an apology should be accepted, whether the affair should go before a court of justice, and many other points of that description. I knew my father too well to doubt that he would be averse to see the matter end without a duel: but I held my peace; for I had learned from him before, that women should not meddle in such things. For the rest, it did not strike me as if any thing had passed between the friends, in which my interests were specially concerned; but my father soon communicated to my mother the purport of their further conversation. Narciss, he said, appeared to be exceedingly affected at the help afforded by me; had embraced him, declared himself my debtor forever, signified that he desired no happiness except what he could share with me, and concluded by entreating that he might presume to ask my hand. All this mamma repeated to me, but subjoined the safe reflection, that, "as for what was said in the first agitation of mind in such a case, there was little trust to be placed in it." — "Of course, none," I answered with affected coldness; though all the while I was feeling, Heaven knows what.

Narciss continued sick for two months; owing to the wound in his right hand, he could not even write. Yet, in the mean time, he showed me his regard by the most obliging courtesies. All these unusual attentions I combined with what my mother had disclosed to me, and constantly my head was full of fancies. The whole city talked of the occurrence. With me they spoke of it in a peculiar tone: they drew inferences, which, greatly as I struggled to avoid them, touched me very close. What had formerly been habitude and trifling, was now grown seriousness and inclination. The anxiety in which I lived was the more violent, the more carefully I studied to conceal it from every one. The idea of losing him frightened me: the possibility of any closer union made me tremble. For a half-prudent girl, there is really something awful in the thought of marriage.

By such incessant agitations I was once more led to recollect myself. The gaudy imagery of a thoughtless life, which used to hover day and night before my eyes, was at once blown away. My soul again began to awaken, but the greatly interrupted intimacy with my invisible friend was not so easy to renew. We still continued at a frigid distance: it was again something, but little to the times of old.

A duel had been fought, and the captain severely wounded, before I ever heard of it. The public feeling was, in all senses, strong on the side of my lover, who at length again appeared upon the scene. But, first of all, he came, with his head tied up and his arm in a sling, to visit us. How my heart beat while he was there! The whole family was present: general thanks and compliments were all that passed on either side. Narciss, however, found an opportunity to show some secret tokens of his love to me; by which means my inquietude was but increased. After his recovery he visited us throughout the winter on the former footing; and in spite of all the soft, private marks of tenderness which he contrived to give me, the whole affair remained unsettled, undiscussed.

In this manner was I kept in constant practice. I could trust my thoughts to no mortal, and from God I was too far removed. Him I had quite forgotten those four wild years: I now again began to think of him occasionally, but our acquaintance had grown cool; they were visits of mere ceremony, these; and as, moreover, in waiting on him, I used to dress in fine apparel, to set before him self-complacently my virtue, honor, and superiorities to others, he did not seem to notice me, or know me in that finery.

A courtier would have been exceedingly distressed, if the prince who held his fortune in his hands had treated him in this way; but, for me, I did not sorrow at it. I had what I required, — health and conveniences: if God should please to think of me, well; if not, I reckoned I had done my duty.

Narciss in a duel

This, in truth, I did not think at that period; yet it was the true figure of my soul. But, to change and purify my feelings, preparations were already made.

The spring came on: Narciss once visited me unannounced, and at a time when I happend to be quite alone. He now appeared in the character of lover, and asked me if I could bestow on him my heart, and, so soon as he should obtain some lucrative and honorable place, my hand along with it.

He had been received into our service; but at first they kept him back, and would not rapidly promote him, because they dreaded his ambition. Having some little fortune of his own, he was left with a slender salary.

Notwithstanding my regard for him, I knew that he was not a man to treat with altogether frankly. I drew up, therefore, and referred him to my father. About my father he did not seem to doubt, but wished first to be at one with me, now and here. I at last said, Yes; but stipulated, as an indispensable condition, that my parents should concur. He then spoke formally with both of them; they signified their satisfaction: mutual promises were given, on the faith of his advancement, which it was expected would be speedy. Sisters and aunts were informed of this arrangement, and the strictest secrecy enjoined on them.

Thus had my lover become my bridegroom, and great was the difference between the two. If one could change the lovers of all honorable maidens into bridegrooms, it would be a kindness to our sex, even though marriage should not follow the connection. The love between two persons does not lessen by the change, but it becomes more reasonable. Innumerable little follies, all coquetries and caprices, disappear. If the bridegroom tells us that we please him better in a morning-cap than in the finest headdress, no discreet young woman will disturb herself about her hair-dressing; and nothing is more natural than that he, too, should think solidly, and rather wish to form a housewife for himself than a gaudy doll for others. And thus it is in every province of the business.

Should a young woman of this kind be fortunate enough to have a bridegroom who possesses understanding and acquirements, she learns from him more than universities and foreign lands can teach. She not only willingly receives instruction when he offers it, but she endeavors to elicit more and more from him. Love makes much that was impossible possible. By degrees, too, that subjection, so necessary and so graceful for the female sex, begins: the bridegroom does not govern like the husband; he only asks: but his mistress seeks to discover what he wants, and to offer it before he asks it.

So did experience teach me what I would not for much have missed. I was happy, truly happy as a woman could be in the world, — that is to say, for a while.

Amid these quiet joys, a summer passed away. Narciss gave not the slightest reason to complain of him: he daily became more dear to me; my whole soul was his. This he well knew, and knew also how to prize it. Meanwhile, from seeming trifles, something rose, which by and by grew hurtful to our union.

Narciss behaved to me as to a bride, and never dared to ask of me such favors as were yet forbidden us. But, about the boundaries of virtue and decorum, we were of very different opinions. I meant to walk securely, and so never granted him the smallest freedom which the whole world might not have witnessed. He, used to dainties, thought this diet very strict. On this point there was continual variance: he praised my modesty, and sought to undermine my resolution.

The *serious* of my old French teacher now occurred to me, as well as the defence which I had once suggested in regard to it.

With God I had again become a little more acquainted. He had given me a bridegroom whom I loved, and for this I felt some thankfulness. Earthly love itself concentrated my soul, and put its powers in motion; nor did it contradict my intercourse with God. I naturally complained to him of what alarmed me, but I did not perceive that I myself was wishing and desiring it. In my own eyes I was strong: I did not pray, "Lead us not into temptation!" My thoughts were far beyond temptation. In this flimsy tinselwork of virtue I came to God. He did not drive me back. On the smallest movement towards him, he left a soft impression in my soul; and this impression caused me always to return.

Except Narciss, the world was altogether dead to me: excepting him, there was nothing in it that had any charm. Even my love for dress was but the wish to please him: if I knew that he was not to see me, I could spend no care upon it. I liked to dance; but, if he was not beside me, it seemed as if I could not bear the motion. At a brilliant festival, if he was not invited, I could neither take the trouble of providing new things, nor of putting on the old according to the mode. To me they were alike agreeable, or rather, I might say, alike burdensome. I used to reckon such an evening very fairly spent when I could join myself to any ancient card-party, though formerly I had not the smallest taste for such things; and, if some old acquaintance came and rallied me about it, I would smile, perhaps for the first time all that night. So, likewise, it was with promenades, and every social entertainment that can be imagined: —

> "Him had I chosen from all others;
> His would I be, and not another's:
> To me his love was all in all."

Thus was I often solitary in the midst of company, and real solitude was generally acceptable to me. But my busy soul could neither sleep nor dream: I felt and thought, and acquired by degrees some faculty to speak about my feelings and my thoughts with God. Then were feelings of another sort unfolded, but these did not contradict the former feelings: my affection to Narciss accorded with the universal scheme of nature; it nowhere hindered the performance of a duty. They did not contradict each other, yet they were immensely different. Narciss was the only living form which hovered in my mind, and to which my love was all directed; but the other feeling was not directed towards any form, and yet it was unspeakably agreeable. I no longer have it: I no longer can impart it.

My lover, whom I used to trust with all my secrets, did not know of this. I soon discovered that he thought far otherwise: he often gave me writings which opposed, with light and heavy weapons, all that can be called connection with the Invisible. I used to read the books because they came from him; but, at the end, I knew no word of all that had been argued in them.

Nor, in regard to sciences and knowledge, was there want of contradiction in our conduct. He did as all men do, — he mocked at learned women; and yet he kept continually instructing me. He used to speak with me on all subjects, law excepted; and, while constantly procuring books of every kind for me, he frequently repeated the uncertain precept, "That a lady ought to keep the knowledge she might have more secret than the Calvinist his creed in Catholic countries." And while I, by natural consequence, endeavored not to show myself more wise or learned than formerly before the world, Narciss himself was commonly the first who yielded to the vanity of speaking about me and my superiorities.

A nobleman of high repute, and at that time valued for his influence, his talents, and accomplishments, was living at our court with great applause. He bestowed especial notice on Narciss, whom he kept continually about him. They once had an argument about the virtue of women. Narciss repeated to me what had passed between them: I was not wanting with my observations, and my friend required of me a written essay on the subject. I could write French fluently enough: I had laid a good foundation with my teacher. My correspondence with Narciss was likewise carried on in French: except in French books, there was then no elegant instruction to be had. My essay pleased the count: I was obliged to let him have some little songs, which I had lately been composing. In short, Narciss appeared to revel without stint in the renown of his beloved: and the story, to his great contentment, ended with a French epistle in heroic verse, which the count transmitted to him on departing; in which their argument was mentioned, and my friend reminded of his happiness in being destined, after all his doubts and errors, to learn most certainly what virtue was, in the arms of a virtuous and charming wife.

He showed this poem first of all to me, and then to almost every one; each thinking of the matter what he pleased. Thus did he act in several cases: every stranger, whom he valued, must be made acquainted in our house.

A noble family was staying for a season in the place, to profit by the skill of our physician. In this house, too, Narciss was looked on as a son; he introduced me there; we found among these worthy persons the most pleasant entertainment for mind and heart. Even the common pastimes of society appeared less empty here than elsewhere. All knew how matters stood with us: they treated us as circumstances would allow, and left the main relation unalluded to. I mention this one family; because, in the after-period of my life, it had a powerful influence upon me.

Almost a year of our connection had elapsed; and, along with it, our spring was over. The summer came, and all grew drier and more earnest.

By several unexpected deaths, some offices fell vacant, which Narciss might make pretensions to. The instant was at hand when my whole destiny must be decided; and while Narciss, and all our friends, were making every effort to efface some impressions which obstructed him at court, and to obtain for him the wished-for situation, I turned with my request to my Invisible Friend. I was received so kindly, that I gladly came again. I confessed, without disguise, my wish that Narciss might obtain the place; but my prayer was not importunate, and I did not require that it should happen for the sake of my petition.

The place was obtained by a far inferior competitor. I was dreadfully troubled at this news: I hastened to my room, the door of which I locked behind me. The first fit of grief went off in a shower of tears: the next thought was, "Yet it was not by chance that it happened"; and instantly I formed the resolution to be well content with it, seeing even this apparent evil would be for my true advantage. The softest emotions then pressed in upon me, and divided all the clouds of sorrow. I felt, that, with help like this, there was nothing one might not endure. At dinner I appeared quite cheerful, to the great astonishment of all the house.

Narciss had less internal force than I, and I was called upon to comfort him. In his family, too, he had many crosses to encounter, some of which afflicted him considerably; and, such true confidence subsisting between us, he intrusted me with all. His negotiations for entering on foreign service were not more fortunate; all this I felt deeply on his account and mine; all this, too, I ultimately carried to the place where my petitions had already been so well received.

The softer these experiences were, the oftener did I endeavor to renew them: I hoped continually to meet with comfort where I had so often met with it. Yet I did not always meet with it: I was as one that goes to warm him in the sunshine, while there is something standing in the way that makes a shadow. "What is this?" I asked myself. I traced the matter zealously, and soon perceived that it all depended on the situation of my soul: if this was not turned in the straightest direction towards God, I still continued cold; I did not feel his counter-influence; I could obtain no answer. The second question was, "What hinders this direction?" Here I was in a wide field: I perplexed myself in an inquiry which lasted nearly all the second year of my attachment to Narciss. I might have ended the investigation sooner, for it was not long till I had got upon the proper trace; but I would not confess it, and I sought a thousand outlets.

I very soon discovered that the straight direction of my soul was marred by foolish dissipations, and employment with unworthy things. The how and the where were clear enough to me. Yet by what means could I help myself, or extricate my mind from the calls of a world where every thing was either cold indifference or hot insanity? Gladly would I have left things standing as they were, and lived from day to day, floating down with the stream, like other people whom I saw quite happy; but I durst not: my inmost feelings contradicted me too often. Yet if I determined to renounce society, and alter my relations to others, it was not in my power. I was hemmed in as by a ring drawn round me; certain connections I could not dissolve; and, in the matter which lay nearest to my heart, fatalities accumulated and oppressed me more and more. I often went to bed with tears, and, after a sleepless night, arose again with tears: I required some strong support; and God would not vouchsafe it me while I was running with the cap and bells.

I proceeded now to estimate my doings, all and each: dancing and play were first put upon their trial. Never was there any thing spoken, thought, or written, for or against these practices, which I did not examine, talk of, read, weigh, reject, aggravate, and plague myself about. If I gave up these habits, I was certain that Narciss would be offended; for he dreaded exceedingly the ridicule which any look of straitlaced conscientiousness gives one in the eyes of the world. And doing what I now looked upon as folly, noxious folly, out of no taste of my own, but merely to gratify him, it all grew wofully irksome to me.

Without disagreeable prolixities and repetitions, it is not in my power to represent what pains I took, in trying so to counteract those occupations which distracted my attention and disturbed my peace of mind, that my heart, in spite of them, might still be open to the influences of the Invisible Being. But at last, with pain, I was compelled to admit, that in this way the quarrel could not be composed. For no sooner had I clothed myself in the garment of folly, than it came to be something more than a mask, than the foolishness pierced and penetrated me through and through.

May I here overstep the province of a mere historical detail, and offer one or two remarks on what was then taking place within me? What could it be which so changed my tastes and feelings, that, in my twenty-second year, nay, earlier, I lost all relish for the recreations with which people of that age are harmlessly delighted? Why were they not harmless for me? I may answer, just because they were not harmless; because I was not, like others of my years, unacquainted with my soul. No! I knew, from experiences which had reached me unsought, that there are loftier emotions, which afford us a contentment such as it is vain to seek in the amusements of the world; and that, in these higher joys, there is also kept a secret treasure for strengthening the spirit in misfortune.

But the pleasures of society, the dissipations of youth, must needs have had a powerful charm for me; since it was not in my power to engage in them without participation, to act among them as if they were not there. How many things could I now do, if I liked, with entire coldness, which then dazzled and confounded me, nay, threatened to obtain the mastery over me! Here there could no medium be observed: either those delicious amusements, or my nourishing and quickening internal emotions, must be given up.

But, in my soul, the strife had, without my own consciousness, already been decided. Even if there still was any thing within me that longed for earthly pleasures, I had now become unfitted for enjoying them. Much as a man might hanker after wine, all desire of drinking would forsake him, if he should be placed among full barrels in a cellar, where the foul air was like to suffocate him. Free air is more than wine; this I felt but too keenly: and, from the first, it would have cost me little studying to prefer the good to the delightful, if the fear of losing the affection of Narciss had not restrained me. But at last, when after many thousand struggles, and thoughts continually renewed, I began to cast a steady eye upon the bond which held me to him, I discovered that it was but weak, that it might be torn asunder. I at once perceived it to be only as a glass bell, which shut me up in the exhausted, airless space: one bold stroke to break the bell in pieces, and thou art delivered!

No sooner thought than tried. I drew off the mask, and on all occasions acted as my heart directed. Narciss I still cordially loved: but the thermometer, which formerly had stood in hot water, was now hanging in the natural air; it could rise no higher than the warmth of the atmosphere directed.

Unhappily it cooled very much. Narciss drew back, and began to assume a distant air: this was at his option, but my thermometer descended as he drew back. Our family observed this, questioned me, and seemed to be surprised. I explained to them, with stout defiance, that heretofore I had made abundant sacrifices; that I was ready, still farther and to the end of my life, to share all crosses that befell him; but that I required full freedom in my conduct, that my doings and avoidings must depend upon my own conviction; that, indeed, I would never bigotedly cleave to my own opinion, but, on the other hand, would willingly be reasoned with; yet, as it concerned my own happiness, the decision must proceed from myself, and be liable to no manner of constraint. The greatest physician could not move me, by his reasonings, to take an article of food, which perhaps was altogether wholesome and agreeable to many, so soon as my experience had shown, that on all occasions it was noxious to me; as I might produce coffee for an instance: and just as little, nay, still less, would I have any sort of conduct which misled me, preached up and demonstrated upon me as morally profitable.

Having so long prepared myself in silence, these debates were rather pleasant than vexatious to me. I gave vent to my soul: I felt the whole worth of my determination. I yielded not a hair's-breadth, and those to whom I owed no filial respect were sharply handled and despatched. In the family I soon prevailed. My mother from her youth had entertained these sentiments, though in her they had never reached maturity; for no necessity had pressed upon her, and exalted her courage to achieve her purpose. She rejoiced in beholding her silent wishes fulfilled through me. My younger sisters seemed to join themselves with me: the second was attentive and quiet. Our aunt had the most to object. The arguments which she employed appeared to her irrefragable; and they were irrefragable, being altogether common-place. At last I was obliged to show her, that she had no voice in the affair in any sense; and, after this, she seldom signified that she persisted in her views. She was, indeed, the only person that observed this transaction close at hand, without in some degree experiencing its influence. I do not calumniate her, when I say that she had no character, and the most limited ideas.

My father had acted altogether in his own way. He spoke not much, but often, with me on the matter: his arguments were rational; and, being *his* arguments, they could not be impugned. It was only the deep feeling of my right that gave me strength to dispute against him. But the scenes soon changed: I was forced to make appeal to his heart. Straitened by his understanding, I came out with the most pathetic pleadings. I gave free course to my tongue and to my tears. I showed him how much I loved Narciss; how much constraint I had for two years been enduring; how certain I was of being in the right, that I was ready to testify that certainty, by the loss of my beloved bridegroom and prospective happiness, — nay, if it were necessary, by the loss of all that I possessed on earth; that I would rather leave my native country, my parents, and my friends, and beg my bread in foreign lands, than act against these dictates of my conscience. He concealed his emotion: he said nothing on the subject for a while, and at last he openly declared in my favor.

During all this time Narciss forbore to visit us; and my father now gave up the weekly club, where he was used to meet him. The business made a noise at court, and in the town. People talked about it, as is common in such cases, which the public takes a vehement interest in, because its sentence has usurped an influence on the resolutions of weak minds. I knew enough about the world to understand that one's conduct is often censured by the very persons who would have advised it, had one consulted them; and independently of this, with my internal composure, I should have looked on all such transitory speculations just as if they had not been.

On the other hand, I hindered not myself from yielding to my inclination for Narciss. To me he had become invisible, and to him my feelings had not altered. I loved him tenderly; as it were anew, and much more steadfastly than before. If he chose to leave my conscience undisturbed, then I was his: wanting this condition, I would have refused a kingdom with him. For several months I bore these feelings and these thoughts about with me; and, finding at last that I was calm and strong enough to go peacefully and firmly to work, I wrote him a polite but not a tender note, inquiring why he never came to see me.

As I knew his manner of avoiding to explain himself in little matters, but of silently doing what seemed good to him, I purposely urged him in the present instance. I got a long, and, as it seemed to me, pitiful, reply, in vague style and unmeaning phrases, stating, that, without a better place, he could not fix himself, and offer me his hand; that I best knew how hard it had fared with him hitherto; that as he was afraid lest a fruitless intercourse, so long continued, might prove hurtful to my reputation, I would give him leave to continue at his present distance; so soon as it was in his power to make me happy, he would look upon the word which he had given me as sacred.

I answered him on the spot, that, as our intercourse was known to all the world, it might, perhaps, be rather late to spare my reputation; for which, at any rate, my conscience and my innocence were the surest pledges; however, that I hereby freely gave him back his word, and hoped the change would prove a happy one for him. The same hour I received a short reply, which was, in all essential particulars, entirely synonymous with the first. He adhered to his former statement, that, so soon as he obtained a situation, he would ask me, if I pleased, to share his fortune with him.

This I interpreted as meaning simply nothing. I signified to my relations and acquaintances, that the affair was altogether settled; and it was so in fact. Having, nine months afterwards, obtained the much-desired preferment, he offered me his hand, but under the condition, that, as the wife of a man who must keep house like other people, I should alter my opinions. I returned him many thanks, and hastened with my heart and mind away from this transaction, as one hastens from the playhouse when the curtain falls. And as he, a short time afterwards, had found a rich and advantageous match, a thing now easy for him; and as I now knew him to be happy in the way he liked, — my own tranquillity was quite complete.

I must not pass in silence the fact, that several times before he got a place, and after it, there were respectable proposals made to me; which, however, I declined without the smallest hesitation, much as my father and my mother could have wished for more compliance on my part.

At length, after a stormy March and April, the loveliest May weather seemed to be allotted me. With good health, I enjoyed an indescribable composure of mind: look around me as I pleased, my loss appeared a gain to me. Young and full of sensibility, I thought the universe a thousand times more beautiful than formerly, when I required to have society and play, that in the fair garden tedium might not overtake me. And now, as I did not conceal my piety, I likewise took heart to own my love for the sciences and arts. I drew, painted, read, and found enough of people to support me: instead of the great world, which I had left, or, rather, which had left me, a smaller one formed itself about me, which was infinitely richer and more entertaining. I had a turn for social life; and I do not deny, that, on giving up my old acquaintances, I trembled at the thought of solitude. I now found myself abundantly, perhaps excessively, indemnified. My acquaintances erelong were very numerous, not at home only, but likewise among people at a distance. My story had been noised abroad, and many persons felt a curiosity to see the woman who had valued God above her bridegroom. There was a certain pious tone to be observed, at that time, generally over Germany. In the families of several counts and princes, a care for the welfare of the soul had been awakened. Nor were there wanting noblemen who showed a like attention; while, in the inferior classes, sentiments of this kind were diffused on every side.

The noble family, whom I mentioned above, now drew me nearer to them. They had, in the mean while, gathered strength; several of their relations having settled in the town. These estimable persons courted my familiarity, as I did theirs. They had high connections: I became acquainted, in their house, with a great part of the princes, counts, and lords of the empire. My sentiments were not concealed from any one: they might be honored or be tolerated; I obtained my object, — none attacked me.

There was yet another way by which I was again led back into the world. About this period a step-brother of my father, who till now had never visited the house except in passing, staid with us for a considerable time. He had left the service of his court, where he enjoyed great influence and honor, simply because all matters were not managed quite according to his mind. His intellect was just, his character was rigid. In these points he was very like my father: only the latter had withal a certain touch of softness, which enabled him with greater ease to yield a little in affairs, and though not to do, yet to permit, some things against his own conviction; and then to evaporate his anger at them, either in silence by himself, or in confidence amid his family. My uncle was a great deal younger, and his independence of spirit had been favored by his outward circumstances. His mother had been very rich, and he still had large possessions to expect from her near and distant relatives; so he needed no foreign increase: whereas my father, with his moderate fortune, was bound to his place by the consideration of his salary.

My uncle had become still more unbending from domestic sufferings. He had early lost an amiable wife and a hopeful son; and, from that time, he appeared to wish to push away from him every thing that did not hang upon his individual will.

In our family it was whispered now and then with some complacency, that probably he would not wed again, and so we children might anticipate inheriting his fortune. I paid small regard to this, but the demeanor of the rest was not a little modified by their hopes. In his own imperturbable firmness of character, my uncle had grown into the habit of never contradicting any one in conversation. On the other hand, he listened with a friendly air to every one's opinion, and would himself elucidate and strengthen it by instances and reasons of his own. All who did not know him fancied that he thought as they did; for he was possessed of a preponderating intellect, and could transport himself into the mental state of any man, and imitate his manner of conceiving. With me he did not prosper quite so well; for here the question was about emotions, of which he had not any glimpse: and, with whatever tolerance and sympathy and rationality he spoke about my sentiments, it was palpable to me, that he had not the slightest notion of what formed the ground of all my conduct.

With all his secrecy, we by and by found out the aim of his unusual stay with us. He had, as we at length discovered, cast his eyes upon our youngest sister, with the view of giving her in marriage, and rendering her happy as he pleased; and certainly, considering her personal and mental attractions, particularly when a handsome fortune was laid into the scale along with them, she might pretend to the first matches. His feelings towards me he likewise showed us pantomimically, by procuring me a post of canoness, the income of which I very soon began to draw.

My sister was not so contented with his care as I. She now disclosed to me a tender secret, which hitherto she had very wisely kept back; fearing, as in truth it happened, that I would by all means counsel her against connection with a man who was not suited to her. I did my utmost, and succeeded. The purpose of my uncle was too serious and too distinct: the prospect for my sister, with her worldly views, was too delightful to be thwarted by a passion which her own understanding disapproved; she mustered force to give it up.

On her ceasing to resist the gentle guidance of my uncle, the foundation of his plan was quickly laid. She was appointed maid of honor at a neighboring court, where he could commit her to the oversight and the instructions of a lady, his friend, who presided there as governess with great applause. I accompanied her to the place of her new abode. Both of us had reason to be satisfied with the reception we met with; and frequently I could not help, in secret, smiling at the character, which now as canoness, as young and pious canoness, I was enacting in the world.

In earlier times a situation such as this would have confused me dreadfully, perhaps have turned my head; but now, in the midst of all the splendors that surrounded me, I felt extremely cool. With great quietness I let them frizzle me, and deck me out for hours, and thought no more of it than that my place required me to wear that gala livery. In the thronged saloons I spoke with all and each, though no shape or character among them made any impression on me. On returning to my house, nearly all the feeling I brought back with me was that of tired limbs. Yet my understanding drew advantage from the multitude of persons whom I saw: and I became acquainted with some ladies, patterns of every virtue, of a noble and good demeanor; particularly with the governess, under whom my sister was to have the happiness of being formed.

At my return, however, the consequences of this journey, in regard to health, were found to be less favorable. With the greatest temperance, the strictest diet, I had not been, as I used to be, completely mistress of my time and strength. Food, motion, rising, and going to sleep, dressing and visiting, had not depended, as at home, on my own conveniency and will. In the circle of social life you cannot stop without a breach of courtesy: all that was needful I had willingly performed; because I looked upon it as my duty, because I knew that it would soon be over, and because I felt myself completely healthy. Yet this unusual, restless life must have had more effect upon me than I was aware of. Scarcely had I reached home, and cheered my parents with a comfortable narrative, when I was attacked by a hemorrhage, which, although it did not prove dangerous or lasting, yet left a weakness after it, perceptible for many a day.

Here, then, I had another lesson to repeat. I did it joyfully. Nothing bound me to the world, and I was convinced that here the true good was never to be found; so I waited in the cheerfullest and meekest state: and, after having abdicated life, I was retained in it.

A new trial was awaiting me: my mother took a painful and oppressive ailment, which she had to bear five years, before she paid the debt of nature. All this time we were sharply proved. Often, when her terror grew too strong, she would have us all summoned, in the night, to her bed, that so at least she might be busied, if not bettered, by our presence. The load grew heavier, nay, scarcely to be borne, when my father, too, became unwell. From his youth he had frequently had violent headaches, which, however, at longest never used to last beyond six and thirty hours. But now they were continual; and, when they mounted to a high degree of pain, his moanings tore my very heart. It was in these tempestuous seasons that I chiefly felt my bodily weakness; because it kept me from my holiest and dearest duties, or rendered the performance of them hard to an extreme degree.

It was now that I could try whether the path which I had chosen was the path of fantasy or truth; whether I had merely thought as others showed me, or the object of my trust had a reality. To my unspeakable support, I always found the latter. The straight direction of my heart to God, the fellowship of the "Beloved Ones,"[1] I had

---

[1] So in the original. — ED.

sought and found; and this was what made all things light to me. As a traveller in the dark, my soul, when all was pressing on me from without, hastened to the place of refuge; and never did it return empty.

In later times some champions of religion, who seem to be animated more by zeal than feeling for it, have required of their brethren to produce examples of prayers actually heard; apparently as wishing to have seal and signature, that so they might proceed juridically in the matter. How unknown must the true feeling be to these persons! how few real experiences can they themselves have made!

I can say that I never returned empty, when in straits and oppression I called on God. This is saying infinitely much: more I must not and can not say. Important as each experience was at the critical moment for myself, the recital of them would be flat, improbable, and insignificant, were I to specify the separate cases. Happy was I, that a thousand little incidents in combination proved, as clearly as the drawing of my breath proved me to be living, that I was not without God in the world. He was near to me: I was before him. This is what, with a diligent avoidance of all theological systematic terms, I can with the greatest truth declare.

Much do I wish, that, in those times too, I had been entirely without system. But which of us arrives early at the happiness of being conscious of his individual self, in its own pure combination, without extraneous forms? I was in earnest with religion. I timidly trusted in the judgments of others: I entirely gave in to the Hallean system of conversion, but my nature would by no means tally with it.

According to this scheme of doctrine, the alteration of the heart must begin with a deep terror on account of sin: the heart in this agony must recognize, in a less or greater degree, the punishment which it has merited, must get a foretaste of hell, and so embitter the delight of sin. At last it feels a very palpable assurance of grace; which, however, in its progress often fades away, and must again be sought with earnest prayer.

Of all this no jot or tittle happened with me. When I sought God sincerely, he let himself be found of me, and did not reproach me about by-gone things. On looking back, I saw well enough where I had been unworthy, where I still was so; but the confession of my faults was altogether without terror. Not for a moment did the fear of hell occur to me; nay, the very notion of a wicked spirit, and a place of punishment and torment after death, could nowise gain admission into the circle of my thoughts. I considered the men who lived without God, whose hearts were shut against the trust in and the love of the Invisible, as already so unhappy, that a hell and external pains appeared to promise rather an alleviation than an increase of their misery. I had but to look upon the persons, in this world, who in their breasts gave scope to hateful feelings; who hardened their hearts against the good of whatever kind, and strove to force the evil on themselves and others; who shut their eyes by day, that so they might deny the shining of the sun. How unutterably wretched did these persons seem to me! Who could have formed a hell to make their situation worse?

This mood of mind continued in me, without change, for half a score of years. It maintained itself through many trials, even at the moving death-bed of my beloved mother. I was frank enough, on this occasion, not to hide my comfortable frame of mind from certain pious but rigorously orthodox people; and I had to suffer many a friendly admonition on that score. They reckoned they were just in season, for explaining with what earnestness one should be diligent to lay a right foundation in the days of health and youth.

In earnestness I, too, determined not to fail. For the moment I allowed myself to be convinced; and fain would I have grown, for life, distressed and full of fears. But what was my surprise on finding that I absolutely could not. When I thought of God, I was cheerful and contented: even at the painful end of my dear mother, I did not shudder at the thought of death. Yet I learned many and far other things than my uncalled teachers thought of, in these solemn hours.

By degrees I grew to doubt the dictates of so many famous people, and retained my own sentiments in silence. A certain lady of my friends, to whom I had at first disclosed too much, insisted always on interfering with my business. Of her, too, I was obliged to rid myself: I at last firmly told her, that she might spare herself this labor, as I did not need her counsel; that I knew my God, and would have no guide but him. She was greatly offended: I believe she never quite forgave me.

Such determination to withdraw from the advices and the influence of my friends, in spiritual matters, produced the consequence, that also in my temporal affairs I gained sufficient courage to obey my own persuasions. But for the assistance of my faithful, invisible Leader, I could not have prospered here. I am still gratefully astonished at his wise and happy guidance. No one knew how matters stood with me: even I myself did not know.

The thing, the wicked and inexplicable thing, which separates us from the Being to whom we owe our life, and in whom all that deserves the name of life must find its nourishment, — the thing which we call sin I yet knew nothing of.

In my intercourse with my invisible Friend, I felt the sweetest enjoyment of all my powers. My desire of constantly enjoying this felicity was so predominant, that I abandoned without hesitation whatever marred our intercourse; and here experience was my best teacher. But it was with me as with sick persons who have no medicine, and try to help themselves by diet: something is accomplished, but far from enough.

I could not always live in solitude, though in it I found the best preservative against the dissipation of my thoughts. On returning to the tumult, the impression it produced upon me was the deeper for my previous loneliness. My most peculiar advantage lay in this, that love for quiet was my ruling passion, and that in the end I still drew back to it. I perceived, as in a kind of twilight, my weakness and my misery, and tried to save myself by avoiding danger and exposure.

For seven years I had used my dietetic scheme. I held myself not wicked, and I thought my state desirable. But for some peculiar circumstances and occurrences I had remained in this position: it was by a curious path that I got farther. Contrary to the advice of all my friends, I entered on a new connection. Their objections, at first, made me pause. I turned to my invisible Leader; and, as he permitted me, I went forward without fear.

A man of spirit, heart, and talents had bought a property beside us. Among the strangers whom I grew acquainted with, were this person and his family. In our manners, domestic economy, and habits we accorded well; and thus we soon approximated to each other.

Philo, as I propose to call him, was already middle-aged: in certain matters he was highly serviceable to my father, whose strength was now decaying. He soon became the friend of the family: and finding in me, as he was pleased to say, a person free alike from the extravagance and emptiness of the great world, and from the narrowness and aridness of the still world in the country, he courted intimacy with me; and erelong we were in one another's confidence. To me he was very pleasing and useful.

Though I did not feel the smallest inclination or capacity for mingling in public business, or seeking any influence on it, yet I liked to hear about such matters, — liked to know whatever happened far and near. Of worldly things, I loved to get a clear though unconcerned perception; feeling, sympathy, affection, I reserved for God, for my people, and my friends.

The latter were, if I may say so, jealous of Philo, in my new connection with him. In more than one sense, they were right in warning me about it. I suffered much in secret, for even I could not consider their remonstrances as altogether empty or selfish. I had been accustomed, from of old, to give a reason for my views and conduct; but in this case my conviction would not follow. I prayed to God, that here, as elsewhere, he would warn, restrain, and guide me; and, as my heart on this did not dissuade me, I went forward on my way with comfort.

Philo, on the whole, had a remote resemblance to Narciss: only a pious education had more enlivened and concentrated his feelings. He had less vanity, more character; and in business, if Narciss was delicate, exact, persevering, indefatigable, the other was clear, sharp, quick, and capable of working with incredible ease. By means of him I learned the secret history of almost every noble personage with whose exterior I had got acquainted in society. It was pleasant for me to behold the tumult, off my watch-tower from afar. Philo could now hide nothing from me: he confided to me, by degrees, his own concerns, both inward and outward. I was in fear because of him, for I foresaw certain circumstances and entanglements; and the mischief came more speedily than I had looked for. There were some confessions he had still kept back, and even at last he told me only what enabled me to guess the worst.

What an effect had this upon my heart! I attained experiences which to me were altogether new. With infinite sorrow I beheld an

Agathon, who, educated in the groves of Delphi, still owed his school-fees, which he was now obliged to pay with their accumulated interest; and this Agathon was my especial friend. My sympathy was lively and complete; I suffered with him; both of us were in the strangest state.

After having long occupied myself with the temper of his mind, I at last turned round to contemplate my own. The thought, "Thou art no better than he," rose like a little cloud before me, and gradually expanded till it darkened all my soul.

I now not only thought myself no better than he: I felt this, and felt it as I should not wish to do again. Nor was it any transitory mood. For more than a year, I was compelled to feel, that, had not an unseen hand restrained me, I might have become a Girard, a Cartouche, a

Damiens, or any wretch you can imagine. The tendencies to this I traced too clearly in my heart. Heavens, what a discovery!

If hitherto I had never been able, in the faintest degree, to recognize in myself the reality of sin by experience, its possibility was now become apparent to me by anticipation, in the frightfullest manner. And yet I knew not evil; I but feared it: I felt that I might be guilty, and could not accuse myself of being so.

Deeply as I was convinced that such a temperament of soul, as I now saw mine to be, could never be adapted for that union with the invisible Being which I hoped for after death, I did not, in the smallest, fear that I should finally be separated from him. With all the wickedness which I discovered in my heart, I still loved *Him*: I hated what I felt, nay, wished to hate it still more earnestly; my whole desire was, to be delivered from this sickness, and this tendency to sickness; and I was persuaded that the great Physician would at length vouchsafe his help.

The sole question was, What medicine will cure this malady? The practice of virtue? This I could not for a moment think. For ten years I had already practised more than mere virtue; and the horrors now first discovered had, all the while, lain hidden at the bottom of my soul. Might they not have broken out with me, as they did with David when he looked on Bathsheba? Yet was not he a friend of God! and was not I assured, in my inmost heart, that God was my friend?

Was it, then, an unavoidable infirmity of human nature? Must we just content ourselves in feeling and acknowledging the sovereignty of inclination? And, with the best will, is there nothing left for us but to abhor the fault we have committed, and on the like occasion to commit it again?

From systems of morality I could obtain no comfort. Neither their severity, by which they try to bend our inclinations, nor their attractiveness, by which they try to place our inclinations on the side of virtue, gave me any satisfaction. The fundamental notions, which I had imbibed from intercourse with my invisible Friend, were of far higher value to me.

Once, while I was studying the songs composed by David after that tremendous fall, it struck me very much that he traced his indwelling corruption even in the substance out of which he had been shaped; yet that he wished to be freed from sin, and that he earnestly entreated for a pure heart.

But how was this to be attained? The answer from Scripture I was well aware of: "that the blood of Jesus cleanseth us from all sin," was a Bible truth which I had long known. But now, for the first time, I observed that as yet I had never understood this oft-repeated saying. The questions, What does it mean? How is it to be? were day and night working out their answers in me. At last I thought I saw, as by a gleam of light, that what I sought was to be found in the incarnation of the everlasting Word, by whom all things, even we ourselves, were made. That the Eternal descended as an inhabitant to the depths in which we dwell, which he surveys and comprehends; that he passed through our lot from stage to stage, from conception and birth to the grave; that by this marvellous circuit he again mounted to those shining heights, whither we too must rise in order to be happy: all this was revealed to me, as in a dawning remoteness.

Oh! why must we, in speaking of such things, make use of figures which can only indicate external situations? Where is there in his eyes aught high or deep, aught dark or clear? It is we only that have an Under and Upper, a night and day. And even for this did he become like us, since otherwise we could have had no part in him.

But how shall we obtain a share in this priceless benefit? "By faith," the Scripture says. And what is faith? To consider the account of an event as true, what help can this afford me? I must be enabled to appropriate its effects, its consequences. This appropriating faith must be a state of mind peculiar, and, to the natural man, unknown.

"Now, gracious Father, grant me faith!" so prayed I once, in the deepest heaviness of heart. I was leaning on a little table, where I sat: my tear-stained countenance was hidden in my hands. I was now in the condition in which we seldom are, but in which we are required to be, if God is to regard our prayers.

Oh, that I could but paint what I felt then! A sudden force drew my soul to the cross where Jesus once expired: it was a sudden force, a pull, I cannot name it otherwise, such as leads our soul to an absent loved one; an approximation, which, perhaps, is far more real and true than we imagine. So did my soul approach the Son of man, who died upon the cross; and that instant did I know what faith was.

"This is faith!" said I, and started up as if half frightened. I now endeavored to get certain of my feeling, of my view; and shortly I became convinced that my soul had acquired a power of soaring upwards which was altogether new to it.

Words fail us in describing such emotions. I could most distinctly separate them from all fantasy: they were entirely without fantasy, without image; yet they gave us just such certainty of their referring to some object as our imagination gives us when it paints the features of an absent lover.

When the first rapture was over, I observed that my present condition of mind had formerly been known to me; only I had never felt it in such strength; I had never held it fast, never made it mine. I believe, indeed, every human soul at intervals feels something of it. Doubtless it is this which teaches every mortal that there is a God.

With such faculty, wont from of old to visit me now and then, I had hitherto been well content: and had not, by a singular arrangement of events, that unexpected sorrow weighed upon me for a twelvemonth; had not my own ability and strength, on that occasion, altogether lost credit with me, — I perhaps might have remained content with such a state of matters all my days.

But now, since that great moment, I had, as it were, got wings. I could mount aloft above what used to threaten me; as the bird can fly singing and with ease across the fiercest stream, while the little dog stands anxiously baying on the bank.

My joy was indescribable; and, though I did not mention it to any one, my people soon observed an unaccustomed cheerfulness in me, and could not understand the reason of my joy. Had I but forever held my peace, and tried to nourish this serene temper in my soul; had I not allowed myself to be misled by circumstances, so as to reveal my secret, — I might then have been saved once more a long and tedious circuit.

As in the previous ten years of my Christian course, this necessary force had not existed in my soul, I had just been in the case of other worthy people, — had helped myself by keeping my fancy always full of images, which had some reference to God, — a practice so far truly useful; for noxious images and their baneful consequences are by that means kept away. Often, too, our spirit seizes one or other of these spiritual images, and mounts with it a little way upwards, like a young bird fluttering from twig to twig.

Images and impressions pointing towards God are presented to us by the institutions of the Church, by organs, bells, singing, and particularly by the preaching of our pastors. Of these I used to be unspeakably desirous; no weather, no bodily weakness, could keep me from church; the sound of the Sunday bells was the only thing that rendered me impatient on a sick-bed. Our head court-chaplain, a gifted man, I heard with great pleasure; his colleagues, too, I liked: and I could pick the golden apple of the Word from the common fruit, with which on earthen platters it was mingled. With public ordinances, all sorts of private exercises were combined; and these, too, only nourished fancy and a finer kind of sense. I was so accustomed to this track, I reverenced it so much, that even now no higher one occurred to me. For my soul has only feelers, and not eyes: it gropes, but does not see. Ah! that it could get eyes, and look!

Now again, therefore, I went with a longing mind to sermon; but, alas! what happened? I no longer found what I was wont to find. These preachers were blunting their teeth on the shell, while I enjoyed the kernel. I soon grew weary of them; and I had already been so spoiled, that I could not be content with the little they afforded me. I required images, I wanted impressions from without, and reckoned it a pure spiritual desire that I felt.

Philo's parents had been in connection with the Herrnhuter Community: in his library were many writings of Count Zinzendorf's. He had spoken with me, more than once, very candidly and clearly on the subject; inviting me to turn over one or two of these treatises, if it were but for the sake of studying a psychological phenomenon. I looked upon the count, and those that followed him, as very heterodox; and so the Ebersdorf Hymn-book, which my friend had pressed upon me, lay unread.

However, in this total destitution of external excitements for my soul, I opened the hymn-book, as it were, by chance, and found in it, to my astonishment, some songs which actually, though under a fantastic form, appeared to shadow what I felt. The originality and simplicity of their expression drew me on. It seemed to be peculiar emotions expressed in a peculiar way: no school technology suggested any notion of formality or commonplace. I was persuaded that these people felt as I did: I was very happy to lay hold of here and there a stanza in their songs, to fix it in my memory, and carry it about with me for days.

Since the moment when the truth had been revealed to me, some three months had in this way passed on. At last I came to the resolution of disclosing every thing to Philo, and asking him to let me have those writings, about which I had now become immoderately curious. Accordingly I did so, notwithstanding there was something in my heart which earnestly dissuaded me.

I circumstantially related to him all the story; and as he was himself a leading person in it, and my narrative conveyed the sharpest reprimand on him, he felt surprised and moved to an extreme degree. He melted into tears. I rejoiced; believing that, in his mind also, a full and fundamental change had taken place.

He provided me with all the writings I could require, and now I had excess of nourishment for my imagination. I made rapid progress in the Zinzendorfic mode of thought and speech. And be it not supposed that I am yet incapable of prizing the peculiar turn and manner of the count. I willingly do him justice: he is no empty fantast; he speaks of mighty truths, and mostly in a bold, figurative style; the people who despise him know not either how to value or discriminate his qualities.

At that time I became exceedingly attached to him. Had I been mistress of myself, I would certainly have left my friends and country, and gone to join him. We should infallibly have understood each other, and should hardly have agreed together long.

Thanks to my better genius, that now kept me so confined by my domestic duties! I reckoned it a distant journey if I visited the garden. The charge of my aged, weakly father afforded me employment enough; and in hours of recreation, I had Fancy to procure me pastime. The only mortal whom I saw was Philo; he was highly valued by my father; but, with me, his intimacy had been cooled a little by the late explanation. Its influence on him had not penetrated deep: and, as some attempts to talk in my dialect had not succeeded with him, he avoided touching on this subject; and the rather, as his extensive knowledge put it always in his power to introduce new topics in his conversation.

I was thus a Herrnhut sister on my own footing. I had especially to hide this new turn of my temper and my inclinations from the head court-chaplain, whom, as my father confessor, I had much cause to honor, and whose high merits his extreme aversion to the Herrnhut Community did not diminish, in my eyes, even then. Unhappily this worthy person had to suffer many troubles on account of me and others.

Several years ago he had become acquainted with an upright, pious gentleman, residing in a distant quarter, and had long continued in unbroken correspondence with him, as with one who truly sought God. How painful was it to the spiritual leader, when this gentleman subsequently joined himself to the Community of Herrnhut, where he lived for a long while! How delightful, on the other hand, when at length he quarrelled with the brethren, determined to settle in our neighborhood, and seemed once more to yield himself completely to the guidance of his ancient friend!

The stranger was presented, as in triumph, by the upper pastor, to all the chosen lambs of his fold. To our house alone he was not introduced, because my father did not now see company. The gentleman obtained no little approbation: he combined the polish of the court with the winning manner of the brethren; and, having also many fine qualities by nature, he soon became the favorite saint with all who knew him, — a result at which the chaplain was exceedingly contented. But, alas! it was merely in externals that the gentleman had split with the Community: in his heart he was yet entirely a Herrnhuter. He was, in truth, concerned for the reality of the matter; but yet the gimcracks, which the count had stuck round it, were, at the same time, quite adapted to his state. Besides, he had now become accustomed to this mode of speaking and conceiving: and, if he had to hide it carefully from his old friend, the gladder was he, in any knot of trusty persons, to come forth with his couplets, litanies, and little figures; in which, as might have been supposed, he met with great applause.

I knew nothing of the whole affair, and wandered quietly along in my separate path. For a good while we continued mutually unknown.

Once, in a leisure hour, I happened to visit a lady who was sick. I found several acquaintances with her, and soon perceived that my appearance had cut short their conversation. I affected not to notice any thing, but saw erelong, with great surprise, some Herrnhut figures stuck upon the wall in elegant frames. Quickly comprehending what had passed before my entrance, I expressed my pleasure at the sight, in a few suitable verses.

Conceive the wonder of my friends! We explained ourselves: instantly we were agreed, and in each other's confidence.

I often henceforth sought opportunities of going out. Unhappily I found such only once in the three or four weeks; yet I grew acquainted with our gentleman apostle, and by degrees with all the body. I visited their meetings when I could: with my social disposition, it was quite delightful for me to communicate to others, and to hear from them, the feelings which, till now, I had conceived and harbored by myself.

But I was not so completely taken with my friends, as not to see that few of them could really feel the sense of those affecting words and emblems; and that from these they drew as little benefit as formerly they did from the symbolic language of the Church. Yet, notwithstanding, I went on with them, not letting this disturb me. I thought I was not called to search and try the hearts of others. Had not I, too, by long-continued innocent exercisings of that sort, been prepared for something better? I had my share of profit from our meetings: in speaking, I insisted on attending to the sense and spirit, which, in things so delicate, is rather apt to be disguised by words than indicated by them; and for the rest, I left, with silent tolerance, each to act according to his own conviction.

These quiet times of secret social joy were shortly followed by storms of open bickering and contradiction, — contentions which excited great commotion, I might almost say occasioned not a little scandal, in court and town. The period was now arrived when our chaplain, that stout gainsayer of the Herrnhut Brethren, must discover to his deep, but, I trust, sanctified humiliation, that his best and once most zealous hearers were all leaning to the side of that community. He was excessively provoked: in the first moments he forgot all moderation, and could not, even if he had inclined it, retract afterwards. Violent debates took place, in which, happily, I was not mentioned, both as being an accidental member of those hated meetings, and then because, in respect of certain civic matters, our zealous preacher could not safely disoblige either my father or my friend. With silent satisfaction I continued neutral. It was irksome to me to converse about such feelings and objects, even with well-affected people, when they could not penetrate the deepest sense, and lingered merely on the surface. But to strive with adversaries, about things on which even friends could scarcely understand each other, seemed to me unprofitable, nay, pernicious. For I soon perceived, that many amiable noblemen, who on this occurrence could not shut their hearts to enmity and hatred, had rapidly passed over to injustice, and, in order to defend an outward form, had almost sacrificed their most substantial duties.

Far as the worthy clergyman might, in the present case, be wrong; much as others tried to irritate me at him, — I could never hesitate to give him my sincere respect. I knew him well: I could candidly transport myself into his way of looking at these matters. I have never seen a man without his weaknesses: only in distinguished men they strike us more. We wish, and will at all rates have it, that persons privileged as they are should at the same time pay no tribute, no tax whatever. I honored him as a superior man, and hoped to use the influence of my calm neutrality to bring about, if not a peace, at least a truce. I know not what my efforts might have done; but God concluded the affair more briefly, and took the chaplain to himself. On his coffin all wept, who had lately been striving with him about words. His uprightness, his fear of God, no one had ever doubted.

I, too, was erelong forced to lay aside this Herrnhut dollwork, which, by means of these contentions, now appeared before me in a rather different light. Our uncle had, in silence, executed his intentions with my sister. He offered her a young man of rank and fortune as a bridegroom, and showed, by a rich dowry, what might be expected of himself. My father joyfully consented: my sister was free and forewarned; she did not hesitate to change her state. The bridal was appointed at my uncle's castle: family and friends were all invited, and we came together in the cheerfullest mood.

For the first time in my life, the aspect of a house excited admiration in me. I had often heard of my uncle's taste, of his Italian architect, of his collections and his library; but, comparing this with what I had already seen, I had formed a very vague and fluctuating picture of it in my thoughts. Great, accordingly, was my surprise at the earnest and harmonious impression which I felt on entering the house, and which every hall and chamber deepened. If elsewhere pomp and decoration had but dissipated my attention, I felt here concentrated and drawn back upon myself. In like manner the preparatives for these solemnities and festivals produced a silent pleasure, by their air of dignity and splendor; and to me it seemed as inconceivable that one man could have invented and arranged all this, as that more than one could have worked together in so high a spirit. Yet, withal, the landlord and his people were entirely natural: not a trace of stiffness or of empty form was to be seen.

The wedding itself was managed in a striking way: an exquisite strain of vocal music came upon us by surprise, and the clergyman went through the ceremony with a singular solemnity. I was standing by Philo at the time; and, instead of a congratulation, he whispered in my ear, "When I saw your sister give away her hand, I felt as if a stream of boiling water had been poured over me." — "Why so?" I inquired. "It is always the way with me," said he, "when I see two people joined." I laughed at him, but I have often since had cause to recollect his words.

The revel of the party, among whom were many young people, looked particularly glittering and airy; as every thing around us was dignified and serious. The furniture, plate, table-ware, and table-ornaments accorded with the general whole; and if in other houses you would say the architect was of the school of the confectioner, it here appeared as if even our confectioner and butler had taken lessons from the architect.

We staid together several days, and our intelligent and gifted landlord had variedly provided for the entertainment of his guests. I did not in the present case repeat the melancholy proof, which has so often in my life been forced upon me, how unhappily a large mixed company are situated, when, altogether left to themselves, they have to select the most general and vapid pastimes, that the fools of the party may not want amusement, however it may fare with those that are not such.

My uncle had arranged it altogether differently. Two or three marshals, if I may call them so, had been appointed by him: one of them had charge of providing entertainment for the young. Dances, excursions, little games, were of his invention and under his direction: and as young people take delight in being out-of-doors, and do not fear the influences of the air, the garden and garden-hall had been assigned to them; while some additional pavilions and galleries had been erected and appended to the latter, formed of boards and canvas merely, but in such proportions, so elegant and noble, they reminded one of nothing but stone and marble.

How rare is a festivity in which the person who invites the guests feels also that it is his duty to provide for their conveniences and wants of every kind!

Hunting and card parties, short promenades, opportunities for trustful private conversations, were afforded the elder persons; and whoever wished to go earliest to bed was sure to be lodged the farthest from noise.

By this happy order, the space we lived in appeared to be a little world: and yet, considered narrowly, the castle was not large; without an accurate knowledge of it, and without the spirit of its owner, it would have been impossible to entertain so many people here, and quarter each according to his humor.

As the aspect of a well-formed person pleases us, so also does a fair establishment, by means of which the presence of a rational, intelligent mind is manifested. We feel a joy in entering even a cleanly house, though it may be tasteless in its structure and its decorations, because it shows us the presence of a person cultivated in at least one sense. Doubly pleasing is it, therefore, when, from a human dwelling, the spirit of a higher though merely sensual culture speaks to us.

All this was vividly impressed on my observation at my uncle's castle. I had heard and read much of art; Philo, too, was lover of pictures, and had a fine collection: I myself had often practised drawing; but I had been too deeply occupied with my emotions, striving exclusively after the one thing needful, which alone I was bent on carrying to perfection; and then, such objects of art as I had hitherto seen, appeared, like all other worldly objects, to distract my thoughts. But now, for the first time, outward things had led me back upon myself:

I now first perceived the difference between the natural charm of the nightingale's song, and that of a four-voiced anthem pealed from the expressive organs of men.

My joy over this discovery I did not hide from my uncle, who, when all the rest settled at their posts, was wont to come and talk with me in private. He spoke with great modesty of what he possessed and had produced here, with great decision of the views in which it had been gathered and arranged: and I could easily observe that he spoke with a forbearance towards me; seeming, in his usual way, to rate the excellence, which he himself possessed below that other excellence, which, in my way of thinking, was the best and properest.

"If we can conceive it possible," he once observed, "that the Creator of the world himself assumed the form of his creature, and lived in that manner for a time upon earth, this creature must appear to us of infinite perfection, because susceptible of such a combination with its Maker. Hence, in our idea of man, there can be no inconsistency with our idea of God; and if we often feel a certain disagreement with him and remoteness from him, it is but the more on that account our duty, not like advocates of the wicked Spirit, to keep our eyes continually upon the nakedness and weakness of our nature, but rather to seek out every property and beauty by which our pretension to a similarity with the Divinity may be made good."

I smiled, and answered, "Do not make me blush, dear uncle, by your complaisance in talking in my language! What you have to say is of such importance to me, that I wish to hear it in your own most peculiar style; and then what parts of it I cannot quite appropriate I will endeavor to translate."

"I may continue," he replied, "in my own most peculiar way, without any alteration of my tone. Man's highest merit always is, as much as possible to rule external circumstances, and as little as possible to let himself be ruled by them. Life lies before us, as a huge quarry lies before the architect: he deserves not the name of architect, except when, out of this fortuitous mass, he can combine, with the greatest economy and fitness and durability, some form, the pattern of which originated in his spirit. All things without us, nay, I may add, all things on us, are mere elements; but deep within us lies the creative force, which out of these can produce what they were meant to be, and which leaves us neither sleep nor rest, till, in one way or another, without us or on us, that same have been produced. You, my dear niece, have, it may be, chosen the better part; you have striven to bring your moral being, your earnest, lovely nature, into accordance with itself and with the Highest: but neither ought we to be blamed, when we strive to get acquainted with the sentient man in all his comprehensiveness, and to bring about an active harmony among his powers."

By such discoursing, we in time grew more familiar; and I begged of him to speak with me as with himself, omitting every sort of condescension. "Do not think," replied my uncle, "that I flatter you when I commend your mode of thinking and acting. I reverence the individual who understands distinctly what it is he wishes; who unweariedly advances, who knows the means conducive to his object, and can seize and use them. How far his object may be great or little, may merit praise or censure, is the next consideration with me. Believe me, love, most part of all the misery and mischief, of all that is denominated evil in the world, arises from the fact, that men are too remiss to get a proper knowledge of their aims, and, when they do know them, to work intensely in attaining them. They seem to me like people who have taken up a notion that they must and will erect a tower, and who yet expend on the foundation not more stones and labor than would be sufficient for a hut. If you, my friend, whose highest want it was to perfect and unfold your moral nature, had, instead of those bold and noble sacrifices, merely trimmed between your duties to yourself and to your family, your bridegroom, or perhaps your husband, you must have lived in constant contradiction with your feelings, and never could have had a peaceful moment."

"You employ the word sacrifice," I answered here: "and I have often thought, that to a higher purpose, as to a divinity, we offer up by way of sacrifice a thing of smaller value; feeling like persons who should willingly and gladly bring a favorite lamb to the altar for the health of a beloved father."

"Whatever it may be," said he, "reason or feeling, that commands us to give up the one thing for the other, to choose the one before the other, decision and perseverance are, in my opinion, the noblest qualities of man. You cannot have the ware and the money both at the same time; and he who always hankers for the ware without having heart to give the money for it, is no better off than he who repents him of the purchase when the ware is in his hands. But I am far from blaming men on this account: it is not they that are to blame; it is the difficult, entangled situation they are in: they know not how to guide themselves in its perplexities. Thus, for instance, you will on the average find fewer bad economists in the country than in towns, and fewer again in small towns than in great; and why? Man is intended for a limited condition; objects that are simple, near, determinate, he comprehends, and he becomes accustomed to employ such means as are at hand; but, on entering a wider field, he now knows neither what he would nor what he should; and it amounts to quite the same, whether his attention is distracted by the multitude of objects, or is overpowered by their magnitude and dignity. It is always a misfortune for him when he is induced to struggle after any thing with which he cannot connect himself by some regular exertion of his powers.

"Certainly," pursued he, "without earnestness there is nothing to be done in life; yet, among the people whom we name cultivated men, little earnestness is to be found: in labors and employments, in arts, nay, even in recreations, they proceed, if I may say so, with a sort of self-defence; they live, as they read a heap of newspapers, only to have done with it; they remind one of that young Englishman at Rome, who said, with a contented air one evening in some company, that to-day he had despatched six churches and two galleries. They wish to know and learn a multitude of things, and precisely those they have the least concern with; and they never see that hunger is not stilled by snapping at the air. When I become acquainted with a man, my first inquiry is, With what does he employ himself, and how, and with what degree of perseverance? The answer regulates the interest I shall take in him for life."

"My dear uncle," I replied, "you are, perhaps, too rigorous: you perhaps withdraw your helping hand from here and there a worthy man to whom you might be useful."

"Can it be imputed as a fault," said he, "to one who has so long and vainly labored on them and about them? How much we have to suffer in our youth from men who think they are inviting us to a delightful pleasure-party, when they undertake to introduce us to the Danaides or Sisyphus! Heaven be praised! I have rid myself of these people: if one of them unfortunately comes within my sphere, I forthwith, in the politest manner, compliment him out again. It is from such persons that you hear the bitterest complaints about the miserable course of things, the aridity of science, the levity of artists, the emptiness of poets, and much more of that sort. They do not recollect that they, and the many like them, are the very persons who would never read a book which had been written just as they require it; that true poetry is alien to them; that even an excellent work of art can never gain their approbation except by means of prejudice. But let us now break off, for this is not the time to rail or to complain."

He directed my attention to the different pictures hanging on the wall: my eye dwelt on those whose look was beautiful or subject striking. This he permitted for a while: at last he said, "Bestow a little notice on the spirit manifested in these other works. Good minds delight to trace the finger of the Deity in nature: why not likewise pay some small regard to the hand of his imitator?" He then led my observation to some unobtrusive figures; endeavoring to make me understand that it was the history of art alone which could give us an idea of the worth and dignity of any work of art; that we should know the weary steps of mere handicraft and mechanism, over which the man of talents has struggled in the course of centuries, before we can conceive how it is possible for the man of genius to move with airy freedom on the pinnacle whose very aspect makes us giddy.

With this view he had formed a beautiful series of works; and, whilst he explained it, I could not help conceiving that I saw before me a similitude of moral culture. When I expressed my thought to him, he answered, "You are altogether right; and we see from this, that those do not act well, who, in a solitary, exclusive manner, follow moral cultivation by itself. On the contrary, it will be found, that he whose spirit strives for a development of that kind, has likewise every reason, at the same time, to improve his finer sentient powers; that so he may not run the risk of sinking from his moral height by giving way to the enticements of a lawless fancy, and degrading his moral nature by allowing it to take delight in tasteless baubles, if not in something worse."

I did not suspect him of levelling at me; but I felt myself struck, when I reflected how many insipidities there might be in the songs that used to edify me, and how little favor the figures which had joined themselves to my religious ideas would have found in the eyes of my uncle.

Philo, in the mean time, had frequently been busied in the library: he now took me along with him. We admired the selection, as well as the multitude, of books. They had been collected on my uncle's general principle: there were none to be found among them but such as either lead to correct knowledge, or teach right arrangement; such as either give us fit materials, or further the concordance of our spirit.

In the course of my life I had read very largely; in certain branches, there was almost no work unknown to me: the more pleasant was it here to speak about the general survey of the whole; to mark deficiencies, and not, as elsewhere, see nothing but a hampered confusion or a boundless expansion.

Here, too, we became acquainted with a very interesting, quiet man. He was a physician and a naturalist: he seemed rather one of the *Penates* than of the inmates. He showed us the museum, which, like the library, was fixed in glass cases to the walls of the chambers, adorning and ennobling the space, which it did not crowd. On this occasion I recalled with joy the days of my youth, and showed my father many of the things he had been wont to lay upon the sick-bed of his little child, just opening its little eyes to look into the world then. At the same time the physician, in our present and following conversations, did not scruple to avow how near he approximated to me in respect of my religious sentiments: he warmly praised my uncle for his tolerance, and his esteem of all that testified or forwarded the worth and unity of human nature; admitting, also, that he called for a similar return from others, and would shun and condemn nothing else so heartily as individual pretension and narrow exclusiveness.

Since the nuptials of my sister, joy had sparkled in the eyes of our uncle: he often spoke with me of what he meant to do for her and for her children. He had several fine estates: he managed them himself, and hoped to leave them in the best condition to his nephews. Regarding the small estate where we at present were, he appeared to entertain peculiar thoughts. "I will leave it to none," said he, "but to a person who can understand and value and enjoy what it contains, and who feels how loudly every man of wealth and rank, especially in Germany, is called on to exhibit something like a model to others."

Most of his guests were now gone: we, too, were making ready for departure, thinking we had seen the final scene of this solemnity, when his attention in affording us some dignified enjoyment produced a new surprise. We had mentioned to him the delight which the chorus of voices, suddenly commencing without accompaniment of any instrument, had given us, at my sister's marriage. We hinted, at the same time, how pleasant it would be were such a thing repeated; but he seemed to pay no heed to us. The livelier was our surprise, when he said, one evening, "The music of the dance has died away; our transitory, youthful friends have left us; the happy pair themselves have a more serious look than they had some days ago. To part at such a time, when, perhaps, we shall never meet again, certainly never without changes, exalts us to a solemn mood, which I know not how to entertain more nobly than by the music you were lately signifying a desire to have repeated."

The chorus, which had in the mean while gathered strength, and by secret practice more expertness, was accordingly made to sing to us a series of four- and of eight-voiced melodies, which, if I may say so, gave a real foretaste of bliss. Till then I had only known the pious mode of singing, as good souls practice it, frequently with hoarse pipes, imagining, like wild birds, that they are praising God, while they procure a pleasant feeling to themselves. Or, perhaps, I had listened to the vain music of concerts, in which you are at best invited to admire the talent of the singer, and very seldom have even a transient enjoyment. Now, however, I was listening to music, which, as it originated in the deepest feeling of the most accomplished human beings, was, by suitable and practised organs in harmonious unity, made again to address the deepest and best feelings of man, and to impress him at that moment with a lively sense of his likeness to the Deity. They were all devotional songs, in the Latin language: they sat like jewels in the golden ring of a polished intellectual conversation; and, without pretending to edify, they elevated me and made me happy in the most spiritual manner.

At our departure he presented all of us with handsome gifts. To me he gave the cross of my order, more beautifully and artfully worked and enamelled than I had ever seen it before. It was hung upon a large brilliant, by which also it was fastened to the chain: this he gave me, he said, "as the noblest stone in the cabinet of a collector."

My sister, with her husband, went to their estates, the rest of us to our abodes; appearing to ourselves, so far as outward circumstances were concerned, to have returned to quite an every-day existence. We had been, as it were, dropped from a palace of the fairies down upon the common earth, and were again obliged to help ourselves as we best could.

The singular experiences which this new circle had afforded left a fine impression on my mind. This, however, did not long continue in its first vivacity: though my uncle tried to nourish and renew it by sending me certain of his best and most pleasing works of art; changing them, from time to time, with others which I had not seen.

I had been so much accustomed to be busied with myself, in regulating the concerns of my heart and temper, and conversing on these matters with persons of a like mind, that I could not long study any work of art attentively without being turned by it back upon myself. I was used to look at a picture or copper-plate merely as at the letters of a book. Fine printing pleases well, but who would read a book for the beauty of the printing? In like manner I required of each pictorial form that it should tell me something, should instruct, affect, improve me; and, after all my uncle's letters to expound his works of art, say what he would, I continued in my former humor.

Yet not only my peculiar disposition, but external incidents and changes in our family, still farther drew me back from contemplations of that nature; nay, for some time even from myself. I had to suffer and to do more than my slender strength seemed fit for.

My maiden sister had, till now, been as a right arm to me. Healthy, strong, unspeakably good-natured, she had managed all the housekeeping; I myself being busied with the personal nursing of our aged father. She was seized with a catarrh, which changed to a disorder of the lungs: in three weeks she was lying in her coffin. Her death inflicted wounds on me, the scars of which I am not yet willing to examine.

I was lying sick before they buried her: the old ailment in my breast appeared to be awakening; I coughed with violence, and was so hoarse I could not speak beyond a whisper.

My married sister, out of fright and grief, was brought to bed before her time. Our old father thought he was about to lose at once his children and the hope of their posterity; his natural tears increased my sorrow: I prayed to God that he would give me back a sufferable state of health. I asked him but to spare my life till my father should die. I recovered: I was what I reckoned well, being able to discharge my duties, though with pain.

My sister was again with child. Many cares, which in such cases are committed to the mother, in the present instance fell to me. She was not altogether happy with her husband; this was to be hidden from our father: I was often made judge of their disputes, in which I could decide with the greater safety, as my brother trusted in me; and the two were really worthy persons, only each of them, instead of humoring, endeavored to convince, the other, and, out of eagerness to live in constant harmony, never could agree. I now learned to mingle seriously in worldly matters, and to practise what of old I had but sung.

My sister bore a son: the frailty of my father did not hinder him from travelling to her. The sight of the child exceedingly enlivened and cheered him: at the christening, contrary to his custom, he seemed as if inspired; nay, I might say like a Genius with two faces. With the one, he looked joyfully forward to those regions which he soon hoped to enter; with the other, to the new, hopeful, earthly life which had arisen in the boy descended from him. On our journey home he never wearied talking to me of the child, its form, its health, and his wish that the gifts of this new denizen of earth might be rightly cultivated. His reflections on the subject lasted when we had arrived at home: it was not till some days afterwards that I observed a kind of fever in him, which displayed itself, without shivering, in a sort of languid heat commencing after dinner. He did not yield, however: he went out as usual in the mornings, faithfully attending to the duties of his office, till at last continuous serious symptoms kept him within doors.

I never shall forget with what distinctness, clearness, and repose of mind he settled in the greatest order the concerns of his house, nay, the arrangements of his funeral, as he would have done a business of some other person.

With a cheerfulness which he never used to show, and which now mounted to a lively joy, he said to me, "Where is the fear of death which I once felt? Shall I shrink at departing? I have a gracious God; the grave awakens no terror in me; I have an eternal life."

To recall the circumstances of his death, which shortly followed, forms one of the most pleasing entertainments of my solitude: the visible workings of a higher Power in that solemn time, no one shall ever argue from me.

The death of my beloved father altogether changed my mode of life. From the strictest obedience, the narrowest confinement, I passed at once into the greatest freedom: I enjoyed it like a sort of food from which one has long abstained. Formerly I very seldom spent two hours from home: now I very seldom lived a day there. My friends, whom I had been allowed to visit only by hurried snatches, wished now to have my company without interruption, as I did to have theirs. I was often asked to dinner: at walks and pleasure-jaunts I never failed. But, when once the circle had been fairly run, I saw that the invaluable happiness of liberty consisted, not in doing what one pleases and what circumstances may invite to, but in being able, without hinderance or restraint, to do in the direct way what one regards as right and proper; and, in this instance, I was old enough to reach a valuable truth, without smarting for my ignorance.

One pleasure I could not deny myself: it was, as soon as might be, to renew and strengthen my connection with the Herrnhut Brethren. I hastened, accordingly, to visit one of their establishments at no great distance; but here I by no means found what I had been anticipating. I was frank enough to signify my disappointment, which they tried to soften by alleging that the present settlement was nothing to a full and fitly organized community. This I did not take upon me to deny; yet, in my thought, the genuine spirit of the matter might have displayed itself in a small body as well as in a great one.

One of their bishops, who was present, a personal disciple of the count, took considerable pains with me. He spoke English perfectly; and as I, too, understood a little of it, he reckoned this a token that we both belonged to one class. I, however, reckoned nothing of the kind: his conversation did not in the least satisfy me. He had been a cutler; was a native of Moravia; his mode of thought still savored of the artisan. With Herr von L——, who had been a major in the French service, I got upon a better footing: yet I could never bring myself to the submissiveness he showed to his superiors; nay, I felt as if you had given me a box on the ear, when I saw the major's wife, and other women more or less like ladies, take the bishop's hand and kiss it. Meanwhile a journey into Holland was proposed; which, however, doubtless for my good, did not take place.

My sister had been delivered of a daughter; and now it was the turn of us women to exult, and consider how the little creature should be bred like one of us. The husband, on the other hand, was not so satisfied, when in the following year another daughter saw the light: with his large estates, he wanted to have boys about him, who in future might assist him in his management.

My health was feeble: I kept myself in peace, and, by a quiet mode of life, in tolerable equilibrium. I was not afraid of death; nay, I wished to die: yet I secretly perceived that God was granting time for me to prove my soul, and to advance still nearer to himself. In my many sleepless nights, especially, I have at times felt something which I cannot undertake to describe.

It was as if my soul were thinking separately from the body: she looked upon the body as a foreign substance, as we look upon a garment. She pictured with extreme vivacity events and times long past, and felt, by means of this, events that were to follow. Those times are all gone by; what follows likewise will go by; the body, too, will fall to pieces like a vesture; but I, the well-known I, I am.

The thought is great, exalted, and consoling; yet an excellent friend, with whom I every day became more intimate, instructed me to dwell on it as little as I could. This was the physician whom I met in my uncle's house, and who had since accurately informed himself about the temper of my body and my spirit. He showed me how much these feelings, when we cherish them within us independently of outward objects, tend, as it were, to excavate us, and to undermine the whole foundation of our being. "To be active," he would say, "is the primary vocation of man: all the intervals in which he is obliged to rest, he should employ in gaining clearer knowledge of external things; for this will in its turn facilitate activity."

This friend was acquainted with my custom of looking on my body as an outward object: he knew also that I pretty well understood my constitution, my disorder, and the medicines of use for it; nay, that, by continual sufferings of my own or other people's, I had really grown a kind of half-doctor: he now carried forward my attention from the human body, and the drugs which act upon it, to the kindred objects of creation; he led me up and down as in the paradise of the first man; only, if I may continue my comparison, allowing me to trace, in dim remoteness, the Creator walking in the garden in the cool of the evening.

How gladly did I now see God in nature, when I bore him with such certainty within my heart! How interesting to me was his handi-work! how thankful did I feel that he had pleased to quicken me with the breath of his mouth!

We again had hopes that my sister would present us with a boy: her husband waited anxiously for that event, but did not live to see it. He died in consequence of an unlucky fall from horseback; and my sister followed him, soon after she had brought into the world a lovely boy. The four orphans they had left I could not look at but with sadness. So many healthy people had been called away before poor, sickly me; might I not also have blights to witness among these fair and hopeful blossoms? I knew the world sufficiently to understand what dangers threaten the precarious breeding of a child, especially a child of quality; and it seemed as if, since the period of my youth, these dangers had increased. I felt that, weakly as I was, I could not be of much, perhaps of any, service to the little ones; and I rejoiced the more on finding that my uncle, as indeed might have been looked for, had determined to devote his whole attention to the education of these amiable creatures. And this they doubtless merited in every sense: they were handsome; and, with great diversities, all promised to be well-conditioned, reasonable persons.

Since my worthy doctor had suggested it, I loved to trace out family likenesses among our relatives and children. My father had carefully preserved the portraits of his ancestors, and got his own and those of his descendants drawn by tolerable masters; nor had my mother and her people been forgotten. We accurately knew the characters of all the family; and, as we had frequently compared them with each other, we now endeavored to discover in the children the same pe-culiarities outward or inward. My sister's eldest son, we thought, resembled his paternal grandfather, of whom there was a fine youthful picture in my uncle's collection: he had been a brave soldier; and in this point, too, the boy took after him, liking arms above all things, and busying himself with them whenever he paid me a visit. For my father had left a very pretty armory; and the boy got no rest till I had given him a pair of pistols and a fowling-piece, and he had learned the proper way of using them. At the same time, in his conduct or bearing, there was nothing like rudeness: far from that, he was always meek and sensible.

The eldest daughter had attracted my especial love; of which, perhaps, the reason was, that she resembled me, and of all the four seemed to like me best. But I may well admit, that, the more closely I observed her as she grew, the more she shamed me: I could not look on her without a sentiment of admiration, nay, I may almost say, of reverence. You would scarcely have seen a nobler form, a more peaceful spirit, an activity so equable and universal. No moment of her life was she unoccupied, and every occupation in her hands became dignified. All seemed indifferent to her, so that she could but accomplish what was proper in the place and time; and, in the same manner, she could patiently continue unemployed, when there was nothing to be done. This activity without need of occupation I have never elsewhere met with. In particular, her conduct to the suffering and destitute was, from her earliest youth, inimitable. For my part, I freely confess I never had the gift to make a business of beneficence: I was not niggardly to the poor; nay, I often gave too largely for my means; yet this was little more than buying myself off: and a person needed to be made for me, if I was to bestow attention on him. Directly the reverse was the conduct of my niece. I never saw her give a poor man money: whatever she obtained from me for this purpose, she failed not in the first place to change for some necessary article. Never did she seem more lovely in my eyes, than when rummaging my clothes-presses: she was always sure to light on something which I did not wear and did not need; to sew these old cast-off articles together, and put them on some ragged child, she thought her highest happiness.

Her sister's turn of mind appeared already different: she had much of her mother; she promised to become very elegant and beautiful, and she now bids fair to keep her promise. She is greatly taken up with her exterior: from her earliest years she could decorate and carry herself in a way that struck you. I still remember with what ecstasy, when quite a little creature, she saw herself in a mirror, decked in certain precious pearls, once my mother's, which she had by chance discovered, and made me try upon her.

Reflecting on these diverse inclinations, it was pleasant for me to consider how my property would, after my decease, be shared among them, and again called into use. I saw the fowling-pieces of my father once more travelling round the fields on my nephew's shoulder, and birds once more falling from his hunting-pouch: I saw my whole wardrobe issuing from the church, at Easter Confirmation, on the persons of tidy little girls; while the best pieces of it were employed to decorate some virtuous burgher maiden on her marriage-day. In furnishing such children and poor little girls, Natalia had a singular delight; though, as I must here remark, she showed not the smallest love, or, if I may say it, smallest need, of a dependence upon any visible or invisible Being, such as I had in my youth so strongly manifested.

When I also thought that the younger sister, on that same day, would wear my jewels and pearls at court, I could see with peace my possessions, like my body, given back to the elements.

The children waxed apace: to my comfort, they are healthy, handsome, clever creatures. That my uncle keeps them from me, I endure without repining: when staying in the neighborhood, or even in town, they seldom see me.

A singular personage, regarded as a French clergyman, though no one rightly knows his history, has been intrusted with the oversight of all these children. He has them taught in various places: they are put to board now here, now there.

At first I could perceive no plan whatever in this mode of education; till at last our doctor told me the abbé had convinced my uncle, that, in order to accomplish any thing by education, we must first become acquainted with the pupil's tendencies and wishes; that, these once ascertained, he ought to be transported to a situation where he may, as speedily as possible, content the former and attain the latter, and so, if he have been mistaken, may still in time perceive his error, and at last, having found what suits him, may hold the faster by it, may the more diligently fashion himself according to it. I wish this strange experiment may prosper: with such excellent natures it is, perhaps, possible.

But there is one peculiarity in these instructors, which I never shall approve of: they study to seclude the children from whatever might awaken them to an acquaintance with themselves and with the invisible, sole, faithful Friend. I often take it ill of my uncle, that, on this account, he considers me dangerous for the little ones. Thus in practice there is no man tolerant! Many assure us that they willingly leave each to take his own way, yet all endeavor to exclude from action every one that does not think as they do.

This removal of the children troubles me the more, the more I am convinced of the reality of my belief. How can it fail to have a heavenly origin, an actual object, when in practice it is so effectual? Is it not by practice alone that we prove our own existence? Why, then, may we not, by a like mode, prove to ourselves the influence of that Power who gives us all good things?

That I am still advancing, never retrograding; that my conduct is approximating more and more to the image I have formed of perfection; that I every day feel more facility in doing what I reckon proper, even while the weakness of my body so obstructs, me, — can all this be accounted for upon the principles of human nature, whose corruption I have so clearly seen into? For me, at least, it cannot.

I scarcely remember a commandment: to me there is nothing that assumes the aspect of law; it is an impulse that leads me, and guides me always aright. I freely follow my emotions, and know as little of constraint as of repentance. God be praised that I know to whom I am indebted for such happiness, and that I cannot think of it without humility! There is no danger I should ever become proud of what I myself can do or can forbear to do: I have seen too well what a monster might be formed and nursed in every human bosom, did not higher Influence restrain us.

Book Seven

S PRING had come in all its brilliancy; a storm that had been lowering all day went fiercely down upon the hills; the rain drew back into the country; the sun came forth in all its splendor, and upon the dark vapor rose the lordly rainbow. Wilhelm was riding towards it: the sight made him sad. "Ah!" said he within himself, "must it be that the fairest hues of life appear to us only on a ground of black? And must drops fall, if we are to be enraptured? A bright day is like a dull day, if we look at it unmoved; and what can move us but some silent hope that the inborn inclination of our soul shall not always be without an object? The recital of a noble action moves us; the sight of every thing harmonious moves us: we feel then as if we were not altogether in a foreign land; we fancy we are nearer the home towards which our best and inmost wishes impatiently strive."

Meanwhile a pedestrian overtook him, and, walking with a stout step by the side of the horse, began to keep him company. After a few common words, he looked at the rider, and said, "If I am not mistaken, I must have already seen you somewhere."

"I, too, remember you," said Wilhelm: "had we not some time ago a pleasant sail together?" — "Right!" replied the other.

Wilhelm looked at him more narrowly, then, after a pause, observed, "I do not know what alteration has occurred in you. Last time we met, I took you for a Lutheran country clergyman: you now seem to me more like a Catholic priest."

"To-day, at least, you are not wrong," replied the other, taking off his hat, and showing him the tonsure. "Where is your company gone? Did you stay long with them?"

"Longer than was good: on looking back upon the period which I passed in their society, it seems as if I looked into an endless void; nothing of it has remained with me."

"Here you are mistaken," said the stranger: "every thing that happens to us leaves some trace behind it; every thing contributes imperceptibly to form us. Yet often it is dangerous to take a strict account of that. For either we grow proud and negligent, or downcast and dispirited; and both are equally injurious in their consequences. The safe plan is, always simply to do the task that lies nearest us; and this in the present case," added he, with a smile, "is to hasten to our quarters."

Wilhelm asked how far Lothario's house was distant: the stranger answered that it lay behind the hill. "Perhaps I shall meet you there," continued he: "I have merely a small affair to manage in the neighborhood. Farewell till then!" And, with this, he struck into a steep path that seemed to lead more speedily across the hill.

"Yes, the man is right!" said Wilhelm to himself, as he proceeded: "we should think of what is nearest; and for me, at present, there is nothing nearer than the mournful errand I have come to do. Let me see whether I can still repeat the speech, which is to put that cruel man to shame."

He then began reciting to himself this piece of oratory: not a syllable was wanting; and the more his recollection served him, the higher grew his passion and his courage. Aurelia's sorrows and her death were vividly present to his soul.

"Spirit of my friend!" exclaimed he, "hover round me, and, if thou canst, give some sign to me that thou art softened, art appeased!"

Amid such words and meditations, he had reached the summit of the hill; and, near the foot of its declivity, he now beheld a curious building, which he at once took to be Lothario's dwelling. An old, irregular castle, with several turrets and peaked roofs, appeared to have been the primitive erection; but the new additions to it, placed near the main structure, looked still more irregular. A part of them stood close upon the main edifice: others, at some distance, were combined with it by galleries and covered passages. All external symmetry, every shade of architectural beauty, appeared to have been sacrificed to the convenience of the interior. No trace of wall or trench was to be seen; none of avenues or artificial gardens. A fruit and pot-herb garden reached to the very buildings, and little patches of a like sort showed themselves even in the intermediate spaces. A cheerful village lay at no great distance: the fields and gardens everywhere appeared in the highest state of cultivation.

Sunk in his own impassioned feelings, Wilhelm rode along, not thinking much of what he saw: he put up his horse at an inn, and, not without emotion, hastened to the castle.

An old serving-man received him at the door, and signified, with much good-nature, that to-day it would be difficult to get admission to his lordship, who was occupied in writing letters, and had already refused some people that had business with him. Our friend became more importunate: the old man was at last obliged to yield, and announce him. He returned, and conducted Wilhelm to a spacious, ancient hall; desiring him to be so good as wait, since perhaps it might be some time before his lordship could appear. Our friend walked up and down unrestfully, casting now and then a look at the knights and dames whose ancient figures hung round him on the walls. He repeated the beginning of his speech: it seemed, in presence of these ruffs and coats of mail, to answer even better. Every time there rose any stir, he put himself in posture to receive his man with dignity; meaning first to hand him the letter, then assail him with the weapons of reproach.

More than once mistaken, he was now beginning to be really vexed and out of tune, when at last a handsome man, in boots and light surtout, stepped in from a side-door. "What good news have you for me?" said he to Wilhelm, with a friendly voice: "pardon me, that I have made you wait."

Wilhelm has strange dreams

So speaking, he kept folding a letter which he held in his hand. Wilhelm, not without embarrassment, delivered him Aurelia's paper, and replied, "I bring you the last words of a friend, which you will not read without emotion."

Lothario took it, and returned to his chamber with it; where, as Wilhelm through the open door could very easily observe, he addressed and sealed some letters before opening Aurelia's. He appeared to have perused it once or twice; and Wilhelm, though his feelings signified that the pathetic speech would sort but ill with such a cool reception, girded up his mind, went forward to the threshold, and was just about beginning his address, when a tapestry-door of the cabinet opened, and the clergyman came in.

"I have got the strangest message you can think of," cried Lothario to him. "Pardon me," continued he, addressing Wilhelm, "if I am not in a mood for speaking further with you at this moment. You remain with us to-night: you, abbé, see the stranger properly attended to."

With these words, he made his guest a bow: the clergyman took Wilhelm by the hand, who followed, not without reluctance.

They walked along some curious passages in silence, and at last reached a very pretty chamber. The abbé led him in, then left him, making no excuses. Erelong an active boy appeared: he introduced himself as Wilhelm's valet, and brought up his supper. In waiting, he had much to say about the order of the house, about their breakfasting and dining, labors and amusements; interspersing many things in commendation of Lothario.

Pleasant as the boy was, Wilhelm endeavored to get rid of him as soon as possible. He wished to be alone, for he felt exceedingly oppressed and straitened in his new position. He reproached himself with having executed his intention so ill, with having done his errand only half. One moment, he proposed to undertake next morning what he had neglected to-night; the next, he saw, that, by Lothario's presence, he would be attuned to quite a different set of feelings. The house, too, where he was, seemed very strange to him: he could not be at home in his position. Intending to undress, he opened his travelling-bag: with his night-clothes, he took out the Spirit's veil, which Mignon had packed in along with them. The sight of it increased the sadness of his humor. "Flee, youth! flee!" cried he. "What means this mystic word? What am I to flee, or whither? It were better had the Spirit called to me, Return to thyself!" He cast his eyes on some English copper-plates hung round the room in frames; most of them he looked at with indifference: at last he met with one, in which a ship was represented sinking in a tempest; a father, with his lovely daughters, was awaiting death from the intrusive billows. One of the maidens had a kind of likeness to the Amazon: an indescribable compassion seized our friend; he felt an irresistible necessity to vent his feelings; tears filled his eyes, he wept, and did not recover his composure till slumber overpowered him.

Strange dreams arose upon him towards morning. He was in a garden, which in boyhood he had often visited: he looked with pleasure at the well-known alleys, hedges, flower-beds. Mariana met him: he spoke to her with love and tenderness, recollecting nothing of any by-gone grievance. Erelong his father joined them, in his week-day dress; with a look of frankness that was rare in him, he bade his son fetch two seats from the garden-house; then took Mariana by the hand, and led her into a grove.

Wilhelm hastened to the garden-house, but found it altogether empty: only at a window in the farther side he saw Aurelia standing. He went forward, and addressed her, but she turned not round; and, though he placed himself beside her, he could never see her face. He looked out from the window: in an unknown garden, there were several people, some of whom he recognized. Frau Melina, seated under a tree, was playing with a rose which she had in her hand: Laertes stood beside her, counting money from the one hand to the other. Mignon and Felix were lying on the grass, the former on her back, the latter on his face. Philina came, and clapped her hands above the children: Mignon lay unmoved; Felix started up and fled. At first he laughed while running, as Philina followed; but he screamed in terror when he saw the harper coming after him with large, slow steps. Felix ran directly to a pond. Wilhelm hastened after him: too late; the child was lying in the water! Wilhelm stood as if rooted to the spot. The fair Amazon appeared on the other side of the pond: she stretched her right hand towards the child, and walked along the shore. The child came through the water, by the course her finger pointed to; he followed her as she went round; at last she reached her hand to him, and pulled him out. Wilhelm had come nearer: the child was all in flames; fiery drops were falling from his body. Wilhelm's agony was greater than ever; but instantly the Amazon took a white veil from her head, and covered up the child with it. The fire was at once quenched. But, when she lifted up the veil, two boys sprang out from under it, and frolicsomely sported to and fro; while Wilhelm and the Amazon proceeded hand in hand across the garden, and noticed in the distance Mariana and his father walking in an alley, which was formed of lofty trees, and seemed to go quite round the garden. He turned his steps to them, and, with his beautiful attendant, was moving through the garden, when suddenly the fair-haired Friedrich came across their path, and kept them back with loud laughter and a thousand tricks. Still, however, they insisted on proceeding; and Friedrich hastened off, running towards Mariana and the father. These seemed to flee before him; he pursued the faster, till Wilhelm saw them hovering down the alley almost as on wings. Nature and inclination called on him to go and help them, but the hand of the Amazon detained him. How gladly did he let himself be held! With this mingled feeling he awoke, and found his chamber shining with the morning beams.

CHAPTER TWO

OUR FRIEND was called to breakfast by the boy: he found the abbé waiting in the hall; Lothario, it appeared, had ridden out. The abbé was not very talkative, but rather wore a thoughtful look: he inquired about Aurelia's death, and listened to our friend's recital of it with apparent sympathy. "Ah!" cried he, "the man that discerns, with lively clearness, what infinite operations art and nature must have joined in before a cultivated human being can be formed; the man that himself as much as possible takes interest in the culture of his fellow-men, — is ready to despair when he sees how lightly mortals will destroy themselves, will blamelessly or blamably expose themselves to be destroyed. When I think of these things, life itself appears to me so uncertain a gift, that I could praise the man who does not value it beyond its worth."

Scarcely had he spoken, when the door flew violently up: a young lady came rushing in; she pushed away the old servant, who attempted to restrain her. She made right to the abbé, and seized him by the arm: her tears and sobs would hardly let her speak these words: "Where is he? Where have you put him? 'Tis a frightful treachery! Confess it now! I know what you are doing: I will after him, — will know where you have sent him!"

"Be calm, my child," replied the abbé, with assumed composure; "come with me to your room: you shall know it all; only you must have the strength to listen, if you ask me to relate." He offered her his hand, as if he meant to lead her out. "I will not return to my room," cried she: "I hate the walls where you have kept me prisoner so long. I know it already: the colonel has challenged him; he is gone to meet his enemy: perhaps this very moment he — once or twice I thought I heard the sound of shots! I tell you, order out a coach, and come along with me, or I will fill the house and all the village with my screaming."

Weeping bitterly, she hastened to the window: the abbé held her back, and sought in vain to soothe her.

They heard a sound of wheels: she threw up the window, exclaiming, "He is dead! They are bringing home his body." — "He is coming out," replied the abbé: "you perceive he lives." — "He is wounded," said she wildly, "else he would have come on horseback. They are holding him! The wound is dangerous!" She ran to the door, and down the stairs: the abbé hastened after her; and Wilhelm, following, observed the fair one meet her lover, who had now dismounted.

Lothario leaned on his attendant, whom Wilhelm at once knew as his ancient patron, Jarno. The wounded man spoke very tenderly and kindly to the tearful damsel: he rested on her shoulder, and came slowly up the steps, saluted Wilhelm as he passed, and was conducted to his cabinet.

Jarno soon returned, and, going up to Wilhelm, "It appears," said he, "you are predestined everywhere to find a theatre and actors.

We have here commenced a play which is not altogether pleasant."

"I rejoice to find you," answered Wilhelm, "in so strange an hour: I am astonished, frightened; and your presence already quiets my mind. Tell me, is there danger? Is the baron badly wounded?"

"I imagine not," said Jarno.

It was not long till the young surgeon entered from the cabinet. "Now, what say you?" cried Jarno to him. "That it is a dangerous piece of work," replied the other, putting several instruments into his leathern pouch. Wilhelm looked at the band, which was hanging from the pouch: he fancied he knew it. Bright, contrary colors, a curious pattern, gold and silver wrought in singular figures, marked this band from all the bands in the world. Wilhelm was convinced he beheld the very pouch of the ancient surgeon who had dressed his wounds in the green of the forest; and the hope, so long deferred, of again finding traces of the lovely Amazon, struck like a flame through all his soul.

"Where did you get that pouch?" cried he. "To whom did it belong before you? I beg of you, tell me." — "I bought it at an auction," said the other: "what is it to me whom it belonged to?" So speaking, he went out; and Jarno said, "If there would come but one word of truth from our young doctor's mouth!" — "Then, he did not buy the pouch?" said Wilhelm. "Just as little as Lothario is in danger," said the other.

Wilhelm stood, immersed in many reflections: Jarno asked how he had fared of late. Wilhelm sketched an outline of his history; and when he at last came to speak of Aurelia's death, and his message to the place, his auditor exclaimed, "Well! it is strange! most strange!"

The abbé entered from Lothario's chamber, beckoned Jarno to go in instead of him, and said to Wilhelm, "The baron bids me ask you to remain with us a day or two, to share his hospitality, and, in the present circumstances, contribute to his solacement. If you need to give any notice to your people, your letter shall be instantly despatched. Meanwhile, to make you understand this curious incident, of which you have been witness, I must tell you something, which, indeed, is no secret. The baron had a small adventure with a lady, which excited more than usual attention; the lady having taken him from a rival, and wishing to enjoy her victory too ostentatiously. After a time he no longer found the same delight in her society; which he, of course, forsook: but, being of a violent temper, she could not bear her fate with patience. Meeting at a ball, they had an open quarrel: she thought herself irreparably injured, and would be revenged. No knight stepped forth to do battle for her; till her husband, whom for years she had not lived with, heard of the affair and took it up. He challenged the baron, and to-day he has wounded him; yet, as I hear, the gallant colonel has himself come still worse off."

From this hour our friend was treated in the house as if he had belonged to it.

CHAPTER THREE

AT TIMES they had read a little to the patient: Wilhelm joyfully performed this service. Lydia stirred not from Lothario's bed: her care for him absorbed her whole attention. But to-day the patient himself seemed occupied with thought: he bade them lay aside their book. "To-day," said he, "I feel through my whole heart how foolishly we let our time pass on. How many things have I proposed to do, how many have I planned; yet how we loiter in our noblest purposes! I have just read over the scheme of the changes which I mean to make in my estates; and it is chiefly, I may say, on their account that I rejoice at the bullet's not having gone a deadlier road."

Lydia looked at him with tenderness, with tears in her eyes; as if to ask if *she*, if his friends, could not pretend to any interest in his wish to live. Jarno answered, "Changes such as you project require to be considered well on every side before they are resolved on."

"Long considerations," said Lothario, "are commonly a proof that we have not the point to be determined clearly in our eye; precipitate proceedings, that we do not know it. I see distinctly, that, in managing my property, there are several particulars in which the services of my dependents cannot be remitted; certain rights which I must rigidly insist on: but I also see that there are other articles, advantageous to me, but by no means indispensable, which might admit of relaxation. Do I not profit by my lands far better than my father did? Is not my income still increasing? And shall I alone enjoy this growing benefit? Shall not those who labor with and for me partake, in their degree, of the advantages which expanding knowledge, which a period of improvement, are procuring for us?"

" 'Tis human nature!" cried Jarno: "I do not blame myself when I detect this selfish quality among the rest. Every man desires to gather all things round him, to shape and manage them according to his own pleasure: the money which he himself does not expend, he seldom reckons well expended."

"Certainly," observed Lothario, "much of the capital might be abated if we consumed the interest less capriciously."

"The only thing I shall mention," said the other, "the only reason I can urge against your now proceeding with those alterations, which, for a time at least, must cause you loss, is, that you yourself are still in debt, and that the payment presses hard on you. My advice is, therefore, to postpone your plan till you are altogether free."

"And in the mean while leave it at the mercy of a bullet, or the fall of a tile, to annihilate the whole result of my existence and activity! O my friend! it is ever thus: it is ever the besetting fault of cultivated men, that they wish to spend their whole resources on some idea, scarcely any part of them on tangible, existing objects. Why was it that I contracted debts, that I quarrelled with my uncle, that I left my sisters to themselves so long? Purely for the sake of an idea. In America I fancied I might accomplish something; over seas, I hoped to become useful and essential: if any task was not begirt with a thousand dangers, I considered it trivial, unworthy of me. How differently do matters now appear! How precious, how important, seems the duty which is nearest me, whatever it may be!"

"I recollect the letter which you sent me from the Western world," said Jarno: "it contains the words, 'I will return; and in my house, amid my fields, among my people, I will say, *Here or nowhere is America!*' "

"Yes, my friend; and I am still repeating it, and still repining at myself that I am not so busy here as I was there. For certain equable,

continuous modes of life, there is nothing more than judgment necessary, and we study to attain nothing more: so that we become unable
to discern what extraordinary services each vulgar day requires of us;
or, if we do discern them, we find abundance of excuses for not doing
them. A judicious man is valuable to himself, but of little value for
the general whole."

"We will not," said Jarno, "bear too hard upon judgment: let
us grant, that, whenever extraordinary things are done, they are generally foolish."

"Yes! and just because they are not done according to the proper
plan. My brother-in-law, you see, is giving up his fortune, so far as in
his power, to the Community of Herrnhut: he reckons, that, by doing
so, he is advancing the salvation of his soul. Had he sacrificed a small
portion of his revenue, he might have rendered many people happy,
might have made for them and for himself a heaven upon earth. Our
sacrifices are rarely of an active kind: we, as it were, abandon what we
give away. It is not from resolution, but despair, that we renounce our
property. In these days, I confess it, the image of the count is hovering
constantly before me: I have firmly resolved on doing from conviction
what a crazy fear is forcing upon him. I will not wait for being cured.
Here are the papers: they require only to be properly drawn out.
Take the lawyer with you; our guest will help: what I want, you
know as well as I; recovering or dying, I will stand by it, and say,
Here or nowhere is Herrnhut!"

When he mentioned dying, Lydia sank before his bed: she hung
upon his arm, and wept bitterly. The surgeon entered: Jarno gave our
friend the papers, and made Lydia leave the room.

"For Heaven's sake! what is this about the count?" cried Wilhelm, when they reached the hall and were alone. "What count is it
that means to join the Herrnhuters?"

"One whom you know very well," said Jarno. "You yourself are
the ghost who have frightened the unhappy wiseacre into piety: you
are the villain who have brought his pretty wife to such a state that
she inclines accompanying him."

"And she is Lothario's sister?" cried our friend.

"No other!" — "And Lothario knows" —

"The whole!"

"Oh, let me fly!" cried Wilhelm. "How shall I appear before him? What can he say to me?"

"That no man should cast a stone at his brother; that when one composes long speeches, with a view to shame his neighbors, he should speak them to a looking-glass."

"Do you know that too?"

"And many things beside," said Jarno, with a smile. "But in the present case," continued he, "you shall not get away from me so easily as you did last time. You need not now be apprehensive of my bounty-money: I have ceased to be a soldier; when I was one, you might have thought more charitably of me. Since you saw me, many things have altered. My prince, my only friend and benefactor, being dead, I have now withdrawn from busy life and its concerns. I used to have pleasure in advancing what was reasonable; when I met with any despicable thing, I hesitated not to call it so; and men had never done with talking of my restless head and wicked tongue. The herd of people dread sound understanding more than any thing: they ought to dread stupidity, if they had any notion what was really dreadful. Understanding is unpleasant, they must have it pushed aside; stupidity is but pernicious, they can let it stay. Well, be it so! I need to live: I will by and by communicate my plans to you; if you incline, you shall partake in them. But tell me first how things have gone with you. I see, I feel, that you are changed. How is it with your ancient maggot of producing something beautiful and good in the society of gypsies?"

"Do not speak of it!" cried Wilhelm: "I have been already punished for it. People talk about the stage, but none that has not been upon it can form the smallest notion of it. How utterly these men are unacquainted with themselves, how thoughtlessly they carry on their trade, how boundless their pretensions are, no mortal can conceive. Each would be not only first, but sole; each wishes to exclude the rest, and does not see that even with them he can scarcely accomplish any thing. Each thinks himself a man of marvellous originality; yet, with a ravening appetite for novelty, he cannot walk a footstep from the beaten track. How vehemently they counterwork each other! It is only the pitifullest self-love, the narrowest views of interest, that unite them. Of reciprocal accommodation they have no idea: backbiting and hidden spitefulness maintain a constant jealousy among them. In their lives they are either rakes or simpletons. Each claims the loftiest re-spect, each writhes under the slightest blame. 'All this he knew al-ready,' he will tell you! Why, then, did he not do it? Ever needy, ever unconfiding, they seem as if their greatest fear were reason and good taste; their highest care, to secure the majesty of their self-will."

Wilhelm drew breath, intending to proceed with his eulogium, when an immoderate laugh from Jarno interrupted him. "Poor actors!" cried he; threw himself into a chair, and laughed away. "Poor, dear actors! Do you know, my friend," continued he, recovering from his fit, "that you have been describing, not the playhouse, but the world; that, out of all ranks, I could find you characters and doings in abund-ance to suit your cruel pencil? Pardon me: it makes me laugh again, that you should think these amiable qualities existed on the boards alone."

Wilhelm checked his feelings. Jarno's extravagant, untimely laughter had in truth offended him. "It is scarcely hiding your mis-anthropy," said he, "when you maintain that faults like these are universal."

"And it shows your acquaintance with the world, when you impute them to the theatre in such a heinous light. I pardon, in the player, every fault that springs from self-deception and the desire to please. If he seem not something to himself and others, he is nothing. To seem is his vocation; he must prize his moment of applause, for he gets no other recompense; he must try to glitter, — he is there to do so."

"You will give me leave at least to smile, in my turn," answered Wilhelm. "I should never have believed that you could be so merciful, so tolerant."

"I swear to you I am serious, fully and deliberately serious. All faults of the man I can pardon in the player: no fault of the player can I pardon in the man. Do not set me upon chanting my lament about the latter: it might have a sharper sound than yours."

The surgeon entered from the cabinet; and, to the question how his patient was, he answered, with a lively air of complaisance, "Ex-tremely well, indeed: I hope soon to see him quite recovered." He hastened through the hall, not waiting Wilhelm's speech, who was preparing to inquire again with greater importunity about his leathern case. His anxiety to gain some tidings of his Amazon inspired him with confidence in Jarno: he disclosed his case to him, and begged his help. "You that know so many things," said he, "can you not discover this?"

Jarno reflected for a moment; then, turning to his friend, "Be calm," said he, "give no one any hint of it: we shall come upon the fair one's footsteps, never fear. At present I am anxious only for Lothario: the case is dangerous; the kindliness and comfortable talking of the doctor tells me so. We should be quit of Lydia, for here she does no good; but how to set about the task I know not. To-night I am looking for our old physician: we shall then take further counsel."

CHAPTER FOUR

THE PHYSICIAN came: it was the good, old, little doctor whom we know already, and to whom we were obliged for the communication of the pious manuscript. First of all, he visited the wounded man, with whose condition he appeared to be by no means satisfied. He had next a long interview with Jarno, but they made no allusion to the subject of it when they came to supper.

Wilhelm saluted him in the kindest manner, and inquired about the harper. "We have still hopes of bringing round the hapless creature," answered the physician. "He formed a dreary item in your limited and singular way of life," said Jarno. "How has it fared with him? Tell me."

Having satisfied Jarno's curiosity, the physician thus proceeded: "I have never seen another man so strangely circumstanced. For many years he has not felt the smallest interest in any thing without him, scarcely paid the smallest notice to it: wrapped up in himself, he has looked at nothing but his own hollow, empty Me, which seemed to him like an immeasurable abyss. It was really touching when he spoke to us of this mournful state. 'Before me,' cried he, 'I see nothing; behind me nothing but an endless night, in which I live in the most horrid solitude. There is no feeling in me but the feeling of my guilt; and this appears but like a dim, formless spirit, far before me. Yet here there is no height, no depth, no forwards, no backwards: no words can express this never-changing state. Often in the agony of this sameness I exclaim with violence, Forever! Forever! and this dark, incomprehensible word is clear and plain to the gloom of my condition. No ray of Divinity illuminates this night: I shed all my tears by myself and for myself. Nothing is more horrible to me than friendship and love, for they alone excite in me the wish that the apparitions which surround me might be real. But these two spectres also have arisen from the abyss to plague me, and at length to tear from me the precious consciousness of my existence, unearthly though it be.'

"You should hear him speak," continued the physician, "when in hours of confidence he thus alleviates his heart. I have listened to him often with the deepest feelings. When pressed by any thing, and, as it were, compelled for an instant to confess that a space of time has passed, he looks astounded, then again refers the alteration to the things about him, considering it as an appearance of appearances, and so rejecting the idea of progress in duration. One night he sung a song about his gray hairs: we all sat round him weeping."

"Oh, get it for me!" cried Wilhelm.

"But have you not discovered any trace of what he calls his crime?" inquired Jarno: "nor found out the reason of his wearing such a singular garb; of his conduct at the burning of the house; of his rage against the child?"

"It is only by conjectures that we can approximate to any knowledge of his fate: to question him directly contradicts our principle. Observing easily that he was of the Catholic religion, we thought perhaps confession might afford him some assuagement; but he shrinks away with the strangest gestures every time we try to introduce the priest to him. However, not to leave your curiosity respecting him entirely unsatisfied, I may communicate our suppositions on the subject. In his youth, we think, he must have been a clergyman: hence probably his wish to keep his beard and long cloak. The joys of love appear to have remained for many years unknown to him. Late in life, as we conceive, some aberration with a lady very nearly related to him; then her death, the consequence of an unlucky creature's birth, — have altogether crazed his brain.

"His chief delusion is a fancy that he brings misfortune everywhere along with him; and that death, to be unwittingly occasioned by a boy, is constantly impending over him. At first he was afraid of Mignon, not knowing that she was a girl; then Felix frightened him; and as, with all his misery, he has a boundless love of life, this may, perhaps, have been the origin of his aversion to the child."

"What hopes have you of his recovery?" inquired our friend.

"It advances slowly," answered the physician, "yet it does advance. He continues his appointed occupations: we have now accustomed him to read the newspapers; he always looks for them with eagerness."

"I am curious about his songs," said Jarno.

"Of these I can engage to get you several," replied the doctor. "Our parson's eldest son, who frequently writes down his father's sermons, has, unnoticed by the harper, marked on paper many stanzas of his singing; out of which some songs have gradually been pieced together."

Next morning Jarno met our friend, and said to him, "We have to ask a kindness of you. Lydia must, for some time, be removed: her violent, unreasonable love and passionateness hinder the baron's recovery. His wound requires rest and calmness, though with his healthy temperament it is not dangerous. You see how Lydia tortures him with her tempestuous anxieties, her ungovernable terrors, her never-drying tears; and — Enough!" he added with a smile, after pausing for a moment, "our doctor expressly requires that she must quit us for a while. We have got her to believe that a lady, one of her most intimate friends, is at present in the neighborhood, wishing and expecting instantly to see her. She has been prevailed upon to undertake a journey to our lawyer's, which is but two leagues off. This man is in the secret: he will wofully lament that Fräulein Theresa should just have left him again; he will seem to think she may still be overtaken. Lydia will hasten after her, and, if you prosper, will be led from place to place. At last, if she insist on turning back, you must not contradict her; but the night will help you: the coachman is a cunning knave, and we shall speak with him before he goes. You are to travel with her in the coach, to talk to her, and manage the adventure."

"It is a strange and dubious commission that you give me," answered Wilhelm. "How painful is the sight of true love injured! And am I to be the instrument of injuring it? I have never cheated any person so; for it has always seemed to me, that if we once begin deceiving, with a view to good and useful purposes, we run the risk of carrying it to excess."

"Yet you cannot manage children otherwise," said Jarno.

"With children it may do," said Wilhelm; "for we love them tenderly, and take an open charge of them. But with our equals, in behalf of whom our heart is not so sure to call upon us for forbearance, it might frequently be dangerous. Yet do not think," he added, after pausing for a moment, "that I purpose to decline the task on this account. Honoring your judgment as I do, feeling such attachment to your noble friend, such eagerness to forward his recovery by whatever means, I willingly forget myself and my opinions. It is not enough that we can risk our life to serve a friend: in the hour of need, we should also yield him our convictions. Our dearest passions, our best wishes, we are bound to sacrifice in helping him. I undertake the charge; though it is easy to foresee the pain I shall have to suffer, from the tears, from the despair, of Lydia."

"And, for this, no small reward awaits you," answered Jarno: "Fräulein Theresa, whom you get acquainted with, is a lady such as you will rarely see. She puts many a man to shame; I may say, she is a genuine Amazon: while others are but pretty counterfeits, that wander up and down the world in that ambiguous dress."

Wilhelm was struck: he almost fancied that in Theresa he would find his Amazon again; especially as Jarno, whom he importuned to tell him more, broke off abruptly, and went away.

The new, near hope of once more seeing that beloved and honored being awoke a thousand feelings in his heart. He now looked upon the task which had been given him as the intervention of a special Providence: the thought that he was minded treacherously to carry off a helpless girl from the object of her sincerest, warmest love dwelt but a moment in his mind, as the shadow of a bird flits over the sunshiny earth.

The coach was at the door: Lydia lingered for a moment, as she was about to mount. "Salute your lord again for me," said she to the old servant: "tell him that I shall be home before night." Tears were standing in her eyes as she again looked back when the carriage started. She then turned round to Wilhelm, made an effort to compose herself, and said, "In Fräulein Theresa you will find a very interesting person. I wonder what it is that brings her hither; for, you must know, Lothario and she once passionately loved each other. In spite of the distance, he often used to visit her: I was staying with her then; I thought they would have lived and died for one another. But all at once it went to wreck, no creature could discover why. He had seen me, and I must confess that I was envious of Theresa's fortune; that I scarcely hid my love from him; that, when he suddenly appeared to choose me in her stead, I could not but accept of him. She behaved to me beyond my wishes, though it almost seemed as if I had robbed her of this precious lover. But, ah! how many thousand tears and pains that love of his has cost me! At first we met only now and then, and by stealth, at some appointed place: but I could not long endure that kind of life; in his presence only was I happy, wholly happy! Far from him, my eyes were never dry, my pulse was never calm. Once he staid away for several days: I was altogether in despair; I ordered out my carriage, and surprised him here. He received me tenderly; and, had not this unlucky quarrel happened, I should have led a heavenly life with him. But, since the time he began to be in danger and in pain, I shall not say what I have suffered: at this moment I am bitterly reproaching myself that I could leave him for a single day."

Wilhelm was proceeding to inquire about Theresa, when they reached the lawyer's house. This gentleman came forward to the coach, lamenting wofully that Fräulein Theresa was already gone. He invited them to breakfast; signifying, however, that the lady might be overtaken in the nearest village. They determined upon following her: the coachman did not loiter; they had soon passed several villages, and yet come up with nobody. Lydia now gave orders for returning: the coachman drove along, as if he did not understand her. As she insisted with redoubled vehemence, Wilhelm called to him, and gave the promised token. The coachman answered that it was not necessary to go back by the same road: he knew a shorter, and, at the same time, greatly easier one. He turned aside across a wood, and over large commons. At last, no object they could recognize appearing, he confessed that unfortunately he had lost his way; declaring, at the same time, that he would soon get right again, as he saw a little town before him. Night came on: the coachman managed so discreetly, that he asked everywhere, and nowhere waited for an answer. He drove along all night: Lydia never closed an eye; in the moonshine she was constantly detecting similarities, which as constantly turned out to be dissimilar. In the morning things around seemed known to her, and but more strange on that account. The coach drew up before a neat little country-house: a young lady stepped out, and opened the carriage-door. Lydia looked at her with a stare of wonder, looked around, looked at her again, and fainted in the arms of Wilhelm.

CHAPTER FIVE

WILHELM was conducted to a little upper room: the house was new, as small nearly as it could be, and extremely orderly and clean. In Theresa, who had welcomed him and Lydia at the coach, he had not found his Amazon: she was another and altogether different woman. Handsome, and but of middle stature, she moved about with great alertness; and it seemed as if her clear, blue, open eyes let nothing that occurred escape them.

She entered Wilhelm's room, inquiring if he wanted any thing. "Pardon me," said she, "for having lodged you in a chamber which the smell of paint still renders disagreeable: my little dwelling is but just made ready; you are handselling this room, which is appointed for my guests. Would that you had come on some more pleasant errand! Poor Lydia is like to be a dull companion: in other points, also, you will have much to pardon. My cook has run away from me, at this unseasonable time; and a serving-man has bruised his hand. The case might happen I had to manage every thing myself; and if it were so, why, then we should just put up with it. One is plagued so with nobody as with one's servants: none of them will serve you, scarcely even serve himself."

She said a good deal more on different matters: in general she seemed to like speaking. Wilhelm inquired for Lydia, — if he might not see her, and endeavor to excuse himself.

"It will have no effect at present," said Theresa: "time excuses, as it comforts. Words, in both cases, are of little effect. Lydia will not see you. 'Keep him from my sight,' she cried, when I was leaving her: 'I could almost despair of human nature. Such an honorable countenance, so frank a manner, and this secret guile!' Lothario she has quite forgiven: in a letter to the poor girl, he declares, 'My friends persuaded me, my friends compelled me!' Among these she reckons you, and she condemns you with the rest."

"She does me too much honor in so blaming me," said Wilhelm: "I have no pretension to the friendship of that noble gentleman; on this occasion, I am but a guiltless instrument. I will not praise what I have done: it is enough that I could do it. It concerned the health, it concerned the life, of a man whom I value more than any one I ever knew before. Oh, what a man is he, Fräulein! and what men are they that live about him! In their society, I for the first time, I may well say, carried on a conversation; for the first time, was the inmost sense of my words returned to me, more rich, more full, more comprehensive, from another's mouth; what I had been groping for was rendered clear to me; what I had been thinking I was taught to see. Unfortunately this enjoyment was disturbed, at first by numerous anxieties and whims, and then by this unpleasant task. I undertook it with submission; for I reckoned it my duty, even though I sacrificed my feelings, to comply with the request of this gifted company of men."

While he spoke, Theresa had been looking at him with a very friendly air. "Oh, how sweet is it to hear one's own opinion uttered by a stranger tongue! We are never properly ourselves until another thinks entirely as we do. My own opinion of Lothario is perfectly the same as yours: it is not every one that does him justice, and therefore all that know him better are enthusiastic in esteem of him. The painful sentiment that mingles with the memory of him in my heart cannot hinder me from thinking of him daily." A sigh heaved her bosom as she spoke thus, and a lovely tear glittered in her right eye. "Think not," continued she, "that I am so weak, so easy to be moved. It is but the eye that weeps. There was a little wart upon the under eyelid; they have happily removed it, but the eye has been weak ever since; the smallest cause brings a tear into it. Here sat the little wart: you cannot see a vestige of it now."

He saw no vestige, but he saw into her eye; it was clear as crystal: he almost imagined he could see to the very bottom of her soul.

"We have now," said she, "pronounced the watchword of our friendship: let us get entirely acquainted as fast as possible. The history of every person paints his character. I will tell you what my life has been: do you, too, place a little trust in me, and let us be united even when distance parts us. The world is so waste and empty, when we figure only towns and hills and rivers in it; but to know of some one here and there whom we accord with, who is living on with us, even in silence, — this makes our earthly ball a peopled garden."

She hastened off, engaging soon to take him out to walk. Her presence had affected him agreeably: he wished to be informed of her relation to Lothario. He was called: she came to meet him from her room. While they descended, necessarily one by one, the straight and even steepish stairs, she said, "All this might have been larger and grander, had I chosen to accept the offers of your generous friend; but, to continue worthy of him, I must study to retain the qualities which gave me merit in his eyes. Where is the steward?" asked she, stepping from the bottom of the stairs. "You must not think," continued she, "that I am rich enough to need a steward: the few acres of my own little property I myself can manage well enough. The steward is my new neighbor's, who has bought a fine estate beside us, every point of which I am acquainted with. The good old gentleman is lying ill of gout: his men are strangers here; I willingly assist in settling them."

They took a walk through fields, meadows, and some orchards. Everywhere Theresa kept instructing the steward; nothing so minute but she could give account of it: and Wilhelm had reason to wonder at her knowledge, her precision, the prompt dexterity with which she suggested means for ends. She loitered nowhere, always hastened to the leading-points; and thus her task was quickly over. "Salute your master," said she, as she sent away the man: "I mean to visit him as soon as possible, and wish him a complete recovery. There, now," she added with a smile, as soon as he was gone, "I might soon be rich: my good neighbor, I believe, would not be disinclined to offer me his hand."

"The old man with the gout?" cried Wilhelm: "I know not how, at your years, you could bring yourself to make so desperate a determination." — "Nor am I tempted to it!" said Theresa. "Whoever can administer what he possesses has enough, and to be wealthy is a burdensome affair, unless you understand it."

Wilhelm testified his admiration at her skill in husbandry concerns. "Decided inclination, early opportunity, external impulse, and continued occupation in a useful business," said she, "make many things, which were at first far harder, possible in life. When you have learned what causes stimulated me in this pursuit, you will cease to wonder at the talent you now think strange."

On returning home, she sent him to her little garden. Here he could scarcely turn himself, so narrow were the walks, so thickly was it sown and planted. On looking over to the court, he could not help smiling: the firewood was lying there, as accurately sawed, split, and piled, as if it had been part of the building, and had been intended to continue permanently there. The tubs and implements, all clean, were standing in their places: the house was painted white and red; it was really pleasant to behold. Whatever can be done by handicraft, which knows not beautiful proportions, but labors for convenience, cheerfulness, and durability, appeared united in this spot. They served him up dinner in his own room: he had time enough for meditating. Especially it struck him, that he should have got acquainted with another person of so interesting a character, who had been so closely related to Lothario. "It is just," said he to himself, "that a man so gifted should attract round him gifted women. How far the influence of manliness and dignity extends! Would that others did not come so wofully short, compared with him! Yes, confess thy fear. When thou meetest with thy Amazon, this woman of women, in spite of all thy hopes and dreaming, thou wilt find her, in the end, to thy humiliation and thy shame, — his bride."

WILHELM had passed a restless afternoon, not altogether without tedium, when towards evening his door opened, and a handsome hunter-boy stepped forward with a bow. "Shall we have a walk?" said the youth; and in the instant Wilhelm recognized Theresa by her lovely eyes.

"Pardon me this masquerade," said she; "for now, alas! it is nothing more. But, as I am going to tell you of the time when I so enjoyed the world, I will recall those days by every method to my fancy. Come along! Even the place where we have rested so often from our hunts and promenades shall help me."

They went accordingly. On their way Theresa said to her attendant, "It is not fair that I alone should speak: you already know enough of me, I nothing about you. Tell me, in the mean while, something of yourself, that I may gather courage to submit to you my history and situation." — "Alas!" said Wilhelm, "I have nothing to relate but error on the back of error, deviation following deviation; and I know none from whom I would more gladly hide my present and my past embarrassments than from yourself. Your look, the scene you move in, your whole temperament and manner, prove to me that you have reason to rejoice in your by-gone life; that you have travelled by a fair, clear path in constant progress; that you have lost no time; that you have nothing to reproach yourself withal."

Theresa answered with a smile, "Let us see if you will think so after you have heard my history." They walked along: among some general remarks, Theresa asked him, "Are you free?" — "I think I am," said he, "and yet I do not wish it." — "Good!" said she: "that indicates a complicated story: you also will have something to relate."

Conversing thus, they ascended the hill, and placed themselves beside a lofty oak, which spread its shade far out on every side. "Here," said she, "beneath this German tree, will I disclose to you the history of a German maiden: listen to me patiently.

"My father was a wealthy nobleman of this province, — a cheerful, clear-sighted, active, able man; a tender father, an upright friend, an excellent economist. I knew but one fault in him: he was too compliant to a wife who did not know his worth. Alas that I should have to say so of my mother! Her nature was the opposite of his. She was quick and changeful; without affection either for her home or for me, her only child; extravagant, but beautiful, sprightly, full of talent, the delight of a circle she had gathered round her. Her society, in truth, was never large; nor did it long continue the same. It consisted principally of men, for no woman could like to be near her; still less could *she* endure the merit or the praise of any woman. I resembled my father, both in form and disposition. As the duckling, with its first footsteps, seeks the water; so, from my earliest youth, the kitchen, the storeroom, the granaries, the fields, were my selected element. Cleanliness and order in the house seemed, even while I was playing in it, to be my peculiar instinct, my peculiar object. This tendency gave my father pleasure; and he directed, step by step, my childish endeavor into the suitablest employments. On the contrary, my mother did not like me; and she never for a moment hid it.

"I waxed in stature: with my years increased my turn for occupation, and my father's love to me. When we were by ourselves, when walking through the fields, when I was helping to examine his accounts, it was then I could see how glad he was. While gazing on his eyes, I felt as if I had been looking in upon myself; for it was in the eyes that I completely resembled him. But, in the presence of my mother, he lost this energy, this aspect: he excused me mildly when she blamed me unjustly and violently; he took my part, not as if he would protect me, but as if he would extenuate the demerit of my good qualities. To none of her caprices did he set himself in opposition. She began to be immensely taken with a passion for the stage: a theatre was soon got up; of men of all shapes and ages, crowding to display themselves along with her upon her boards, she had abundance; of women, on the other hand, there was often a scarcity. Lydia, a pretty girl who had been brought up with me, and who promised from the first to be extremely beautiful, had to undertake the secondary parts; the mothers and aunts were represented by an ancient chambermaid; while the leading heroines, lovers, and shepherdesses of every kind were seized on by my mother. I cannot tell you how ridiculous it seemed to me to see the people, every one of whom I knew full well, standing on their scaffold, and pretending, after they had dressed themselves in other clothes, to pass for something else than what they were. In my eyes they were never any thing but Lydia and my mother, this baron and that secretary, whether they appeared as counts and princes, or as peasants; and I could not understand how they meant to make me think that they were sad or happy, that they were indifferent or in love, liberal or avaricious, when I well knew the contrary to be the case. Accordingly I very seldom staid among the audience: I always snuffed their candles, that I might not be entirely without employment; I prepared the supper; and next morning, before they rose, I used to have their wardrobe all sorted, which commonly, the night before, they had left in a chaotic state.

"To my mother this activity appeared quite proper, but her love I could not gain. She despised me; and I know for certain that she more than once exclaimed with bitterness, 'If the mother could be as uncertain as the father, you would scarcely take this housemaid for my daughter!' Such treatment, I confess, at length entirely estranged me from her: I viewed her conduct as the conduct of a person unconnected with me; and, being used to watch our servants like a falcon (for this, be it said in passing, is the ground of all true housekeeping), the proceedings of my mother and her friends at the same time naturally forced themselves upon my observation. It was easy to perceive that she did not look on all men alike: I gave sharper heed, and soon found out that Lydia was her confidant, and had herself, by this opportunity, become acquainted with a passion, which, from her earliest youth, she had so often represented. I was aware of all their meetings; but I held my tongue, hinting nothing to my father, whom I was afraid of troubling. At last, however, I was obliged to speak. Many of their enterprises could not be accomplished without corrupting the servants. These now began to grow refractory: they despised my father's regulations, disregarded my commands. The disorders which arose from this I could not tolerate: I discovered all, complained of all to my father.

"He listened to me calmly. 'Good girl!' replied he with a smile; 'I know it all: be quiet, bear it patiently; for it is on thy account alone that I endure it.'

"I was not quiet: I had not patience. I in secret blamed my

father, for I did not think that any reason should induce him to endure such things. I called for regularity from all the servants: I was bent on driving matters to extremity.

"My mother had been rich before her marriage, yet she squandered more than she had a right to; and this, as I observed, occasioned many conferences between my parents. For a long time the evil was not helped, till at last the passions of my mother brought it to a head.

"Her first gallant became unfaithful in a glaring manner: the house, the neighborhood, her whole condition, grew offensive to her. She insisted on removing to a different estate; there she was too solitary: she insisted on removing to the town; there she felt herself eclipsed among the crowd. Of much that passed between my father and her I know nothing: however, he at last determined, under stipulations which I did not learn, to consent that she should take a journey, which she had been meditating, to the south of France.

"We were now free; we lived as if in heaven: I do believe my father could not be a loser, had he purchased her absence by a considerable sum. All our useless domestics were dismissed, and fortune seemed to smile on our undertakings: we had some extremely prosperous years; all things succeeded to our wish. But, alas! this pleasing state was not of long continuance: altogether unexpectedly my father had a shock of palsy; it lamed his right side, and deprived him of the proper use of speech. We had to guess at every thing that he required, for he never could pronounce the word that he intended. There were times when this was dreadfully afflicting to us: he would require expressly to be left alone with me; with earnest gestures, he would signify that every one should go away; and, when we saw ourselves alone, he could not speak the word he meant. His impatience mounted to the highest pitch: his situation touched me to the inmost heart. Thus much seemed certain: he had something which he wished to tell me, which especially concerned my interest. What longing did I feel to know it! At other times I could discover all things in his eyes, but now it was in vain. Even his eyes no longer spoke. Only this was clear: he wanted nothing, he desired nothing; he was striving to discover something to me, which unhappily I did not learn. His malady revisited him: he grew entirely inactive, incapable of motion; and a short time afterwards he died.

"I know not how it had got rooted in my thoughts, that somewhere he had hid a treasure which he wished at death to leave me rather than my mother; I searched about for traces of it while he lived, but I could meet with none: at his death a seal was put on every thing. I wrote to my mother, offering to continue in the house, and manage for her: she refused, and I was obliged to leave the place. A mutual testament was now produced: it gave my mother the possession and the use of all; and I was left, at least throughout her life, dependent on her. It was now that I conceived I rightly understood my father's beckonings: I pitied him for having been so weak; he had let himself be forced to do unjustly to me even after he was dead. Certain of my friends maintained that it was little better than if he had disinherited me: they called upon me to attack the will by law, but this I never could resolve on doing. I reverenced my father's memory too much: I trusted in destiny; I trusted in myself.

"There was a lady in the neighborhood possessed of large property, with whom I had always been on good terms: she gladly received me; I engaged to superintend her household, and erelong the task grew very easy to me. She lived regularly, she loved order in every thing; and I faithfully assisted her in struggling with her steward and domestics. I am neither of a niggardly nor grudging temper; but we women are disposed to insist, more earnestly than men, that nothing shall be wasted. Embezzlement of all sorts is intolerable to us: we require that each enjoy exactly in so far as right entitles him.

"Here I was in my element once more: I mourned my father's death in silence. My protectress was content with me: one small circumstance alone disturbed my peace. Lydia returned: my mother had been harsh enough to cast the poor girl off, after having altogether spoiled her. Lydia had learned with her mistress to consider passions as her occupation: she was wont to curb herself in nothing. On her unexpected re-appearance, the lady whom I lived with took her in: she wished to help me, but could train herself to nothing.

"About this time the relatives and future heirs of my protectress often visited the house, to recreate themselves with hunting. Lothario was frequently among them: it was not long till I had noticed, though without the smallest reference to myself, how far he was superior to the rest. He was courteous towards all, and Lydia seemed erelong to have

Wilhelm and Theresa

attracted his attention to her. Constantly engaged in something, I was seldom with the company: while he was there I did not talk so much as usual; for, I will confess it, lively conversation, from of old, had been to me the finest seasoning of existence. With my father I was wont to talk of every thing that happened. What you do not speak of, you will seldom accurately think of. No man had I ever heard with greater pleasure than I did Lothario, when he told us of his travels and campaigns. The world appeared to lie before him clear and open, as to me the district was in which I lived and managed. We were not entertained with marvellous personal adventures, the extravagant half-truths of a shallow traveller, who is always painting out himself, and not the country he has undertaken to describe. Lothario did not tell us his adventures: he led us to the place itself. I have seldom felt so pure a satisfaction.

"But still higher was my pleasure when I heard him talk, one evening, about women. The subject happened to be introduced: some ladies of the neighborhood had come to see us, and were speaking, in the common style, about the cultivation of the female mind. Our sex, they said, was treated unjustly: every sort of higher education men insisted on retaining for themselves; they admitted us to no science, they required us either to be dolls or family drudges. To all this Lothario said not much; but, when the party was a little thinned, he gave us his opinion more explicitly. 'It is very strange,' cried he, 'that men are blamed for their proceeding here: they have placed woman on the highest station she is capable of occupying. And where is there any station higher than the ordering of the house? While the husband has to vex himself with outward matters, while he has wealth to gather and secure, while perhaps he takes part in the administration of the state, and everywhere depends on circumstances; ruling nothing, I may say, while he conceives that he is ruling much; compelled to be but politic where he would willingly be reasonable, to dissemble where he would be open, to be false where he would be upright; while thus, for the sake of an object which he never reaches, he must every moment sacrifice the first of objects, harmony with himself, — a reasonable housewife is actually governing in the interior of her family; has the comfort and activity of every person in it to provide for, and make possible. What is the highest happiness of mortals, if not to execute what we consider right and good, — to be really masters of the means conducive to our aims? And where should or can our nearest aims be, but in the interior of our home? All those indispensable and still to be renewed supplies, where do we expect, do we require, to find them, if not in the place where we rise and where we go to sleep, where kitchen and cellar, and every species of accommodation for ourselves and ours, is to be always ready? What unvarying activity is needed to conduct this constantly recurring series in unbroken living order! How few are the men to whom it is given to return regularly like a star, to command their day as they command their night; to form for themselves their household instruments, to sow and to reap, to gain and to expand, and to travel round their circle with perpetual success and peace and love! It is when a woman has attained this inward mastery, that she truly makes the husband whom she loves, a master: her attention will acquire all sorts of knowledge; her activity will turn them all to profit. Thus is she dependent upon no one; and she procures her husband genuine independence, that which is interior and domestic: whatever he possesses, he beholds secured; what he earns, well employed: and thus he can direct his mind to lofty objects; and, if fortune favors, he may act in the state the same character which so well becomes his wife at home.'

"He then described to us the kind of wife he wished. I reddened; for he was describing me, as I looked and lived. I silently enjoyed my triumph; and the more, as I perceived, from all the circumstances, that he had not meant me individually, that, indeed, he did not know me. I cannot recollect a more delightful feeling in my life than this, when a man whom I so highly valued gave the preference, not to my person, but to my inmost nature. What a recompense did I consider it! What encouragement did it afford me!

"So soon as they were gone, my worthy benefactress with a smile observed to me, 'Pity that men often think and speak of what they will never execute, else here were a special match, the exact thing for my dear Theresa!' I made sport of her remark, and added, that indeed men's understanding gave its vote for household wives, but that their heart and imagination longed for other qualities; and that we household people could not stand a rivalry with beautiful and lovely women. This was spoken for the ear of Lydia; she did not hide from us that Lothario had made a deep impression on her heart: and, in reality, he seemed at each new visit to grow more and more attentive to her. She was poor, and not of rank; she could not think of marriage; but she was unable to resist the dear delight of charming and of being charmed. I had never loved, nor did I love at present; but though it was unspeakably agreeable to see in what light my turn of mind was viewed, how high it was ranged by such a man, I will confess I still was not altogether satisfied. I now wished that he should be acquainted with me, and should take a personal interest in me. This wish arose, without the smallest settled thought of any thing that could result from it.

"The greatest service I did my benefactress was in bringing into order the extensive forests which belonged to her. In this precious property, whose value time and circumstances were continually increasing, matters still went on according to the old routine, — without regularity, without plan, no end to theft and fraud. Many hills were standing bare: an equal growth was nowhere to be found but in the oldest cuttings. I personally visited the whole of them, with an experienced forester. I got the woods correctly measured: I set men to hew, to sow, to plant; in a short time, all things were in progress. That I might mount more readily on horseback, and also walk on foot with less obstruction, I had a suit of men's clothes made for me: I was present in many places, I was feared in all.

"Hearing that our young friends, with Lothario, were purposing to have another hunt, it came into my head, for the first time in my life, to make a figure, or, that I may not do myself injustice, to pass in the eyes of this noble gentleman for what I was. I put on my men's clothes, took my gun upon my shoulder, and went forward with our hunters, to await the party on our marches. They came: Lothario did not know me; a nephew of the lady introduced me to him as a clever forester, joked about my youth, and carried on his jesting in my praise, till at last Lothario recognized me. The nephew seconded my project, as if we had concocted it together. He circumstantially and gratefully described what I had done for the estates of his aunt, and consequently for himself.

"Lothario listened with attention: he talked with me, inquired concerning all particulars of the estates and district. I, of course, was glad to have such an opportunity of showing him my knowledge: I stood my ordeal very well; I submitted certain projects of improvement to him, which he sanctioned, telling me of similar examples, and strengthening my arguments by the connection which he gave them. My satisfaction grew more perfect every moment. Happily, however, I merely wished that he should be acquainted with me, not that he should love me. We came home; and I observed, more clearly than before, that the attention he showed Lydia seemed expressive of a secret attachment. I had reached my object, yet I was not at rest: from that day he showed a true respect for me, a fine trust in me; in company he usually spoke to me, asked my opinion, and appeared to be persuaded, that, in household matters, nothing was unknown to me. His sympathy excited me extremely: even when the conversation was of general finance and political economy, he used to lead me to take part in it; and, in his absence, I endeavored to acquire more knowledge of our province, nay, of all the empire. The task was easy for me: it was but repeating on the great scale what I knew so accurately on the small.

"From this period he visited our house oftener. We talked, I may say, of every thing; yet in some degree our conversation always in the end grew economical, if even but in a secondary sense. What immense effects a man, by the continuous application of his powers, his time, his money, even by means which seem but small, may bring about, was frequently and largely spoken of.

"I did not withstand the tendency which drew me towards him; and, alas! I felt too soon how deep, how cordial, how pure and genuine, was my love, as I believed it more and more apparent that Lydia, and not myself, was the occasion of these visits. She, at least, was most vividly persuaded so: she made me her confidant; and this, again, in some degree, consoled me. For, in truth, what she explained so much to her advantage, I reckoned nowise of importance: there was not a trace of any serious lasting union being meditated, but the more distinctly did I see the wish of the impassioned girl to be his at any price.

"Thus did matters stand, when the lady of the house surprised me with an unexpected message. 'Lothario,' said she, 'offers you his hand, and desires through life to have you ever at his side.' She enlarged upon my qualities, and told me, what I liked sufficiently to hear, that in me Lothario was persuaded he had found the person whom he had so long been seeking for.

"The height of happiness was now attained for me: my hand was asked by a man for whom I had the greatest value, beside whom, and along with whom, I might expect a full, expanded, free, and profitable enployment of my inborn tendency, of my talent perfected by practice. The sum of my existence seemed to have enlarged itself into infinitude. I gave my consent: he himself came, and spoke with me in private; he held out his hand to me; he looked into my eyes, he clasped me in his arms, and pressed a kiss upon my lips. It was the first and the last. He confided to me all his circumstances; told me how much his American campaign had cost him, what debts he had accumulated on his property; that, on this score, he had in some measure quarrelled with his grand-uncle; that the worthy gentleman intended to relieve him, though truly in his own peculiar way, being minded to provide him with a rich wife, whereas, a man of sense would choose a household wife, at all events; that, however, by his sister's influence, he hoped his noble relative would be persuaded. He set before me the condition of his fortune, his plans, his prospects, and requested my co-operation. Till his uncle should consent, our promise was to be a secret.

"Scarcely was he gone when Lydia asked me whether he had spoken of her. I answered no, and tired her with a long detail of economical affairs. She was restless, out of humor; and his conduct, when he came again, did not improve her situation.

"But the sun, I see, is bending to the place of rest. Well for you, my friend! You would otherwise have had to hear this story, which I often enough go over by myself, in all its most minute particulars. Let me hasten: we are coming to an epoch on which it is not good to linger.

"By Lothario I was made acquainted with his noble sister; and she, at a convenient time, contrived to introduce me to the uncle. I gained the old man: he consented to our wishes, and I returned with happy tidings to my benefactress. The affair was now no secret in the house: Lydia heard of it; she thought the thing impossible. When she could no longer doubt of it, she vanished all at once: we knew not whither she had gone.

"Our marriage-day was coming near: I had often asked him for his portrait; just as he was going off, I reminded him that he had promised it. He said, 'You have never given me the case you want to have it fitted into.' This was true: I had got a present from a female friend, on which I set no ordinary value. Her name, worked from her own hair, was fastened on the outer glass: within, there was a vacant piece of ivory, on which her portrait was to have been painted, when a sudden death snatched her from me. Lothario's love had cheered me at the time her death lay heavy on my spirits, and I wished to have the void which she had left me in her present filled by the picture of my friend.

"I ran to my chamber, fetched my jewel-box, and opened it in his presence. Scarcely had he looked into it, when he noticed a medallion with the portrait of a lady. He took it in his hand, considered it attentively, and asked me hastily whose face it was. 'My mother's,' answered I. 'I could have sworn,' said he, 'that it was the portrait of a Madame Saint Alban, whom I met some years ago in Switzerland.' — 'It is the same,' replied I, smiling, 'and so you have unwittingly become acquainted with your stepmother. Saint Alban is the name my mother has assumed for travelling with: she passes under it in France at present.'

" 'I am the miserablest man alive!' exclaimed he, as he threw the portrait back into the box, covered his eyes with his hand, and hurried from the room. He sprang on horseback: I ran to the balcony, and called out after him; he turned, waved his hand to me, went speedily away, — and I have never seen him more."

The sun went down: Theresa gazed with unaverted looks upon the splendor, and both her fine eyes filled with tears.

Theresa spoke not: she laid her hand upon her new friend's hands; he kissed it with emotion: she dried her tears, and rose. "Let us return, and see that all is right," said she.

The conversation was not lively by the way. They entered the garden-door, and noticed Lydia sitting on a bench: she rose, withdrew before them, and walked in. She had a paper in her hand: two little girls were by her. "I see," observed Theresa, "she is still carrying her only comfort, Lothario's letter, with her. He promises that she shall live with him again so soon as he is well: he begs of her till then to stay in peace with me. On these words she hangs, with these lines she solaces herself; but with his friends she is extremely angry."

Meanwhile the two children had approached. They courtesied to Theresa, and gave her an account of all that had occurred while she was absent. "You see here another part of my employment," said Theresa. "Lothario's sister and I have made a league: we educate some little ones in common; such as promise to be lively, serviceable housewives I take charge of, she of such as show a finer and more quiet talent: it is right to provide for the happiness of future husbands, both in household and in intellectual matters. When you become acquainted with my noble friend, a new era in your life will open. Her beauty, her goodness, make her worthy of the reverence of the world." Wilhelm did not venture to confess, that unhappily the lovely countess was already known to him; that his transient connection with her would occasion him perpetual sorrow. He was well pleased that Theresa let the conversation drop, that some business called for her within. He was now alone: the intelligence which he had just received of the young and lovely countess being driven to replace, by deeds of benevolence, her own lost comfort, made him very sad; he felt, that, with her, it was but a need of self-oblivion, an attempt to supply, by the hopes of happiness to others, the want of a cheerful enjoyment of existence in herself. He thought Theresa happy, since, even in that unexpected melancholy alteration which had taken place in her prospects, there was no alteration needed in herself. "How fortunate beyond all others," cried he, "is the man, who, in order to adjust himself to fate, is not required to cast away his whole preceding life!"

Theresa came into his room, and begged pardon for disturbing him. "My whole library," said she, "is in the wall-press here: they are rather books which I do not throw aside, than which I have taken up. Lydia wants a pious book: there are one or two of that sort among them. Persons who throughout the whole twelve months are worldly, think it necessary to be godly at a time of straits: all moral and religious matters they regard as physic, which is to be taken with aversion when they are unwell; in a clergyman, a moralist, they see nothing but a doctor, whom they cannot soon enough get rid of. Now, I confess, I look upon religion as a kind of diet, which can only be so when I make a constant practice of it, when throughout the whole twelve months I never lose it out of sight."

She searched among the books: she found some edifying works, as they are called. "It was of my mother," said Theresa, "that poor Lydia learned to have recourse to books like these. While her gallant continued faithful, plays and novels were her life: his departure brought religious writings once more into credit. I, for my share, cannot understand," continued she, "how men have made themselves believe that God speaks to us through books and histories. The man to whom the universe does not reveal directly what relation it has to him, whose heart does not tell him what he owes to himself and others, that man will scarcely learn it out of books, which generally do little more than give our errors names."

She left our friend alone: he passed his evening in examining the little library; it had, in truth, been gathered quite at random.

Theresa, for the few days Wilhelm spent with her, continued still the same: she related to him at different times the consequences of that singular incident with great minuteness. Day and hour, place and name, were present to her memory: we shall here compress into a word or two so much of it as will be necessary for the information of our readers.

The reason of Lothario's quick departure was, unhappily, too easy to explain. He had met Theresa's mother on her journey: her charms attracted him; she was no niggard of them; and this luckless transitory aberration came at length to shut him out from being united to a lady whom nature seemed to have expressly made for him. As for Theresa, she continued in the pure circle of her duties. They learned that Lydia had been living in the neighborhood in secret. She was happy that the marriage, though for unknown causes, had not been completed. She endeavored to renew her intimacy with Lothario; and more, as it seemed, out of desperation than affection, by surprise than with consideration, from tedium than of purpose, he had met her wishes.

Theresa was not uneasy on this account; she waived all further claims; and, if he had even been her husband, she would probably have had sufficient spirit to endure a matter of this kind, if it had not troubled her domestic order: at least, she often used to say, that a wife who properly conducted her economy should take no umbrage at such little fancies of her husband, but be always certain that he would return.

Erelong Theresa's mother had deranged her fortune: the losses fell upon the daughter, whose share of the effects, in consequence, was small. The old lady, who had been Theresa's benefactress, died, leaving her a little property in land, and a handsome sum by way of legacy. Theresa soon contrived to make herself at home in this new, narrow circle. Lothario offered her a better property, Jarno endeavoring to negotiate the business; but she refused it. "I will show," said she, "in this little, that I deserved to share the great with him; but I keep this before me, that, should accident embarrass me, on my own account or that of others, I will betake myself without the smallest hesitation to my generous friend."

There is nothing less liable to be concealed and unemployed than well-directed practical activity. Scarcely had she settled in her little property, when her acquaintance and advice began to be desired by many of her neighbors; and the proprietor of the adjacent lands gave her plainly enough to understand that it depended on herself alone whether she would take his hand, and be heiress of the greater part of his estates. She had already mentioned the matter to our friend: she often jested with him about marriages, suitable and unsuitable.

"Nothing," said she once, "gives a greater loose to people's tongues than when a marriage happens which they can denominate unsuitable: and yet the unsuitable are far more common than the suitable; for, alas! with most marriages, it is not long till things assume a very piteous look. The confusion of ranks by marriage can be called unsuitable only when the one party is unable to participate in the manner of existence which is native, habitual, and which at length grows absolutely necessary, to the other. The different classes have different ways of living, which they cannot change or communicate to one another; and this is the reason why connections such as these, in general, were better not formed. Yet exceptions, and exceptions of the happiest kind, are possible. Thus, too, the marriage of a young woman with a man advanced in life is generally unsuitable; yet I have seen some such turn out extremely well. For me, I know but of one kind of marriage that would be entirely unsuitable, — that in which I should be called upon to make a show, and manage ceremonies: I would rather give my hand to the son of any honest farmer in the neighborhood."

Wilhelm at length made ready for returning. He requested of Theresa to obtain for him a parting word with Lydia. The impassioned girl at last consented: he said some kindly things to her, to which she answered, "The first burst of anguish I have conquered. Lothario will be ever dear to me: but for those friends of his, I know them; and it grieves me that they are about him. The abbé, for a whim's sake, could leave a person in extreme need, or even plunge one into it; the doctor would have all things go on like clock-work; Jarno has no heart; and you — at least no force of character! Just go on: let these three people use you as their tool; they will have many an execution to commit to you. For a long time, as I know well, my presence has been hateful to them. I had not found out their secret, but I had observed that they had one. Why these bolted rooms, these strange passages? Why can no one ever reach the central tower? Why did they banish me, whenever they could, to my own chamber? I will confess, jealousy at first incited me to these discoveries: I feared some lucky rival might be hid there. I have now laid aside that suspicion: I am well convinced that Lothario loves me, that he means honorably by me; but I am quite as well convinced that his false and artful friends betray him. If you would really do him service, if you would ever be forgiven for the injury which I have suffered from you, free him from the hands of these men. But what am I expecting! Give this letter to him; repeat what it contains, — that I will love him forever, that I depend upon his word. Ah!" cried she, rising, and throwing herself with tears upon Theresa's neck: "he is surrounded by my foes; they will endeavor to persuade him that I have sacrificed nothing for his sake. Oh! Lothario may well believe that he is worthy of any sacrifice, without needing to be grateful for it."

Wilhelm's parting with Theresa was more cheerful: she wished they might soon meet again. "Me you wholly know," said she: "I alone have talked while we have been together. It will be your duty, next time, to repay my candor."

During his return he kept contemplating this new and bright phenomenon with the liveliest recollection. What confidence had she inspired him with. He thought of Mignon and Felix, and how happy they might be if under her direction; then he thought of himself, and felt what pleasure it would be to live beside a being so entirely serene and clear. As he approached Lothario's castle, he observed, with more than usual interest, the central tower and the many passages and side-buildings: he resolved to question Jarno or the abbé on the subject, by the earliest opportunity.

CHAPTER SEVEN

ON ARRIVING at the castle, Wilhelm found its noble owner in the way of full recovery: the doctor and the abbé had gone off; Jarno alone was there. It was not long till the patient now and then could ride, sometimes by himself, sometimes with his friends. His conversation was at once courteous and earnest, instructive and enlivening: you could often notice in it traces of a tender sensibility; although he strove to hide it, and almost seemed to blame it, when, in spite of him, it came to view.

One evening while at table he was silent, though his look was very cheerful.

"To-day," said Jarno, "you have met with an adventure; and, no doubt, you relished it."

"I give you credit for your penetration," said Lothario. "Yes, I have met with a very pleasing adventure. At another time, perhaps, I should not have considered it so charming as to-day, when it came upon me so attractively. Towards night I rode out beyond the river, through the hamlets, by a path which I had often visited in former years. My bodily ailings must have reduced me more than I supposed: I felt weak; but, as my strength was re-awakening, I was, as it were, new-born. All objects seemed to wear the hues they had in earlier times: all looked graceful, lovely, charming, as they have not looked to me for many years. I easily observed that it was mere debility, yet I continued to enjoy it: I rode softly onwards, and could now conceive how men may grow to like diseases which attune us to those sweet emotions. You know, perhaps, what used of old so frequently to lead me that way?"

"If I mistake not," answered Jarno, "it was a little love-concern you were engaged in with a farmer's daughter."

"It might be called a great one," said Lothario; "for we loved each other deeply, seriously, and for a long time. To-day, it happened, every thing combined to represent before me in its liveliest color the earliest season of our love. The boys were again shaking may-bugs from the trees: the ashen grove had not grown larger since the day I saw her first. It was now long since I had met with Margaret. She is married at a distance; and I had heard by chance that she was come with her children, some weeks ago, to pay a visit to her father."

"This ride, then, was not altogether accidental?"

"I will not deny," replied Lothario, "that I wished to meet her. On coming near the house, I saw her father sitting at the door: a child of probably a year old was standing by him. As I approached, a female gave a hasty look from an upper window; and a minute afterwards I heard some person tripping down-stairs. I thought surely it was she; and, I will confess, I was flattering myself that she had recognized me, and was hastening to meet me. But what was my surprise and disappointment, when she bounded from the door, seized the child, to whom the horses had come pretty close, and took it in! It gave me a painful twinge: my vanity, however, was a little solaced when I thought I saw a tint of redness on her neck and on the ear, which were uncovered.

"I drew up, and, while speaking with the father, glanced sideways over all the windows, to observe if she would not appear at some of them; but no trace of her was visible. Ask I would not, so I rode away. My displeasure was a little mollified by wonder; though I had not seen the face, it appeared to me that she was scarcely changed; and ten years are a pretty space! Nay, she looked even younger, quite as slim, as light of foot; her neck, if possible, was lovelier than before; her cheeks as quick at blushing; yet she was the mother of six children, perhaps of more. This apparition suited the enchantment which surrounded me so well, that I rode along with feelings grown still younger; and I did not turn till I was at the forest, when the sun was going down. Strongly as the falling dew and the prescription of our doctor called upon me to proceed direct homewards, I could not help again going round by the farmhouse. I observed a woman walking up and down the garden, which is fenced by a light hedge. I rode along the footpath to it, and found myself at no great distance from the person whom I wanted.

"Though the evening sun was glancing in my eyes, I saw that she was busy with the hedge, which only slightly covered her. I thought I recognized my mistress. On coming up, I halted, not without a palpitation at the heart. Some high twigs of wild roses, which a soft air was blowing to and fro, made her figure indistinct to me. I spoke to her, asked her how she was. She answered, in an under-tone, 'Quite well.' In the mean time I perceived a child behind the hedge, engaged in plucking roses; and I took the opportunity of asking where her other children were. 'It is not my child,' said she: 'that were rather early!' And at this moment it happened that the twigs were blown aside, and her face could be distinctly seen. I knew not what to make of the affair. It was my mistress, and it was not. Almost younger, almost lovelier, than she used to be ten years before. 'Are not you the farmer's daughter?' inquired I, half confused. 'No,' said she: 'I am her cousin.'

" 'You resemble one another wonderfully,' added I.

" 'Yes, so says every one that knew her half a score of years ago.'

"I continued putting various questions to her: my mistake was pleasant to me, even after I had found it out. I could not leave this living image of by-gone blessedness that stood before me. The child, meanwhile, had gone away: it had wandered to the pond in search of flowers. She took her leave, and hastened after it.

"I had now, however, learned that my former love was really in her father's house. While riding forward, I employed myself in guessing whether it had been her cousin or she that had secured the child from harm. I more than once, in thought, repeated all the circumstances of the incident: I can remember few things that have affected me more gratefully. But I feel that I am still unwell: we must ask the doctor to deliver us from the remains of this pathetic humor."

With confidential narratives of pretty love adventures, it often happens as with ghost stories: when the first is told, the others follow of themselves.

Our little party, in recalling other times, found numerous passages of this description. Lothario had the most to tell. Jarno's histories were all of one peculiar character: what Wilhelm could disclose we already know. He was apprehensive they might mention his adventure with the countess; but it was not hinted at, not even in the remotest manner.

"It is true," observed Lothario, "there can scarcely any feeling in the world be more agreeable than when the heart, after a pause of indifference, again opens to love for some new object; yet I would forever have renounced that happiness, had fate been pleased to unite me with Theresa. We are not always youths: we ought not always to be children. To the man who knows the world, who understands what he should do in it, what he should hope from it, nothing can be more desirable than meeting with a wife who will everywhere co-operate with him, who will everywhere prepare his way for him; whose diligence takes up what his must leave; whose occupation spreads itself on every side, while his must travel forward on its single path. What a heaven had I figured for myself beside Theresa! Not the heaven of an enthusiastic bliss, but of a sure life on earth; order in prosperity, courage in adversity, care for the smallest, and a spirit capable of comprehending and managing the greatest. Oh! I saw in her the qualities which, when developed, make such women as we find in history, whose excellence appears to us far preferable to that of men, — this clearness of view, this expertness in all emergencies, this sureness in details, which brings the whole so accurately out, although they never seem to think of it. You may well forgive me," added he, and turning to Wilhelm, with a smile, "that I forsook Aurelia for Theresa: with the one I could expect a calm and cheerful life, with the other not a happy hour."

"I will confess," said Wilhelm, "that, in coming hither, I had no small anger in my heart against you; that I proposed to censure with severity your conduct to Aurelia."

"It was really censurable," said Lothario: "I should not have exchanged my friendship for her with the sentiment of love; I should not, in place of the respect which she deserved, have intruded an attachment she was neither calculated to excite nor to maintain. Alas! she was not lovely when she loved, — the greatest misery that can befall a woman."

"Well, it is past!" said Wilhelm. "We cannot always shun the things we blame; in spite of us, our feelings and our actions sometimes strangely swerve from their natural and right direction; yet there are certain duties which we never should lose sight of. Peace be to the ashes of our friend! Without censuring ourselves or her, let us with sympathizing hearts strew flowers upon her grave. But, at the grave in which the hapless mother sleeps, let me ask why you acknowledge not the child, — a son whom any father might rejoice in, and whom you appear entirely to overlook? With your pure and tender nature, how can you altogether cast away the instinct of a parent? All this while you have not spent one syllable upon that precious creature, of whose attractions I could say so much."

"Whom do you speak of?" asked Lothario: "I do not understand you."

"Of whom but of your son, Aurelia's son, the lovely child, to whose good fortune there is nothing wanting, but that a tender father should acknowledge and receive him."

"You mistake, my friend!" exclaimed Lothario; "Aurelia never had a son, at least by me: I know of no child, or I would with joy acknowledge it; and, even in the present case, I will gladly look upon the little creature as a relic of her, and take charge of educating it. But did she ever give you to believe that the boy was hers, was mine?"

"I cannot recollect that I ever heard a word from her expressly on the subject; but we took it up so, and I never for a moment doubted it."

"I can give you something like a clew to this perplexity," said Jarno. "An old woman, whom you must have noticed often, gave Aurelia the child: she accepted it with passion, hoping to alleviate her sorrows by its presence; and, in truth, it gave her many a comfortable hour."

This discovery awoke anxieties in Wilhelm: he thought of his dear Mignon and his beautiful Felix with the liveliest distinctness. He expressed his wish to remove them both from the state in which they were.

"We shall soon arrange it," said Lothario. "The little girl may be committed to Theresa: she cannot be in better hands. As for the boy, I think you should yourself take charge of him: what in us the women leave uncultivated, children cultivate when we retain them near us."

"But first, I think," said Jarno, "you will once for all renounce the stage, as you have no talent for it."

Our friend was struck: he had to curb himself, for Jarno's harsh sentence had not a little wounded his self-love. "If you convince me of that," replied he, forcing a smile, "you will do me a service, though it is but a mournful service to rouse one from a pleasing dream."

"Without enlarging on the subject," answered Jarno, "I could merely wish you would go and fetch the children. The rest will come in course."

"I am ready," answered Wilhelm: "I am restless, and curious to see if I can get no further knowledge of the boy: I long to see the little girl who has attached herself so strangely to me."

It was agreed that he should lose no time in setting out. Next day he had prepared himself: his horse was saddled; he only waited for Lothario to take leave of him. At the dinner-hour they went as usual to table, not waiting for the master of the house. He did not come till late, and then sat down by them.

"I could bet," said Jarno, "that to-day you have again been making trial of your tenderness of heart: you have not been able to withstand the curiosity to see your quondam love."

"Guessed!" replied Lothario.

"Let us hear," said Jarno, "how it went: I long to know."

"I confess," replied Lothario, "the affair lay nearer my heart than it reasonably ought: so I formed the resolution of again riding out, and actually seeing the person whose renewed young image had affected me with such a pleasing illusion. I alighted at some distance from the house, and sent the horses to a side, that the children, who were playing at the door, might not be disturbed. I entered the house: by chance she met me just within the threshold; it was herself; and I recognized her, notwithstanding the striking change. She had grown stouter, and seemed to be larger; her gracefulness was shaded by a look of staidness; her vivacity had passed into a calm reflectiveness. Her head, which she once bore so airily and freely, drooped a little: slight furrows had been traced upon her brow.

"She cast down her eyes on seeing me, but no blush announced any inward movement of the heart. I held out my hand to her, she gave me hers; I inquired about her husband, he was absent; about her children, she stepped out and called them; all came in and gathered round her. Nothing is more charming than to see a mother with a child upon her arm; nothing is more reverend than a mother among many children. That I might say something, I asked the name of the youngest. She desired me to walk in and see her father; I agreed; she introduced me to the room, where every thing was standing almost just as I had left it; and, what seemed stranger still, the fair cousin, her living image, was sitting on the very seat behind the spinning-wheel, where I had found my love so often in the self-same form. A little girl, the very figure of her mother, had come after us; and thus I stood in the most curious scene, between the future and the past, as in a grove of oranges, where within a little circle flowers and fruits are living, in successive stages of their growth, beside each other. The cousin went away to fetch us some refreshment : I gave the woman I had loved so much my hand, and said to her, 'I feel a true joy in seeing you again.' — 'You are very good to say so,' answered she; 'but I also can assure you I feel the highest joy. How often have I wished to see you once more in my life! I have wished it in moments which I regarded as my last.' She said this with a settled voice, without appearance of emotion, with that natural air which of old delighted me so much. The cousin returned, the father with her; and I leave you to conceive with what feelings I remained, and with what I came away."

CHAPTER EIGHT

IN HIS JOURNEY to the town, our friend was thinking of the lovely women whom he knew or had heard of : their curious fortunes, which contained so little happiness, were present to him with a sad distinct-ness. "Ah!" cried he, "poor Mariana! What shall I yet learn of thee? And thou, noble Amazon, glorious, protecting spirit, to whom I owe so much, whom I everywhere expect to meet, and nowhere see, in what mournful circumstances may I find thee, shouldst thou again appear before me!"

On his arrival in the town, there was not one of his acquaintances at home : he hastened to the theatre; he supposed they would be rehearsing. Here, however, all was still; the house seemed empty : one little door alone was open. Passing through it to the stage, he found Aurelia's ancient serving-maid, employed in sewing linen for a new decoration : there was barely light enough to let her work. Felix and Mignon were sitting by her on the floor : they had a book between them; and, while Mignon read aloud, Felix was repeating all the words, as if he, too, knew his letters, — as if he, too, could read.

The children started up, and ran to him : he embraced them with the tenderest feelings, and brought them closer to the woman. "Art thou the person," said he to her with an earnest voice, "from whom Aurelia received this child?" She looked up from her work, and turned her face to him: he saw her in full light; he started back in terror, — it was old Barbara.

"Where is Mariana?" cried he. "Far from here," replied the crone.

"And Felix" —

"Is the son of that unhappy and too true and tender-hearted girl. May you never feel what you have made us suffer! May the treasure which I now deliver you make you as happy as he made us wretched!"

She arose to go away: Wilhelm held her fast. "I mean not to escape you," said she: "let me fetch a paper that will make you glad and sorrowful."

She retired, and Wilhelm gazed upon the child with a painful joy: he durst not reckon him his own. "He is thine!" cried Mignon, "he is thine!" and passed the child to Wilhelm's knee.

Barbara came back, and handed him a letter. "Here are Mariana's last words," said she.

"She is dead!" cried he.

"Dead," said the old woman. "I wish to spare you all reproaches."

Astonished and confounded, Wilhelm broke up the letter; but scarcely had he read the first words of it when a bitter grief took hold of him: he let the letter fall, and sank upon a seat. Mignon hurried to him, trying to console him. In the mean time Felix had picked up the letter: he teased his playmate till she yielded, till she knelt beside him and read it over. Felix repeated the words, and Wilhelm was compelled to hear them twice. "If this sheet should ever reach thee, then lament thy ill-starred friend. Thy love has caused her death. The boy, whose birth I survive but a few days, is thine: I die faithful to thee, much as appearances may be against me; with thee I lost every thing that bound me to life. I die content, for they have assured me that the child is healthy and will live. Listen to old Barbara; forgive her: farewell, and forget me not."

What a painful, and yet, to his comfort, half-enigmatic letter! Its contents pierced through his heart, as the children, stuttering and stammering, pronounced and repeated them.

"That's what has come of it!" said the crone, not waiting till he had recovered. "Thank Heaven, that, having lost so true a love, you have still left you so fine a child. Your grief will be unequalled when you learn how the poor, good girl stood faithful to you to the end, how miserable she became, and what she sacrificed for your sake."

"Let me drain the cup of sorrow and of joy at once!" cried Wilhelm. "Convince me, even persuade me, that she was a good girl, that she deserved respect as well as love: then leave me to my grief for her irreparable loss."

"It is not yet time," said Barbara: "I have work to do, and I would not we were seen together. Let it be a secret that Felix is your son: I should have too much abuse to suffer from the company, for having formerly deceived them. Mignon will not betray us: she is good and close."

"I have known it long, and I said nothing," answered Mignon. "How is it possible?" cried Barbara. "Whence?" cried Wilhelm.

"The spirit told it me."

"Where? Where?"

"In the vault, when the old man drew his knife, it called to me, 'Bring his father;' and I thought it must be thou."

"*Who* called to thee?"

"I know not: in my heart, in my head, I was terrified; I trembled, I prayed; then it called, and I understood it."

Wilhelm pressed her to his heart, recommended Felix to her, and retired. He had not observed till then that she was grown much paler and thinner than when he left her. Madam Melina was the first acquaintance he met: she received him in the friendliest manner.

"Oh that you might find every thing among us as you wished!" exclaimed she.

"I doubt it," answered Wilhelm: "I do not expect it. Confess that they have taken all their measures to dispense with me."

"Why would you go away?" replied his friend.

"We cannot soon enough convince ourselves," said he, "how very simply we may be dispensed with in the world. What important personages we conceive ourselves to be! We think that it is we alone who animate the circle we move in; that, in our absence, life, nourishment, and breath will make a general pause: and, alas! the void which occurs is scarcely remarked, so soon is it filled up again; nay, it is often but the place, if not for something better, at least for something more agreeable."

"And the sorrows of our friends we are not to take into account?"

"For our friends, too, it is well, when they soon recover their composure, when they say each to himself, there where thou art, there where thou remainest, accomplish what thou canst; be busy, be courteous, and let the present scene delight thee."

On a narrower inquiry, he found what he had looked for: the opera had been set up, and was exclusively attracting the attention of the public. His parts had in the mean while been distributed between Horatio and Laertes, and both of them were in the habit of eliciting from the spectators far more liberal applause than he had ever been enabled to obtain.

Laertes entered: and Madam Melina cried, "Look you here at this lucky fellow; he is soon to be a capitalist, or Heaven knows what!" Wilhelm, in embracing him, discovered that his coat was superfine: the rest of his apparel was simple, but of the very best materials.

"Solve me the riddle!" cried our friend.

"You are still in time to learn," replied Laertes, "that my running to and fro is now about to be repaid; that a partner in a large commercial house is turning to advantage my acquirements from books or observation, and allowing me a share with him. I would give something, could I purchase back my confidence in women: there is a pretty niece in the house; and I see well enough, that, if I pleased, I might soon be a made man."

"You have not heard," said Frau Melina, "that a marriage has already taken place among ourselves? Serlo is actually wedded to the fair Elmira: her father would not tolerate their secret correspondence."

They talked in this manner about many things that had occurred while he was absent: nor was it difficult for him to observe, that, according to the present temper and constitution of the company, his dismissal had already taken place.

He impatiently expected Barbara, who had appointed him to wait for her far in the night. She was to come when all were sleeping: she required as many preparations as if she had been the youngest maiden gliding in to her beloved. Meanwhile he read a hundred times the letter she had given him,— read with unspeakable delight the word *faithful* in the hand of his darling, with horror the announcement of her death, whose approaches she appeared to view unmoved.

Midnight was past, when something rustled at the half-open door, and Barbara came in with a little basket. "I am to tell you the story of our woes," said she: "and I must believe that you will sit unmoved at the recital; that you are waiting for me but to satisfy your curiosity; that you will now, as you did formerly, retire within your cold selfishness, while our hearts are breaking. But look you here! Thus, on that happy evening, did I bring you the bottle of champagne; thus did I place the three glasses on the table: and as you then began, with soft nursery tales, to cozen us and lull us asleep; so will I now with stern truths instruct you and keep you waking."

Wilhelm knew not what to say, when the old woman, in fact, let go the cork, and filled the three glasses to the brim.

"Drink!" cried she, having emptied at a draught her foaming glass. "Drink, ere the spirit of it pass! This third glass shall froth away untasted to the memory of my unhappy Mariana. How red were her lips when she then drank your health! Ah, and now forever pale and cold!"

"Sibyl! Fury!" cried Wilhelm, springing up, and striking the table with his fist, "what evil spirit possesses thee and drives thee? For what dost thou take me, that thou thinkest the simplest narrative of Mariana's death and sorrows will not harrow me enough, but usest these hellish arts to sharpen my torment? If thy insatiable greediness is such, that thou must revel at the funeral-table, drink and speak! I have loathed thee from of old; and I cannot reckon Mariana guiltless while I even look upon thee, her companion."

"Softly, mein Herr!" replied the crone: "you shall not ruffle me. Your debts to us are deep and dark: the railing of a debtor does not anger one. But you are right: the simplest narrative will punish you sufficiently. Hear, then, the struggle and the victory of Mariana striving to continue yours."

"Continue mine?" cried Wilhelm: "what fable dost thou mean to tell me?"

"Interrupt me not," said she; "hear me, and then give what belief you list: to me it is all one. Did you not, the last night you were with us, find a letter in the room, and take it with you?"

"I found the letter *after* I had taken it with me: it was lying in the neckerchief, which, in the warmth of my love, I had seized and carried off."

"What did the sheet contain?"

"The expectation of an angry lover to be better treated on the next than he had been on the preceding evening. And that you kept your word to him, I need not be told; for I saw him with my own eyes gliding from your house before daybreak."

"You may have seen him; but what occurred within, how sadly Mariana passed that night, how fretfully I passed it, you are yet to learn. I will be altogether candid: I will neither hide nor palliate the fact, that I persuaded Mariana to yield to the solicitations of a certain Norberg; it was with repugnance that she followed my advice, nay, that she even heard it. He was rich; he seemed attached: I hoped he would be constant. Soon after, he was forced to go upon his journey; and Mariana became acquainted with you. What had I then to abide! What to hinder, what to undergo! 'Oh!' cried she often, 'hadst thou spared my youth, my innocence, but four short weeks, I might have found a worthy object of my love; I had then been worthy of him; and love might have given, with a quiet conscience, what now I have sold against my will.' She entirely abandoned herself to her affection for you:

"I need not ask if you were happy. Over her understanding I had an unbounded power, for I knew the means of satisfying all her little inclinations: but over her heart I had no control; for she never sanctioned what I did for her, what I counselled her to do, when her heart said nay. It was only to irresistible necessity that she would yield, but erelong the necessity appeared to her extremely pressing. In the first period of her youth, she had never known want; by a complication of misfortunes, her people lost their fortune; the poor girl had been used to have a number of conveniences; and upon her young spirit certain principles of honor had been stamped, which made her restless, without much helping her. She had not the smallest skill in worldly matters: she was innocent in the strictest meaning of the word. She had no idea that one could buy without paying; nothing frightened her more than being in debt: she always rather liked to give than take. This, and this alone, was what made it possible that she could be constrained to give herself away, in order to get rid of various little debts which weighed upon her."

"And couldst not thou," cried Wilhelm, in an angry tone, "have saved her?"

"Oh, yes!" replied the beldame, "with hunger and need, with sorrow and privation; but for this I was not disposed."

"Abominable, base procuress! So thou hast sacrificed the hapless creature! Offered her up to thy throat, to thy insatiable maw!"

"It were better to compose yourself, and cease your reviling," said the dame. "If you will revile, go to your high, noble houses: there you will meet with many a mother, full of anxious cares to find out for some lovely, heavenly maiden the most odious of men, provided he be the richest. See the poor creature shivering and faltering before her fate, and nowhere finding consolation, till some more experienced female lets her understand, that, by marriage, she acquires the right, in future, to dispose of her heart and person as she pleases."

"Peace!" cried Wilhelm. "Dost thou think that one crime can be the excuse of another? To thy story, without further observations!"

"Do you listen, then, without blaming! Mariana became yours against my will. In this adventure, at least, I have nothing to reproach myself with. Norberg returned; he made haste to visit Mariana: she received him coldly and angrily, — would not even admit him to a kiss. I employed all my art in apologizing for her conduct, — gave him to understand that her confessor had awakened her conscience; that, so long as conscientious scruples lasted, one was bound to respect them. I at last so far succeeded that he went away, I promising to do my utmost for him. He was rich and rude; but there was a touch of goodness in him, and he loved Mariana without limit. He promised to be patient, and I labored with the greatest ardor not to try him too far.

"With Mariana I had a stubborn contest: I persuaded her, nay, I may call it forced her, by the threat of leaving her, to write to Norberg, and invite him for the night. You came, and by chance picked up his answer in the neckerchief. Your presence broke my game. For scarcely were you gone, when she anew began her lamentation: she swore she would not be unfaithful to you; she was so passionate, so frantic, that I could not help sincerely pitying her. In the end, I promised, that for this night also I would pacify her lover, and send him off, under some pretence or other. I entreated her to go to bed, but she did not seem to trust me: she kept on her clothes, and at last fell asleep, without undressing, agitated and exhausted with weeping as she was.

"Norberg came; representing in the blackest hues her conscientious agonies and her repentance, I endeavored to retain him: he wished to see her, and I went into the room to prepare her; he followed me, and both of us at once came forward to her bed. She awoke, sprang wildly up, and tore herself from our arms: she conjured and begged, she entreated, threatened, and declared she would not yield. She was improvident enough to let fall some words about the true state of her affections, which poor Norberg had to understand in a spiritual sense. At length he left her, and she locked her door. I kept him long with me, and talked with him about her situation. I told him that she was with child; that, poor girl, she should be humored. He was so delighted with his fatherhood, with his prospect of a boy, that he granted every thing she wished: he promised rather to set out and travel for a time, than vex his dear, and injure her by these internal troubles. With such intentions at an early hour he glided out; and if you, mein Herr, stood sentry by our house, there was nothing wanting to your happiness, but to have looked into the bosom of your rival, whom you thought so favored and so fortunate, and whose appearance drove you to despair."

"Art thou speaking truth?" said Wilhelm.

"True," said the crone, "as I still hope to drive you to despair.

"Yes: certainly you would despair, if I could rightly paint to you the following morning. How cheerfully did she awake! how kindly did she call me in, how warmly thank me, how cordially press me to her bosom! 'Now,' said she, stepping up to her mirror with a smile, 'can I again take pleasure in myself, and in my looks, since once more I am my own, am his, my one beloved friend's. How sweet is it to conquer! How I thank thee for taking charge of me; for having turned thy prudence and thy understanding, once, at least, to my advantage! Stand by me, and devise the means of making me entirely happy!'

"I assented, would not irritate her: I flattered her hopes, and she caressed me tenderly. If she retired but a moment from the window, I was made to stand and watch: for you, of course, would pass; for she at least would see you. Thus did we spend the restless day. At night, at the accustomed hour, we looked for you with certainty. I was already out waiting at the staircase: I grew weary, and came in to her again. With surprise I found her in her military dress: she looked cheerful and charming beyond what I had ever seen her. 'Do I not deserve,' said she, 'to appear to-night in man's apparel? Have I not struggled bravely? My dearest shall see me as he saw me for the first time: I will press him as tenderly and with greater freedom to my heart than then; for am I not his much more than I was then, when a noble resolution had not freed me? But,' added she, after pausing for a little, 'I have not yet entirely won him; I must still risk the uttermost, in order to be worthy, to be certain of possessing him; I must disclose the whole to him, discover to him all my state, then leave it to himself to keep or to reject me. This scene I am preparing for my friend, preparing for myself; and, were his feelings capable of casting me away, I should then belong again entirely to myself; my punishment would bring me consolation, I would suffer all that fate could lay upon me.'

"With such purposes and hopes, mein Herr, this lovely girl expected you: you came not. Oh! how shall I describe the state of watching and of hope? I see thee still before me, — with what love, what heartfelt love, thou spokest of the man whose cruelty thou hadst not yet experienced."

"Good, dear Barbara!" cried Wilhelm, springing up, and seizing the old woman by the hand, "we have had enough of mummery and preparation! Thy indifferent, thy calm, contented tone betrays thee. Give me back my Mariana! She is living, she is near at hand. Not in vain didst thou choose this late, lonely hour to visit me; not in vain hast thou prepared me by thy most delicious narrative. Where is she? Where hast thou hidden her? I believe all, I will promise to believe all, so thou but show her to me, so thou give her to my arms. The shadow of her I have seen already: let me clasp her once more to my bosom. I will kneel before her, I will entreat forgiveness; I will congratulate her upon her victory over herself and thee; I will bring my Felix to her. Come! Where hast thou concealed her? Leave *her*, leave me no longer in uncertainty! Thy object is attained. Where hast thou hidden her? Let me light thee with this candle, let me once more see her fair and kindly face!"

He had pulled old Barbara from her chair: she stared at him; tears started into her eyes, wild pangs of grief took hold of her. "What luckless error," cried she, "leaves you still a moment's hope? Yes, I have hidden her, but beneath the ground: neither the light of the sun nor any social taper shall again illuminate her kindly face. Take the boy Felix to her grave, and say to him, 'There lies thy mother, whom thy father doomed unheard.' The heart of Mariana beats no longer with impatience to behold you: not in a neighboring chamber is she waiting the conclusion of my narrative or fable; the dark chamber has received her, to which no bridegroom follows, from which none comes to meet a lover."

She cast herself upon the floor beside a chair, and wept bitterly. Wilhelm now, for the first time, felt entirely convinced that Mariana was no more: his emotions it is easy to conceive. The old woman rose: "I have nothing more to tell you," cried she, and threw a packet on the table. "Here are some writings that will put your cruelty to shame: peruse these sheets with unwet eyes, if you can." She glided softly out. Our friend had not the heart to open the pocket-book that night: he had himself presented it to Mariana; he knew that she had carefully preserved in it every letter he had sent her. Next morning he prevailed upon himself: he untied the ribbon; little notes came forward written with pencil in his own hand, and recalled to him every situation, from the first day of their graceful acquaintance to the last of their stern separation. In particular, it was not without acute anguish that he read a small series of billets which had been addressed to himself, and to which, as he saw from their tenor, Werner had refused admittance.

"No one of my letters has yet penetrated to thee; my entreaties, my prayers, have not reached thee; was it thyself that gave these cruel orders? Shall I never see thee more? Yet again I attempt it: I entreat thee, come, oh come! I ask not to retain thee, if I might but once more press thee to my heart."

"When I used to sit beside thee, holding thy hands, looking in thy eyes, and with the full heart of love and trust to call thee 'Dear, dear good Wilhelm!' it would please thee so, that I had to repeat it over and over. I repeat it once again: 'Dear, dear good Wilhelm! Be good as thou wert: come, and leave me not to perish in my wretchedness.'"

"Thou regardest me as guilty: I am so, but not as thou thinkest. Come, let me have this single comfort, to be altogether known to thee, let what will befall me afterwards."

"Not for my sake alone, for thy own too, I beg of thee to come. I feel the intolerable pains thou art suffering, whilst thou fleest from me. Come, that our separation may be less cruel! Perhaps I was never worthy of thee till this moment, when thou art repelling me to boundless woe."

"By all that is holy, by all that can touch a human heart, I call upon thee! It involves the safety of a soul, it involves a life, two lives, one of which must ever be dear to thee. This, too, thy suspicion will discredit: yet I will speak it in the hour of death; the child which I carry under my heart is thine. Since I began to love thee, no other man has even pressed my hand. Oh that thy love, that thy uprightness, had been the companions of my youth!"

"Thou wilt not hear me? I must even be silent. But these letters will not die: perhaps they will speak to thee, when the shroud is covering my lips, and the voice of thy repentance cannot reach my ear. Through my weary life, to the last moment, this will be my only comfort, that, though I cannot call myself blameless, towards thee I am free from blame."

Wilhelm could proceed no farther: he resigned himself entirely to his sorrow, which became still more afflicting; when, Laertes entering, he was obliged to hide his feelings. Laertes showed a purse of ducats, and began to count and reckon them, assuring Wilhelm that there could be nothing finer in the world than for a man to feel himself on the way to wealth; that nothing then could trouble or detain him. Wilhelm bethought him of his dream, and smiled; but at the same time, he remembered with a shudder, that in his vision Mariana had forsaken him, to follow his departed father, and that both of them at last had moved about the garden, hovering in the air like spirits.

Laertes forced him from his meditations: he brought him to a coffee-house, where, immediately on Wilhelm's entrance, several persons gathered round him. They were men who had applauded his performance on the stage: they expressed their joy at meeting him;

lamenting that, as they had heard, he meant to leave the theatre. They spoke so reasonably and kindly of himself and his acting, of his talent, and their hopes from it, that Wilhelm, not without emotion, cried at last, "Oh, how infinitely precious would such sympathy have been to me some months ago! How instructive, how encouraging! Never had I turned my mind so totally from the concerns of the stage, never had I gone so far as to despair of the public."

"So far as this," said an elderly man who now stepped forward, "we should never go. The public is large: true judgment, true feeling, are not quite so rare as one believes; only the artist ought not to demand an unconditional approval of his work. Unconditional approval is always the least valuable: conditional you gentlemen are not content with. In life, as in art, I know well, a person must take counsel with himself when he purposes to do so or to produce any thing: but, when it is produced or done, he must listen with attention to the voices of a number; and, with a little practice, out of these many votes he will be able to collect a perfect judgment. The few who could well have saved us this trouble for the most part hold their peace."

"This they should not do," said Wilhelm. "I have often heard people, who themselves kept silence in regard to works of merit, complain and lament that silence was kept."

"To-day, then, we will speak aloud," cried a young man. "You must dine with us; and we will try to pay off a little of the debt which we have owed to you, and sometimes also to our good Aurelia."

This invitation Wilhelm courteously declined: he went to Frau Melina, whom he wished to speak with on the subject of the children, as he meant to take them from her.

Old Barbara's secret was not too religiously observed by him. He betrayed himself so soon as he again beheld the lovely Felix. "Oh my child!" cried he: "my dear child!" He lifted him, and pressed him to his heart.

"Father! what hast thou brought for me?" cried the child. Mignon looked at both, as if she meant to warn them not to blab.

"What new phenomenon is this?" said Frau Melina. They got the children sent away; and Wilhelm, thinking that he did not owe old Barbara the strictest secrecy, disclosed the whole affair to Frau Melina. She viewed him with a smile. "Oh, these credulous men!" exclaimed she. "If any thing is lying in their path, it is so easy to impose it on them; while in other cases they will neither look to the right nor left, and can value nothing which they have not previously impressed with the stamp of an arbitrary passion!" She sighed, against her will: if our friend had not been altogether blind, he must have noticed in her conduct an affection for him which had never been entirely subdued.

He now spoke with her about the children, — how he purposed to keep Felix with him, and to place Mignon in the country. Madam Melina, though sorry at the thought of parting with them, said the plan was good, nay, absolutely necessary. Felix was becoming wild with her, and Mignon seemed to need fresh air and other occupation: she was sickly, and was not yet recovering.

"Let it not mislead you," added Frau Melina, "that I have lightly hinted doubts about the boy's being really yours. The old woman, it is true, deserves but little confidence; yet a person who invents untruths for her advantage, may likewise speak the truth when truths are profitable to her. Aurelia she had hoodwinked to believe that Felix was Lothario's son; and it is a property of us women, that we cordially like the children of our lovers, though we do not know the mothers, or even hate them from the heart." Felix came jumping in: she pressed him to her with a tenderness which was not usual to her.

Wilhelm hastened home, and sent for Barbara, who, however, would not undertake to meet him till the twilight. He received her angrily. "There is nothing in the world more shameful," said he, "than establishing one's self on lies and fables. Already thou hast done much mischief with them; and now, when thy word could decide the fortune of my life, now must I stand dubious, not venturing to call the child my own, though to possess him without scruple would form my highest happiness. I cannot look upon thee, scandalous creature, without hatred and contempt."

"Your conduct, if I speak with candor," said the old woman, "appears to me intolerable. Even if Felix were not yours, he is the fairest and the loveliest child in nature: one might purchase him at any price, to have him always near one. Is he not worthy your acceptance? Do not I deserve for my care, for the labor I have had with him, a little pension for the small remainder of my life? Oh, you gentlemen who know no want! It is well for you to talk of truth and honor; but how the miserable being whose smallest necessity is unprovided for, who sees in her perplexities no friend, no help, no counsel, how she is to press through the crowd of selfish men, and to starve in silence, you are seldom at the trouble to consider. Did you read Mariana's letters? They are the letters she wrote to you at that unhappy season. It was in vain that I attempted to approach you to deliver you these sheets: your savage brother-in-law had so begirt you, that craft and cunning were of no avail; and at last, when he began to threaten me and Mariana with imprisonment, I had then to cease my efforts and renounce all hope. Does not every thing agree with what I told you? And does not Norberg's letter put the story altogether out of doubt?"

"What letter?" asked he.

"Did you not find it in the pocket-book?" said Barbara.

"I have not yet read all of them."

"Give me the pocket-book: on that paper every thing depends. Norberg's luckless billet caused this sorrowful perplexity: another from his hand may loose the knots, so far as aught may still depend upon unravelling them." She took a letter from the book: Wilhelm recognized that odious writing; he constrained himself, and read, —

"Tell me, girl, how hast thou got such power over me? I would not have believed that a goddess herself could make a sighing lover of me. Instead of hastening towards me with open arms, thou shrankest back from me: one might have taken it for aversion. Is it fair that I should spend the night with old Barbara, sitting on a trunk, and but two doors between me and my pretty Mariana? It is too bad, I tell thee! I have promised to allow thee time to think, not to press thee unrelentingly: I could run mad at every wasted quarter of an hour. Have not I given thee gifts according to my power? Dost thou still doubt of my love? What wilt thou have? Do but tell me: thou shalt want for nothing. Would the Devil had the priest that put such stuff into thy head! Why didst thou go to such a churl? There are plenty of them that allow young people somewhat. In short, I tell thee, things must alter: in two days I must have an answer, for I am to leave the town; and, if thou become not kind and friendly to me, thou shalt never see me more. . . ."

In this style the letter spun itself to great length; turning, to Wilhelm's painful satisfaction, still about the same point, and testifying for the truth of the account which he had got from Barbara. A second letter clearly proved that Mariana, in the sequel, also had maintained her purpose; and it was not without heartfelt grief, that, out of these and other papers, Wilhelm learned the history of the unlucky girl to the very hour of her death.

Barbara had gradually tamed rude, regardless Norberg, by announcing to him Mariana's death, and leaving him in the belief that Felix was his son. Once or twice he had sent her money, which, however, she retained for herself; having talked Aurelia into taking charge of the child. But, unhappily, this secret source of riches did not long endure. Norberg, by a life of riot, had impaired his fortune; and, by repeated love-affairs, his heart was rendered callous to his supposed first-born.

Probable as all this seemed, beautifully as it all agreed, Wilhelm did not venture to give way to joy. He still appeared to dread a present coming from his evil Genius.

"Your jealous fears," said Barbara, who guessed his mood of mind, "time alone can cure. Look upon the child as a stranger one; take stricter heed of him on that account; observe his gifts, his temper, his capacities; and if you do not, by and by, discover in him the exact resemblance of yourself, your eyes must certainly be bad. Of this I can assure you, — were I a man, no one should foist a child on me; but it is a happiness for women, that, in these cases, men are not so quick of sight."

These things over, Wilhelm and Barbara parted: he was to take Felix with him; she, to carry Mignon to Theresa, and afterwards to live in any place she pleased, upon a small annuity which he engaged to settle on her.

He sent for Mignon, to prepare her for the new arrangement. "Master," said she, "keep me with thee: it will do me good, and do me ill."

He told her, that, as she was now grown up, there should be something further done for her instruction. "I am sufficiently instructed," answered she, "to love and grieve."

He directed her attention to her health, and showed that she required continuous care, and the direction of a good physician. "Why care for me," said she, "when there are so many things to care for?"

After he had labored greatly to persuade her that he could not take her with him, that he would conduct her to a place where he might often see her, she appeared as if she had not heard a word of it. "Thou wishest not to have me with thee," said she. "Perhaps it is better: send me to the old harper; the poor man is lonely where he is."

Wilhelm tried to show her that the old man was in comfortable circumstances. "Every hour I long for him," replied the child.

"I did not see," said Wilhelm, "that thou wert so fond of him when he was living with us."

"I was frightened for him when he was awake; I could not bear his eyes: but, when he was asleep, I liked so well to sit by him! I used to chase the flies from him! I could not look at him enough. Oh! he has stood by me in fearful moments: none knows how much I owe him. Had I known the road, I should have run away to him already."

Wilhelm set the circumstances in detail before her: he said that she had always been a reasonable child, and that, on this occasion also, she might do as she desired. "Reason is cruel," said she; "the heart is better: I will go as thou requirest, only leave me Felix."

After much discussion her opinion was not altered; and Wilhelm at last resolved on giving Barbara both the children, and sending them together to Theresa. This was the easier for him, as he still feared to look upon the lovely Felix as his son. He would take him on his arm, and carry him about: the child delighted to be held before the glass; Wilhelm also liked, though unavowedly, to hold him there, and seek resemblances between their faces. If for a moment any striking similarity appeared between them, he would press the boy in his arms; and then, at once affrightened by the thought that he might be mistaken, he would set him down, and let him run away. "Oh," cried he, "if I were to appropriate this priceless treasure, and it were then to be snatched from me, I should be the most unhappy man on earth!"

The children had been sent away; and Wilhelm was about to take a formal leave of the theatre, when he felt that in reality he had already taken leave, and needed but to go. Mariana was no more: his two guardian spirits had departed, and his thoughts hied after them. The fair boy hovered like a beautiful uncertain vision in the eyes of his imagination: he saw him, at Theresa's hand, running through the fields and woods, forming his mind and person in the free air, beside a free and cheerful foster-mother. Theresa had become far dearer to him since he figured her in company with Felix. Even while sitting in the theatre, he thought of her with smiles; he was almost in her own case: the stage could now produce no more illusion in him.

Serlo and Melina were excessively polite to him, when they observed that he was making no pretensions to his former place. A portion of the public wished to see him act again: this he could not accede to; nor in the company did any one desire it, saving Frau Melina.

Of this friend he now took leave; he was moved at parting with her: he exclaimed, "Why do we presume to promise any thing depending on an unknown future? The most slight engagement we have not the power to keep, far less a purpose of importance. I feel ashamed in recollecting what I promised to you all, in that unhappy night, when we were lying plundered, sick, and wounded, crammed into a miserable tavern. How did misfortune elevate my courage! what a treasure did I think I had found in my good wishes! And of all this not a jot has taken effect! I leave you as your debtor; and my comfort is, that our people prized my promise at its actual worth, and never more took notice of it."

"Be not unjust to yourself," said Frau Melina: "if no one acknowledges what you have done for us, I at least will not forget it. Our whole condition had been different, if you had not been with us. But it is with our purposes as with our wishes. They seem no longer what they are, when they have been accomplished, been fulfilled; and we think we have done, have wished for, nothing."

"You shall not, by your friendly statement," answered Wilhelm, "put my conscience to peace. I shall always look upon myself as in your debt."

"Nay, perhaps you are so," said Madam Melina, "but not in the manner you suppose. We reckon it a shame to fail in the fulfilment of a promise we have uttered with the voice. O my friend! a worthy person by his very presence promises us much. The confidence he elicits, the inclination he inspires, the hopes he awakens, are unbounded: he is and continues in our debt, although he does not know it. Fare you well! If our external circumstances have been happily repaired by your direction, in my mind there is, by your departure, produced a void which will not be filled up again so easily."

Before leaving the city, Wilhelm wrote a copious sheet to Werner. He had before exchanged some letters; but, not being able to agree, they had at length ceased to write. Now, however, Wilhelm had again approximated to his brother: he was just about to do what Werner had so earnestly desired. He could say, "I am abandoning the stage: I mean to join myself with men whose intercourse, in every sense, must lead me to a sure and suitable activity." He inquired about his property; and it now seemed strange to him, that he had never, for so long a time, disturbed himself about it. He knew not that it is the manner of all persons who attach importance to their inward cultivation altogether to neglect their outward circumstances. This had been Wilhelm's case: he now for the first time seemed to notice, that, to work effectively, he stood in need of outward means. He entered on his journey, this time, in a temper altogether different from that of last; the prospects he had in view were charming; he hoped to meet with something cheerful by the way.

CHAPTER NINE

ON RETURNING to Lothario's castle, Wilhelm found that changes had occurred. Jarno met him with the tidings, that, Lothario's uncle being dead, the baron had himself set out to take possession of the heritage. "You come in time," said he, "to help the abbé and me. Lothario has commissioned to to purchase some extensive properties of land in this quarter: he has long contemplated the bargain, and we have now got cash and credit just in season. The only point which made us hesitate was, that a distant trading-house had also views upon the same estates: at length we have determined to make common cause with it, as otherwise we might outbid each other without need or reason. The trader seems to be a prudent man. At present we are making estimates and calculations: we must also settle economically how the lands are to be shared, so that each of us may have a fine estate." The papers were submitted to our friend: the fields, meadows, houses, were inspected; and, though Jarno and the abbé seemed to understand the matter fully, Wilhelm could not help desiring that Theresa had been with them.

In these labors several days were spent, and Wilhelm had scarcely time to tell his friends of his adventures and his dubious fatherhood. This incident, to him so interesting, they treated with indifference and levity.

He had noticed, that they frequently in confidential conversation, while at table or in walks, would suddenly stop short, and give their words another application; thereby showing, at least, that they had on the anvil many things which were concealed from him. He bethought him of what Lydia had said; and he put the greater faith in it, as one entire division of the castle had always been inaccessible to him. The way to certain galleries, particularly to the ancient tower, with which externally he was so well acquainted, he had often sought, and hitherto in vain.

One evening Jarno said to him, "We can now consider you as ours, with such security, that it were unjust if we did not introduce you deeper into our mysteries. It is right that a man, when he first enters upon life, should think highly of himself, should determine to attain many eminent distinctions, should endeavor to make all things possible; but, when his education had proceeded to a certain pitch, it is advantageous for him, that he learn to lose himself among a mass of men, that he learn to live for the sake of others, and to forget himself in an activity prescribed by duty. It is then that he first becomes acquainted with himself, for it is conduct alone that compares us with others. You shall soon see what a curious little world is at your very hand, and how well you are known in it. To-morrow morning before sunrise be dressed and ready."

Jarno came at the appointed hour: he led our friend through certain known and unknown chambers of the castle, then through several galleries; till at last they reached a large old door, strongly framed with iron. Jarno knocked: the door went up a little, so as to admit one person. Jarno shoved in our friend, but did not follow him. Wilhelm found himself in an obscure and narrow stand: all was dark around him; and, when he tried to go a step forward, he found himself hemmed in. A voice not altogether strange to him cried, "Enter!" and he now discovered that the sides of the place where he was were merely hung with tapestry, through which a feeble light glimmered in to him. "Enter!" cried the voice again: he raised the tapestry, and entered.

The hall in which he now stood appeared to have at one time been a chapel: instead of the altar, he observed a large table raised some steps above the floor, and covered with a green cloth hanging over it.

On the top of this, a drawn curtain seemed as if it hid a picture; on the sides were spaces beautifully worked, and covered in with fine wire-netting, like the shelves of a library; only here, instead of books, a multitude of rolls had been inserted. Nobody was in the hall: the rising sun shone through the window, right on Wilhelm, and kindly saluted him as he came in.

"Be seated!" cried a voice, which seemed to issue from the altar. Wilhelm placed himself in a small arm-chair, which stood against the tapestry where he had entered. There was no seat but this in the room: Wilhelm had to be content with it, though the morning radiance dazzled him; the chair stood fast, he could only keep his hand before his eyes.

But now the curtain, which hung down above the altar, went asunder with a gentle rustling, and showed, within a picture-frame, a dark, empty aperture. A man stepped forward at it, in a common dress, saluted the astonished looker-on, and said to him, "Do you not recognize me? Among the many things which you would like to know, do you feel no curiosity to learn where your grandfather's collection of pictures and statues are at present? Have you forgot the painting which you once so much delighted in? Where, think you, is the sick king's son now languishing?" Wilhelm, without difficulty, recognized the stranger, whom, in that important night, he had conversed with at the inn. "Perhaps," continued his interrogator, "we should now be less at variance in regard to destiny and character."

Wilhelm was about to answer, when the curtain quickly flew together. "Strange!" said Wilhelm to himself: "can chance occurrences have a connection? Is what we call Destiny but Chance? Where *is* my grandfather's collection? and why am I reminded of it in these solemn moments?"

He had not leisure to pursue his thoughts: the curtain once more parted; and a person stood before him, whom he instantly perceived to be the country clergyman that had attended him and his companions on that pleasure-sail of theirs. He had a resemblance to the abbé, though he seemed to be a different person. With a cheerful countenance, in a tone of dignity, he said, "To guard from error is not the instructor's duty, but to lead the erring pupil; nay, to let him quaff his error in deep, satiating draughts, this is the instructor's wisdom. He who only tastes his error, will long dwell with it, will take delight in it as in a singular felicity; while he who drains it to the dregs will, if he be not crazy, find it out." The curtain closed again, and Wilhelm had a little time to think. "What error can he mean," said he within himself, "but the error which has clung to me through my whole life, — that I sought for cultivation where it was not to be found; that I fancied I could form a talent in me, while without the smallest gift for it?"

The curtain dashed asunder faster than before: an officer advanced, and said in passing, "Learn to know the men who may be trusted!" The curtain closed; and Wilhelm did not long consider, till he found this officer to be the one who had embraced him in the count's park, and had caused his taking Jarno for a crimp. How that stranger had come hither, who he was, were riddles to our friend. "If so many men," cried he, "took interest in thee, know thy way of life, and how it should be carried on, why did they not conduct thee with greater strictness, with greater seriousness? Why did they favor thy silly sports, instead of drawing thee away from them?"

"Dispute not with us!" cried a voice. "Thou art saved, thou art on the way to the goal. None of thy follies wilt thou repent; none wilt thou wish to repeat; no luckier destiny can be allotted to a man." The curtain went asunder, and in full armor stood the old king of Denmark in the space. "I am thy father's spirit," said the figure; "and I depart in comfort since my wishes for thee are accomplished, in a higher sense than I myself contemplated. Steep regions cannot be surmounted save by winding paths: on the plain, straight roads conduct from place to place. Farewell, and think of me when thou enjoyest what I have provided for thee."

Wilhelm was exceedingly amazed and struck: he thought it was his father's voice; and yet in truth it was not: the present and the past alike confounded and perplexed him.

He had not meditated long when the abbé came to view, and placed himself behind the green table. "Come hither!" cried he to his marvelling friend. He went, and mounted up the steps. On the green cloth lay a little roll. "Here is your indenture," said the abbé: "take it to heart; it is of weighty import." Wilhelm lifted, opened it, and read: —

"Here is your indenture"

INDENTURE

Art is long, life short, judgment difficult, opportunity transient. To act is easy, to think is hard; to act according to our thought is troublesome. Every beginning is cheerful: the threshold is the place of expectation. The boy stands astonished, his impressions guide him: he learns sportfully, seriousness comes on him by surprise. Imitation is born with us: what should be imitated is not easy to discover. The excellent is rarely found, more rarely valued. The height charms us, the steps to it do not: with the summit in our eye, we love to walk along the plain. It is but a part of art that can be taught: the artist needs it all. Who knows it half, speaks much, and is always wrong: who knows it wholly, inclines to act, and speaks seldom or late. The former have no secrets and no force: the instruction they can give is liked baked bread, savory and satisfying for a single day; but flour cannot be sown, and seed-corn ought not to be ground. Words are good, but they are not the best. The best is not to be explained by words. The spirit in which we act is the highest matter. Action can be understood and again represented by the spirit alone. No one knows what he is doing while he acts aright, but of what is wrong we are always conscious. Whoever works with symbols only is a pedant, a hypocrite, or a bungler. There are many such, and they like to be together. Their babbling detains the scholar: their obstinate mediocrity vexes even the best. The instruction which the true artist gives us opens the mind; for, where words fail him, deeds speak. The true scholar learns from the known to unfold the unknown, and approaches more and more to being a master.

"Enough!" cried the abbé: "the rest in due time. Now look round you among these cases."

Wilhelm went, and read the titles of the rolls. With astonishment he found, "Lothario's Apprenticeship," "Jarno's Apprenticeship," and his own Apprenticeship placed there, with many others whose names he did not know.

"May I hope to cast a look into these rolls?"

"In this chamber there is now nothing hid from you."

"May I put a question?"

"Without scruple; and you may expect a positive reply, if it concerns a matter which is nearest your heart, and ought to be so."

"Good, then! Ye marvellous sages, whose sight has pierced so many secrets, can you tell me whether Felix is in truth my son?"

"Hail to you for this question!" cried the abbé, clapping hands for joy. "Felix is your son! By the holiest that lies hid among us, I swear to you Felix is your son; nor, in our opinion, was the mother that is gone unworthy of you. Receive the lovely child from our hands: turn round, and venture to be happy."

Wilhelm heard a noise behind him: he turned round, and saw a child's face peeping archly through the tapestry at the end of the room; it was Felix. The boy playfully hid himself so soon as he was noticed. "Come forward!" cried the abbé: he came running; his father rushed towards him, took him in his arms, and pressed him to his heart. "Yes! I feel it," cried he, "thou art mine! What a gift of Heaven have I to thank my friends for! Whence or how comest thou, my child, at this important moment?"

"Ask not," said the abbé. "Hail to thee, young man! Thy Apprenticeship is done: Nature has pronounced thee free."

Book Eight

CHAPTER ONE

FELIX skipped into the garden; Wilhelm followed him with rapture: a lovely morning was displaying every thing with fresh charms; our friend enjoyed the most delightful moment. Felix was new in the free and lordly world, nor did his father know much more than he about the objects concerning which the little creature was repeatedly and unweariedly inquiring. At last they joined the gardener, who had to tell them the names and uses of a multitude of plants. Wilhelm looked on nature as with unscaled eyes: the child's new-fangled curiosity first made him sensible how weak an interest he himself had taken in external things, how small his actual knowledge was. Not till this day, the happiest of his life, did his own cultivation seem to have commenced: he felt the necessity of learning, being called upon to teach.

Jarno and the abbé did not show themselves again till evening, when they brought a guest along with them. Wilhelm viewed the stranger with amazement; he could scarce believe his eyes: it was Werner, who likewise, for a moment, hesitated in his recognition. They embraced each other tenderly: neither of them could conceal that he thought the other greatly altered. Werner declared that his friend was taller, stronger, straighter; that he had become more polished in his looks and carriage. "Something of his old true-heartedness I miss, however," added he. "That, too, will soon appear again," said Wilhelm, "when we have recovered from our first astonishment."

The impression Werner made upon his friend was by no means so favorable. The honest man seemed rather to have retrograded than advanced. He was much leaner than of old; his peaked face appeared to have grown sharper, his nose longer; brow and crown had lost their hair; the voice, clear, eager, shrill, the hollow breast and stooping shoulders, the sallow cheeks, announced indubitably that a melancholic drudge was there.

Wilhelm was discreet enough to speak but sparingly of these great changes; while the other, on the contrary, gave free course to his friendly joy. "In truth," cried he, "if thou hast spent thy time badly, and, as I suppose, gained nothing, it must be owned thou art grown a piece of manhood such as cannot fail to turn to somewhat. Do not waste and squander me this, too, again: with such a figure thou shalt buy some rich and beautiful heiress." — "I see," said Wilhelm, smiling, "thou wilt not belie thy character. Scarcely hast thou found thy brother after long absence, when thou lookest on him as a piece of goods, a thing to speculate on and make profit by."

Jarno and the abbé did not seem at all astonished at this recognition: they allowed the two to expatiate on the past and present as they pleased. Werner walked round and round his friend, turned him to this side and to that, so as almost to embarrass him. "No!" cried he, "such a thing as this I never met with, and yet I know that I am not mistaken. Thy eyes are deeper, thy brow is broader; thy nose has grown finer, thy mouth more lovely. Do but look at him, how he stands; how it all suits and fits together! Well, idling is the way to grow. But for me, poor devil," said he, looking at himself in the glass, "if I had not all this while been making store of money, it were over with me altogether."

Werner had got Wilhelm's last letter: the distant trading-house, in common with which Lothario meant to purchase the estates, was theirs. On that business Werner had come hither, not dreaming that he should meet with Wilhelm on the way. The baron's lawyer came: the papers were produced; Werner reckoned the conditions reasonable. "If you mean well," said he, "as you seem to do, with this young man, you will of yourselves take care that our part be not abridged: it shall be at my friend's option whether he will take the land and lay out a portion of his fortune on it." Jarno and the abbé protested that they did not need this admonition. Scarcely had the business been discussed in general terms, when Werner signified a longing for a game at ombre; to which, in consequence, Jarno and the abbé set themselves along with him. He was now grown so accustomed to it, that he could not pass the evening without cards.

The two friends, after supper, being left alone, began to talk and question one another very keenly, touching every thing they wished to have communicated. Wilhelm spoke in high terms of his situation, of his happiness in being received among such men. Werner shook his head, and said, "Well, I see, we should believe nothing that we do not see with our eyes. More than one obliging friend assured me thou wert living with a wild young nobleman, wert supplying him with actresses, helping him to waste his money; that, by thy means, he had quarrelled with every one of his relations." — "For my own sake, and the sake of these worthy gentlemen, I should be vexed at this," said Wilhelm, "had not my theatrical experience made me tolerant to every sort of calumny. How can men judge rightly of our actions, which appear but singly or in fragments to them; of which they see the smallest portion; while good and bad take place in secret, and for most part nothing comes to light but an indifferent show? Are not the actors and actresses in a play set up on boards before them; lamps are lit on every side; the whole transaction is comprised within three hours; yet scarcely one of them knows rightly what to make of it?"

Our friend proceeded to inquire about his family, his young comrades, his native town. Werner told, with great haste, of changes that had taken place, of changes that were still in progress. "The women in our house," said he, "are satisfied and happy: we are never short of money. One half of their time they spend in dressing, the other in showing themselves when dressed. They are as domestic as a reasonable man could wish. My boys are growing up to prudent youths. I already, as in vision, see them sitting, writing, reckoning, running, trading, trucking: each of them, as soon as possible, shall have a business of his own. As to what concerns our fortune, thou wilt be contented with the state of it. When we have got these lands in order, thou must come directly home with me; for it now appears as if thou, too, couldst mingle with some skill in worldly undertakings, thanks to thy new friends, who have set thee on the proper path. I am certainly a fool: I never knew till now how well I liked thee, — now when I cannot gape and gaze at thee enough, so well and handsome thou lookest. That is, in truth, another form than the portrait which was sent thy sister, which occasioned such disputes at home. Both mother and daughter thought young master very handsome indeed, with his slack collar, half-open breast, large ruff, sleek, pendent hair, round hat, short waistcoat, and wide pantaloons; while I, on the other hand, maintained that the costume was scarce two finger-breadths from that of harlequin. But now thou lookest like a man: only the cue is wanting, in which I beg of thee to bind thy hair; else, some time or other, they will seize thee as a Jew, and demand toll and tribute of thee."

Felix, in the mean time, had come into the room; and, as they did not mind him, he had laid himself upon the sofa, and was fallen asleep. "What urchin is this?" said Werner. Wilhelm at that moment had not the heart to tell the truth, nor did he wish to lay a still ambiguous narrative before a man who was by nature any thing but credulous.

The whole party now proceeded to the lands, to view them, and conclude the bargain. Wilhelm would not part with Felix from his side: for the boy's sake, he rejoiced exceedingly in the intended purchase. The longing of the child for cherries and berries, the season for which was at hand, brought to his mind the days of his own youth, and the manifold duties of a father, to prepare, to procure, and to maintain for his family a constant series of enjoyments. With what interest he viewed the nurseries and the buildings! How zealously he contemplated repairing what had been neglected, restoring what had fallen! He no longer looked upon the world with the eyes of a bird of passage: an edifice he did not now consider as a grove that is hastily put together, and that withers ere one leaves it. Every thing that he proposed commencing was to be completed for his boy: every thing that he erected was to last for several generations. In this sense his apprenticeship was ended: with the feeling of a father, he had acquired all the virtues of a citizen. He felt this, and nothing could exceed his joy. "O needless strictness of morality!" exclaimed he, "while Nature in her own kindly manner trains us to all that we require to be. O strange demands of civil society! which first perplexes and misleads us, then asks of us more than Nature herself. Woe to every sort of culture which destroys the most effectual means of all true culture, and directs us to the end, instead of rendering us happy on the way!"

Much as he had already seen in his life, it seemed as if the observation of the child afforded him his first clear view of human nature. The theatre, the world, had appeared before him, only as a multitude of thrown dice, every one of which upon its upper surface indicates a greater or a smaller value, and which, when reckoned up together, make a sum. But here in the person of the boy, as we might say, a single die was laid before him, on the many sides of which the worth and worthlessness of man's nature were legibly engraved.

The child's desire to have distinctions made in his ideas grew stronger every day. Having learned that things had names, he wished to hear the name of every thing: supposing that there could be nothing which his father did not know, he often teased him with his questions, and caused him to inquire concerning objects which, but for this, he would have passed without notice. Our innate tendency to pry into the origin and end of things was likewise soon developed in the boy. When he asked whence came the wind, and whither went the flame, his father for the first time truly felt the limitation of his own powers, and wished to understand how far man may venture with his thoughts, and what things he may hope ever to give account of to himself or others. The anger of the child, when he saw injustice done to any living thing, was extremely grateful to the father, as the symptom of a generous heart. Felix once struck fiercely at the cook for cutting up some pigeons. The fine impression this produced on Wilhelm was, indeed, erelong disturbed, when he found the boy unmercifully tearing sparrows in pieces and beating frogs to death. This trait reminded him of many men, who appear so scrupulously just when without passion, and witnessing the proceedings of other men.

The pleasant feeling, that the boy was producing so fine and wholesome an influence on his being, was, in a short time, troubled for a moment, when our friend observed, that in truth the boy was educating him more than he the boy. The child's conduct he was not qualified to correct: its mind he could not guide in any path but a spontaneous one. The evil habits which Aurelia had so violently striven against had all, as it seemed, on her death, assumed their ancient privileges. Felix still never shut the door behind him, he still would not eat from a plate; and no greater pleasure could befall him than when he happened to be overlooked, and could take his bit immediately from the dish, or let the full glass stand, and drink out of the bottle. He delighted also very much when he could set himself in a corner with a book, and say with a serious air, "I must study this scholar stuff!" though he neither knew his letters, nor would learn them.

Thus, when Wilhelm thought how little he had done for Felix, how little he was capable of doing, there arose at times a restlessness within him, which appeared to counterbalance all his happiness. "Are we men, then," said he, "so selfishly formed, that we cannot possibly take proper charge of any one without us? Am I not acting with the boy exactly as I did with Mignon? I drew the dear child towards me: her presence gave me pleasure, yet I cruelly neglected her. What did I do for her education, which she longed for with such earnestness? Nothing! I left her to herself, and to all the accidents to which, in a society of coarse people, she could be exposed. And now for this boy, who seemed so interesting before he could be precious to thee, has thy heart ever bid thee do the smallest service to him? It is time that thou shouldst cease to waste thy own years and those of others: awake, and think what thou shouldst do for thyself, and for this good being, whom love and nature have so firmly bound to thee."

This soliloquy was but an introduction to admit that he had already thought and cared, and tried and chosen: he could delay no longer to confess it. After sorrow, often and in vain repeated, for the loss of Mariana, he distinctly felt that he must seek a mother for the boy; and also that he could not find one equal to Theresa. With this gifted lady he was thoroughly acquainted. Such a spouse and help-mate seemed the only one to trust one's self to in such circumstances. Her generous affection for Lothario did not make him hesitate. By a singular destiny, they two had been forever parted: Theresa looked upon herself as free; she had talked of marrying, with indifference, indeed, but as of a matter understood.

After long deliberation he determined on communicating to her every thing he knew about himself. She was to be made acquainted with him, as he already was with her. He accordingly began to take a survey of his history; but it seemed to him so empty of events, and in general so little to his credit, that he more than once was on the point of giving up his purpose. At last, however, he resolved on asking Jarno for the Roll of his Apprenticeship, which he had noticed lying in the tower: Jarno said it was the very time for that, and Wilhelm consequently got it.

It is a feeling of awe and fear which seizes on a man of noble mind when conscious that his character is just about to be exhibited before him. Every transition is a crisis, and a crisis presupposes sickness. With what reluctance do we look into the glass after rising from a sick-bed! The recovery we feel: the effects of the past disease are all we see. Wilhelm had, however, been sufficiently prepared: events had already spoken loudly to him, and his friends had not spared him. If he opened the roll of parchment with some hurry, he grew calmer and calmer the farther he read. He found his life delineated with large, sharp strokes; neither unconnected incidents, nor narrow sentiments, perplexed his view; the most bland and general reflections taught, without shaming him. For the first time his own figure was presented to him, not, indeed, as in a mirror, a second self, but as in a portrait, another self: we do not, it is true, recognize ourselves in every feature; but we are delighted that a thinking spirit has so understood us, that such gifts have been employed in representing us, that an image of what we were exists, and may endure when we ourselves are gone.

Wilhelm next employed himself in setting forth the history of his life, for the perusal of Theresa: all the circumstances of it were recalled to memory by what he had been reading; he almost felt ashamed that to her great virtues he had nothing to oppose which indicated a judicious activity. He had been minute in his written narrative: he was brief in the letter which he sent along with it. He solicited her friendship, her love if it were possible: he offered her his hand, and entreated for a quick decision.

After some internal contest, whether it were proper to impart this weighty business to his friends, — to Jarno and the abbé, — he determined not to do so. His resolution was so firm, the business was of such importance, that he could not have submitted it to the decision of the wisest and best of men. He was even cautious enough to carry his letter with his own hand to the nearest post. From his parchment-roll it appeared with certainty enough, that in very many actions of his life, in which he had conceived himself to be proceeding freely and in secret, he had been observed, nay, guided; and perhaps the thought of this had given him an unpleasant feeling: and he wished at least, in speaking to Theresa's heart, to speak purely from the heart, — to owe his fate to her decision and determination only. Hence, in this solemn point, he scrupled not to give his overseers the slip.

CHAPTER TWO

SCARCELY was the letter gone, when Lothario returned. Every one was gladdened at the prospect of so speedily concluding the important business which they had in hand. Wilhelm waited with anxiety to see how all these many threads were to be loosed, or tied anew, and how his own future state was to be settled. Lothario gave a kindly salutation to them all: he was quite recovered and serene; he had the air of one who knows what he should do, and who finds no hinderance in the way of doing it.

His cordial greeting Wilhelm could scarcely repay. "This," he had to own within himself, "is the friend, the lover, bridegroom, of Theresa: in his stead thou art presuming to intrude. Dost thou think it possible for thee to banish, to obliterate, an impression such as this?" Had the letter not been sent away, perhaps he would not have ventured sending it at all. But happily the die was cast: it might be, Theresa had already taken up her resolution, and only distance shrouded with its veil a happy termination. The winning or the losing must soon be decided. By such considerations he endeavored to compose himself, and yet the movements of his heart were almost feverish. He could give but little attention to the weighty business, on which, in some degree, the fate of his whole property depended. In passionate moments how trivial do we reckon all that is about us, all that belongs to us!

Happily for him, Lothario treated the affair with magnanimity, and Werner with an air of ease. The latter, in his violent desire of gain, experienced a lively pleasure in contemplating the fine estate which was to be his friend's. Lothario, for his part, seemed to be revolving very different thoughts. "I cannot take such pleasure in the acquirement of property," said he, "as in the justness of it."

"And, in the name of Heaven," cried Werner, "is not this of ours acquired justly?"

"Not altogether," said Lothario.

"Are we not giving hard cash for it?"

"Doubtless," replied Lothario; "and most probably you will consider what I am now hinting at as nothing but a whim. No property appears to me quite just, quite free of flaw, except it contribute to the state its due proportion."

"What!" said Werner. "You would rather that our lands, which we have purchased free from burden, had been taxable?"

"Yes," replied Lothario, "in a suitable degree. It is only by this equality with every other kind of property, that our possession of it can be made secure. In these new times, when so many old ideas are tottering, what is the grand reason why the peasant reckons the possession of the noble less equitable than his own? Simply that the noble is not burdened, and lies a burden on him."

"But how would the interest of our capital agree with that?" said Werner.

"Perfectly well," returned the other; "if the state, for a regular and fair contribution, would relieve us from the feudal hocus-pocus; would allow us to proceed with our lands according to our pleasure: so that we were not compelled to retain such masses of them undivided, so that we might part them more equally among our children, whom we might thus introduce to vigorous and free activity, instead of leaving them the poor inheritance of these our limited and limiting privileges, to enjoy which we must ever be invoking the ghosts of our forefathers. How much happier were men and women in our rank of life, if they might, with unforbidden eyes, look round them, and elevate by their selection, here a worthy maiden, there a worthy youth, regarding nothing further than their own ideas of happiness in marriage! The state would have more, perhaps better citizens, and would not so often be distressed for want of heads and hands."

"I can assure you honestly," said Werner, "I never in my life thought about the state: my taxes, tolls, and tributes I have paid, because it was the custom."

"Still, however," said Lothario, "I hope to make a worthy patriot of you. As he alone is a good father who at table serves his children first; so is he alone a good citizen who, before all other outlays, discharges what he owes the state."

By such general reflections their special business was accelerated rather than retarded. It was nearly over, when Lothario said to Wilhelm, "I must send you to a place where you are needed more than here. My sister bids me beg of you to go to her as soon as possible. Poor Mignon seems to be decaying more and more, and it is thought your presence might allay the malady. Besides telling me in person, my sister has despatched this note after me: so that you perceive she reckons it a pressing case." Lothario handed him a billet. Wilhelm, who had listened in extreme perplexity, at once discovered in these hasty pencil-strokes the hand of the countess, and knew not what to answer.

"Take Felix with you," said Lothario: "the little ones will cheer each other. You must be upon the road to-morrow morning early: my sister's coach, in which my people travelled hither, is still here; I will give you horses half the way, the rest you post. A prosperous journey to you! Make many compliments from me, when you arrive: tell my sister I shall soon be back, and that she must prepare for guests. Our grand-uncle's friend, the Marchese Cipriani, is on his way to visit us: he hoped to find the old man still in life; they meant to entertain each other with their common love of art, and the recollection of their early intimacy. The marchese, much younger than my uncle, owed to him the greater part of his accomplishments. We must exert all our endeavors to fill up, in some measure, the void which is awaiting him; and a larger party is the readiest means."

Lothario went with the abbé to his chamber; Jarno had ridden off before; Wilhelm hastened to his room. There was none to whom he could unbosom his distress, none by whose assistance he could turn aside the project, which he viewed with so much fear. The little servant came, requesting him to pack: they were to put the luggage on to-night, meaning to set out by daybreak. Wilhelm knew not what to do: at length he cried, "Well, I shall leave this house at any rate; on the road I may consider what is to be done; at all events, I will halt in the middle of my journey; I can send a message hither, I can write what I recoil from saying, then let come of it what will." In spite of this resolution, he spent a sleepless night: a look on Felix resting so serenely was the only thing that gave him any solace. "Oh, who knows," cried he, "what trials are before me! who knows how sharply by-gone errors will yet punish me, how often good and reasonable projects for the future shall miscarry! But this treasure, which I call my own, continue it to me, thou exorable or inexorable Fate! Were it possible that this best part of myself were taken from me, that this heart could be torn from my heart, then farewell sense and understanding; farewell all care and foresight; vanish thou tendency to perseverance! All that distinguishes us from the beasts, pass away! And, if it is not lawful for a man to end his heavy days by the act of his own hand, may speedy madness banish consciousness, before death, which destroys it forever, shall bring on his own long night."

He seized the boy in his arms, kissed him, clasped him, and wetted him with plenteous tears.

The child awoke: his clear eye, his friendly look, touched his father to the inmost heart. "What a scene awaits me," cried he, "when I shall present thee to the beautiful, unhappy countess, when she shall press thee to her bosom, which thy father has so deeply injured! Ought I not to fear that she will push thee from her with a cry, when a touch of thee renews her real or fancied pain?" The coachman did not leave him time for further thought or hesitation, but forced him into the carriage before day. Wilhelm wrapped his Felix well; the morning was cold but clear: the child, for the first time in his life, saw the sun rise. His astonishment at the first fiery glance of the luminary, at the growing power of the light; his pleasure and his strange remarks, — rejoiced the father, and afforded him a glimpse into the heart of the boy, before which, as over a clear and silent sea, the sun was mounting and hovering.

In a little town the coachman halted, unyoked his horses, and rode back. Wilhelm took possession of a room, and asked himself seriously whether he would stay or proceed. Thus irresolute, he ventured to take out the little note, which hitherto he had never had the heart to look on: it contained the following words: "Send thy young friend very soon: Mignon for the last two days has been growing rather worse. Sad as the occasion is, I shall be happy to get acquainted with him."

The concluding words Wilhelm, at the first glance, had not seen. He was terrified on reading them, and instantly determined not to go. "How?" cried he, "Lothario, knowing what occurred between us, has not told her who I am? She is not, with a settled mind, expecting an acquaintance, whom she would rather not see: she expects a stranger, — and I enter! I see her shudder and start back, I see her blush! No, it is impossible for me to encounter such a scene!" Just then his horses were led out and yoked: Wilhelm was determined to take off his luggage and remain. He felt extremely agitated. Hearing the maid running up stairs to tell him, as he thought, that all was ready, he began on the spur of the instant to devise some pretext for continuing: his eyes were fixed, without attention, on the letter which he still held in his hand. "In the name of Heaven!" cried he, "what is this? It is not the hand of the countess: it is the hand of the Amazon!"

The maid came in, requested him to walk down, and took Felix with her. "Is it possible," exclaimed he, "is it true? What shall I do? Remain, and wait, and certify myself? Or hasten, hasten, and rush into an explanation? Thou art on the way to her, and thou canst loiter? This night thou mayest see her, and thou wilt voluntarily lock thyself in prison? It is her hand; yes, it is hers! This hand calls thee: her coach is yoked to lead thee to her! Now the riddle is explained: Lothario has two sisters; my relation to the one he knows, how much I owe to the other is unknown to him. Nor is she aware that the wounded stroller, who stands indebted to her for his health, if not his life, has been received with such unmerited attention in her brother's house."

Felix, who was swinging to and fro in the coach, cried up to him, "Father! Come, oh come! Look at the pretty clouds, the pretty colors!" — "Yes, I come," cried Wilhelm, springing down-stairs; "and all the glories of the sky, which thou, good creature, so admirest, are as nothing to the moment which I look for."

Sitting in the coach, he recalled all the circumstances of the matter to his memory. "So this is the Natalia, then, Theresa's friend!

What a discovery! what hopes, what prospects! How strange that the fear of speaking about the one sister should have altogether concealed from me the existence of the other!" With what joy he looked on Felix! He anticipated for the child, as for himself, the best reception.

Evening at last came on; the sun had set; the road was not the best; the postilion drove slowly; Felix had fallen asleep, and new cares and doubts arose in the bosom of our friend. "What delusion, what fantasies, are these that rule thee!" said he to himself. "An uncertain similarity of handwriting has at once assured thee, and given thee matter for the strangest castles in the air." He again brought out the paper; in the departing light he again imagined that he recognized the hand of the countess: his eyes could no longer find in the parts what his heart had at once shown him in the whole. "These horses, then, are running with thee to a scene of terror! Who knows but in a few hours they may have to bring thee back again? And if thou shouldst meet with her alone! But perhaps her husband will be there, perhaps the baroness! How altered will she be! Shall I not fail, and sink to the earth, at sight of her?"

Yet a faint hope that it might be his Amazon would often gleam through these gloomy thoughts. It was now night: the carriage rolled into a court-yard, and halted; a servant with a link stepped out of a stately portal, and came down the broad steps to the carriage-door. "You have been long looked for," said he, opening it. Wilhelm dismounted, took the sleeping Felix in his arms: the first servant called to a second, who was standing in the door with a light, "Show the gentleman up to the baroness."

Quick as lightning, it went through Wilhelm's soul, "What a happiness! Be it by accident or of purpose, the baroness is here! I shall see her first: apparently the countess has retired to rest. Ye good spirits, grant that the moment of deepest perplexity may pass tolerably over!"

He entered the house: he found himself in the most earnest, and, as he almost felt, the holiest, place that he had ever trod. A pendent, dazzling lustre threw its light upon a broad and softly rising flight of stairs, which lay before him, and which parted into two divisions at a turn above. Marble statues and busts were standing upon pedestals, and arranged in niches: some of them seemed known to

Mignon as an angel

him. The impressions of our childhood abide with us, even in their minutest traces. He recognized a Muse, which had formerly belonged to his grandfather, not indeed by its form or worth, but by an arm which had been restored, and some new-inserted pieces of the robe. He felt as if a fairy-tale had turned out to be true. The child was heavy in his arms: he lingered on the stairs, and knelt down, as if to place him more conveniently. His real want, however, was to get a moment's breathing-time. He could scarcely raise himself again. The servant, who was carrying the light, offered to take Felix; but Wilhelm could not part with him. He had now mounted to an ante-chamber, in which, to his still greater astonishment, he observed the well-known picture of the sick king's son hanging on the wall. He had scarcely time to cast a look on it: the servant hurried him along through two rooms into a cabinet. Here, behind a light-screen, which threw a shadow on her, sat a young lady reading. "Oh that it were she!" said he within himself at this decisive moment. He set down the boy, who seemed to be awakening; he meant to approach the lady; but the child sank together, drunk with sleep; the lady rose and came to him. It was the Amazon! Unable to restrain himself, he fell upon his knee, and cried, "It is she!" He seized her hand, and kissed it with unbounded rapture. The child was lying on the carpet between them, sleeping softly.

Felix was carried to the sofa: Natalia sat down beside him; she directed Wilhelm to the chair which was standing nearest them. She proposed to order some refreshments; these our friend declined: he was altogether occupied convincing himself that it was she, closely examining her features, shaded by the screen, and accurately recognizing them. She told him of Mignon's sickness, in general terms; that the poor child was gradually consuming under the influence of a few deep feelings; that with her extreme excitability, and her endeavoring to hide it, her little heart often suffered violent and dangerous pains; that, on any unexpected agitation of her mind, this primary organ of life would suddenly stop, and no trace of the vital movement could be felt in the good child's bosom; that, when such an agonizing cramp was past, the force of nature would again express itself in strong pulses, and now torment the child by its excess, as she had before suffered by its defect.

Wilhelm recollected one spasmodic scene of that description; and Natalia referred him to the doctor, who would speak with him at large on the affair, and explain more circumstantially why he, the friend and benefactor of the child, had been at present sent for. "One curious change," Natalia added, "you will find in her: she now wears women's clothes, to which she had once such an aversion."

"How did you succeed in this?" said Wilhelm.

"If it was, indeed, a thing to be desired," said she, "we owe it all to chance. Hear how it happened. Perhaps you are aware that I have constantly about me a number of little girls, whose opening minds I endeavor, as they grow in strength, to train to what is good and right. From my mouth they learn nothing but what I myself regard as true: yet I can not and would not hinder them from gathering, among other people, many fragments of the common prejudices and errors which are current in the world. If they inquire of me about them, I attempt, as far as possible, to join these alien and intrusive notions to some just one, and thus to render them, if not useful, at least harmless. Some time ago my girls had heard, among the peasants' children, many tales of angels, of Knecht Rupert, and such shadowy characters, who, they understood, appeared at certain times in person, to give presents to good children, and to punish naughty ones. They had an idea that these strange visitants were people in disguise; in this I confirmed them: and, without entering into explanations, I determined, on the first opportunity, to let them see a spectacle of that sort. It chanced that the birthday of two twin-sisters, whose behavior had been always very good, was near: I promised, that, on this occasion, the little present they had so well deserved should be delivered to them by an angel. They were on the stretch of curiosity regarding this phenomenon. I had chosen Mignon for the part; and accordingly, at the appointed day, I had her suitably equipped in a long, light, snow-white dress. She was, of course, provided with a golden girdle round her waist, and a golden fillet on her hair. I at first proposed to omit the wings; but the young ladies who were decking her insisted on a pair of large golden pinions, in preparing which they meant to show their highest art. Thus did the strange apparition, with a lily in the one hand, and a little basket in the other, glide in among the girls: she surprised even me. 'There comes the angel!' said I. The children all shrank back: at last they cried, 'It is Mignon!' yet they durst not venture to approach the wondrous figure.

" 'Here are your gifts,' said she, putting down the basket. They gathered around her, they viewed, they felt, they questioned her.

" 'Art thou an angel?' asked one of them.

" 'I wish I were,' said Mignon.

" 'Why dost thou bear a lily?'

" 'So pure and so open should my heart be: then were I happy.'

" 'What wings are these? Let us see them?'

" 'They represent far finer ones, which are not yet unfolded.'

"And thus significantly did she answer all their other childlike, innocent inquiries. The little party having satisfied their curiosity, and the impression of the show beginning to abate, we were for proceeding to undress the little angel. This, however, she resisted: she took her cithern; she seated herself here, on this high writing-table, and sang a little song with touching grace: —

> " 'Such let me seem, till such I be:
>   Take not my snow-white dress away!
> Soon from this dusk of earth I flee
>   Up to the glittering lands of day.
>
> There first a little space I rest,
>   Then wake so glad, to scenes so kind:
> In earthly robes no longer drest,
>   This band, this girdle, left behind.
>
> And those calm, shining sons of morn,
>   They ask not who is maid or boy:
> No robes, no garments, there are worn;
>   Our body pure from sin's alloy.
>
> Through little life not much I toiled,
>   Yet anguish long this heart has wrung;
> Untimely woe my blossom spoiled:
>   Make me again forever young!'

"I immediately determined upon leaving her the dress," proceeded Natalia, "and procuring her some others of a similar kind.

These she now wears; and in them, I think, her form has quite a different expression."

As it was already late, Natalia let the stranger go: he parted from her not without anxiety. "Is she married, or not?" asked he within himself. He had been afraid, at every rustling, that the door would open, and her husband enter. The serving-man, who showed him to his room, went off before our friend had mustered resolution to inquire regarding this. His unrest held him long awake: he kept comparing the figure of the Amazon with the figure of his new acquaintance. The two would not combine: the former he had, as it were, himself fashioned; the latter seemed as if it would almost new-fashion *him*.

CHAPTER THREE

NEXT MORNING, while all was yet quiet, he went about, viewing the house. It was the purest, finest, stateliest piece of architecture he had ever seen. "True art," cried he, "is like good company: it constrains us in the most delightful way to recognize the measure by which, and up to which, our inward nature has been shaped by culture." The impression which the busts and statues of his grandfather made upon him was exceedingly agreeable. With a longing mind he hastened to the picture of the sick king's son, and he still felt it to be charming and affecting. The servant opened to him various other chambers: he found a library, a museum, a cabinet of philosophical instruments. In much of this he could not help perceiving his extreme ignorance. Meanwhile Felix had awakened, and come running after him. The thought of how and when he might receive Theresa's letter gave him pain: he dreaded seeing Mignon, and in some degree Natalia. How unlike his present state was his state at the moment when he sealed the letter to Theresa, and with a glad heart wholly gave himself to that noble being!

Natalia sent for him to breakfast. He proceeded to a room where several tidy little girls, all apparently below ten years, were occupied in furnishing a table; while another of the same appearance brought in various sorts of beverage.

Wilhelm cast his eye upon a picture hung above the sofa: he could not but recognize in it the portrait of Natalia, little as the execution satisfied him. Natalia entered, and the likeness seemed entirely to vanish. To his comfort, it was painted with the cross of a religious order on its breast; and he now saw another such upon Natalia's.

"I have just been looking at the portrait here," said he; "and it seems surprising that a painter could have been at once so true and so false. The picture resembles you, in general, extremely well; and yet it neither has your features nor your character."

"It is rather matter of surprise," replied Natalia, "that the likeness is so good. It is not my picture, but the picture of an aunt, whom I resembled even in childhood, though she was then advanced in years. It was painted when her age was just about what mine is: at the first glance, every one imagines it is meant for me. You should have been acquainted with that excellent lady. I owe her much. A very weak state of health, perhaps too much employment with her own thoughts, and, withal, a moral and religious scrupulosity, prevented her from being to the world what, in other circumstances, she might have become. She was a light that shone but on a few friends, and on me especially."

"Can it be possible," said Wilhelm, after thinking for a moment, while so many circumstances seemed to correspond so well, "can it be possible that the fair and noble Saint, whose meek confessions I had liberty to study, was your aunt?"

"You read the manuscript?" inquired Natalia.

"Yes," said Wilhelm, "with the greatest sympathy, and not without effect upon my life. What most impressed me in this paper was, if I may term it so, the purity of being, not only of the writer herself, but of all that lay round her; that self-dependence of nature, that impossibility of admitting any thing into her soul which would not harmonize with its own noble, lovely tone."

"You are more tolerant to this fine spirit," said Natalia, "nay, I will say more just, than many other men to whom the narrative has been imparted. Every cultivated person knows how much he has to strive against a certain coarseness, both in himself and others; how much his culture costs him; how apt he is, after all, in certain cases, to recollect himself alone, forgetting what he owes to others. How often has a worthy person to reproach himself for having failed to act with proper delicacy! And when a fair nature too delicately, too conscientiously, cultivates, nay, if you will, overcultivates, itself, there seems to be no toleration, no indulgence, for it in the world. Yet such persons are, without us, what the ideal of perfection is within us, — models, not for being imitated, but for being aimed at. We laugh at the cleanliness of the Dutch; but would our friend Theresa be what she is, if some such notion were not always present to her in her housekeeping?"

"I see before me, then," cried Wilhelm, "in Theresa's friend, the same Natalia whom her amiable relative was so attached to; the Natalia, who, from her youth, was so affectionate, so sympathizing, and helpful! It was only out of such a line that such a being could proceed. What a prospect opens before me, while I at once survey your ancestors, and all the circle you belong to!"

"Yes," replied Natalia, "in a certain sense, the story of my aunt would give you the faithfullest picture of us. Her love to me, indeed, has made her praise the little girl too much: in speaking of a child, we never speak of what is present, but of what we hope for."

Wilhelm, in the mean time, was rapidly reflecting that Lothario's parentage and early youth were now likewise known to him. The fair countess, too, appeared before him in her childhood, with the aunt's pearls about her neck: he himself had been near those pearls, when her soft, lovely lips bent down to meet his own. These beautiful remembrances he sought to drive away by other thoughts. He ran through the characters to whom that manuscript had introduced him. "I am here, then," cried he, "in your worthy uncle's house! It is no house, it is a temple; and you are the priestess, nay, the Genius, of it: I shall recollect for life my impression yesternight, when I entered, and the old figures of my earliest days were again before me. I thought of the compassionate marble statues in Mignon's song: but these figures had not to lament about me; they looked upon me with a lofty earnestness, they brought my first years into immediate contact with the present moment. That ancient treasure of our family, the joy of my grandfather, I find here placed among so many other noble works of art; and myself, whom nature made the darling of the good old man, my unworthy self I find here also, Heavens! in what society, in what connections!"

The girls had, by degrees, gone out to mind their little occupations. Natalia, left alone with Wilhelm, asked some further explanation of his last remark. The discovery, that a number of her finest paintings and statues had at one time been the property of Wilhelm's grandfather, did not fail to give a cheerful stimulus to their discourse. As by that manuscript he had got acquainted with Natalia's house; so now he found himself too, as it were, in his inheritance. At length he asked for Mignon. His friend desired him to have patience till the doctor, who had been called out into the neighborhood, returned. It is easy to suppose that the doctor was the same little, active man whom we already know, and who was spoken of in the "Confessions of a Fair Saint."

"Since I am now," said Wilhelm, "in the middle of your family circle, I presume the abbé whom that paper mentions is the strange, inexplicable person whom, after the most singular series of events, I met with in your brother's house? Perhaps you can give some more accurate conception of him?"

"Of the abbé there might much be said," replied Natalia: "what I know best about him, is the influence which he exerted on our education. He was, for a time at least, convinced that education ought, in every case, to be adapted to the inclinations: his present views of it I know not. He maintained, that with man the first and last consideration was activity, and that we could not act on any thing without the proper gifts for it, without an instinct impelling us to it. 'You admit,' he used to say, 'that poets must be born such; you admit this with regard to all professors of the fine arts; because you must admit it, because those workings of human nature cannot very plausibly be aped. But, if we consider well, we shall find that every capability, however slight, is born with us; that there is no vague, general capability in men. It is our ambiguous, desultory education that makes men uncertain: it awakens wishes when it should be animating tendencies; instead of forwarding our real capacities, it turns our efforts towards objects which are frequently discordant with the mind that aims at them. I augur better of a child, a youth, who is wandering astray on a path of his own, than of many who are walking aright upon paths which are not theirs. If the former, either by themselves or by the guidance of others, ever find the right path, that is to say, the path which suits their nature, they will never leave it; while the latter are in danger every moment of shaking off a foreign yoke, and abandoning themselves to unrestricted license.' "

"It is strange," said Wilhelm, "that this same extraordinary man should likewise have taken charge of me; should, as it seems, have, in his own fashion, if not led, at least confirmed, me in my errors, for a time. How he will answer to the charge of having joined with others, as it were, to make game of me, I wait patiently to see."

"Of this whim, if it is one," said Natalia, "I have little reason to complain: of all the family I answered best with it. Indeed, I see not how Lothario could have got a finer breeding: but for my sister, the countess, some other treatment might have suited better; perhaps they should have studied to infuse more earnestness and strength into her nature. As to brother Friedrich, what is to become of him cannot be conjectured: he will fall a sacrifice, I fear, to this experiment in pedagogy."

"You have another brother, then?" cried Wilhelm.

"Yes," replied Natalia: "and a light, merry youth he is; and, as they have not hindered him from roaming up and down the world, I know not what the wild, dissipated boy will turn to. It is a great while since I saw him. The only thing which calms my fears is, that the abbé, and the whole society about my brother, are receiving constant notice where he is and what he does."

Wilhelm was about to ask Natalia her opinion more precisely on the abbé's paradoxes, as well as to solicit information about that mysterious society; but the physician entering changed their conversation. After the first compliments of welcome, he began to speak of Mignon.

Natalia then took Felix by the hand; saying she would lead the child to Mignon, and prepare her for the entrance of her friend.

The doctor, now alone with Wilhelm, thus proceeded: "I have wondrous things to tell you, such as you are not anticipating. Natalia has retired, that we might speak with greater liberty of certain matters, which, although I first learned them by her means, her presence would prevent us from discussing freely. The strange temper of the child seems to consist almost exclusively of deep longing: the desire of re-visiting her native land, and the desire for you, my friend, are, I might almost say, the only earthly things about her. Both these feel-ings do but grasp towards an immeasurable distance, both objects lie before her unattainable. The neighborhood of Milan seems to be her home: in very early childhood she was kidnapped from her parents by a company of rope-dancers. A more distinct account we cannot get from her, partly because she was then too young to recollect the names of men and places, but especially because she has made an oath to tell no living mortal her abode and parentage. For the strolling-party, who came up with her when she had lost her way, and to whom she so accurately described her dwelling, with such piercing entreaties to conduct her home, but carried her along with them the faster; and at night in their quarters, when they thought the child was sleeping, joked about their precious capture, declaring she would never find the way home again. On this a horrid desperation fell upon the miserable creature; but at last the Holy Virgin rose before her eyes, and prom-ised that she would assist her. The child then swore within herself a sacred oath, that she would henceforth trust no human creature, would disclose her history to no one, but live and die in hope of immediate aid from Heaven. Even this, which I am telling you, Natalia did not learn expressly from her, but gathered it from detached expressions, songs, and childlike inadvertencies, betraying what they meant to hide."

Wilhelm called to memory many a song and word of this dear child, which he could now explain. He earnestly requested the phy-sician to keep from him none of the confessions or mysterious poetry of this peculiar being.

"Prepare yourself," said the physician, "for a strange confession; for a story with which you, without remembering it, have much to do, and which, as I greatly fear, has been decisive for the death and life of this good creature."

"Let me hear," said Wilhelm: "my impatience is unbounded."

"Do you recollect a secret nightly visit from a female," said the doctor, "after your appearance in the character of Hamlet?"

"Yes, I recollect it well," cried Wilhelm, blushing; "but I did not look to be reminded of it at the present moment."

"Do you know who it was?"

"I do not! You frighten me! In the name of Heaven, not Mignon, surely? Who was it? Tell me, pray."

"I know it not myself."

"Not Mignon, then?"

"No, certainly not Mignon; but Mignon was intending at the time to glide in to you, and saw with horror, from a corner where she lay concealed, a rival get before her."

"A rival!" cried our friend. "Speak on: you more and more confound me."

"Be thankful," said the doctor, "that you can arrive at the result so soon through means of me. Natalia and I, with but a distant interest in the matter, had distress enough to undergo before we could thus far discover the perplexed condition of the poor, dear creature, whom we wished to help. By some wanton speeches of Philina and the other girls, by a certain song which she had heard Philina sing, the child's attention had been roused: she longed to pass a night beside the man she loved, without conceiving anything to be implied in this beyond a happy and confiding rest. A love for you, my friend, was already keen and powerful in her little heart. In your arms, the child had found repose from many a sorrow; she now desired this happiness in all its fulness. If at one time she purposed requesting it as a favor, at another a secret horror would hold her back. At last that merry night and the excitement of abundant wine inspired her with the courage to attempt the adventure, and glide in to you on that occasion. Accordingly she ran before, to hide herself in your apartment, which was standing open; but just when she had reached the top of the stairs, having heard a rustling, she concealed herself, and saw a female in a white dress slip into your chamber. You yourself arrived soon after, and she heard you push the large bolt.

"Mignon's agony was now unutterable: all the violent feelings of a passionate jealousy mingled themselves with the unacknowledged longing of obscure desire, and seized her half-developed nature with tremendous force. Her heart, which hitherto had beaten violently with eagerness and expectation, now at once began to falter and stop; it pressed her bosom like a heap of lead: she could not draw her breath, she knew not what to do; she heard the sound of the old man's harp, hastened to the garret where he was, and passed the night at his feet in horrible convulsions."

The physician paused a moment: then, as Wilhelm still kept silence, he proceeded, "Natalia told me, nothing in her life had so alarmed and touched her as the state of Mignon while relating this; indeed, our noble friend accused herself of cruelty in having, by her questions and management, drawn this confession from her, and re-newed by recollection the violent sorrows of the poor little girl.

" 'The dear creature,' said Natalia, 'had scarcely come so far with her recital, or, rather, with her answers to my questions, when she sank all at once before me on the ground, and, with her hand on her bosom, piteously moaned that the pain of that excruciating night was come back. She twisted herself like a worm upon the floor; and I had to summon all my composure, that I might remember and apply such means of remedy for mind and body as were known to me.' "

"It is a painful predicament you put me in," cried Wilhelm, "by impressing me so vividly with the feeling of my manifold injustice towards this unhappy and beloved being, at the very moment when I am again to meet her. If she is to see me, why do you deprive me of the courage to appear with freedom? And shall I confess it to you? Since her mind is so affected, I perceive not how my presence can be advantageous to her. If you, as a physician, are persuaded that this double longing has so undermined her being as to threaten death, why should I renew her sorrows by my presence, and perhaps accelerate her end?"

"My friend," replied the doctor, "where we cannot cure, it is our duty to alleviate; and how much the presence of a loved object tends to take from the imagination its destructive power, how it changes an impetuous longing to a peaceful looking, I could prove by the most convincing instances. Every thing in measure and with purpose! For, in other cases, this same presence may rekindle an affection nigh extinguished. But do you go and see the child; behave to her with kindness, and let us wait the consequence."

Natalia, at this moment coming back, bade Wilhelm follow her to Mignon. "She appears to feel quite happy with the boy," observed Natalia, "and I hope she will receive our friend with mildness." Wilhelm followed, not without reluctance: he was deeply moved by what he had been hearing; he feared a stormy scene of passion. It was altogether the reverse that happened on his entrance.

Mignon, dressed in long, white, women's clothes, with her brown, copious hair partly knotted, partly clustering out in locks, was sitting with the boy Felix on her lap, and pressing him against her heart. She looked like a departed spirit, he like life itself: it seemed as if Heaven and Earth were clasping one another. She held out her hand to Wilhelm with a smile, and said, "I thank thee for bringing back the child to me: they had taken him away, I know not how; and since then I could not live. So long as my heart needs any thing on earth, thy Felix shall fill up the void."

The quietness which Mignon had displayed on meeting with her friend produced no little satisfaction in the party. The doctor signified that Wilhelm should go frequently and see her; that in body as in mind, she should be kept as equable as possible. He himself departed, promising to return soon.

Wilhelm could now observe Natalia in her own circle: one would have desired nothing better than to live beside her. Her presence had the purest influence on the girls, and young ladies of various ages, who resided with her in the house, or came to pay her visits from the neighborhood.

"The progress of your life," said Wilhelm once to her, "must always have been very even: your aunt's delineation of you in your childhood seems, if I mistake not, still to fit. It is easy to see that you never were entangled in your path. You have never been compelled to retrograde."

"This I owe to my uncle and the abbé," said Natalia, "who so well discriminated my prevailing turn of mind. From my youth upwards, I can recollect no livelier feeling than that I was constantly observing people's wants, and had an irresistible desire to make them up. The child that had not learned to stand on its feet, the old man that could no longer stand on his; the longing of a rich family for children, the inability of a poor one to maintain their children; each silent wish for some particular species of employment; the impulse towards any talent; the natural gifts for many little necessary arts of life, — were sure to strike me: my eyes seemed formed by nature for detecting them. I saw such things where no one had directed my attention: I seemed born for seeing them alone. The charms of inanimate nature, to which so many persons are exceedingly susceptible, had no effect on me: the charms of art, if possible, had less. My most delightful occupation was and is, when a deficiency, a want, appeared before me anywhere, to set about devising a supply, a remedy, a help for it.

"If I saw a poor creature in rags, the superfluous clothes I had noticed hanging in the wardrobes of my friends immediately occurred to me; if I saw children wasting for want of care, I was sure to recollect some lady I had found oppressed with tedium amid riches and conveniences; if I saw too many persons crammed into a narrow space, I thought they should be lodged in the spacious chambers of palaces and vacant houses. This mode of viewing things was altogether natural, without the least reflection: so that in my childhood I often made the strangest work of it, and more than once embarrassed people by my singular proposals. Another of my peculiarities was this: I did not learn till late, and after many efforts, to consider money as a means of satisfying wants; my benefits were all distributed in kind: and my simplicity, I know, was frequently the cause of laughter. None but the abbé seemed to understand me: he met me everywhere; he made me acquainted with myself, with these wishes, these tendencies, and taught me how to satisfy them suitably."

"Do you, then," said Wilhelm, "in the education of your little female world, employ the method of these extraordinary men? Do you, too, leave every mind to form itself? Do you, too, leave your girls to search and wander, to pursue delusions, happily to reach the goal, or miserably lose themselves in error?"

"No," replied Natalia: "such treatment as that would altogether contradict my notions. To my mind, he who does not help us at the needful moment, never helps; he who does not counsel at the needful moment, never counsels. I also reckon it essential, that we lay down and continually impress on children certain laws, to operate as a kind of hold in life. Nay, I could almost venture to assert, that it is better to be wrong by rule, than to be wrong with nothing but the fitful caprices of our disposition to impel us hither and thither; and, in my way of viewing men, there always seems to be a void in their nature, which cannot be filled up, except by some decisive and distinctly settled law."

"Your manner of proceeding, then," said Wilhelm, "is entirely different from the manner of our friends?"

"Yes," replied Natalia; "and you may see the unexampled tolerance of these men, from the fact, that they nowise disturb me in my practice, but leave me on my own path, simply because it is my own, and even assist me in every thing that I require of them."

A more minute description of Natalia's plans in managing her children we reserve for some other opportunity.

Mignon often asked to be of their society; and this they granted her with greater readiness, as she appeared to be again accustoming herself to Wilhelm, to be opening her heart to him, and in general to have become more cheerful, and contented with existence. In walking, being easily fatigued, she liked to hang upon his arm. "Mignon," she would say, "now climbs and bounds no more; yet she still longs to mount the summits of the hills, to skip from house to house, from tree to tree. How enviable are the birds! and then so prettily and socially they build their nests too!"

Erelong it became habitual for her to invite her friend, more than once every day, into the garden. When Wilhelm was engaged or absent, Felix had to take his place; and, if poor Mignon seemed at times quite loosened from the earth, there were other moments when she would again hold fast to father and son, and seem to dread a separation from them more than any thing beside.

Natalia wore a thoughtful look. "We meant," said she, "to open her tender little heart, by sending for you hither. I know not whether we did prudently." She stopped, and seemed expecting Wilhelm to say something. To him also it occurred, that, by his marriage with Theresa, Mignon, in the present circumstances, would be fearfully offended: but, in his uncertainty, he did not venture mentioning his project; he had no suspicion that Natalia knew of it.

As little could he talk with freedom, when his noble friend began to speak about her sister, to praise her good qualities, and to lament her hapless situation. He felt exceedingly embarrassed when Natalia told him he would shortly see the countess here. "Her husband," said she, "has now no object but replacing Zinzendorf in the Community, and, by insight and activity, supporting and extending that establishment. He is coming with his wife, to take a sort of leave: he then purposes visiting the various spots where the Community have settled. They appear to treat him as he wishes: and I should not wonder if, in order to be altogether like his predecessor, he ventured, with my sister, on a voyage to America; for, being already well-nigh convinced that a little more would make a saint of him, the wish to superadd the dignity of martyrdom has probably often enough flitted through his mind."

CHAPTER FOUR

THEY HAD OFTEN spoken of Theresa, often mentioned her in passing; and Wilhelm almost every time was minded to confess that he had offered her his heart and hand. A certain feeling, which he was not able to explain, restrained him: he paused and wavered, till at length Natalia, with the heavenly, modest, cheerful smile she often wore, said to him, "It seems, then, I at last must break silence, and force myself into your confidence! Why, my friend, do you keep secret from me an affair of such importance to yourself, and so closely touching my concerns? You have made my friend the offer of your hand: I do not mix uncalled in the transaction; here are my credentials; here is the letter which she writes to you, which she sends you through my hands."

"A letter from Theresa!" cried he.

"Yes, mein Herr! Your destiny is settled: you are happy. Let me congratulate my friend and you on your good fortune."

Wilhelm spoke not, but gazed out before him. Natalia looked at him: she saw that he was pale. "Your joy is strong," continued she: "it takes the form of terror, it deprives you of the power to speak. My participation is not the less cordial that I show it you in words. I hope you will be grateful, for I may say my influence on the decision of your bride has not been small: she asked me for advice; and as it happened, by a singular coincidence, that you were here just then, I was enabled to destroy the few scruples she still entertained. Our messages went swiftly to and fro: here is her determination; here is the conclusion of the treaty! And now you shall read her other letters: you shall have a free, clear look into the fair heart of your Theresa."

Wilhelm opened the letter, which she handed him unsealed. It contained these friendly words: —

"I am yours, as I am and as you know me. I call you mine, as you are and as I know you. What in ourselves, what in our connection, wedlock changes, we shall study to adjust by reason, cheerfulness, and mutual good will. As it is no passion, but trust and inclination, for each other that is leading us together, we run less risk than thousands of others. You will forgive me, will you not, if I still think often and kindly of my former friend: in return, I will press your Felix to my heart, as if I were his mother. If you choose to share my little mansion straightway, we are lord and master there; and in the mean while the purchase of your land might be concluded. I could wish that no new arrangements were made in it without me. I could wish at once to prove that I deserve the confidence you repose in me. Adieu, dear, dear friend! Beloved bridegroom, honored husband! Theresa clasps you to her breast with hope and joy. My friend will tell you more, will tell you all."

Wilhelm, to whose mind this sheet recalled the image of Theresa with the liveliest distinctness, had now recovered his composure. While reading, thoughts had rapidly alternated within his soul. With terror he discovered in his heart the most vivid traces of an inclination to Natalia: he blamed himself, declaring every thought of that description to be madness; he represented to himself Theresa in her whole perfection: he again perused the letter, he grew cheerful, or, rather, he so far regained his self-possession that he could appear cheerful. Natalia handed him the letters which had passed between Theresa and herself: out of Theresa's we propose extracting one or two passages.

After delineating her bridegroom in her own peculiar way, Theresa thus proceeded: —

"Such is the notion I have formed of the man who now offers

me his hand. What he thinks of himself, thou shalt see by and by in the papers he has sent me, where he altogether candidly draws his own portrait: I feel persuaded that I shall be happy with him."

"As for rank, thou knowest what my ideas have always been on this point. Some people look on disagreement of external circumstances as a fearful thing, and cannot remedy it. I wish not to persuade any one, I wish to act according to my own persuasion. I mean not to set others an example, nor do I act without example. It is interior disagreements only that frighten me: a frame that does not fit what it is meant to hold, much pomp and little real enjoyment, wealth and avarice, nobility and coarseness, youth and pedantry, poverty and ceremonies, these are the things which would annihilate me, however it may please the world to stamp and rate them."

"If I hope that we shall suit each other, the hope is chiefly founded upon this, that he resembles thee, my dear Natalia, thee whom I so highly prize and reverence. Yes: he has thy noble searching and striving for the better, whereby we of ourselves produce the good which we suppose we find. How often have I blamed thee, not in silence, for treating this or that person, for acting in this or that case, otherwise than I should have done; and yet, in general, the issue showed that thou wert right. 'When we take people,' thou wouldst say, 'merely as they are, we make them worse: when we treat them as if they were what they should be, we improve them as far as they can be improved.' To see or to act thus, I know full well is not for me. Skill, order, discipline, direction, that is my affair. I always recollect what Jarno said: 'Theresa trains her pupils, Natalia forms them.' Nay, once he went so far as to assert that of the three fair qualities, faith, love, and hope, I was entirely destitute. 'Instead of faith,' said he, 'she has penetration; instead of love, she has steadfastness; instead of hope, she has trust.' Indeed, I will confess, that, till I knew thee, I knew nothing higher in the world than clearness and prudence: it was thy presence only that persuaded, animated, conquered me; to thy fair, lofty soul I willingly give place. My friend, too, I honor on the same principle: the description of his life is a perpetual seeking without finding, — not empty seeking, but wondrous, generous seeking; he fancies others may give him what can proceed from himself alone.

So, love, the clearness of my vision has not injured me on this occasion more than others: I know my husband better than he knows himself, and I value him the more. I see him, yet I see not over him: all my skill will not enable me to judge of what he can accomplish. When I think of him, his image always blends itself with thine: I know not how I have deserved to belong to two such persons. But I will deserve it, by endeavoring to do my duty by fulfilling what is looked for from me."

"If I recollect of Lothario? Vividly and daily. In the company which in thought surrounds me, I cannot want him for a moment. Oh, what a pity for this noble character, related by an error of his youth to me, that nature has related him to thee! A being such as thou, in truth, were worthier of him than I. To thee I could, I would, surrender him. Let us be to him all we can, till he find a proper wife; and then, too, let us be, let us abide, together."

"But what shall we say to our friends?" began Natalia. "Your brother does not know of it?" — "Not a hint; your people know as little; we women have, on this occasion, managed the affair ourselves. Lydia had put some whims into Theresa's head concerning Jarno and the abbé. There are certain plans and secret combinations, with the general scheme of which I am acquainted, and into which I never thought of penetrating farther. With regard to these, Theresa has, through Lydia, taken up some shadow of suspicion: so in this decisive step she would not suffer any one but me to influence her. With my brother it had been already settled that they should merely announce their marriages to one another, not giving or asking counsel on the subject."

Natalia wrote a letter to her brother: she invited Wilhelm to subjoin a word or two, Theresa having so desired it. They were just about to seal, when Jarno unexpectedly sent up his name. His reception was, of course, as kind as possible: he wore a sportful, merry air; he could not long forbear to tell his errand. "I am come," said he, "to give you very curious and very pleasing tidings: they concern Theresa. You have often blamed us, fair Natalia, for troubling our heads about so many things; but now you see how good it is to have one's spies in every place. Guess, and let us see your skill for once!"

The self-complacency with which he spoke these words, the roguish mien with which he looked at Wilhelm and Natalia, persuaded both of them that he had found their secret. Natalia answered, smiling, "We are far more skilful than you think: before we even heard your riddle, we had put the answer to it down in black and white."

With these words she handed him the letter to Lothario, satisfied at having met, in this way, the little triumph and surprise he had meant for them. Jarno took the sheet with some astonishment, ran it quickly over, started, let it drop from his hands, and stared at both his friends with an expression of amazement, nay, of fright, which, on his countenance, was rare. He spoke no word.

Wilhelm and Natalia were not a little struck: Jarno stepped up and down the room. "What shall I say?" cried he, "or shall I say it all? But it must come out: the perplexity is not to be avoided. So secret for secret, surprise against surprise! Theresa is not the daughter of her reputed mother! The hinderance is removed: I came to ask you to prepare her for a marriage with Lothario."

Jarno saw the shock which he had given his friends: they cast their eyes upon the ground. "The present case," said he, "is one of those which are worse to bear in company. What each has to consider in it, he considers best in solitude: I, at least, require an hour of leave." He hastened to the garden: Wilhelm followed him mechanically, yet without approaching near.

At the end of an hour they were again assembled. Wilhelm opened the conversation. "Formerly," said he, "while I was living without plan or object, in a state of carelessness, or, I may say, of levity, friendship, love, affection, trust, came towards me with open arms, they pressed themselves upon me; but now, when I am serious, destiny appears to take another course with me. This resolution, of soliciting Theresa's hand, is probably the first that has proceeded altogether from myself. I laid my plan considerately; my reason fully joined in it: by the consent of that noble maiden, all my hopes were crowned. But now the strangest fate puts back my outstretched hand: Theresa reaches hers to me, but from afar, as in a dream; I cannot grasp it, and the lovely image leaves me forever. So fare thee well, thou lovely image! and all ye images of richest happiness that gathered round it!"

He was silent for a moment, looking out before him: Jarno was about to speak. "Let me have another word," cried Wilhelm, "for the lot is drawing which is to decide the destiny of all my life. At this moment, I am aided and confirmed by the impression which Lothario's presence made upon me at the first glance, and which has ever since continued with me. That man well merits every sort of friendship and affection; and, without sacrifices, friendship cannot be imagined. For his sake, it was easy for me to delude a hapless girl; for his sake, it shall be possible for me to give away the worthiest bride. Return, relate the strange occurrence to him, and tell him what I am prepared for."

"In emergencies like this," said Jarno, "I hold that every thing is done, if one do nothing rashly. Let us take no step till Lothario has agreed to it. I will go to him: wait patiently for my return or for his letter."

He rode away, and left his friends in great disquiet. They had time to reconsider these events, to think of them maturely. It now first occurred to them, that they had taken Jarno's statement simply by itself, and without inquiring into any of the circumstances. Wilhelm was not altogether free from doubts; but next day their astonishment, nay, their bewilderment, arose still higher, when a messenger, arriving from Theresa, brought the following letter to Natalia.

"Strange as it may seem, after all the letters I have sent, I am obliged to send another, begging that thou wouldst despatch my bridegroom to me instantly. He shall be my husband, what plans soever they may lay to rob me of him. Give him the enclosed letter, only not before witnesses, whoever they may be!"

The enclosed letter was as follows: "What opinion will you form of your Theresa, when you see her all at once insisting passionately on a union which calm reason alone appeared to have appointed? Let nothing hinder you from setting out the moment you have read this letter. Come, my dear, dear friend; now three times dearer, since they are attempting to deprive me of you."

"What is to be done?" cried Wilhelm, after he had read the letter.

"In no case that I remember," said Natalia, after some reflection, "have my heart and judgment been so dumb as in this: what to do or to advise I know not."

"Can it be," cried Wilhelm vehemently, "that Lothario does not know of it? or, if he does, that he is but like us, the sport of hidden plans? Has Jarno, when he saw our letter, devised that fable on the spot? Would he have told us something different, if we had not been so precipitate? What can they mean? What intentions can they have? What plan can Theresa mean? Yes, it must be owned, Lothario is begirt with secret influences and combinations: I myself have found that they are active, that they take a certain charge of the proceedings, of the destiny, of several people, and contrive to guide them. The ulterior objects of these mysteries I know not; but their nearest purpose, that of snatching my Theresa from me, I perceive but too distinctly. On the one hand, this prospect of Lothario's happiness, which they exhibit to me, may be but a hollow show: on the other hand, I see my dear, my honored bride inviting me to her affection. What shall I do? What shall I forbear?"

"A little patience!" said Natalia: "a little time for thought. In these singular perplexities I know but this, that what can never be recalled should not be done in haste. To a fable, to an artful plan, we have steadfastness and prudence to oppose: whether Jarno has been speaking true or false must soon appear. If my brother has actually hopes of a union with Theresa, it were hard to cut him off forever from that prospect at the moment when it seems so kindly inviting him. Let us wait at least till we discover whether he himself knows any thing of it, whether he believes and hopes."

These prudent counsels were confirmed by a letter from Lothario. "I do not send Jarno," he wrote: "a line from my hand is more to thee than the minutest narrative in the mouth of a messenger. I am certain Theresa is not the daughter of her reputed mother; and I cannot renounce hope of being hers, till she, too, is persuaded, and can then decide between my friend and me, with calm consideration. Let him not leave thee, I entreat it! The happiness, the life, of a brother is at stake. I promise thee, this uncertainty shall not be long."

"You see how the matter stands," said she to Wilhelm, with a friendly air: "give me your word of honor that you will not leave the house!"

"I give it!" cried he, stretching out his hand: "I will not leave this house against your will. I thank Heaven, and my better Genius, that on this occasion I am led, and led by you."

Natalia wrote Theresa an account of every thing, declaring that she would not let her friend away. She sent Lothario's letter also.

Theresa answered, "I wondered not a little that Lothario is himself convinced: to his sister he would not feign to this extent. I am vexed, greatly vexed. It is better that I say no more. But I will come to thee, so soon as I have got poor Lydia settled: they are treating her cruelly. I fear we are all betrayed, and shall be so betrayed that we shall never reach the truth. If my friend were of my opinion, he would give thee the slip after all, and throw himself into the arms of his Theresa, whom none shall take away from him. But I, as I dread, shall lose him, and not regain Lothario. From the latter they are taking Lydia by showing him, afar off, the prospect of obtaining me. I will say no more: the entanglement will grow still deeper. Whether, in the mean time, these delightful positions in which we stand to each other may not be so pushed awry, so undermined and broken down, that, when the darkness passes off, the mischief can no longer admit of remedy, time will show. If my friend do not break away, in a few days I myself will come and seek him out beside thee, and hold him fast. Thou marvellest how this passion can have gained the mastery of thy Theresa. It is no passion, but conviction: it is a belief, that, since Lothario can never be mine, this new friend will make me happy. Tell him so, in the name of the little boy that sat with him underneath the oak, and thanked him for his sympathy. Tell it him in the name of

Theresa, who met his offers with a hearty openness. My first dream of living with Lothario has wandered far away from my soul: the dream of living with my other friend is yet wholly present to me. Do they hold me so light as to think that it were easy to exchange the former with the latter?"

"I depend on you," said Natalia to Wilhelm, handing him the letter: "you will not leave me. Consider that the comfort of my life is in your hands. My being is so intimately bound and interwoven with my brother's, that he feels no sorrow which I do not feel, no joy which does not likewise gladden me. Nay, I may truly say, through him alone I have experienced that the heart can be affected and exalted; that in the world there may be joy, love, and an emotion which contents the soul beyond its utmost want."

She stopped: Wilhelm took her hand, and cried, "Oh, continue! This is the time for a true, mutual disclosure of our thoughts: it never was more necessary for us to be well acquainted with each other."

"Yes, my friend!" said she, smiling, with her quiet, soft, indescribable dignity: "perhaps it is not out of season, if I tell you that the whole of what so many books, of what the world, holds up to us and names love, has always seemed to me a fable."

"You have never loved?" cried Wilhelm.

"Never or always!" said Natalia.

CHAPTER FIVE

During this conversation they kept walking up and down the garden; and Natalia gathered various flowers of singular forms, entirely unknown to Wilhelm, who began to ask their names, and occupy himself about them.

"You know not," said Natalia, "for whom I have been plucking these? I intend them for my uncle, whom we are to visit. The sun is

shining even now so bright on the Hall of the Past, I must lead you in
this moment; and I never go to it without a few of the flowers which my
uncle liked particularly, in my hand. He was a peculiar man, susceptible of very strange impressions. For certain plants and animals, for
certain neighborhoods and persons, nay, for certain sorts of minerals,
he had an especial love, which he was rarely able to explain. 'Had I
not,' he would often say, 'from youth, withstood myself, and striven
to form my judgment upon wide and general principles, I had been the
narrowest and most intolerable person living. For nothing can be more
intolerable than circumscribed peculiarity, in one from whom a pure
and suitable activity might be required.' And yet he was obliged to
confess that life and breath would, as it were, leave him, if he did not
now and then indulge himself, not from time to time allow himself a
brief and passionate enjoyment of what he could not always praise and
justify. 'It is not my fault,' said he, 'if I have not brought my inclinations and my reason into perfect harmony.' On such occasions he
would joke with me, and say, 'Natalia may be looked upon as happy
while she lives: her nature asks nothing which the world does not wish
and use.' "

So speaking, they arrived again at the house. Natalia led him
through a spacious passage to a door, before which lay two granite
sphinxes. The door itself was in the Egyptian fashion, somewhat narrower above than below; and its brazen leaves prepared one for a
serious or even a gloomy feeling. Wilhelm was, in consequence, agreeably surprised, when his expectation issued in a sentiment of pure,
cheerful serenity, as he entered a hall where art and life took away all
recollection of death and the grave. In the walls all round, a series of
proportionable arches had been hollowed out, and large sarcophaguses
stood in them: among the pillars in the intervals between them smaller
openings might be seen, adorned with urns and similar vessels. The
remaining spaces of the walls and vaulted roof were regularly divided;
and between bright and variegated borders, within garlands and other
ornaments, a multitude of cheerful and significant figures had been
painted upon grounds of different sizes. The body of the edifice was
covered with that fine, yellow marble, which passes into reddish:
clear blue stripes of a chemical substance, happily imitating azure
stone, while they satisfied the eye with contrast, gave unity and com-

Wilhelm and Natalia in the Hall of the Past

bination to the whole. All this pomp and decoration showed itself in the chastest architectural forms: and thus every one who entered felt as if exalted above himself; while the co-operating products of art, for the first time, taught him what man is and what he may become.

Opposite the door, on a stately sarcophagus, lay a marble figure of a noble-looking man, reclined upon a pillow. He held a roll before him, and seemed to look at it with still attention. It was placed so that you could read with ease the words which stood there: *Think of living.*

Natalia took away a withered bunch of flowers, and laid the fresh one down before the figure of her uncle. For it was her uncle whom the marble represented. Wilhelm thought he recognized the features of the venerable gentleman whom he had seen when lying wounded in the green of the forest. "Here he and I passed many an hour," said Natalia, "while the hall was getting ready. In his latter years, he had gathered several skilful artists round him; and his chief delight was to invent or superintend the drawings and cartoons for these pictures."

Wilhelm could not satisfy himself with looking at the objects which surrounded him. "What a life," exclaimed he, "in this Hall of the Past! One might with equal justice name it Hall of the Present and the Future. Such all were, such all will be. There is nothing transitory but the individual who looks at and enjoys it. Here, this figure of the mother pressing her infant to her bosom will survive many generations of happy mothers. Centuries hence, perhaps some father will take pleasure in contemplating this bearded man, who has laid aside his seriousness, and is playing with his son. Thus shame-faced will the bride sit for ages, and, amid her silent wishes, need that she be comforted, that she be spoken to; thus impatient will the bridegroom listen on the threshold whether he may enter."

The figures Wilhelm was surveying with such rapture were of almost boundless number and variety. From the first jocund impulse of the child, merely to employ its every limb in sport, up to the peaceful, sequestered earnestness of the sage, you might, in fair and living order, see delineated how man possesses no capacity or tendency without employing and enjoying it. From the first soft, conscious feeling, when the maiden lingers in pulling up her pitcher, and looks with satisfaction at her image in the clear fountain, to those high solemnities when kings and nations invoke the gods at the altar to witness their alliances, all was depicted, all was forcible and full of meaning.

It was a world, it was a heaven, that in this abode surrounded the spectator; and beside the thoughts which those polished forms suggested, beside the feelings they awoke, there still seemed something further to be present, something by which the whole man felt himself laid hold of. Wilhelm, too, observed this, though unable to account for it. "What is this," exclaimed he, "which independently of all signification, without any sympathy that human incidents and fortunes may inspire us with, acts on me so strongly and so gracefully? It speaks to me from the whole, it speaks from every part; though I have not fully understood the former, though I do not specially apply the latter to myself. What enchantment breathes from these surfaces, these lines, these heights and breadths, these masses and colors! What is it that makes these figures so delightful, even when slightly viewed, and merely in the light of decorations? Yes, I feel it: one might tarry here, might rest, might view the whole, and be happy; and yet feel and think something altogether different from aught that stood before his eyes."

And certainly, if we were able to describe how happily the whole was subdivided, how every thing determined by its place, by combination or by contrast, by uniformity or by variety, appeared exactly as it should have done, producing an effect as perfect as distinct, we should transport the reader to a scene from which he would not be in haste to stir.

Four large marble candelabras rose in the corners of the hall: four smaller ones were in the midst of it, around a very beautifully worked sarcophagus, which, judging from its size, might once have held a young person of middle stature.

Natalia paused beside this monument: she laid her hand upon it as she said, "My worthy uncle had a great attachment to this fine antique. 'It is not,' he would often say, 'the first blossoms alone that drop; such you can keep above, in these little spaces; but fruits also, which, hanging on their twigs, long give us the fairest hope, whilst a secret worm is preparing their too early ripeness and their quick decay.' I fear," continued she, "his words have been prophetic of that dear little girl, who seems withdrawing gradually from our cares, and bending to this peaceful dwelling."

As they were about to go, Natalia stopped, and said, "There is something still which merits your attention. Observe these half-round openings aloft on both sides. Here the choir can stand concealed while singing: these iron ornaments below the cornice serve for fastening on the tapestry, which, by order of my uncle, must be hung round at every burial. Music, particularly song, was a pleasure he could not live without; and it was one of his peculiarities, that he wished the singer not to be in view. 'In this respect,' he would say, 'they spoil us at the theatre: the music there is, as it were, subservient to the eye; it accompanies movements, not emotions. In oratorios and concerts, the form of the musician constantly disturbs us; true music is intended for the ear alone: a fine voice is the most universal thing that can be figured; and, while the narrow individual that uses it presents himself before the eye, he cannot fail to trouble the effect of that pure universality. The person whom I am to speak with, I must see; because it is a solitary man, whose form and character give worth or worthlessness to what he says: but, on the other hand, whoever sings to me must be invisible; his form must not confuse me, or corrupt my judgment. Here it is but one human organ speaking to another: it is not spirit speaking to spirit, not a thousand-fold world to the eye, not a heaven to the man.' On the same principles, in respect of instrumental music, he required that the orchestra should as much as possible be hid; because, by the mechanical exertions, by the mean and awkward gestures of the performers, our feelings are so much dispersed and perplexed. Accordingly, he always used to shut his eyes while hearing music; thereby to concentrate his whole being on the single pure enjoyment of the ear."

They were about to leave the hall, when they heard the children running hastily along the passage, and Felix crying, "No, I! No, I!"

Mignon rushed in at the open door: she was foremost, but out of breath, and could not speak a word. Felix, still at some distance, shouted out, "Mamma Theresa is come!" The children had run a race, as it seemed, to bring the news. Mignon was lying in Natalia's arms: her heart was beating vehemently.

"Naughty child," said Natalia, "art thou not forbidden to make violent exertions? See how thy heart is beating!"

"Let it break!" said Mignon with a deep sigh: "it has beat too long."

They had scarcely composed themselves from this surprise, this sort of consternation, when Theresa entered. She flew to Natalia, clasped her and Mignon in her arms. Then, turning round to Wilhelm, she looked at him with her clear eyes, and said "Well, my friend, how is it with you? You have not let them cheat you?" He made a step towards her: she sprang to him, and hung upon his neck. "O my Theresa!" cried he.

"My friend, my love, my husband! Yes, forever thine!" cried she, amid the warmest kisses.

Felix pulled her by the gown, and cried, "Mamma Theresa, I am here too!" Natalia stood, and looked before her: Mignon on a sudden clapped her left hand on her heart, and, stretching out the right arm violently, fell with a shriek at Natalia's feet, as dead.

The fright was great: no motion of the heart or pulse was to be traced. Wilhelm took her on his arm, and hastily carried her away: the body hung lax over his shoulders. The presence of the doctor was of small avail: he and the young surgeon, whom we know already, strove in vain. The dear little creature could not be recalled to life.

Natalia beckoned to Theresa: the latter took her friend by the hand, and led him from the room. He was dumb, not uttering a word: he durst not meet her eyes. He sat down with her upon the sofa, where he had first found Natalia. He thought with great rapidity along a series of fateful incidents, or, rather, he did not think, but let his soul be worked on by the thoughts which would not leave it. There are moments in life when past events, like winged shuttles, dart to and fro before us, and by their incessant movements weave a web which we ourselves, in a greater or less degree, have spun and put upon the loom. "My friend, my love!" said Theresa, breaking silence, as she took him by the hand, "let us stand together firmly in this hour, as we perhaps shall often have to do in similar hours. These are occurrences which it takes two united hearts to suffer. Think, my friend, feel, that thou art not alone: show that thou lovest thy Theresa by imparting thy sorrows to her!" She embraced him, and drew him softly to her bosom: he clasped her in his arms, and pressed her strongly towards him. "The poor child," cried he, "used in mournful moments to seek shelter and protection in my unstable bosom: let the stability of thine assist me in this heavy hour." They held each other fast; he felt her heart beat against his breast; but in his spirit all was desolate and void: only the figures of Mignon and Natalia flitted like shadows across the waste of his imagination.

Natalia entered. "Give us thy blessing!" cried Theresa: "let us, in this melancholy moment, be united before thee!" Wilhelm had hid his face upon Theresa's neck: he was so far relieved that he could weep. He did not hear Natalia come; he did not see her; but, at the sound of her voice, his tears redoubled. "What God has joined I will not part," she answered, smiling, "but to unite you is not in my power: nor am I gratified to see that sorrow and sympathy seem altogether to have banished from your hearts the recollection of my brother." At these words, Wilhelm started from Theresa's arms. "Whither are you going?" cried the ladies. "Let me see the child," said he, "whom I have killed! Misfortune, when we look upon it with our eyes, is smaller than when our imagination sinks the evil down into the recesses of the soul. Let us view the departed angel! Her serene countenance will say to us that it is well with her." As his friends could not restrain the agitated youth, they followed him; but the worthy doctor with the surgeon met them, and prevented them from coming near the dead. "Keep away from this mournful object," said he, "and allow me, so far as I am able, to give some continuance to these remains. On this dear and singular being I will now display the beautiful art, not only of embalming bodies, but of retaining in them a look of life. As I foresaw her death, the preparations are already made: with these helps I shall undoubtedly succeed. Give me but a few days, and ask not to see the child again till I have brought her to the Hall of the Past."

The young surgeon had in his hands that well-known case of instruments. "From whom can he have got it?" Wilhelm asked the doctor. "I know it very well," replied Natalia: "he has it from his father, who dressed your wounds when we found you in the forest."

"Then, I have not been mistaken! I recognized the band at once!" cried Wilhelm. "Oh, get it for me! It was this that first gave me any hint of my unknown benefactress. What weal and woe will such a thing survive! Beside how many sorrows has this band already been, and its threads still hold together! How many men's last moments has it witnessed, and its colors are not yet faded! It was near me in one of the fairest hours of my existence, when I lay wounded on the ground, and your helpful form appeared before me, and the child whom we are now lamenting sat with its bloody hair, busied with the tenderest care to save my life!"

It was not long that our friends could converse about this sad occurrence, that Theresa could inquire about the child, and the probable cause of its unexpected death; for strangers were announced, who, on making their appearance, proved to be well-known strangers. Lothario, Jarno, and the abbé entered. Natalia met her brother: among the rest there was a momentary silence. Theresa, smiling on Lothario, said, "You scarcely expected to find me here: of course, it would not have been advisable that we should visit one another at the present time: however, after such an absence, take my cordial welcome."

Lothario took her hand, and answered, "If we are to suffer and renounce, it may as well take place in the presence of the object whom we love and wish for. I desire no influence on your determination: my confidence in your heart, in your understanding, and clear sense, is still so great, that I willingly commit to your disposal my fate and that of my friend."

The conversation turned immediately to general, nay, we may say, to trivial topics. The company soon separated into single pairs, for walking. Natalia was with her brother, Theresa with the abbé: our friend was left with Jarno in the castle.

The appearance of the guests at the moment when a heavy sorrow was oppressing Wilhelm had, instead of dissipating his attention, irritated him, and made him worse: he was fretful and suspicious, and unable or uncareful to conceal it, when Jarno questioned him about his sulky silence. "What is the use of saying more?" cried Wilhelm. "Lothario with his helpers is come; and it were strange if those mysterious watchmen of the tower, who are constantly so busy, did not now exert their influence on us, to effect I know not what strange purpose. So far as I have known these saintly gentlemen, it seems to be in every case their laudable endeavor to separate the united and to unite the separated. What sort of web their weaving will produce may probably to unholy eyes be forever a riddle."

"You are cross and bitter," said the other: "that is as it should be. Would you get into a proper passion, it were still better."

"That, too, might come about," said Wilhelm: "I fear much some of you are in the mind to load my patience, natural and acquired, beyond what it will bear."

"In the meantime," said the other, "till we see what *is* to be the issue of the matter, I could like to tell you somewhat of the tower which you appear to view with such mistrust."

"It stands with you," said Wilhelm, "whether you will risk your eloquence on an attention so distracted. My mind is so engaged at present, that I know not whether I can take a proper interest in these very dignified adventures."

"Your pleasing humor shall not hinder me," said Jarno, "from explaining this affair to you. You reckon me a clever fellow; I want to make you reckon me an honest one: and, what is more, on this occasion I am bidden speak." — "I could wish," said Wilhelm, "that you did it of yourself, and with an honest purpose to inform me; but, as I cannot hear without suspicion, wherefore should I hear at all?" — "If I have nothing better to do," said Jarno, "than tell you stories, you, too, have time to listen to me; and to this you may perhaps feel more inclined, when I assure you, that all you saw in the tower was but the relics of a youthful undertaking, in regard to which the greater part of the initiated were once in deep earnest, though all of them now view it with a smile."

"So, with these pompous signs and words, you do but mock?" cried Wilhelm. "With a solemn air, you lead us to a place inspiring reverence by its aspect; you make the strangest visions pass before us; you give us rolls full of glorious mystic apothegms, of which, in truth, we understand but little; you disclose to us, that hitherto we have been pupils; you solemnly pronounce us free; and we are just as wise as we were." — "Have you not the parchment by you?" said the other. "It contains a deal of sense: those general apothegms were not picked at random, though they seem obscure and empty to a man without experience to recollect while reading them. But give me the Indenture, as we call it, if it is at hand." — "Quite at hand," cried Wilhelm: "such an amulet well merits being worn upon one's breast." — "Well," said Jarno, smiling, "who knows whether the contents of it may not one day find place in your head and heart?"

He opened the roll, and glanced over the first half of it. "This," said he, "regards the cultivation of our gifts for art and science, of which let others speak: the second treats of life; here I am more at home."

He then began to read passages, speaking between whiles, and connecting them with his remarks and narrative. "The taste of youth for secrecy, for ceremonies, for imposing words, is extraordinary, and frequently bespeaks a certain depth of character. In those years we wish to feel our whole nature seized and moved, even though it be but vaguely and darkly. The youth who happens to have lofty aspirations and forecastings thinks that secrets yield him much, that he must depend much on secrets, and effect much by means of them. It was with such views that the abbé favored a certain society of young men, partly according to his principle of aiding every tendency of nature, partly out of habit and inclination; for in former times he had himself been joined to an association which appears to have accomplished many things in secret. For this business I was least of all adapted. I was older than the rest; from youth I had thought clearly; I wished in all things nothing more than clearness; I felt no interest in men but to know them as they were. With the same taste I gradually infected all the best of our associates, and this circumstance had almost given a false direction to our plan of culture. For we now began to look at nothing but the errors and the narrowness of others, and to think ourselves a set of highly gifted personages. Here the abbé came to our assistance: he taught us that we never should inspect the conduct of men, unless we at the same time took an interest in improving it; and that through action only could we ever be in a condition to inspect and watch ourselves. He advised us, however, to retain the primary forms of the society: hence there was still a sort of law in our proceedings; the first mystic impressions might be traced in the constitution of the whole. At length, as by a practical similitude, it took the form of a corporate trade, whose business was the arts. Hence came the names of apprentices, assistants, and masters. We wished to see with our own eyes, and to form for ourselves, a special record of our own experience in the world. Hence those numerous confessions which in part we ourselves wrote, in part made others write, and out of which the several *Apprenticeships* were afterwards compiled. The formation of his character is not the chief concern with every man. Many merely wished to find a sort of recipe for comfort, directions for acquiring riches, or whatever good they aim at. All such, when they would not be instructed in their proper duties, we were wont to mystify, to treat with juggleries, and every sort of hocus-pocus, and at length to shove aside. We advanced none to the rank of masters, but such as clearly felt and recognized the purpose they were born for, and had got enough of practice to proceed along their way with a certain cheerfulness and ease."

"In my case, then," cried Wilhelm, "your ceremony has been very premature; for, since the day when you pronounced me free, what I can, will, or shall do has been more unknown to me than ever." — "We are not to blame for this perplexity: perhaps good fortune will deliver us. In the mean time, listen: 'He in whom there is much to be developed will be later in acquiring true perceptions of himself and of the world. There are few who at once have Thought and the capacity of Action. Thought expands, but lames: Action animates, but narrows.' "

"I beg of you," cried Wilhelm, "not to read me any more of that surprising stuff. These phrases have sufficiently confused me before." — "I will stick by my story, then," said Jarno, half rolling up the parchment, into which, however, he kept casting frequent glances. "I myself have been of less service to the cause of our society, and of my fellow-men, than any other member. I am but a bad school-master: I cannot bear to look on people making awkward trials; when I see a person wander from his path, I feel constrained to call him, although it were a night-walker going straight to break his neck. On this point I had a continual struggle with the abbé, who maintains that error can never be cured, except by erring. About you, too, we often argued. He had taken an especial liking to you, and it is saying something to have caught so much of his attention. For me, you must admit, that every time we met I told you just the naked truth." — "Certainly, you spared me very little," said the other; "and I think you still continue faithful to your principles." — "What is the use of sparing," answered

Jarno, "when a young man of many good endowments is taking a quite false direction?" — "Pardon me," said Wilhelm: "you have rigorously enough denied me any talent for the stage; I confess to you, though I have entirely renounced the art, I cannot think myself entirely incapable." — "And with me," said Jarno, "it is well enough decided, that a person who can only play himself is no player. Whoever cannot change himself, in temper and in form, into many forms, does not deserve the name. Thus you, for example, acted Hamlet, and some other characters, extremely well; because, in these, your form, your disposition, and the temper of the moment, suited. For an amateur theatre, for any one who saw no other way before him, this would, perhaps, have answered well enough. But," continued Jarno, looking on the roll, " 'we should guard against a talent which we cannot hope to practise in perfection. Improve it as we may, we shall always, in the end, when the merit of the master has become apparent to us, painfully lament the loss of time and strength devoted to such botching.' "

"Do not read!" cried Wilhelm: "I entreat you earnestly, speak on, tell, inform me! So, the abbé aided me in Hamlet: he provided me a Ghost?" — "Yes; for he asserted that it was the only way of curing you, if you were curable." — "And on this account he left the veil, and bade me flee?" — "Yes: he hoped, that, having fairly acted Hamlet, your desire of acting would be satiated. He maintained that you would never go upon the stage again: I believed the contrary, and I was right. We argued on the subject that very evening, when the play was over." — "You saw me act, then?" — "I did indeed." — "And who was it that played the Ghost?" — "That I cannot tell you: either the abbé or his twin-brother; but I think the latter, for he is a little taller." — "You, then, have secrets from each other?" — "Friends may and must *have* secrets from, but they *are* not secrets to, each other."

"The very thought of that perplexity perplexes me. Let me understand the man to whom I owe so many thanks as well as such reproaches."

"What gives him such a value in our estimation," answered Jarno, "what, in some degree, secures him the dominion over all of us, is the free, sharp eye that nature has bestowed on him, for all the powers which dwell in man, and are susceptible of cultivation, each according to its kind. Most men, even the most accomplished, are but limited: each prizes certain properties in others and himself; these alone he favors, these alone will he have cultivated. Directly the reverse is the procedure of our abbé: for every gift he has a feeling; every gift he delights to recognize and forward. But I must look into my roll again! 'It is all men that make up mankind, all powers taken together that make up the world. These are frequently at variance; and, as they endeavor to destroy each other, Nature holds them together, and again produces them. From the first animal tendency to handicraft attempts, up to the highest practising of intellectual art; from the inarticulate crowings of the happy infant, up to the polished utterance of the orator and singer; from the first bickerings of boys, up to the vast equipments by which countries are conquered and retained; from the slightest kindliness, and the most transitory love, up to the fiercest passion, and the most earnest covenant; from the merest perception of sensible presence, up to the faintest presentiments and hopes of the remotest spiritual future, — all this, and much more also, lies in man, and man must be cultivated, yet not in one, but in many. Every gift is valuable, and ought to be unfolded. When one encourages the beautiful alone, and another encourages the useful alone, it takes them both to form a man. The useful encourages itself; for the multitude produce it, and no one can dispense with it: the beautiful must be encouraged; for few can set it forth, and many need it.' "

"Hold! Hold!" cried Wilhelm: "I have read it all." — "Yet a line or two!" said Jarno. "Here is our worthy abbé to a hair's-breadth: 'One power rules another, none can cultivate another: in each endowment, and not elsewhere, lies the force which must complete it; this many people do not understand, who yet attempt to teach and influence.' " — "Nor do I understand it," answered Wilhelm. — "You will often hear the abbé preach on this text; and, therefore, 'Let us merely keep a clear and steady eye on what is in ourselves, on what endowments of our own we mean to cultivate: let us be just to others, for we ourselves are only to be valued in so far as we can value.' " — "For Heaven's sake, no more of these wise saws! I feel them to be but a sorry balsam for a wounded heart. Tell me, rather, with your cruel settledness, what you expect of me, how, and in what manner, you intend to sacrifice me." — "For every such suspicion, I assure you, you will afterwards beg our pardon. It is your affair to try and choose: it is ours to aid you. A man is never happy till his vague striving has itself marked out its proper limitation. It is not to me that you must look, but to the abbé: it is not of yourself that you must think, but of what surrounds you. Thus, for instance, learn to understand Lothario's superiority; how his quick and comprehensive vision is inseparably united with activity; how he constantly advances; how he expands his influence, and carries every one along with him. Wherever he may be, he bears a world about with him: his presence animates and kindles. Observe our good physician, on the other hand. His nature seems to be directly the reverse. If the former only works upon the general whole, and at a distance, the latter turns his piercing eye upon the things that are beside him: he rather furnishes the means for being active, than himself displays or stimulates activity. His conduct is exactly like the conduct of a good domestic manager: he is busied silently, while he provides for each in his peculiar sphere; his knowledge is a constant gathering and expanding, a taking in and giving out on a small scale. Perhaps Lothario in a single day might overturn what the other had for years been employed in building up; but perhaps Lothario also might impart to others, in a moment, strength sufficient to restore a hundred-fold what he had overturned." — "It is but a sad employment," answered Wilhelm, "to contemplate the sublime advantages of others, at a moment when we are at variance with ourselves. Such contemplations suit the man at ease, not him whom passion and uncertainty are agitating." — "Peacefully and reasonably to contemplate is at no time hurtful," answered Jarno: "and, while we use ourselves to think of the advantages of others, our own mind comes insensibly to imitate them; and every false activity, to which our fancy was alluring us, is then willingly abandoned. Free your mind, if you can, from all suspicion and anxiety. Here comes the abbé: be courteous towards him, till you have learned still further what you owe him. The rogue! There he goes between Natalia and Theresa: I could bet he is contriving something. As in general he rather likes to act the part of Destiny; so he does not fail to show a taste for making matches when he finds an opportunity."

Wilhelm, whose angry and fretful humor all the placid, prudent words of Jarno had not bettered, thought his friend exceedingly indelicate for mentioning marriage at a moment like the present: he answered, with a smile indeed, but a rather bitter one, "I thought the taste for making matches had been left to those that had a taste for one another."

CHAPTER SIX

THE COMPANY had met again: the conversation of our friends was necessarily interrupted. Erelong a courier was announced, as wishing to deliver with his own hand a letter to Lothario. The man was introduced: he had a vigorous, sufficient look; his livery was rich and hand-some. Wilhelm thought he knew him, nor was he mistaken; for it was the man whom he had sent to seek Philina and the fancied Mariana, and who never came back. Our friend was about to address him, when Lothario, who had read the letter, asked the courier with a serious, almost angry, tone, "What is your master's name?"

"Of all questions," said the other, with a prudent air, "this is the one which I am least prepared to answer. I hope the letter will communicate the necessary information: verbally I have been charged with nothing."

"Be it as it will," replied Lothario with a smile: "since your master puts such trust in me as to indite a letter so exceedingly facetious, he shall be welcome to us." — "He will not keep you long waiting for him," said the courier, with a bow, and withdrew.

"Do but hear the distracted, stupid message," said Lothario. " 'As of all guests, Good Humor is believed to be the most agreeable where he appears, and as I always keep that gentleman beside me by way of travelling companion, I feel·persuaded that the visit I intend to pay your noble lordship will not be taken ill: on the contrary, I hope the whole of your illustrious family will witness my arrival with complete satisfaction, and in due time also my departure; being always, *et cœtera*, Count of Snailfoot.' "

" 'Tis a new family," said the abbé.

"A vicariat count, perhaps," said Jarno.

"The secret is easy to unriddle," said Natalia: "I wager it is none but brother Friedrich, who has threatened us with a visit ever since my uncle's death."

"Right, fair and skilful sister!" cried a voice from the nearest thicket; and immediately a pleasant, cheerful youth stepped forward. Wilhelm could scarcely restrain a cry of wonder. "What!" exclaimed he: "does our fair-haired knave, too, meet me here?" Friedrich looked attentively, and, recognizing Wilhelm, cried, "In truth, it would not have astonished me so much to have beheld the famous pyramids, which still stand fast in Egypt, or the grave of King Mausolus, which, as I am told, does not exist, here placed before me in my uncle's garden, as to find you in it, my old friend, and frequent benefactor. Accept my best and heartiest service!"

After he had kissed and complimented the whole circle he again sprang towards Wilhelm, crying, "Use him well, this hero, this leader of armies, and dramatical philosopher! When we became acquainted first, I dressed his hair indifferently, I may say execrably; yet he after-

wards saved me from a pretty load of blows. He is magnanimous as
Scipio, munificent as Alexander: at times he is in love, yet he never
hates his rivals. Far from heaping coals of fire on the heads of his enemies, — a piece of service, I am told, which we can do for any one, —
he rather, when his friends have carried off his love, despatches good
and trusty servants after them, that they may not strike their feet
against a stone."

In the same style he ran along with a volubility which baffled all
attempts to restrain it; and, as no one could reply to him in that vein,
he had the conversation mostly to himself. "Do not wonder," cried
he, "that I am so profoundly versed in sacred and profane writers: you
shall hear by and by how I attained my learning." They wished to
know how matters stood with him, — where he had been; but crowds
of proverbs and old stories choked his explanation.

Natalia whispered to Theresa, "His gayety afflicts me: I am sure
at heart he is not merry."

As, except a few jokes which Jarno answered, Friedrich's merriment was met by no response from those about him, he was obliged at
last to say, 'Well, there is nothing left for me, but, among so many
grave faces, to be grave myself. And as, in such a solemn scene, the
burden of my sins falls heavy on my soul, I must honestly resolve upon
a general confession; for which, however, you, my worthy gentlemen
and ladies, shall not be a jot the wiser. This honorable friend already
knows a little of my walk and conversation; he alone shall know the
rest; and this the rather, as he alone has any cause to ask about it. Are
not you," continued he to Wilhelm, "curious about the how and where,
the when and wherefore? And how it stands with the conjugation of
the Greek verb φιλέω, φιλῶ, and the derivatives of that very amiable
part of speech?"

He then took Wilhelm by the arm, and led him off, pressing him
and skipping round him with the liveliest air of kindness.

Scarcely had they entered Wilhelm's room, when Friedrich noticed, in the window, a powder-knife, with the inscription, *Think of
me.* "You keep your valuables well laid up!" said he. "This is the
powder-knife Philina gave you, when I pulled your locks for you. I
hope, in looking at it, you have diligently thought of that fair damsel;
I assure you, she has not forgotten you: if I had not long ago obliter-

ated every trace of jealousy from my heart, I could not look on you without envy."

"Talk no more of that creature," answered Wilhelm. "I confess it was a while before I could get rid of the impression which her looks and manner made on me, but that was all."

"Fie, Fie!" cried Friedrich. "Would any one deny his deary? You loved her as completely as a man could wish. No day passed without your giving her some present; and, when a German gives, you may be sure he loves. No alternative remained for me but whisking her away from you, and in this the little red officer at last succeeded."

"What! you were the officer whom we discovered with her, whom she travelled off with?"

"Yes," said Friedrich, "whom you took for Mariana. We had sport enough at the mistake."

"What cruelty," cried Wilhelm, "to leave me in such suspense!"

"And, besides, to take the courier, whom you sent to catch us, into pay!" said Friedrich. "He is a very active fellow: we have kept him by us ever since. And the girl herself I love as desperately as ever. She has managed me in some peculiar style: I am almost in a mythologic case; every day I tremble at the thought of being metamorphosed."

"But tell me, pray," said Wilhelm, "where have you acquired this stock of erudition? It surprises me to hear the strange way you have assumed of speaking always with a reference to ancient histories and fables."

"It was by a pleasant plan," said Friedrich, "that I got my learning. Philina lives with me at present: we have got a lease of an old, knightly castle from the farmer in whose ground it is; and there we live, with the hobgoblins of the place, as merrily as possible. In one of the rooms we found a small, but choice, library, consisting of a Bible in folio, 'Gottfried's Chronicle,' two volumes of the 'Theatrum Europæum,' and 'Acerra Philologica,' 'Gryphius' Writings,' and some other less important works. As we now and then, when tired of romping, felt the time hang heavy on our hands, we proposed to read some books; and, before we were aware, the time hung heavier than ever. At last Philina hit upon the royal plan of laying all the tomes, opened at once, upon a large table. We sat down opposite to one another: we read to one another, — always in detached passages, first from this book, then from that. We had a jolly time of it. We felt now as if we were in good society, where it is reckoned unbecoming to dwell on any subject, or search it to the bottom: we thought ourselves in witty, gay society, where none will let his neighbor speak. We regularly treat ourselves with this diversion every day, and the erudition we obtain from it is quite surprising. Already there is nothing new for us under the sun: on every thing we see or hear, our learning offers us a hint. This method of instruction we diversify in many ways. Frequently we read by an old, spoiled sand-glass, which runs in a minute or two. The moment it is down, the silent party turns it round like lightning, and commences reading from his book; and no sooner is it down again, than the other cuts him short, and starts the former topic. Thus we study in a truly academic manner, with this difference, that our hours are shorter, and our studies extremely varied."

"This rioting is quite conceivable," said Wilhelm, "when a pair like you two are together; but how a pair so full of frolic stay together does not seem so easily conceivable."

"It is our good fortune," answered Friedrich, "and our bad. Philina dare not let herself be seen, — she cannot bear to see herself: she is with child. Nothing ever was so ludicrous and shapeless in the world. A little while before I came away, she chanced to cast an eye upon the looking-glass in passing. 'Faugh!' cried she, and turned away her face: 'the living picture of the Frau Melina! Shocking figure! One looks entirely deplorable!'"

"I confess," said Wilhelm, with a smile, "it must be rather farcical to see a father and a mother, such as you and she, together."

"'Tis a foolish business," answered Friedrich, "that I must at last be raised to the paternal dignity. But she asserts, and the time agrees. At first that cursed visit which she paid you after 'Hamlet' gave me qualms."

"What visit?"

"I suppose you have not quite slept off the memory of it yet? The pretty, flesh-and-blood spirit of that night, if you do not know it, was Philina. The story was, in truth, a hard dower for me; but, if we cannot be content with such things, we should not be in love. Fatherhood, at any rate, depends entirely upon conviction: I am convinced, and so I am a father. There, you see, I can employ my logic in the proper season too. And, if the brat do not laugh itself to death so soon as it is born, it may prove, if not a useful, at least a pleasant, citizen of this world."

Whilst our friends were talking thus of mirthful subjects, the rest of the party had begun a serious conversation. Scarcely were Friedrich and Wilhelm gone, when the abbé led his friends, as if by chance, into a garden-house, and, having got them seated, thus addressed them: —

"We have in general terms asserted that Fräulein Theresa was not the daughter of her reputed mother: it is fit that we should now explain ourselves on this matter, in detail. I shall relate the story to you, which I undertake to prove and to elucidate in every point.

"Frau von —— spent the first years of her wedlock in the utmost concord with her husband; but they had this misfortune, that the children she brought him came into the world dead: and, on occasion of the third, the mother was declared by the physicians to be on the verge of death, and to be sure of death if she should ever have another. The parties were obliged to take their resolution: they would not break the marriage; it was too suitable to both, in a civil point of view. Frau von —— sought in the culture of her mind, in a certain habit of display, in the joys of vanity, a compensation for the happiness of motherhood, which was refused her. She cheerfully indulged her husband, when she noticed in him an attachment to a young lady, who had sole charge of their household, a person of beautiful exterior, and very solid character. Frau von —— herself, erelong, assisted in procuring an arrangement, by which the lady yielded to the wishes of Theresa's father; continuing to discharge her household duties, and testifying to the mistress of the family, if possible, a more submissive zeal to serve her than before.

"After a while she declared herself with child; and both the father and his wife, on this occasion, though from very different causes, fell upon the same idea. Herr von —— wished to have the offspring of his mistress educated in the house as his lawful child; and Frau von ——, angry that the indiscretion of her doctor had allowed some whisper of her condition to go abroad, proposed by a supposititious child to counteract this, and likewise to retain, by such compliance, the superiority in her household, which otherwise she was like to lose.

However, she was more discreet than her husband: she observed his purpose, and contrived, without any formal question, to facilitate his explanation. She made her own terms, obtaining almost every thing that she required; and hence the will in which so little care was taken of the child. The old doctor was dead: they applied to a young, active, and discreet successor; he was well rewarded; he looked forward to the credit of exposing and remedying the unskilfulness and premature decision of his deceased colleague. The true mother not unwillingly consented: they managed the deception very well; Theresa came into the world, and was surrended to a stepmother, while her mother fell a victim to the plot; having died by venturing out too early, and left the father inconsolable.

"Frau von —— had thus attained her object; in the eyes of the world she had a lovely child, which she paraded with excessive vanity: and she had also been delivered from a rival whose fortune she envied, and whose influence, at least in prospect, she beheld with apprehension. The infant she loaded with her tenderness: and by affecting, in trustful hours, a lively feeling for her husband's loss, she gained a mastery of his heart; so that in a manner he surrendered all to her, laid his own happiness and that of his child in her hands: nor was it till a short while prior to his death, and, in some degree, by the exertions of his grown-up daughter, that he again assumed the rule in his own house. This, fair Theresa, was in all probability the secret which your father, in his last sickness, so struggled to communicate: this is what I wished to lay circumstantially before you, at a moment when our young friend, who by a strange concurrence has become your bridegroom, happens to be absent. Here are the papers which will prove in the most rigorous manner every thing that I have stated. You will also see from them how long I have been following the trace of this discovery; though, till now, I could never attain certainty respecting it. I did not risk imparting to my friend the possibility of such a happiness: it would have wounded him too deeply had this hope a second time deceived him. You will understand poor Lydia's suspicion: I readily confess, I nowise favored our friend's attachment to her, when I began again to look forward to his union with Theresa."

To this recital no one replied. The ladies, some days afterwards, returned the papers, not making any further mention of them.

There were other matters in abundance to engage the party when they were together; and the scenery around was so delightful, that our friends, singly or in company, on horseback, in carriages, or on foot, delighted to explore it. On one of these excursions, Jarno took an opportunity of opening the affair to Wilhelm: he delivered him the papers; not, however, seeming to require from him any resolution in regard to them.

"In this most singular position in which I am," said our friend, "I need only repeat to you what I said at first, in presence of Natalia, and with the clear intention to fulfil it. Lothario and his friends may require of me every sort of self-denial; I here abandon in their favor all pretension to Theresa: do you procure me in return a formal discharge. There requires no great reflection to decide. For some days I have noticed that Theresa has to make an effort in retaining any show of the vivacity with which she welcomed me at first. Her affection is gone from me; or, rather, I have never had it."

"Such affairs are more conveniently explained," said Jarno, "by a gradual process, in silence and expectation, than by many words, which always cause a sort of fermentation and embarrassment."

"I rather think," said Wilhelm, "that precisely this affair admits of the most clear and calm decision on the spot. I have often been reproached with hesitation and uncertainty: why will you now, when I do not hesitate, commit against myself the fault you have often blamed in me? Do people take such trouble with our training only to let us feel that they themselves will not be trained? Yes: grant me soon the cheerful thought that I am out of a mistaken project, into which I entered with the purest feelings in the world."

Notwithstanding this request, some days elapsed without his hearing any more of the affair, or observing any further alteration in his friends. The conversation, on the contrary, was general, and of indifferent matters.

JARNO and Wilhelm were sitting one day by Natalia. "You are thoughtful, Jarno," said the lady: "I have seen it in your looks for some time."

"I am so," answered Jarno: " a weighty business is before me, which we have for years been meditating, and must now begin to execute. You already know the outline of it: I may speak of it before our friend; for it will depend on himself whether he, too, shall not share in it. You are going to get rid of me before long: I mean to take a voyage to America."

"To America?" said Wilhelm, smiling: "such an adventure I did not anticipate from you, still less that you would have selected me for a companion."

"When you rightly understand our plan," said Jarno, "you will give it a more honorable name, and, perhaps, yourself be tempted to embark in it. Listen to me. It requires but a slight acquaintance with the business of the world to see that mighty changes are at hand, that property is almost nowhere quite secure."

"Of the business of the world I have no clear notion," interrupted Wilhelm; "and it is but of late that I ever thought about my property. Perhaps I had done well to drive it out of my head still longer: the care of securing it appears to give us hypochondria."

"Hear me out," said Jarno. "Care beseems ripe age, that youth may live, for a time, free from care: in the conduct of poor mortals, equilibrium cannot be restored except by contraries. As matters go, it is any thing but prudent to have property in only one place, to commit your money to a single spot; and yet it is difficult to guide it well in many. We have, therefore, thought of something else. From our old tower there is a society to issue, which must spread itself through every quarter of the world, and to which members from every quarter of the world shall be admissible. We shall insure a competent subsistence to each other, in the single case of a revolution happening, which might drive any part of us entirely from their possessions. I am now proceeding to America to profit by the good connections which our friend established while he staid there. The abbé means to go to Russia: if you like to join us, you shall have the choice of continuing in Germany to help Lothario, or of accompanying me. I conjecture you will choose the latter: to take a distant journey is extremely serviceable to a young man."

Wilhelm thought a moment, and replied, "The offer well deserves consideration; for erelong the word with me must be, The farther off, the better. You will let me know your plan, I hope, more perfectly. It is, perhaps, my ignorance of life that makes me think so; but such a combination seems to me to be attended with insuperable difficulties."

"The most of which, till now, have been avoided," answered Jarno, "by the circumstance that we have been but few in number, honorable, discreet, determined people, animated by a certain general feeling, out of which alone the feeling proper for societies can spring." — "And if you speak me fair," said Friedrich, who hitherto had only listened, "I, too, will go along with you."

Jarno shook his head.

"Well, what objections can you make?" cried Friedrich. "In a new colony, young colonists will be required; these I bring with me: merry colonists will also be required; of these I make you certain. Besides, I recollect a certain damsel, who is out of place on this side of the water, — the fair, soft-hearted Lydia. What is the poor thing to do with her sorrow and mourning, unless she get an opportunity to throw it to the bottom of the sea, unless some brave fellow take her by the hand? You, my benefactor," said he, turning towards Wilhelm, "you have a taste for comforting forsaken persons: what withholds you now? Each of us might take his girl under his arm, and trudge with Jarno."

This proposal struck Wilhelm offensively. He answered with affected calmness, "I know not whether she is unengaged; and, as in general I seem to be unfortunate in courtship, I shall hardly think of making the attempt."

"Brother Friedrich," said Natalia, "though thy own conduct is so full of levity, it does not follow that such sentiments will answer others. Our friend deserves a heart that shall belong to him alone, that shall not, at his side, be moved by recollections of some previous attachment. It was only with a character as pure and reasonable as Theresa's that such a venture could be risked."

"Risk!" cried Friedrich: "in love it is all risk. In the grove or at the altar, with a clasp of the arms or a golden ring, by the chirping of the cricket or the sound of trumpets and kettle-drums, it is all but a risk: chance does it all."

"I have often noticed," said Natalia, "that our principles are just a supplement to our peculiar manner of existence. We delight to clothe our errors in the garb of universal laws, to attribute them to irresistibly appointed causes. Do but think by what a path thy dear will lead thee, now that she has drawn thee towards her, and holds thee fast there."

"She herself is on a very pretty path," said Friedrich, — "on the path to saintship. A by-path, it is true, and somewhat roundabout, but the pleasanter and surer for that. Maria of Magdala travelled it, and who can say how many more? But, on the whole, sister, when the point in hand is love, thou shouldst not mingle in it. In my opinion, thou wilt never marry, till a bride is lacking somewhere: in that case, thou wilt give thyself, with thy habitual charity, to be the supplement of some peculiar manner of existence, not otherwise. So let us strike a bargain with this soul-broker, and agree about our travelling-company."

"You come too late with your proposals," answered Jarno: "Lydia is disposed of." "And how?" cried Friedrich.

"I myself have offered her my hand," said Jarno.

"Old gentleman," said Friedrich, "you have done a feat to which, if we regard it as a substantive, various adjectives might be appended; various predicates, if we regard it as a subject."

"I must honestly confess," replied Natalia, "it appears a dangerous experiment to make a helpmate of a woman, at the very moment when her love for another man is like to drive her to despair."

"I have ventured," answered Jarno: "under a certain stipulation she is to be mine. And, believe me, there is nothing in the world more precious than a heart susceptible of love and passion. Whether it has loved, whether it still loves, are points which I regard not. The love of which another is the object charms me almost more than that which is directed to myself. I see the strength, the force, of a tender soul; and my self-love does not trouble the delightful vision."

"Have you, then, talked with Lydia of late?" inquired Natalia.

Jarno smiled and nodded: Natalia shook her head, and said as he rose, "I really know not what to make of you; but me you shall not mystify, I promise you."

She was about retiring, when the abbé entered with a letter in his hand. "Stay, if you please," said he to her: "I have a proposal here, respecting which your counsel will be welcome. The marchese, your late uncle's friend, whom for some time we have been expecting, will be here in a day or two. He writes to me, that German is not so familiar to him as he had supposed; that he needs a person who possesses this and other languages, to travel with him; that, as he wishes to connect himself with scientific rather than political society, he cannot do without some such interpreter. I can think of no one better suited for the post than our young friend here. He knows the language, is acquainted with many things beside; and, for himself, it cannot but be advantageous to travel over Germany in such society and such circumstances. Till we have seen our native country, we have no scale to judge of other countries by. What say you, my friend? What say you, Natalia?"

Nobody objected to the scheme: Jarno seemed to think his transatlantic project would not be a hinderance, as he did not mean to sail directly. Natalia did not speak, and Friedrich uttered various saws about the uses of travel.

This new project so provoked our friend, that he could hardly conceal his irritation. He saw in this proposal a concerted plan for getting rid of him as soon as possible; and, what was worse, they went so openly to work, and seemed so utterly regardless of his feelings. The suspicions Lydia had excited in him, all that he himself had witnessed, rose again upon his mind: the simple manner in which every thing had been explained by Jarno now appeared to him another piece of artifice.

He constrained himself, and answered, "At all events, the offer will require mature deliberation."

"A quick decision may, perhaps, be necessary," said the abbé.

"For that I am not prepared," answered Wilhelm. "We can wait till the marchese comes, and then observe if we agree together. One condition must, however, be conceded first of all, — that I take Felix with me."

"This is a condition," said the abbé, "which will scarcely be conceded."

"And I do not see," cried Wilhelm, "why I should let any man prescribe conditions to me, or why, if I choose to view my native country, I must go in company with an Italian."

"Because a young man," said the abbé, with a certain imposing earnestness, "is always called upon to form connections."

Wilhelm, feeling that he could not long retain his self-command, as it was Natalia's presence only which, in some degree, assuaged his indignation, hastily made answer, "Give me a little while to think. I imagine it will not be very hard to settle whether I am called upon to form additional connections; or ordered irresistibly, by heart and head, to free myself from such a multiplicity of bonds, which seem to threaten me with a perpetual, miserable thraldom."

Thus he spoke, with a deeply agitated mind. A glance at Natalia somewhat calmed him: her form and dignity, in this impassioned moment, stamped themselves more deeply on his mind than ever.

"Yes," said he, so soon as he was by himself, "confess it, thou lovest her: thou once more feelest what it means to love with thy whole soul. Thus did I love Mariana, and deceive myself so dreadfully; I loved Philina, and could not help despising her; Aurelia I respected, and could not love; Theresa I reverenced, and paternal tenderness assumed the form of an affection for her. And now, when all the feelings that can make a mortal happy meet within my heart, now am I compelled to flee! Ah! why should these feelings and convictions be combined with an insuperable longing? Why, without the hope of its fulfilment, should they utterly subvert all other happiness? Shall the sun and the world, society or any other gift of fortune, ever henceforth yield me pleasure? Wilt thou not forever say, Natalia is not here? And yet, alas! Natalia will be always present to thee! If thou closest thy eyes, she will appear to thee: if thou openest them, her form will flit before all outward things, like the image which a dazzling object leaves behind it in the eye. Did not the swiftly passing figure of the Amazon dwell continually in thy imagination? And yet thou hadst but seen her, thou didst not know her. Now when thou knowest her, when thou hast been so long beside her, when she has shown such care about thee, — now are her qualities impressed as deeply upon thy soul as her form was then upon thy fancy. It is painful to be always seeking, but far more painful to have found, and to be forced to leave. What now shall I ask for further in the world? What now shall I look for further? Is there a country, a city, that contains a treasure such as this? And I must travel on, and ever find inferiority? Is life, then, like a race-course, where a man must rapidly return when he has reached the utmost end? Does the good, the excellent, stand before us like a firm, unmoving goal, from which, with fleet horses, we are forced away the instant we appeared to have attained it? Happier are they who strive for earthly wares! They find what they are seeking in its proper climate, or they buy it in the fair.

"Come, my darling boy!" cried he to Felix, who now ran frisking towards him: "be thou and remain thou all to me! Thou wert given me as a compensation for thy loved mother; thou wert to replace the second mother whom I meant for thee; and now thou hast a loss still greater to make good. Occupy my heart, occupy my spirit, with thy beauty, thy loveliness, thy capabilities, and thy desire to use them!"

The boy was busied with a new plaything: his father tried to put it in a better state for him; just as he succeeded, Felix had lost all pleasure in it. "Thou art a true son of Adam!" cried Wilhelm. "Come, my child! Come, my brother! let us wander, playing without object, through the world, as we best may."

His resolution to remove, to take the boy along with him, and recreate his mind by looking at the world, had now assumed a settled form. He wrote to Werner for the necessary cash and letters of credit; sending Friedrich's courier on the message, with the strictest charges to return immediately. Much as the conduct of his other friends had grieved him, his relation to Natalia remained serene and clear as ever.

He confided to her his intention. She took it as a settled thing that he would go; and, if this seeming carelessness in her chagrined him, her kindly manner and her presence made him calm. She counselled him to visit various towns, that he might get acquainted with certain of her friends. The courier returned, and brought the letter which our friend required; though Werner did not seem content with this new whim. "My hope that thou wert growing reasonable," so the letter ran, "is now again deferred. Where are you all gadding? And where lingers the lady who thou saidst was to assist us in arranging these affairs?

Thy other friends are also absent. They have thrown the whole concern upon the shoulders of the lawyer and myself. Happy that he is as expert a jurist as I am a financier, and that both of us are used to business. Fare thee well! Thy aberrations shall be pardoned thee, since but for them our situation here could not have been so favorable."

So far as outward matters were concerned, Wilhelm might now have entered on his journey; but there were still for his heart two hinderances that held him fast. In the first place, they flatly refused to show him Mignon's body till the funeral the abbé meant to celebrate; and, for this solemnity, the preparations were not ready. There had also been a curious letter from the country clergyman, in consequence of which the doctor had gone off. It related to the harper, of whose fate Wilhelm wanted to have further information.

In these circumstances, day or night he found no rest for mind or body. When all were asleep, he wandered up and down the house. The presence of the pictures and statues, which he knew so well of old, alternately attracted and repelled him. Nothing that surrounded him could he lay hold of or let go; all things reminded him of all: the whole ring of his existence lay before him; but it was broken into fragments, and seemed as if it would never unite again. These works of art, which his father had sold, appeared to him an omen that he himself was destined never to obtain a lasting, calm possession of any thing desirable in life, or always to be robbed of it so soon as gained, by his own or other people's blame. He waded so deep in these strange and dreary meditations, that often he almost thought himself a disembodied spirit; and, even when he felt and handled things without him, he could scarcely keep himself from doubting whether he was really there and alive.

Nothing but the piercing grief which often seized him, but the tears he shed at being forced, by causes frivolous as they were irresistible, to leave the good which he had found, and found after having lost it, restored him to the feeling of his earthly life. It was in vain to call before his mind his happy state in other respects. "All is nothing, then," exclaimed he, "if the one blessing, which appears to us worth all the rest, is wanting!"

The abbé told the company that the marchese was arrived. "You have determined, it appears," said he to Wilhelm, "to set out upon your travels with your boy alone. Get acquainted with this nobleman, however: he will be useful to you if you meet him by the way." The marchese entered. He was a person not yet very far advanced in years, — a fine, handsome, pleasing, Lombard figure. In his youth, while in the army and afterwards in public business, he had known Lothario's uncle; they had subsequently travelled through the greater part of Italy together: and many of the works of art, which the marchese now again fell in with, had been purchased in his presence, and under various happy circumstances, which he still distinctly recollected.

The Italians have in general a deeper feeling for the high dignity of art than any other nation. In Italy, whoever follows the employment tries to pass at once for artist, master, and professor; by which pretensions he acknowledges at least that it is not sufficient merely to lay hold of some transmitted excellency, or to acquire by practice some dexterity, but that a man who aims at art should have the power to think of what he does, to lay down principles, and make apparent to himself and others how and wherefore he proceeds in this way or in that.

The stranger was affected at again beholding these productions when the owner of them was no more, and cheered to see the spirit of his friend surviving in the gifted persons left behind him. They discussed a series of works: they found a lively satisfaction in the harmony of their ideas. The marchese and the abbé were the speakers; Natalia felt herself again transported to the presence of her uncle, and could enter without difficulty into their opinions and criticisms; Wilhelm could not understand them, except as he translated their technology into dramatic language. Friedrich's facetious vein was sometimes rather difficult to keep in check. Jarno was seldom there.

It being observed that excellent works of art were very rare in latter times, it was remarked by the marchese, "We can hardly think or estimate how many circumstances must combine in favor of the artist: with the greatest genius, with the most decisive talent, the demands which he must make upon himself are infinite, the diligence required in cultivating his endowments is unspeakable. Now, if circumstances are not in his favor, if he observe that the world is very easy to be satisfied, requiring but a slight, pleasing, transitory show, it were a matter of surprise if indolence and selfishness did not keep him fixed at mediocrity: it were strange if he did not rather think of bartering modish wares for gold and praises than of entering on the proper path, which could not fail in some degree to lead him to a sort of painful martyrdom. Accordingly, the artists of our time are always offering and never giving. They always aim at charming, and they never satisfy: every thing is merely indicated; you can nowhere find foundation or completion. Those for whom they labor, it is true, are little better. If you wait a while in any gallery of pictures, and observe what works attract the many, what are praised and what neglected, you have little pleasure in the present, little hope in the future."

"Yes," replied the abbé: "and thus it is that artists and their judges mutually form each other. The latter ask for nothing but a general, vague enjoyment; a work of art is to delight them almost as a work of nature; they imagine that the organs for enjoying works of art may be cultivated altogether of themselves, like the tongue and the palate; they try a picture or a poem as they do an article of food. They do not understand how very different a species of culture it requires to raise one to the true enjoyment of art. The hardest part of it, in my opinion, is that sort of separation which a man that aims at perfect culture must accomplish in himself. It is on this account that we observe so many people partially cultivated, and yet every one of them attempting to pronounce upon the general whole."

"Your last remark is not quite clear to me," said Jarno, who came in just then.

"It would be difficult," replied the abbé, "to explain it fully without a long detail. Thus much I may say: When any man pretends to mix in manifold activity or manifold enjoyment, he must also be enabled, as it were, to make his organs manifold, and independent of each other. Whoever aims at doing or enjoying all and every thing with his entire nature, whoever tries to link together all that is without him by such a species of enjoyment, will only lose his time in efforts that can never be successful. How difficult, though it seems so easy, is it to contemplate a noble disposition, a fine picture, simply in and for itself; to watch the music for the music's sake; to admire the actor in the actor; to take pleasure in a building for its own peculiar harmony and durability. Most men are wont to treat a work of art, though fixed and done, as if it were a piece of soft clay. The hard and polished marble is again to mould itself, the firm-walled edifice is to contract or to expand itself, according as their inclinations, sentiments, and whims may dictate: the picture is to be instructive, the play to make us better, — every thing is to do all. The reason is, that most men are themselves uninformed, they cannot give themselves and their being any certain shape; and thus they strive to take from other things their proper shape, that all they have to do with may be loose and wavering like themselves. Every thing is, in the long-run, reduced by them to what they call effect: every thing is relative, say they; and so, indeed, it is: every thing with them grows relative, except absurdity and platitude, which truly are absolute enough."

"I understand you," answered Jarno; "or, rather, I perceive how what you have been saying follows from the principles you hold so fast by. Yet with men, poor devils, we should not go to quest so strictly. I know enow of them in truth, who, beside the greatest works of art and nature, forthwith recollect their own most paltry insufficiency; who take their conscience and their morals with them to the opera; who bethink them of their loves and hatreds in contemplating a colonnade. The best and greatest that can be presented to them from without, they must first, as far as possible, diminish in their way of representing it, that they may in any measure be enabled to combine it with their own sorry nature."

CHAPTER EIGHT

THE ABBÉ called them in the evening to attend the exequies of Mignon. The company proceeded to the Hall of the Past: they found it magnificently ornamented and illuminated. The walls were hung with azure tapestry almost from ceiling to floor, so that nothing but the friezes and socles, above and below, were visible. On the four candelabras in the corner large wax-lights were burning: smaller lights were in the four smaller candelabras placed by the sarcophagus in the middle. Near this stood four boys, dressed in azure with silver: they had broad fans of ostrich-feathers, which they waved above a figure that was resting upon the sarcophagus. The company sat down: two invisible choruses began in a soft, musical recitative to ask, "Whom bring ye us to the still dwelling?" The four boys replied with lovely voices, " 'Tis a tired playmate whom we bring you: let her rest in your still dwelling, till the songs of her heavenly sisters once more awaken her."

CHORUS

"Firstling of youth in our circle, we welcome thee! With sadness welcome thee! May no boy, no maiden, follow! Let age only, willing and composed, approach the silent hall, and in the solemn company, repose this one dear child!

BOYS

Ah, reluctantly we brought her hither! Ah, and she is to remain here! Let us, too, remain: let us weep, let us weep upon her bier!

CHORUS

Yet look at the strong wings; look at the light, clear robe. How glitters the golden band upon her head! Look at the beautiful, the noble, repose.

BOYS

Ah! the wings do not raise her; in the frolic game, her robe flutters to and fro no more; when we bound her head with roses, her looks on us were kind and friendly.

CHORUS

Cast forward the eye of the spirit. Awake in your souls the imaginative power, which carries forth what is fairest, what is highest, life, away beyond the stars.

BOYS

But, ah! We find her not here; in the garden she wanders not; the flowers of the meadow she plucks no longer. Let us weep, we are leaving her here! Let us weep, and remain with her!

CHORUS

Children, turn back into life! Your tears let the fresh air dry, which plays upon the rushing water. Flee from Night! Day and Pleasure and Continuance are the lot of the living.

BOYS

Up! Turn back into life! Let the day give us labor and pleasure, till the evening brings us rest, and the nightly sleep refreshes us.

CHORUS

Children! Hasten into life! In the pure garments of beauty, may Love meet you with heavenly looks and with the wreath of immortality!"

The boys had retired: the abbé rose from his seat, and went behind the bier. "It is the appointment," said he, "of the man who prepared this silent abode, that each new tenant of it shall be introduced with a solemnity. After him, the builder of this mansion, the founder of this establishment, we have next brought a young stranger hither; and thus already does this little space contain two altogether different victims of the rigorous, arbitrary, and inexorable Death-goddess. By appointed laws we enter into life: the days are numbered which make us ripe to see the light, but for the duration of our life there is no law. The weakest thread will spin itself to unexpected length; and the strongest is cut suddenly asunder by the scissors of the Fates, delighting, as it seems, in contradictions. Of the child whom we have here committed to her final rest, we can say but little. It is still uncertain whence she came; her parents we know not; the years of her life we can only conjecture. Her deep and closely shrouded soul allowed us scarce to guess at its interior movements: there was nothing clear in her, nothing open but her affection for the man who had snatched her from the hands of a barbarian. This impassioned tenderness, this vivid gratitude, appeared to be the flame which consumed the oil of her life: the skill of the physician could not save that fair life, the most anxious friendship could not lengthen it. But, if art could not stay the departing spirit, it has done its utmost to preserve the body, and withdraw it from decay. A balsamic substance has been forced through all the veins, and now tinges, in place of blood, these cheeks too early faded. Come near, my friends, and view this wonder of art and care!"

He raised the veil: the child was lying in her angel's dress, as if asleep, in the most soft and graceful posture. They approached, and admired this show of life. Wilhelm alone continued sitting in his place; he was not able to compose himself: what he felt he durst not think, and every thought seemed ready to destroy his feeling.

For the sake of the marchese, the speech had been pronounced in French. That nobleman came forward with the rest, and viewed the figure with attention. The abbé thus proceeded. "With a holy confidence, this kind heart, shut up to men, was continually turned to its God. Humility, nay, an inclination to abase herself externally, seemed natural to her. She clave with zeal to the Catholic religion, in which she had been born and educated. Often she expressed a still wish to sleep on consecrated ground; and, according to the usage of the Church, we have, therefore, consecrated this marble coffin, and the little earth which is hidden in the cushion that supports her head. With what ardor did she, in her last moments, kiss the image of the Crucified, which stood beautifully figured on her tender arm, with many hundred points!" So saying, he stripped up her right sleeve; and a crucifix, with marks and letters round it, showed itself in blue upon the white skin.

The marchese looked at this with eagerness, stooping down to view it more intensely. "O God!" cried he, as he stood upright, and raised his hands to heaven. "Poor child! Unhappy niece! Do I meet thee here? What a painful joy to find thee, whom we had long lost hope of; to find this dear frame, which we had long believed the prey of fishes in the ocean, here preserved, though lifeless! I assist at thy funeral, splendid in its external circumstances, still more splendid from the noble persons who attend thee to thy place of rest. And to these," added he, with a faltering voice, "so soon as I can speak, I will express my thanks."

Tears hindered him from saying more. By the pressure of a spring, the abbé sank the body into the cavity of the marble. Four youths, dressed as the boys had been, came out from behind the tapestry, and lifting the heavy, beautifully ornamented lid upon the coffin, thus began their song:

THE YOUTHS

"Well is the treasure now laid up, — the fair image of the Past! Here sleeps it in the marble, undecaying: in your hearts, too, it lives, it works. Travel, travel back into life! Take along with you this holy earnestness, for earnestness alone makes life eternity."

The invisible chorus joined in with the last words, but no one heard the strengthening sentiment: all were too much busied with themselves, and the emotions which these wonderful disclosures had excited. The abbé and Natalia conducted the marchese out: Theresa and Lothario walked by Wilhelm. It was not till the music had altogether died away, that their sorrows, thoughts, meditations, curiosity, again fell on them with all their force, and made them long to be transported back into that exalting scene.

CHAPTER NINE

THE MARCHESE avoided speaking of the matter, but had long, secret conversations with the abbé. When the company was met, he often asked for music, — a request to which they willingly assented, as each was glad to be delivered from the charge of talking. Thus they lived for some time, till it was observed that he was making preparations for departure. One day he said to Wilhelm, "I wish not to disturb the remains of this beloved child; let her rest in the place where she loved and suffered: but her friends must promise to visit me in her native country, in the scene where she was born and bred; they must see the pillars and statues, of which a dim idea remained with her. I will lead you to the bays where she liked so well to roam, and gather pebbles. You, at least, young friend, shall not escape the gratitude of a family that stands so deeply indebted to you. To-morrow I set out on my journey. The abbé is acquainted with the whole history of this matter: he will tell it you again. He could pardon me when grief interrupted my recital: as a third party, he will be enabled to narrate the incidents with more connection. If, as the abbé had proposed, you like to follow me in travelling over Germany, you shall be heartily welcome. Leave not your boy behind: at every little inconvenience which he causes us, we will again remember your attentive care of my poor niece."

The same evening our party was surprised by the arrival of the countess. Wilhelm trembled in every joint as she entered: she herself, though forewarned, kept close by her sister, who speedily reached a chair. How singularly simple was her attire, how altered was her form! Wilhelm scarcely dared to look at her: she saluted him with a kindly air; a few general words addressed to him did not conceal her sentiments and feelings. The marchese had retired betimes; and, as the company were not disposed to part so early, the abbé now produced a manuscript. "The singular narrative which was intrusted to me," said he, "I forthwith put on paper. The case where pen and ink should least of all be spared, is in recording the particular circumstances of remarkable events." They informed the countess of the matter; and the abbé read as follows, in the name of the marchese: —

"Many men as I have seen, I still regard my father as a very extraordinary person. His character was noble and upright; his ideas were enlarged, I may even say great; to himself he was severe: in all his plans there was a rigid order, in all operations an unbroken perseverance. In one sense, therefore, it was easy to transact and live with him: yet, owing to the very qualities which made it so, he never could accommodate himself to life; for he required from the state, from his neighbors, from his children, and his servants, the observance of all the laws which he had laid upon himself. His most moderate demands became exorbitant by his rigor; and he never could attain to enjoyment, for nothing ever was completed as he had forecast it. At the moment when he was erecting a palace, laying out a garden, or acquiring a large estate in the highest cultivation, I have seen him inwardly convinced, with the sternest ire, that Fate had doomed him to do nothing but abstain and suffer. In his exterior he maintained the greatest dignity: if he jested, it was but displaying the preponderancy of his understanding. Censure was intolerable to him: the only time I ever saw him quite transported with rage was once when he heard that one of his establishments was spoken of as something ludicrous. In the same spirit he had settled the disposal of his children and his fortune. My eldest brother was educated as a person that had large estates to look for. I was to embrace the clerical profession: the youngest was to be a soldier. I was of a lively temper, fiery, active, quick, apt for corporeal exercises: the youngest rather seemed inclined to an enthusiastic quietism, — devoted to the sciences, to music, and poetry. It was not till after the hardest struggle, the maturest conviction of the impossibility of his project, that our father, still reluctantly, agreed to let us change vocations; and, although he saw us both contented, he could never suit himself to this arrangement, but declared that nothing good would come of it. The older he grew, the more isolated did he feel from all society. At last he came to live almost entirely alone. One old friend, who had served in the German armies, who had lost his wife in the campaign, and brought a daughter of about ten years of age along with him, remained his only visitor. This person bought a fine little property beside us: he used to come and see my father on stated days of the week, and at stated hours; his little daughter came along with him. He was never heard to contradict my father, who at length grew perfectly habituated to him, and endured him as the only tolerable company he had. After our father's death, we easily observed that this old gentleman had not been visiting for naught, — that his compliances had been rewarded by an ample settlement. He enlarged his estates: his daughter might expect a handsome portion. The girl grew up, and was extremely beautiful: my elder brother often joked with me about her, saying I should go and court her.

"Meanwhile brother Augustin, in the seclusion of his cloister, had been spending his years in the strangest state of mind. He abandoned himself wholly to the feeling of a holy enthusiasm, to those half-spiritual, half-physical emotions which, as they for a time exalted him to the third heaven, erelong sank him down to an abyss of powerlessness and vacant misery. While my father lived, no change could be contemplated: what, indeed, could we have asked for or proposed? After the old man's death, our brother visited us frequently: his situation, which at first afflicted us, in time became much more tolerable; for his reason had at length prevailed. But, the more confidently reason promised him complete recovery and contentment on the pure path of nature, the more vehemently did he require of us to free him from his vows. His thoughts, he let us know, were turned upon Sperata, our fair neighbor.

"My elder brother had experienced too much suffering from the harshness of our father to look on the condition of the youngest without sympathy. He spoke with the family confessor, a worthy old man: we signified to him the double purpose of our brother, and requested him to introduce and expedite the business. Contrary to custom he delayed; and at last, when Augustin pressed us, and we recommended the affair more keenly to the clergyman, he had nothing left but to impart the strange secret to us.

"Sperata was our sister, and that by both her parents. Our mother had declared herself with child at a time when both she and our father were advanced in years: a similar occurrence had shortly before been made the subject of some merriment in our neighborhood; and our father, to avoid such ridicule, determined to conceal this late lawful fruit of love as carefully as people use to conceal its earlier accidental fruits. Our mother was delivered secretly: the child was carried to the country; and the old friend of the family, who, with the confessor, had alone been trusted with the secret, easily engaged to give her out for his daughter. The confessor had reserved the right of disclosing the secret in case of extremity. The supposed father was now dead: Sperata was living with an old lady; we were aware that a love of song and music had already led our brother to her; and on his again requiring us to undo his former bond, that he might engage himself by a new one, it was necessary that we should, as soon as possible, apprise him of the danger he stood in.

"He viewed us with a wild, contemptuous look. 'Spare your idle tales,' cried he, 'for children and credulous fools: from me, from my heart, they shall not tear Sperata; she is mine. Recall, I pray you, instantly, your frightful spectre, which would but harass me in vain. Sperata is not my sister: she is my wife!' He described to us, in rapturous terms, how this heavenly girl had drawn him out of his unnatural state of separation from his fellow-creatures into true life; how their spirits accorded like their voices; how he blessed his sufferings and errors, since they had kept clear of him women, till the moment when he wholly and forever gave himself to this most amiable being. We were shocked at the discovery, we deplored his situation, but we knew not how to help ourselves; for he declared, with violence, that Sperata was with a child by him. Our confessor did whatever duty could suggest to him, but by this means he only made the evil worse. The demands of nature and religion, moral rights and civil laws, were vehemently attacked and spurned at by our brother. He considered nothing holy but his relation to Sperata, nothing dignified but the names of father and wife. 'These alone,' cried he, 'are suitable to nature: all else is caprice and opinion. Were there not noble nations which admitted marriage with a sister? Name not your gods! You never name them but when you wish to befool us, to lead us from the paths of nature, and, by scandalous constraint, to transform the noblest inclinations into crimes. Unspeakable are the perplexities, abominable the abuses, into which you force the victims whom you bury alive.

" 'I may speak, for I have suffered like no other, — from the highest, sweetest feeling of enthusiasm, to the frightful deserts of utter powerlessness, vacancy, annihilation, and despair; from the loftiest aspirations of preternatural existence, to the most entire unbelief, — unbelief in myself. All these horrid grounds of the cup, so flattering at the brim, I have drained; and my whole being was poisoned to its core. And now, when kind Nature, by her greatest gift, by love, has healed me; now, when in the arms of a heavenly creature I again feel that I am, that she is, that out of this living union a third shall arise and smile in our faces, — now ye open up the flames of your hell, of your purgatory, which can only singe a sick imagination: ye oppose them to the vivid, true, indestructible enjoyment of pure love. Meet us under these cypresses, which turn their solemn tops to heaven; visit us among those espaliers where the citrons and pomegranates bloom beside us, where the graceful myrtle stretches out its tender flowers to us, — and then venture to disturb us with your dreary, paltry nets which men have spun!'

"Thus for a long time he persisted in a stubborn disbelief of our story; and when we assured him of its truth, when the confessor himself asseverated it, he did not let it drive him from his point. 'Ask not the echoes of your cloisters, not your mouldering parchments, not your narrow whims and ordinances! Ask Nature and your heart: she will teach you what you should recoil from; she will point out to you with the strictest finger over what she has pronounced her everlasting curse. Look at the lilies: do not husband and wife shoot forth on the same stalk? Does not the flower which bore them hold them both? And is not the lily the type of innocence? Is not their sisterly union fruitful? When Nature abhors, she speaks it aloud; the creature that shall not be, is not produced; the creature that lives with a false life, is soon destroyed. Unfruitfulness, painful existence, early destruction, these are her curses, the marks of her displeasure. It is only by immediate consequences that she punishes. Look around you; and what is prohibited, what is accursed, will force itself upon your notice. In the silence of the convent, in the tumult of the world, a thousand practices are consecrated and revered, while her curse rests on them. On stagnant idleness as on overstrained toil, on caprice and superfluity as on constraint and want, she looks down with mournful eyes; her call is to moderation; true are all her commandments, peaceful all her influences. The man who has suffered as I have done, has a right to be free. Sperata is mine: death alone shall take her from me. How I shall retain her, how I may be happy, these are your cares. This instant I go to her, and part from her no more.'

"He was for proceeding to the boat, and crossing over to her: we restrained him, entreating that he would not take a step which might produce the most tremendous consequences. He should recollect, we told him, that he was not living in the free world of his own thoughts and ideas, but in a constitution of affairs, the ordinances and conditions of which had become as inflexible as laws of nature. The confessor made us promise not to let him leave our sight, still less our house: after this he went away, engaging to return erelong. What we had foreseen took place: reason had made our brother strong, but his heart was weak; the earlier impressions of religion rose on him, and dreadful doubts along with them. He passed two fearful nights and days: the confessor came again to his assistance, but in vain. His enfranchised understanding acquitted him: his feelings, religion, all his usual ideas, declared him guilty.

"One morning we found his chamber empty: on the table lay a note, in which he signified, that, as we kept him prisoner by force, he felt himself entitled to provide for his freedom; that he meant to go directly to Sperata; he expected to escape with her, and was prepared for the most terrible extremities should any separation be attempted.

"The news, of course, affrighted us exceedingly; but the confessor bade us be at rest. Our poor brother had been narrowly enough observed: the boatman, in place of taking him across, proceeded with him to his cloister. Fatigued with watching for the space of four and twenty hours, he fell asleep, as the skiff began to rock him in the moonshine; and he did not awake till he saw himself in the hands of his spiritual brethren: he did not recover from his amazement till he heard the doors of the convent bolting behind him.

"Sharply touched at the fate of our brother, we reproached the confessor for his cruelty; but he soon silenced or convinced us by the surgeon's reason, that our pity was destructive to the patient. He let us know that he was not acting on his own authority, but by order of the bishop and his chapter; that by this proceeding they intended to avoid all public scandal, and to shroud the sad occurrence under the veil of a secret course of discipline prescribed by the Church. Our sister they would spare: she was not to be told that her lover was her brother. The charge of her was given to a priest, to whom she had before disclosed her situation. They contrived to hide her pregnancy and her delivery. As a mother she felt altogether happy in her little one.

"Like most of our women, she could neither write, nor read writing: she gave the priest many verbal messages to carry to her lover. The latter, thinking that he owed this pious fraud to a suckling mother, often brought pretended tidings from our brother, whom he never saw; recommending her, in his name, to be at peace; begging of her to be careful of herself and of her child, and for the rest to trust in God.

"Sperata was inclined by nature to religious feelings. Her situation, her solitude, increased this tendency: the clergyman encouraged it, in order to prepare her by degrees for an eternal separation. Scarcely was her child weaned, scarcely did he think her body strong enough for suffering agony of mind, when he began to paint her fault to her in most terrific colors, to treat the crime of being connected with a priest as a sort of sin against nature, as a sort of incest. For he had taken up the strange thought of making her repentance equal in intensity to what it would have been had she known the true circumstances of her error. He thereby produced so much anxiety and sorrow in her mind; he so exalted the idea of the Church and of its head before her; showed her the awful consequences, for the weal of all men's souls, should indulgence in a case like this be granted, and the guilty pair rewarded by a lawful union; signifying, too, how wholesome it was to expiate such sins in time, and thereby gain the crown of immortality, — that at last, like a poor criminal, she willingly held out her neck to the axe, and earnestly entreated that she might forever be divided from our brother. Having gained so much, the clergy left her the liberty (reserving to themselves a certain distant oversight) to live at one time in a convent, at another in her house, according as she afterwards thought good.

"Her little girl, meanwhile, was growing: from her earliest years she had displayed an extraordinary disposition. When still very young, she could run and move with wonderful dexterity: she sang beautifully, and learned to play upon the cithern almost of herself. With words, however, she could not express herself; and the impediment seemed rather to proceed from her mode of thought than from her organs of speech. The feelings of the poor mother to her, in the mean time, were of the most painful kind: the expostulations of the priest had so perplexed her mind, that, though she was not quite deranged, her state was far from being sane. She daily thought her crime more terrible and punishable: the clergyman's comparison of incest, frequently repeated, had impressed itself so deeply, that her horror was not less than if the actual circumstances had been known to her. The priest took no small credit for his ingenuity, with which he had contrived to tear asunder a luckless creature's heart. It was miserable to behold maternal love, ready to expand itself in joy at the existence of her child, contending with the frightful feeling that this child should not exist. The two emotions warred with each other in her soul: love was often weaker than aversion.

"The child had long ago been taken from her, and committed to a worthy family residing on the seashore. In the greater freedom which the little creature enjoyed here, she soon displayed her singular delight in climbing. To mount the highest peaks, to run along the edges of the ships, to imitate in all their strangest feats the rope-dancers whom she often saw in the place, seemed a natural tendency in her.

"To practise these things with the greater ease, she liked to change clothes with boys; and, though her foster-parents thought this highly blamable and unbecoming, we bade them indulge her as much as possible. Her wild walks and leapings often led her to a distance: she would lose her way, and be long from home, but she always came back. In general, as she returned, she used to set herself beneath the columns in the portal of a country house in the neighborhood: her people now had ceased to look for her; they waited for her. She would there lie resting on the steps, then run up and down the large hall, looking at the statues; after which, if nothing specially detained her, she used to hasten home.

"But at last our confidence was balked, and our indulgence punished. The child went out, and did not come again: her little hat was found swimming on the water near the spot where a torrent rushes down into the sea. It was conjectured, that, in clambering among the rocks, her foot had slipped: all our searching could not find the body.

"The thoughtless tattle of her housemates soon communicated the occurrence to Sperata: she seemed calm and cheerful when she heard it; hinting not obscurely at her satisfaction that God had pleased to take her poor child to himself, and thus preserved it from suffering, or causing some more dreadful misery.

"On this occasion all the fables which are told about our waters came to be the common talk. The sea, it was said, required every year an innocent child: yet it would endure no corpse, but sooner or later throw it to the shore; nay, the last joint, though sunk to the lowest bottom, must again come forth. They told the story of a mother, inconsolable because her child had perished in the sea, who prayed to God and his saints to grant her at least the bones for burial. The first storm threw ashore the skull, the next the spine; and, after all was gathered, she wrapped the bones in a cloth, and took them to the church: but, oh! miraculous to tell! as she crossed the threshold of the temple, the packet grew heavier and heavier; and at last, when she laid it on the steps of the altar, the child began to cry, and issued living from the cloth. One joint of the right-hand little finger was alone wanting: this, too, the mother anxiously sought and found; and, in memory of the event, it was preserved among the other relics of the church.

"On poor Sperata these recitals made a deep impression: her imagination took a new flight, and favored the emotion of her heart. She supposed that now the child had expiated, by its death, both its own sins and the sins of its parents; that the curse and penalty which hitherto had overhung them all was at length wholly removed; that nothing more was necessary could she only find the child's bones, that she might carry them to Rome, where, upon the steps of the great altar in St. Peter's, her little girl, again covered with its fair, fresh skin, would stand up alive before the people. With its own eyes it would once more look on father and mother; and the pope, convinced that God and his saints commanded it, would, amid the acclamations of the people, remit the parents their sins, acquit them of their oaths, and join their hands in wedlock.

"Her looks and her anxiety were henceforth constantly directed to the sea and the beach. When at night, in the moonshine, the waves were tossing to and fro, she thought every glittering sheet of foam was bringing out her child; and some one about her had to run off, as if to take it up when it should reach the shore.

"By day she walked unweariedly along the places where the pebbly beach shelved slowly to the water: she gathered in a little basket all the bones she could find. None durst tell her that they were the bones of animals: the larger ones she buried, the little ones she took along with her. In this employment she incessantly persisted. The clergyman, who, by so unremittingly discharging what he thought his duty, had reduced her to this condition, now stood up for her with all his might. By his influence the people in the neighborhood were made to look upon her, not as a distracted person, but as one entranced: they stood in reverent attitudes as she walked by, and the children ran to kiss her hand.

"To the old woman, her attendant and faithful friend, the secret of Sperata's guilt was at length imparted by the priest, on her solemnly engaging to watch over the unhappy creature, with untiring care, through all her life. And she kept this engagement to the last, with admirable conscientiousness and patience.

"Meanwhile we had always had an eye upon our brother. Neither the physicians nor the clergy of his convent would allow us to be seen by him; but, in order to convince us of his being well in some sort, we had leave to look at him as often as we liked in the garden, the passages, or even through a window in the roof of his apartment.

"After many terrible and singular changes, which I shall omit, he had passed into a strange state of mental rest and bodily unrest. He never sat but when he took his harp and played upon it, and then he usually accompanied it with singing. At other times he kept continually in motion; and in all things he was grown extremely guidable and pliant, for all his passions seemed to have resolved themselves into the single fear of death. You could persuade him to do any thing by threatening him with dangerous sickness or with death.

"Besides this singularity of walking constantly about the cloister, a practice which he hinted it were better to exchange for wandering over hill and dale, he talked about an apparition which perpetually tormented him. He declared, that, on awakening at whatever hour of the night, he saw a beautiful boy standing at the foot of his bed, with a bare knife, and threatening to destroy him. They shifted him to various other chambers of the convent, but he still asserted that the boy pursued him. His wandering to and fro became more unrestful: the people afterwards remembered, too, that at this time they had often seen him stand at the window, and look out upon the sea.

"Our poor sister, on the other hand, seemed gradually wasting under the consuming influence of her single thought, of her narrow occupation. It was at last proposed by the physician, that, among the bones she had gathered, the fragments of a child's skeleton should by degrees be introduced, and so the hapless mother's hopes kept up. The experiment was dubious; but this at least seemed likely to be gained by it, that, when all the parts were got together, she would cease her weary search, and might be entertained with hopes of going to Rome.

"It was accordingly resolved on. Her attendant changed, by imperceptible degrees, the small remains committed to her with the bones Sperata found. An inconceivable delight arose in the poor, sick woman's heart, when the parts began to fit each other, and the shape of those still wanting could be marked. She had fastened every fragment in its proper place with threads and ribbons; filling up the vacant spaces with embroidery and silk, as is usually done with the relics of saints.

"In this way nearly all the bones had been collected: none but a few of the extremities were wanting. One morning, while she was asleep, the physician having come to ask for her, the old attendant, with a view to show him how his patient occupied herself, took away these dear remains from the little chest where they lay in poor Sperata's bedroom. A few minutes afterwards they heard her spring upon the floor: she lifted up the cloth, and found the chest empty. She threw herself upon her knees: they came, and listened to her joyful, ardent prayer. 'Yes,' exclaimed she, 'it is true! it was no dream, it is real! Rejoice with me, my friends! I have seen my own beautiful, good little girl again alive.' She arose, and threw the veil from off her; her splendor enlightened all the room; her beauty was transfigured to celestial loveliness; she could not tread the ground, although she wished it. Lightly was she borne aloft: she had not even time to stretch her hand to me. '*There!*' cried she to me, and pointed to the road where I am soon to go. 'Yes, I will follow her, — soon follow her: my heart is light to think of it. My sorrows are already vanished: the sight of my risen little one has given me a foretaste of the heavenly joys.'

"From that time her soul was wholly occupied with prospects of the brightest kind; she gave no further heed to any earthly object; she took but little food; her spirit by degrees cast off the fetters of the body. At last this imperceptible gradation reached its head unexpectedly: her attendants found her pale and motionless; she opened not her eyes; she was what we call dead.

"The report of her vision quickly spread abroad among the people; and the reverential feeling, which she had excited in her lifetime, soon changed, at her death, to the thought that she should be regarded as in bliss, — nay, as in sanctity.

"When we were bearing her to be interred, a crowd of persons pressed with boundless violence about the bier: they would touch her hand, they would touch her garment. In this impassioned elevation, various sick persons ceased to feel the pains by which at other times they were tormented: they looked upon themselves as healed; they declared it; they praised God and his new saint. The clergy were obliged to lay the body in a neighboring chapel: the people called for opportunity to offer their devotion. The concourse was incredible: the mountaineers, at all times prone to lively and religious feelings, crowded forward from their valleys; the reverence, the wonder, the adoration, daily spread, and gathered strength. The ordinances of the bishop, which were meant to limit, and in time abolish, this new worship, could not be put in execution: every show of opposition raised the people into tumults; every unbeliever they were ready to assail with personal violence. 'Did not Saint Borromæus,' cried they, 'dwell among our forefathers? Did not his mother live to taste the joy of his canonization? Was not that great figure on the rocks at Arona meant to represent to us, by a sensible symbol, his spiritual greatness? Do not the descendants of his kindred live among us to this hour? And has not God promised ever to renew his miracles among a people that believe?'

"As the body, after several days, exhibited no marks of putrefaction, but grew whiter, and, as it were, translucent, the general faith rose higher and higher. Among the multitude were several cures which even the sceptical observer was unable to account for, or ascribe entirely to fraud. The whole country was in motion: those who did not go to see it, heard at least no other topic talked of.

"The convent where my brother live resounded, like the land at large, with the noise of these wonders; and the people felt the less restraint in speaking of them in his presence, as in general he seemed to pay no heed to any thing, and his connection with the circumstance was known to none of them. But on this occasion it appeared he had listened with attention. He conducted his escape with such dexterity and cunning, that the manner of it still remains a mystery. We learned afterwards, that he had crossed the water with a number of travellers, and charged the boatman, who observed no other singularity about him, above all to have a care lest their vessel overset. Late in the night he reached the chapel, where his hapless loved one was resting from her woes. Only a few devotees were kneeling in the corners of the place: her old friend was sitting at the head of the corpse; he walked up to her, saluted her, and asked how her mistress was. 'You see it,' answered she, with some embarrassment. He looked at the corpse with a sidelong glance. After some delay he took its hand. Frightened by its coldness, he in the instant let it go: he looked unrestfully around him; then, turning to the old attendant, 'I cannot stay with her at present,' said he: 'I have a long, long way to travel; but at the proper time I shall be back: tell her so when she awakens.'

"With this he went away. It was a while before we got intelligence of these occurrences: we searched, but all our efforts to discover him were vain. How he worked his way across the mountains none can say. A long time after he was gone we came upon a trace of him among the Grisons, but we were too late: it quickly vanished. We supposed that he was gone to Germany, but his weak footprints had been speedily obliterated by the war."

CHAPTER TEN

THE ABBÉ ceased to read. No one had listened without tears. The countess scarcely ever took her handkerchief from her eyes: at last she rose, and, with Natalia, left the room. The rest were silent, till the abbé thus began: "The question now arises, whether we shall let the good marchese leave us without telling him our secret. For who can doubt a moment that our harper and his brother Augustin are one? Let us consider what is to be done, both for the sake of that unhappy man himself and of his family. My advice is, not to hurry, but to wait till we have heard what news the doctor, who has gone to see him, brings us back."

All were of the same opinion; and the abbé thus proceeded: "Another question, which perhaps may be disposed of sooner, still remains. The marchese is affected to the bottom of his heart at the kindness which his poor niece experienced here, particularly from our young friend. He made me tell him again and again every circumstance connected with her, and he shows the liveliest gratitude. 'Her young benefactor,' he said, 'refused to travel with me, while he knew not the connection that subsists between us. I am not now a stranger, of whose manner of existence, of whose humors, he might be uncertain: I am his associate, his relation; and, as his unwillingness to leave his boy behind was the impediment which kept him from accompanying me, let this child now become a fairer bond to join us still more closely. Beyond the obligations he has already placed me under, let him be of service to me on my present journey; let him, then, return along with me; my elder brother will receive him as he ought. And let him not despise the heritage of his unhappy foster-child; for, by a secret stipulation of our father with his military friend, the fortune which he gave Sperata has returned to us: and certainly we will not cheat our niece's benefactor of the recompense he has merited so well.' "

Theresa, taking Wilhelm by the hand, now said to him, "We have here another beautiful example that disinterested well-doing yields the highest and best return. Follow the call which so strangely comes to you, and, while you lay a double load of gratitude on the marchese, hasten to a fair land, which has already often drawn your heart and your imagination towards it."

"I leave myself entirely to the guidance of my friends and you," said Wilhelm: "it is vain to think, in this world, of adhering to our individual will. What I purposed to hold fast, I must let go; and benefits which I have not deserved descend upon me of their own accord."

Pressing Theresa's hand, Wilhelm took his own away. "I give you full permission," said he to the abbé, "to decide about me as you please. Since I shall not need to leave my Felix, I am ready to go any-whither, and to undertake whatever you think good."

Thus authorized, the abbé forthwith sketched out his plan. The marchese, he proposed, should be allowed to depart: Wilhelm was to wait for tidings from the doctor; he might then, when they had settled what was to be done, set off with Felix. Accordingly, under the pre-tence that Wilhelm's preparations for his journey would detain him, he advised the stranger to employ the mean while in examining the curi-osities of the city, which he meant to visit. The marchese did in con-sequence depart, and not without renewed and strong expressions of his gratitude; of which indeed the presents left by him, including jewels, precious stones, embroidered stuffs, afforded a sufficient proof.

Wilhelm, too, was at length in readiness for travelling; and his friends began to be distressed that the doctor sent them no news. They feared some mischief had befallen the poor old harper, at the very moment when they were in hopes of radically improving his condition.

They sent the courier off; but he was scarcely gone, when the doctor in the evening entered with a stranger, whose form and aspect were expressive, earnest, striking, and whom no one knew. Both stood silent for a space: the stranger at length went up to Wilhelm, and, holding out his hand, said, "Do you no longer know your old friend?" It was the harper's voice, but of his form there seemed to remain no vestige. He was in the common garb of a traveller, cleanly and genteelly equipped; his beard had vanished; his hair was dressed with some attention to the mode; and what particularly made him quite irrecognizable was, that in his countenance the look of age was no longer visible. Wilhelm embraced him with the liveliest joy: he was presented to the rest, and behaved with great propriety, not knowing that the party had a little while before become so well acquainted with him. "You will have patience with a man," continued he, with great composure, "who, grown up as he appears, is entering on the world, after long sorrows, inexperienced as a child. To this skilful gentleman I stand indebted for the privilege of again appearing in the company of my fellow-men."

They bade him welcome: the doctor motioned for a walk, to interrupt the conversation, and lead it to indifferent topics.

In private the doctor gave the following explanation: "It was by the strangest chance that we succeeded in the cure of this man. We have long treated him, morally and physically, as our best consideration dictated: in some degree the plan was efficacious; but the fear of death continued powerful in him, and he would not lay aside his beard and cloak. For the rest, however, he appeared to take more interest in external things than formerly; and both his songs and his conceptions seemed to be approaching nearer life. A strange letter from the clergyman, as you already know, called me from you. I arrived: I found our patient altogether changed; he had voluntarily given up his beard; he had let his locks be cut into a customary form; he asked for common clothes; he seemed to have all at once become another man. Though curious to penetrate the reason of this sudden alteration, we did not risk inquiring of himself: at last we accidentally discovered it. A glass of laudanum was missing from the parson's private laboratory: we thought it right to institute a strict inquiry; every one endeavored to ward off suspicion, and the sharpest quarrels rose among the inmates of the house. At last this man appeared before us, and admitted that he had the laudanum: we asked if he had swallowed any of it. 'No,' said he, 'but it is to this that I owe the recovery of my reason. It is at your choice to take the vial from me, and to drive me back, inevitably, to my former state. The feeling, that it was desirable to see the pains of life terminated by death, first put me on the way of cure: before long the thought of terminating them by voluntary death arose in me, and with this intention I took the glass of poison. The possibility of casting off my load of griefs forever gave me strength to bear them; and thus have I, ever since this talisman came into my possession, forced myself back into life by a contiguity with death. Be not anxious lest I use the drug, but resolve, as men acquainted with the human heart, by granting me an independence of life, to make me properly and wholesomely dependent on it.' After mature consideration, we determined not to meddle further with him; and he now carries with him, in a firm little ground-glass vial, this poison, of which he has so strangely made an antidote.''

The doctor was informed of all that had become known in the

mean time: towards Augustin it was determined that they should observe the deepest silence in regard to it. The abbé undertook to keep beside him, and to lead him forward on the healthful path he had entered.

Meanwhile Wilhelm was to set about his journey over Germany with the marchese. If it should appear that Augustin could be again excited to affection for his native country, the circumstances were to be communicated to his friends, and Wilhelm might conduct him thither.

Wilhelm had at last made every preparation for his journey. At first the abbé thought it strange that Augustin rejoiced in hearing of his friend and benefactor's purpose to depart, but he soon discovered the foundation of this curious movement. Augustin could not subdue his fear of Felix; and he longed, as soon as possible, to see the boy removed.

By degrees so many people had assembled, that the castle and adjoining buildings could scarcely accommodate them all, and the less, as such a multitude of guests had not originally been anticipated. They breakfasted, they dined, together: each endeavored to persuade himself they were living in a comfortable harmony; but each, in secret, longed in some degree to be away. Theresa frequently rode out, attended by Lothario, and oftener alone: she had already got acquainted with all the landladies and landlords in the district; for she held it as a principle of her economy, in which, perhaps, she was not far mistaken, that it is essential to be in good acceptance with one's neighbors, male and female, and to maintain with them a constant interchange of civilities. Of an intended marriage with Lothario, she appeared to have no thought. Natalia and the countess often talked with one another; the abbé seemed to covet the society of Augustin; Jarno had frequent conversations with the doctor; Friedrich held by Wilhelm; Felix ran about wherever he could meet with most amusement. It was thus, too, that in general they paired themselves in walking when the company broke up: when it was obliged to be together, recourse was quickly had to music, to unite them all by giving each back to himself.

Unexpectedly the count increased the party; intending to remove his lady, and, as it appeared, to take a solemn farewell of his worldly friends. Jarno hastened to the coach to meet him: the count inquired what guests they had; to which the other answered, in a fit of wild humor that would often seize him, "We have all the nobility in nature, — marcheses, marquises, milords, and barons: we wanted nothing but a count." They came up-stairs: Wilhelm was the first who met them in the ante-chamber. "Milord," said the count to him in French, after looking at him for a moment, "I rejoice very much in the unexpected pleasure of renewing my acquaintance with your lordship: I am very much mistaken if I did not see you at my castle in the prince's suite." "I had the happiness of waiting on your Excellence at that time," answered Wilhelm; "but you do me too much honor when you take me for an Englishman, and that of the first quality. I am a German, and" — "And a fine young fellow," interrupted Jarno. The count looked at Wilhelm with a smile, and was about to make some reply, when the rest of the party entered, and saluted him with many a friendly welcome. They excused themselves for being unable at the moment to show him to a proper chamber, promising without delay to make the necessary room for him.

"Ay, ay!" said he, smiling: "we have left Chance, I see, to act as our purveyor. Yet with prudence and arrangement, how much is possible! For the present I entreat you not to stir a slipper from its place: the disorder, I perceive, would otherwise be great. Every one would be uncomfortably lodged; and this no one shall be on my account, if possible, not even for an hour. You can testify," said he to Jarno, "and you, too, Meister," turning to Wilhelm, "how many people I commodiously stowed that time in my castle. Let me have the list of persons and servants; let me see how they are lodged at present: I will make a plan of dislocation, such that, with the very smallest inconvenience, every one shall find a suitable apartment; and there shall be room enough to hold another guest if one should accidentally arrive."

Jarno at once offered the count his assistance, procured him all the necessary information; taking great delight, as usual, if he could now and then contrive to lead him astray, and leave him in awkward difficulties. The old gentleman at last, however, gained a signal triumph The arrangement was completed: he caused the names to be written on their several doors, himself attending; and it could not be denied, that, by a very few changes and substitutions, the object had been fully gained. Jarno, among other things, had also managed, that the persons who at present took an interest in each other should be lodged together.

"Will you help me," said the count to Jarno, after every thing was settled, "to clear up my recollections of the young man there, whom you call Meister, and who you tell me is a German?" Jarno was silent; for he knew very well that the count was one of those people who, in asking questions, merely wish to show their knowledge. The count, accordingly, continued, without waiting for an answer, "You, I recollect, presented him to me, and warmly recommended him in the prince's name. If his mother was a German woman, I'll be bound for it his father is an Englishman, and one of rank too: who can calculate the English blood that has been flowing these last thirty years in German veins! I will not insist on knowing more: I know you have always family secrets of that kind, but in such cases it is in vain to think of cheating me." He then proceeded to detail a great variety of things as having taken place with Wilhelm at the castle, to the whole of which Jarno, as before, made no reply; though the count was altogether in the wrong, confounding Wilhelm more than once with a young Englishman of the prince's suite. The truth was, the good old gentleman had in former years possessed a very excellent memory, and was still proud of being able to remember the minutest circumstances of his youth; but, in regard to late occurrences, he used to settle in his mind as true, and utter with the greatest certainty, whatever fables and fantastic combinations, in the growing weakness of his powers, imagination might present to him. For the rest, he was become extremely mild and courteous: his presence had a very favorable influence upon the company. He would call on them to read some useful book together; nay, he often gave them little games, which, without participating in them, he directed with the greatest care. If they wondered at his condescension, he would reply, that it became a man who differed from the world in weighty matters to conform to it the more anxiously in matters of indifference.

In these games our friend had, more than once, an angry and unquiet feeling to endure. Friedrich, with his usual levity, took frequent opportunity of giving hints that Wilhelm entertained a secret passion for Natalia. How could he have found it out? What entitled him to say so? And would not his friends think, that, as they two were often together, Wilhelm must have made a disclosure to him, — so thoughtless and unlucky a disclosure?

One day, while they were merrier than common at some such joke, Augustin, dashing up the door, rushed in with a frightful look; his countenance was pale, his eyes were wild; he seemed about to speak, but his tongue refused its office. The party were astounded: Lothario and Jarno, supposing that his madness had returned, sprang up and seized him. With a choked and faltering voice, then loudly and violently, he spoke, and cried, "Not me! Haste! Help! Save the child! Felix is poisoned!"

They let him go; he hastened through the door: all followed him in consternation. They called the doctor; Augustin made for the abbé's chamber; they found the child, who seemed amazed and frightened, when they called to him from a distance, "What hast thou been doing?"

"Dear papa!" cried Felix, "I did not drink from the bottle, I drank from the glass: I was very thirsty."

Augustin struck his hands together: "He is lost!" cried he, then pressed through the by-standers, and hastened away.

They found a glass of almond-milk upon the table, with a bottle near it more than half empty. The doctor came, was told what they had seen and heard: with horror he observed the well-known laudanum-vial lying empty on the table. He called for vinegar: he summoned all his art to his assistance.

Natalia had the little patient taken to a room: she busied herself with painful care about him. The abbé had run out to seek Augustin, and draw some explanation from him. The unhappy father had been out upon the same endeavor, but in vain: he returned, to find anxiety and fear on every face. The doctor, in the mean time, had been examining the almond-milk in the glass; he found it to contain a powerful mixture of opium: the child was lying on the sofa, seeming very sick; he begged his father "not to let them pour more stuff into him, not to let them plague him any more." Lothario had sent his people, and had ridden off himself, endeavoring to find some trace of Augustin. Natalia sat beside the child; he took refuge in her lap, and entreated earnestly for her protection, earnestly for a little piece of sugar: the vinegar, he said, was biting sour. The doctor granted his request; the child was in a frightful agitation; they were obliged to let him have a moment's rest. The doctor said that every means had been adopted: he would continue to do his utmost. The count came near, with an air of displeasure; his look was earnest, even solemn; he laid his hands upon the child, turned his eyes to heaven, and remained some moments in that attitude. Wilhelm, who was lying inconsolable on a seat, sprang up, and, casting a despairing look at Natalia, left the room. Shortly afterwards the count, too, left it.

"I cannot understand," said the doctor, having paused a little, "how it comes that there is not the smallest trace of danger visible about the child. At a single gulp he must have swallowed an immense dose of opium; yet I find no movement in his pulse but what may be ascribed to our remedies, and to the terror we have put him into."

In a few minutes Jarno entered, with intelligence that Augustin had been discovered in the upper story, lying in his blood: a razor had been found beside him; to all appearance he had cut his throat. The doctor hastened out: he met the people carrying down the body. The unhappy man was laid upon a bed, and accurately examined: the cut had gone across the windpipe; a copious loss of blood had been succeeded by a swoon; yet it was easy to observe that life, that hope, was still there. The doctor put the body in a proper posture, joined the edges of the wound, and bandaged it. The night passed sleepless and full of care to all. Felix would not quit Natalia; Wilhelm sat before her on a stool; he had the boy's feet upon his lap; the head and breast were lying upon hers. Thus did they divide the pleasing burden and the painful anxiety, and continue, till the day broke, in their uncomfortable, sad position. Natalia had given her hand to Wilhelm; they did not speak a word; they looked at the child, and then at one another. Lothario and Jarno were sitting at the other end of the room, and carrying on a most important conversation, — which, did not the pressure of events forbid us, we would gladly lay before our readers. The boy slept softly: he awoke quite cheerful early in the morning, and demanded a piece of bread and butter.

So soon as Augustin had in some degree recovered, they endeavored to obtain some explanation from him. They learned with difficulty, and by slow degrees, that having, by the count's unlucky shifting, been appointed to the same chamber with the abbé, he had found the manuscript in which his story was recorded. Struck with horror on perusing it, he felt that it was now impossible for him to live, on which he had recourse, as usual, to the laudanum: this he poured into a glass of almond-milk, and raised it to his mouth; but he shuddered when it reached his lips: he set it down untasted, went out to walk once more across the garden, and behold the face of nature; and, on his return, he found the child employed in filling up the glass out of which it had been drinking.

They entreated the unhappy creature to be calm: he seized Wilhelm by the hand with a spasmodic grasp, and cried, "Ah! why did I not leave thee long ago? I knew well that I should kill the boy, and he me." — "The boy lives!" said Wilhelm. The doctor, who had listened with attention, now inquired of Augustin if all the drink was poisoned. "No," replied he, "nothing but the glass." — "By the luckiest chance, then," cried the doctor, "the boy has drunk from the bottle! A benignant genius has guided his hand, that he did not catch at death, which stood so near and ready for him." — "No, no!" cried Wilhelm, with a groan, and clapping both his hands upon his eyes. "How dreadful are the words! Felix said expressly that he drank, not from the bottle, but the glass. His health is but a show: he will die among our hands." Wilhelm hastened out: the doctor went below, and taking Felix up, with much caressing, asked, "Now, did not you, my pretty boy? You drank from the bottle, not the glass?" The child began to cry. The doctor secretly informed Natalia how the matter stood: she also strove in vain to get the truth from Felix, who but cried the more, — cried till he fell asleep.

Wilhelm watched by him: the night went peacefully away. Next morning Augustin was found lying dead in bed: he had cheated his attendants by a seeming rest, had silently loosened the bandages, and bled to death. Natalia went to walk with Felix: he was sportful as in his happiest days. "You are always good to me," said Felix, "you never scold, you never beat, me: I will tell you the truth, I did drink from the bottle. Mamma Aurelia used to rap me over the fingers every time I touched the bottle: father looked so sour, I thought he would beat me."

With winged steps Natalia hastened to the castle: Wilhelm came, still overwhelmed with care, to meet her. "Happy father!" cried she, lifting up the child, and throwing it into his arms: "there is thy son again! He drank from the bottle: his naughtiness has saved him."

They told the count the happy issue; but he listened with a smiling, silent, modest air of knowingness, like one tolerating the error of worthy men. Jarno, attentive to all, could not explain this lofty self-complacency, till, after many windings, he at last discovered it to be his lordship's firm belief, that the child had really taken poison, and that he himself, by prayer and the laying on of hands, had miraculously counteracted the effects of it. After such a feat, his lordship now determined on departing. Every thing, as usual with him, was made ready in a moment: the fair countess, when about to go, took Wilhelm's hand before parting with her sister's; she then pressed both their hands between her own, turned quickly round, and stepped into the carriage.

So many terrible and strange events, crowding one upon the back of another, inducing an unusual mode of life, and putting every thing into disorder and perplexity, had brought a sort of feverish movement into all departments of the house. The hours of sleep and waking, of eating, drinking, and social conversation, were inverted. Except Theresa, none of them had kept in their accustomed course. The men endeavored, by increased potations, to recover their good-humor; and, thus communicating to themselves an artificial vivacity, they drove away that natural vivacity which alone imparts to us true cheerfulness, and strength for action.

Wilhelm, in particular, was moved and agitated by the keenest feelings. Those unexpected, frightful incidents had thrown him out of all condition to resist a passion which had so forcibly seized his heart. Felix was restored to him, yet still it seemed that he had nothing: Werner's letters, the directions for his journey, were in readiness; there was nothing wanting but the resolution to remove. Every thing conspired to hasten him. He could not but conjecture that Lothario and Theresa were awaiting his departure, that they might be wedded. Jarno was unusually silent: you would have said that he had lost a portion of his customary cheerfulness. Happily the doctor helped our friend, in some degree, from this embarrassment: he declared him sick, and set about administering medicine to him.

The company assembled always in the evening: Friedrich, the wild madcap, who usually drank more wine than was meet, took possession of the talk, and by a thousand frolicsome citations, fantasies, and waggish allusions, often kept the party laughing, often, also, threw them into awkward difficulties, by the liberty he took to think aloud.

In the sickness of his friend he seemed to have little faith. Once, when they were all together, "Pray, doctor," cried he, "how is it you call the malady our friend is laboring under? Will none of the three thousand names with which you decorate your ignorance apply to it? The disease at least is not without examples. There is one such case," continued he, with an emphatic tone, "in the Egyptian or Babylonian history."

The company looked at one another, and smiled.

"What call you the king?" — cried he, and stopped short a moment. "Well, if you will not help me, I must help myself." He threw the door-leaves up, and pointed to the large picture in the ante-chamber. "What call you the goat-beard there, with the crown on, who is standing at the foot of the bed, making such a rueful face about his sick son? How call you the beauty who enters, and in her modest, roguish eyes, at once brings poison and antidote? How call you the quack of a doctor, who at this moment catches a glimpse of the reality, and, for the first time in his life, takes occasion to prescribe a reasonable recipe, to give a drug which cures to the very heart, and is at once salutiferous and savory?"

In this manner he continued babbling. The company took it with as good a face as might be, hiding their embarrassment behind a forced laugh. A slight blush overspread Natalia's cheeks, and betrayed the movements of her heart. By good fortune she was walking up and down with Jarno: on coming to the door, with a cunning motion she slipped out, walked once or twice across the ante-chamber, and retired to her room.

The company were silent: Friedrich began to dance and sing, —

"O ye shall wonders see!
What has been is not to be;
What is said is not to say,
Before the break of day
Ye shall wonders see!"

Theresa had gone out to find Natalia: Friedrich pulled the doctor forward to the picture, pronounced a ridiculous eulogium on medicine, and glided from the room.

Lothario had been standing all the while in the recess of a window: he was looking, without motion, down into the garden. Wilhelm was in the most dreadful state. Left alone with his friend, he still kept silence for a time; he ran with a hurried glance over all his history, and at last, with shuddering, surveyed his present situation: he started up, and cried, "If I am to blame for what is happening, for what you and I are suffering, punish me. In addition to my other miseries, deprive me of your friendship, and let me wander, without comfort, forth into the wide world, in which I should have mingled, and withdrawn myself from notice, long ago. But if you see in me the victim of a cruel entanglement of chance, out of which I could not thread my way, then give me the assurance of your love, of your friendship, on a journey which I dare not now postpone. A time will come when I may tell you what has passed of late within me. Perhaps this is but a punishment which I am suffering, because I did not soon enough disclose myself to you, because I hesitated to display myself entirely as I was: you would have assisted me, you would have helped me out in proper season. Again and again have my eyes been opened to my conduct; but it was ever too late, it was ever in vain! How richly do I merit Jarno's censure! I imagined I had seized it: how firmly did I purpose to employ it, to commence another life! Could I, might I, have done so? It avails not for mortals to complain of fate or of themselves. We are wretched, and appointed for wretchedness; and what does it matter whether blame of ours, higher influence or chance, virtue or vice, wisdom or folly, plunge us into ruin? Farewell! I will not stay another moment in a house where I have so fearfully violated the rights of hospitality. Your brother's indiscretion is unpardonable: it aggravates my suffering to the highest pitch, it drives me to despair."

"And what," replied Lothario, taking Wilhelm by the hand, "what if your alliance with my sister were the secret article on which depended my alliance with Theresa? This amends that noble maiden has appointed for you: she has vowed that these two pairs should appear together at the altar. 'His reason has made choice of me,' said she; 'his heart demands Natalia: my reason shall assist his heart.' We agreed to keep our eyes upon Natalia and yourself: we told the abbé of our plan, who made us promise not to intermeddle with this union, or at-tempt to forward it, but to suffer every thing to take its course. We have done so: Nature has performed her part; our mad brother only shook the ripe fruit from the branch. And now, since we have come together so unusually, let us lead no common life: let us work together in a noble manner, and for noble purposes! It is inconceivable how much a man of true culture can accomplish for himself and others, if, without attempting to rule, he can be the guardian over many; can induce them to do that in season which they are at any rate disposed enough to do; can guide them to their objects, which in general they see with due distinctness, though they miss the road to them. Let us make a league for this: it is no enthusiasm, but an idea which may be fully executed, which, indeed, is often executed, only with imperfect consciousness, by people of benevolence and worth. Natalia is a living instance of it. No other need attempt to rival the plan of conduct which has been prescribed by Nature for that pure and noble soul."

He had more to say, but Friedrich with a shout came jumping in. "What a garland have I earned!" cried he: "how will you reward me? Myrtle, laurel, ivy, leaves of oak, the freshest you can find, come twist them: I have merits far beyond them all. Natalia is thine! I am the conjurer who raised this treasure for thee."

"He raves," said Wilhelm: "I must go."

"Art thou empowered to speak?" inquired Lothario, holding Wil-helm from retiring.

"By my own authority," said Friedrich, "and the grace of God. It was thus I was the wooer, thus I am the messenger: I listened at the door; she told the abbé every thing."

"Barefaced rogue! who bade thee listen?" said Lothario.

"Who bade her bolt the door?" cried Friedrich. "I heard it all: she was in a wondrous pucker. In the night when Felix seemed so ill, and was lying half upon her knees, and thou wert sitting comfortless before her, sharing the beloved load, she made a vow, that, if the child died, she would confess her love to thee, and offer thee her hand. And now, when the child lives, why should she change her mind? What we promise under such conditions, we keep under any. Nothing want-ing but the parson! He will come, and marvel what strange news he brings."

The abbé entered. "We know it all," cried Friedrich; "be as brief as possible; it is mere formality you come for, — they never send for you or me on any other score."

"He has listened," said the baron. "Scandalous!" exclaimed the abbé.

"Now, quick!" said Friedrich. "How stands it with the ceremonies? These we can reckon on our fingers. You must travel: the marchese's invitation answers to a hair's-breadth. If we had you once beyond the Alps, it will all be right: the people are obliged to you for undertaking any thing surprising; you procure them an amusement which they are not called to pay for. It is as if you gave a free ball: all ranks partake in it."

"In such popular festivities," replied the abbé, "you have done the public much service in your time; but to-day, it seems, you will not let me speak at all."

"If it is not just as I have told it," answered Friedrich, "let us have it better. Come round, come round: we must see them both together."

Lothario embraced his friend, and led him to Natalia, who, with Theresa, came to meet them. All were silent.

"No loitering!" cried Friedrich. "In two days you may be ready for your travels. Now, think you, friend," continued he, addressing Wilhelm, "when we first scraped acquaintance, and I asked you for the pretty nosegay, who could have supposed you were ever to receive a flower like this from me?"

"Do not, at the moment of my highest happiness, remind me of those times!"

"Of which you need not be ashamed, any more than one need be ashamed of his descent. The times were very good times: only I cannot but laugh to look at thee; to my mind thou resemblest Saul the son of Kish, who went out to seek his father's asses, and found a kingdom."

"I know not the worth of a kingdom," answered Wilhelm; "but I know I have attained a happiness which I have not deserved, and which I would not change with any thing in life."